AWS®
Certified Advanced
Networking
Study Guide
Second Edition

AWS®
Certified Advanced Networking
Study Guide
Specialty (ANS-C01) Exam
Second Edition

Todd Montgomery

SYBEX®
A Wiley Brand

This book is dedicated to My Nguyen for all her support and patience.

Acknowledgments

First off, I would like to acknowledge and thank you, the readers of this book. You are the reason for all the long hours of research and writing to complete this rather large undertaking. I truly want to give back to the tech community, and this is my contribution to the networking community that I have spent my life in. I hope that by allowing me to transfer some of my knowledge to you, you can be more successful in your career and, of course, pass the AWS Advanced Networking exam. If you become a better networking engineer because of something you picked up reading this book, then I will feel satisfied.

To my wonderful daughter, who is now in college at Georgia State University, I want to thank you for the support and giving me encouragement when yet another weekend was consumed writing this book. My Nguyen was so understanding and supportive, it just never stops amazing me. She understood the sacrifices made and our missed time together as I hid out in libraries around the city pounding out text to complete yet another chapter. She is an amazing woman and helped me across the finish line of completing this book. Thank you, My!

There is the whole team at Wiley that I want to acknowledge and thank for all the support and assistance they gave me through this project. Thank you, Ken Brown, helping me through every project I undertake with Wiley; you have helped me so much over the years and I really appreciate everything you do. Kelly Talbot was the force behind the scenes as the development editor who tried to keep me out of the ditch as much as possible. Kelly, thank you for all the hours you dedicated to making this book as professional and accurate as we possibly could, I know it was not easy. I want to thank the managing editor, Pete Gaughan, for all his hard work. As always, there is a team of Wiley professionals in offices coast to coast who work behind the scenes to edit and produce quality books. To all the hidden Wiley professionals, thank you for all the great work you do!

—Todd Montgomery

About the Author

Todd Montgomery has been in the networking industry for more than 40 years. Todd holds many AWS, CompTIA, Cisco, and Juniper certifications. Todd has spent most of his career in the field working on-site in data centers throughout North America and around the world. He has worked on the most advanced networks of equipment manufacturers, systems integrators, and end users in the data center and cloud computing environments of the private sector, service providers, and the government sector. Todd currently works as a data center network automation engineer in Austin, Texas. He is involved in network implementation and support of emerging data center technologies and AWS public cloud services. Todd lives in Austin, Texas, and in his free time enjoys auto racing, traveling, general aviation, and Austin's live music venues. He can be reached at `toddmont@tipofthehat.com`.

About the Technical Editor

Doug Holland is a software engineer and architect at SnapLogic and previously spent 13 years at Microsoft Corporation. He holds a master's degree in software engineering from the University of Oxford. Before joining Microsoft, he was awarded the Microsoft MVP and Intel Black Belt Developer awards.

Contents at a Glance

Contents

Introduction

There is a lot to know to really understand advanced networking in general and specifically how to configure and manage all the networking services AWS offers us in their cloud. As I was researching and performing deep dives into all the topics I needed to cover for the exam, I kept thinking, this could really be a massive book that would take years to put together and then still not cover everything with as much detail as I wanted. However, that is the business we are in; it's very complex, and the technologies, protocols, and service offerings change all the time. Maybe that's why we find networking so interesting. I have been a hands-on networking engineer for my whole career and have worked on some of the largest networks in the world and helped bring many new networking technologies to the global market. I have also taken more than 50 networking certification exams over the last 30 or so years. The AWS Advanced Networking Specialty Exam ranks as one of the most difficult tests I have ever taken. I came from the enterprise networking world and spent many years working with many AWS cloud services and still found it to be a difficult exam. This exam is very different than a networking vendor's certification test track. I cannot stress this enough: you must learn networking from a cloud perspective and know the material in the exam blueprint at a deep and detailed level. This is not an associate level certification; it goes very deep into networking, and you must know the material well if you expect to pass the exam.

Every effort has been made to include as much detail as possible in the guide. However, I strongly suggest that you also read the FAQ, developer guides, and white papers that AWS has posted on the services covered in the exam. As is often said, the more, the better. Many of the services covered in this book are chargeable in AWS; however, I urge you to get as much console time as you can to better understand the topics. You do not have to enable everything; just "take a look" in the console to get a better understanding of the services.

The exam goes way beyond just identifying the services and their basic functions. There will be detailed scenario questions that really make you think. Read the questions carefully and take the time to really understand what is being asked before you select the best answer. There may be several answers that look plausible, but read each one closely and select the most appropriate answer from the options given. Remember, one word in the question or answer can change everything.

Interactive Online Learning Environment and Test Bank

Studying the material in the *AWS Certified Advanced Networking Study Guide Specialty (ANS-C01) Exam Second Edition* is an important part of preparing for the AWS Certified Advanced Networking - Specialty (ANS-C01) exam, but we provide additional tools to help you prepare. The online test bank will help you understand the types of questions that will appear on the certification exam.

The Sample Tests in the test bank include all the questions in each chapter as well as the questions from the assessment test that appears after this introduction. In addition, there are two practice exams with 50 questions each. You can use these tests to evaluate your understanding and identify areas that may require additional study.

The flashcards in the test bank will push the limits of what you should know for the certification exam. There are 100 questions provided in digital format. Each flashcard has one question and one correct answer.

The online glossary is a searchable list of key terms introduced in this exam guide that you should know for the AWS Certified Advanced Networking - Specialty (ANS-C01) exam.

To start using these to study for the AWS Certified Advanced Networking - Specialty (ANS-C01) exam, go to www.wiley.com/go/sybextestprep, register your book to receive your unique PIN, and then once you have the PIN, return to www.wiley.com/go/sybextestprep; find your book and click register or log in and follow the link to register a new account or add this book to an existing account.

Like all exams, the Advanced Networking certification from AWS is updated periodically and may eventually be retired or replaced. At some point after AWS is no longer offering this exam, the old editions of our books and online tools will be retired. If you have purchased this book after the exam was retired or are attempting to register in the Sybex online learning environment after the exam was retired, please know that we make no guarantees that this exam's online tools will be available once the exam is no longer available.

AWS Certified Advanced Networking - Specialty (ANS-C01) Study Guide Exam Objectives

This table provides the extent, by percentage, that each section is represented on the actual examination.

Section	% of Examination
Domain 1: Network Design	30%
Domain 2: Network Implementation	26%
Domain 3: Network Management and Operations	20%
Domain 4: Network Security, Compliance, and Governance	24%
Total	100%

Exam objectives are subject to change at any time without prior notice and at AWS's sole discretion. Please visit the AWS Certified Advanced Networking - Specialty (ANS-C01) website at `https://aws .amazon.com/certification/certified-advanced-networking-specialty` for up-to-date information on the certification and details on taking the exam. It is important to be familiar with the current exam objectives that can be downloaded here: `https://d1.awsstatic.com/ training-and-certification/docs-advnetworking-spec/AWS-Certified-Advanced-Networking-Specialty_Exam-Guide.pdf`.

Objective Map

Objective	Chapter
Domain 1: Network Design	
1.1: Design a solution that incorporates edge network services to optimize user performance and traffic management for global architectures.	1
1.2: Design DNS solutions that meet public, private, and hybrid requirements.	2
1.3: Design solutions that integrate load balancing to meet high availability, scalability, and security requirements.	4
1.4: Define logging and monitoring requirements across AWS and hybrid networks.	5
1.5: Design a routing strategy and connectivity architecture between on-premises networks and the AWS cloud.	6
1.6: Design a routing strategy and connectivity architecture that include multiple AWS accounts, AWS regions, and VPCs to support different connectivity patterns.	6
Domain 2: Network Implementation	
2.1: Implement routing and connectivity between on-premises networks and the AWS cloud.	7
2.2: Implement routing and connectivity across multiple AWS accounts, regions, and VPCs to support different connectivity patterns.	8
2.3: Implement complex hybrid and multi-account DNS architectures.	3
2.4: Automate and configure network infrastructure.	10

How to Contact the Publisher

If you believe you've found a mistake in this book, please bring it to our attention. At John Wiley & Sons, we understand how important it is to provide our customers with accurate content, but even with our best efforts an error may occur.

To submit your possible errata, please email it to our Customer Service Team at wileysupport@wiley.com with the subject line "Possible Book Errata Submission."

Assessment Test

1. You have deployed AWS Lambda@edge to run code that gets triggered by CloudFront events. You want to validate that the Lambda function is triggered when a specific header is present in the request. Which action should you take?

    A.   Modify your CloudFront distribution to forward the specific header to the origin

    B.   Modify your CloudFront distribution to add a custom header and prepend the value of true

    C.   Modify CloudFront to whitelist the specific header

    D.   Code the Lambda function to check for the presence of the specific header in the request

    E.   Implement the AWS WAF service to create a rule that allows requests with the specific header

2. You are deploying the AWS Elastic Load Balancer service to distribute inbound traffic across multiple EC2 instances. You want to verify that the load balancer is routing traffic to instances in multiple availability zones. Which action can you take to accomplish this?

    A.   Modify the load balancer to use the cross-zone algorithm

    B.   Create a load balancer all-at-once routing policy

    C.   Launch the backend EC2 instances in multiple availability zones and register them with the load balancer

    D.   Use the weighted routing policy on the load balancer

    E.   Enable Route 53 latency-based routing to route traffic to instances in multiple availability zones

3. You are the senior cloud networking engineer for an international e-commerce company. You manage a global network of web servers that are hosted in six different AWS regions. The current task is to configure Route 53 to route traffic to the web servers in the region that have the lowest latency for each user. Which routing policy would you use to accomplish this?

    A.   Simple routing

    B.   Failover routing

    C.   Geolocation routing

    D.   Geo-proximity routing with traffic biasing

    E.   Latency routing

4. You manage the public hosted zone for your domain tipofthehat.com and want to configure Route 53 to route traffic for the www.tipofthehat.com subdomain to a new EC2 instance you are deploying in us-east-1. Which option is the correct configuration?

    A.   Create an NS record for the www.tipofthehat.com subdomain that points to the name servers for the public hosted zone

    B.   Create an A record for the www.tipofthehat.com subdomain that points to the public IP address of the EC2 instance

    C. Create an MX record for the `www.tipofthehat.com` subdomain that points to the mail servers for the public hosted zone

    D. Create a TXT record for the `www.tipofthehat.com` subdomain that contains the public IP address of the EC2 instance

    E. Create a CNAME record for the `www.tipofthehat.com` subdomain that points to the public IP address of the EC2 instance

5. Your company has a pool of EC2 instances running web applications. You plan to use the AWS Network Load Balancer service to distribute traffic across the EC2 instances. You must architect the network to ensure that the load balancer is able to handle spikes in traffic and that it is highly available. Which configuration should you use?

    A. Deploy a single network load balancer with a single subnet

    B. Configure a single network load balancer with multiple subnets in the same availability zone

    C. Use a single network load balancer with multiple subnets in different availability zones

    D. Deploy a multi-AZ network load balancer with a single subnet in each availability zone

    E. Deploy a multi-AZ network load balancer with multiple subnets in each availability zone

6. You are a cloud networking engineer for a large financial services company. The firm has a fleet of EC2 instances that are all running a web application. You plan on using Cloud-Watch to monitor the network performance of the EC2 instances. Your plan is to generate CloudWatch alerts if the network performance drops below a defined threshold that you configure. Which metrics would be the best to monitor for the network performance of the EC2 instances?

    A. NetworkIn

    B. NetworkOut

    C. PercentPacketLoss

    D. PacketsReceived

    E. PacketsSent

7. Your company has a VPC that contains a fleet of EC2 instances running a web application. You are planning to configure CloudTrail to log all API calls that are made to the EC2 instances. You also want to use VPC Flow Logs to capture information about the network traffic that is flowing to and from the EC2 instances. Which one of the following options will enable you to capture the source and destination IP addresses, the ports, and the protocols of the network traffic that are associated with the API calls?

    A. Configure CloudTrail to log all API calls to the EC2 instances and configure VPC Flow Logs to export the logs to CloudWatch Logs

    B. Configure CloudTrail to log all API calls to the EC2 instances and configure VPC Flow Logs to export the logs to Amazon S3

    C. Configure CloudTrail to log all API calls to the EC2 instances and configure VPC Flow Logs to export the logs to a Lambda function

    D. Configure CloudTrail to log all API calls to the EC2 instances and configure VPC Flow Logs to export the logs to a CloudWatch Logs Insights query

8. You are setting up AWS GuardDuty for a large construction company in Austin, Texas. They have multiple accounts and VPCs in the company. You need to ensure that all findings are sent to a central security operations center account for correlation, analysis, and a unified response. Which option would best fit this requirement?

A. Enable GuardDuty in each account and configure it to send findings to the SOC account using Amazon SNS

B. Enable GuardDuty in the SOC account and monitor all the accounts using cross-account access

C. Enable GuardDuty in each account and configure it to send findings to the SOC account using Amazon SQS

D. Enable GuardDuty in the SOC account and configure it to assume an IAM role in each monitored account

E. Enable GuardDuty in each account and configure it to send findings to the SOC account using AWS Lambda

9. Your company has a default VPC running in the ap-northeast-2 Seoul region that hosts a fleet of EC2 instances running a web application. You want to use AWS Direct Connect to connect the VPC to your on-premises data center in Goyang. You must establish a connection that is highly available. Which of the following offers the highest level of availability?

A. Establish a single Direct Connect connection with a single 10 Gbps port

B. Establish a single Direct Connect connection with two 10 Gbps ports

C. Establish two Direct Connect connections, each with a single 10 Gbps port

D. Establish two Direct Connect connections, each with two 10 Gbps ports

10. You are a senior networking engineer at a large bank that has a VPC that contains a fleet of EC2 instances running a web application. You also have data center servers that need to be able to communicate with the EC2 instances. You want to use AWS Transit Gateway to connect your VPC to your data center. You must ensure that the connection is highly available, and you can scale the network as needed. Which of the following will meet this requirement?

A. Create a single Transit Gateway attachment with a single 10 Gbps BGP session

B. Create a single Transit Gateway attachment with two 10 Gbps BGP sessions

C. Create two Transit Gateway attachments, each with a single 10 Gbps BGP session

D. Create two Transit Gateway attachments, each with two 10 Gbps BGP sessions

11. You work for a construction company that has a VPC that contains a fleet of EC2 instances running a web application in the eu-west-2 London region. You want to use the AWS Reachability Analyzer to verify that the EC2 instances are reachable from the Internet. You need to be able to trace the path the network traffic takes from the Internet to the EC2 instances. Which option should you use to configure AWS Reachability Analyzer?

A. Configure AWS Reachability Analyzer to analyze the path from a specific IP address on the Internet to the EC2 instances

B. Configure AWS Reachability Analyzer to analyze the path from a specific CIDR block on the Internet to the EC2 instances

C. Configure AWS Reachability Analyzer to analyze the path from a specific EC2 instance to the Internet

D. Configure AWS Reachability Analyzer to analyze the path from a specific VPC to the Internet

12. Your company has two VPCs, one for production and one for development. You want to allow the EC2 instances in the production VPC to communicate with the EC2 instances in the development VPC. Your CIO has asked you to do this without using a VPN or Direct Connect. Which option should you use to configure VPC peering?

    A. Create a VPC peering connection between the production VPC and the development VPC

    B. Create a VPN connection between the production VPC and the development VPC

    C. Create a Direct Connect connection between the production VPC and the development VPC

    D. Create a Bastion host in the production VPC and allow the EC2 instances in the development VPC to connect to the Bastion host

13. Your company has a microservices architecture that is deployed on AWS. They are requesting that you use AWS App Mesh to control the traffic between the microservices. You must ensure that the traffic is routed in a way that minimizes latency and maximizes availability. Which of the following options should you use to configure App Mesh?

    A. Create a virtual service for each microservice and use a service mesh router to route the traffic between the virtual services

    B. Create a virtual service for each of the microservices and use a service mesh router to route the traffic between the microservices

    C. Create a virtual service for each microservice and use a service mesh proxy to route the traffic between the microservices

    D. Create a single virtual service for all the microservices and use a service mesh proxy to route the traffic between the microservices

14. Your company has a VPC that runs six EC2 instances hosting a custom web application. You want to use CloudFormation to create a new subnet in the VPC and then launch a new EC2 instance in the subnet. Which of the following options best fits this requirement?

    A. Create the new subnet in the VPC using the AWS CLI. Then, deploy the new EC2 instance to the subnet using the AWS CLI

    B. Create the subnet in the VPC using the AWS Management Console. Then, deploy the new EC2 instance to the subnet using the AWS Management Console

    C. Create a new subnet and deploy the new EC2 instance using a CloudFormation template

    D. Create the new subnet using the AWS CLI and deploy the new EC2 instance using a CloudFormation template

15. The research organization that you work for has deployed a cluster of EC2 instances that are running a high-performance computing application. You want to implement the AWS Elastic Fabric Adapter interface to increase the performance of the application. Which options would provide the best performance improvement?

    A. Create a single Elastic Fabric Adapter interface and attach it to all the cluster EC2 instances

    B. Create multiple Elastic Fabric Adapter interfaces and attach one EFA to each EC2 instance in the cluster

    C. Create a single Elastic Fabric Adapter interface and attach it to a subset of the cluster EC2 instances

    D. Create multiple Elastic Fabric Adapter interfaces and attach one EFA to a subset of the EC2 instances in the cluster

16. You are the senior network engineer for a large shipping company. The company's production VPC hosts a fleet of EC2 instances running a custom web application. You are planning on configuring Traffic Mirroring to capture all ingress and egress traffic from the EC2 instances and storing the captured traffic into a CloudWatch Logs log group. What is the best way to configure VPC Traffic Mirroring?

    A. Create a VPC traffic mirror session that mirrors all the traffic to a network interface in the VPC. Then, enable your CloudWatch Logs subscription for the network interface

    B. Configure a VPC traffic mirror session that mirrors all the traffic to a CloudWatch Logs log group

    C. Set up a VPC traffic mirror session that mirrors all the traffic to an AWS S3 bucket Next, configure a CloudWatch Logs subscription for the S3 bucket

    D. Configure a VPC traffic mirror session that mirrors all the traffic into a Kinesis Data Firehose stream. Then, create a CloudWatch Logs subscription for the Kinesis Data Firehose

17. You work as the senior cloud network engineer for a data analytics company. The company's eu-west-1 Ireland test VPC hosts six large EC2 instances that are all running an AI application. You want to use an AWS Elastic Network Interface (ENI) to create a dedicated network interface for each of the EC2 instances. Which option should you use to create dedicated network interfaces for each EC2 instance?

    A. Create a single ENI and attach it to all the EC2 instances in the VPC

    B. Create multiple ENIs and attach one each to the EC2 instance in the VPC

    C. Create a single ENI and attach it to a subset of the EC2 instances in the VPC

    D. Create multiple ENIs and attach one ENI to a subset of the EC2 instances in the VPC

18. You are a network engineer for a large university. It has a website that is hosted in the AWS us-west-1 California region. You are concerned about the website being attacked by a DDoS attack and are planning on using the AWS Shield service to protect your website. Which of the following provides the best protection against a DDoS attack?

    A. Enable AWS Shield Standard

    B. Enable AWS Shield Advanced

    C. Enable AWS Shield Standard and AWS Shield Advanced

    D. Enable AWS Shield Advanced and configure custom DDoS protection rules

19. Your company has a fleet of EC2 instances running a critical web application. You are planning on using the AWS Firewall Manager to create a centralized firewall policy for all of the EC2 instances. Which option allows you to create a centralized firewall policy?

    A. Create a firewall policy in each VPC that the EC2 instances are in

    B. Create a firewall policy in a single VPC and attach it to all the EC2 instances

    C. Create a firewall policy in AWS Firewall Manager and attach it to all the EC2 instances

    D. Create a firewall policy in AWS Firewall Manager and attach it to the VPCs that the EC2 instances are in

20. You are a network engineer for a chain of retail stores in eastern Canada. The company has deployed a fleet of EC2 instances running a secure web application. You plan to use the AWS Certificate Manager to create a certificate to secure the web application. Which option allows you to create a certificate that will be trusted by all major browsers?

    A. Create a self-signed certificate

    B. Create a certificate that is signed by a third-party certificate authority

    C. Create a certificate that is signed by AWS Certificate Manager

    D. Create a certificate that is signed by Amazon Trust Services

Answers to Assessment Test

1. D. To accomplish this requirement, you would need to modify the Lambda function to check for the presence of the specific header in the request. The Lambda function will trigger only when a specific header is present in the request. You must modify the Lambda function code to check for the presence of the header, and if the header is present, the function will continue processing; otherwise, it can return the appropriate response that you define. The other options are not correct because they do not provide a way to trigger the Lambda function based on the presence of a specific header. Forwarding headers and adding custom headers do not affect how Lambda functions are triggered. Whitelisting headers can allow CloudFront to forward headers to the origin but does not affect how Lambda functions are triggered. The AWS Web Application Firewall is used to protect against web exploits but does not affect how Lambda functions are triggered.

2. C. To ensure that Elastic Load Balancer routes traffic to instances in multiple availability zones, launch the backend EC2 instances in multiple availability zones and register them with the load balancer. Once this has been completed, the load balancer will automatically distribute incoming traffic across the registered instances in all availability zones. The other options are incorrect because they do not provide a way to route traffic to instances in multiple availability zones. Cross-zone load balancing and routing policies will affect how traffic is distributed across registered instances but do not ensure that instances are launched in multiple availability zones. Using Amazon's Route 53 DNS latency-based routing can route traffic based on the lowest network latency but does not affect how the Elastic Load Balancer routes traffic.

3. D. Geo-proximity routing with traffic biasing is the best routing policy to use to accomplish this requirement. Geo-proximity routing with traffic biasing routes traffic to the resource that is closest to the user's location, but it also allows you to configure bias routing so that traffic is more likely to be routed to a particular region. This ensures that traffic is routed to a region that has the lowest latency for a particular user. Geo-proximity routing with traffic biasing uses the source IP address of the user's request to determine the closest AWS resource. The user's IP address is used to calculate the distance between the user and the resource. The resource that is closest to the user is then routed to. If you have configured Route 53 traffic biasing, it will also consider the weight that you have assigned to each region. This means you can bias the routing so that traffic is more likely to be routed to a particular region. Simple routing is the simplest routing policy. It routes traffic to the first resource that is listed in the record and does not consider the location of the user. Failover routing is used to route traffic to a backup resource if the primary resource is unavailable and is not the best routing policy to use in this case. Geolocation routing routes traffic to the resource that is closest to the user's location, and latency routing routes traffic to the resource that has the lowest latency; however, neither of these routing policies allow you to bias the routing.

4. E. A CNAME record maps a subdomain to another domain name or IP address. In this requirement, you must map the `www.tipofthehat.com` subdomain to the public IP address of the EC2 instance. The NS record specifies the name servers for a hosted zone and is not used to route traffic to a specific IP address. The A record is used to specify the IP address for a domain name and is not used to route traffic to a subdomain. MX records

specify the mail servers for a domain name. TXT records are used to specify text associated with a domain name. MX and txt records are not used to route traffic to a specific IP address.

5.   E. The multi-AZ network load balancer has two load balancers that are in different availability zones. Deploying the multi-AZ network load balancer with multiple subnets in each availability zone is the best configuration to use to meet your requirements. The multi-AZ network load balancer is highly available because it has two load balancers each in a different availability zone. If one availability zone goes down, the other availability zone will still be able to handle traffic. Also, using multiple subnets in each availability zone will help to distribute traffic across the subnets, which will improve performance. Using a single NLB with a single subnet is not highly available. If the subnet goes down, the load balancer will also go down. Using a single NLB with multiple subnets in the same availability zone is not as highly available as a multi-AZ NLB. If the availability zone goes down, all subnets in the availability zone will also go down. Deploying a single NLB with multiple subnets in different availability zones is not a good option because it does not distribute traffic across the subnets. Configuring the multi-AZ NLB with a single subnet in each availability zone is not a good option because it does not distribute traffic across the subnets.

6.   C. PercentPacketLoss would be the preferred metric for monitoring the network performance of the EC2 instances. PercentPacketLoss measures the percentage of packets that are lost in transit. If the metric is high, it means that there is a problem with the network performance. A high packet loss metric indicates that there is a problem with the network performance. This could be because of a congested network, a faulty network device, or a software bug. NetworkIn measures the number of bytes that are received by the EC2 instance. NetworkOut measures the number of bytes that are sent by the EC2 instance. PacketsReceived measures the number of packets that are received by the EC2 instance and PacketsSent measures the number of packets that are sent by the EC2 instance. These metrics are not as useful for monitoring network performance as PercentPacketLoss because they do not consider the number of packets that are lost.

7.   A. The best option is to configure CloudTrail to log all API calls to the EC2 instances and enable VPC Flow Logs and export the logs to CloudWatch Logs. CloudTrail will log the source and destination IP addresses, the ports, and the protocols of the API calls. VPC Flow Logs will log the source and destination IP addresses, the ports, and the protocols of the network traffic. When you combine the logs from CloudTrail and VPC Flow Logs, you will be able to see the source and destination IP addresses, the ports, and the protocols of the network traffic that is associated with the API calls. CloudTrail allows you to track AWS API calls made on your behalf. VPC Flow Logs enables you to capture information about the network traffic that is flowing to and from your VPC. By combining the logs from CloudTrail and VPC Flow Logs, you can get a complete picture of the activity that is happening in your VPC.

Configuring CloudTrail to log all API calls to the EC2 instances and configuring VPC Flow Logs to export the logs to Amazon S3 is not as good an option as configuring the logs to export to CloudWatch Logs. By using CloudWatch Logs, you have a centralized location to store and analyze your log data, which makes it easier to troubleshoot problems. Configuring CloudTrail to log all API calls to the EC2 instances and configuring VPC Flow Logs to export the logs to a Lambda function is not as desirable an option as configuring the logs to export to CloudWatch Logs. Lambda functions are a powerful tool that can be used to automate tasks, but they are not as good a solution for storing and analyzing log data as CloudWatch Logs. Configuring CloudTrail to log all API calls to the EC2 instances and configuring VPC Flow Logs to export the logs to a CloudWatch Logs Insights query is not as good an option as configuring the logs to export to CloudWatch Logs. CloudWatch Logs Insights is a powerful tool that allows you to query your log data, but it is not as easy to use as CloudWatch Logs.

8. B. GuardDuty supports cross-account access enabling you to designate one AWS account as a master account that can view and manage GuardDuty findings from member accounts. This enables you to centralize the management of GuardDuty findings in a single SOC account. SNS, SQS, and Lambda are not used for sending GuardDuty findings between accounts, assuming an IAM role is not necessary for cross-account access with GuardDuty.

9. C. AWS Direct Connect is a service that allows you to create a dedicated network connection between your on-premises network and AWS. Establishing two Direct Connect connections, each with a single 10 Gbps port, will provide the highest availability. If one connection goes down, the other connection will still be available. Creating a single Direct Connect connection with a single 10 Gbps port will not provide the highest level of availability. Establishing a single Direct Connect connection with two 10 Gbps ports would also not provide the highest level of availability. In both options, if the connection goes down, you will lose connectivity to AWS. Creating two Direct Connect connections, each with two 10 Gbps ports, will provide more bandwidth at a higher cost than option C.

10. D. AWS Transit Gateway service allows you to create a central hub for your network traffic. Transit Gateway attachments allow you to connect your VPCs and on-premises networks to the gateway. BGP sessions are used to establish communication between the Transit Gateway and your networks. Creating two Transit Gateway attachments, each with two 10 Gbps BGP sessions, will meet the requirements of the scenario. This is because it will provide the highest level of availability and the ability to scale the network as needed. Creating a single Transit Gateway attachment with a single 10 Gbps BGP session will not meet the requirements of the scenario because it will not provide high availability. Creating a single Transit Gateway attachment with two 10 Gbps BGP sessions does not provide the ability to scale the network as needed. Creating two Transit Gateway attachments, each with a single 10 Gbps BGP session, will not provide the highest level of availability.

11. B. AWS Reachability Analyzer service allows you to analyze network paths between two points in your AWS network. You can use Reachability Analyzer to troubleshoot connectivity issues and to verify that your network is configured correctly. Configuring AWS Reachability Analyzer to analyze the path from a specific CIDR block from the Internet to the EC2 instances is the best option in this case. This is because it will allow you to see the path that the network traffic takes from the Internet to the EC2 instances, regardless of the specific IP address that is used to access the EC2 instances.

Configuring AWS Reachability Analyzer to analyze the path from a specific IP address on the Internet to the EC2 instances is not as good an option as configuring the analysis to analyze the path from a specific CIDR block on the Internet to the EC2 instances. This is because if the IP address that is used to access the EC2 instances changes, the analysis will need to be updated. Configuring AWS Reachability Analyzer to analyze the path from a specific EC2 instance to the Internet is not as good an option as configuring the analysis to analyze the path from a specific CIDR block on the Internet to the EC2 instances because if the EC2 instance is moved to a different subnet, the analysis will need to be updated. Configuring AWS Reachability Analyzer to analyze the path from a specific VPC to the Internet is not as good an option as configuring the analysis to analyze the path from a specific CIDR block in the Internet to the EC2 instances because, if the VPC is expanded, the analysis will need to be updated.

12. A. VPC peering allows you to connect two VPCs together so that they can communicate with each other as if they were in the same network. VPC peering is a simple and cost-effective way to connect two VPCs and does not require any additional hardware. Creating a VPC peering connection between the production VPC and the development VPC is the best option in this case.

Creating a VPN connection between the production VPC and the development VPC is not as good an option as creating a VPC peering connection because VPN connections can be more complex to configure and manage than VPC peering connections. Creating a Direct Connect connection between the production VPC and the development VPC is not as good an option as creating a VPC peering connection because Direct Connect connections are more expensive than VPC peering connections. Creating a Bastion host in the production VPC and allowing the EC2 instances in the development VPC to connect to the Bastion host is not the best option because Bastion hosts can be a single point of failure and may introduce security risks if not configured correctly.

13. C. AWS App Mesh is a service that allows you to control the traffic between microservices. App Mesh uses virtual services to represent microservices, and it uses service mesh proxies to route the traffic between the virtual services. Service mesh proxies are deployed alongside the microservices, and they provide features such as traffic routing, observability, and fault tolerance. Creating a virtual service for each microservice and using a service mesh proxy to route the traffic between the microservices is the best option in this case. This is because it will allow you to control the traffic between the microservices in a granular way, and it will also provide you with visibility into the traffic.

Creating a single virtual service for all the microservices and using a service mesh router to route the traffic between the microservices is not as good an option as creating a virtual service for each microservice and using a service mesh proxy to route the traffic between the microservices. This is because it will not allow you to control the traffic between the microservices in a granular way. Creating a single virtual service for all the microservices and using a service mesh proxy to route the traffic between the microservices is not as good an option because it will not provide you with as much visibility into the traffic. Using a service mesh router to route the traffic between the microservices is not as good of an option as using a service mesh proxy to route the traffic between the microservices because service mesh proxies provide features that service mesh routers do not, including observability and fault tolerance.

14. C. CloudFormation is used to create a variety of AWS resources, including VPCs, subnets, and EC2 instances. CloudFormation templates define the resources that you want to create. Creating a new subnet and deploying the new EC2 instance using a CloudFormation template is the best option.

Creating a new subnet in the VPC using the CLI or Management Console and deploying the new EC2 instance using the CLI or the Management Console is not as good an option as creating a new subnet and deploying the new EC2 instance using a CloudFormation template. These options will not be as easy to automate. Creating a new subnet using the AWS CLI and deploying the new EC2 instance using a CloudFormation template is not as good an option because it is more difficult to manage the two templates.

15. B. Creating multiple Elastic Fabric Adapter interfaces and attaching one EFA to each EC2 instance in the cluster will provide the best performance improvement. This enables each EC2 instance to have its own dedicated network interface for inter-node communication. The AWS Elastic Fabric Adapter (EFA) is a high-performance network interface that is designed for high-performance computing (HPC) applications. EFAs deliver low latency and high bandwidth for inter-node communication.

Creating a single EFA and attaching it to all the EC2 instances in the cluster or creating multiple EFAs and attaching one EFA to a subset of the EC2 instances in the cluster are not good solutions because the EC2 instances will have to share the bandwidth of the single EFA. If you create multiple EFAs and attach one EFA to a subset of the EC2 instances in the cluster, it will not give you the optimal performance improvement because the EC2 instances are not attached to the EFA and will not be able to communicate with each other as efficiently.

16. B. The AWS VPC Traffic Mirroring service allows you to mirror all the traffic going to and from a specific source or destination in your VPC. The mirrored traffic is then stored in a specified destination. Creating a VPC traffic mirror session that mirrors all the traffic into a CloudWatch Logs log group is the best option because it allows you to store the captured traffic in a central location where it can be accessed.

Creating a VPC mirror that sends all the traffic to a network interface in the VPC, Kinesis Firehose, or an S3 bucket and then creating a CloudWatch Logs subscription for the network interface, data stream, or S3 bucket is not as good as creating a VPC traffic mirror session that mirrors all of the traffic to a CloudWatch Logs log group because it requires you to manage two separate resources.

17. B. The AWS Elastic Network Interface (ENI) is a virtual network interface that allows you to connect an EC2 instance to a VPC. ENIs can be attached to multiple EC2 instances, but each EC2 instance can be attached to only a single ENI. The correct answer is to create multiple ENIs and attach one ENI to each EC2 instance in the VPC. This allows you to create a dedicated network interface for each EC2 instance. Each EC2 instance will have its own dedicated ENI, which will prevent them all from sharing the bandwidth of a single ENI.

Creating a single ENI and attaching it to all the EC2 instances in the VPC will not allow you to create a dedicated network interface for each EC2 instance because the EC2 instances will have to share the bandwidth of the single ENI. Configuring a single ENI and attaching it to a subset of the EC2 instances in the VPC does not allow you to create a dedicated network interface for each EC2 instance because the EC2 instances that are not attached to the ENI will not be able to communicate with the Internet as efficiently. If you create multiple ENIs and attach one ENI to a subset of the EC2 instances in the VPC that will not create dedicated network interfaces for each EC2 instance because the EC2 instances that are not attached to the ENI will not be able to communicate with the Internet as efficiently.

18. B. AWS Shield is an AWS managed DDoS protection service that protects your AWS resources from distributed denial-of-service attacks. Enabling AWS Shield Advanced will provide the best protection against DDoS attacks. AWS Shield Advanced provides more comprehensive protections than AWS Shield Standard and includes features such as automatic detection and mitigation of DDoS attacks, custom protection rules, and 24/7 monitoring and support.

Enabling AWS Shield Standard will provide some protection against DDoS attacks but is not as complete a service as Shield Advanced. If you enable both AWS Shield Standard and Advanced, it will provide the same level of protection as enabling AWS Shield Advanced alone. If you configure a custom DDoS protection rule, it can provide additional protection against DDoS attacks; however, it may not be as comprehensive as AWS Shield Advanced.

19. C. AWS Firewall Manager protects your AWS resources from common web attacks. Firewall Manager enables you to create and manage firewall policies that are applied to your EC2 instances, ELBs, and other AWS resources. The AWS Firewall Manager is a centralized service that creates and manages firewall policies. Creating a firewall policy using the AWS Firewall Manager and then attaching it to all the EC2 instances allows you to create a centralized firewall policy.

If you create a firewall policy in each VPC that the EC2 instances are in that will not allow a centralized firewall policy because you will have to manage multiple firewall policies, which can be difficult to track and maintain. If you create a firewall policy in a single VPC and attach it to all the EC2 instances that will not allow you to create a centralized firewall policy because you will have to manage the firewall policy in the single VPC. If you create firewall policies with the Firewall Manager and attach them to the VPCs that the EC2 instances are in that will not allow you to create centralized firewall policies because you will have to manage the firewall policy in each VPC.

20. C. Creating an SSL/TLS certificate signed by the AWS Certificate Manager allows you to create certificates that are trusted by all major browsers because AWS Certificate Manager uses a variety of trusted root CAs to sign its certificates. AWS Certificate Manager (ACM) is an AWS service that enables you to provision, manage, and deploy public and private SSL/TLS certificates for your AWS deployments. Certificates created by ACM are trusted by all major browsers, including Chrome, Firefox, Edge, and Safari.

Creating a self-signed certificate does not allow you to create a certificate that will be trusted by all major browsers because self-signed certificates are not trusted by default by most browsers. If you create a certificate that is signed by a third-party CA, it may or may not be trusted by all the major browsers. You will need to ensure that the CA is trusted by the browsers you are using. Using the AWS Trust Service, ATS, allows you to create a certificate that will be trusted by all major browsers. However, ATS is a premium service that is not available in all regions.

Network Design

Chapter 1: Edge Networking

Chapter 2: Domain Name Services

Chapter 3: Hybrid and Multi-Account DNS

Chapter 4: Load Balancing

Chapter 5: Logging and Monitoring

Chapter 1

Edge Networking

THE AWS CERTIFIED ADVANCED NETWORKING - SPECIALTY EXAM OBJECTIVES COVERED IN THIS CHAPTER MAY INCLUDE, BUT ARE NOT LIMITED TO, THE FOLLOWING:

✓ **Domain 1: Network Design**

- Objective 1.1: Design a solution that incorporates edge network services to optimize user performance and traffic management for global architectures.

Content Distribution Networking

In this chapter, we will cover edge networking, APIs, and content distribution offerings that are specific to AWS. We will start at the beginning of the exam blueprint in Domain 1, which is about AWS network design. This chapter covers services offered at the edge of the global AWS network, including CloudFront, Global Accelerator, Load Balancing API Gateway, and the other edge offerings from AWS.

CloudFront

CloudFront is the AWS global content distribution network that is a pay-as-you-go service with minimum fees and no contracts that lock you into time-length windows.

CloudFront content is stored, or *cached*, at AWS edge locations. Edge locations are located throughout the world and contain large storage arrays to store the cached data. Edge locations also host AWS Lambda, DNS, API Gateway compression, and transfer acceleration endpoints.

AWS has more than 400 edge locations in more than 90 cities in 47 countries as of this writing. New edge locations are constantly being added as the network expands throughout the world. Figure 1.1 illustrates how these edge locations are spread throughout the world in major cities that do not have AWS regional data centers.

The base design for publishing content on the Internet is to host the data in either a cloud or private data center and have users access the information over the Internet from these centralized locations. While this design has been the standard for many years, there are several limitations. Users who are in geographically distant locations might have to contend with network round-trip latency and sometimes slow Internet links causing poor transfer speeds.

By using *content distribution networks* (CDNs), this data can be distributed over the AWS backbone network and cached at locations worldwide that are closer to the people and systems requesting the information. Now, using the same connection strings including the URLs, the data is served much closer to the destination and does not have to go back to the originating location to fetch the content. CloudFront is most effective when servicing frequently accessed content. This content can be either static or dynamic and can include web pages, images, software update files, and both audio and video media. Protocols supported include HTTP, HTTPS, PHP, and WebSockets as well as live or on-demand video streaming services running over HTTP.

FIGURE 1.1   AWS global CloudFront network

The originating, or *origin*, data can be stored in an AWS region or private data center, as shown in Figure 1.2. Static content can use storage systems such as an AWS S3 bucket, and dynamic content can use a web server running on EC2, for example. The *origin* is defined as the location where the source data is located.

FIGURE 1.2   AWS CloudFront edge distributions

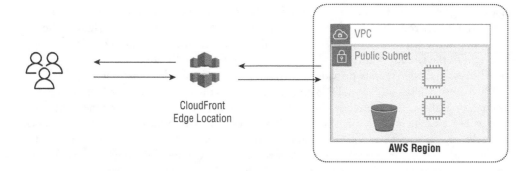

CloudFront Implementation

When creating a CloudFront implementation, sites are registered with CloudFront using configuration objects called *distributions*. Origins and all other configuration items are stored in the distributions.

The CloudFront distributions will be assigned a DNS name by AWS that uses the `cloudfront.net` domain. We can then map our own domain name to the distribution by creating a CNAME record in DNS that references the AWS CloudFront domain name. When connecting to the URL, connections are directed to the nearest location that can provide the best performance and not back to the origin, which may be on the other side of the world.

Origin redundancy can be configured to use a backup to your primary source of data. If your main source origin fails, a failover can occur based on HTTP status codes such as the 400 and 500 series. Both AWS hosted and on-premise origins are supported and will back up each other based on the design requirements.

Creating a CloudFront distribution can be done from API calls, with the AWS command-line interface, with the AWS web graphical user interface, or as infrastructure as code using CloudFormation.

Route 53 is the AWS DNS service. CloudFront domains will always use the `cloudfront.net` DNS name by default. However, you can use CNAME pointers to map your company DNS name to the CloudFront distribution DNS for clarity. Also, Route 53 supports the mapping of zone apex names free of charge. This allows you to map a top domain such as `helloworld.com` to your CloudFront distribution such as `abcdef12345678.cloudfront.net`.

Caching and Object Retention

There is also a regional CloudFront component that contains less frequently accessed data and has a larger storage capacity than edge locations. *Regional edge caches* serve content to a subset of the edge locations. Regional edges have larger cache storage capacities and longer retention times than the smaller edge locations. This way, if the content should time out on the edge storage sites because of the data not being requested for a period of time, the edge location does not have to request the data from the origin. Instead, the edge will query the regional edge cache, and if the data is stored in the regional cache, then it is returned to the edge with a faster response than having to retrieve the information from the origin. If the data is not in the regional cache, then a regional fetch is performed to pull the object from the origin to the CloudFront regional cache and on to the edge location. Figure 1.3 shows how the regional edge servers provide cached data closer to the edge locations.

When a user makes a request, DNS will route them to the nearest edge location to serve the content. If this is the first request or if there has not been a request for the time-out period, there will be a cache miss. In this case, CloudFront will go back to the origin if it is S3 data or regional cache to retrieve all the other data. The data is delivered to the end user and stored locally in the edge cache. Any new requests at this location will be serviced quickly as the data is now stored at the CloudFront edge location. Figure 1.4 shows the traffic flow.

FIGURE 1.3 AWS CloudFront regional edge nodes

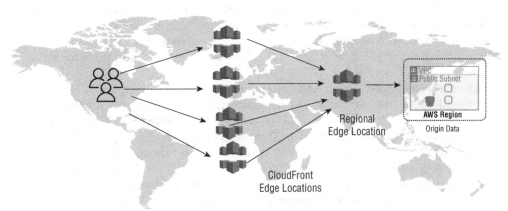

1. The user makes a request for an object from the CloudFront edge location.

2. If the object is not stored in the CloudFront edge, there is a cache miss; the edge will then check with the regional edge location to see if it is stored there, which is closer to the source.

3. If there is a cache miss at the regional edge, the regional edge will download the data from the origin and forward it to the edge location to reply to the requester and add to its cache.

4. There is an origin fetch of the object from the regional edge that then sends the object to the edge location where it is cached for future requests and also sent to the user requesting the object.

FIGURE 1.4 Caching data at CloudFront edge locations

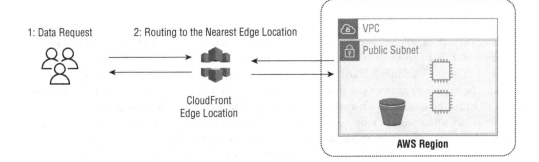

Data retention in the edge cache has a default value of 24 hours. It is a best practice to have a longer retention time if the content does not change very often and to use a versioning system to track updates to objects. If the edge receives a user request for an object that has been cached for more than 24 hours, the origin is checked to see if the content has changed. If it has, the new object will be uploaded and the expiration timer set back to the TTL value. File cache control headers are used to instruct the edge location on how often to check for a new object version at the origin or regional cache. If it is S3, then the origin location will be checked; however, for other content, the regional cache is checked first. If the value of the cache control header is 0, then the check for a newer object is made for every request.

Each edge location views an object as current if it is within its time-to-live (TTL) range. When the TTL of an object stored in an edge location counts down to zero, it becomes stale but is not deleted from its local cache. Instead, the edge checks with the origin to see if there is an updated version of the object. If the origin returns a response code of 304 Not Modified, the edge location marks the locally stored object as current. If there is a newer version, the origin will forward the data to the edge to replace the stale data stored locally and flagged as current data. The default validity period is defined for each distribution with the default value set at 24 hours. Per-object TTL values can be defined for an object that will override the default of 24 hours. There are also minimum and maximum TTL values that can be configured per distribution that set absolute high and low values that cannot be exceeded when configuring TTL values, either default or custom.

HTTP headers can be configured to control the TTL values when making a request. The Cache-Control max-age (seconds) and Cache-Control s-max-age (seconds) defines the TTL for the object, and both serve the same function. Next is the Expires (date and time) header, which is self-explanatory. As we discussed, the values that are defined either in seconds or as a date-time format are limited by the minimum and maximum age global TTL values. If the header values are below the minimum or maximum timers, then the default is used, either high or low. The headers are defined differently depending on the origin being used. If the origin is an S3 bucket, then the values are stored in the object metadata. The second option is to have the application or web server insert the values.

Invalidations

Cache invalidations are configured for all edge locations at the distribution level. A cache invalidation will expire all objects in the edge cache even if there are TTL values that have not expired. It is a forced deletion of the object from cache. Invalidation can define a specific file or be expanded using wildcards. Since this is a chargeable operation, another approach that can be used is to rename the new files with a version number and change the application to point to the new version. This will force the edge cache to be updated and the older version to expire and eventually be removed from the edge cache without incurring any charges. Other advantages of versioning include more accurate logging information given that the filenames are different when updated and that browser caches will automatically update to the new object. Also with versioning, you will be able to retain copies of the older objects since they will have a different version number in the object filename.

To clear the edge cache and remove unwanted objects, we can delete, or *invalidate*, the object from the origin and let it age out in the edge cache based on its expiration value in each object's HTTP header. Forcing the cache removal of an object before its expiration time is accomplished by calling the invalidation API of the object. AWS will charge you every time you invalidate an object. Up to 3,000 invalidation requests can be performed for each distribution at any given time. Up to 15 invalidation wildcards are supported simultaneously. The best practice is to limit the use of invalidation requests and instead use an object versioning approach or shorten the header's expiration time.

The Origin Shield service reduces the read load on the origin by adding an additional cache layer between the regional and edge locations and the origin, as shown in Figure 1.5. This is accomplished by directing all requests for the same content from the edge and regional locations to a central cache server to increase the cache hit ratio of the edge locations. If the object is not in the Origin Shield cache, all of the requests for the same object will be consolidated into a single object request to the origin to reduce the traffic and workload from the origin. Origin Shield is enabled when creating a distribution and incurs additional charges.

FIGURE 1.5   Origin Shield

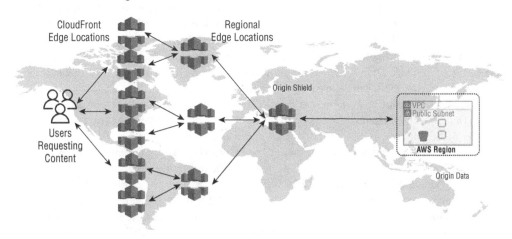

Protocol Support

CloudFront supports the WebSockets protocol that enables real-time bidirectional communications that are used by chat, multimedia meeting applications, collaboration applications, gaming, financial trading systems, and many other newer Internet-based services. WebSockets connections are often active for long periods of time, which enables low-latency bidirectional HTTP connections since there is no need to constantly create new connections. WebSockets connections are enabled using the `upgrade: WebSockets` header value. The server will accept the WebSockets request by returning an HTTP status code of 101 to signal a switch to use WebSockets. SSL/TLS encryption is supported in CloudFront when using the WebSockets protocol if requested at the initial connection request.

HTTP responses to errors can be customized using your corporate branding and messaging. These are supported for 4xx and 5xx response codes.

CloudFront supports compression by enabling automatic object compression in the CloudFront console. The compression format is gzip and works for both text and binary data. The client must include, in the HTTP header, `accept-encoding: gzip` to complete the process, which is the default value for all newer browsers.

Streaming content is another supported CloudFront feature. HTTP real-time streaming using Adobe, Apple, MPEG, and Microsoft delivers data in real time and includes bidirectional services for stop, forward, rewind, and other controls for both video and audio streams.

CloudFront Encryption Using SSL/TLS and SNI

Encrypting data in transit over the Internet is the recommended transport method for web traffic. This relies on the Secure Sockets Layer (SSL)/Transport Layer Security (TLS) services. SSL has been deprecated and replaced by TLS even though the SSL name lives on and is widely used in the industry even when TLS is actually the protocol being used. AWS includes a security certificate at all CloudFront edge locations that is bound to the `cloudfront` `.net` domain that is globally used by AWS as the default domain name for CloudFront. If you choose to connect to the edge nodes using this default domain, all you need to do is to enable it in the CloudFront distribution configuration settings.

However, it is common to use your own domain and map it to the CloudFront domain in DNS using a CNAME. DNS will be covered in the next two chapters; however, at this stage, just understand that DNS can redirect one domain name to another. This allows you to use your company's descriptive domain name and hide the rather convoluted AWS CloudFront domain that is in the format of `https://a123456789abcd.cloudfront.net`, as an example. By default, the `*.cloudfront.net` certificate is installed and supported.

To use your own certificate, such as `www.tipofthehat.com`, for example, you can create it at any number of security authorities that offer certificates or choose to use the AWS certificate services called *Amazon Certificate Manager* (ACM). Regardless of how you create the certificate for your domain, you will need to import it into ACM. ACM certificates are usually AWS region–dependent, which means you must create the certificate in the AWS region you intend to use it in. However, since CloudFront is a global service, all CloudFront certificates are managed in the AWS us-east-1 region in Northern Virginia.

Incoming traffic to the edge location can be either HTTPS and use the certificate or unencrypted HTTP. There is a commonly used option to redirect unencrypted connection requests using HTTP port 80 to HTTPS port 443 to force encrypted traffic regardless if the client is making an HTTP or HTTPS request. This forces the user's connection to be encrypted. It is important to understand that the certificate being used must match the domain name of the distribution. If they are different, the SSL/TLS handshake will fail.

There are actually two encrypted sessions negotiated for every connection when using CloudFront. The first is from the user to the edge, which will terminate the encrypted connection. Then the edge will initiate the second connection to the origin on the back end using another SSL/TLS connection. This is often referred to as a *proxy connection*.

There are two categories of certificates; the first is created internally in your organization and is often referred to as *self-signed*. These are not used on the Internet as there is no proof of ownership in the public key infrastructure to confirm that it's a valid certificate. The validation check is supported only by public certificates that are created by a well-known public certificate authority. CloudFront will only support public certificates and not those that are self-signed. At the origin locations, public signed certificates are also required. S3 supports this natively. Application load balancers, EC2, and on-premise servers also require public certificates.

Originally every website that used SSL/TLS was required to have its own dedicated IP address. This forced web servers to only be able to host a single website's IP address. With the expansion of web server capabilities, now each server can host hundreds of websites. This created an issue with SSL/TLS because of the requirement to use the domain name in the digital certificate. With many different domains now using a single IP address on the web server, a method was created to distinguish the incoming connection requests and connect them to the correct certificate for each domain. In the header of the connection request, a field was added that includes the domain name being requested. This allows the server to match the connection request with the proper digital certificate for each domain. *Server Name Indication* (SNI) is an extension to TLS where the client tells the server which domain to connect to using a single IP address that supports many certificates. This is done before the TLS security negotiation is started, and the connect request is handed off to the proper certificate based on its domain and negotiation proceeds. Be aware that older browsers do not support SNI, but this issue will decrease over time. Single IP addresses are supported by CloudFront at an additional charge, and SNI is the default configuration at no additional charge.

CloudFront Security

CloudFront supports multiple security options. Front-end Internet-based denial-of-service protection is included at no cost when deploying a CloudFront distribution. AWS uses its *Shield* service in front of all edge locations. Shield will protect the edge from distributed denial-of-service (DDoS) attacks. Shield includes automatic inline attack mitigation support to protect your site from common attacks at no additional charge.

The *Web Application Firewall* (WAF) and many third-party firewalls can be combined with CloudFront for application-level perimeter security.

Field-level encryption for CloudFront allows sensitive user data to be uploaded to the edge location in a secure manner. Sensitive data can include medical or financial records. With field-level encryption, data will be encrypted in transit to the origin site using customer-provided keys. Field-level encryption complements SSL/TLS encryption in that it can encrypt fields in the stream such as credit card numbers that only a small group of users or microservices need to access. This prevents sensitive data from being exposed when it is decrypted after arriving to the origin over a TLS connection. The CloudFront edge locations will encrypt sensitive fields such as credit card numbers using the origin's public key. When the origin receives the traffic from the edge, it will use its private key to decrypt the data. This allows for a granular security approach at the origin of your data.

CloudFront edge interfaces support SNI or SSL/TLS. SNI includes the domain or server name in the connection request and is an extension of the TLS specification. This allows a single IP address to support multiple domains, each with its own SSL/TLS certificate, as was described earlier. When an SSL/TLS connection request is processed at the edge, there may be many different domains associated with its IP address, and each domain will have its own SSL/TLS certificate. By using SNI, the TLS header is read, and the connection request is forwarded to the correct domain to complete the secure connection handshake.

CloudFront supports HTTP cookies to enable customized or dynamic content. Cloud-Front will analyze the cookies and determine if the object can be serviced from its local cache or need to be forwarded to the origin for processing. Performance is enhanced by serving objects at the edge where possible and custom content from the origin. All requests can be tracked and recorded by using the CloudFront monitoring service.

Headers can be created or modified by CloudFront before they are sent to the origin. This allows for enhanced security by validating that the information was received from Cloud-Front and not a bogus imposter. The origin can be configured to only accept requests from CloudFront. Custom header configurations are offered at no charge and configured using the management interface or API calls.

Dynamic content such as search results often includes the query string in the URL. These strings can be used as a key to identify objects in the local edge cache. Dynamic content can then be stored at the edge; for example, changing sports scores or short-term search values can be served from the edge cache based on the values in the URL query string. To filter up to 10 specific values in the URL parameters, the whitelisting feature is used. This narrows the match to a subset of the values in the cache key and forwards all of the parameters to the origin. Supported parameter types are between the HTTP GET after the ? character and the & delimiter character. These types are noted in RFC 3986.

When you set up CloudFront and use an S3 bucket as the origin of your content, the S3 URL may still be exposed to the Internet, allowing users to bypass CloudFront and pull data directly from S3, which can be a major security violation.

Internet users can source data directly from the S3 origin if not blocked from doing so. This can be prevented by configuring Origin Access Identity (OAI). To restrict users' direct S3 access and require them to use only CloudFront, a signed URL can be configured. Also, by forcing all requests through CloudFront edge locations, additional features can be leveraged such as restricting access by IP address or location. Also, more detailed logging and metrics are collected in CloudWatch. Up to 100 CloudFront OAIs can be applied to any number of distributions. This feature is enabled in the CloudFront console under the S3 bucket access tab or the `CreateCloudFrontOriginAccessIdentity` API. S3 bucket policies can also be used to give the OAI access to the bucket. Since the OAI is attached to the CloudFront distribution and uniquely identifies it, an S3 bucket policy can be applied to allow only that OAI and deny all other connection requests. Origins such as EC2 and application load balancers do not support OAIs. The solution for this is to create a custom HTTP/HTTPS header in the origin request configured in CloudFront. If the custom header is not configured and is not received at the origin, it will refuse the connection. Another option is to use the IP address blocks used by AWS, which they publish to restrict access. Access control lists can then be defined at the availability zone level to only allow access to the content from the IP edge location address blocks.

Billing

Billing is for the actual usage of CloudFront and does not require minimum charges or any time commitments. Billing is based on the amount of data you transmit out from the edge locations to the Internet and is charged by the gigabyte. Charges from the CloudFront services to the origins, either AWS or in a private data center, are also billed by the gigabyte transferred. The number of HTTP/HTTPS requests and, finally, invalidation requests made to remote objects from the cache are also chargeable.

The first TB of data transferred out each month is at no cost, and HTTP/HTTPS billing is in 10,000-request increments. Large volume customers transmitting more than 10TB per month are eligible for a discount with the AWS volume pricing plans.

Lambda@edge

In addition to CloudFront serving content, it also supports the AWS Lambda microservice compute platform. Lambda@edge supports local processing at the edge location of Node.js and Python Lambda runtimes, as shown in Figure 1.6. This allows processing to be done closer to the user requests and eliminates the need to provision servers at the origin. Lambda can also be used to modify CloudFront requests and responses at the endpoint closest to the user making the request. This results in a much faster response time. For example, processing can be done locally at the edge origin to inspect cookies and take action based on the content and to rewrite URLs. Different objects can be returned to the requester based on header information such as the user-agent that identifies the device type such as a mobile phone or tablet. Lambda@edge is used for header inspection for authorization to perform access control closer to the source of the request. Headers can be modified by Lambda to direct the connection requests to different objects stored in the cache. Unauthenticated users can be redirected to sign-up pages by using Lambda to generate responses based on the viewer requests.

FIGURE 1.6   Lambda@edge

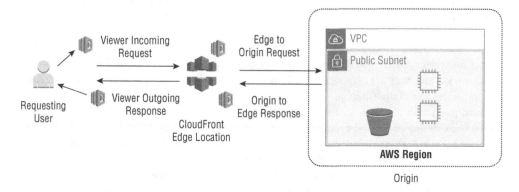

Geo-restriction and Geolocation

CloudFront is a global service with edge locations all over the planet. When a distribution is created, all the edge locations are included, and there are no restrictions placed on who can access that information at the CloudFront level. Access to the CloudFront CDN edge locations can be restricted for security or compliance reasons by using *geo-restrictions*, as shown in Figure 1.7. CloudFront will monitor incoming connection requests and based on the geo-restriction configuration either allow or deny the connections. When the service is enabled, the edge location will query a GeoIP database to see if the source IP (which maps to a country) is either allowed or denied. If it is allowed, the connection is allowed to proceed as usual. However, if it is not allowed, a 403 forbidden status code is returned to the requester.

FIGURE 1.7   Geo-restriction

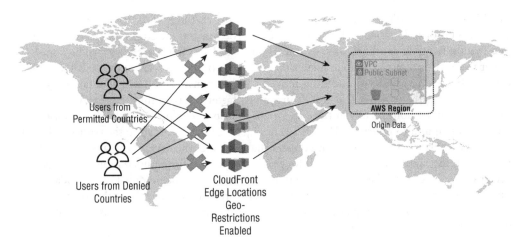

The first and most basic feature that is built into the standard CloudFront service allows for either a whitelist (permit only what is on this list and deny all others) or blacklist (deny based on the blacklist and allow all others). The GeoIP database uses restrictions based on country codes that map to assigned IP address blocks for each country. With the basic geo-restriction service, either you define all country codes allowed with a whitelist or you define the country codes that are blocked and allow all others with a backlist. These apply across all edge nodes in the distribution.

Third-party companies offer extensions to CloudFront that vary depending on each company's offerings and that are often referred to as *geolocations*. CloudFront will check a database for restrictions that are provided by the services offered, as shown in Figure 1.8. This can, for example, include attributes such as login status, profiles, header information, information in cookies, and licensing. Check the AWS Marketplace for current products being offered. Third-party geo-restrictions are much more flexible than the fixed-country-only geo-restriction model offered by AWS. With geolocations, the architecture is significantly different than geo-restrictions. The third-party application servers receive the connection requests in front of the AWS edge nodes. These application servers terminate the connection and query their database to either allow or block with a 403 restricted error. In this case, the third-party providers use CloudFront as a front end and use the AWS Cloud-Front network as a private backend network. If the connections are permitted, then a signed URL or cookie is returned to the requester, and a connection is made directly with the edge location. Given that they terminate the connection, they can allow for deep inspection of many different parameters beyond just the country code to allow you to granularly meet your geolocation requirements.

FIGURE 1.8   Geolocation

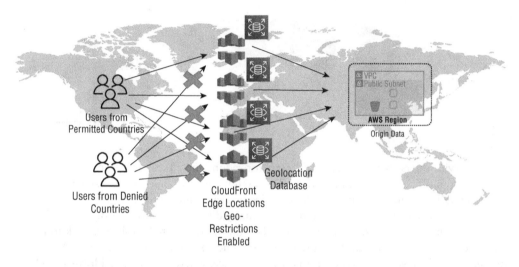

Global Accelerator

When accessing AWS resources over the Internet, traffic is routed from your local connection over the Internet to the region requested over many hops and, often, across many different Internet providers and backbone carriers. This can cause additional latency and suboptimal performance. The AWS *Global Accelerator* service can greatly improve network performance by routing traffic to the nearest edge location and transporting the traffic over the AWS internal high-speed backbone network to its destination. By using Global Accelerator, traffic flows are optimized from the requester to the AWS services being accessed by having users connect to the AWS at the closest location possible, as illustrated in Figure 1.9.

The service offers a single IP anycast address as an entry point that maps to multiple AWS regions and services. By using the same IP address at many locations, the user connections can be connected as close to the source as possible.

The global edge network is constantly being expanded by AWS and currently includes 102 access points in 47 countries. See the AWS Global Accelerator page for updates: https://aws.amazon.com/global-accelerator/features.

FIGURE 1.9   Global Accelerator high-level architecture

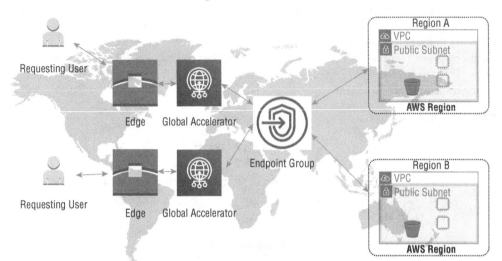

The service offers two IP *anycast addresses* for redundancy; these act as entry points that map to multiple regions and services. This architecture also allows for resiliency by providing failover and rerouting should a service or availability zone go offline. An Anycast address is an IP address that can be assigned to many different locations or devices and advertised simultaneously from all locations. This allows the routed public network to pick the closest Anycast address to the source thereby reducing hop counts and latency. A normal IP unicast address would be assigned to only one device, whereas Anycast addresses can be assigned to any number of devices and the source requester selects the Global Accelerator edge location that is closest. This allows traffic to move off of the public Internet and onto the AWS backbone network at a closer entry point to increase network performance by reducing the delays and hop counts from source to the AWS destination. By using the AWS global backbone network, there will be fewer router hops and better performance.

When you configure a Global Accelerator service, two IP addresses for redundancy will be assigned for your use and advertised into the public Internet. Upon entering the AWS global backbone network, you will transit over the AWS high-speed inter-region network optical connections.

While this may sound a lot like CloudFront, there are significant differences between the two services. CloudFront moves the content closer to the users using edge location caching (it is a content distribution network), whereas Global Accelerator locates the AWS network entry point closer to your end users for a faster network connection to your content and services in AWS regions. Think of CloudFront as caching and Global Accelerator as data transport. Also, CloudFront is used for caching HTTP/HTTPS data, whereas Global Accelerator transports any kind of TCP or UDP traffic. Since Global Accelerator is a network-layer product, it does not recognize service ports such as HTTP/80 or HTTPS/443, and it does not cache data at the edge.

A speed comparison tool is available to compare the advantages of using Global Accelerator over the public Internet: https://speedtest.globalaccelerator.aws/#. Figure 1.10 shows a sample speed comparison test.

FIGURE 1.10 Global Accelerator speed comparison test

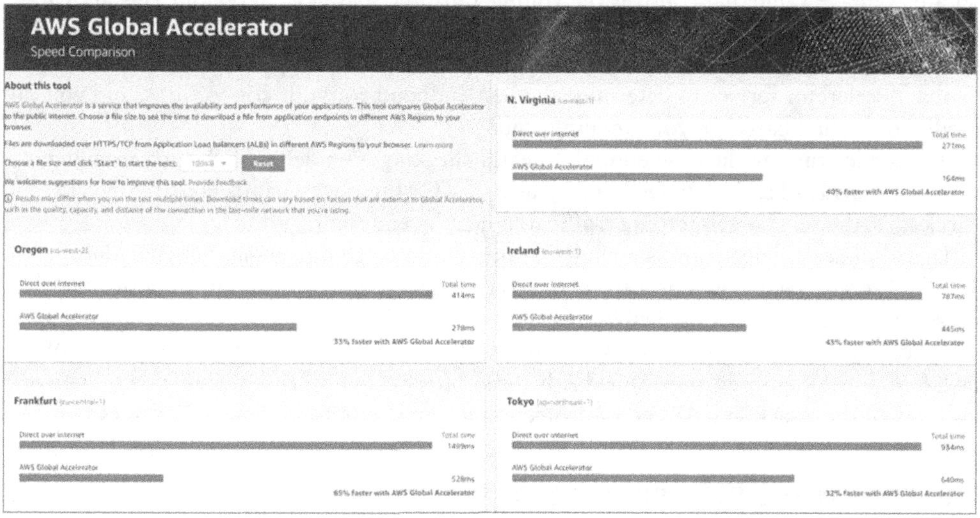

Global Accelerator Architecture

The Anycast IP addresses are injected into the Internet's BGP tables to advertise each public interface into the AWS network. The same IP address is advertised for each edge location to allow traffic to enter the network at its closest entry point from the user by using BGP reachability metrics. This reduces the number of hops over the public Internet to increase speed and decrease network latency by entering and traversing the AWS internal network as soon as possible. These IP addresses are publicly accessible front ends to your AWS services such as EC2 instance, elastic and network load balancers, and Elastic IP addresses.

High availability is achieved with fault tolerance using networking zones. These zones isolate the failure domain with separate network infrastructure inside the AWS backbone network. If one of the Anycast IP addresses goes offline because of a zone issue, the other remains available to route traffic. Remember, two IP addresses are assigned when creating a Global Accelerator instance. The end user is connected to the nearest location, and a TCP three-way handshake is performed from the AWS network edge to the client. TCP traffic is terminated at the point of presence or endpoint. Then a second TCP connection is created from the edge to the AWS application endpoint. This increases the end-to-end performance between the user and the application.

If your requirements are to use your own IPv4 address blocks, you can allocate up to two /24 blocks to the Global Accelerator service. This is often referred to as *bring-your-own IP* (BYOIP) and has a maximum of 512 addresses. Your public addresses can be assigned to endpoints when you create your accelerator. Two blocks are usually used for redundancy, but there is an option to use one of your own address blocks and the second from the AWS pool.

Traffic engineering allows you to define flow allocations to specific regions. These "dials" set a percentage value that controls the volume of traffic sent to each region. This allows you to do blue/green deployments of new or updated code releases or to use them in failover scenarios. The default setting of 100 percent for each region's endpoint groups allows the Global Accelerator service to determine the best endpoint for your connections, and you can modify the values based on your requirements.

The service runs application endpoint health checking with definable health-checking values such as HTTP/HTTPS GETs or by using a TCP three-way handshake. If a health check fails, the service will reroute traffic to a healthy endpoint.

Denial-of-service detection is included at no additional charge using the *AWS Shield* Standard service. Shield acts as a front end to the edge locations by monitoring the data flows and blocking incoming denial-of-service exploits. For an additional charge, AWS Shield Advanced can be purchased; it adds features such as 24/7 technical support from the AWS DDoS response support group. Shield Advanced offers many other features such as network visibility of the attack and AWS cost protection for any additional incurred charges.

Custom Routing Accelerator

Custom routing accelerators extend the capabilities to allow you to map specific application IP ports to destinations in one or more AWS regions that you define. This capability allows you to control the destination devices across the AWS network as compared to standard accelerators that do not support routing to a specific destination. Specific ports are configured on your accelerator, and that port gets mapped to a destination you define. Custom accelerators allow you to define global entry locations into the AWS network with Anycast, and then you control the destination region and service.

If your application requires that an incoming request to be connected to a specific EC2 instance, for example, a custom routing accelerator can be used to route that connection request, regardless of where it enters the AWS network, to that instance and the application running on it.

The connection coming into the custom accelerator gets statically mapped to a specific endpoint's private IP address based on the entry point's port number.

AWS Global Accelerator Pricing

AWS Global Accelerator has two pricing components, a flat hourly rate and a premium data transport fee.

The hourly or partial hourly flat rate is charged regardless of the status of the accelerator; if it is either enabled or disabled, it will be charged. Traffic pricing is based on the dominant flow direction of the traffic. If your traffic patterns are greater for outbound to the customer, then that is what the billing will be based on. Conversely, if inbound volumes are highest, then inbound will be dominant and used for billing. See https://aws.amazon.com/global-accelerator/pricing for more detailed information.

Elastic Load Balancers

Load balancing addresses the issues found when cloud workloads and connections increase to the point where a single server can no longer handle the workload or performance requirements of the web, DNS, and FTP servers; firewalls; and other network services. Load balancer functions include offloading applications and tasks from the application servers, such as the processing for SSL/TLS, compression, and TCP handshakes. With load balancing, you can configure the cloud for many servers working together and sharing the load. Therefore, redundancy and scalability can be achieved.

A *load balancer* is commonly found in front of web servers. The website's IP address is advertised on the network via DNS. This IP address is not of the real web server but instead is an interface on the load balancer. The load balancer allocates the traffic by distributing the connections to one of many servers connected to it. Load balancing allows a website to scale by allocating many servers in the cloud to handle the workload. Also, a load balancer can check the health of each server and remove a server from the network; if there is a hardware, network, or application issue, they can also terminate secure connections such as SSL/TLS to offload security processing from the web servers.

Users can experience a consistent experience by leveraging the elastic nature of the AWS ELB services. For example, if a website is having a special event and the connections increase beyond the existing servers' ability to handle the workload, *autoscaling* can be used to add servers during this period and remove them when the workload returns to normal. If a web server should fail, it can be removed, deleted, restarted, or reinstalled.

Load Balancer Architectures

ELB architectures include Internet-facing or internal configurations. When assigned a public IP address and configured to be reachable from the Internet, an AWS Elastic Load Balancer instance can service public connections by acting as a front end to the backend services that can be inaccessible to the public and be in a private VPC for security.

ELBs can be used for internal VPC architectures to load balance inside your environment in a private VPC, for example.

Listeners

A *listener* is an IP address/port number combination that accepts incoming connections to the load balancer. When configuring listeners, you set how the connection requests are processed and sent to the backend services called *targets*.

Listeners support HTTP and HTTPS connections on a port that you define between 1 and 65535. TCP offload can be set to decrypt SSL/TLS connections on the ELB to eliminate the server decryption workload. Listeners support WebSockets HTTP/2 and can service up to 128 parallel requests per connection.

A listener must have a rule assigned to it to set the priority, actions to be performed, and any conditions. Rules can be added, removed, or edited after the ELB has been brought online. If there are no custom rules defined, then the default rule is used. Conditions in the rules can be applied using a large number of parameters such as source IP, header values, and methods such as GET or PUT or URL, plus many others.

Actions include how authentication is to be handled such as using AWS *Cognito* and who the identity providers will be, HTTP responses, x-forwarded headers, redirects, and subdomain and top-level domain names.

Target Groups

A *target group* is a listing of endpoint targets used to make backend connections to. Target groups are defined when setting a rule for the listener. When conditions are met in the rule, traffic is forwarded to the target groups. Different target groups get created for different request types and applications running on the backend target and servers.

Health checks are created in the target group as they may need to be compatible with the specific configurations for the servers in the group. If the health checks are healthy, connections are allowed to the target servers.

Health Checking

One of the advantages of using a load balancer is to achieve high availability by checking to see if the backend servers are healthy before sending connections to them. For example, if you have 10 web servers in a pool, the ELB will send periodic health check requests to them to make sure they respond. If there is no response, the server is considered to be down and removed from the pool.

Sticky Connections

Sticky connections bind a user's connections though the ELB to a specific target for the duration of the connection. All connections from the user for the session will always be directed to the same backend target. Some applications maintain state information at the server level such as checkout carts or other session tracking data. If the ELB were to direct a user's connection to different servers during a session, that information could be lost. Sticky, or, as it is often called, *session affinity*, allows for connection persistence to the target for the duration of the session. Cookie support must be enabled to ensure the client can be identified and directed to the current connection on a specific target. Cookies can be either ELB or application generated.

Application load balancers allow for cookies that are duration based or application based. When configuring a target group, combinations of duration, application based, and no stickiness are supported. ELB-generated cookies are locally encrypted with a rotating key, and you are not allowed to decrypt them or to modify the AWS load balancer–generated cookies.

Stickiness using a duration-based configuration directs requests to a specific target, or server, in a target group for the duration of the session using a load balancer–generated cookie. The cookie is used to map the client connection to the same target server. The session duration time value is defined in the target group. When a request is first received from the client, the ELB uses its configured connection algorithm (such as round-robin) to make the initial connection to the target server. The ELB also generates a cookie named AWSALB that contains information about the target. This cookie is encrypted by AWS and sent to the client in the HTTP response. This cookie manages the sticky connection and has an expiration date of 7 days, which cannot be changed. If the target should fail during the session, a new target is selected, and the cookie is updated and sent to the client. When cross-origin resource sharing (CORS) is used in combination with sticky sessions, a second cookie is generated called AWSALBCORS that contains the same information as the original except for the different domain name.

Stickiness based on applications is also supported on the AWS application load balancer. As with other sticky types, when a request is first received from the client, the ELB uses its configured connection algorithm (such as round-robin) to make the initial connection to the target server. Then a server-based cookie is used to maintain client to target affinity. Note that this cookie is not generated by the application load balancer. However, the load balancer will then take the application-received cookie and automatically create a new application cookie that is AWS encrypted. Both the application cookie and the load balancer cookies are sent to the client for the session. All following requests will use both cookies, with the load balancer using its generated cookie, and the application references the cookie it created for the session.

Most browsers support cookie sizes of up to 4Kb. If the cookies are larger than this, the ELB will fragment them into shards and reference the shard number in the cookie such as AWSALBAPP-0 and then AWSALBAPP-1, incrementing to the size of the cookies in 4Kb blocks.

Proxy Connections

Proxy protocol connections are used by the classic load balancer to inject source and destination IP addresses and port numbers into the connection request by the load balancer before sending it to the target server. Both TCP and SSL/TLS support is standard. Many applications require this data to not be modified by the load balancer, so the proxy protocol was created to allow the source information to pass through the load balancer and into the web target servers.

Since the application load balancer inserts X-Forwarded_For HTTP headers, proxy protocol support is not required on that platform. On network load balancers, the IP source information is passed through, so there is no need to support the proxy protocol. Only on the classic load balancer is proxy protocol supported. Note that if you are already running the proxy protocol on another device in front of the classic load balancer, you do not enable it on the ELB as they will interfere with each other.

Load Balancing Across Different Availability Zones

AWS availability zones are physically and logically separated data centers in a region. By placing groups of servers into different availability zones and load balancing the workloads between them, resiliency can be achieved. If an AZ should go offline for whatever reason, then the workload can shift to the remaining AZ for continuity.

Cross-zone load balancing is supported in both the application and classic load balancers, as shown in Figure 1.11. This feature allows you to load balance across AZs and not have standby servers in a separate availability zone for fault tolerance.

FIGURE 1.11   Cross-zone load balancing

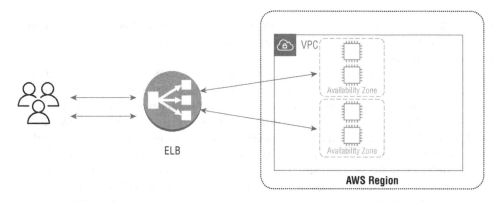

Layer 7 application load balancing allows us to make connection decisions based on many different data points such as URLs, headers, cookies, or any other attribute.

Deployments can be either internal when configured with an internal VPC IP address or external to the Internet with a public, Internet-facing IP address. Security groups and access control lists can be configured in your VPC for security. When the ALB is external facing, AWS Shield or Shield Advanced protects your data from Internet exploits.

ALB supports the latest SSL/TLS security transforms and current features such as HTTP/2 that can use 256 sessions on a single connection from the client. Inter-service microservice communications can leverage the gRPC now available in the ALB using HTTP/2.

HTTPS support is integrated with AWS Certificate Manager and Identity and Access Manager (IAM). SSL/TLS offload allows the load balancer to perform all encrypt and decrypt operations on the platform to reduce the encryption burden normally assumed by the target servers. Predefined policies can be used to simplify the configuration process.

Connection Draining

When a server is being taken offline or disabled, connection draining can be implemented to allow existing connections to complete their operations and prevent any new connections from being made to the server. This allows for a nondisruptive operation that is transparent to the end users. Connection draining is sometimes called a *deregistration delay*. When enabling this feature, you will need to specify a time period that the ELB will maintain the connections before deregistration takes effect. The default value is 300 seconds (5 minutes) with a supported range of 1 to 3,600 seconds (one hour). When the time value is reached, the connections are forced off the device.

AWS Load Balancer Offerings

AWS offers three types of elastic load balancers with each designed for a specific use case. In this section we will learn about these AWS service offerings, what they do, how they are different, and which load balancer in the family is the best fit for a given requirement.

Tables 1.1 through 1.6 show a side-by-side feature comparison of the load balancer products currently offered by AWS.

TABLE 1.1   AWS ELB Product Comparisons: ELB Types

Feature	Application Load Balancer	Network Load Balancer	Gateway Load Balancer	Classic Load Balancer
Load balancer type	Layer 7	Layer 4	Layer 3 gateway + layer 4 load balancing	Layer 4/7
Target type	IP, instance, Lambda	IP, instance, Application Load Balancer	IP, instance	
Terminates flow/ proxy behavior	Yes	Yes	No	Yes
Protocol listeners	HTTP, HTTPS, gRPC	TCP, UDP, TLS	IP	TCP, SSL/TLS, HTTP, HTTPS
Reachable via	VIP	VIP	Route table entry	VIP

TABLE 1.2   AWS ELB Product Comparisons: Layer 7

Feature	Application Load Balancer	Network Load Balancer	Gateway Load Balancer	Classic Load Balancer
Load balancer type	Layer 7	Layer 4	Layer 3 gateway + layer 4 load balancing	Layer 4/7
Redirects	✔			

continues

TABLE 1.2   AWS ELB Product Comparisons: Layer 7 *(continued)*

Feature	Application Load Balancer	Network Load Balancer	Gateway Load Balancer	Classic Load Balancer
Fixed response	✔			
Desync mitigation mode	✔			
HTTP header-based routing	✔			
HTTP/2gRPC	✔			

TABLE 1.3   AWS ELB Product Comparisons: Characteristics

Feature	Application Load Balancer	Network Load Balancer	Gateway Load Balancer	Classic Load Balancer
Load balancer type	Layer 7	Layer 4	Layer 3 gateway + layer 4 load balancing	Layer 4/7
Common configurations and characteristics				
Slow start	✔			
Outpost support	✔			
Local zone	✔			
IP address - static, elastic		✔		
Connection draining (deregistration delay)	✔	✔	✔	✔
Configurable idle connection timeout	✔			✔
PrivateLink support		✔ (TCP, TLS)	✔ (GWLBe)	
Zonal Isolation		✔	✔	
Session resumption	✔	✔		

TABLE 1.3   AWS ELB Product Comparisons: Characteristics *(continued)*

Feature	Application Load Balancer	Network Load Balancer	Gateway Load Balancer	Classic Load Balancer
Long-lived TCP connection		✔	✔	
Load balancing to multiple ports on the same instance	✔	✔	✔	
Load balancer deletion protection	✔	✔	✔	
Preserve source IP address	✔	✔	✔	
WebSockets	✔	✔	✔	
Supported network/platforms	VPC	VPC	VPC	EC2-Classic, VPC
Cross-zone load balancing	✔	✔	✔	✔
IAM permissions (resource, tag based)	✔	✔	✔	✔ (Only resource-based)
Flow stickiness (All packets of a flow are sent to one target, and return traffic comes from same target)	Symmetric	Symmetric	Symmetric	Symmetric
Target failure behavior	Fail close on targets, unless all targets are unhealthy (fail open)	Fail close on targets, unless all targets are unhealthy (fail open)	Existing flows continue to go to existing target appliances, new flows are rerouted to healthy target appliances	
Health checks	HTTP, HTTPS, gRPC	TCP, HTTP, HTTPS	TCP, HTTP, HTTPS	TCP, SSL/TLS, HTTP, HTTPS
Security				
SSL offloading	✔	✔		✔

continues

TABLE 1.3   AWS ELB Product Comparisons: Characteristics *(continued)*

Feature	Application Load Balancer	Network Load Balancer	Gateway Load Balancer	Classic Load Balancer
Server Name Indication (SNI)	✔	✔		
Backend server encryption	✔	✔		✔
User authentication	✔			
Custom security policy				✔
ALPN	✔	✔		

TABLE 1.4   AWS ELB Security

Feature	Application Load Balancer	Network Load Balancer	Gateway Load Balancer	Classic Load Balancer
Load balancer type	Layer 7	Layer 4	Layer 3 gateway + layer 4 load balancing	Layer 4/7
Security				
SSL offloading	✔	✔		✔
Server Name Indication (SNI)	✔	✔		
Backend server encryption	✔	✔		✔
User authentication	✔			
Custom security policy				✔
ALPN	✔	✔		

TABLE 1.5　AWS ELB Kubernetes Controller

Feature	Application Load Balancer	Network Load Balancer	Gateway Load Balancer	Classic Load Balancer
Load balancer type	Layer 7	Layer 4	Layer 3 gateway + layer 4 load balancing	Layer 4/7
Kubernetes controller				
Direct-to-pod	✔	✔ (Fargate pods)		
Load balance to multiple namespaces	✔			
Support for fully private EKS clusters	✔	✔		

TABLE 1.6　AWS ELB Logging and Monitoring

Feature	Application Load Balancer	Network Load Balancer	Gateway Load Balancer	Classic Load Balancer
Load balancer type	Layer 7	Layer 4	Layer 3 gateway + layer 4 load balancing	Layer 4/7
Logging and monitoring				
CloudWatch metrics	✔	✔	✔	✔
Logging	✔	✔	✔	✔

Application Load Balancers

The AWS application load balancer (ALB) is at the high end of the ELB family of load balancers. As the name indicates, it operates at the application layer, or layer 7, of the OSI stack and has a long list of features, as outlined in Figure 1.12. The listener supports unencrypted HTTP or encrypted HTTPS SSL/TLS traffic. On the back end, targets can include micro-services such as Lambda, containers such as Kubernetes or Docker, EC2 virtual servers, IP addresses, and both local and remote services inside and external to the AWS cloud. The ALB is supported in all AWS regions on the outposts on-premise AWS racks.

FIGURE 1.12   ALB features

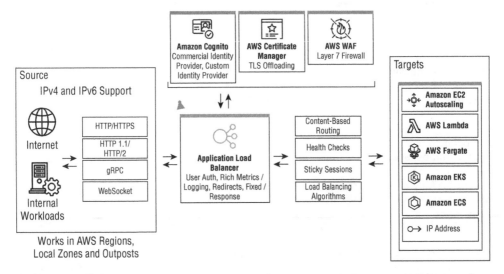

Layer 7 application load balancing allows us to make connection decisions based on many different data points such as the URL, headers, cookies, or any other attribute.

ALBs can be either internal when configured with an internal VPC IP address or external to the Internet with a public-facing IP address. Security groups and access control lists can be configured in your VPC for security. When the ALB is external facing, AWS services such as Shield and Shield Advanced protect your deployment from external exploits from the Internet.

ALB supports the latest SSL/TLS security transforms and current features such as HTTP/2 that can use 256 sessions of a single connection from the client. Inter-service microservice communications can leverage the gRPC support now available in the application load balancer using HTTP/2.

HTTPS support is integrated with AWS Certificate Manager and IAM. SSL/TLS offload allows the load balancer to perform all encrypt and decrypt operations on the platform to reduce the encryption burden normally assumed by the target servers. Predefined policies can be used to simplify the security configuration process.

For sites that have multiple domains and secure websites behind a single IP address, there is SNI, which supports multiple SSL/TLS certificates. As we discussed previously, sticky session support is part of the ALB. Inside a VPC, IPv4 and IPv6 are supported. Application support includes trace support by using the x-Amzn-Trace-Id HTTP header and allows us to trace the data through the AWS site for troubleshooting and monitoring at the request level. Redirects from one URL to another are included and often used to redirect unencrypted

HTTP port 80 traffic to HTTPS port 443 listeners to force client SSL/TLS connection encryption or from an old site to a new website under the same URL. WebSocket support, as we covered, is supported. IP addresses can be assigned as targets to route connections to on-site data center web targets or to specific interfaces on a large server that may have many IP addresses and interfaces. Lambda function invocation by the ALB allows Lambda services to be spun up based on the content of the incoming request. The load balancers can connect to the various microservices and change IP and port numbers dynamically to allow for completely serverless application deployments.

Content-based routing directs incoming requests to the desired backend locations by switching based on the host field, URL path, HTTP header, HTTP method, source IP address, or query string.

Container supports load balancing over many ports on the same EC2 instance. ALB is integrated with the Elastic Container Service (ECS) that is completely managed by AWS. There is an ECS scheduler that automatically adds a dynamic port in a container task definition.

The WAF can be implemented as a front end to the ALB for web protection from common exploits. Connections are round-robin with slow start connection support to prevent the web servers coming online from being overwhelmed with a flood of new connection requests.

User authentication on the load balancer offloads the operations from the individual target servers and centralizes administration from many servers to a single load balancer. Cloud authentication services are supported by Facebook, Google, and Amazon using Cognito as well as enterprise identities such as Auth and Microsoft Active Directory services using SAML and OpenID connectors.

ALB pricing is based on the hours (or partial hour) that the load balancer is operational and the number of capacity units used per hour.

Gateway Load Balancers

Gateway load balancers are used with virtual network appliances at the network layer 3 of the OSI model. The listener uses a transparent network gateway to distribute traffic across networking devices such as intrusion detection/prevention systems, firewalls, compliance validation, policy enforcement, and deep packet inspection appliances. On-demand scaling allows for the dynamic allocation of these resources based on the current traffic load. Figure 1.13 lists the gateway load balancer feature sets.

The gateway load balancer listens across all ports in an IP flow and forwards the traffic you define in a listener rule to target groups. Sticky connections are used for session persistence, and UDP and TCP connections are supported. Generic Network Virtualization Encapsulation (GENEVE) is supported; GENEVE is a network encapsulation protocol that uses port 6081. GENEVE encapsulates frames in a special header that overcomes some of the limitations of VxLAN and Generic Routing Encapsulation (GRE) for use in large multitenant cloud deployments such as AWS. The main difference is that the header can contain system state information and is extensible so it can evolve over time to meet future use cases.

Load balancer endpoints are used to exchange traffic across VPC boundaries. This allows a service provider and customer to securely exchange traffic across VPCs. The gateway load balancer is deployed in the VPC where the virtual appliances reside and the appliances are registered with the load balancer using target groups. The traffic flows to the gateway load balancer in the service provider's VPC from the customer's VPCs and are routed using standard routing. Figure 1.14 shows the interconnect model.

FIGURE 1.13   Gateway load balancer features

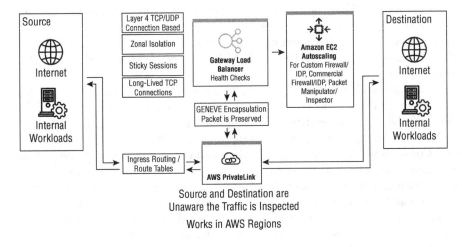

FIGURE 1.14   Gateway load balancer VPC interconnections

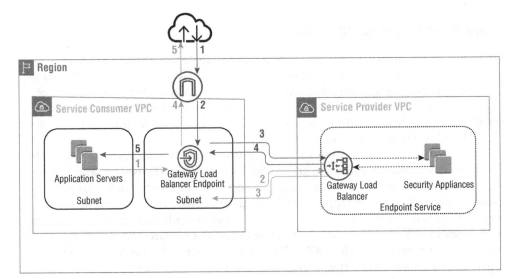

There are many AWS networking security partners that offer a wide variety of services that are integrated with the gateway load balancer. A current list can be found at `https://aws.amazon.com/elasticloadbalancing/partners`.

Gateway load balancer pricing is based on each hour (or partial hour) that the load balancer is running and the number of gateway load balancing capacity units consumed per hour. Charges for the gateway load balancer endpoint that is a VPC private link endpoint and partner service offerings are billed separately.

Network Load Balancer

The AWS *network load balancer* (NLB) is used for very high-performance use cases and operates at the network layer, layer 4, of the OSI model. The service has a lengthy list of features, as illustrated in Figure 1.15. The NLB can handle millions of connections per second and is used in very demanding and large implementations that benefit from high-throughput, low-latency connections. It supports large connection bursts and highly variable traffic patterns and uses a single IP address per availability zone. Targets can include EC2 instances, microservices, Lambda, and containers such as ECS and EKS. Both TCP and UDP IP connections are supported.

FIGURE 1.15   NLB features

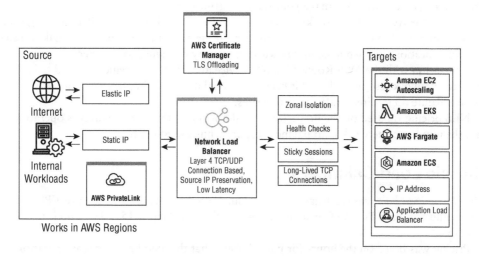

When an NLB is created in an availability zone, the ELB node gets created in that AZ to service local nodes that are only in that AZ. Cross-zone load balancing is also supported, and the NLB, when configured in this mode, will also load balance targets in other availability zones external to where it is configured. By configuring multiple availability zone targets in a target group, high availability is achieved and will continue to operate even if the AZ goes offline by utilizing DNS to route traffic to load balancers in other zones. Targets can be added or removed during production operations. The service can scale up or down by adding and removing targets dynamically to meet load requirements.

High performance is achieved by using a hash for each connection that is based on the TCP protocol, source and destination IP addresses and port numbers, and the TCP sequence number. Each session based on its unique hash value is routed to a single target for the duration of the session. UDP traffic also sets up connections based on hashes, but since UDP does not contain sequence numbers, it uses source and destination IP addresses and port numbers.

The load balancer will create a new network interface in every availability zone it is configured to operate in and receives a static IP address. If the load balancer is Internet-facing, one Classic IP for each subnet can be associated with its listener interface.

Health checks are configured to monitor the targets, so connections are forwarded only to healthy endpoints.

The ELB is integrated with other AWS services such as AWS Certificate Manager, ECS container services, autoscaling, CloudTrail, Elastic Beanstalk, CloudWatch, CodeDeploy, and CloudFormation.

SSL/TLS client session termination acts as an SSL offload for the backend targets. SSL/TLS security policies are predefined and offer a large selection to meet your specific security requirements and allow for older browser support. Amazon Certificate Manager and IAM are options you can use to manage your digital certificates.

As with the ALB, SNI and sticky session features are included. Source IP addressing is preserved and passed to the target servers. You can use static IP addressing, which makes security configurations and whitelisting/blacklisting security configurations easier.

Integration with the AWS Route 53 DNS service allows DNS to remove a load balancer from the network resources should it become unavailable. By using DNS for failover, you can use Route 53 to direct traffic to active sites.

NLB pricing is based on the hours (or partial hour) that the load balancer is operational and the number of network load balancer capacity units used per hour.

Classic Load Balancers

The *classic load balancer* is a legacy service from AWS that was used on the pre-VPC EC2 classic and Standard EC2 VPC instances. It was retired on August 15, 2022, and is no longer available.

Pricing was based on the hours (or partial hour) that the load balancer was operational with an additional charge for each GB of data passing through the classic load balancer.

Configuring Elastic Load Balancers

It's interesting to find the load balancer service's main configuration screen in the AWS console under the EC2 tab, but that's where you will find it.

Configuration support can be accomplished in many different ways, including the AWS graphical user interface, CLI, APIs, and CloudFormation.

API Gateway

API Gateway is the AWS managed serverless service that acts as a front end to your data, services, and backend servers. While the topic of APIs is in the developer realm and covered in the AWS Certified Developer Associate and Professional certifications, it is important to understand. You should know how the networking architectures are used to properly deploy them in your environment.

An API is a standard data interchange format primarily used by applications to communicate with each other. This prevents the need to design custom software interfaces for each service or application. API Gateway is a suite of protocols defining a standardized structure for one process to send and receive information with another. The API Gateway is a server front end that receives API requests in a standardized format and passes the request to backend services and returns the response to the requester. Additional features such as rate limiting, caching, and security are also part of this AWS service. API Gateway acts as a front-end software interface for many applications and services such as Lambda, EC2, ELB, containers, microservices, databases, and on-premise servers, to name a few examples. The service is low cost and scales automatically based on traffic loads.

APIs allow each API endpoint to be sent to a different backend target where each can be a totally different service. Think of API Gateway as a single front door to all of your backend AWS services.

APIs operate behind the scenes when communicating with applications and services. For example, all AWS console and web functions are user front ends to API calls. If you click a console operation, it makes an API call to invoke the action. Creating and deploying APIs can be rather complex and require a lot of up-front programming. With API Gateway, AWS offers this functionality as a service; AWS manages the API application instead of having to create it internally in your organization.

API Gateway allows you to create and configure APIs by using the AWS Management Console, the AWS CLI, APIs, CloudFormation, or language-specific SDKs. Usage of your APIs is logged and integrated with AWS management tools such as CloudWatch and CloudTrail. To restrict the impact of outside attacks or unintended large bills, the APIs can be configured to throttle requests. Versioning is supported, so you can, for example, have TEST/DEV/PROD versions. User authentication is also supported.

REST API

REST stands for Representational State Transfer. The REST architecture, or *RESTful API*, is a well-defined schema that allows dissimilar devices and services to interact with each other. The REST API makes calls to the API gateway, which, in turn, proxies the request to backend services in any format required.

The REST API's main elements are a client that is the software that makes the request, the server (or gateway) that is the access point to the data, and the resource that is the content or data being requested such as an image, data file, or video clip.

The REST requests include the HTTP method (GET, PUT, POST, or DELETE) endpoint information that is in a URL format that is the pointer to where the resource is located on the Internet, the headers, and the body of information. The headers contain data about the request such as authentication information, the IP address, or the name of the computer where the data is located and formatting information. The body contains information to the servers such as what data you are requesting and if you want to add or replace it.

HTTP API

An updated version of the REST API was created by AWS in 2019 and is known as the *HTTP API*; it is now a standard option of the service. The REST and HTTP APIs are both RESTful services, with the HTTP API available at a lower cost with a more limited feature set than the REST version. The HTTP APIs are commonly used for Lambda and HTTP back ends. The HTTP APIs include native support of the OpenID connect OAuth 2.0 authorization methods. CORS and automatic deployment are also included in the service.

WebSocket Protocol

WebSocket support for API Gateway adds the ability to use persistent connection APIs for bidirectional real-time streaming, chat, financial trading, collaboration, or multiplayer gaming applications. Services supported include Lambda, HTTP, and many AWS services that require either bidirectional, stateful, or streaming data. A single WebSocket API call is established, and not only is data sent to the application, the application can stream voice and video back to the requester over the same connection without the browser having to first make the request. WebSocket URLs are identified with WSS:// and support encryption for data in transit.

API Gateway Configuration

In the AWS console or using the CLI, you define a container for the API you are creating. Resources are configured, and for each, you select an HTTP method such as GET, PUT, POST, PATCH, or DELETE. Security is then configured. The next step is to define the back-end target and how to communicate with its interface. Targets can be any type of service such as DynamoDB, RDS, EC2, Lambda, etc. The API request from the client to the services and its response can be transformed between data formats as required.

The service supports HTTPS and uses its own domain name for all requests. However, you can also use your own domain name if desired. AWS Security Manager is supported, and SSL/TLS certificates are included at no additional cost.

External APIs can be imported into the gateway with support for the OpenAPI/Swagger format. OpenAPI (OAS) was originally called Swagger and was OpenAPI version 2. It was superseded by version 3 and is now only called OpenAPI. *OpenAPI* is a standard interface specification for the RESTful API that defines what the API structure is. The specification defines the formats for endpoints, operations such as GET and PUT, both input and output parameters, and authentication. It also describes the API's contact information, licensing, and terms of use. The data format is either YAML or JSON, which makes it rather easy to understand by us humans. To migrate your APIs into and out of API gateway, you can generate OpenAPI output code or import it in either JSON or YAML format. Both operations are completed in the API Gateway console or CLI with various options to add extensions for AWS or Postman formats.

After you complete your API Gateway configurations, they will not take effect until you select Deploy API from the pull-down menu to activate it.

API Gateway Caching

To reduce the number of calls to the endpoints and improve response times, caching can be configured to locally store frequent requests on the gateway. API Gateway will cache response for the TTL period. API Gateway will then first check the cache for the response before making an endpoint request if there is a cache miss.

Endpoint Types

For global connection requirements, the AWS CloudFront edge locations are used as API endpoints, as shown in Figures 1.16 and 1.17. Using edge locations improves latency by reducing the number of hops that may be required over the public Internet from distant locations. For instance, a user in Germany that is accessing your API endpoint in the us-east-1 Northern Virginia region will be connected to the nearest edge location and traverse the AWS dedicated backbone network to the us-east-1 region. AWS Gateway will still reside in the region you created it in, but the edge network can improve performance across the global network to connect to the gateway.

FIGURE 1.16   Edge API gateways

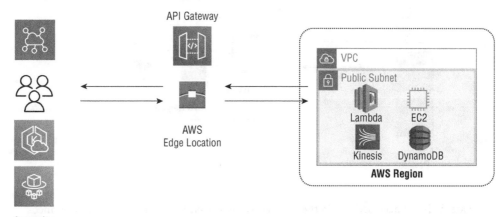

FIGURE 1.17   Regional API gateways

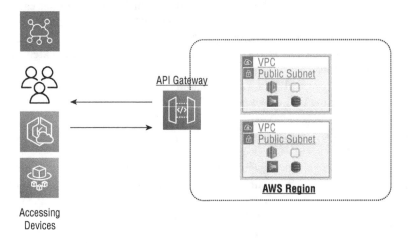

Accessing
Devices

Regional endpoints are used by users connecting to API interfaces at the regional level, as shown Figure 1.17.

Another deployment option is to create a VPC gateway that is reachable only from inside your VPC, as shown in Figure 1.18, using a VPC endpoint network interface (ENI). Access will be controlled with a resource policy being applied.

FIGURE 1.18   API Gateway deployed in a VPC

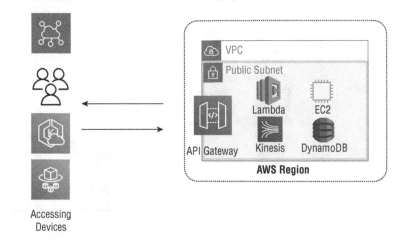

Accessing
Devices

Private APIs are accessed inside the VPC or systems that have remote network connectivity to the VPC, as shown in Figure 1.19.

FIGURE 1.19   Private API gateways

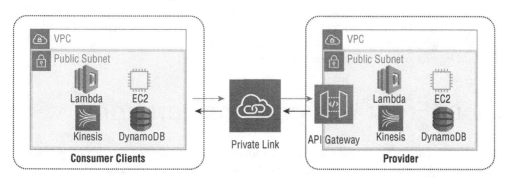

Security

Web security models enforce what is known as a *same-origin policy*. This was implemented to prevent cross-site scripting (XSS) attacks. Same origin allows any scripts running from a web page to call or access data in a second web page only if they have the same origin. If they are of different domains, the calls will be dropped by the browsers unless they are configured to allow XSS operations by enabling cross origin resource sharing, or CORS. With CORS enabled, your AWS deployments can call the S3, cloudfront.net, and amazonaws.com domains that are different but are now allowed at the browser level. When a browser asks the API for HTTP OPTIONS, it will reply with the approved names of domains to interact with. If you see "Error - Origin policy cannot be read at the remote resource," CORS is disabled and needs to be set to allow in the API Gateway console.

Authentication and Authorization

When accessing the API gateway from inside AWS, IAM is used to provide authentication support for API Gateway, and, as is always the case, there are a large number of policies preconfigured and also the ability to create custom polices as required. IAM requests are sent from the requester to API Gateway using Sigv4 security headers that contain the IAM credentials, which are then passed to IAM from API Gateway.

Another option is to use resource policies, which are JSON documents that define the rights to access API gateway and its backend services. Resource policies combined with IAM security are often used with cross-account access.

For external clients, such as those on the Internet that access your web resources using the API gateway, Cognito user pools are created and allowed access to your APIs. Users authenticate using Cognito user pools, and authorization is granted to access the APIs at the methods level you specify. The client receives a token from Cognito user pools, and the client passes the token to API Gateway to be granted access to the backend services. The token is single use with an expiration timer for onetime access.

For maximum flexibility, Lambda authorizers can be integrated with API Gateway. This token-based authorization service evaluates the request and returns an IAM policy to the requester to grant access. This method uses external, or third-party, authentication and Lambda authorization. This approach is more complex than the other methods but gives us the flexibility to meet all use case requirements.

CloudFront Design Considerations

Design requirements for connecting to AWS CloudFront locations should take geography, technical, and political constraints into consideration. Global Internet connectivity is controlled by the BGP routing protocol that is widely distributed and divided into autonomous systems that are controlled by different entities. This leaves us with little influence on how traffic gets routed with BGP across the Internet and ultimately to our content stored in AWS. What BGP does offer us is resiliency with the ability to route around failed nodes or suboptimal paths but no direct end-user control of steering the data over a path we may prefer.

At the political level, many regulations control where user data can be stored. These are often referred to as *data sovereignty laws*, and with more than 100 countries having laws that protect user's data, we must take into consideration where the data is stored and accessed when evaluating CloudFront designs.

What we can do is leverage the extensive AWS CloudFront edge footprint of more than 400 locations throughout the world. This gives us the capability to connect to a preferred edge node based on our requirements and off of the public Internet. Once in the AWS network, we gain a higher level of control as to how and where our data is accessed.

In Chapter 2, "Domain Name Services," and Chapter 3, "Hybrid and Multi-Account DNS," we will go into detail about the AWS DNS service called Route 53 and how to leverage its extended capabilities to connect to your CloudFront locations using routing policies. CloudFront supports geo-restrictions and geolocation that can be used to allow or prevent connections based on location and that are useful when meeting data sovereignty requirements.

As we discussed earlier in this chapter, Global Accelerator is used to route traffic onto the AWS network from the Internet as soon as possible for traffic engineering. For private networks, the AWS Cloud WAN services allow you to do traffic engineering using software-defined networking. Cloud WAN is a managed wide-area networking service that allows you to build and manage networks that connect your private network with the AWS global cloud network. Multiregional VPC connections and the ability to replace parts of your internal network with the AWS backbone are advantages of using this service. Cloud WAN has a single point of control and dynamic routing with a single dashboard for monitoring and event displays. Cloud WAN offers dynamic routing that is not part of the Transit Gateway and can be integrated with SD-WAN vendors such as Cisco, DXC, VMware Fortinet, and others.

Summary

In this first chapter, we introduced you to the Domain 1, Network Design, objectives for the Advanced Networking specialty certification. We started with a deep dive into the AWS CloudFront global content distribution network.

The CloudFront architecture was explained in detail including the edge locations, regional edge caches, and content sources.

You learned about content caching at the edge locations, protocols supported, and encryption using SSL/TLS, as well as security and how to invalidate data stored in cache.

From there, this chapter covered global traffic management with the Global Accelerator network service, including what it is, how it operates along with the variants of the service, and the custom routing accelerator.

Next we went into detail on the family of ELB services offered by AWS. We detailed the application, network, and gateway load balancers. You learned which is the best load balancer to use based on your requirements.

Finally, you learned about how applications communicate using standard APIs. We covered the details of the AWS Managed API service called API Gateway.

Exam Essentials

Understand the architecture of AWS CloudFront. Know that cached data is stored at edge locations based on demand. Regional edge caches are intermediate data stores for the local edge location to refresh content without having to go back to the originating source.

Know the details of CloudFront invalidations and the protocols supported. Know that CloudFront supports SSL/TLS session termination and uses the Web Application Firewall in front of the edge locations to protect against denial-of-service attacks. Know that Cloud-Front can support additional services such as processing at the edge using the Lambda serverless services from AWS.

Understand how Global Accelerator works. Know that it is used to receive traffic from the Internet into the AWS global network as close to the source as possible to offer better performance and lower latency than traversing the Internet to the intended AWS region. Know that Anycast IP addresses are used and that they can be assigned to more than one endpoint and advertised to the Internet using BGP. This allows users to connect to the nearest edge Global Accelerator access location. Understand how custom routing accelerators are different from global accelerators in that they offer more specific endpoint policies and configurations.

Remember the different types of load balancers. Application load balancers operate at layer 7 of the OSI model and can switch content based on information in the HTTP headers and URL. The listener supports unencrypted HTTP or encrypted HTTPS SSL/TLS traffic. On the backend, targets can include microservices such as Lambda, containers such as Kubernetes or Docker, EC2 virtual servers, IP addresses, and both local and remote services inside and external to the AWS cloud.

Understand the details of ELB listeners.   Target groups and health checking are basic load balancer configuration settings. Listeners are the entry point from the Internet, target groups define the backend services such as web servers, and health checks make sure the targets are healthy and able to receive connections. Sticky connections ensure that all source to destination connections terminate on the same target for the duration of the connection and are also referred to as session affinity.

Understand that network load balancers are used for very high-performance use cases. Network load balancers operate at the network layer, layer 4, of the OSI model. An NLB can handle millions of connections per second and is used in demanding and large implementations that benefit from high-throughput, low-latency connections. Targets can include EC2 instances, microservices, Lambda, and containers such as ECS and EKS. Both TCP and UDP IP connections are supported.

Know API Gateway in detail.   Understand how all the features fit together. Know the differences between the RESTful and HTTP API types and what the WebSocket protocol is and where it can be used.

Exercises

1. In the AWS management console, navigate to the CloudFront service. Read the Getting Started and FAQ documentation.

2. Search the CloudFront documentation page at `https://docs.aws.amazon.com/cloudfront` and review the developer guide.

3. In the AWS management console, navigate to the Global Accelerator service. Read the Getting Started and FAQ documentation.

4. Search the Global Accelerator documentation page at `https://docs.aws.amazon.com/global-accelerator` and review the developer guide.

5. Read the "How customer routing accelerators work" documentation at `https://docs.aws.amazon.com/global-accelerator/latest/dg/work-with-custom-routing-accelerators.html`.

6. Search the Elastic Load Balancing documentation page at `https://docs.aws.amazon.com/elasticloadbalancing` and review the most current user guide.

7. In the AWS management console, navigate to the API Gateway service. Read the Getting Started and FAQ documentation.

8. Search the API Gateway documentation page at `https://docs.aws.amazon.com/apigateway` and review the developer guide and API references.

Written Lab

Written Lab 1.1: Create an HTTP API by Using the AWS Management Console

1. Open the AWS web management console, and under the services search box, search for and select API Gateway.

2. Under Choose API, type **HTTP API** and then select Build.

3. Select Add Integration, and then choose an AWS Lambda function in the region it resides in using the drop-down box or enter a full HTTP endpoint URL with an ANY method.

4. For Name, enter a name for your API; this is a marker name and only used for your reference.

5. Click Review And Create.

6. Click Create.

7. Now your API is ready to invoke. You can test your API by entering its invoke URL in a browser or by using Curl.

8. Select and copy the URL from the details screen and paste it into your browser to test.

    ```
    https://l030ogly41.execute-api.us-west-2.amazonaws.com (for example)
    curl https://l030ogly41.execute-api.us-west-2.amazonaws.com (for example)
    ```

    Note: Since there is not a live web server, you will not see any data.

9. To complete the lab, delete the API Gateway instance that was created by selecting the gateway by name and, in the Actions drop-down box, selecting Delete.

Review Questions

The following questions are designed to test your understanding of this chapter's material. For more information on how to obtain additional questions, please see this book's introduction.

1. Content in the Brussels edge location needs to be updated as soon as possible because of an error in a product pricing update. What would be the best way to update the content?

   A. Manually set the TTL to zero

   B. Replace the file at the origin, and the edge will see that it's newer and automatically update its local cache

   C. Call the invalidation API of the object

   D. Use the file management utilities in the CloudFront CLI to manually delete the file, which forces the edge to update from the origin

2. The `index.html` file in the Asia CloudFront edge locations has become stale with the TTL reaching zero seconds. Where does the CloudFront edge in Singapore go to fetch an updated `index.html` file?

   A. The closest edge peer, which happens to be in Kuala Lumpur

   B. The origin data stored in the defined region's availability zone

   C. The regional edge cache location

   D. Nowhere; the TTL of the file automatically resets

3. Chuck is an AWS networking consultant hired to optimize response times for a company that needs to push a new version of its application to its global base. Because of locality variances in the code such as language support and embedded encryption types, he wants to minimize download times and make sure the correct updates are delivered. What is an approach Chuck could consider?

   A. Implement Global Accelerator to speed up network response times

   B. Use CloudFront with the geolocation feature enabled

   C. Store the updates in all AWS regions worldwide

   D. Use a multi-RW RDS instance with multiple red replicas

4. Global Widgets customers need to download manuals from their Texas FTP server. The download requests originated from Asia-Pacific and Middle East customers, and users are complaining about slow download speeds. What can be done to optimize the download speeds to these remote locations?

   A. Use a CloudFront content distribution network to cache the FTP files at edge locations near the customers

   B. Place a network load balancer in the us-west-2 region to balance the FTP request across multiple servers that scale based on workload

   C. Use the AWS Global Accelerator service to transport traffic over the AWS global network and not the Internet

   D. Use API Gateway with the HTTP API type to increase response times

5. Global Widgets has a requirement to have its global customers access its download servers in the Ohio region with low latency but has a security policy to limit the use of IP addresses allowed in its internal networks. What can be recommended to meet this security policy?

    A. Use their own public IP addresses on a Global Accelerator instance

    B. Use AWS-assigned Anycast addresses

    C. This cannot be done; use a CloudFront distribution instead

    D. Implement a Web Application Firewall with the BYOIP option enabled

6. A customer has specific routing and endpoint connectivity requirements for its global customer base to support its disaster recovery policies. The delays from Australia and South Africa locations are highly noticeable, and users are complaining about long download times for large files. What can be recommended to allow for faster connection speeds to the remote sites and still have the endpoint mappings required?

    A. Implement a custom Global Accelerator instance

    B. Use the standard AWS Global Accelerator service

    C. Use API gateways in AWS regional availability zones closest to the remote users

    D. Deploy classic load balancers in Australia and South Africa

7. You want to optimize what AWS charges and still meet the requirement of hosting multiple web domains on an AWS load balancer with a single listener. What feature set can you enable to meet this requirement and still be able to make secure Internet connections?

    A. Deploy SNI on the ALB listener

    B. Use URL mapping on the ALB

    C. Use a network load balancer with content switching based on HTTP header information

    D. Terminate the SSL/TLS connections using CloudFront

8. A website hosting custom content that is formatted differently based on the device their users are connecting with has a global footprint. They are upgrading their site that uses a CloudFront distribution network and desire to modify certain HTTP headers at the edge to provide custom content to Android and iOS phones. This requires a rewrite before the content is requested from the origin S3 buckets. What is a good method to use to meet this requirement?

    A. Send all requests to an EC2 instance in the region where the content is located to modify the headers before passing the request to the buckets

    B. Use API Gateway to transform the requests based on the type of device making the request

    C. Use Lambda@edge to preprocess the request based on device type

    D. Implement an application load balancer with policies to rewrite the headers before forwarding the request to the backend server pools

9. Tip Of The Hat Enterprises is preparing for its annual Black Friday sales event and antici- pates a heavy load on its front-end web servers with a high connection count and bursting connections. You have been brought on to the project to recommend a cloud-based net- working solution that will not slow down during peak usage. What would you recommend to the design team to account for the additional traffic during the sales event?

   A. Convert all of your EC2 fleet to Lambda serverless with provisioned concurrency

   B. Add read replicas to your RDS backend database

   C. Deploy a network load balancer

   D. Use API Gateway as the application front end

10. Your company is designing a new financial trading application that is browser based. You are exploring new protocols and architectures to maximize the application's performance. From a networking perspective, what would you recommend for the standards-based front end to the application?

    A. Use Global Accelerator to reduce network latency from the customer to your trading data

    B. Deploy API Gateway using the WebSockets protocol

    C. Deploy an application load balancer with sticky connections to the backend container services

    D. Use CloudFront to distribute the content at edge locations closer to requesters

11. Your e-commerce website is designed to host shopping carts on individual web servers instead of using a centralized database. There have been support cases where users have lost the contents of their shopping cart due to poor Internet connections that cause random drops and reconnects. This is causing your company lost revenue and low customer retention. What can be done at the network level to help resolve the issue? (Choose two.)

    A. Implement sticky sessions on the ELB

    B. Configure the target groups to re-establish user connections to the server hosting their shopping cart

    C. Enable session affinity on the load balancer

    D. Verify that health checking is enabled at the session level and to sync incoming connec- tions to the original web server hosting the shopping cart

12. You are investigating options to protect your CloudFront deployment from external attacks. Which two options would you investigate?

    A. CloudFront DDoS

    B. AWS Shield

    C. AWS Control Tower

    D. Web Application Firewall

13. Your applications access API Gateway from inside your VPC. IAM is used to provide authentication support for API Gateway. How are the IAM requests passed from the requester to the gateway?

  A. User pools

  B. Sigv4

  C. Cognito

  D. AD connector

14. What interface contains an IP address and port number combination that accepts incoming connections to the load balancer?

  A. Cognito

  B. Target group

  C. User pool

  D. Transfer accelerator

  E. Listener

15. Which AWS load balancer listens across all ports in an IP flow and forwards the traffic you define in a listener rule to target groups without modifying the original packet?

  A. Classic load balancer

  B. Network load balancer

  C. Application load balancer

  D. Gateway load balancer

16. You want to reduce the number of calls to the endpoints and improve the response times of AWS API Gateway. What single solution can you implement to achieve this?

  A. Use a gateway load balancer in front of API Gateway

  B. Gateway caching

  C. Use a CloudFront distribution

  D. Implement a network load balancer

17. The gateway load balancer listens across all ports in an IP flow and forwards the traffic you define in a listener rule to target groups. Which protocol encapsulates frames in a special header for use in large multitenant cloud deployments such as AWS?

  A. VxLAN

  B. GENEVE protocol

  C. Proxy protocol

  D. WebSockets

18. Which design requirements should be considered for connection to AWS CloudFront locations? (Choose two.)

    A. Geography

    B. Internet BGP policies

    C. Political constraints

    D. Encryption limitations

19. Four servers in your PROD target group need to be taken offline for updates. However, you do not want to disrupt existing user connections by forcefully downing the servers. What options do you have to take these servers offline without dropping user sessions? (Choose two.)

    A. Set the deregistration delay

    B. Configure proxy connections

    C. Enable session affinity

    D. Enable configuration draining

20. You are looking to integrate a token-based authentication method into your API gateway that will give you maximum flexibility to evaluate a request and return an IAM policy to the requester to grant access using a third-party service. What would be a good solution to implement?

    A. Enable Kerberos-based AD authentication

    B. Lambda authorizers

    C. IAM authorization

    D. Make an OAuth API call

Chapter

2

Domain Name Services

THE AWS CERTIFIED ADVANCED
NETWORKING - SPECIALTY EXAM
OBJECTIVES COVERED IN THIS CHAPTER
MAY INCLUDE, BUT ARE NOT LIMITED TO,
THE FOLLOWING:

✓ **Domain 1: Network Design**

   ▪ Objective 1.2: Design DNS solutions that meet public, private,
     and hybrid requirements.

DNS and Route 53

Before we go into all of the details of DNS and Route 53 needed to ace the Advanced Networking exam, let's first set a DNS knowledge baseline and then get into the specifics of the AWS DNS service known as *Route 53*.

The *Domain Name System* (DNS) is key to the efficient operation of all IP-based networks including the Internet and Amazon Web Services. Its primary function is to store and disseminate the mappings from a human-readable domain name to the IP address used by the actual systems on the network. It is easy to think of DNS as the "phone book" of the Internet. DNS also has many extended and advanced features that we will explore here and in Chapter 3, "Hybrid and Multi-account DNS."

The Internet runs on numbers, and we humans are not all that good at remembering them. To make networking more user-friendly, the Domain Name System is used so that all devices, including smartphones, tablets, and laptops all the way up to the largest server farms on the Internet, use human-understandable domain names. DNS then maps the human-readable name to the IP address used by the machines running on the AWS cloud, private networks, and the Internet. This name-to-numbers mapping would, for example, translate www.tipofthehat.com when typed into a browser to an IP address of 172.16.36.221, which is returned to the requester so that the computers can then use it to connect to each other. This process is known as a *DNS query*. DNS is a universal service and absolutely critical for the operation of the AWS cloud, the Internet, and private networks.

The AWS DNS service is known as Route 53 and is a play on the TCP/UDP port number of 53 that DNS uses. Route 53 has a large feature set and is much more than just a database mapping from domain to IP address, as we will learn. There are many DNS applications available to use, including the popular BIND server created in the early days of DNS at University of California, Berkeley. You can set up your own DNS system running on either Linux or Windows servers. The application service model used by AWS offers many advantages over a do-it-yourself method including a fully managed DNS service with 100 percent uptime service-level agreements, a web configuration interface, and APIs, eliminating the need to manage the underlying servers, software updates, redundancy, and global distribution. Route 53 features close integration with many other AWS services, advanced feature sets including domain name registration services, security enhancements, and more.

Route 53 maps requests to services running in the AWS cloud such as EC2 instances, load balancers, RDS databases, containers, CloudWatch, or any other service. Route 53 operations are not exclusive to AWS and can be used to access any device containing an IP address on the public Internet or your private devices. Route 53 is a global network of DNS servers located at AWS edge locations and regions and is not specific to any single region. The global DNS server network offers high availability and fast response times to users regardless of their location.

As we will cover later in the chapter, Route 53 has many advanced features such as routing requests based on latency, geographic proximity of the origin to the destination, and round-robin responses. These routing policies can be then combined with failover options for flexibility in setting up a low-latency and fault-tolerant deployment. Multiple policies can be configured based on delay, proximity, and health. These policies can be stored and enabled or disabled based on your specific requirements.

Hybrid architectures to interconnect Route 53 to your internal DNS infrastructure are offered including Direct Connect, VPC resolutions, VPN services managed by AWS, and private and on-premise data centers.

Route 53 can be set up and managed using the web console, the command line, Cloud-Formation, or APIs for automation. Billing is based on what you use, and AWS includes service-level agreements for peace of mind. Security is provided with *Identity and Access Management* (IAM) integration and DNS firewall integration.

Since Route 53 runs as a service, AWS maintains all the underlying infrastructure worldwide and scales the services to meet demand without the customers needing to manage performance.

DNS Overview

DNS is a distributed service that operates globally in all IP-based networks. DNS clients run on networking devices such as smartphones, tablets, laptops, all the way to huge server clusters running in AWS. DNS services the client requests for information to connect to devices given a domain name and returning an IP address. DNS has been enhanced and extended over the years to add the functionality and security required by modern IP-based networks.

Domain names, including the names of domains, hosted zones, and records, consist of a series of labels separated by dots and can be up to 63 bytes long. The total length of a domain name cannot be longer than 255 bytes. When registering a public domain name, the rules are that it can only use the characters a–z, 0–9, and a hyphen. The hyphen cannot be at the beginning or end of the name. Hosted zones and records are more open and allow any ASCII character to be used except for spaces.

Amazon Route 53 supports any valid domain name. DNS supports lowercase characters only. Route 53 will automatically convert uppercase characters to the lowercase format. Asterisks for hosted zones are treated as regular characters and not as any wildcard. The asterisk cannot be at the beginning of a hosted zone but can be inside the label, for example, `*.tipofthehhat.com` is not valid, but `t*pofthehat.com` is. For a DNS record, the asterisk is treated as a wildcard character that means the standard "anything." So,

`*.tipofthehat.com` will include all subdomains under `tipofthehat.com`, and DNS will use the more specific domain name over the more general asterisk wildcard.

Architecture

The domain name is the human-readable text that is sent to the DNS servers when a query is made to be translated into an IP address and returned to the client. The *Uniform Resource Record* (URL) is the standard format used by a browser to create a DNS query and is shown in Figure 2.1.

FIGURE 2.1   URL format

https://www.tipofthehat.com

Protocol   Subdomain   Domain   Top-Level Domain

The DNS architecture is distributed and divided into specific functional areas and we will go into more detail shortly. This architecture adds resiliency by distributing the DNS service across thousands of servers throughout the world managed by different organizations. If any component, cloud region, or section of the Internet were to fail or suffer from performance degradation, the DNS service is designed to keep running. There have been many denial-of-service (DoS) attacks on DNS, but the service has been robust enough to stay operational.

DNS Hierarchy

DNS is a highly distributed database that contains a hierarchy that flows from very general information at the top of the stack to specific host information at the bottom, as shown in Figure 2.2. Distributed *root servers* are at the top of the DNS hierarchy and are used to direct queries to the *top-level name servers* based on the URL. Examples of top-level domains include `.com`, `.net`, `.io`, `.edu`, and many others. The root servers store the records of these TLD servers. The TLD servers store the domain records for the specific top-level domains and respond to the query with the name of the TLD server where the next level in the domain structure can be found. TLDs contain the information after the last dot in a URL. Below the TLD servers are the name servers where the information on how to reach the servers for each domain is stored.

Each level is separated by a period, for example, `www.amazon.com`. There is actually a period after `.com` that is rarely shown. This period is the pointer to the root servers and is inserted by the application software, so we never have to type `www.amazon.com.` with the period at the end even though, in reality, it's there.

As a relic of the distant past, there are only 13 IP addresses allocated for all of the root servers in the world. Management responsibility for the Internet root servers is with the Internet Corporation for Assigned Names and Numbers (ICANN). While this may seem like a huge limitation, each IPv4 address, and also some IPv6 servers, have more than 600 root servers sitting behind them. Also, these root IP addresses are anycast, so the same address is used at many locations all over the world. The 13 IP addresses of the root servers are built into the code of all DNS resolvers and operate hidden from view.

There are more than 1,500 top-level domains (TLDs) operating on the Internet supporting more than 340 million domains. The number of TLDs and unique domains is constantly growing.

FIGURE 2.2   DNS server hierarchy

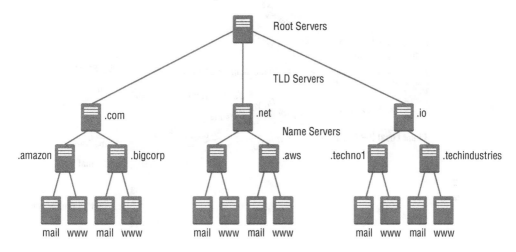

Zones

Each zone includes one or more domains or subdomains. The zone contains the name servers that store a zone file of resource records. The *primary zone* is authoritative for the domain that acts as the final authority over the domain records and sends updates to other zones as needed. There are also *secondary zones* for which a server can respond to a query but does not have the final determination of the records. The secondary zone periodically polls, or queries, the primary zone to see if there are any updates and that its records are correct. It is a read-only copy of the primary zone that is stored on a different server. The secondary zone can retrieve updates only from the primary zone. Secondary zones are used to reduce the load on primary DNS servers and for preventing a single point of failure.

Resource records are stored on DNS servers across the Internet. The master copy of the resource record is stored in a specific zone, or portion of the DNS namespace, that is the primary source of the data. A zone includes one or more domains and subdomains. The zone contains name servers that have a zone file containing individual resource records. Each record has a name, type, and time-to-live (TTL).

DNS Resolution Process

Figure 2.3 illustrates the steps involved with a standard DNS query and the interactions from the different levels of the DNS hierarchy as the client types a URL into a browser window until the IP address is returned.

The client types in the browser a web page to load such as www.tipofthehat.com. The computer queries its local DNS server for www.tipofthehat.com.

FIGURE 2.3   DNS resolution process

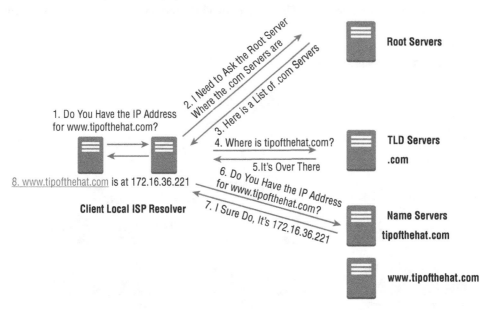

The ISP resolver will look at its locally cached records to see if the domain to IP mapping is stored locally; if it is, the IP address is returned to the client.

If the ISP resolver does not contain the data, it will look at its local configuration to get the IP address of a root server and ask it where the .com TLD servers are.

The root server will respond with the IP addresses it can use to contact a TLD .com server.

The resolver queries the .com server asking for the tipofthehat domain. The TLD server will reply with the tipofthehat.com DNS name server address.

The resolver will have the information to contact the tipofthehat.com DNS server, which contains the www A record. The tipofthehat.com IP address is returned to the local resolver and in turn is sent to the client that originally made the request.

Now the client's browser has the IP address to contact www.tipofthehat.com, which then initiates the connection.

Notice that the local resolver coordinated all of the lookup work on the client's behalf, and the client waited for the answer to be returned after its request.

Resource Records

Resource records are at the core of DNS functionality. They contain the actual data about DNS resources. Each record contains a name, type, and TTL information, as shown in Figure 2.4. The master copy of each group of resource records is stored in a specific zone, which is a portion of the DNS namespace, and can be distributed throughout the Internet's

DNS system. While there are more than 90 different types of resource records, most are rarely seen. Here, we will cover the records most commonly used in DNS.

FIGURE 2.4   Sample resource record

- *A record*: Associates an IPv4 address with a hostname.
- *AAAA record*: Same as an A record but for IPv6.
- *MX record*: Mail Exchange Record, identifies mail servers for the domain.
- *NS record*: Name server that points to the authoritative DNS server for a zone.
- *PTR record*: A reverse DNS lookup where given an IP address, a domain name is returned.
- *SPF record*: Determines if the email sender is authorized to send emails from this domain.
- *SRV record*: Service locator, a generic service pointer used to show a server's hostname and the ports it is listening on.
- *CNAME record*: Canonical name, an alias that references one host by multiple domain names.

- *DNAME record*: Delegation of an entire part of a DNS tree to a new name. Compare this to a CNAME, which is a single record.

- *LOC record*: Location record, has physical geographic location information including latitude, longitude, and altitude of where the domain resides.

- *SOA record*: The start of authority record, has information about the domain that includes information that other servers for the zone can use to identify changes, the primary name server information, refresh intervals for data freshness, information on the domain administrator such as the contact's email address.

- *TXT record*: Used to store data in the domain for outside services to query. TXT records provide data for validation, proof of domain ownership, and many other uses.

Timers

Since DNS is a distributed database, there must be a mechanism to ensure that the data remains fresh in the nonauthoritative servers. When a resolver requests a record, it will store that information locally in case it is needed again. However, if it remains in the local cache, the primary, or authoritative, server may have been updated, and the resolver's data becomes stale. There are timers, often called TTL *or time to live,* that tell the nonauthoritative servers how long to keep the data before requesting a refresh. For example, if the TTL is set for 1,800 seconds, then the resolver must go back every 30 minutes and request a refresh of the records to keep it from getting stale. The TTL values are sent from the authoritative to nonauthoritative servers when a DNS record is delivered.

Sites that make frequent changes would benefit from a short TTL so the clients receive accurate and updated information. However, if a site seldom changes, then a longer TTL would offer a higher level of performance since the DNS record data would be cached closer to the clients and the DNS servers would not have to take the time to refresh the cached data.

Delegations

When resolving a DNS query, each DNS server that answers the queries needs a path to every zone in that namespace. *Delegations* provide this purpose. The delegation is a record stored in the parent zone that lists authoritative name servers at the next level down in the hierarchy. This allows for servers in one zone to direct clients to servers in other zones. For example, the root zones delegate to the `.com` servers below them, which in turn delegate to the company domain below them, such as `tipofthehat.com`.

DNSSEC Overview

Traditionally the basic Route 53 service did not implement any security and the DNS records traditionally sent data in the clear. This was the case since DNS was first used in 1983 to replace host files with a dynamic database for name resolution. To implement tighter security measures when using DNS, the *Domain Name System Security Extension* (DNSSEC) specification was developed in 2010 and was added to Route 53 in 2021. The Route 53 DNSSEC implementation can be enabled for all existing and new public hosted zones and for resolver validations to guarantee the authenticity and integrity of the DNS data. Security mandates from FedRAMP and others are adding encryption compliance requirements for DNS. DNS-SEC is the tool that enables the security required under these mandates.

DNSSEC enables authentication for data origins and verification for the integrity of the data by using asymmetric digital signatures and the *Public Key Cryptography* (PKI) infrastructure. The data owner applies the cryptography to the actual DNS data and not the queries and responses.

Route 53 performs the crypto signatures on each record in its hosted zones. The key is managed by Route 53 and can be managed through the *Key Management Services* (KMS) of AWS. The Route 53 Resolver in each VPC guarantees that the DNS responses have not been tampered with during transmission. When a server does a recursive lookup, it will use the public key of the zone to validate the authenticity of the DNS data. This proves that the data was received from the actual zone where the DNS records are and not a fake or imposter zone. The data integrity part of DNSSEC confirms to the resolver that the data was not changed or tampered with in transit and that it was originally signed by the zone administrator using its private key.

Route 53 DNSSEC uses two types of keys. The first is the *key-signing key* (KSK), as shown in Figures 2.5 and 2.6. Each KSK is an asymmetric customer-managed public/private key pair that is owned by you and stored in the AWS Key Management Service (KMS) for your account. All KSK operations are your responsibility including rotating and replacing the keys as required. The *zone-signing key* (ZSK) is managed by AWS and will be transparent to your AWS administrators. The Route 53 hosted zones have a hard-coded TTL value for DNSSEC implementations of one week. Also, be careful with multivendor DNSSEC implementations to check if interoperability is supported with Route 53.

DNS Logging and Monitoring

Amazon Web Services has integrated Route 53 into its management applications for ease of use and insight into its operations. Since all interactions with Route 53 are an API call behind the scenes, these records can be natively sent to *CloudTrail* for a record of activities and analysis. The *CloudWatch* monitoring service can be used to collect and graphically view metrics and trigger actions based on rules you configure.

With the growth of artificial intelligence, these DNS records can be scanned, and trends can be tracked for normal and abnormal usage. For example, the Redshift service can be used to analyze Route 53 records stored in S3 using standard SQL queries.

CloudTrail

Route 53 has native integration with CloudTrail for recording API calls from the console, CLI, SDK, and applications directly to Route 53, and exporting the records to CloudTrail. Users, roles, and services of AWS will capture the API calls occurring in Route 53 and record them in CloudTrail. If you create a trail in CloudTrail, then all Route 53 IP records can be stored in an S3 storage bucket for analysis, troubleshooting, and historical archives. This will collect data on who made the request, what the requested domain name was, the IP address, date/time, and more. Since CloudTrail is enabled when you create your AWS account, Route 53 records DNS logs in event history by default. API access information can be globally collected from all AWS regions and stored in a single consolidated CloudTrail S3 bucket.

FIGURE 2.5 DNSSEC key creation

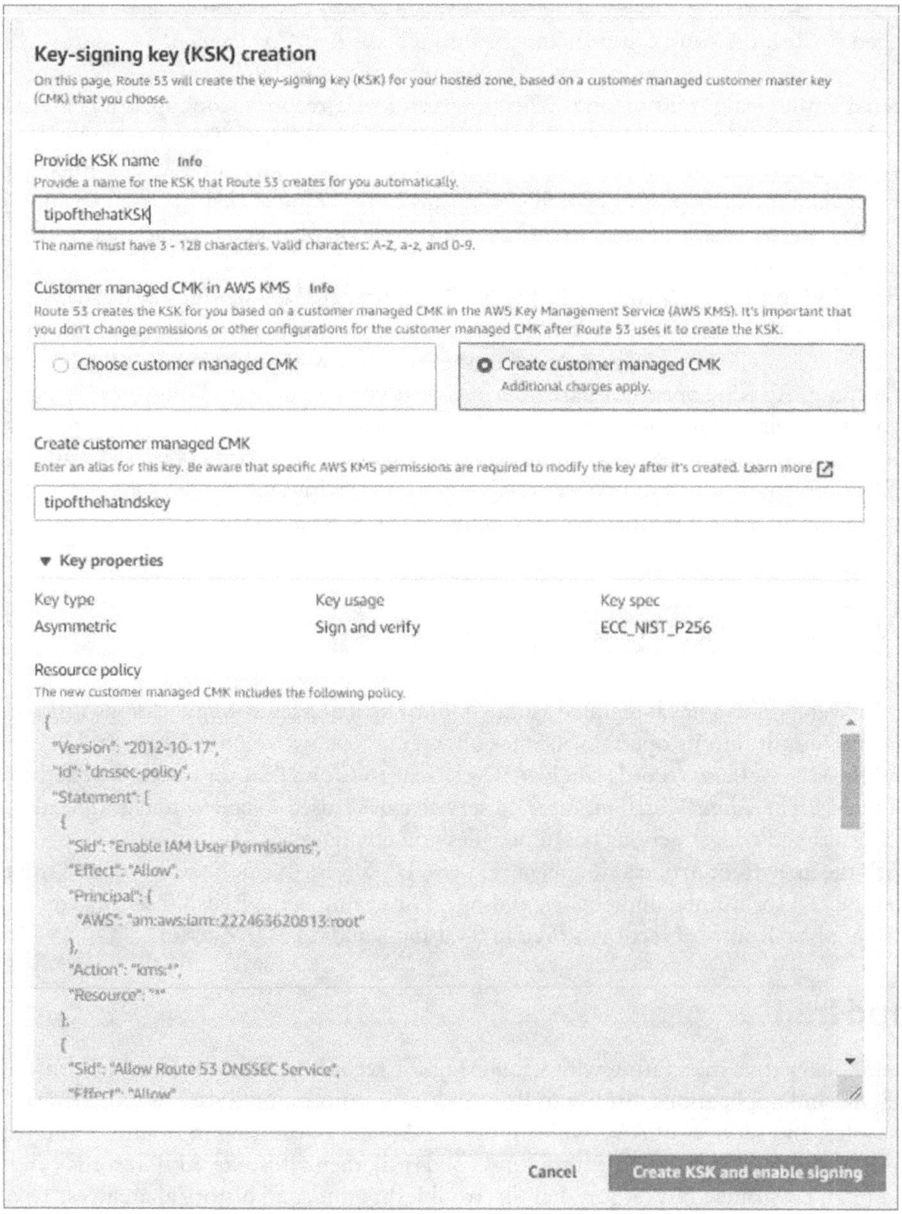

FIGURE 2.6   DNSSEC KSK generation

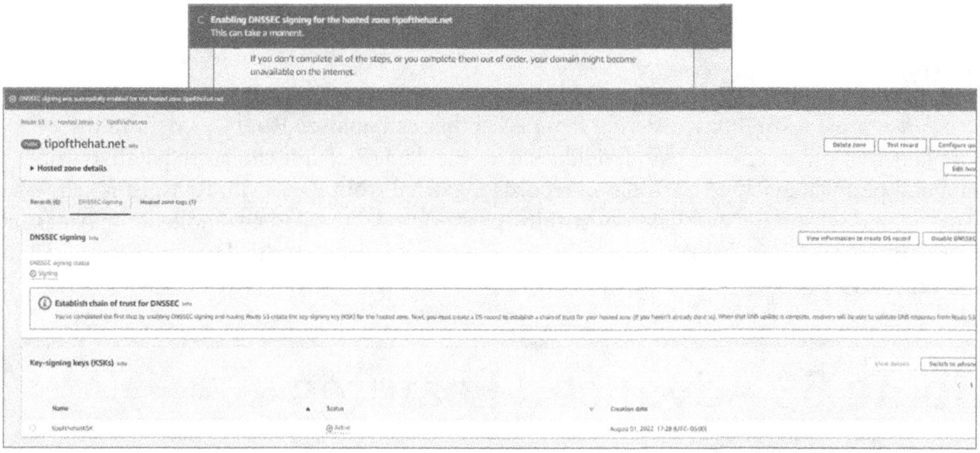

CloudWatch

CloudWatch is an AWS event monitoring service that can collect Route 53 data in near real time for monitoring and producing insights into your DNS operations. By default, data is sent from Route 53 into CloudWatch in 1-minute intervals and stored for 14 days. Cloud-Watch can be configured to store the data for a longer periods of time in S3 for historical analysis and data retention if desired.

CloudWatch can monitor the health checking of endpoints by Route 53. Hosted zone metrics include DNS queries for all records in each hosted zone. You set the number of queries Route 53 responds to in time intervals that you specify. These are delivered as either a total or a sample count. Note that Route 53 is a global service and not part of any AWS region; therefore, to collect hosted zone metrics, the U.S. East Northern Virginia region is the central repository region specified. DNSSEC internal failures are reported as either a 1 for a failure or a 0 if there is no failure. `DNSSECKeySigningKeysNeedingAction` reports if action is needed due to KMS failures. `DNSSECKeySigningKeyMaxNeedingActionAge` and `DNSSECKeySigningKeyAge` are also reported to CloudWatch from Route 53. If a resolver is configured to forward DNS queries to and from your network, these metrics can be reported to CloudWatch in 5-minute intervals. There are a large number of metrics that can be collected and analyzed. Refer to the Route 53 documentation for the latest information on what is available.

CloudWatch can monitor Route 53 Resolver DNS firewall rule groups at 5-minute inter-vals. When a Route 53 Resolver firewall rule group is set up in a VPC, it will filter DNS queries. The DNS firewall will then send the metric to CloudWatch.

Artificial Intelligence and Machine Learning

Since CloudTrail and CloudWatch collect logging and metric data from Route 53 operations, this can be stored and analyzed with AI/ML tools offered by AWS and its business partners.

Companies such as Splunk and others offer services in this space. Check the AWS Marketplace for the latest information.

Redshift

Redshift is a data warehouse offering from AWS that can analyze Route 53 data in the data lake and run queries to gain intelligence on the data. Redshift can store petabytes of data and perform machine learning on records exported from Route 53. Redshift is self-learning and self-tuning and has robust third-party support services available in the Amazon Marketplace. Redshift uses standard SQL to analyze and visualize the data from Route 53 and other sources.

Route 53 Advanced Features and Policies

Route 53 has added to the basic DNS service to enhance its performance, add resiliency, and better integrate with many internal AWS services.

Alias Records

Amazon *Alias records* in Route 53 are a specific DNS extension that allow for the routing of traffic to select AWS resources, such as S3 or CloudFront. Specifically, they allow one record in a hosted zone to be routed to another record in the same zone.

The Alias record is a unique record type that points your domain name to a hostname in the same zone. This is referred to as the *zone apex* such as `tipofthehat.com`. While not allowed when created by a CNAME, the Alias records allow us to point the zone apex to a specific hostname. For example, `tipofthehat.com` can be pointed to `www.tipofthehat.com`.

One of the features of using Alias records in your AWS deployment is that when an Alias record is used to route the traffic in DNS, Route 53 can automatically learn about changes in the resource. An example of this would be if you created an Alias for `tipofthehat.com` that points to a load balancer in your VPC running in the us-west-1 region. If we have an ELB running in us-west-2 with a DNS name of `internal-tests08032022- 411436634.us-west-2.elb.amazonaws.com`, we could create an Alias in Route 53 from the `tipofthehat.com` zone apex to the ELB in our VPC to hide the complex AWS ELB URL. Now all the connections to `tipofthehat.com` will resolve to the ELB. If the ELB address were to change, Route 53 would note the change and reply with the new IP address of the ELB without your intervention.

In the previous example, we pointed the Alias record to an internal AWS resource, the ELB service. In this case, you will not be able to adjust the TTL value. Route 53 will take the default TTL for the targeted resource. Also, if the Alias points to another record in the same hosted zone, the TTL value will be taken from that resource and cannot be configured locally.

Alias records are supported by many AWS services including the following:

- API Gateway custom, regional, or edge-optimized API.
- VPC interface endpoint.
- CloudFront distribution.
- Elastic Beanstalk environment; Route 53 responds with one or more IP addresses for the environment.
- ELB load balancer; Route 53 responds with one or more IP addresses for the load balancer. This includes the application, classic, and, network load balancers.
- Global Accelerator.
- S3 bucket that is configured as a static website.
- A Route 53 record in the same hosted zone.
- AppSync domain name.

Alias records can point only to Route 53 resources. AWS will not charge for queries to an Alias record that points to an AWS resource. However, all CNAME queries will be charged to your account.

Resolvers

DNS *resolvers* are at the heart of DNS functionality. Resolvers, also known as *recursive resolvers*, receive queries that contain the hostname and reply with the IP address of that hostname, as shown in Figure 2.7. The Route 53 Resolver acts as a bridge between your on-premise DNS infrastructure and the AWS VPC. Route 53 Resolvers in hybrid clouds enable DNS query responses in a hybrid cloud. DNS endpoints and conditional forwarding rules are used to allow the resolution for DNS between the VPC and your internal data center.

FIGURE 2.7   DNS Resolver

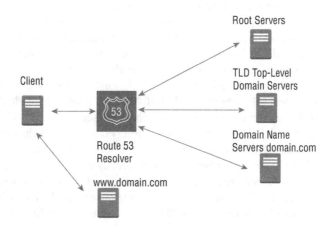

The AWS resolver enables bidirectional name resolution between on-premise and VPC resources. On-premise DNS records can now be queried from the AWS VPC, and the on-premise devices can query and resolve DNS records in a VPC.

A Route 53 Resolvers consists of an Amazon-provided DNS server and is provided by default as part of every AWS VPC. This DNS server fields DNS queries for AWS public resources, Route 53 private hosted zones, and names that are specific to the VPC DNS names. Resolver rules can be configured to conditionally forward DNS requests originating inside a VPC directed to an on-premise DNS resolver. By establishing a direct connection between your data center and a VPC using a VPN or Direct Connect, a VPC resolver endpoint acts as the forwarding target server of the on-premise DNS server to reply to on-premise requests to VPC resources.

Route 53 Resolver DNS Firewall

Route 53 has integrated firewall capabilities that filter outbound DNS traffic from a VPC based on rules you define. Rules are created and placed in groups that can be reused throughout your deployment. The Route 53 firewall rule groups are associated with a VPC for filtering. Firewall activity is displayed in logs and metrics that can be monitored and used to adjust your rules to filter the DNS replies. The DNS firewall allows you to monitor and control which domains your servers can query by denying access to the domains that you specify and allowing all others to be allowed to be forwarded. The opposite is also supported where you can specify which domains are trusted and allowed and block all others. Requests for specific EC2 instances can be blocked in either public or private subnets, and VPC endpoint resolution requests to resources in your VPC can also be allowed or blocked.

Health Checks

An extension for the Route 53 functionality is to *health check* the resources in a record before responding to queries. This prevents Route 53 DNS from delivering an IP address of a service that is down and not responding to health checks.

These health checks can be performed on any type of endpoint including web, FTP, and email servers or load balancers, as shown in Figure 2.8. Notifications of failed health checks can be configured in CloudWatch to perform any number of actions including restarting the service, running a Lambda application, or sending out alert emails.

When configuring health checking in Route 53, you must specify the endpoint service and what actions to take if the health check should fail. You will need to provide the IP address of the endpoint and the protocol to use for health checking such as HTTP, HTTPS, or TCP (three-way handshake). The failure threshold is the interval to perform the check and how many failures in a row are OK before declaring that the service is down.

Once health checking has been configured in a record, as shown in Figures 2.9 and 2.10, Route 53 will perform the checks based on its configuration. If there is a positive response, no further actions are taken. However, if there is no response from the endpoint, then Route 53 will track the number of failed responses. When the failure threshold is reached, the endpoint is declared to be in the failed state, and the defined actions are taken. However, if there is a positive response before the failure threshold, then the failure counter gets reset to zero, and no failure actions are taken.

FIGURE 2.8   Route 53 health checks

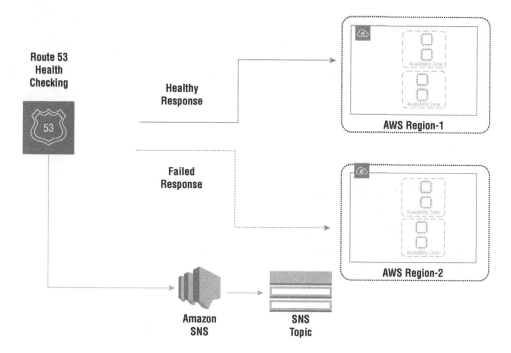

Traffic Routing Policies

Routing policies are a Route 53 extension to DNS that allows you to customize query responses to affect how your content gets delivered. Routing policies shape the traffic based on our requirements in a number of different use cases. We can send all traffic to a single site, give multiple responses to a single request, enable load balancing, set percentages of where the user requests are sent, failover, and modify responses based on geographical locations.

When a record is created in Route 53, you must select a routing policy that will tell Route 53 what IP address to respond with when a query is made to that record, as shown in Figure 2.11. There are a number of policies that we will cover to better explain this concept. Policies include just a basic "what is the IP address of www.tipofthehat.com; here is its IP address" all the way to regional restrictions, network delays to determine proximity, and failover options.

Simple Routing

Simple routing is the most basic of the Route 53 policies and is also its default for all new resources that you configure. It is a single record for a single resource. When a query is made, for example, for www.tipofthehat.com, a simple routing policy will return the A record's single IP address, as shown in Figure 2.12. Simple routing is also used for other record types such as MX, TXT, and CNAMEs. If there are multiple records for a given domain name, simple routing will return only a single value that is chosen at random from multiple defined IP addresses.

FIGURE 2.9   Route 53 health check configuration

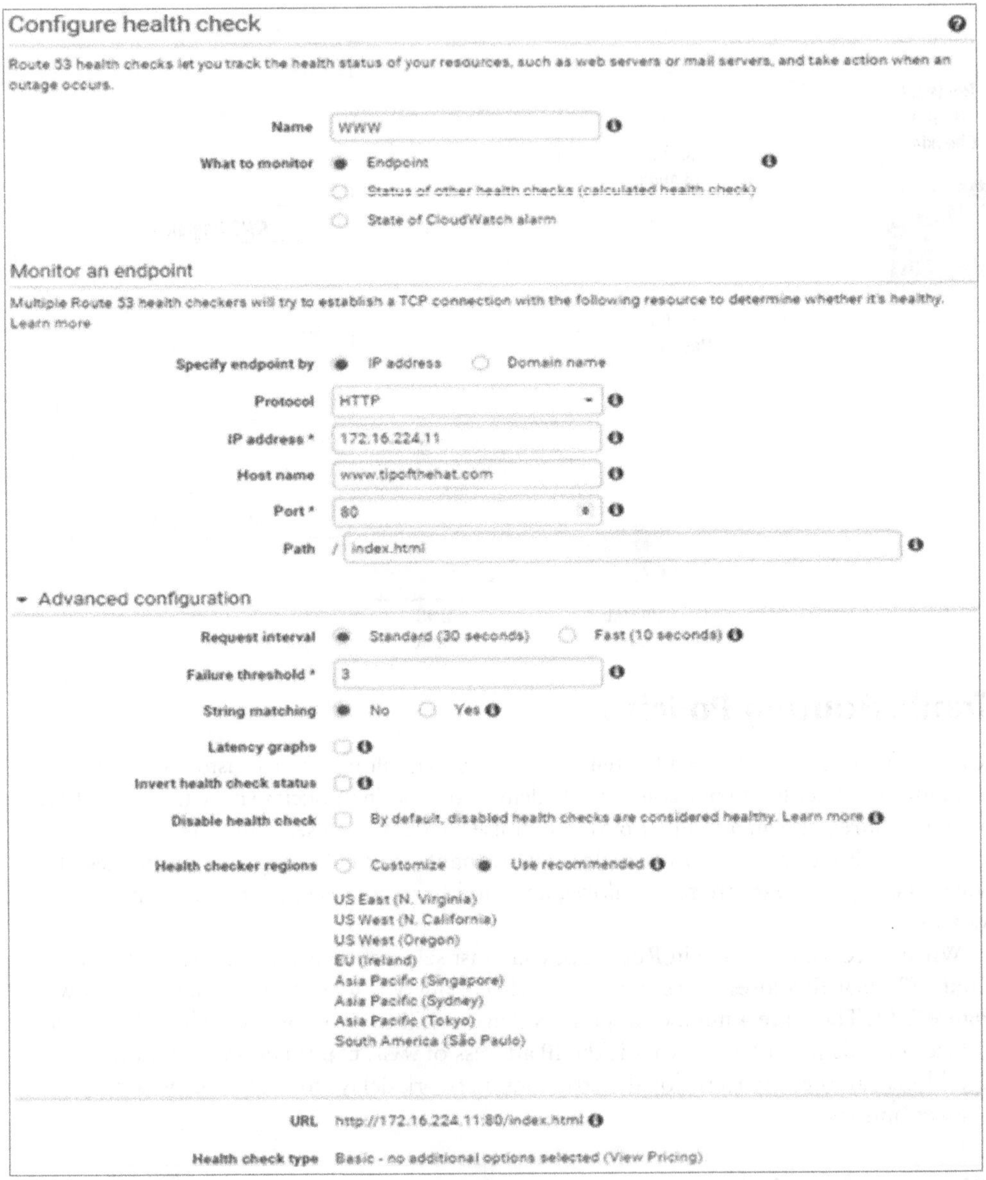

Configure health check   ?

Route 53 health checks let you track the health status of your resources, such as web servers or mail servers, and take action when an outage occurs.

Name   WWW   ⓘ

What to monitor   ⦿ Endpoint   ⓘ
                   ○ Status of other health checks (calculated health check)
                   ○ State of CloudWatch alarm

Monitor an endpoint

Multiple Route 53 health checkers will try to establish a TCP connection with the following resource to determine whether it's healthy. Learn more

Specify endpoint by   ⦿ IP address   ○ Domain name

Protocol   HTTP   ▾ ⓘ

IP address *   172.16.224.11   ⓘ

Host name   www.tipofthehat.com   ⓘ

Port *   80   ⓘ

Path   / index.html   ⓘ

▾ Advanced configuration

Request interval   ⦿ Standard (30 seconds)   ○ Fast (10 seconds) ⓘ

Failure threshold *   3   ⓘ

String matching   ⦿ No   ○ Yes ⓘ

Latency graphs   ☐ ⓘ

Invert health check status   ☐ ⓘ

Disable health check   ☐   By default, disabled health checks are considered healthy. Learn more ⓘ

Health checker regions   ○ Customize   ⦿ Use recommended ⓘ

US East (N. Virginia)
US West (N. California)
US West (Oregon)
EU (Ireland)
Asia Pacific (Singapore)
Asia Pacific (Sydney)
Asia Pacific (Tokyo)
South America (São Paulo)

URL   http://172.16.224.11:80/index.html ⓘ

Health check type   Basic - no additional options selected (View Pricing)

To review the process, a client types www.tipofthehat.com into her browser, and a DNS query is made from her local machine to its locally configured resolver. The resolver will ask the DNS infrastructure for the IP address of www.tipofthehat.com if it is not cached locally. The first query is made to the root DNS server for the .com top-level domain that gets returned; then the resolver will ask the top-level domain servers where it can find `tipofthehat.com`. Then the `tipofthehat.com` domain server will be queried for the IP address of www under that domain. A simple, single IP address is returned, and the browser now knows how to make a connection to the `www.tipofthehat.com` web server.

FIGURE 2.10   Route 53 health check notification

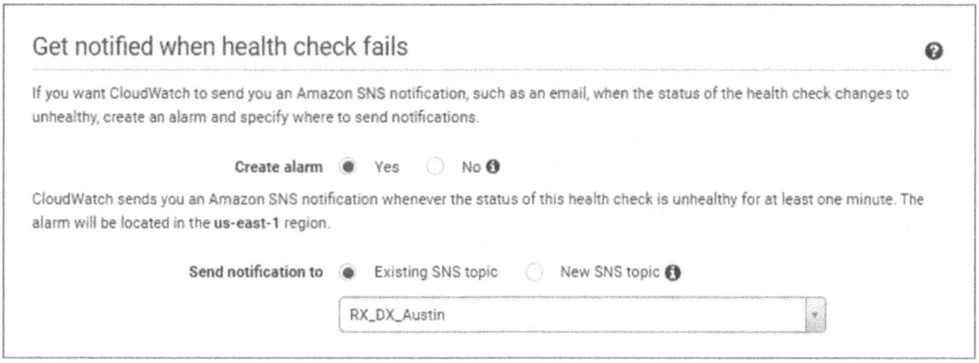

Get notified when health check fails   ❷

If you want CloudWatch to send you an Amazon SNS notification, such as an email, when the status of the health check changes to unhealthy, create an alarm and specify where to send notifications.

                    Create alarm ⦿ Yes   ◯ No ❶

CloudWatch sends you an Amazon SNS notification whenever the status of this health check is unhealthy for at least one minute. The alarm will be located in the **us-east-1** region.

              Send notification to ⦿ Existing SNS topic   ◯ New SNS topic ❶

                    RX_DX_Austin   ▾

Multivalue Responses

Multivalue responses are an extension to the simple routing policy. Instead of returning just a single IP address, multivalue will return any number up to eight responses of IP address for the same domain name and can be used as a form of host redundancy. This allows the client to choose which IP address to use as the domain is active on all of the IP addresses. Route 53 will also perform health checks on each endpoint and, if one should fail, remove that IP from its pool of responses. Multivalue responses are illustrated in Figure 2.13.

Latency-Based Routing

To enhance response times, a *latency-based routing* policy can be used. Route 53 will test the response times in the background of all the configured endpoints for a domain name. Route 53 determines the quickest response time between the origin and destination. This is the best destination value that is returned in the DNS response to the requester, as shown in Figure 2.14. Latency-based routing is helpful when servicing traffic from multiple AWS regions by directing user requests to the site with the lowest latency from their location.

After configuring a latency-based routing policy in multiple regions, Route 53 will examine a DNS request and compare its stored latency values from the requester's location to the configured regions. The region with the lowest latency from the user's location will be the value returned from the request. The latency values are collected by Route 53 over a period of time and updated as delays on the Internet vary over time. This means a region delivered by a DNS request using a latency policy may be different over time based on traffic conditions on the Internet. The latency measurements are from the requester, and the AWS region, and do not account for any delays inside or beyond the region. If there is additional latency in a container or database, for example, that latency is not calculated by Route 53 latency-based routing policies.

FIGURE 2.11   Route 53 routing policies

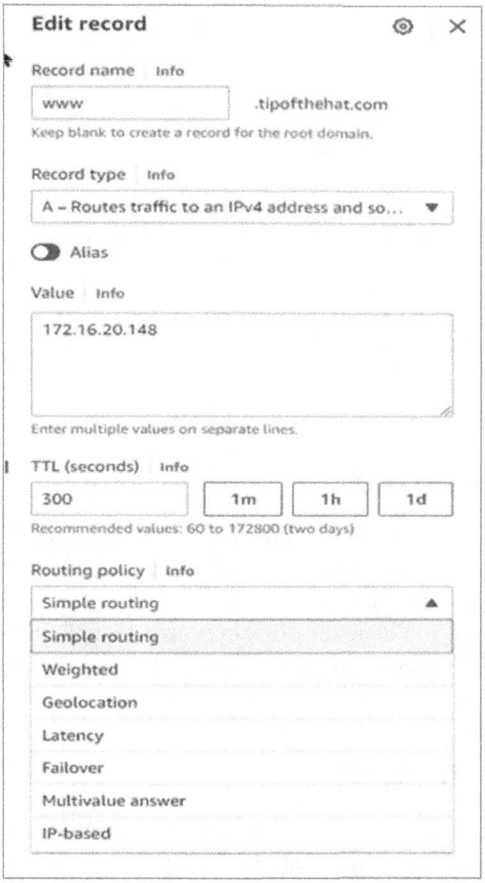

> **Edit record**   ◎   ✕
>
> Record name   Info
>
> | www | .tipofthehat.com
>
> Keep blank to create a record for the root domain.
>
> Record type   Info
>
> | A – Routes traffic to an IPv4 address and so... ▼ |
>
> ◯ Alias
>
> Value   Info
>
> | 172.16.20.148 |
>
> Enter multiple values on separate lines.
>
> TTL (seconds)   Info
>
> | 300 | | 1m | | 1h | | 1d |
>
> Recommended values: 60 to 172800 (two days)
>
> Routing policy   Info
>
> | Simple routing   ▲ |
> | Simple routing |
> | Weighted |
> | Geolocation |
> | Latency |
> | Failover |
> | Multivalue answer |
> | IP-based |

FIGURE 2.12   Route 53 simple routing policy

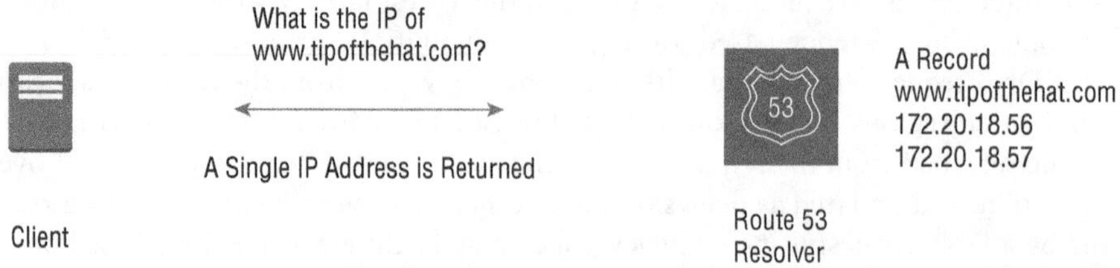

Client

What is the IP of
www.tipofthehat.com?

⟵──────────────⟶

A Single IP Address is Returned

Route 53
Resolver

A Record
www.tipofthehat.com
172.20.18.56
172.20.18.57

FIGURE 2.13   Route 53 Multivalue response

What is the IP of
www.tipofthehat.com?

←——————————→

Multiple IP Addresses are Returned
172.20.18.56
172.20.18.57

Client

A Record
www.tipofthehat.com
172.20.18.56
172.20.18.57

Route 53
Resolver

FIGURE 2.14   Route 53 latency-based routing policy

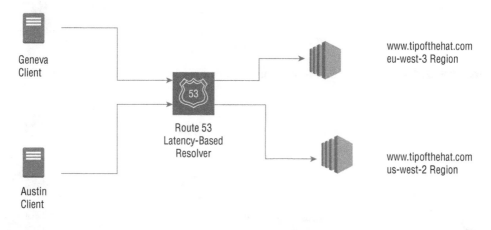

Geneva
Client

Route 53
Latency-Based
Resolver

Austin
Client

www.tipofthehat.com
eu-west-3 Region

www.tipofthehat.com
us-west-2 Region

Failover Routing

Route 53 *failover routing* is used when high availability is desired and you want one site to act as a backup should the primary site fail, as illustrated in Figure 2.15. In normal operations all traffic is directed to the primary site by serving its IP address to queries. Should health checks to the primary fail, then Route 53 will failover to the backup by now sending out the IP address of the standby servers when queried.

Two record sets are defined for the same host. One host is configured as the primary and the other as the backup. So, with failover configured, 100 percent of the traffic will go to the primary until it fails health checks, and then 100 percent of the traffic gets directed to the standby site.

Round-Robin Routing

Round-robin routing is a simple method to use Route 53 to load balance using the values returned from queries, as shown in Figure 2.16. Instead of just returning a single value as a simple routing policy does, round-robin will sequentially respond with IP addresses from a pool in a circular fashion. This will equally distribute connection requests across all the hosts in the pool.

FIGURE 2.15   Route 53 failover routing policy

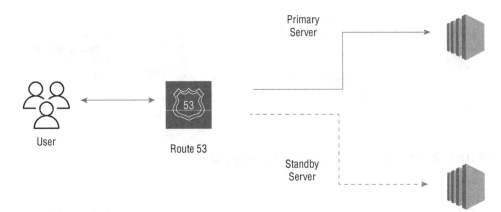

FIGURE 2.16   Route 53 round-robin routing policy

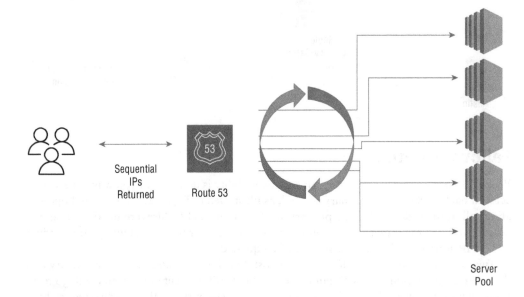

Weighted Routing

Weighted routing is based on the round-robin policy but adds a weighted feature to affect how the load gets distributed. Multiple hosts with different IP addresses all serve the same content. Each host will then have a weight assigned to it between 0 and 255. If they are all set to the value of 0, then traffic is distributed evenly across all the servers just like round-robin does. However, by changing the weights, each record is assigned a value that is the weight, and the load is dispersed as a percentage of the total value to the total weight assigned, as shown in Figure 2.17.

FIGURE 2.17   Route 53 weighted routing policy

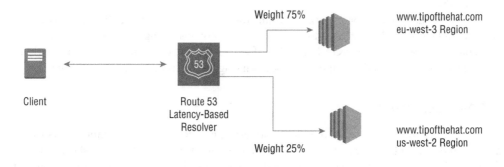

Geolocation

Geolocation policies will examine the user's source IP address, determine where it is physically located, and serve traffic based on their location. Then a lookup is done, and the reply will direct them to the defined location. Restrictions can be placed at the country, state (in the United States), or continent level. Geolocation can direct users to local websites that host content in their local language or where regulations restrict traffic to originate from. Geolocation maps IP addresses to locations by using the mapping and learning the location routing decisions based on the policy configured, as shown in Figure 2.18.

FIGURE 2.18   Route 53 geolocation routing policy

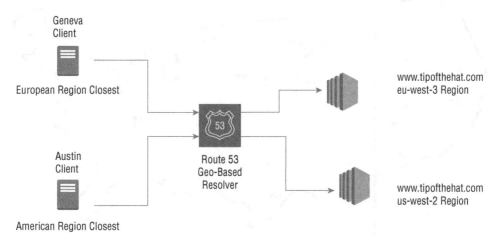

You can configure geolocation by continent and then be more granular by country. The country level will take precedence over the more broadly defined continent. Also, if a continent is defined, geolocation will favor the smaller region. For example, if there is a geolocation policy for Europe and you have web servers in AWS regions located in Ireland and Germany, Ireland would take precedence since it is the smaller geographic region. This policy can then be modified to add country codes to send traffic from the defined country to the AWS Frankfurt region.

In the case that geolocation cannot determine the location of the source IP address, two actions can be taken. The first is to drop the request by not answering the query and not allow it to connect since there is no record provided of where to route the traffic. The second option is to create a default record that routes the unknown originating traffic to the region you specify.

Geo-proximity

Geo-proximity routes traffic based on location just as geolocation, with enhancements to allow you to adjust how the traffic gets routed based on a value called *bias*, as shown in Figure 2.19. The bias increases or decreases the geographical size of the region that traffic gets routed to. Geo-proximity works for both AWS and non-AWS resources. If the resource resides in an AWS region, then the region is defined in the policy. If the resource is in a non-AWS location such as a corporate data center, then latitude and longitude values are used. Once the resources are defined in the policy, the size of the region can be expanded by adding a positive number between 1 and 99, and it can be shrunk with a negative value between –1 to –99.

FIGURE 2.19   Route 53 geo-proximity routing policy

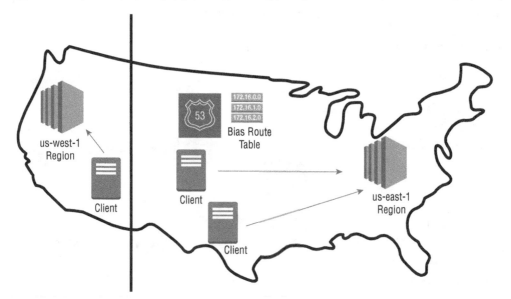

Route 53 Service Integrations

There are many hooks and integrations between the many AWS service offerings. Since Route 53 is a very fundamental networking service that is used extensively within AWS to route traffic, there are many features added to Route 53 to integrate features and make configurations easier for the customer. Amazon does not charge for Alias queries for internal services, which is nice.

VPC

DNS is supported in a VPC using Route 53's resolver features. Since Route 53 is a global service, its servers sit outside of the VPC using the IP address of 169.254.169.253, which is the base CIDR IP of the VPC's subnet +2. So, if you have a subnet of 172.16.200.0 /24, the DNS IP address would be 172.16.200.2. If the instance is configured with a private IP address, AWS will assign a hostname and IP address and register with DNS. If it is a public IP, then a public hostname will be registered along with its public IP address. Route 53 creates a private hosted zone for name resolution. Network access control lists and security groups will not work as filters of Route 53 communications, and the Route 53 Resolver only supports recursive lookups.

For public name resolution, DNS default names are in two different formats. The first for the us-east-1 (Virginia) region looks like `ec2-<public IP address>-compute-1 .amazonaws.com`; for all other regions, it will be `ec2-<public IP address>-region .compute.amazonaws.com`. Each EC2 instance can query at a rate of 1,024 packets per second. When this quota is exceeded, the service is throttled.

The resolver matches the public domain name with the public IP address of the outside instance interface and to the private IP of the inside, or private, instance interface.

To support public name resolution, the `enableDnsHostnames` attribute enables assigning public DNS hostnames to instances with public IP addresses. This attribute is enabled by default for the default VPC and disabled for all other VPCs. `enableDnsSupport`, enabled by default, allows the use of the Amazon DNS service in the VPC. Virtual machine interface address and names can be obtained through the web GUI under EC2, the CLI using the `describe-network-interfaces` command, and in PowerShell using the `Get_ EC2VpcAttribute` command.

CloudFront

Route 53 is integrated with CloudFront using routing policies including latency, geo-based, and failover routing. Zone apex support allows you to access your CloudFront edge locations using the apex name of, for example, `tipofthehat.com` along with `www.tipofthehat .com`. Alias records allow you to use your company domain name in place of the more convoluted AWS CloudFront names.

Load Balancers

The use of the Alias record is also used in directing traffic via Route 53 to the Elastic Load Balancing (ELB) service. Since the ELB address is a domain, an Alias can be configured to point your company's domain name to the AWS load balancer virtual server's DNS name. These integrations work for all of the different ELB offerings.

Route 53 Application Recovery Controller

Application availability can be increased by using the Application Recovery Controller, which is a feature of Route 53 that monitors your endpoints and is used to determine if they have availability and are ready for recovery. You can use the routing control and readiness checking to manage failover using DNS responses to queries. The feature can be used in all regions and availability zones as well as your on-premise applications. It acts as a single control point in the AWS console to manage Route 53's recovery features. Recoveries can be either active-active and/or active standby. Recoveries can be automated or manually executed.

With built-in intelligence that enhances the Route 53 services beyond basic DNS, it monitors your resource quotas, routing policies, and defined capacity. It will suggest options on how to improve your configurations and when making changes during recovery operations. policies can be configured to prevent premature recovery from happening either manually or with automation. You can configure safety rules to ensure that defined policies are enforced during a failover that prevents automated recovery actions impacting application availability.

Hybrid Route 53

Hybrid DNS with Route 53 allows you to interconnect DNS systems from your corporate on-premise servers with Route 53 running in the AWS cloud for end-to-end name resolution. DNS queries originating from AWS can be sent to your corporate DNS for resolution, and corporate DNS requests can be sent to a Route 53 Resolver to access your AWS VPC resources. This allows DNS to work across your entire network. The Route 53 Resolver allows for seamless interconnection of your Route 53 and on-premise systems, as shown in Figure 2.20.

FIGURE 2.20   Hybrid DNS architecture

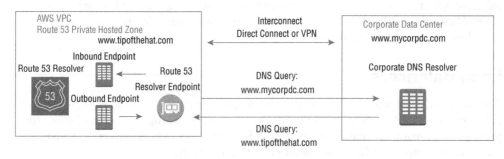

The Route 53 Resolver is a fully managed AWS service that supports 10,000 queries per second both inbound and outbound. Query metrics are displayed in CloudWatch. The on-premise and AWS cloud are required to be directly connected either by Direct Connect or by a VPN service.

Multi-account Route 53

Route 53 is supported when using multiple AWS accounts. It is common for organizations to set up a master AWS account and then create separate accounts for different environments such as production, development, and test, as shown in Figure 2.21. These can all share the same primary domain with subdomains delegated to each account such as `prod.tipofthehat.com`, `dev.tipofthehat.com`, and `test.tipofthehat.com`. Each account can own and manage its own subdomain records and not the others. With the root domain hosted in the master AWS account, the subdomains will be owned by each unique environment's account.

FIGURE 2.21　Multi-account DNS

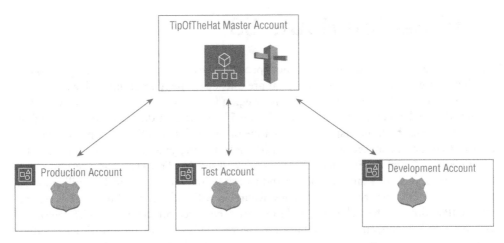

When you create the subdomains in each account, an NS record will be created. Copy these NS records and add them to the master account's Route 53 zone. The master account will then reference the NS records for each of the subdomains. What this accomplishes is that the ownership and administration of its hosted zoned is delegated to each specific account so the accounts own the subdomains and do not require administration from the master account. With multi-account Route 53 configured, different teams can now make changes to their individual records, and access is restricted at the account level.

When a DNS request is made for a host in the `test.tipofthehat.com` domain, a query is made to the `tipofthehat.com` domain, and its name server will respond with the addresses of the delegated name server for `test.tipofthehat.com`. The `test.tipofthehat.com` domain receives a query from the resolver and will then resolve the hostname to an IP address since `test.tipofthehat.com` contains the host A records are contained. This name server will reply with the requested IP address. This process is shown in Figure 2.22.

FIGURE 2.22 Multi-account forward requests

Multi-Region Route 53

Route 53 is a global AWS service and is not specific to any region. You can configure zone records that are hosted in any region or that are outside of the AWS cloud such as your own data center. Route 53 extensions allow Multi-Region failovers by enabling health checking.

Multi-Region latency-based routing is a Route 53 feature that directs users to the region hosting the service with the fastest response time or lowest latency. For example, if a user in Zurich requests a connection to `www.tipofthehat.com`, as we discussed earlier, Route 53 with latency-based routing enabled will check and see that Frankfurt has a response time of 125 milliseconds, for example, and Ireland is responding on average in 150 milliseconds. Given that Frankfurt has the lowest latency, Route 53 will reply to the Zurich user's request with the IP address of the web server in Frankfurt. Geo-based directs use an AWS region based on their location, and weighted route-robin responds to DNS queries with a rotating list of IP addresses across the regions you define to evenly disperse the load between multiple regions. Route 53 DNS failover will direct all traffic to a primary region, and should that not respond to health checks, it begins replying with IP addresses for the backup region.

Using Route 53 Public Hosted Zones

A public hosted zone is used in Route 53 to route traffic over the Internet for a specific domain such as `tipofthehat.com` and all of its subdomains such as `dev.tipofthehat`

.com, `test.tipofthehat.com`, and `prod.tipofthehat.com`. Hosted zones are created when you register a domain in Route 53 or when you transfer an externally registered domain into AWS. A public hosted zone contains your defined instructions about how you direct traffic on the Internet to your domain by defining records. When a public zone is created, Route 53 will automatically create the name server (NS) and start of authority (SOA) records.

Using Route 53 Private Hosted Zones

Private hosted zones are used to store records for your internal, non-Internet, hosts. Route 53 will respond to queries that are for resources running inside of your VPC. Every zone can support services and servers in multiple VPCs if the zone is associated with the VPC.

The private hosted zone is used strictly to route internally to your VPC and can connect to services such as ELB, an EC2 instance, or any service that has an IP address endpoint. Once the private hosted zone is created, then resource records can be added to define your endpoint records. For Internet-bound DNS queries, use the public hosted zone.

Using Route 53 Resolver Endpoints in Hybrid and AWS Architectures

Resolvers in a VPC can be configured as either inbound, outbound, or both. Inbound allows queries from your internal DNS deployment to the DNS server in your VPC. Outbound enables VPC DNS queries to your on-premise DNS, and both enable queries in both directions. When configuring an outbound endpoint, one or more forwarding rules are created to enable the domain names to route the DNS queries inside the on-premise network. The outbound endpoints specify the VPC used for the queries. Figure 2.23 shows a Route 53 Resolver interconnected with an on-premise data center.

Outbound resolver endpoints require the following values:

- The name of the endpoint, which can be any name you specify to help identify the endpoint and make it easy to identify in the AWS console.
- The VPC used for outbound DNS queries, which is the VPC that connects to your network.
- A security group for the endpoint that defines access control to the VPC. Specify an inbound rule that opens DNS on UDP and TCP port 53. Outbound rules will enable access to your on-premise DNS server from the VPC, and it is common to use UDP and TCP port 53, which is the standard port number for DNS. More than one security group can be applied.

- IP addresses inside your VPC that the resolver will forward DNS queries to reach your internal DNS resolvers. For redundancy, specify an IP address in two or more availability zones.

- When the IP addresses are defined, a VPC *Elastic Network Interface* (ENI) is created that resides in the VPC availability zone in the subnet you specified. If you are using multiple IP addresses to an endpoint, the order is not important, and for forwarded queries, the resolver will pick any IP address from the list.

- The availability zone that DNS queries will traverse in transit to your network.

- The subnet that the IP address resides in that DNS queries are originating from.

- The IP address that the DNS queries are originating from; these can be selected for you form the subnet pool of the availability zone or statically configured.

FIGURE 2.23   Resolver endpoints

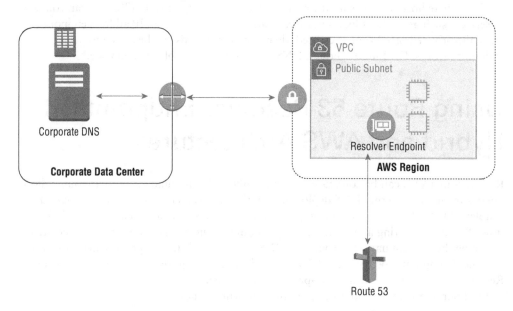

There can be four resolver endpoints per region and each endpoint can be assigned six IP addresses. There is a maximum of 1,000 rules per region and each endpoint can service up to 10,000 queries per second.

Using Route 53 for Global Traffic Management

DNS can be used in high-availability architectures of your AWS deployment. Multiregional failover can be achieved with the proper Route 53 configurations to detect a failure and reroute traffic to an operational region or availability zone. To ensure that your applications are available through natural disasters or planned outages at the regional or availability zone level and to enable cross-region replications, the advanced features of Route 53 can assist in maintaining your uptime metrics.

Route 53 Failover

Once all of the application-related tasks have been completed for the backup location, Route 53 needs to be configured with health checking, as shown in Figure 2.24. This allows for Route 53 to continuously check that the primary location is up, and should it stop responding to the checks, it will be considered failed. Traffic will be rerouted to the backup location by changing the DNS record's IP address to the backup site. Because of the design of DNS and its use of caching, there will be a delay as the backup IP addresses propagate. This is because of the TTL values associated with each A record and the time it takes for changes to spread across the global DNS framework. You can help reduce the propagation by setting the TTL to a lower value such as 60 seconds in an attempt to force the server to decrease the update frequency of refreshes.

FIGURE 2.24   Route 53 regional failover

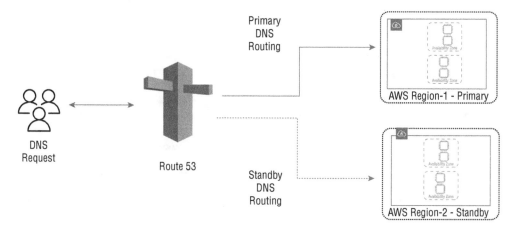

For a failover to be successful, much of the success will require that the applications in the backup region are able to accept and handle the load delivered during a failure. This requires that standard disaster recovery planning takes place to have the destination servers running and able to accept the connections from the failed primary.

Domain Registration

Amazon Route 53 includes a domain registration service that allows you to purchase public domains for use with Route 53 or other DNS service providers' services. In addition to creating a new domain, you can transfer an existing domain that you own into AWS and manage it from the AWS Route 53 console. You can also export your domain to another registrar if desired.

From the AWS Route 53 console, check to see if the domain is available for purchase, as shown in Figures 2.25 and 2.26.

FIGURE 2.25   Domain lookup

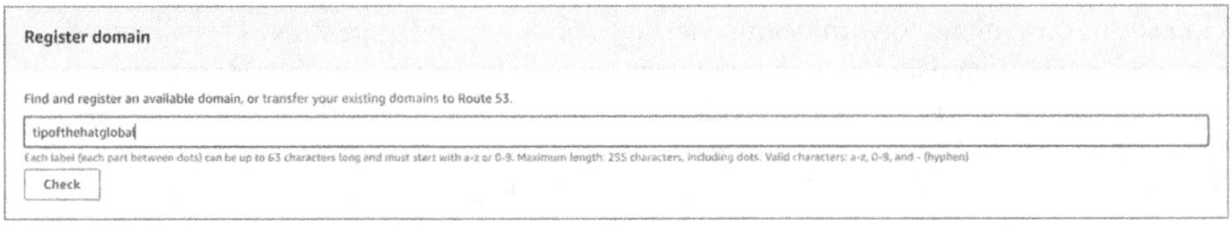

FIGURE 2.26   Domain choice

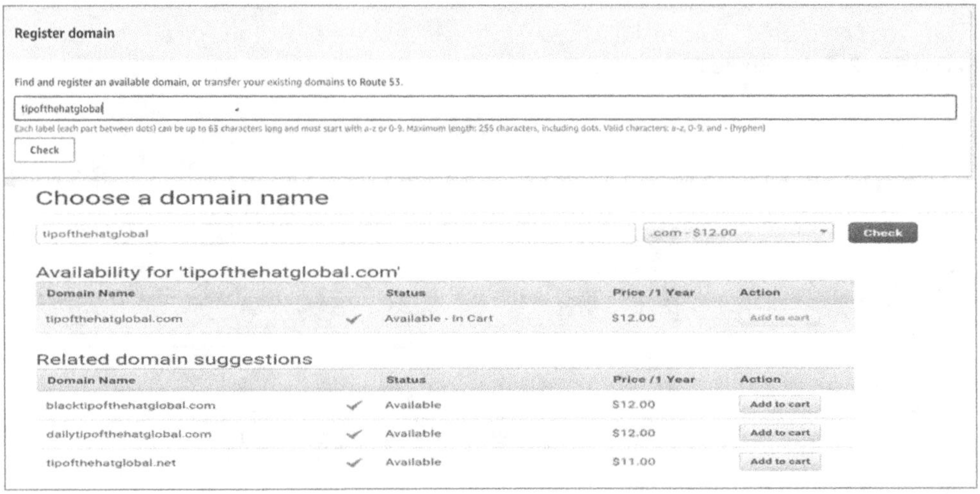

Required Information to Register a Domain

You are required to have a contact type, which can be either an individual or an organization, which includes the first and last names of the contact.

You must specify the same contact information for the registrant of the domain, the administrative contact, and the technical contact, as shown in Figure 2.27.

The contact information includes the following:

- The name of the organization registering the domain
- Contact email
- Street address

- City
- State (or province)
- Zip or postal code
- Country

FIGURE 2.27   Route 53 domain registration contact information

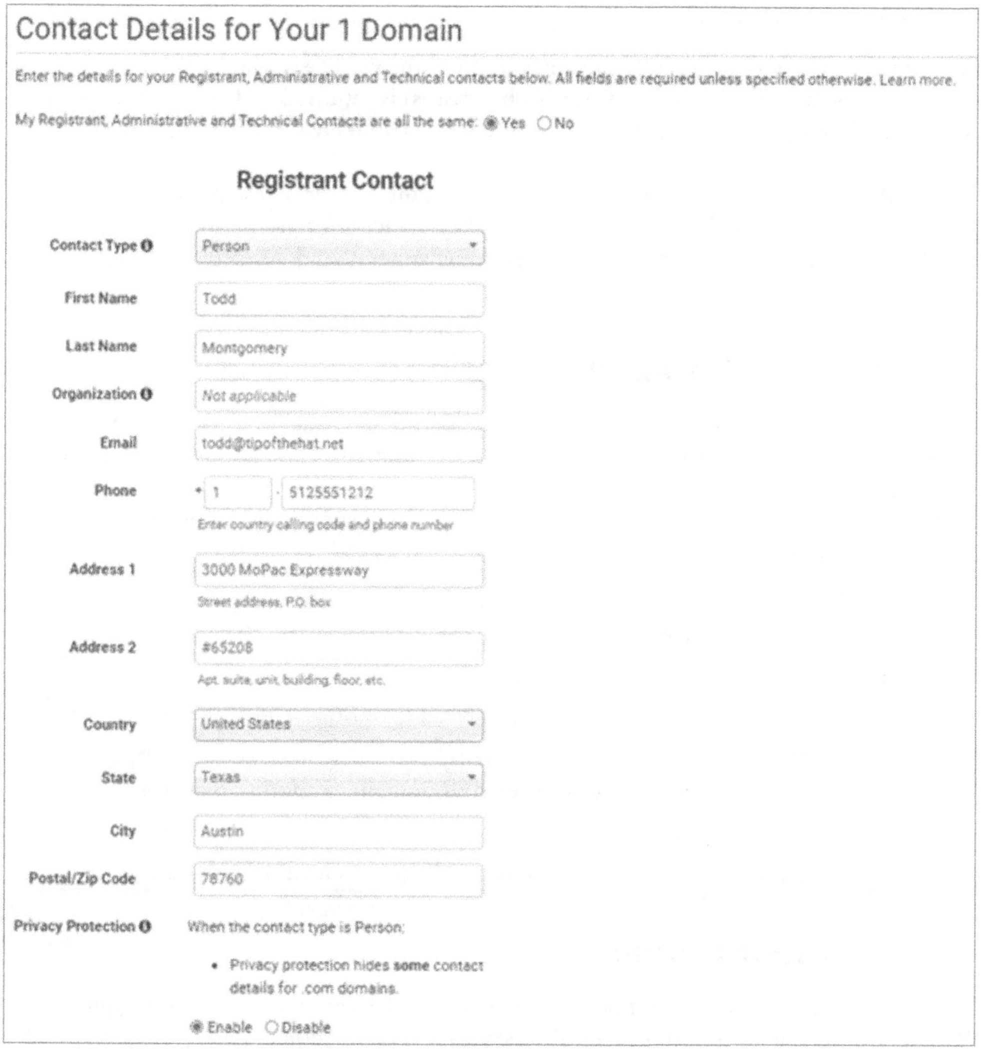

Contact Details for Your 1 Domain

Enter the details for your Registrant, Administrative and Technical contacts below. All fields are required unless specified otherwise. Learn more.

My Registrant, Administrative and Technical Contacts are all the same: ◉ Yes ○ No

Registrant Contact

Contact Type ❶	Person ▾
First Name	Todd
Last Name	Montgomery
Organization ❶	Not applicable
Email	todd@tipofthehat.net
Phone	* 1 - 5125551212
	Enter country calling code and phone number
Address 1	3000 MoPac Expressway
	Street address, P.O. box
Address 2	#65208
	Apt, suite, unit, building, floor, etc.
Country	United States ▾
State	Texas ▾
City	Austin
Postal/Zip Code	78760
Privacy Protection ❶	When the contact type is Person:

- Privacy protection hides **some** contact details for .com domains.

◉ Enable ○ Disable

Some TLDs will need extra information such as tax and legal documents based on local regulations. Some examples of TLDs that will require additional information include the following: `.com`, `.au` and `.net.au`, `.ca`, `.es`, `.fi`, `.fr`, `.it`, `.ru`, `.se`, `.sg`, `.co.uk`, `.me`

.uk, and .org.uk. See the AWS documentation for details on what is needed for each top-level domain.

The contact email must be active and monitored. Failure to respond to a verification email can cause your domain to be deactivated and no longer reachable from the Internet. If you change who administers the domain, proof must be provided using this email to approve the change before a change will be applied.

Privacy Protection

You can elect to hide your WHOIS information from the public so when a WHOIS query is made, the registrar information (Amazon Web Services) is returned and not your personal data. If you do not hide your personal data, you will most likely get a fair amount of spam in your inbox.

WHOIS is widely used and available to anyone on the Internet. Anyone can perform a WHOIS query for a domain and get back all of the contact information for that domain. The WHOIS command is available in many operating systems, and it's also available as a web application on many websites.

Route 53 Registration Information

The ICANN is the organization that manages and coordinates the Internet namespaces and IP addressing for the Internet. ICANN coordinates all domain registrations for the Internet worldwide.

After your registration is completed with AWS, they will supply the following information to you:

- The date the domain was registered
- The expiration date, which is usually one year but can be up to 10 years
- The status of the domain using an ICANN status code
- If the domain is locked and cannot be transferred to another registrar or unlocked allowing a transfer
- The authorization code needed to transfer your domain to another registrar
- If autorenew is turned on
- The AWS name servers that will be used for DNS queries for this domain

Renewing Your Domain

You can set the domain to autorenew, and the renewal charges will be applied to your AWS account. If you disable autorenewals, then, as it says, the domain will not be renewed and will expire on the expiration date, making it no longer available on the Internet. If the domain has expired, the name will be available for anyone to register and use.

Summary

In this chapter, you learned about DNS and the Amazon-specific offering called Route 53. DNS is a name-to-IP resolution service that is used extensively in both public and private networks. You learned about the DNS architecture and hierarchy and the basic functions of DNS systems including the root, top-level, and domain name servers. We discussed what a resolver is and how it queries various name servers to obtain an IP when given a domain name. Zones were also introduced as containers that store records for the domain, and then you learned about the various types of records used in DNS.

Route 53 is a fully managed service that includes a 100 percent uptime service-level agreement and many advanced features that extend its functionality beyond basic DNS services.

Various DNS internals were discussed such as TTL timers and the delegation of zones to distribute DNS operations. DNSSEC is a feature that was added to DNS to provide encryption and authentication for security. As a part of DNSSEC, we briefly discussed public key encryption and the types of security keys that are used in DNSSEC.

Route 53 is integrated with many AWS services for logging and monitoring its operations. These services include CloudTrail, CloudWatch, and Redshift. Advanced features of Route 53 include the addition of Alias records, resolvers, health checking, and a Route 53 firewall.

Traffic routing policies determine how resolution records are returned to the resolver and include simple, multivalue, latency, failover, weighted, and round-robin routing options. Geolocation and geo-proximity routing were discussed as a method to route requests to specific locations based on where the originator and destination are located from each other.

We also learned about service integrations with Route 53 and other services such as VPCs, CloudFront, load balancers, health checking, and the Application Recovery Controller.

Hybrid Route 53 is when we interconnect your on-premise DNS system to Route 53 in a VPC for both internal and external name resolution using public and private hosted zones. Next, we discussed how Route 53 can be implemented in multi-account and multiregion AWS deployments.

Global traffic operations were discussed, and failure architectures were introduced.

Finally, you learned how to use Route 53 to register a domain for your use.

Exam Essentials

Know the DNS resolution steps.   Understand the resolution steps that DNS takes to resolve a URL that a user types in a browser to resolve the DNS name to an IP address.

Know what a zone is.   A zone is a subset of your domain records that contains your DNS records such as the A record, which is an IPv4 address, an MX record for Mail, a TXT record for basic information about the domain, and many others. Familiarize yourself with the record types given in this chapter with a special focus on the Alias record.

Know in detail the DNS hierarchies and what they represent.   Understand the various server types such as root, top-level, and domain servers and the role of the resolver.

Understand the Route 53 DNS extensions that go beyond basic DNS name resolution services. You must know these in detail for the exam. These include traffic policies and service integrations with other AWS services. Understand the logging and security aspects of the service.

Know what internal and public zones are and when to use each one. Internal zones provide name resolution inside of a VPC, and public zones are Internet-facing.

Understand the interconnection with Route 53 to your internal DNS system in a hybrid configuration.   Take the time to watch videos and read the internal AWS documentation that goes into detail on how this operates and how to set it up.

Know that Route 53 is a domain registrar.   Understand the steps required to transfer or register a domain name for your use.

Exercises

Setting up Route 53 requires the use of a registered domain. This will incur charges for you to get hands-on with the service. While it is encouraged to do so, if you do not want to be billed, then reviewing the documentation is recommended.

1. Read the DNS and Route 53 overview to understand basic DNS operation and the resolution process: `https://docs.aws.amazon.com/Route53/latest/Developer Guide/welcome-dns-service.html`.

2. Read the documents under Route 53 best practices: `https://docs.aws.amazon .com/Route53/latest/DeveloperGuide/best-practices.html`.

3. Read the documentation on the Route 53 health-checking process: `https://docs .aws.amazon.com/Route53/latest/DeveloperGuide/welcome-health-checks.html`.

4. Become familiar with the Route 53 DNS firewall: `https://docs.aws.amazon.com/ Route53/latest/DeveloperGuide/resolver-dns-`.

5. Know the different routing policies and how they are used: `https://docs.aws .amazon.com/Route53/latest/DeveloperGuide/routing-policy.html`.

6. Read the overview of Route 53 integrations with other AWS services: `https://docs .aws.amazon.com/Route53/latest/DeveloperGuide/integration-with-other-services.html`.

7. In the AWS management console, navigate the Transit Gateway documentation and become familiar with its functions and use cases. See `https://aws.amazon.com/ blogs/networking-and-content-delivery/centralized-dns-management-of-hybrid-cloud-with-amazon-route-53-and-aws-transit-gateway`.

8. Read and have a basic understanding of DNSSEC and how it is implemented in Route 53: `https://docs.aws.amazon.com/Route53/latest/DeveloperGuide/domain-configure-dnssec.html`.

9. Read the short document on domain registration: `https://docs.aws.amazon.com/Route53/latest/DeveloperGuide/welcome-domain-registration.html`.

Review Questions

The following questions are designed to test your understanding of this chapter's material. For more information on how to obtain additional questions, please see this book's introduction.

1. Your production FTP services are running across four separate servers in two regions for resiliency and to enable support for peak load times during end of month processing. The application support team is reporting that all connections are being sent to one server and the other three have no FTP sessions. You have been tasked to find a method to evenly disperse the connection load. What would be a good solution to implement?

    A. Enable simple routing to serve IP records across all four FTP servers

    B. Use latency-based routing and configure the load to be delivered at 25 percent for each of three servers

    C. Deploy the AWS CloudFront content distribution network

    D. Enable a round-robin Route 53 policy

    E. Deploy a weighted routing Route 53 policy

2. A critical application is being migrated to AWS, and there is a mandate from the corporate management team that a hot standby site be set up in the Asia-Pacific Mumbai region to back up the primary server fleet in Asia-Pacific Jakarta. As the cloud network specialist on the project, you are looking at DNS solutions to facilitate failover. What feature of Route 53 would meet this requirement?

    A. Monitor CloudWatch metrics for a failure and trigger an SNS and Lambda process to failover to the backup site

    B. Configure Route 53 failover routing to health check the Jakarta servers, and if they stop responding, change the DNS response to point to Mumbai

    C. Use a Route 53 public hosted zone with a multivalue response of both locations

    D. Configure an Alias record for the standby and have it take effect if the primary site's health checks fail three consecutive times

    E. Trigger a CloudTrail event notification to page the on-call engineer to activate the standby site in Mumbai

3. Your corporate DNS server is running BIND and connects to your Route 53 private zone over a direct connection for their data center to your VPC running is the Ireland region. Your VPC resolver is configured for resolution, but systems in the corporate data center cannot resolve to EC2 instances in your VPC. What would need to be changed to enable AWS private zone support from the corporate network?

    A. Configure the BIND server to source AWS zone records

    B. Configure the VPC for enableDnsHostnames and enableDnsSupport to be true.

    C. Configure the Route 53 firewall to allow inbound traffic from the BIND server UDP/TCP port 53

    D. Make sure the zone has Internet connectivity with a NAT instance and Internet gateway configured.

    E. Create an IAM role for the DNS resolver in the corporate network

4. What statements are accurate about Route 53 resource records? (Choose two.)

    A. Alias records can point to a DNS record regardless of where it is hosted.

    B. Alias records can map one domain name to another.

    C. Zone apex names can be created in CNAMEs.

    D. Alias records support changing the TTL value.

    E. Route 53 CNAME records can point to other records regardless of location.

5. You have been tasked as the cloud network engineer to give architecture advice on a new project that includes network load balancers in the Northern Virginia region. One requirement is to point the domain apex of `tipofthehat.com` to the external-facing interface of the ELB configured as `www.tipofthehat.com`. How would you accomplish this?

    A. Configure an A record for the ELB

    B. Configure an AAAA record for the ELB

    C. Use the Route 53 Alias record

    D. Use the Route 53 CNAME record

6. A member of the accounting staff enters `www.tipofthehat.com` into their web browser. The resolver does not have this record in cache and must do a lookup to find the IP address. What are two of the servers it would query to resolve this domain name?

    A. TLD

    B. Alias

    C. Root

    D. Apex

    E. Public zone server

7. You server fleet has a mixture of EC2 instances that are used to serve content to your customers. There is a large performance difference, and the older instances can accept only a limited number of connections as compared to the newer EC2 deployments that can serve hundreds of requests. You would need to make a static network configuration change to account for the difference in server performance. What policy would help resolve this issue?

    A. Latency-based routing

    B. Simple routing

    C. Multivalue responses

    D. Weighted routing

    E. Round-robin routing

8. A new project is starting for the development group, and they plan to add a new VPC to host EC2 instances to support their programming tools. A requirement is to use the existing Route 53 private zone for name resolution. What steps would you need to accomplish this task? (Choose two.)

    A. This is not possible; a new Route 53 private zone would need to be created in the new VPC.

    B. Set the DHCP option in the new VPC's subnet to deliver the Route 53 Resolver address.

    C. Configure a host file on the EC2 instances for local name resolution.

    D. Associate the Route 53 private hosted zones' VPC to the new VPC.

    E. Connect the private data centers forwarders to connect to the Route 53 Resolver.

9. Your operations teams want to collect metrics on DNS activity in your AWS operations. What would you recommend as a base server to accomplish this request?

    A. CloudTrail

    B. Amazon Macie

    C. Control Tower

    D. CloudFront

    E. CloudWatch

10. What is the name of the organization that tracks registered domains?

    A. IANA

    B. ICANN

    C. ARIN

    D. ENISA

11. You are in the process of configuring Route 53 DNS services for both your Internet accessible servers and servers in an availability zone that has no NAT gateway. What two types of zones would you need to configure?

    A. Private hosted zone

    B. Single AZ zone

    C. Public hosted zone

    D. Internet zone

12. What Route 53 feature is used to monitor your endpoints and is used to determine if they have the ability and are ready for reinstatement in DNS responses to queries?

    A. Hybrid Route 53

    B. Route 53 failover

    C. Application Recovery Controller

    D. Transfer acceleration

13. When resolving a DNS query, each DNS server that answers the queries needs a path to every zone in that namespace. What is the name given to this process?

    A. Delegation

    B. Zone

    C. Multivalue

    D. Health checking

14. What AWS data warehouse offering can analyze Route 53 logging data in a data lake and SQL queries to gain insight on the data?

   A. Elastic Map Reduce

   B. Hadoop

   C. Redshift

   D. Spark

15. Which extension of the simple routing policy returns any number up to eight responses of IP addresses for the same domain name?

   A. Latency

   B. Multivalue

   C. Round-robin

   D. Weighted

16. What is stored in a zone that contains host-specific data and information about the zone?

   A. Resource records

   B. Alias records

   C. Resolvers

   D. Host's file

17. What is the term used to describe when you interconnect Route 53 with the DNS system from your corporate on-premise operations for end-to-end name resolution?

   A. Public hosted zones

   B. Hybrid Route 53

   C. Multi-account

   D. Private hosted zones

18. Which AWS Route 53 component allows for seamless interconnection of your Route 53 and on-premise systems?

   A. CloudFront

   B. Hybrid Route 53

   C. Control Tower

   D. Resolver

19. Which DNS resource record contains a mapping from domain name to IPv6 address?

   A. A

   B. AAAA

   C. MX

   D. CNAME

20. Which Route 53 routing policy uses a bias to affect the records returned from a query?

    A. Regional routing

    B. Geo-proximity

    C. Geo-zone

    D. Geolocation

Chapter

3

Hybrid and Multi-account DNS

THE AWS CERTIFIED ADVANCED NETWORKING - SPECIALTY EXAM OBJECTIVES COVERED IN THIS CHAPTER MAY INCLUDE, BUT ARE NOT LIMITED TO, THE FOLLOWING:

✓ **Domain 2: Network Implementation**

- Objective 2.3: Implement complex hybrid and multi-account DNS architectures.

Implementing Hybrid and Multi-account DNS Architectures

In this chapter, we will expand on the DNS and Route 53 topics covered in Chapter 2, "Domain Name Services," with the primary focus on implementing Route 53 and its features. We will use the AWS web console and configure the many features of Route 53. Since owning a domain name and hosting it on Route 53 is a chargeable service, you will have to decide whether you want to purchase your own domain or just follow along with the examples in this chapter.

You will gain skills in configuring Route 53 zones, records, traffic management, and security, as well as how to work with centralized and decentralized configurations and how to set up Route 53 monitoring and logging. With this practical knowledge, you will have the skills to answer the DNS objectives on the exam and also to work with Route 53 in the real world.

Route 53 Hosted Zones

When working with standard DNS applications, you will configure zone files. A *zone file* is a collection of records that are managed as a group and belong to a single domain name. In Route 53, the concept is the same, but the name is slightly different as it is referred to by AWS as a *hosted zone*. A hosted zone is a container that contains the various types of DNS records. The hosted zone is part of a domain or subdomain such as `tipofthehat.com` or `production.tipofthehat.com`. The hosted zone and domain share the same name in the AWS Route 53 console, as shown in Figure 3.1.

FIGURE 3.1   Route 53 hosted zones

Route 53		Route 53 > Hosted zones								
Dashboard										
Hosted zones		**Hosted zones (3)**					↻	View details	Edit	Delete	**Create hosted zone**
Health checks		Automatic mode is the current search behavior optimized for best filter results. To change modes go to settings.									
▼ IP-based routing		Q Filter hosted zones by property or value								< 1 > ⊚
CIDR collections										
		Domain name ▽	Type ▽	Created by ▽	Record count ▽	Description ▽	Hosted zone ID ▽
▼ Traffic flow		tipofthehat.com	Public	Route 53	11	Main TipofTheHat.com	
Traffic policies		test.tipofthehat.com	Public	Route 53	2	-	
Policy records		tipofthehat.net	Public	Route 53	6	-	

Hosted zones are either external and public-facing or internal to an AWS VPC, called a *private zone*. Public and private hosted zones are defined when configuring the zones in the Route 53 console, CLI, or API.

Private Hosted Zones

In Chapter 2, you learned that private hosted zones are used to store records for your internal, non-Internet hosts. Route 53 will respond to queries that are for resources running inside your VPC. Every zone can support services and servers in multiple VPCs if the zone is associated with the VPC. The *private hosted zone* is used strictly to route internally in your VPC and can connect to services such as ELB, an EC2 instance, or any service that has an IP address endpoint. Once the private hosted zone is created, resource records can be added to define your endpoints.

To route traffic inside your VPC using DNS, you must create a private hosted zone, as shown in Figure 3.2, and place the resource records inside of the zone.

FIGURE 3.2   Route 53 private hosted zones

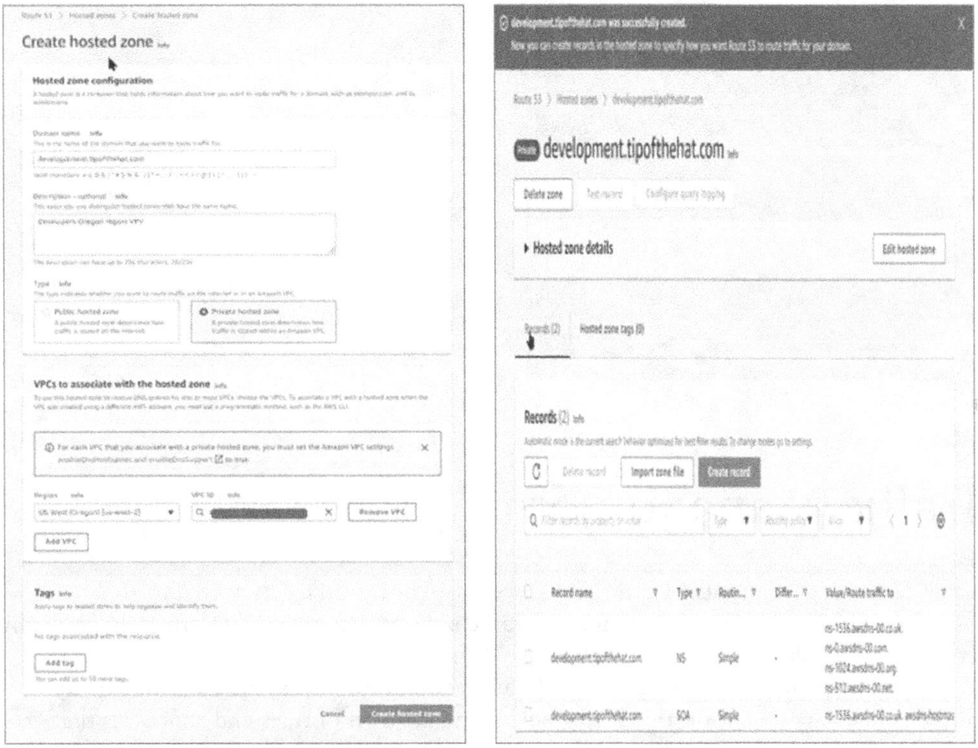

Public Hosted Zones

Public hosted zones are created to deliver name resolution and other Route 53 DNS services on the Internet. In Route 53 a public zone routes traffic on the Internet for a specific domain.

For Internet-based DNS queries, the *public hosted zone* is used. A public hosted zone contains your defined instructions about how you want to direct traffic on the Internet to your domain by defining records. When a public zone is created, Route 53 will automatically create the Name Server (NS) and Start of Authority (SOA) records for you, and you must create the specific resource records needed for your domain. Figure 3.3 shows the fields required to create a public hosted zone in the Route 53 web console.

FIGURE 3.3   Route 53 public hosted zones

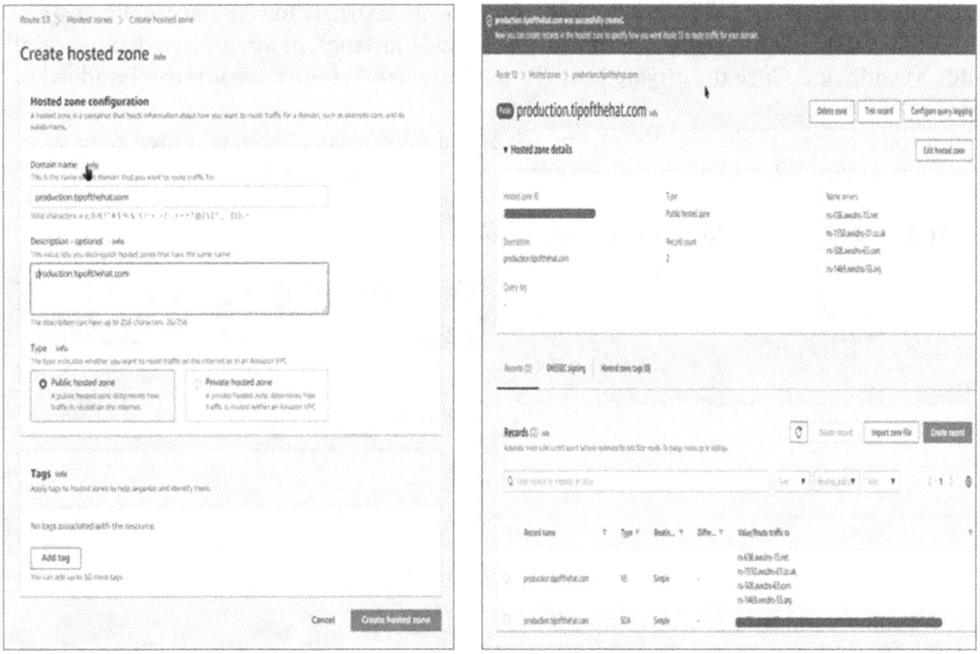

Traffic Management

Route 53 traffic management features let you control how traffic gets routed to your service endpoints. Route 53 supports a number of traffic policies that are used to affect the traffic by returning an IP address based on a policy you define.

By creating policies, you can affect the IP address that Route 53 returns from a query. Traffic policies are used for traffic management and are a set of rules and endpoints that are created by you and applied to the domain name. You can also create a single policy and apply it to more than one domain name.

The policy is the name of the container that contains all of the configurations. The traffic policy record is the domain name with a policy applied to it.

To configure a traffic policy, select Traffic Policies on the left pane of the Route 53 console to open the visual editor, as shown in Figure 3.4. You start by entering a policy name that is user-friendly and easy to understand. The policy name will appear in the console when the policies are listed, and you cannot change the name after it has been created. The version number will be automatically assigned by AWS. The version description allows you to document any changes or notes about this version and will appear in the console when the traffic versions are listed. Click Next, and the Traffic Policy Editor will appear. The DNS Type field is the starting point and lists many of the record types that you can select to configure. If you are connecting to an AWS service such as CloudFront, S3, or an elastic load balancer, use its IP address (A record). The next step is to define what you are connecting to; here you define the failover rules, a geolocation, latency, multivalue, and weighted, an endpoint, and an existing rule or endpoint. Next is the Value type where the options include CloudFront, an ELB, an S3 website, or a DNS type value. Based on your selection, follow the graphical interface configuration steps to fill out the information to complete the traffic policy creation process.

FIGURE 3.4   Traffic policy editor

If you need to update a policy, you can edit an existing policy and AWS will automatically update the version number with the policy name staying the same. The older version will be retained, and you can decide to delete it if it is no longer needed.

Traffic policies can also be defined by creating a JSON document and importing it into the policy editor. Follow the online documentation for how to format the JSON file.

There is a lot of flexibility available to you when defining a policy. In this section, we will use a standard A record that points to an EC2 instance with an attached elastic IP interface, as shown in Figure 3.5. However, note that traffic policies can be applied to any type of record, and the options may be different. Please refer to the online documentation for the specifics of how to work with the different types of policies.

Using the web graphical interface, you build your policy and then apply it when finished. The first step is to define the DNS policy name of the area labeled "Start point." This is usually an A record, the IP address, or a CNAME that points to another domain name. The next step is to define how you want to connect, which can be either weighted, failover, geolocation, latency, multivalue, geo-proximity, or a new endpoint. Then click Create.

FIGURE 3.5 Traffic policy creation step 1

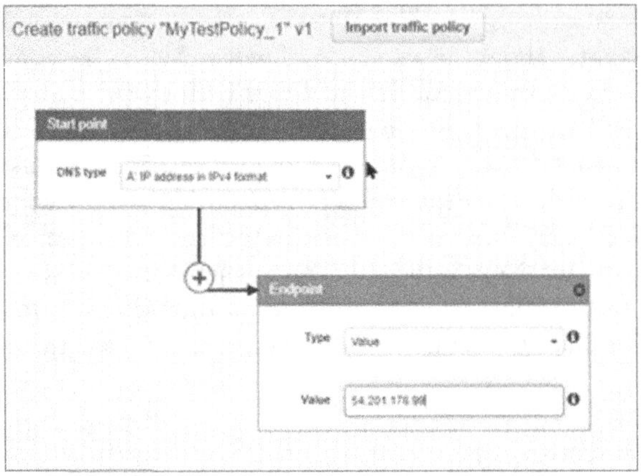

Figure 3.6 shows the final step of creating the policy. After the policy has been created, it will be applied and take immediate effect.

FIGURE 3.6 Traffic policy creation step 2

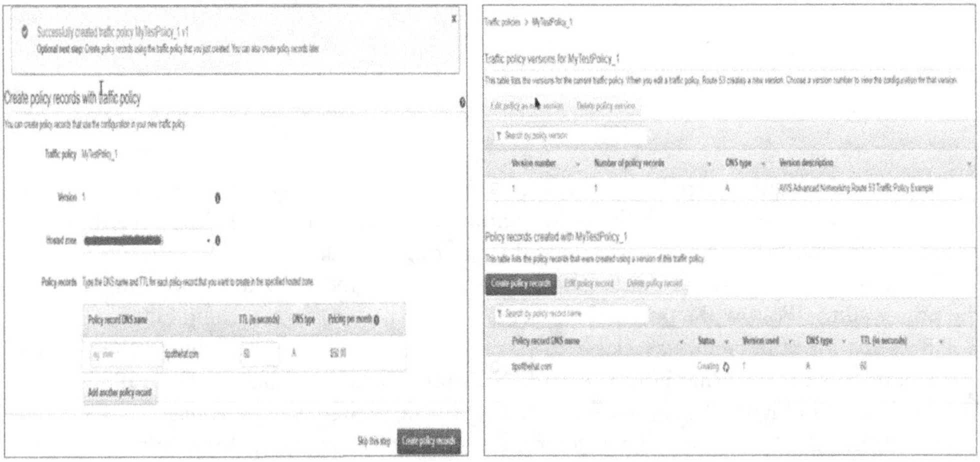

The policies are versioned so you can roll backward or forward as needed and track changes to your policy configurations. All previous versions are automatically saved and can be manually deleted if they are no longer needed.

Latency

Latency-based routing is configured at the record level in the Route 53 console. AWS calculates the delay, or latency, over the Internet from the requesting device to the endpoint in the AWS cloud. However, latency-based routing does not calculate the application's delay such as the latency inherent in a database or backend application. Select the record you want to apply the policy to in the AWS Route 53 hosted zone console. The basic record detail parameters will appear on the right pane; click Edit Record to configure the policy. In the Routing Policy drop-down box, select Latency, fill out the fields for the region, and configure health checking if desired and the ID, which can be anything you choose to define, as shown in Figure 3.7.

FIGURE 3.7   Traffic latency-based routing

Geolocation

In the AWS Route 53 hosted zone console, select the record you want to apply the geo policy to and begin the configuration process. The basic record detail parameters will appear on the right pane; click Edit record to configure the policy. In the Routing Policy drop-down box, select geolocation and fill out the location you are allowing to access this record. The selections can be continent, country, or for the United States, the state, as shown in Figure 3.8. When you are done configuring the policy, it will take effect immediately.

FIGURE 3.8   Geolocation routing

Weighted

Select the record you want to apply the weighted policy to in the AWS hosted zone console. The basic record detail parameters will appear on the right pane; click Edit Record to configure the policy. In the Routing Policy drop-down box, select Weighted and fill out the weight to assign this record. You will need to fill out multiple records and assign different weights to them since using a single weighted policy would still direct 100 percent of the traffic to that endpoint. Figure 3.9 shows the weighted-based routing configuration dialog box.

FIGURE 3.9   Weighted-based routing

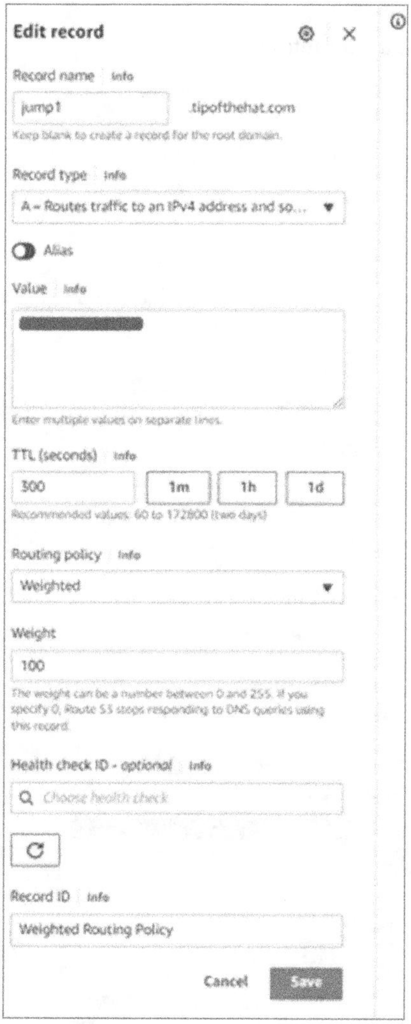

Failover

As you learned in Chapter 2, failover routing policies will direct all traffic to the primary location by serving its IP address as long as it is passing health checks. Should the endpoint stop responding to health checking, a failover will be triggered, and the policy will then begin sending the backup device's IP address in response to DNS queries.

Select the record you want to apply the failover policy to in the AWS hosted zone console. The basic record detail parameters will appear on the right pane; next click Edit Record to configure the policy. In the Routing Policy drop-down box, select Failover Type and the health check policy to be used; then select if you want this record to be the Primary or Secondary endpoint, as shown in Figure 3.10. If the primary should fail, then Route 53 will serve the failover endpoint's IP address.

FIGURE 3.10   Failover-based routing

Multivalue

Multivalue records are similar to simple routing except that you fill out multiple IP addresses, as shown in Figure 3.11. Route 53 will then send out all of the IP addresses in response to a DNS query, and the requesting device will select one from the list to use to initiate the connection. This feature is often used to distribute connections across multiple endpoints without having to implement a load balancer.

FIGURE 3.11   Multivalue-based routing

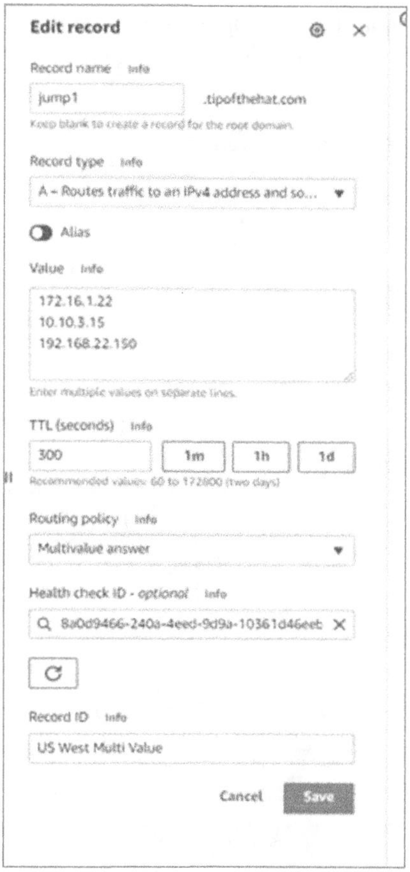

Health Checking

Health checking for Route 53 is used to test that the endpoints are reachable and responding to application requests before returning the IP address in response to a query. Route 53 will send a test connection at regular intervals to either an IP address or domain name that you specify. If a resource does not respond, it is considered to be unhealthy. Route 53 will failover to a backup device by changing the IP address that is returned in a query.

In addition to the DNS record monitoring, CloudWatch metrics can be configured using the large number of metrics that are collected by any AWS service. This allows for application-level monitoring as well as the underlying infrastructure such as EC2 instances or microservices. Other CloudWatch metrics that are used with Route 53 health checking include elastic load balancing metrics, a minimum number of servers that are responding, and backend applications such as RDS databases. These metrics are monitored at the streaming level so they are near real time and do not need to wait for CloudWatch to generate an alarm. Figures 3.12 and 3.13 show the basic health checking configuration in the Route 53 console. There are a lot of additional configuration options because of the flexibility of this feature, and the online documentation covers the details.

FIGURE 3.12   Health check configuration step 1

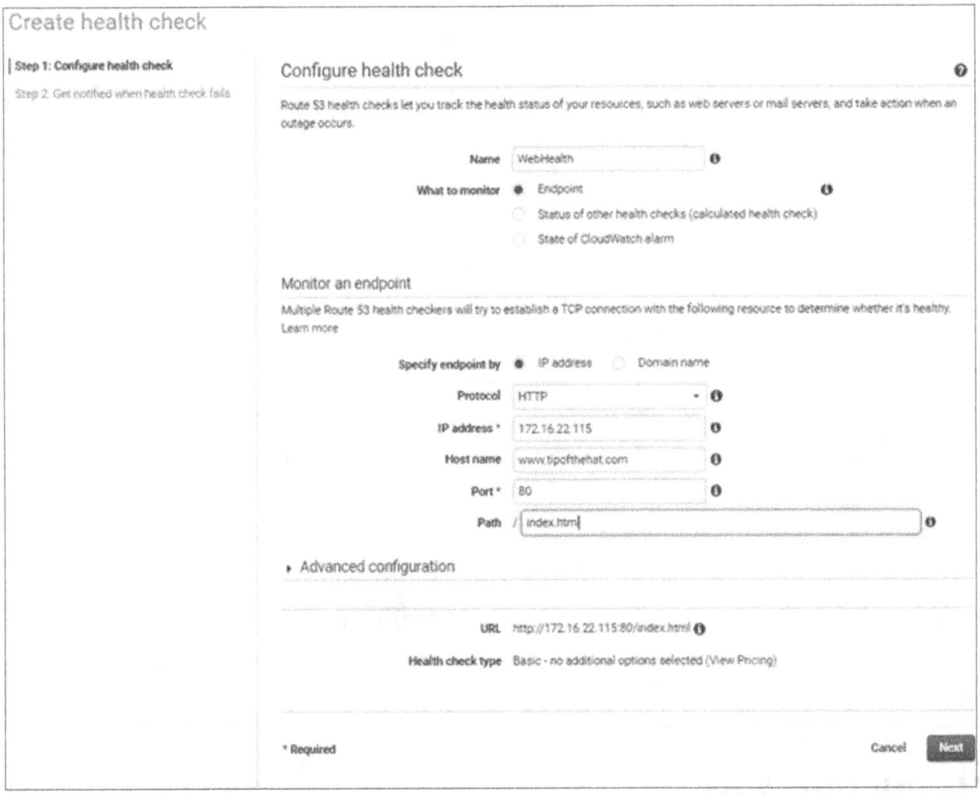

FIGURE 3.13   Health check configuration step 2

Create health check

Step 1: Configure health check
Step 2: Get notified when health check fails

Get notified when health check fails   ❓

If you want CloudWatch to send you an Amazon SNS notification, such as an email, when the status of the health check changes to unhealthy, create an alarm and specify where to send notifications.

Create alarm   ⦿ Yes   ◯ No ❶

CloudWatch sends you an Amazon SNS notification whenever the status of this health check is unhealthy for at least one minute. The alarm will be located in the **us-east-1** region.

Send notification to   ◯ Existing SNS topic   ⦿ New SNS topic ❶

Topic name * | Web_DNS_Check | ❶

Recipient email addresses * | support@tipofthehat.com | ❶

Separate multiple addresses with a comma, a semicolon, or a space.

* Required   Cancel   Previous   Create health check

Domain Delegation and Forwarding

Most large organizations do not configure all of their DNS records, policies, and features from a central point of administration. By dividing the domain up into multiple subdomains such as `production.tipofthehat.com` and `development.tipofthehat.com`, the configuration duties can be delegated to the individual groups by designating authority of part of a namespace to one or more other DNS servers. This is a common scenario, and Route 53 allows you to delegate with a few simple configuration steps.

Delegating Domains

Delegating records involves updating the DNS parent domain with the addition of NS (name server) records for the subdomain.

The steps to configure a subdomain delegation start with creating a new hosted zone in a secondary account such as `production.tipofthehat.com`. Also select if it is a public or private zone in the drop-down box. Click Create and copy the NS records that are assigned to it.

In the main account, create a NS record set from the new delegated zone by selecting the type of name server and enter in the NS records you copied from the new delegated account; click Create to activate the new hosted zone.

Use a tool such as `dig production.tipofthehat.com` to verify the configuration.

You can now create A records or any other parameters in the new subdomain.

The following shows the basic `dig` command response for a domain in AWS:

```
[ec2-user@ip-10-100-1-140 ~]$ dig tipofthehat.com
; <<>> DiG 9.11.4-P2-RedHat-9.11.4-26.P2.amzn2.5.2 <<>> tipofthehat.com
;; global options: +cmd
;; Got answer:
;; ->>HEADER<<- opcode: QUERY, status: NOERROR, id: 2897
;; flags: qr rd ra; QUERY: 1, ANSWER: 1, AUTHORITY: 0, ADDITIONAL: 1

;; OPT PSEUDOSECTION:
; EDNS: version: 0, flags:; udp: 4096
;; QUESTION SECTION:
;tipofthehat.com.                IN      A

;; ANSWER SECTION:
tipofthehat.com.        60      IN      A       54.201.176.99

;; Query time: 18 msec
;; SERVER: 10.100.0.2#53(10.100.0.2)
;; WHEN: Fri Aug 26 21:01:30 UTC 2022
;; MSG SIZE  rcvd: 60
```

Forwarding Rules

Conditional forwarding rules are required to tell the Route 53 Resolver what domain names you want to forward to remote resolvers such as an on-premise DNS server. A forwarding rule is needed for each domain to which you want queries to be forwarded.

In the Route 53 console dashboard, select Rules in the left pane under Resolvers. Click Create Rule and follow the prompts. Figure 3.14 shows an example of the rule creation dialog box in the rule console of Route 53.

Configuring Records in Route 53

Hosted zones act as a container that will hold the various records used in your DNS deployment. While there are more than 90 different types of records, only around 10 are actually used with any frequency. In this section, we will learn how to configure these records in a Route 53 hosted zone. Figure 3.15 shows the web console zones to select when adding records to a hosted zone.

FIGURE 3.14   Resolver forwarding rules

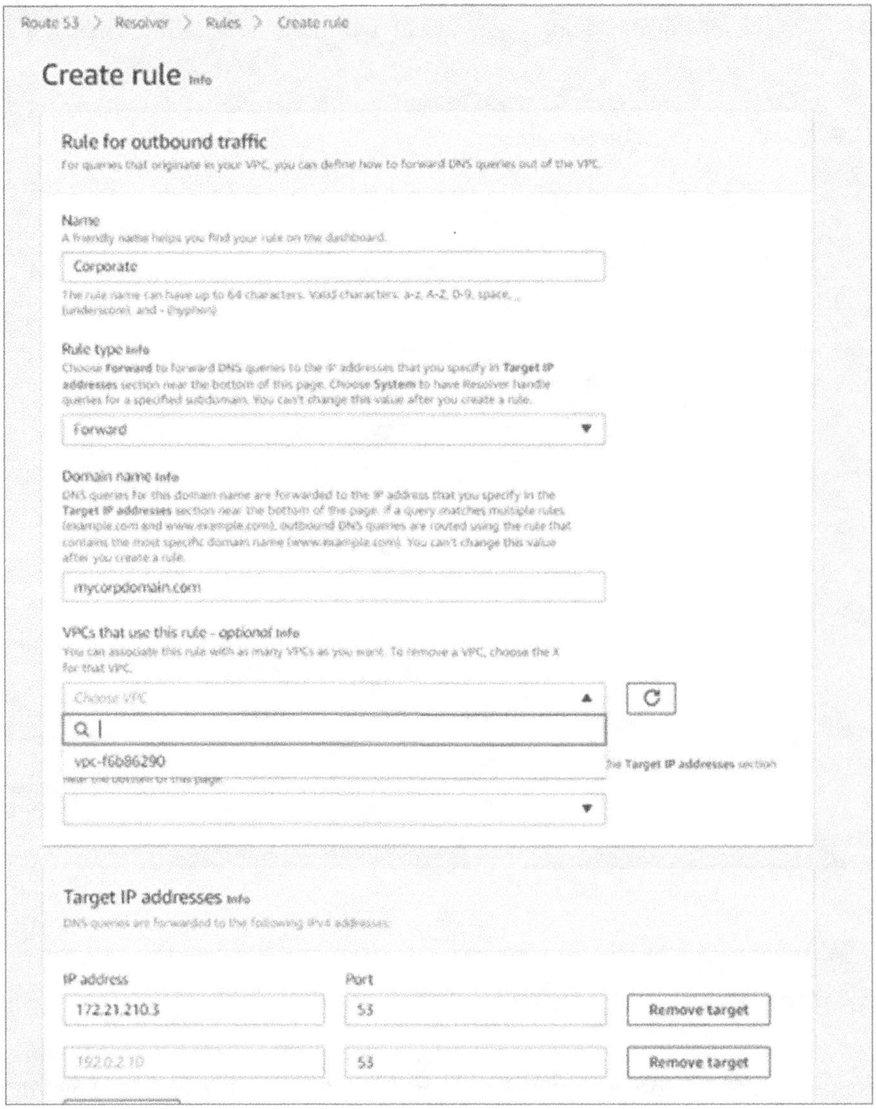

A Record

The most common DNS record type is the A record, which maps a fully qualified domain name to an IP address. Figure 3.16 shows the configuration screen to create an A record, and you will notice that it is very basic. You need the domain name, and the IP address can change the TTL if you desire. When a DNS lookup for an IPv4 host name is received, Route 53 will look at the fully qualified domain name and return the translated IP address in the A record.

FIGURE 3.15 Route 53 record types

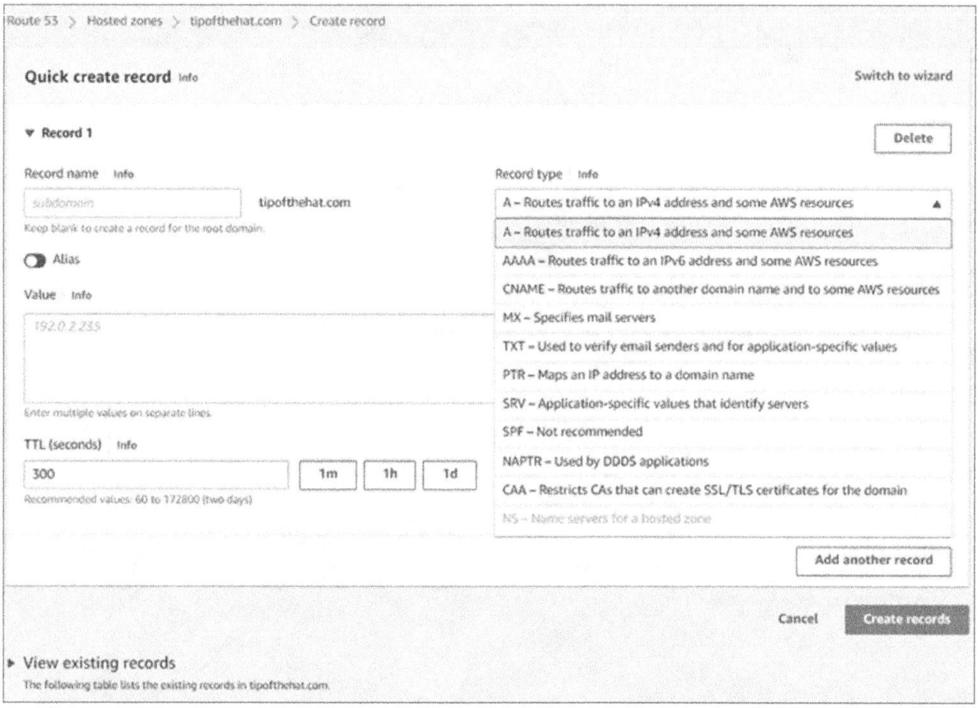

AAAA Record

The AAAA, or as it is often called, the quad A record, is for IPv6 translations. This is the same concept as the A record except it is used for IPv6 addresses. Figure 3.17 shows the AAAA record configuration screen in Route 53.

CNAME

The CNAME, or canonical name, record points one domain name to another domain name or subdomain but never to an IP address. This redirects name lookups to an alternate domain name or AWS resource such as an EC2 or RDS database endpoint. Figure 3.18 shows the configuration dialog in the Route 53 graphical console.

FIGURE 3.16   A record

FIGURE 3.17   AAAA record

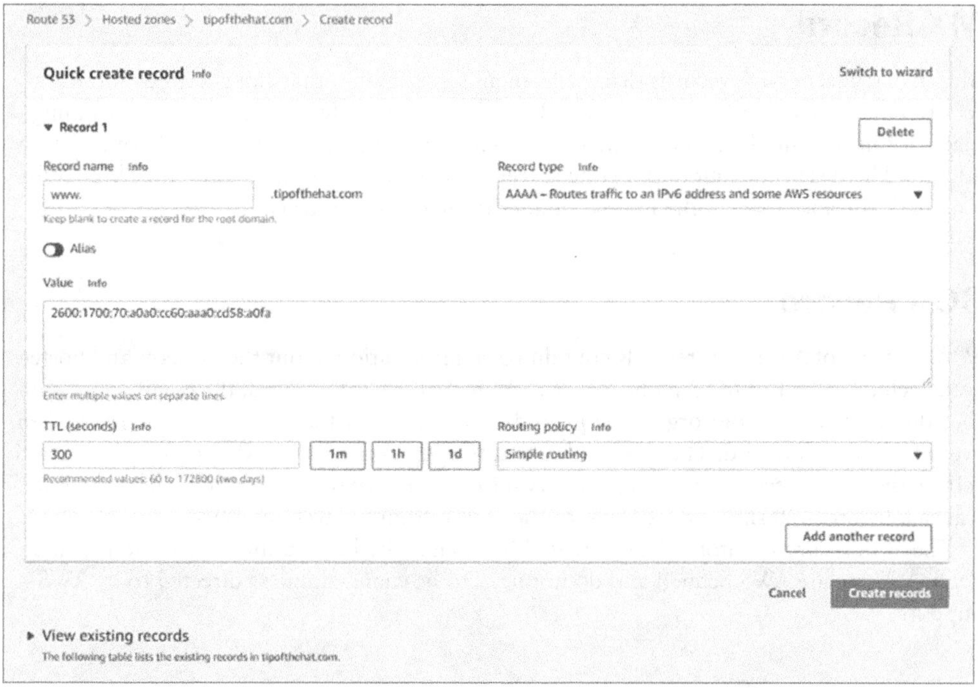

FIGURE 3.18   CNAME record

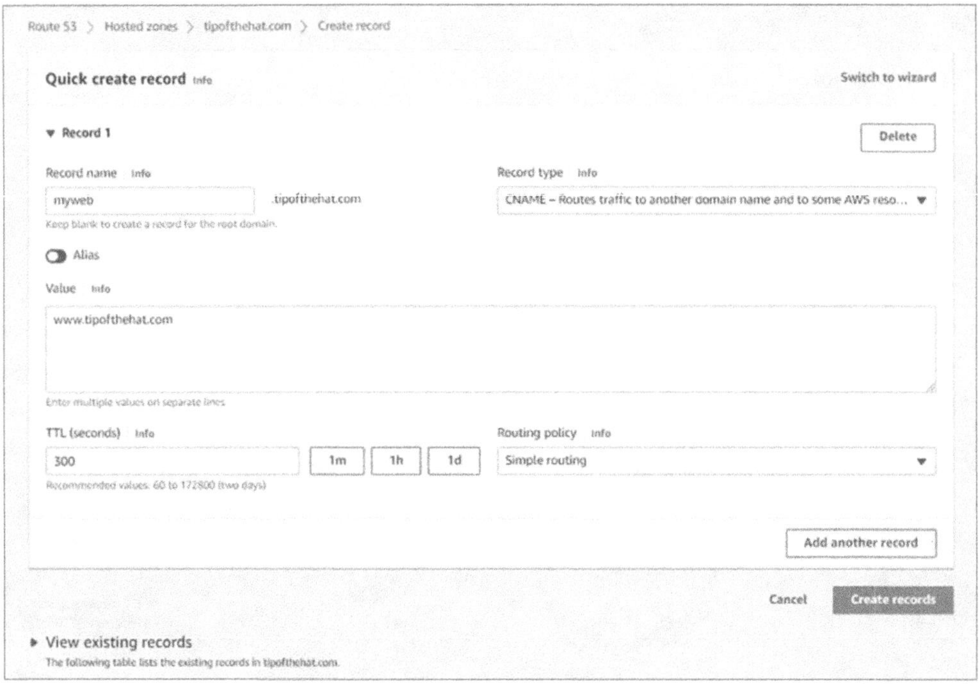

MX Record

Mail Exchange, or MX, records define the email server names that can accept email that's sent to your domain, as shown in Figure 3.19. This record defines where to map incoming mail for this domain. It is a best practice to point to an email server name and not its IP address. There is usually more than one server configured for resiliency, and they are given a numerical priority where the lowest number is the highest priority.

SOA Record

SOA, or Start of Authority, records contain basic information about the domain and hosted zone including the Route 53 name server that created the SOA record, the email address of the administrator for your organization, and a serial number that can be incremented whenever you update a record. There is a value that tells the secondary DNS servers how often to refresh their zone records and a retry interval the secondary server must wait to retry a failed transfer. Figure 3.20 shows the configuration screen from the web interface.

The SOA record is automatically created by Route 53 when a public hosted zone is first defined. These are AWS defined and do not need to be changed unless directed to by AWS Support.

FIGURE 3.19 MX record

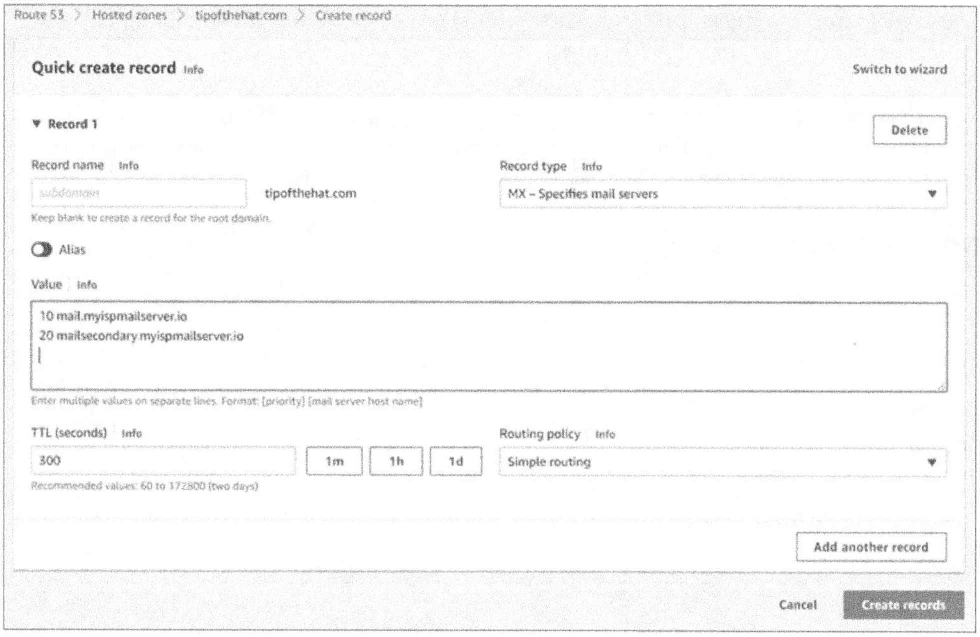

Route 53 > Hosted zones > tipofthehat.com > Create record

Quick create record Info   Switch to wizard

▼ Record 1   [Delete]

Record name Info   Record type Info

[subdomain] tipofthehat.com   [MX – Specifies mail servers   ▼]
Keep blank to create a record for the root domain.

🔘 Alias

Value Info

```
10 mail.myispmailserver.io
20 mailsecondary.myispmailserver.io
|
```
Enter multiple values on separate lines. Format: [priority] [mail server host name]

TTL (seconds) Info   Routing policy Info

[300]   [1m] [1h] [1d]   [Simple routing   ▼]
Recommended values: 60 to 172800 (two days)

                                                                        [Add another record]

                                                             Cancel   [Create records]

FIGURE 3.20 Start of Authority record

Edit record   ⚙ ✕

Record name
tipofthehat.com

Record type
SOA – Start of authority record

🔘 Alias

Value Info

```
ns-1774.awsdns-29.co.uk. awsdns-
hostmaster.amazon.com. 1 7200 900 1209600
86400
```
Enter multiple values on separate lines. Format: [authority-
domain] [hostmaster-email-address] [zone-serial-number]
[refresh-time] [retry-time] [expire-time] [negative caching
TTL]

TTL (seconds) Info

[900 ‡]   [1m] [1h] [1d]
Recommended values: 60 to 172800 (two days)

Routing policy Info

[Simple routing   ▼]

TXT Record

Text records are containers used by administrators to attach both human- and machine-readable notes to the zones. TXT records are used to validate, for example, email ownership, application licensing, or any information about a server, network, data center, company, or accounting data. The TXT record is formatted as standard UTF-8 ASCII text data.

All text data in the value field must be enclosed in quotation marks, and many different lines of text can share a single TXT record, as shown in Figure 3.21.

FIGURE 3.21   TXT record

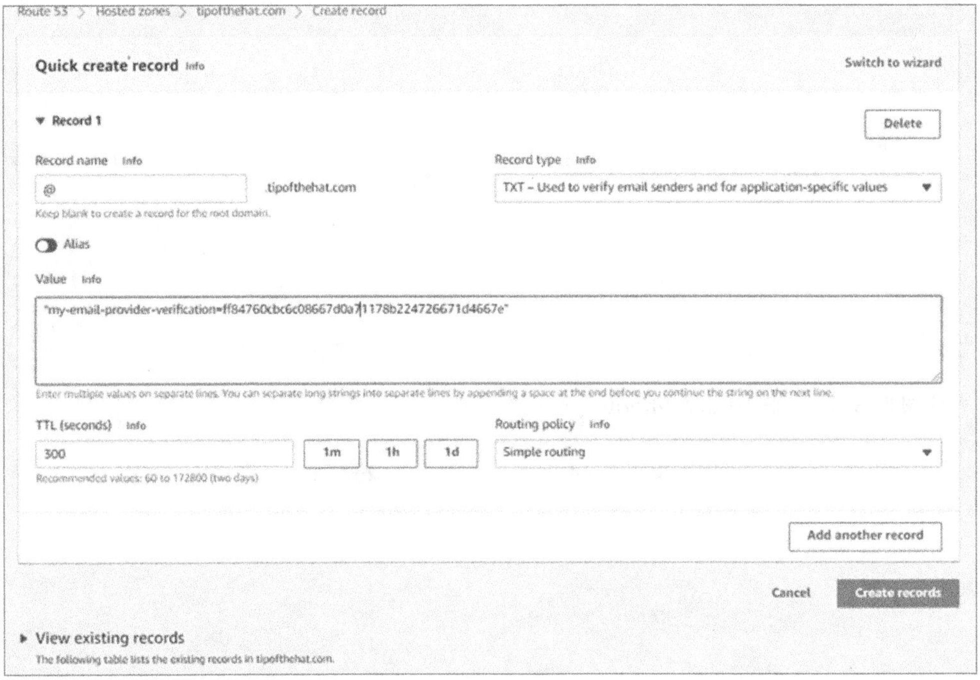

PTR Record

The pointer, or PTR, record is the reverse of what an A or quad A record does. The PTR will return the domain name when given the IP address; it maps the IP address to the domain name instead of the domain name to IP address mapping in standard DNS implementations, as shown in Figure 3.22.

Alias Record

The Alias record is proprietary to AWS and can map a zone apex, which is the raw domain name, to a fully qualified domain. Also, the Alias record maps your company domain name to the AWS internal DNS name. This allows for a user-friendly name that maps to the rather long and sometimes convoluted AWS domains. Another feature of using the Alias record is that Route 53 monitors the Alias record, and if the DNS changes on the backend, traffic will route to the new endpoint. Figure 3.23 shows the setup screen to configure an alias in the Route 53 web console.

FIGURE 3.22   PTR record

SRV Record

The Service, or SRV, record redirects sessions for specific service types, such as VoIP or instant messaging sessions, to specific hosts and port numbers. The syntax is in the format of `[priority] [weight] [port] [server host name]` such as `1 10 5269 xmpp-server1.tipofthehat.com`, as shown in Figure 3.24.

SPF Record

The Sender Policy Framework, or SPF, record was used to limit email spoofing and scammers and was used to validate the identity of the email sender. It has been deprecated and is not in common use because of interoperability issues. TXT records have replaced the use of SPF records. Figure 3.25 shows that Route 53 discourages the implementation of SPF records but still allows you to create them.

FIGURE 3.23   Alias record

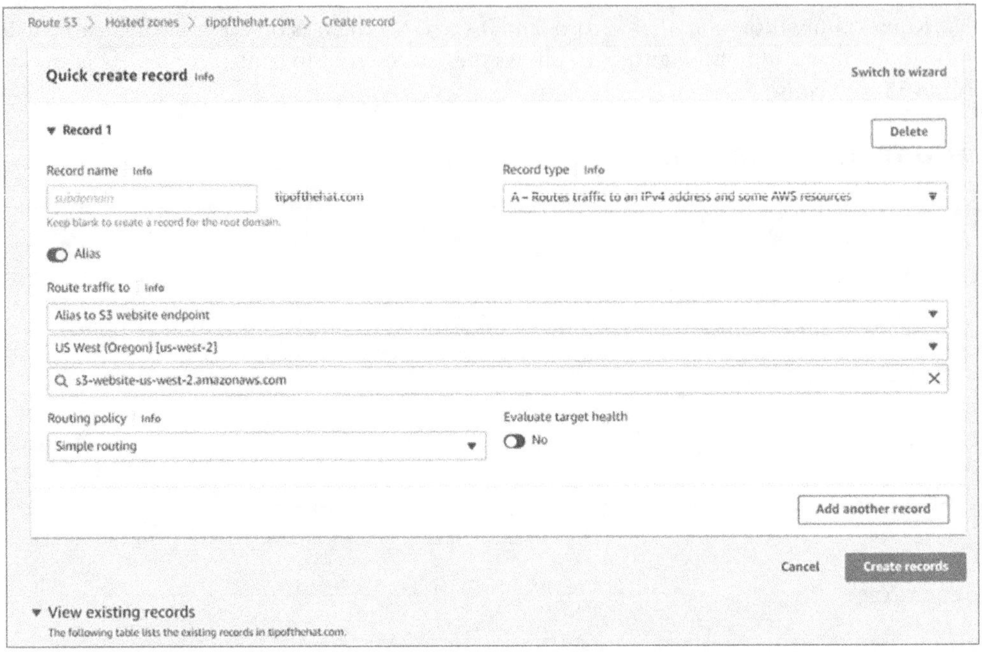

FIGURE 3.24   SRV record

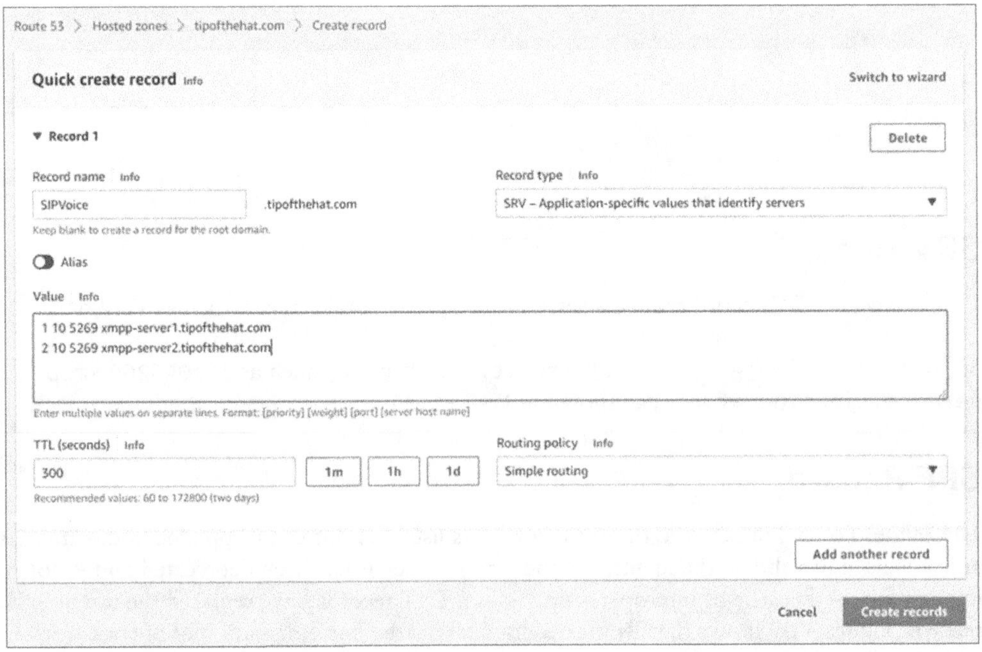

FIGURE 3.25   SPF record

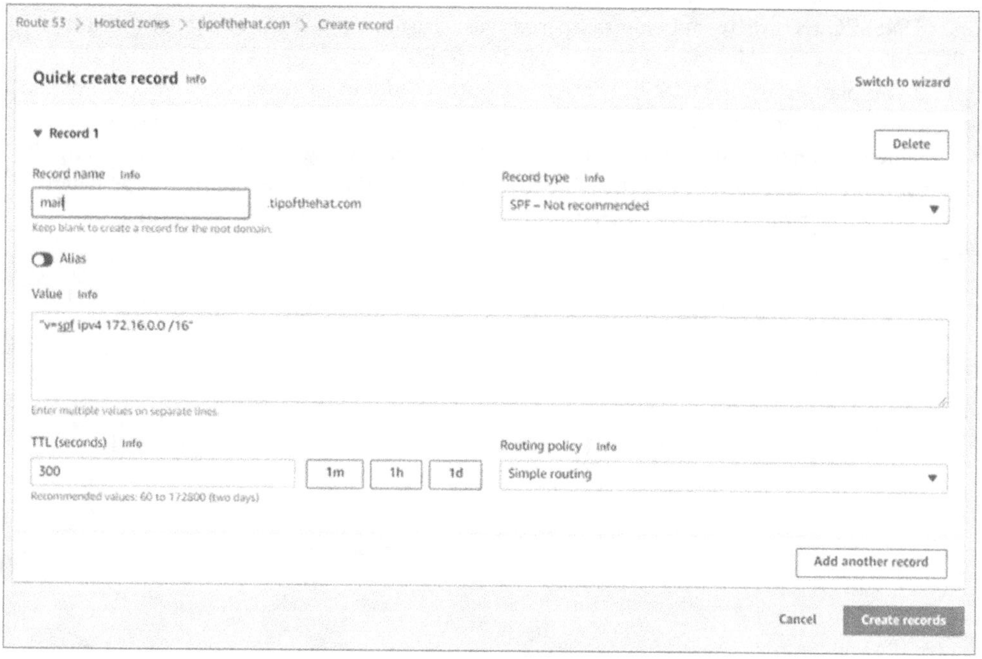

NAPTR Record

The Name Authority Pointer, or NAPTR, record is commonly used for Internet Telephony applications when mapping servers and user addresses in the Session Initiation Protocol (SIP) to convert phone numbers to URIs.

NAPTR record sets are used by Dynamic Delegation Discovery System (DDDS) applications to convert or replace one value with another. Figure 3.26 shows the Route 53 web console screen for the NAPTR record configuration.

CAA Record

The Certificate Authority Authorization, or CAA, record limits the certificate authorities (CAs) that can create TLS/SSL certificates in the domain. This is a whitelist of CAs that you allow to issue certificates for this domain or subdomain. Figure 3.27 shows the basic CAA resource record configuration.

Configuring DNSSEC

As you learned in Chapter 2, DNS Security is a feature added to Route 53 that adds digital signing for public hosted zones, and validation for the Route 53 Resolvers. Data origin, authentication, and integrity verifications are features of this security extension for DNS. Each record in a Route 53 hosted zone is signed with a cryptographic key. This prevents DNSSEC records from being tampered with. Turn on DNSSEC on Route 53 in the VPC you choose, and the resolver will apply the crypto security and keys to enable the feature. If you plan on using DNSSEC between Route 53 and external services, it is important to research the remote application and versions to make sure there is end-to-end compatibility. Since the records in the zone file are cryptographically signed by DNSSEC and apply DNSKEY and RRSIG records in the zone file, follow the AWS-recommended steps when modifying these records to make sure the crypto records are up-to-date with the data in these files.

FIGURE 3.26 NAPTR record

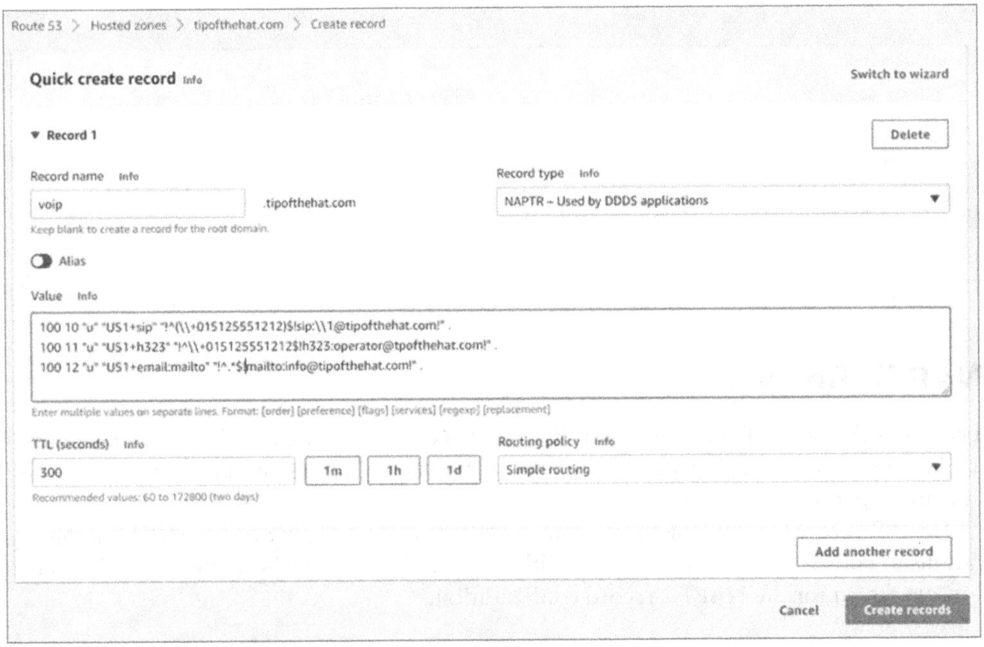

Multi-account Route 53

Many AWS customers divide their operations into multiple accounts for security, operational groups, blast radius reduction, and billing purposes. This allows you to assign a master account and delegate access and operational control to accounts and organizations that belong to the group. The use of organizations also reduces the need to create duplicate resources in each account. This allows you to create a resource one time and share it to accounts you assign by creating shares.

The AWS *Resource Access Manager* (RAM) allows you to share resources across accounts while maintaining security and operational control. You can configure IAM accounts and policies for each account to delegate responsibilities and define what can be accessed in each account by configuring managed permissions for each resource type such as Route 53. The AWS RAM supports Route 53 Resolver rules, monitoring, policies, and all other Route 53 operations that are delegated.

FIGURE 3.27 CAA record

The AWS Resource Access Manager is provided at no cost and is useful for maintaining a clean and organized operation in the AWS cloud.

The AWS RAM works by first creating a resource share to manage the access to resources. Then you select the resources to add to the share, which pushes the resource access to accounts that you define. Next, add the managed permissions that define what actions are allowed to be performed on each resource defined in the share. Then you enter which accounts, organizational units (OUs), IAM roles, and users are allowed to access the share. The resource is accessible based on your configuration.

DNS Endpoints

As you learned in Chapter 2, *DNS endpoints* reside in a VPC and are the connection points for your on-premise resolvers to service DNS queries from your site to AWS or in both directions. Endpoints are also used for VPC-to-VPC resolution in AWS. When configuring resolver endpoints, the requirement is that there be a direct connection between the two networks. This can be either an AWS DX (Direct Connect) or VPN interconnection with appropriate routing to advertise the subnets between the two networks. Resolution can be inbound, outbound, or bidirectional from the perspective of the VPC. Note that bidirectional is actually configuring both inbound and outbound together, as shown in Figure 3.28.

FIGURE 3.28 Inbound/outbound endpoint configuration

Outbound Endpoints

Outbound endpoints allow DNS resolutions originating inside of your VPC to your on-premise DNS deployment or to another VPC. As with all DNS endpoint architectures, a direct connection is required and can be either the DX, Direct Connect, service or by using a VPN connection. Outbound DNS queries require forwarding rules to define the domains hosted on-premise, and the rules define what will be forwarded to the on-premise resolver when a query is made in your VPC.

Figure 3.29 shows the architecture of the outbound endpoint, and Figure 3.30 shows the basic configuration screen. You must give the endpoint a name, the VPC in the region, a security group, and the IP address information. When finished, click Create and validate the changes in the resolver VPC section of the Route 53 console.

FIGURE 3.29   Outbound resolver endpoints

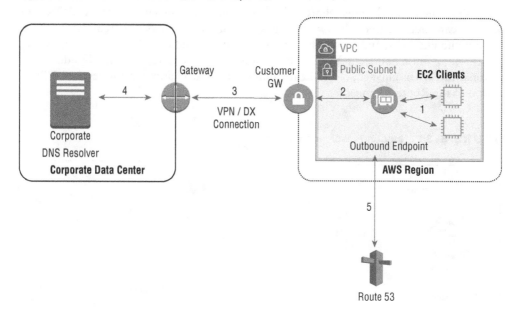

FIGURE 3.30   Outbound endpoint configuration

Inbound Endpoints

Endpoints can be configured as inbound only for DNS resolutions originating outside of the VPC such as from another VPC or from your internal network. The Route 53 Resolver *inbound endpoints* terminate DNS queries from outside of the VPC to the internal Route 53 infrastructure. When connecting your on-premise DNS infrastructure to the VPC, the networks must share a direct connection using either a DX or VPN service that can route between the two networks. Figure 3.31 shows the architecture of the inbound endpoint, and Figure 3.32 shows the basic configuration screen. You must give the endpoint a name, the VPC in the region, a security group, and the IP address information. When finished, click Create and validate the changes in the resolver VPC section of the Route 53 console.

FIGURE 3.31   Inbound resolver endpoints

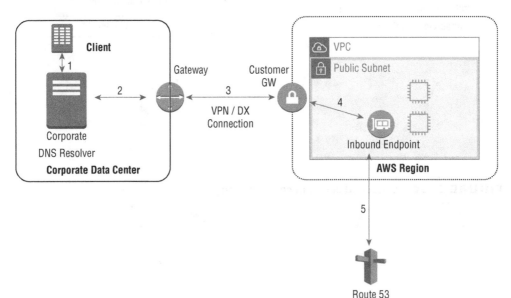

Configuring Route 53 Monitoring and Logging

In this section, you will learn how to configure the many different options available to collect logging and metrics on Route 53 and how to use the collected data to ensure the availability, reliability, security, and performance of your Route 53 deployment.

Before implementing your monitoring strategy, it is valuable to analyze what your needs are. Questions to ask yourself include the following: What is it exactly you are looking to accomplish? Are there any corporate or regulatory requirements for data retention? What Route 53 resources are you intending to monitor? What is the data collection frequency you require? What AWS tools can you use to accomplish your monitoring and logging plan? Which internal groups will be responsible for the day-to-day monitoring and logging operations? Is it better to outsource to an external service company that specializes in this area and has special tools you can leverage? Do you have an escalation plan in place to notify individuals and automation services of critical events?

FIGURE 3.32   Inbound endpoint configuration

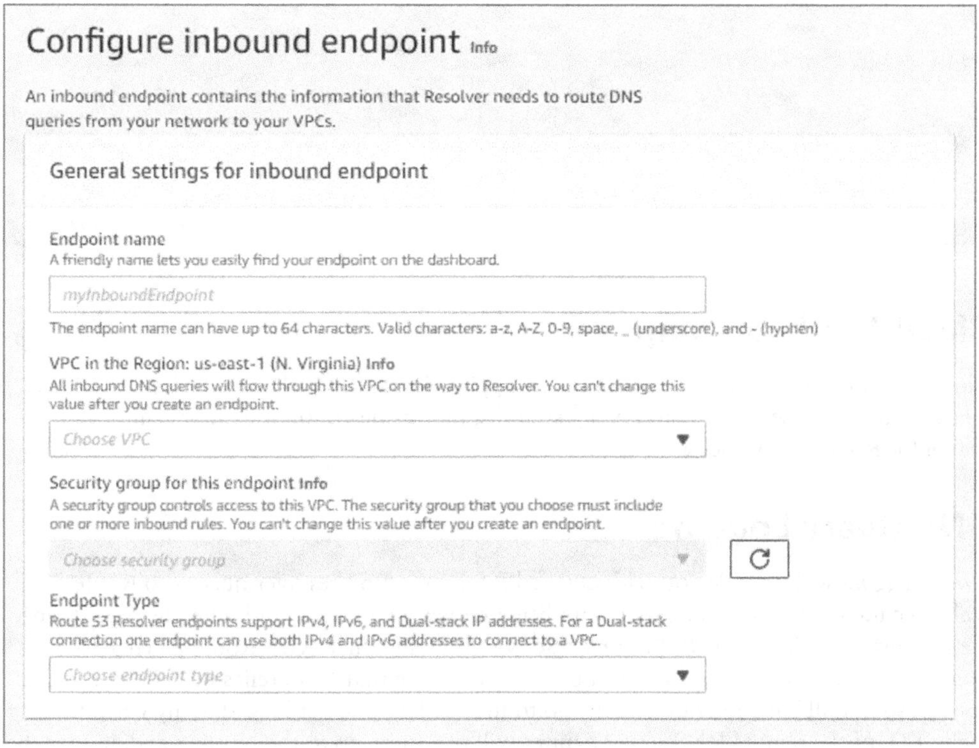

CloudTrail API Logging

CloudTrail is the AWS service that logs activity from users, roles, or other services. If there are console, CLI, or application actions taken, it is an API call behind the scenes, and it gets logged in CloudTrail. Route 53 CloudTrail actions are stored in an S3 bucket that you define for long-term storage and are also cached for the short term in the CloudTrail service in its event history logs.

There is a great deal of event information collected, including the source IP of the request, who made the request, the date and time, and any other pertinent information including what the change was.

The event logging is in the Northern Virginia region since Route 53 is a global and not regional service. See Figure 3.33 for an example of the CloudTrail console for a Route 53 trail.

FIGURE 3.33   CloudTrail event history

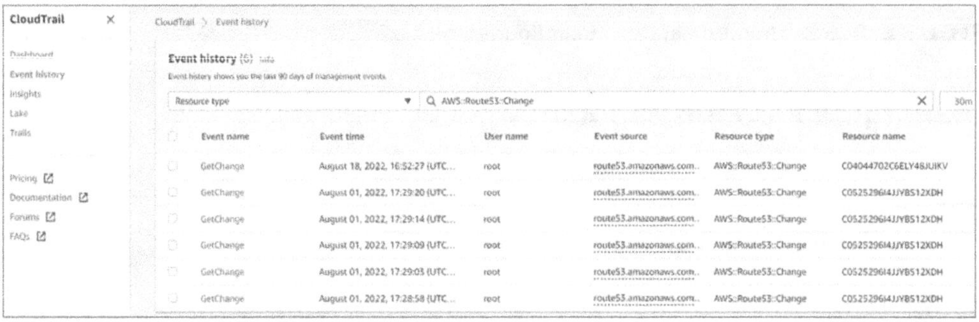

CloudWatch Logging

CloudWatch is the primary AWS monitoring application and is rather extensive in its capabilities and feature sets. In the following sections, the various options available in CloudWatch for Route 53 metrics are explained.

DNS Query Logging

Query logging will provide you with detailed information on resolver queries to Route 53, which includes the domain or subdomain being requested, the date and time, the record type, the response code including NoError or ServFail, and which AWS Route 53 edge location responded to the query if it was a public zone. Note that DNS relies heavily on caching queries, so not all DNS queries actually go to the resolver and get logged. Only when the cache TTL of the remote DNS server expires will the query go to the resolver and, in turn, be logged. It is important to remember that not all DNS queries will be in your logs because of the caching nature of DNS.

Route 53 sends the logs to CloudWatch logs, and they are not directly accessible through Route 53; you must use the CloudWatch console to view them. CloudWatch displays the logging data in near real time and provides search, filter, and export capabilities. A CloudWatch log group creates a stream for each edge location that exports data to the service. The edge ID uses the standard three-character airport codes at its location with a random number appended to the end. For example, the Atlanta edge location would appear as ATL3 in CloudWatch with the numeric 3 given as an example only.

In the Route 53 console, you can see the query logging configuration by going to Hosted zones, selecting the zone name, and then going to Query logging configuration, as shown in Figure 3.34.

FIGURE 3.34   Route 53 query logging configuration

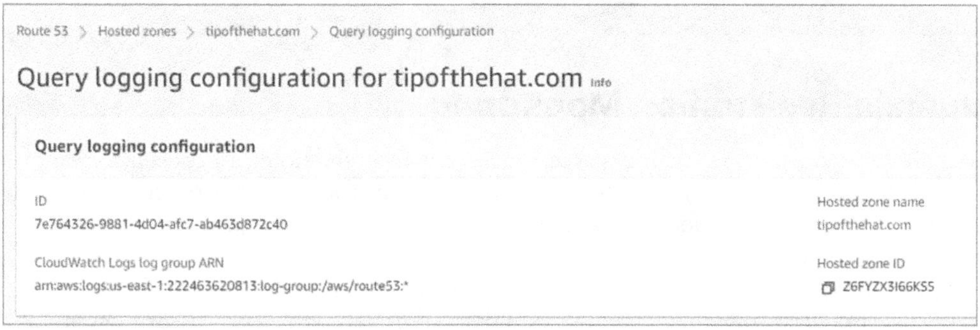

To view the logging data, open the CloudWatch console and go to the Route 53 log group. The following is an example of a log file that was generated by Route 53 and exported to CloudWatch logs:

```
1.0 2022-08-27T17:37:20Z Z6FYZX3I66KS5 tipofthehat.com A NOERROR UDP CDG53-C1
172.70.245.24 -
```

Resolver Query Logging

CloudWatch query logging captures query and response log data that originates in a VPC. Resolver query logging can also log queries from your on-premise systems that query the inbound resolver endpoints in a VPC, outbound resolvers, and DNS firewall rules that either block, allow, or monitor your domain lists.

There is a large amount of data collected in each log, including the AWS region the VPC resides in, VPC ID of the queries' originating VPC, instance IP address and ID of the originator, date/time, record type, response code, and value returned in response to the query. If this is a DNS firewall record, the rule and action data are posted.

Hosted Zone Monitoring

CloudWatch monitors public hosted zone logs in near real time that are accessed through the CloudWatch, and not the Route 53, console. The metric appears in CloudWatch shortly after the DNS query is made in Route 53 with the collection granularity being 1 minute.

To view the metric data in the CloudWatch console, select All Metrics on the Metrics tab in the left panel, select N. Virginia as the region, and enter **Route 53** in the search box.

Resolver Endpoints Monitoring

Data specific to the resolver endpoints is exported to and monitored by CloudWatch. The raw data is collected at 5-minute intervals; converted into readable, near real-time data; and displayed in dashboards and tables you create.

You can use Amazon CloudWatch to monitor the number of DNS queries that are forwarded by Route 53 Resolver endpoints. Amazon CloudWatch collects and processes raw data into readable, near real-time metrics that are stored for 14 days by default.

Domain Registration Monitoring

Domain name registration logging is accessed directly from the Route 53 console and not CloudWatch. This provides you with current details on the status of your registered domains, newly registered domains, domain transfers into Route 53, and the expiration dates of all of your registered domains.

It is a good practice to monitor this console to make sure your domains are in good standing. Also, keep your contact registration data up-to-date so you can receive important notifications from AWS such as the need to renew expiring domains.

Summary

This chapter continued covering DNS and Route 53, which we introduced in Chapter 2. The focus in this chapter was to look at the advanced capabilities of Route 53. You learned about the operation side of Route 53, and we went over many of the configuration options to enable its many features.

We began with hosted zones in either internal, or private, and external, or public, hosted zones. Internal zones are for name resolution services inside a VPC, and external zones provide name resolution for your domain to the Internet. You learned how to create and configure both types of zones using the Route 53 graphical console.

Traffic management was covered in detail, and the various options to direct the traffic in DNS using options such as latency, geography, weighted, failover, and multivalue were covered. To add resiliency and redundancy, health checking was detailed. The AWS *Traffic Policy Editor* is used to create policies using the graphical configuration tool in the console.

In larger organizations, there are often many different groups or organizations that need to administer a section of the domain. You learned about domain delegation and forwarding rules for hybrid DNS deployments.

Traffic records are the fundamental building block of a domain, and how they are configured and administered inside Route 53 was discussed in detail. Each of the primary record type's configuration was covered.

Security was added on to DNS well after it was introduced and it is becoming important to integrate DNSSEC into Route 53 and all DNS services as regulatory and corporate best practices call for a secure DNS service. DNSSEC is the standard solution, and we discussed how it fits into Route 53.

Multi-account Route 53 and how to configure the Route 53 Resolvers for inbound, outbound, and bidirectional name resolution were discussed.

Monitoring and logging options were explained, and some of the common configurations were given. Route 53 uses AWS-based tools such as CloudTrail and CloudWatch. All the various monitoring options were discussed and explained.

Exam Essentials

Know the Route 53 console areas with a focus on hosted zones and routing records. Understand all of the traffic management options in Route 53 such as latency, multivalue, etc., and how they are used. Understand the concept of DNS zones and what information they contain.

Know the difference between public and private hosted zones. Public hosted zones store records that are accessible on the public Internet and contain public IP addressing. A private hosted zone is used internally to your VPC and contains private IP address records.

Know all the types of resource records covered in this chapter in detail. Know what each record contains and what its use case is. For example, know that the A record is for IPv4 records and an MX record is used for email exchange.

Understand the options for logging and monitoring. Know that domain registration is the only management and logging data area in the Route 53 console and then use CloudTrail and CloudWatch as the primary source of information. Also, know that Route 53 is a global service and not region specific. However, in the console it will display as either N. Virginia or Global.

Written Labs

Written Lab 3.1: Configure Logging for DNS Queries

1. Sign in to the Amazon Web Services Management Console and open the Route 53 console at `https://console.amazonaws.cn/route53`.

2. In the navigation pane, choose Hosted Zones.

3. Choose the hosted zone that you want to configure query logging for.

4. In the Hosted Zone Details pane, choose Configure Query Logging.

5. Choose an existing log group or create a new log group.

6. If you receive an alert about permissions (this happens if you haven't configured query logging with the new console before), do one of the following:

   - If you have 10 resource policies already, you can't create any more. Select any of your resource policies, and select Edit. Editing will give Route 53 permissions to write logs to your log groups. Click Save. The alert goes away, and you can continue to the next step.

   - If you have never configured query logging before (or if you haven't created 10 resource policies already), you need to grant permissions to Route 53 to write logs to your CloudWatch logs groups. Choose Grant Permissions. The alert goes away and you can continue to the next step.

7. Choose Permissions - Optional to see a table that shows whether the resource policy matches the CloudWatch log group and whether Route 53 has the permission to publish logs to CloudWatch.

8. Choose Create.

Written Lab 3.2: View DNS Query Metrics for a Public Hosted Zone in the CloudWatch Console

1. Sign in to the Amazon Web Services Management Console and open the CloudWatch console at `https://console.amazonaws.cn/cloudwatch`.

2. In the navigation pane, choose Metrics.

3. On the Amazon region list in the upper-right corner of the console, choose us-east (N. Virginia). Route 53 metrics aren't available if you choose any other Amazon region.

4. On the All Metrics tab, choose Route 53.

5. Choose Hosted Zone Metrics.

6. Select the check box for one or more hosted zones that have the metric name DNSQueries.

7. On the Graphed Metrics tab, change the applicable values to view the metrics in the format that you want.

8. For Statistic, choose Sum or SampleCount; these statistics both display the same value.

Review Questions

The following questions are designed to test your understanding of this chapter's material. For more information on how to obtain additional questions, please see this book's introduction.

1. Connie has been tasked with adding a new record in her Route 53 public zone that is only the raw zone apex domain name of `tipofthehat.com` and not the FQDN record for the `www.tipofthehat.com` domain that was deployed originally to direct traffic to her new application load balancer. The ALB has been deployed in the us-west-2 Oregon region. The load balancer is Internet facing and is configured with both IPv4 and IPv6 publicly routable network addresses. You are the on-site cloud network architect, and she is asking you for advice on how to implement this. How would you suggest she configure this to meet her company's requirements?

   A. Create a new Alias record for `tipofthehat.com` and forward it to the DNS name of the ALB

   B. Create a new CNAME record for `tipofthehat.com` and forward it to `www.tipofthehat.com`

   C. Create an AAAA resource record in the public zone and use the ALB's public address

   D. Create an A resource record in the public zone and use the us-west region's public address that AWS assigns you

2. Your employer's development team is creating automated test scripts for a new application in the eu-north-1 Stockholm region. They are a global organization with developers in Asia-Pacific and South America. The development VPC is in a private availability zone hosting both Docker and EC2 application instances. Because of the dynamic addressing environment, they are asking you to implement a DNS solution that allows them to reference the hosts by their domain name and not their IP address. What type of solution would you deploy?

   A. A public hosted zone for your organization that serves IP address information for queries in the Stockholm VPC

   B. A private hosted zone in the Stockholm region's VPC

   C. Create a geolocation record that restricts development scripts to the VPC in the Stockholm region

   D. Create a multivalue record for the hosts in the Stockholm VPC

3. You are working on a new network design to optimize your company's e-commerce fleet being hosted in AWS. Currently you have five front-end web servers each in the AWS Ohio and California regions. You want to configure your Route 53 record set to optimize the server connection counts. What is a good solution to meet this requirement?

   A. Apply geolocation restrictions to both regions' web servers

   B. Deploy a latency-based routing solution

   C. Create a multivalue record set for the front-end web servers

   D. Deploy a weighted-based routing solution

   E. Deploy a failover-based routing solution

4. Your firm is outsourcing all email operations to a SaaS provider hosting on AWS. You need to make Route 53 changes to redirect traffic to the new provider. What needs to be done?

    A. Modify the Start of Authority records to redirect all port 25 traffic to the new email hosting company

    B. Change the destination values in the hosted zone's MX records

    C. Have the email hosting company add your DNS mail IP addresses in their MX records

    D. The PTR record needs to be modified in your hosted zone to point all email traffic to the new service

5. You are testing IPv6 networking in a test VPC in the Osaka region. What hosted zone record sets would you need to configure?

    A. IPv6 routing

    B. AAAA records

    C. A records

    D. CNAME

    E. IPv6 record

6. The corporate DNS deployment needs to query your new AWS cloud-based operations in the Mumbai region. You are running Route 53 in a private VPC. What do you need to do to interconnect these two DNS systems? (Select two.)

    A. Select hosted zone delegations in the Route 53 console

    B. Make a DX connection from your corporate data center to the Mumbai VPC

    C. Define FWD resource records in the Route 53 private hosted zone

    D. Create an inbound endpoint in the Mumbai VPC

    E. Configure DNS forwarding rules

7. To add high availability to your two-factor authentication server deployment, you placed the two servers in different AWS regions and defined one as the primary and the other as the standby. Your global user base needs to be able to always access these servers. What DNS-based solution would help optimize uptime?

    A. Apply geolocation restrictions to both regions' web servers

    B. Deploy a latency-based routing solution

    C. Create a multivalue record set for the front-end web servers

    D. Deploy a weighted-based routing solution

    E. Deploy a failover-based routing solution

8. What Route 53 feature can be used to test for response of your endpoints? (Select two.)

    A. CloudTrail support

    B. Latency routing

    C. Health checking

    D. Contingency-based records

    E. Using CloudWatch metrics

9. Your production website runs on a combination of EC2 instances that have different CPU and memory capabilities. The user base is complaining that some connections are very responsive while others are terribly slow. What can be done to optimize the connections to your web servers?

   A. Upgrade the slower EC2 instances to match the processing power of the faster virtual machines

   B. Configure latency routing in the private zones

   C. Implement weighted routing on the web server record sets

   D. Add a network ELB to even the response times between the different instance types

   E. Implement CloudWatch metrics

10. As your company's IT operations have expanded, it is becoming increasingly difficult and insecure to manage the Route 53 ongoing administration tasks. What options are available to reduce the administrative burden on the corporate staff?

    A. Implement forwarding rules

    B. Divide the hosted zones into public and private

    C. Delegate domain administration to the different IT group's area of responsibility

    D. Create forwarding rules in the Route 53 console to give other groups in your IT teams the ability to configure Route 53

11. Which AWS routing policy returns query records based on the current traffic conditions on the public Internet?

    A. Latency

    B. Delay

    C. Proximity

    D. Geolocation

12. Which record sets are used by Dynamic Delegation Discovery System (DDDS) applications to convert or replace one value to another such as converting phone numbers to URIs?

    A. SPF

    B. GENEVE

    C. NAPTR

    D. SIP

13. What record type allows you to whitelist authority rights to created digital certificates in your domain?

    A. TLS

    B. CAA

    C. NAPTR

    D. ICANN

14. Which record type redirects sessions for specific service types, such as VoIP or instant messaging sessions, to specific hosts and port numbers?

   A. CAA

   B. SRV

   C. AAAA

   D. NAPTR

15. Which Route 53 feature is used to tell the resolver what domain names you want to forward to remote resolvers such as an on-premise DNS server?

   A. Hybrid DNS

   B. Conditional forwarding

   C. Zone transfer

   D. PTR record

16. Where does Route 53 store query logs?

   A. CloudTrail

   B. CloudWatch

   C. API Gateway

   D. Redshift

17. What monitoring types log the number of DNS queries that are forwarded by a Route 53 Resolver?

   A. Route 53 zone monitoring

   B. Resolver endpoint monitoring

   C. Private hosted zone monitoring

   D. Hybrid Route 53 monitoring

18. Which Route 53 record type contains basic information about the domain and hosted zone including the Route 53 name server that created the record, the email address of the administrator for your organization, and a serial number that can be incremented whenever you update a record?

   A. TXT

   B. SOA

   C. PTR

   D. CAA

19. Which Route 53 interface allows DNS resolutions originating inside of your VPC to your on-premise DNS deployment or to another VPC?

   A. Inbound endpoints

   B. Public hosted zone endpoints

C. Outbound endpoints

D. Private hosted zone endpoints

20. Which DNS record type maps a fully qualified domain name to an IPv4 address?

A. CNAME

B. A

C. AAAA

D. Alias

Chapter

4

Load Balancing

THE AWS CERTIFIED ADVANCED NETWORKING - SPECIALTY EXAM OBJECTIVES COVERED IN THIS CHAPTER MAY INCLUDE, BUT ARE NOT LIMITED TO, THE FOLLOWING:

✓ **Domain 1: Network Design**

  - Objective 1.3: Design solutions that integrate load balancing to meet high availability, scalability, and security requirements.

Elastic Load Balancing

In Chapter 1, "Edge Networking," you learned that the Elastic Load Balancer (ELB) is the AWS family of managed services that distributes request loads across many servers. The ELB family automatically balances and distributes traffic across EC2, Lambda, and micro services. In this chapter, we will take a deeper look into the details of the load balancers to give you an understanding of the features, use cases, security, and integrations to prepare you for the exam. The ELB services include the application load balancer, the network load balancer, and the gateway load balancer. The classic load balancer was introduced in 2009 and was retired in 2022; it's no longer used and has been removed from the AWS console.

You may come across references to version 1 and version 2 of the ELB offerings. Version 1 refers to the classic load balancer that has been deprecated and is no longer available. Everything is now version 2. The advantages of using a version 2 load balancer include a much faster product, lower cost, target groups, rules, and the most recent features in the ELB family.

The primary function of a load balancer is to act as a front end to services, receive connections from customers, and then distribute the connections to backend groups of compute services such as virtual machines or microservices such as Docker containers. This shares the processing workload over more than one server, and if a server in the group should fail, the application can continue to function using the remaining servers.

With this architecture, the backend servers and applications are abstracted from the users. This allows you to add, remove, modify, and reconfigure the backend servers without affecting the user experience.

ELBs allow for a decoupling of services between application tiers and allow for each layer to scale independently of the other layers.

Load scaling can be automated with the CloudWatch integrations to monitor the load on the servers and add or remove servers based on load or to replace a failed server using auto-scaling groups.

ELBs support cross-zone load balancing where servers can be placed in two or more availability zones and requests can be allocated between AZs.

When configuring a load balancer, listeners are created to accept the customer traffic on a user-specified port and protocol. Then, on the backend, the ELB will communicate with the target servers using configured ports and protocols.

The public load balancer backend communications can use either public or private addresses on the target servers. However, there is no requirement that the backend servers be publicly addressed and they can sit in the private address space if that meets your design and security requirements.

ELBs need at least eight IP addresses in the subnet they are assigned. This means that a /28 is the smallest subnet that can be used. However, it is strongly recommended to use a /27 or larger subnet for scalability.

Network Load Balancing

In the Open Systems Interconnection (OSI) model, layer 4 is the transport layer and primarily uses the UDP, TCP, or the SSL/TLS networking protocols. The layer 4 load balancers are in the network load balancer category and are known for their high connection rates, low latency, and overall high-performance characteristics. While you may occasionally see references to a layer 3 load balancer, the load balancing decisions are based on the layer 3 network addressing and layer 4 port number, so keep in mind that when you see either layer 3 or layer 4, we are talking about network load balancers.

The NLB views incoming traffic at the packet level, which means it has no insight into the actual data in the payload for content-based forwarding decisions but, rather, the networking information that includes the source and destination IP addressing and the application port number. A typical NLB configuration would look for a destination port number, for example, port 80, which is for HTTP web traffic. When it sees that the packet is destined for a web server at that destination IP address, it will look at its defined target groups of servers and forward the packet to a server in that group. Multiple groups can be configured for different ports. For example, we could have a second target group for HTTPS port 443 traffic. However, the NLB has no visibility into, or understanding of, HTTP or HTTPS data at application layer 7.

The network load balancer is part of the version 2 AWS ELB product.

When your traffic is burstable, is highly unpredictable, or requires low latency with high performance, a network load balancer is a good solution. NLBs are known for raw performance and scalability that can support millions of connections per second with predictable delays in a secure environment.

The network load balancer supports SSL/TLS encryption offloading on port 443. Traditionally, each server was expected to have a digital SSL/TLS certificate installed for in-flight encryption; then incoming traffic would first connect to the load balancer and then be forwarded to the pools of servers on the backend to terminate the SSL/TLS connection to perform the encrypt/decrypt functions. This architecture was not optimal as it required the server to use processing power for encryption that would be better served to web operations. Also, a digital certificate needed to be installed on each server with no centralized certificate location.

By using the network load balancer, the digital certificate can be installed on the load balancers Internet-facing virtual IP (VIP). Incoming encrypted traffic will terminate SSL/TLS on the VIP to offload the process from the backend servers. This allows a central point of administration, a single certificate to be installed, and centralized logging and monitoring of your in-flight encryption operations. This is called *SSL offload* as the operations are offloaded from the real servers in the backend pool to the load balancer.

Remember that the original security protocol was called Secure Sockets Layer (SSL). SSL has been deprecated and replaced with Transport Layer Security (TLS); however, the terminology for SSL lives on and is often used when TLS would be more accurate. So, if you see SSL, think TLS, as that is the modern version of encrypting traffic in-flight across a network.

NLBs support millions of requests per second at very low latency. Since listeners support static IP addressing, they can be whitelisted on the corporate firewall rules to allow connections into the AWS cloud via the load balancer. If you need to work with protocols that are not either HTTP or HTTPS, then a network load balancer is the solution to implement. The NLB supports a private link that enables you to connect to AWS services in other accounts.

Application Load Balancing

The application load balancer, or layer 7 load balancer, is a version 2 ELB that supports HTTP, HTTPS, and WebSocket protocols. It is important to remember that the ALB does not listen for other protocols such as VOIP, gaming, SSH, FTP, or any others. If you want to work with these protocols, you will need to deploy the network load balancer. However, since it operates at layer 7 of the OSI model, it can inspect content such as cookies, customer headers, and location- and application-specific values. This information can be used to back content-switching decisions.

ALBs support listener-based rules that make them highly customizable. You can have multiple domains connecting to the same application load balancer to simplify your deployments. Host-based rules are created to direct incoming traffic to multiple target groups for processing. Autoscaling groups can then be defined for scalability. A single application load balancer can support many applications for consolidation.

Support for Server Name Indication (SNI) is included and automatically enabled on the listener; it determines the domain of the request to match it with the correct TLS certificate for that domain. Each domain can host a TLS certificate on the same load balancer. If there is only one domain on the listener, then SNI is disabled as it is not required.

Since ALBs inspect the total stack and can read layer 7 information, there can be a large amount of processing involved for every packet that passes through it. This makes them slower than a network load balancer since the NLB uses significantly fewer processing cycles per packet. However, one of the benefits of working at the application layer is that the load balancer can evaluate the health of the application and make intelligent decisions at the application layer.

Rules are defined that process incoming connections to the listener or VIP. Rules can be stacked and processed in priority order with a default rule at the end. Rules have conditions for processing, such as information contained in the host-header, http-header, https-request-method, path-pattern, query-strings, and networking values such as the source IP address. Based on meeting the conditions in a rule, actions are then defined that tell the ALB what to do with the traffic such as where to forward it, where to redirect the connection to somewhere else, where to reply with a fixed-response, how to authenticate it, and other actions that you create.

With the ability to look into the HTTP protocol data, you can customize your web hosting to, for example, inspect for data coming from mobile phones and direct those connections to a web target group that is formatted for low-content mobile devices and then direct all other connection requests to the content-rich hosts in another target group.

Gateway Load Balancing

The AWS gateway load balancer (GWLB) is used to integrate virtual appliances from third-party vendors in a VPC, as shown in Figure 4.1. These appliances can be a wide range of offerings and include firewalls, analytics systems, network visibility, and intrusion detection prevention systems. The key feature is that the GWLB has a single point of ingress and egress for all traffic, performs the load balancing function, scales the virtual appliances, does not modify the packet for transparent flows, and can work with overlapping CIDR address blocks.

FIGURE 4.1   Gateway load balancing

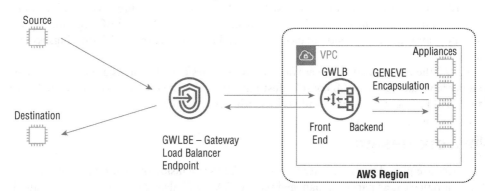

By inserting logic and advanced functions directly into the network flow path, many new advanced features can be implemented. The gateway load balancer is used to insert new functions, features, and services into the network flow path. Since it is an AWS managed service, it manages the complexity, uptime, capacity, and ongoing maintenance of the underlying infrastructure. Services offerings for analytics, security, and Internet of Things, to name a few examples, can leverage the GWLB for better integration with your AWS deployment.

The gateway load balancer is a layer 3 product that uses the GENEVE protocol to encapsulate traffic, which allows the packets to be in the original state when delivered to the appliances that must also support the GENEVE protocol. We will go into GENEVE later in this chapter.

The gateway load balancer is strictly a packet in/out device that does not have any layer 7 application awareness to perform any SSL/TLS encryption/decryption operations. It does not maintain state information. All these features are the responsibility of the target appliances.

The architecture, as shown in Figure 4.1, uses a gateway load balancer endpoint (GWLBE) that connects the GWLB to another VPC. The GWLBE is a VC endpoint. The GWLB can be connected to any number of GWLBEs. The GWLB has a front end that attaches to the GWLBE and to the outside world. The backend is the load balancer section that connects to the virtual appliances with encapsulated packets to preserve the original format with no modifications made by the GWLB. Session stickiness, health checking, and failover are performed on the backend.

Packets that are sent from the source to the destination do not contain the GWLB's listener IP address, and the GWLB is transparent to the flow. Route table modifications direct the traffic into and out of the GWLB.

Classic Load Balancing

For completeness, and to avoid any confusion if you come across the classic load balancer (CLB), it will be briefly mentioned here. The classic load balancer was the first offering within the ELB family of load balancers from AWS. The CLB was deployed to balance EC2 instances before VPCs came into existence. The VPC architecture was introduced in 2013 and quickly became the dominant architecture in AWS. Original EC2 instances predate VPCs, and the classic load balancer was used before the current ELB offerings were released.

In 2022 the classic load balancer was retired. All classic deployments are now retired and no longer available in the ELB console. Just remember that if you see anything related to the classic load balancer, it is legacy and no longer in use.

Network Design

ELB nodes are placed in availability zones, and they scale inside of each AZ. If a node fails, AWS will replace it as part of a managed service. AWS will also scale the nodes as required to meet your workloads and maintain all ongoing maintenance on the compute and load balancer application's software updates.

When the ELB gets created, a node is placed in the subnet, and a single DNS A record is created. The DNS name resolves to all the individual nodes, so all incoming requests are evenly distributed across all of the load balancer nodes.

ELBs support both IPv4 and IPv6 addressing for flexibility in your designs. As we discuss in this chapter, the ELB family is integrated with many other AWS services to add features, flexibility, and capabilities. These include DNS through Route 53, monitoring with CloudTrail and CloudWatch, scalability with autoscaling groups, security with the Web Application Firewall, and IAM security groups.

For high connection counts and throughput where a massive number of connections is normal, the network firewall is usually the best solution. The application load balancer operates at layer 7 and does processing to look in the payload to perform its functions. This offers a great amount of flexibility and capabilities with the trade-off being less throughput than the network load balancer.

The gateway load balancer offers inline transparent flows that allow third-party service providers to insert virtual appliances into the data flow for functions such as data analytics, security, and intrusion detection/prevention services.

High Availability

Elastic load balancers are an integral part of an AWS high availability design. Amazon offers the various ELB architectures as a fully managed service, which means that they are responsible for the underlying hardware and software. There are a great deal of redundancy and recovery mechanisms deployed by AWS to maximize the uptime. This saves your organization from managing, upgrading, and configuring the actual load balancers themselves and enables you to focus on the operations side when deploying high availability load balancing designs.

Without a load balancer, traditional network designs used DNS to resolve the domain names directly to the web servers sitting in a public VPC. An alternative approach was to configure Route 53 with multivalue responses, as you learned about in Chapter 3, "Hybrid and Multi-Account DNS." In this case, a DNS query response would return multiple IP addresses of the servers and could optionally use health checks to ensure the servers were operational.

The client could then initiate a connection to the servers in the IP address pool that you configured using multivalue routing in Route 53.

Using the features available with ELBs integrated with other AWS services, achieving high availability with an AWS ELB architecture is highly resilient, fully featured, offers many design options, and supports automated recovery and failover scenarios.

Security

The application load balancer will terminate all encrypted TLS/SSL connections and allow end-to-end encryption between the client and target server. The incoming TLS session will be terminated on the ALB for inspection and processing. There will be a second connection created on the backend between the ALB and the target. In this case, the ALB will be acting as the client. This means that all ALBs must have TLS/SSL certificates directly installed on them if TLS is being used since it acts as the target server that is terminating the encrypted TLS connections.

You can secure your public-facing listener and reduce the load by using CloudFront as a front-end service and restricting access to the ELB listener to the CloudFront service. When using an application load balancer, you can take advantage of its layer 7 capabilities to have CloudFront insert custom HTTP header values before sending the request to an application load balancer. Then the ALB needs to be configured to process only those requests that contain that header. This prevents users from bypassing CloudFront and going directly to the ALB.

The Web Application Firewall can be placed in front of the ELB's listening interface for public Internet-facing deployments. The WAF reduces the impact of denial-of-service acts, allows you to define access filtering, and is a fully managed and monitored service from AWS.

The VPC security functions of AWS such as access control lists and security groups are available. AWS has a large suite of security services that can detect anomalies and do monitoring such as CloudWatch.

ELB Connectivity Patterns

In this section, we will cover placement options of the load balancers in your deployment such as Internet-facing or for internal designs that enable resiliency, scalability, and service separation.

Internal Load Balancers

Internal load balancers are defined by the VPC subnet the ELB is placed in. If you create an internal load balancer and are using a private listener IP address, then, by definition, this will be an internal load balancer. The IP addressing is the primary difference between a public and private ELB. Other than this distinction, they are the same product with the same feature sets. Figure 4.2 illustrates the placement of the internal load balancer. Remember that internal load balancers are in reference to the placement of the service and not its functionality. An internal load balancer can be any type such as a network or application load balancer.

FIGURE 4.2   Internal load balancing

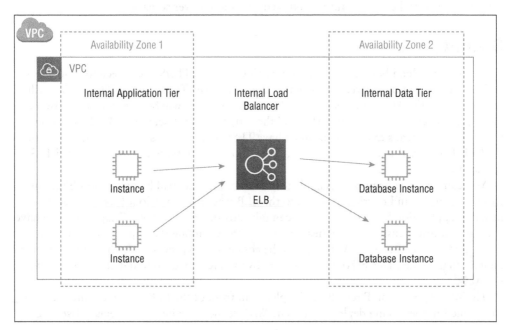

Architecturally a private ELB is the same as a public load balancer except that they have only private IP addresses assigned to their nodes. A multitier architecture may include a public load balancer terminating user requests from the Internet to a pool of backend web servers and then these web servers connecting to internal load balancers with a pool of backend application servers.

Internal load balancers are generally used to separate different tiers of applications in a VPC such as the web tier to the presentation, application, and data tiers.

External Load Balancers

External load balancing is determined by the VPC subnet the ELB is placed in. If you create an Internet-facing load balancer, a public IP address will be assigned to the load balancer node.

External load balancers are accessible from the public Internet and will always have a public IP address assigned to the listener, as shown in Figure 4.3.

FIGURE 4.3   External load balancing

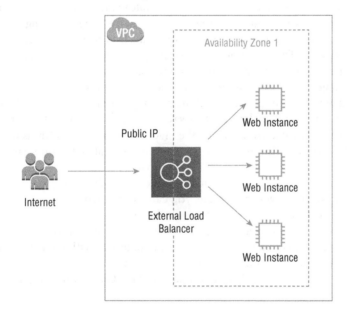

An external load balancer can accept connections from the public Internet with its public IP address and then distribute traffic on the backend with either public- or private-addressed targets. The backend server target groups can be either public or private IP addresses. For example, an EC2 instance does not require a public IP address to work with an external (public) load balancer and can reside in a private subnet in a VPC.

Autoscaling

Autoscaling is an ELB feature that enables you to dynamically add and remove capacity based on your workload. This feature matches the compute servers offered to the current workload to save costs by using only the compute services you need at any given point in time. If your server workload grows as the site becomes more heavily used, autoscaling can automatically add services to meet the workload. Later, when the load drops, those servers will be removed, saving you the cost of paying for unused capacity.

Autoscaling groups can have a minimum and maximum number of servers which allows for redundancy. For example, if you have a web deployment that requires a minimum of four EC2 instances to meet the average workload, you can set the minimum capacity at four and then a maximum to not exceed to control costs of, for example, eight servers. If you should have a server fail and go below the minimum capacity, the server can be automatically replaced.

You set up autoscaling plans in the AWS console to monitor your applications and then automatically add or remove capacity based on the current workload. The console will also give you scaling recommendations. When the scaling plan is created, it uses combined predictive and dynamic scaling to match your workload. Autoscaling can also scan your resources and automatically discover resources to scale saving you the time of having to search your deployment for scaling candidates by consolidating this into one centralized automatic resource discovery area. The service lets you select optimization on either performance or cost, a combination of the two, or a custom policy that you define.

Predictive scaling uses machine learning to scale based on future traffic loads; both daily and weekly load patterns are recorded, and the ML algorithms predict-and-deploy compute services are based on those calculations. This saves research and costs. The capacity planning and provisioning are adjusted over time by the machine learning algorithms that AWS includes with the service. This self-adjusting feature will calculate the optimal resources and immediately add or remove capacity based on your workloads.

CloudWatch alarms can be defined to monitor metrics such as CPU utilization or connection counts to adjust capacity. For example, you can use predictive scaling to monitor the CPU utilization on your EC2 instances. When the hosting web servers reach a sustained 80 percent utilization, add two servers, and then when the utilization drops below 45 percent, remove one server at a time. This matches the compute power with the load on your web servers. Figure 4.4 shows the autoscaling configuration in the web console.

Autoscaling is available at no charge; you pay only for CloudWatch and the underlying services being used.

AWS Service Integrations

AWS makes every effort to integrate its many service offerings for ease of deployment, ease of use, and added flexibility. Because of the nature of the ELB family, there are many networking services that work with the load balancers and are integrated into the ELB console. We will cover the services that are on the exam in this chapter.

FIGURE 4.4　Autoscaling

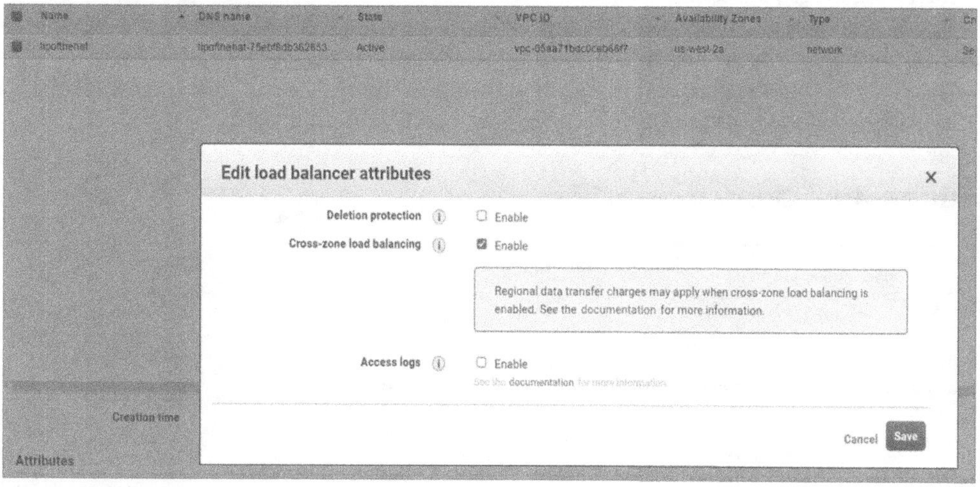

Config

The AWS Config service tracks any changes made to your load balancers or target groups and is integrated into the load balancer console. Config records all changes, and they can be stored in long-term storage for recordkeeping, audits, troubleshooting, and analysis. Automation can be applied to trigger alarms on changes that are outside of the predefined values. The service needs to be enabled in the region where your load balancer resides. By selecting Config on the Integrated Services tab in the ELB web console, you can view all configurations changes that have been made to the service on a searchable timeline. The events data includes the date and time of the change, who the user was, what the event name was such as "create listener," and then a link to the actual CloudTrail event for a highly detailed record of the change. The Config service is charged per record items logged and the total Config rule evaluations. Config also includes conformance packs that, if applied, are chargeable.

Global Accelerator

Global Accelerator has integrations with the AWS application load balancer that is used to route user traffic over the AWS global network to the listener port on the load balancer instead of over the slower public Internet.

Select the Integrated Services tab in the EC2 console to record Global Accelerator's static IP address and DNS name. The DNS record must be updated to route traffic to the Global Accelerator to get to the load balancer. When you create the ALB, you can select to use Global Accelerator to direct traffic over the AWS global network and not traverse the Internet. In the background, AWS integrates the two services together. After creating the accelerator, AWS adds the load balancer as the endpoint and updates the Route 53 DNS records. By using static IP addresses and a global network, this design allows for a single, global entry point into your network to access the load balancer with the added performance of traversing the AWS internal network.

By integrating the two services offerings, you can save the work of creating the accelerator, adding the listener to the accelerator, adding endpoint groups, and attaching the load balancer to the endpoint groups. Figure 4.5 shows the option to add the Global Accelerator service when creating an application load balancer.

FIGURE 4.5   Global Accelerator

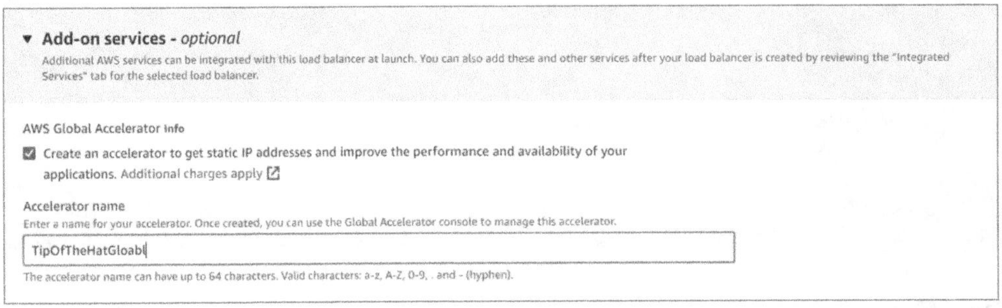

CloudFront

CloudFront can be integrated with Amazon's family of elastic load balancers to act as a front end to the listener and cache content globally for faster response times. By using CloudFront and its global network of edge locations, the content served by the ELB can easily be dispersed worldwide and stored in the local CloudFront cache. When a user requests content, the data is served from the edge location and does not have to reach back to retrieve that content from the region where the ELB is located. This also offloads the workload on the target servers since the data is stored in the edge CloudFront content servers.

CloudFront is most effective when there is a large amount of static content served and the requests come from clients all over the world. The workload on the ALB decreases since it does not have to serve content for every request and the SSL/TLS offload is performed at the CloudFront edge and not the ALB. If the websites are close to the users requesting the content, such as a regional site, the usefulness of CloudFront is diminished because of the proximity of the content to the user's location.

Traffic Mirroring

Network traffic captured in a VPC can be forwarded to a load balancer for analysis and troubleshooting. Mirroring is configured in the VPC and can send the traffic to a network load balancer listener to distribute the captured traffic to target groups associated with the NLB. Gateway load balancing is also supported, which is very useful for service providers as GLB does not modify the original source packets. The ELB web console allows you to create a mirror target in the load balancer you select and is on the Integrated Services tab. Target types can be either the network interface, network load balancer, or gateway load balancer.

VPC Endpoint Services (PrivateLink)

PrivateLink, or the endpoint service, allows outside accounts to share AWS resources with their customers. A network load balancer is created as the entry point in a VPC, and then the endpoint service is assigned to the NLB. Customers are then allowed access to your endpoint connection. PrivateLink allows the load balancer to receive traffic from the customer using the service and, with the use of target groups, routes the traffic on the backend hosts running applicators supporting the services offered. The load balancer console allows you to configure PrivateLink on the Integrated Services tab.

Web Application Firewall

The *Web Application Firewall* (WAF) acts as a front end to your application load balancer to protect web applications and application security breaches. Using the WAF, you set up access controls, rules, or conditions that define what is allowed and blocked before forwarding traffic to the application load balancer. This protects the services on the load balancer from heavy loads caused by attacks sent to the ALB.

It is important to note that the WAF will work with the layer 7 ALB but not with the network load balancer that has visibility only at layer 4. The WAF is integrated with the application load balancer, CloudFront, API Gateway, and AppSync at this time.

Route 53

When an ELB is created, a DNS A record is allocated to it in the format of `name.region.elb.amazonaws.com`.

When domain queries are performed to resolve the host domain name to the IP address of the ELB's listening interface, Route 53 is used to direct domain traffic to the ELB load balancer.

Create an alias record in the Route 53 hosted zone that points to your load balancer. As you learned in Chapter 2, "Domain Name Services," and Chapter 3, an alias record is a Route 53 extension to DNS. Aliases are similar to CNAME records, but they allow you to create an alias record both for the root domain, such as `tipofthehat.com`, and for subdomains, such as `www.tipofthehat.com`. CNAME records are supported only for subdomains and not the root domain.

Amazon Elastic Kubernetes Service

Kubernetes is a containerized microservice and compute service in AWS. For the Advanced Networking exam, we will focus on the networking aspects and how it integrates with AWS networking services. The application load balancer works with the Kubernetes Ingress controller at layer 7 of the OSI model.

Elastic Kubernetes Service (EKS) has integrations with the application load balancer and the network load balancer; however, the classic load balancer services are no longer supported. An EKS cluster and the Ingress controller support ELB services, and the application load balancer controller is installed as a software add-on to the EKS service. For details on installing the controller, reference the user guide at `https://docs.aws.amazon.com/ eks/latest/userguide/aws-load-balancer-controller.html`.

Your first step is to create a Kubernetes cluster and then deploy the load balancer in the cluster using at least two subnets in different availability zones. Both public and private subnets are supported. The load balancer Ingress controller then creates the application load balancer. The Kubernetes Ingress controller configures the application load balancer to route HTTP or HTTPS traffic to different pods within the cluster. The ALB can be deployed at the EC2 instance level or as Fargate IP targets.

The controller manages the ELBs for each Kubernetes cluster. When the controller is created, it will provision the ALB automatically for the Kubernetes Ingress controller. The network load balancer is created when the Kubernetes instance is `LoadBalancer`. Both IP and instance target types are supported.

The AWS load balancer controller is the new name for the AWS ALB Ingress controller, and you may see both terms to describe the same offering. It's actually an open-source project available on GitHub, and you can find installation and operational instructions on the GitHub site. The GitHub site also provides examples to assist in your early deployments.

AWS Certificate Manager

The *AWS Certificate Manager* allows you to create both public and private digital certificates and has integrated the service into the application load balancer, as shown in Figure 4.6. This integration allows you to specify an AWS certificate directly from the ALB configuration GUI, API, and CLI. The Certificate Manager service enables you to provision, manage, and implement TLS certificates for internal- and external-facing ALB listeners. This integration removes much of the manual process of creating, downloading, and installing certificates into the ALB. The Certificate Manager also handles the renewal of certificates, which is critical for uptime of the ALB. There is no charge for public-issued certificates that are implemented on the ALB; you pay only for the ALB incurred charges and not for the certificates. The ACM does charge for its private certificate authority services, and there is a charge for the private certificates themselves.

FIGURE 4.6   Certificate Manager integration with ALB

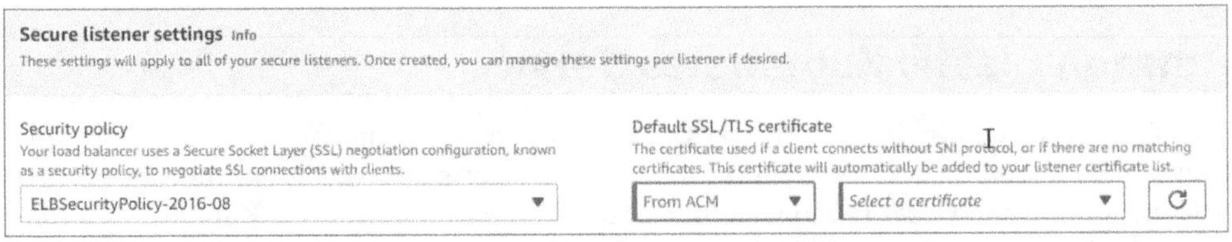

The AWS Certificate Manager creates SSL/TLS certificates per region and logs all certificate transaction logs into CloudTrail. You use the Certificate Manager to generate key pairs without the steps usually required such as generating a certificate-signing request, generating the key pair, and downloading it locally for installation into the ALB service. The Certificate Manager handles all of the backend steps required to install the certificate onto the ALB listener and enables SSL/TLS support in addition to locally generated certificates. The Certificate Manager also allows you to import certificates from outside certificate authorities for central management and logging.

ELB Configuration Options

There are extensive variations to deploy and configure the different load balancer types offered by AWS in the ELB family of services. This section will introduce you to the main topics and give you the background knowledge to successfully design and deploy your solutions as well as to be able to pass the ELB questions on the exam.

Proxy Protocol

To understand where the packet source originates from, you can use processing decisions, accurate connection logging of the source, security, and analytics in your web deployments. However, with the nature of modern networks, the actual source IP address of the end user may not be present in the packet as it arrives at the load balancer. With layer 7 application load balancers, this information can be included in the headers. However, for a network load balancer, there is no insight or knowledge of the information available at the application layer 7. The network load balancer terminates the TCP connection and places a second session to the backend servers. The backend servers will not see the source IP of the client in this scenario; they see only the source of the load balancer. Also, with the use of web proxies and Network Address Translation (NAT) devices in the source to destination path, the source IP can be changed by the network, and the actual origination IP can be lost. The proxy protocol inserts a header at the TCP level, which means it is not application dependent and can support all TCP-based applications in addition to standard HTTP/HTTPS. For example, you can use the proxy protocol for FTP, SMTP, SSH, or any other application that uses TCP connections. The AWS network load balancer supports version 2 of the proxy protocol, which is binary encoded. The application load balancer does not support the proxy protocol.

The proxy protocol header is a feature that inserts the original source IP for the target servers and applications to reference. When enabled, a human-readable header is added to the request header that contains detailed connection information such as source and destination IP addresses and the application port number. This header is sent to the target instance as part of the request and is in a human-readable format. Proxy protocol works with the TCP protocol to identify the IP address of the clients to the backend servers.

The following is an example of the data inside a proxy-protocol header:

```
PROXY_STRING + single space + INET_PROTOCOL + single space + CLIENT_IP +
single space + PROXY_IP + single space + CLIENT_PORT + single space + PROXY_
PORT + "\r\n"
PROXY TCP4 192.168.1.143 172.16.20.45 32623 80\r\n
```

X-Forwarded-For Protocol

Since the application load balancer terminates the connection from the client and establishes a backend session to the target servers, the IP addressing will change along the path. The downside to this is that the target servers do not see who originated the packet since the load balancer has changed the source IP address. To get around this issue, additional data has been added to the HTTP/HTTPS header to append the source IP address and all of the other IP addresses that may be used along the path from the client to the backend server.

The X-Forwarded-For (XFF) protocol is used to deliver the actual source IP address in the header for the destination devices to read. This is a layer 7 extension that works with HTTP and HTTPS only. The proxy or load balancer will add data to tell the server what the actual source IP address of the request is. The client IP address gets added to the list, and as the packet progresses through the network, additional IP addresses are appended as needed. It is important to make sure that the backend server has the ability to read this header, which may require installing a module or upgrading the server application to be able to read the X-Forwarded-For header.

The backend web servers will see the source IP address of the load balancer but can now look inside the HTTP header and see the actual IP address of the client that originated the request. Since this is a web-based protocol at layer 7, only the application load balancer supports the header, and a network load balancer will not since it is only layer 4 aware. Non-HTTP /HTTPS-aware load balancers will use the proxy protocol instead of the X-Forwarded-For protocol.

The ALB looks for the client's IP address at the `routing.http.xff_header_processing.mode` attribute; this is the attribute that can be modified or removed from the X-Forwarded-For header before it is sent from the ALB to the target server.

Cross-Zone Load Balancing

In high availability load balancing designs, it is desirable to spread your instances across multiple availability zones to protect from an AZ failure causing a complete failure of your deployment. The cross-zone load balancing distributes the load across all registered instances in all of the availability zones you define evenly. Route 53 DNS will evenly distribute connections across the availability zones with application load balancer nodes.

This feature is enabled by default with the application load balancer. See Figure 4.7 as an example of a cross-zone load balancer architecture. Notice that availability zone A has two servers and B has four. With cross-zone load balancing disabled, the load would be distributed 50 percent to each AZ. This would create an imbalance as AZ-A has only two servers but gets 50 percent of the traffic resulting in each server processing 25 percent of the load. AZ-B would also get 50 percent of the connections but has four servers in its target group resulting in less server load than AZ-A at 12.5 percent per server.

FIGURE 4.7 Cross-zone load balancing

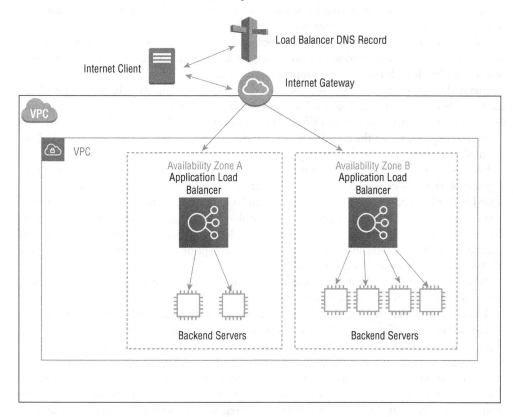

Using the cross-zone load balancing feature, each server will now receive equal amounts of the load. When enabled, the feature takes into consideration the target server count in each AZ and balances the connections automatically to all registered instances in all availability zones, resulting in optimal server load. There is no reason to not leave this enabled on the ALB.

Session Affinity and Sticky Sessions

The application load balancer distributes connections to the backend servers based on the chosen load balancing algorithm such as round-robin or least connections. This may not work in applications that require the source to be bound to a specific server for the duration of the session. An example of this would be in an e-commerce deployment where the shopping cart is on a particular server and the client must remain connected to that server until the checkout process has been completed. If the load balancer were to move the connection to other servers during the session, then the shopping cart could be on a different server with the client no longer having access to it. The method to get around this is to implement sticky session, or often called *session affinity*, to make sure that the client always connects to the same server during the session. This guarantees that all connections are sent to the same target to maintain a steady-state user experience.

Sticky sessions require that you use the application load balancer and have a healthy instance in each availability zone in your deployment. Since sticky sessions require the use of cookies, the client browser must support cookie use.

The ALB supports two modes of stickiness, duration and application based. You enable the sticky feature at the target group level and can combine different methods such as duration, application, and none across different target groups. The duration value gets reset with every new request. When the cookie duration expires, the session is no longer sticky and is handled as a normal connection by the load balancer.

Sticky session cookies map the client source to the server destination and can be from an application that has its own cookies for application-based stickiness or cookies that are generated by the load balancer. In this case, the load balancer tracks the duration in the application cookie. If the load balancer generates the cookie and not the application, it will specify the session duration of the cookie generated by the load balancer. AWS encrypts the load balancer cookies it generates, and you are not able to decrypt or modify them. The name of the AWS-generated cookie is always AWSALB.

When the WebSockets protocol is used, there is no need to enable sticky sessions as this function is inherent to WebSockets and always enabled.

The initial connection from the client to the target server is handled normally by the ALB based on its configuration. After the session is created, the ALB will generate a cookie named AWSALB that includes information such as the target server's identity. The cookie is encrypted and sent to the client by the ALB. The cookie expiration value is 7 days and cannot be modified in the AWS configuration. All requests after this initial exchange require that the client include the AWSALB cookie so the ALB can forward the session to the specified backend server. If the server should fail, or deregister, the ALB will select a new server and update the cookie it returns to the client.

With application-generated cookies, the ALB will generate a new cookie locally that includes the stickiness values for each target group configured to use application-based stickiness. The session will use both the application and ALB cookies and expects the client to return both during the session. The ALB will reference its own cookie, and the application will process its cookie.

The ALB supports cookies sized up to 16KB. However, many browsers can support only 4KB cookies. If this is the case for a session, the ALB will spread the 16KB cookie into multiple 4KB shards named AWSALBAPP-0, AWSALBAPP-1, etc.

When cross-origin resource sharing (CORS) is being used, the ALB will generate a second cookie to note the second URL. This cookie will be named AWSALBCORS and adds the SameSite=None; attribute. The client will now have two cookies from the ALB.

The sticky feature is enabled in the ALB configuration console on the Attributes tab in the Targets section, as shown in Figure 4.8.

FIGURE 4.8   Sticky feature configuration

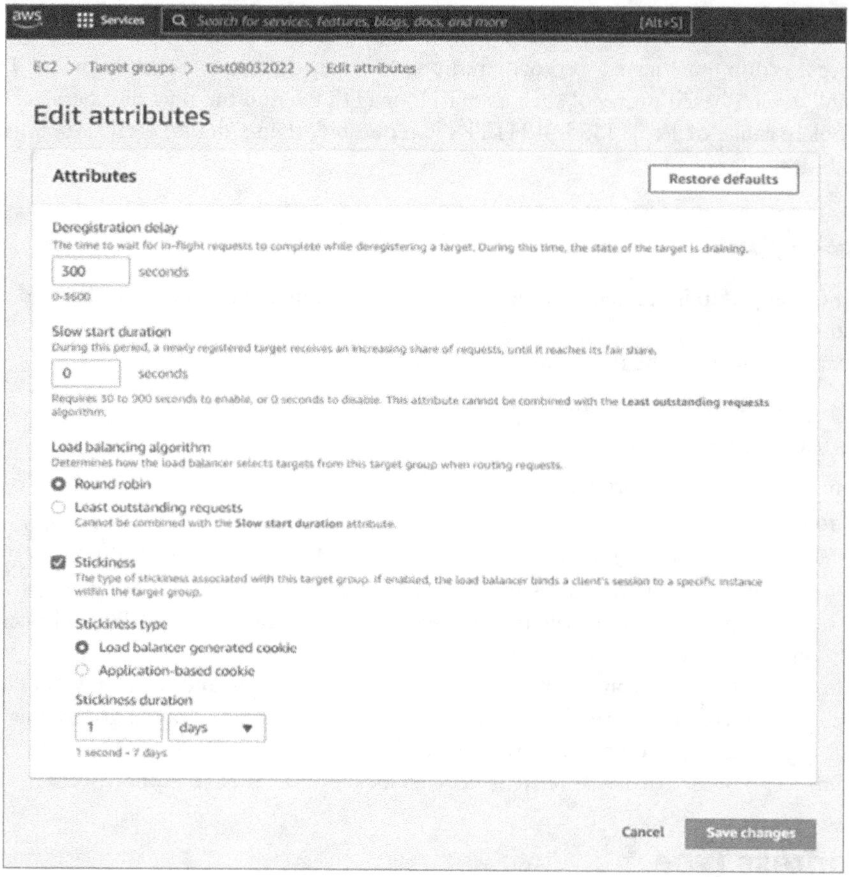

Target Groups

A *target group* is a configuration container that groups targets and is used to route connection requests to one or more of the registered targets. When created, the listener is defined for incoming connections, and the target group lists the devices or servers to connect to on the backend. Also, the target group contains many different conditions that define how you want the ELB to handle the requests. When the conditions of the target group are met, traffic gets forwarded to the matching target group. Multiple target groups can be defined with each one used for a different type of request.

You will add the target servers that can be a microservice such as a container or a virtual server such as an EC2 instance. Health checks are also applied at the target group level, and the targets must pass a health check to receive connections.

Routing

Each target group must have a protocol and port number defined to route traffic to. This is commonly a web-based protocol such as HTTP or HTTPS, and the port numbers are from the complete range of 1 to 65535. If HTTPS is requested, then a digital certificate must be installed on the targets.

Target Types

When a target group is created, a target type must be defined and cannot be changed after creation.

Target types include the following:

- Instance: The target's instance ID
- IP: The target's IP address
- Lambda: Defines the target as a Lambda function

The IP targets are from the private IP address blocks defined in RFCs 1918 and 65598 and include the subnets 10.0.0.0/8, 172.16.0.0/12, 192.168.0.0/16, and 100.64.0.0/10. You cannot use public routable IP addresses in IP-based targets. By using IP addressing, you can specify servers that are in your private data center if it is routable to the VPC and over either a direct connect or a VPN interconnect.

If you specify Lambda, you will register your Lambda function, and the ELB will invoke the Lambda on a per-connection request basis. The Lambda function and target group must be in the same region. Connection content from the ELB to the Lambda are in JSON format with a maximum response size of 1MB. There is no WebSocket or local zone support.

IP Address Type

The IP version needs to be specified in the target group and is usually the IPv4 address type; however, you can also specify IPv6 or both IPv4 and IPv6.

Protocol Version

While the default protocol in the target group is HTTP version 1.1, you can specify HTTP/2 or gRPC.

gRPC is supported only by using HTTP where the target types are instance and IP. Lambda is not supported, and health check responses need to be defined and not automatically populated.

HTTP/2 also is supported only with secure HTTPS connections and for the instance types and IP.

Registered Targets

The ELB listener is the entry point for clients, and the ELB's job is to distribute these connections across the registered and healthy targets. A target can belong to more than one target group, which means that a single server can host multiple applications. To scale your operations, multiple additional targets can be added to the group to meet demand; the servers will start receiving traffic as soon as they register and pass the health check. To remove capacity, you need to deregister the targets from the group to remove them. This does not affect the target server; it just takes it out of the group and stops receiving connection requests.

Routing Algorithms

Depending on your design, you can configure either a round-robin or least outstanding request algorithm to distribute the load to the backend servers in a target group. While the round-robin algorithm is widely used, it does have a few architectural issues to consider. It cannot take into consideration the target server's capacity and utilization when distributing traffic. One web server may be running on a small EC2 instance and others on a faster, more capable server. However, round-robin will not have this awareness and will distribute all connections evenly as if they all had the same capabilities that could create uneven load distributions.

The least outstanding requests algorithm is when each new request will be forwarded to the target server with the least number of requests. Targets with long-lasting connections will not be further loaded with new requests, and the workload is more evenly spread across all targets in a group. Also, if a new server is added, it will receive the majority of the new connections since it has the lowest connection count and will offload the burden from the existing servers.

Deregistration and Connection Draining

When taking a server offline, it's a good practice to not forcefully disconnect the existing sessions but, rather, allow them to complete their sessions while also not allowing any new connections to the servers. The deregistration feature is used to gracefully shut down a target server's connections. The connection draining is defined in the target group and, when enabled, instructs the load balancer to stop sending new connection requests to the servers in the target group. Existing connections will remain and will not be forcefully disconnected until they complete their connection or the deregistration delay time is reached. The timer value can be configured from 0 to 3,600 seconds with a default value of 300 seconds.

Deregistration is configured in the target group on the Group Details tab by selecting Edit attributes, as shown in Figure 4.9.

Deletion Protection

Load balancer deletion protection prevents a load balancer from being deleted when this feature is enabled. Deletion protection is disabled by default, and it's a good practice to enable it. The only way to delete a load balancer when deletion protection is enabled is to disable the feature and then perform the deletion steps.

FIGURE 4.9 Deregistration delay

EC2 > Target groups > test08032022 > Edit attributes
Edit attributes
Attributes
Restore defaults
Deregistration delay
The time to wait for in-flight requests to complete while deregistering a target. During this time, the state of the target is draining.
300
seconds
0-3600

To enable deletion protection, select the load balancer in the web console and click the Edit attributes box. The pop-up allows you to select and save the deletion protection feature.

Figures 4.10 and 4.11 detail enabling deletion protection and the error received when attempting to delete an ELB that has deletion protection enabled.

FIGURE 4.10 ELB deletion protection

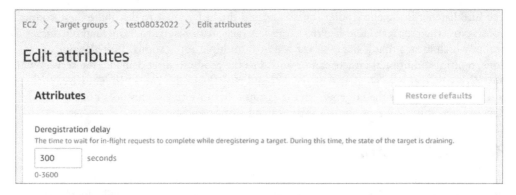

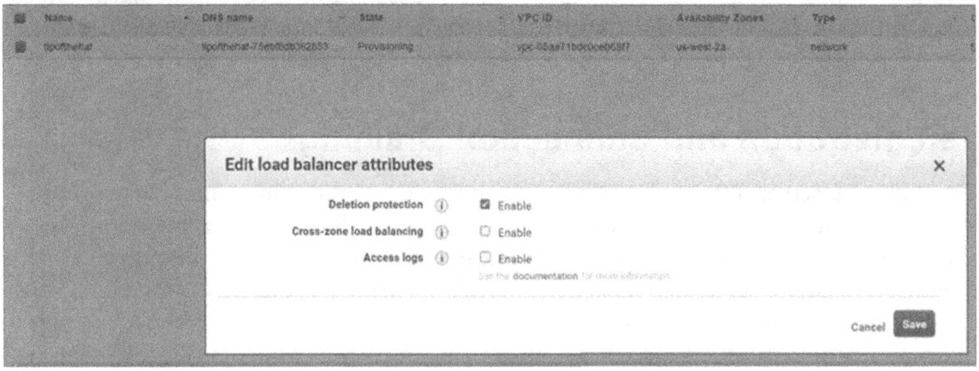
Edit load balancer attributes
Deletion protection
Enable
Cross-zone load balancing
Enable
Access logs
Enable
Cancel
Save

FIGURE 4.11 ELB deletion protection warning

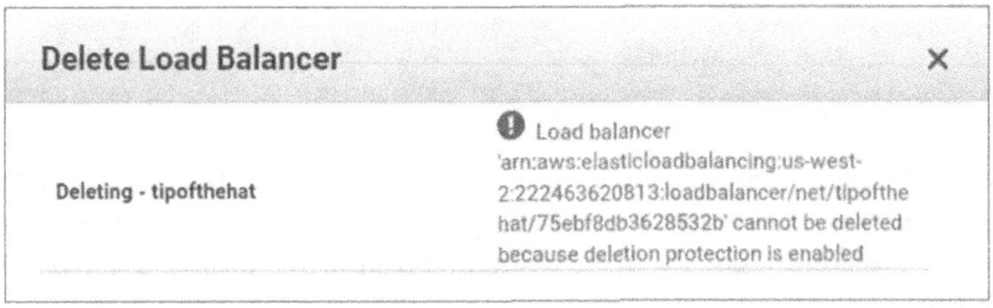
Delete Load Balancer
Deleting - tipofthehat
Load balancer 'arn:aws:elasticloadbalancing:us-west-2:222463620813:loadbalancer/net/tipofthehat/75ebf8db3628532b' cannot be deleted because deletion protection is enabled

Health Checking

Health checking is the determination that the backend servers are operational and able to accept connections from the ELB. The ELB will send out periodic connection requests to each server and listen for a healthy response code to be returned from the server. If the server responds positively, then the ELB will forward connections to it. However, if the server does not respond, it will be taken out of the rotation, and alarms will be generated for remediation.

The health checks are configured in each target group and allow you to define the protocol such as HTTP or HTTPS and advanced features such as TCP port number to check and the URL path on the server, with / being the root of the web server's directory. The healthy threshold defines the number of consecutive health checks that must be successful for the ELB to consider the server healthy. The unhealthy threshold defines the number of consecutive health check failures to take the server offline. The healthy threshold is five checks, and unhealthy is two checks. The time-out value is a default of 5 seconds and is the time the ELB will wait for the server to respond, and the interval is the time between ELB health checks and is set to 30 seconds by default. Finally, the HTTP respond code to listen for is 200, which indicates that the request was successful. See Figure 4.12 for the health check configuration screen in the ELB target group section of the console.

If all of the targets fail health checks in a group, the ELB will fail to open and forward requests to all servers in the group. Also, note that the WebSockets protocol does not support health checking. The actual health checks consist of the ELB making a connection request to the backend target, and after the response is received, the ELB will close the connection request.

Slow Start

To prevent a new target from being overwhelmed with connection requests when it is first brought online, there is a *slow start* feature that allows the server to gradually process new requests after the new target passes its health checking and comes online. This gives the server time to "warm up." The ELB will increase connection requests in a linear manner until the time window is met and the server is fully online.

The GENEVE Protocol

The *GENEVE protocol* is used with the gateway load balancer to preserve the original packet by providing a protocol that supports transparent routing. To make sure that the original packet remains intact, the GENEVE protocol encapsulates the original packet in a new header that the GWLB and appliances both support. This preserves the headers that the appliances need to process and allows for the separation of customer traffic, which may also have overlapping CIDR addresses. GENEVE is similar to VxLAN and Generic Routing Encapsulation (GRE) at layer 3 but does not have the fixed field size limitations of these protocols. This makes it more flexible for load balancing implementations.

The GENEVE protocol is an industry standard defined in RFC 8926.

FIGURE 4.12   Health check configuration

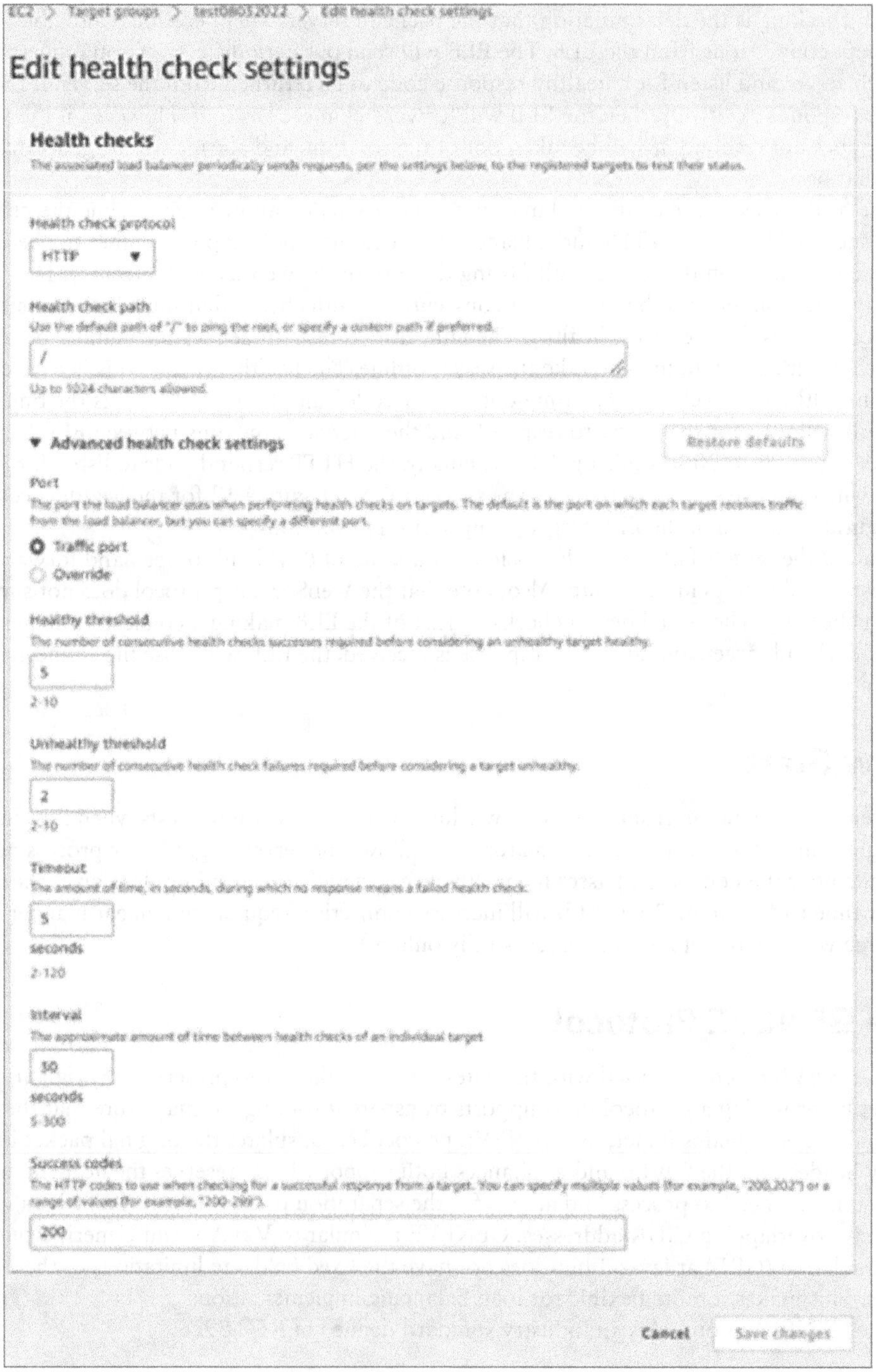

Encryption and Authentication

The ELB can actively support encryption operations to take the workload off the target servers and consolidate security operations in a smaller footprint. Alternatively, the load balancer can be configured to pass through the encrypted in-flight data to the backend servers for processing.

In this section, you will learn about how the load balancers process encrypted in-flight traffic.

The ALB can also process user authentication requests and take that workload off the target servers.

SSL/TLS Offload

In traditional web hosting environments where SSL/TLS encryption is deployed, the web servers terminate the SSL/TLS connections. This architecture is not optimal as it consumes processing power on the web servers to perform the encryption and decryption operations for in-flight packets. Digital certificates needed to be installed on each server, which created operational overhead as the certificates needed to be installed, managed, and periodically rotated across many servers. Also, security operations were spread across all of the servers, where it would be optimal to have them in a central device or, at least, a small number of devices.

With TLS offload, the load balancer takes responsibility for the encrypting and decrypting of in-flight traffic as it sits in the direct path of the traffic flow and is the listener interface that accepts all traffic from the outside. With the offload on the load balancer, the traffic can then be sent to the backend servers for processing without the need for those servers to perform any encryption functions, as shown in Figure 4.13.

When using the load balancer for offload, the digital certificate is bound to the load balancer's outside-facing VIP listener. Incoming encrypted traffic will terminate TLS on the VIP to offload the encryption process from the backend servers. As was previously mentioned in this chapter, this allows for a central point of administration, a single certificate to be installed, and centralized logging and monitoring of your in-flight encryption. The TLS operations are offloaded from the real servers in the backend pool to the load balancer.

TLS Passthrough

TLS passthrough is the more traditional design for load balancers that do not process SSL/TLS traffic on port 443. The load balancer does not have any digital certificates locally installed and just passes all encrypted traffic to the backend servers for them to perform the encryption and decryption functions, as shown in Figure 4.14.

In this case, the load balancer is not aware of and does not look into the encrypted traffic; it just load balances the connections to the servers in the defined target groups.

FIGURE 4.13   SSL/TLS offload

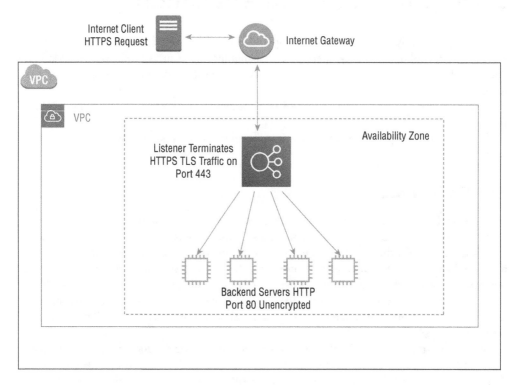

Summary

This chapter's focus was the AWS ELB family of services that includes the network load balancer, the application load balancer, and the gateway load balancer. These were introduced in Chapter 1, and we went into much more detail about the products in this chapter.

You learned about the architectural, deployment, operational, and monitoring specifics and many of the configuration options to enable the many features of the ELB services.

We began with the three types currently offered by AWS, how they operate, and what the use cases are for each type. Next you learned about high availability and security.

Internal load balancers use private IP addressing, and public load balancers are Internet-facing with a public IP on the listener interface. Remember that public load balancers can have EC2 target servers in the private IP address space.

The ELB services are integrated with other AWS services including Global Accelerator, CloudFront, the Web Application Firewall, Route 53, Elastic Kubernetes Service, and the AWS Certificate Manager. We went into some detail about how these services enhance a load balancer's operations and make them easier to deploy and operate.

There are many configuration options available, and you learned about the proxy protocol, X-Forwarded-For, cross-zone, session affinity, and sticky sessions.

FIGURE 4.14   SSL/TLS passthrough

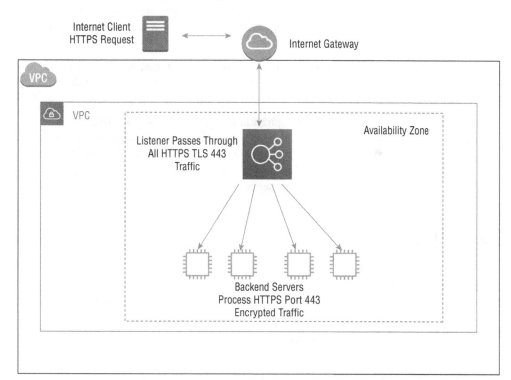

Target groups are configuration containers that define the backend services. There are many options in the target group configurations, and you learned about routing, the different types of targets, IP address types, protocol versions, registering targets, routing algorithms, how to deregister and perform connection draining, deletion protection for the load balancer, what health checks are and what they are used for, how slow starts prevent a new target from being overloaded when it comes online, and the GENEVE protocol that is used in the gateway load balancer.

SSL/TLS handling was detailed, including how the application load balancer can offload the encryption/decryption functions from the target servers and that SSL/TLS passthrough sends the encrypted traffic through the load balancer to the servers where they perform the SSL/TLS encryption/decryption at the server level.

Exam Essentials

Know the different types of load balancers and what makes them different from each other.   Know how they are intended to be used and what problems they are designed to solve.

Know when to use a gateway load balancer for a specific situation.   Know what the gateway load balancer is used for and why it is different from the others. Read the scenarios over, closely looking for key words that may indicate which type of load balancer is needed in the question.

Know that public-facing load balancers can communicate with target servers.   A public load balancer can use either public or private address spaces and have a public IP on the listener interface, and internal load balancers use a private IP for the listener.

Understand autoscaling and the basic configuration options for autoscaling groups.   There are a great deal of configuration options and service integrations with the ELB family given that it sits in the middle of traffic and plays a critical networking role in most AWS deployments. Read in detail about the integrations and configuration options. Visit the AWS console, practice setting up load balancers, and read the documentation in detail.

Exercises

1. Read the application load balancer user guide: `https://docs.aws.amazon.com/elasticloadbalancing/latest/application/introduction.html`.

2. Read the network load balancer user guide: `https://docs.aws.amazon.com/elasticloadbalancing/latest/network/introduction.html`.

3. Read the gateway load balancer user guide: `https://docs.aws.amazon.com/elasticloadbalancing/latest/gateway/introduction.html`.

4. Read the target groups user guide: `https://docs.aws.amazon.com/elasticloadbalancing/latest/network/load-balancer-target-groups.html`.

5. Read the AWS autoscaling documentation: `https://docs.aws.amazon.com/autoscaling/plans/userguide/what-is-a-scaling-plan.html`.

6. Read the AWS cross-zone load balancing documentation: `https://docs.aws.amazon.com/elasticloadbalancing/latest/application/load-balancer-subnets.html`.

7. Read the AWS autoscaling documentation: `https://docs.aws.amazon.com/autoscaling/ec2/userguide/what-is-amazon-ec2-auto-scaling.html`.

8. Read the Kubernetes controller documentation on GitHub: `https://github.com/kubernetes/controller-manager`.

Written Labs

Written Lab 4.1: Create a Network Load Balancer

1. In the AWS web console, go to the EC2 service page at `https://console.aws.amazon.com/ec2`.

2. Select Load Balancers in the navigation panel on the left.

3. Select Create Load Balancer.

4. Click the Create Load Balancer box.

5. Select Create Network Load Balancer.

6. In Basic Configuration, name your load balancer and select Internal IPv4.

7. In Network Mapping, select your VPC to place the load balancer into where the EC2 web servers reside.

8. In Mappings, select one availability zone that is internal.

9. In the Listeners And Routing box, leave the listener protocol at the default and select Create A Target Group.

10. In Target Group Basic configuration, leave the target type as Instances.

11. Name the target group and leave the protocol and port at TCP port 80 (HTTP).

12. Place the target group in the same VPC as the network load balancer and where the EC2 web servers reside.

13. Leave the health checks as TCP.

14. Select one or more EC2 instances and click the Include As Pending box.

15. Select Create Target Group.

16. Back on the load balancer configuration screen, select the default action for listeners and routing to use the target group created earlier.

17. Click Create Load Balancer.

18. Select View Load Balancer.

19. Review the configuration tabs including Description, Listeners, Monitoring, and Integrated Services.

20. When finished, select Actions and delete the network load balancer.

21. Go to Target Groups in the left panel of the EC2 console, deregister the targets, and delete the target group by selecting the target groups and Delete in the Actions pull-down.

Written Lab 4.2: Use the Console to Enable Deletion Protection

1. In the AWS web console, go to the EC2 service page at `https://console.aws.amazon.com/ec2`.

2. Select Load balancers in the navigation panel on the left.

3. Click your configured load balancer.

4. Click the Description tab and the Edit Attributes box.

5. Select Enable for deletion protection on the attributes page and save the changes.

6. Select Save.

Written Lab 4.3: Use the Console to Disable Deletion Protection

1. In the AWS web console, go to the EC2 service page at `https://console.aws.amazon.com/ec2`.

2. Select Load Balancers in the navigation panel on the left.

3. Click your configured load balancer.

4. Click the Description tab and the Edit Attributes box.

5. Clear the Enable box for deletion protection on the attributes page and save the changes.

6. Click Save.

Written Lab 4.4: Enable Application-Based Stickiness

1. In the AWS web console, go to the EC2 service page at `https://console.aws.amazon.com/ec2`.

2. Select Load Balancers in the navigation panel on the left.

3. Click Target Groups.

4. Select the target group you want to modify and open the details page.

5. On the group details tab, go to the Attributes section and click the Edit icon.

6. On the Edit Attributes configuration page, select Stickiness.

7. For the sticky type, select Application-Based Cookie.

8. Select a value of 1 second to 7 days for the stickiness duration.

9. Enter the name of your application-based cookie. Remember that AWSALB, AWSALBAPP, and AWSALBTG are reserved by AWS and cannot be used.

10. Save the changes.

Review Questions

The following questions are designed to test your understanding of this chapter's material. For more information on how to obtain additional questions, please see this book's introduction.

1. Your company will be having flash sales on its popular e-commerce site that is hosted on AWS. Because of high connection rates to backend servers that deliver feature-rich content, it is anticipated that traffic will be sent in bursts with large increases in the connection counts in a short time window. Also, the pages delivered will have motion graphics and high-resolution images delivered to every user. You are part of the architecture team and are reviewing ELB options that would best be able to handle this workload. What would you recommend?

    A. Classic load balancer

    B. Network load balancer

    C. Application load balancer

    D. Gateway load balancer

2. The network analytics application you are offering customers on the Amazon marketplace needs to sit in line with your client's traffic flow but be transparent. The packets cannot be modified in any way, and the packets entering your VPC from the customer must be the same leaving on the egress flow. There is also a possibility that many of your clients will have over-lapping CIDR addressing in the private address space. What AWS solution can you implement to meet this requirement?

    A. Classic load balancer

    B. Network load balancer

    C. Application load balancer

    D. Gateway load balancer

3. The backend target servers for your load balanced application use machine learning and analytics processing based on locality. The connections are getting erroneous IP source information from the incoming packets, and you have been hired to resolve the issue. What would you recommend to resolve the issue?

    A. Implement geo-proximity in Route 53

    B. Enable the X-Forwarded-For protocol on the servers to read the actual source IP in the header

    C. Implement SSL/TLS passthrough so the ALB does not act as a proxy and change the source IP address

    D. Use cross-zone load balancers so the source IP address does not get modified in transit

4. You have been asked to implement an intelligent load balancing solution that will support your company website hosted in the AWS us-west-2 region. There will be a mix of customer devices connecting including smartphones, tablets, and laptops. The web application sources HTML content in either rich or sparse pages based on the connected device type. What solution would be able to do header inspection to determine the device type and direct the traffic to the appropriate target group?

    A. Classic load balancer

    B. Network load balancer

    C. Application load balancer

    D. Gateway load balancer

5. The development team is working on a new e-commerce website, and you have been asked to assist in the networking architecture. The application servers and SQL database replicas need to be able to scale independently of each other and to be able to be upgraded without affecting ongoing operations. What type of load balancer would you use for this design?

    A. External

    B. Internal

    C. Classic

    D. Gateway

    E. Network

6. Your cybersecurity officer has asked you for recommendations to protect your website hosted on AWS using an application load balancer. He is concerned about SYN and denial-of-service attacks originating from the Internet that could affect your company's service offerings. What would you recommend as a solution to protect the ALB listener port?

    A. Route 53

    B. CloudFront

    C. CloudWatch

    D. Web Application Firewall

    E. CloudTrail

7. Your company is planning on expanding its web application services to its European customers. It hosts its server fleet in the Ohio region behind an application load balancer. The deployment team is concerned about network latency from Europe to the United States. What AWS service would reduce these network delays?

    A. Elastic Kubernetes Service

    B. Route 53

    C. CloudTrail

    D. Global Accelerator

    E. Gateway load balancer

8. You are getting trouble tickets about your e-commerce shopping carts suddenly disappearing, and it is affecting revenue and customer satisfaction. The application team has been investigating each application server sitting behind the ALB and can verify that the shopping carts are still present on the server but not on a customer's browser. What can be done to resolve this issue?

A. Enable the GENEVE protocol

B. Use a network load balancer

C. Enable session affinity on the ALB

D. Use cross-zone load balancing

9. Your e-commerce website needs to be able to have multiple servers to support the high connection counts from Internet users. You have been tasked to recommend a load balancer design to front-end the servers from the Internet. What type of load balancer would you use for this design?

A. External

B. Internal

C. Classic

D. Gateway

E. Network

10. The application team needs to take down an application server in an ALB target group to install a critical patch. However, when you check CloudWatch, you notice that there are more than 350 sessions active on the server. Since you do not want to drop active sessions, what solution is offered by AWS to take this server offline without affecting these connections?

A. Slow stop

B. Disable health checking

C. Deletion protection

D. Connection draining

11. What configuration architecture does not have any digital certificates locally installed on the load balancer that passes all encrypted traffic to the backend servers for them to perform the encryption and decryption functions?

A. Offload

B. GENEVE groups

C. Deregistration

D. SSL/TLS passthrough

12. What feature can be enabled to prevent a load balancer from being taken permanently offline?

A. Deletion protection

B. Session affinity

C. Deregistration

D. Forward proxy protection

13. Which protocol preserves the source IP address of the originating host?

    A. Session affinity

    B. Proxy protocol

    C. GENEVE protocol

    D. TLS

14. What ELB feature is enabled to prevent a new target from being overwhelmed with connection requests when it is first brought online?

    A. Session affinity

    B. Slow start

    C. Offload

    D. Connection limiting

15. What is used to determine that the backend servers are operational and able to accept connections from the ELB?

    A. Kubernetes

    B. Round-robin

    C. Offload

    D. Health checking

16. What are two ways to secure the public listener on your application load balancer?

    A. CloudTrail

    B. CloudFront

    C. Web Application Firewall

    D. CloudWatch

17. What target types does an application load balancer support? (Select three.)

    A. Instance ID

    B. IP address

    C. Kinesis

    D. Lambda

    E. Redshift ID

    F. Cognito ID

18. Name two load distribution algorithms used by the AWS ELB family of load balancers.

    A. Latency

    B. Affinity

    C. Round-robin

    D. Least outstanding

19. Which design is where the load balancer takes responsibility for the encrypting and decrypting of in-flight traffic instead of the backend web servers?

    A. Application load balancer

    B. SSL/TLS offload

    C. SSL passthrough

    D. Network load balancer

20. Which ELB feature can dynamically add and remove backend processing capacity based on the current load?

    A. Autoscaling

    B. Autostandby

    C. Autoredundancy

    D. Target groups

Logging and Monitoring

THE AWS CERTIFIED ADVANCED NETWORKING - SPECIALTY EXAM OBJECTIVES COVERED IN THIS CHAPTER MAY INCLUDE, BUT ARE NOT LIMITED TO, THE FOLLOWING:

✓ **Domain 1: Network Design**

- Objective 1.4: Define logging and monitoring requirements across AWS and hybrid networks.

CloudWatch

CloudWatch is the AWS monitoring service used to monitor and manage your AWS deployments. It plays a critical role in providing insight with a wide range of metrics including resource usage and errors that can be used to make sure your services are optimized and, if something should go wrong, generate alarms to trigger remediation steps to restore down or performance-impacted services. CloudWatch plays a critical role in monitoring not just the networking components but all of the AWS offerings including plug-in code to customize the monitoring of your applications. With the installation of agents, on-premises servers can export log and metric data to CloudWatch to allow for a complete AWS monitoring solution.

The service includes integrated tools for analytics to quickly be able to analyze the collected data. With the alerting feature, external systems can be notified of alarms to take actions with your existing network management tools.

In this section, you will learn about the components that are part of the CloudWatch suite of tools and how they are used and integrated to make sure you have complete visibility into your AWS operations. The service supports integration with third-party monitoring systems for log collection, monitoring, graphing, and any other systems management applications.

Metrics

Metrics represent a time-ordered set of data points that are sent to and processed by Cloud-Watch. A metric is a variable value that varies over time such as I/O throughput, CPU utilization, database writes, or any other thousands of data points in AWS. AWS includes a large number of predefined metrics and allows you to define custom metrics.

Metrics and logs are collected by CloudWatch on a regional level and stored in a Cloud-Watch repository. The repository displays data only for the region it's configured for and any data collected from external sources that are exported to the respective regional repository.

Metrics are displayed in the CloudWatch console, as shown in Figure 5.1. Also, the CLI interface, API calls, and the SDK provided by AWS allow access to your collected metrics. This flexibility allows for other systems and tools to be integrated into CloudWatch. Metrics collect data from the systems, subsystems, or resources being used. Every metric records values such as state information or resource usage values including values such as CPU utilization, health check status, disk activities such as read and write operations, network activity, and many other values.

FIGURE 5.1   CloudWatch metrics

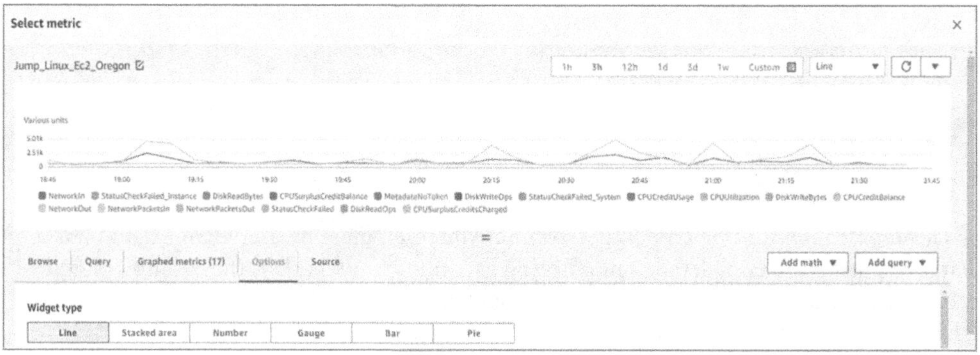

There are three categories of metrics. Standard metrics are the default type and are collected in 5-minute windows and provided by AWS at no cost. Detailed monitoring is recorded in 1-minute windows and must be enabled by the operator. Custom details are configurable down to 1-second intervals. There is an additional cost for detailed metrics.

Data retention times vary based on the metric type. For example, custom metrics recorded in less than 1-minute intervals are stored for 3 hours, 1-minute customer metrics are retained for 15 days, 5-minute metrics are stored for 63 days, and 1-hour metrics are stored for 15 months. It is most common for the systems consuming these metrics to process the data in near real time, so these retention values should be sufficient. Note that based on your cloud deployments and activity levels, CloudWatch can generate a massive amount of data in a short time, so storage costs should be monitored closely. Metrics are aggregated upward. This means that when, for example, the 1-minute detailed metric retention time expires, the data is rolled into 5-minute metrics and then 1-hour metrics with the retention time extended accordingly.

The console gives you a detailed view of the metrics collected for the selected region. You can select different metric groups and get more granular data by clicking into the groups for more specific data. You can also select the time range for which to view the metric data, as shown in Figure 5.2.

Monitoring Categories

There are three different types of monitoring that allow you to pick which one best fits your needs and budget. By selecting either default, detailed, or custom monitoring, you are selecting the time interval between measurements.

Standard monitoring is the default and supported by all AWS services. The interval is 5 minutes, and there is no charge for this service level.

FIGURE 5.2   CloudWatch metric groups

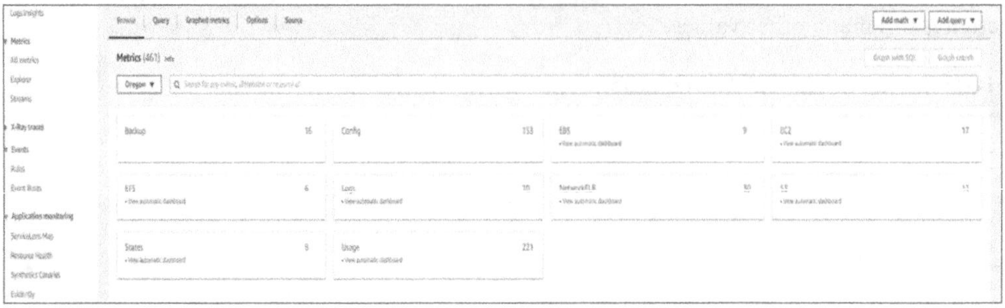

The *detailed monitoring* type is at a 1-minute interval, must be user enabled, and has a charge applied. However, detailed monitoring at 1-minute intervals is the default configuration for the elastic load balancer and relational database services. Custom metrics can be defined down to the 1-second level and are available at an additional cost.

Custom detailed monitoring has a 1-minute interval and can be applied per instance metric, so it does not require you to enable it globally, thereby saving costs. The cost is applied only to the instance that consumes the service to control expenses.

Detailed monitoring is useful where quick responses are required. For example, you may apply detailed monitoring to the CPU utilization for a web server or its connection count to be able to proactively add capacity compared to standard monitoring, which will have a longer measurement window and slower reaction time. Custom monitoring gives you the most granular interfaces down to 1 second. A use case for custom measurements would be when running containers such as ECS or Fargate where it is beneficial to create containers quickly. The 1-second interval increases your response to events and allows you to scale much faster than if you were measuring at 1- or 5-minute intervals. Detailed monitoring is available only on selected services and can be enabled in the EC2 console, as shown in Figure 5.3.

Agents

In addition to the CloudWatch integration with AWS managed services, there is also *Cloud-Watch agent* code that can be installed on your Windows or Linux servers to collect data and forward it to the CloudWatch service.

The agent is installed on your servers and runs in the background. The agent collects logs from EC2 instances and on-premise Linux and Windows servers. Once the agent is installed, internal system metrics are collected using the EC2 instance metrics and custom guest metrics. There is a long list of metrics that can be collected by the agent that can be viewed on the AWS documentation site at `https://docs.aws.amazon.com/AmazonCloudWatch/latest/monitoring/metrics-collected-by-CloudWatch-agent.html`. The agent can be installed on hybrid servers and servers that are not managed by AWS.

The CloudWatch agent is open-source under the MIT license and is hosted on GitHub at `https://github.com/aws/amazon-cloudwatch-agent`. The agent listens on the default socket tcp:25888.

FIGURE 5.3   Enabling detailed monitoring

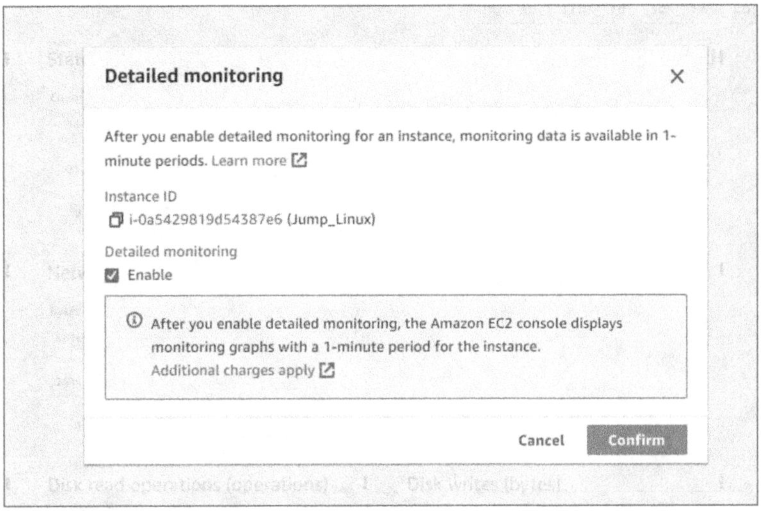

You can store and view the agent metrics that are processed using the CloudWatch service the same as with AWS-generated metrics. The namespace used is CWAgent and can be modified. All logging data collected by the agents can be forwarded to CloudWatch just as with any other logging you are operating. These are stored in CloudWatch logs.

All metrics collected by the agent will be billed as custom metrics.

Logging

CloudWatch acts as a centralized logging collection repository for both system- and application-level logs generated by all of your devices and services and also external services running in your data center with the installation of the CloudWatch logs agent. By centralizing logging into CloudWatch, you have a central repository of all logs generated by all your resources and displayed in a central console, API, SDK, or CLI interface.

CloudWatch Logs can be processed as a complete picture of your operations and not just at the device or application level. This correlation ability gives you not only ongoing visibility but the ability to perform capacity planning and resolve issues as they arise. The logs are collected, combined, and displayed in the web management interface, as shown in Figure 5.4.

CloudWatch can collect log files in many different formats that are generated by dissimilar systems.

Log groups are configured to group log data into similar groupings such as Route 53 logs or load balancing logs. Multiple streams are then sent to each log group. By using the insights search feature, you can create expressions to find the log files of interest. A nice feature of insights is that it can monitor in real time and find new logs that match the filter expressions you define. Based on the match, you can trigger events to generate alerts or call other applications using automation to resolve any issues.

FIGURE 5.4   CloudWatch log groups

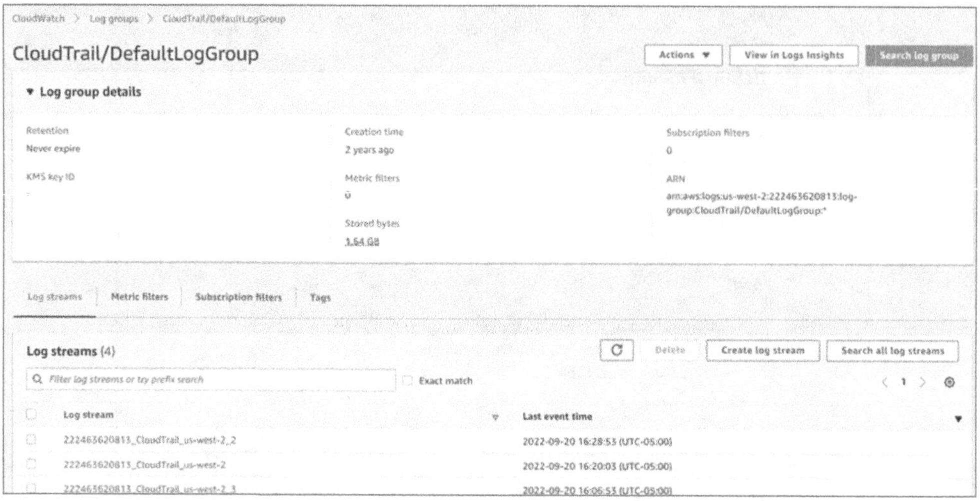

Logs are stored indefinitely and can be exported to S3 with life-cycle management configured to reduce retention costs.

Alarms

Alarms generated by CloudWatch are based on metric conditions, configured thresholds, and log triggers that are defined. These events can trigger notifications to external tools and services. These services can perform actions using automation to notify support personnel using the SNS service, as shown in Figure 5.5. Alarms are configured based on metric values and data patterns in the log files.

CloudWatch alarms are structured to track a condition over a defined time window and then to generate an action. For example, you measure the number of active connections on a web server over a 15-minute interval and add another web server using autoscaling if the connection value exceeds 800 connections. Another example would be to monitor the log files generated by a web server and track 404 errors with 50 errors in a 10-minute window. The action could be to send an alert to the web administrators using the SNS.

Using AWS Lambda microservices gives you a great deal of flexibility to customize alarm actions. You could call a Lambda instance to forward logs to a data lake or Kinesis services to run queries for security intrusions or any other anomalies you track. Lambda can forward data to S3, DynamoDB, and many other services for further processing or storage.

Alert notifications can be configured to call the AWS SNS, which sends the alert to subscribers of the topic and can be used to trigger other downstream services such as SQS, email, and SNS text messaging. This push-based service is real time, which allows for quick response to process events.

FIGURE 5.5   CloudWatch alarms configuration screen

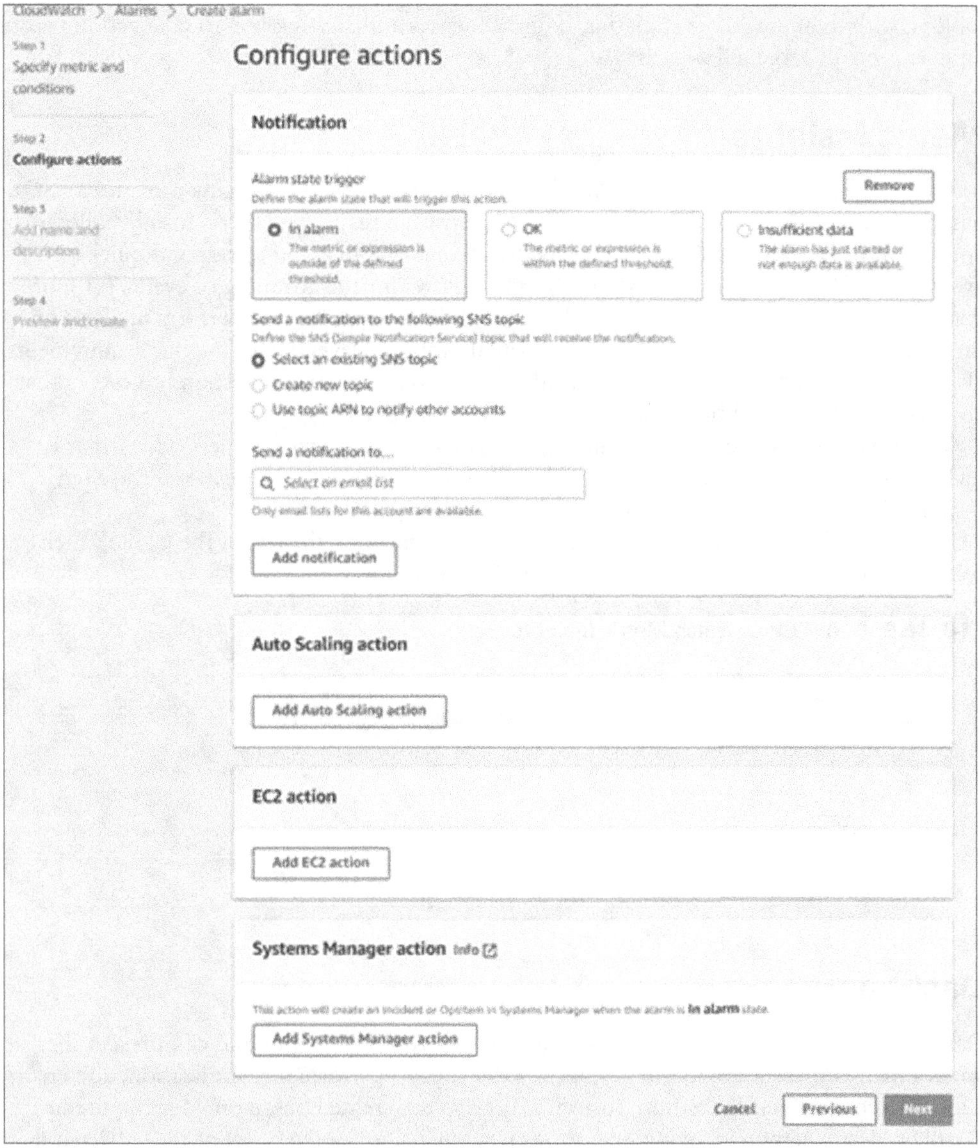

Autoscaling events can be called from CloudWatch alarms. For instance, if a EC2 instance should fail, the alarms from CloudWatch can call an autoscaling group to replace the failed instance without user intervention. Other autoscaling operations include DynamoDB capacity RCUs/WCUs.

Billing alarms are included with CloudWatch to proactively monitor your charges and send out SNS alerts if they exceed your estimated charge limits. These can be forward looking with trending costs estimating future expenses and alerting you to take action before an unexpectedly large bill arrives.

Metric Insights

Metric Insights is part of the CloudWatch service offerings. Metric Insights provides an SQL-based query engine that can search millions of metrics in real time. Metric Insights allows you to capture trends and data patterns as they occur, enabling you to respond quickly to events using SQL-based queries. Metric Insights allows for the grouping of events for more detailed analysis. For example, you could select all EC2 instances and perform analysis on them or drill down to the region, VPC, or availability zone level based on your requirements. Using the data from insights, you could call utilities to automatically respond to events that you define or create real-time graphing for visual dashboards.

The service uses standard SQL language, or you can use the visual query editor that is included in the service. Once you have selected your metrics with the visual editor, Metric Insights will automatically generate the SQL query for you to run.

To run this feature, click the All-Metrics tab in the pane on the left of the CloudWatch console and open the Query tab, as shown in Figure 5.6.

FIGURE 5.6   CloudWatch Metric Insights

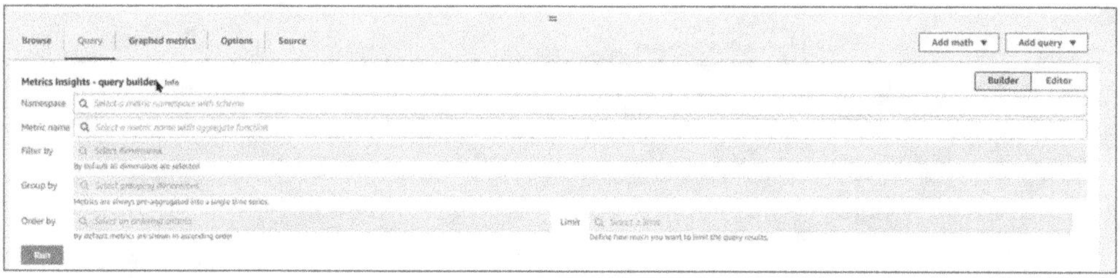

Dashboards

Dashboards allow for a single-pane-of-glass view of your operations and can present the data of many different metrics in graphical form such as performance, utilization, and errors. CloudWatch dashboards are fully customizable and are created based on your requirements. Dashboards are helpful in giving operations personnel a quick overview of the collected metrics of your services.

You can visualize live data about your network and share your visualizations with outside entities even if they do not have an account with AWS or are part of your organization.

Dashboards can present a view of your complete deployment across accounts and regions by aggregating your data into one high-level dashboard. From this global dashboard, you can then drill down to more detailed dashboards without the need to manually change regions or accounts in the console.

Widgets that you create or are supplied by AWS can be added to your dashboards. Examples of widgets include gauges, lines, numbers, alarms, graphs, and more.

Transit Gateway Network Manager

The AWS Transit Gateway Manager is an AWS service used to manage and monitor your global network when using the Transit Gateway service to route your company WAN traffic over the AWS network. The Transit Gateway Manager integrates with SD-WAN branch office devices and gives you network visibility across the AWS network and your private, corporate-connected networks in a single dashboard. The service simplifies the building and ongoing operations of your global network including a dashboard to visualize your network operations. Network metrics and events are monitored and displayed for ongoing network management operations.

To integrate your private network into the AWS Transit Gateway Network Manager, you create AWS Transit Gateways and then add your on-premises networks. The Transit Gateway Network Manager has SD-WAN integrations with HP/Aruba, Aviatrix, Cisco Systems, and Vera networks. With these integrations, your complete cloud and private network can be managed by the Transit Gateway Network Manager. These vendors' management consoles can automatically provision site-to-site VPN connections to AWS from your on-premises networks.

With the graphical dashboard, utilization metrics, including packets and bytes sent and received, packet drops, and alerts, are displayed. Changes in the network topology including routing and up/down connection events are collected, and alerts are generated.

VPC Reachability Analyzer

The *VPC Reachability Analyzer* is used to validate your network connectivity, troubleshoot, identify network configuration issues, and automate validations for connectivity after configuration changes or new deployments. The VPC Reachability Analyzer checks the network path taken by a packet from the source to destination. The tool creates a logical model of the configuration and then checks for connectivity. It is important to note that it does not actually send data over the forwarding plane; the reachability is analyzed in code only.

The VPC Reachability Analyzer traces the network connectivity from the source to destination and is very useful in reachability analysis, configuration validations, and troubleshooting. The service is used inside your VPC to perform connectivity testing and integrates with many AWS services and endpoints to give you a complete picture of the network path and metrics. The VPC Reachability Analyzer provides a hop-by-hop analysis of the path a packet traverses given the source, destination port, and protocol information you define when you set up a trace test. If the test fails, the analyzer will identify where the data is being blocked to assist in troubleshooting. For example, paths can be blocked by network configuration errors, a misconfigured security group, a network ACL deny rule, or a missing route in a route table, to give a few examples.

The Reachability Analyzer supports the following source and destination endpoints: EC2 instances, Internet gateways, network interfaces, Transit Gateways, Transit Gateway attachments, VPC endpoints, VPC peering connections, and VPN gateways. These endpoints must be in the same account and in the same region. Also, they must be in the same VPC or a peered or Transit Gateway VPC. Intermediate devices include network and application load balancers (but not gateway load balancers), NAT gateways, Transit Gateways, Transit Gateway attachments, and VPC peering connections. Reporting on successes and failures can list a large number of AWS components including the following: VPC, EC2 instances, Internet gateways, load balancers (excluding gateway load balancers), NAT gateways, network ACLs, network interfaces, prefix lists, route tables, security groups, subnets, ELB target groups, Transit Gateways, Transit Gateway attachments, Transit Gateway route tables, virtual private gateways, VPC endpoints, and VPC gateway endpoints.

The analyzer can be accessed via the web interface, the CLI, APIs, and SDKs, and is configured and enabled with CloudFormation. In the web console, open the VPC service and select the Reachability Analyzer on the Network Analysis tab in the left panel.

Granular scenarios can be configured; for example, a path is created from the source of the Internet gateway in a VPC to an EC2 instance selected as the destination on TCP port 80. With this test, you can verify that the web server is reachable from the Internet, as shown in Figure 5.7. Figure 5.8 shows the configuration and results of a trace test.

FIGURE 5.7   Network Reachability Analyzer configuration screen

If the test fails and the remote endpoint is not reachable based on your trace parameters, the output will list what is causing the blockage by component or service to direct you to where to begin your troubleshooting.

FIGURE 5.8   Network Reachability Analyzer trace results

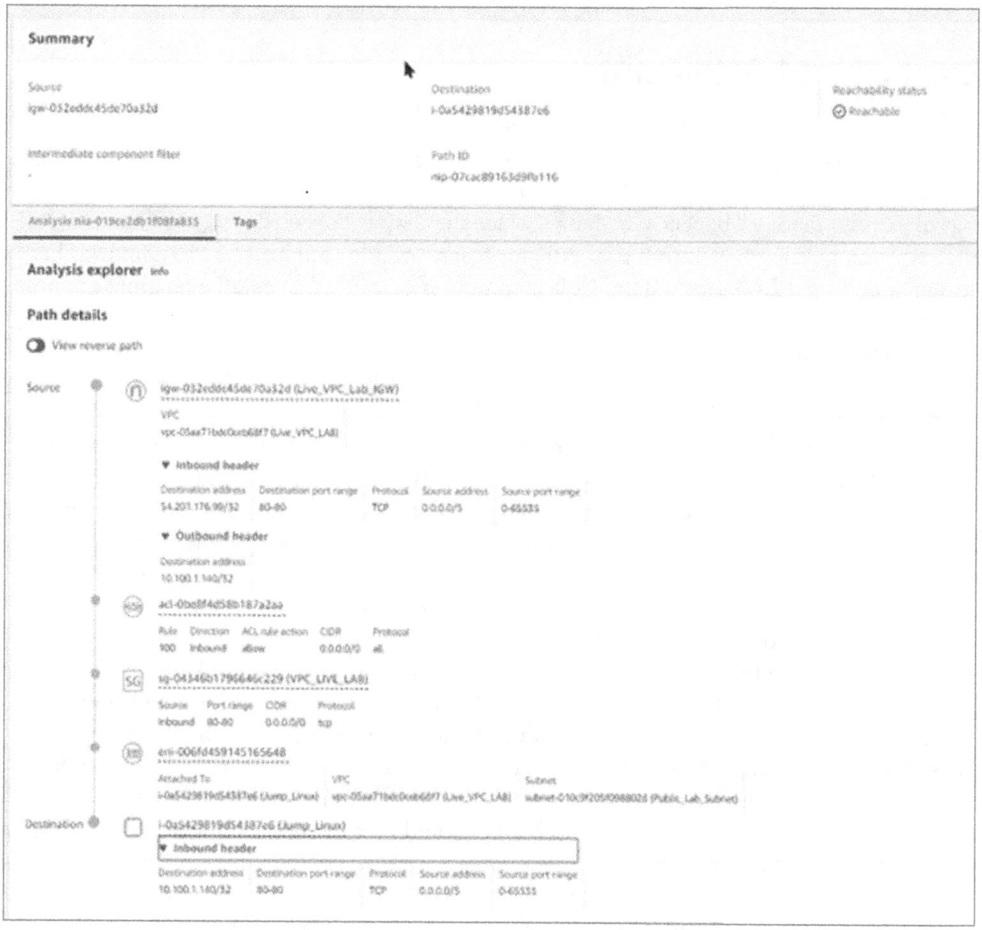

In the case where there is more than one path from the source to the destination, the analyzer will display the shortest path. This can be modified to investigate other alternative paths by specifically listing components in the path to traverse.

Access Logs

Many AWS services record user access and export the data as log files for you to process using backend services. These log files allow you to monitor usage patterns, collect baselines, troubleshoot, and validate any security or compliance mandates your organization may operate under. Analytic services can be used to gain valuable insights into your operations by searching your access logs. In this section, we will discuss the access logs that are specific to networking including load balancing, content distribution, and DNS services.

Elastic Load Balancing

ELB access logs allow you to record and store logging data for every HTTP/HTTPS and TCP request processed by your elastic load balancer. The logs are in plaintext format and are generated as one line per log entry. Logging can be enabled or disabled at any time. These access logs are stored in an S3 bucket you define. Once the data is collected, you can then use AI, analysis, standard logging search tools, or third-party vendor applications to gain insights into your collected ELB access data. Collected data is combined from all availability zones that the ELB is configured for. Data analysis may include the source IP addresses, target server response metrics, and traffic flow from source to target and the return flow. Access logs are disabled by default and can be activated in the LB console, CLI, or with an API call. When configuring access logging, you will need to specify the S3 bucket to store the logs and the desired prefix in the bucket. If you have a very busy site, remember that there can be a large amount of logging data created, and there will be associated charges in S3 to store that data. The logs are collected and exported to CloudWatch at specified time intervals. If a log grows too large before the time interval is complete, multiple logs are generated. So, on busy sites, there may be multiple logs generated for each time interval. It is a good idea to configure log retention time frames and policies; for example, use storage life-cycle rules to migrate older logs to the lower-cost Glacier storage service.

The logging is useful for setting baselines of your deployment and to identify impairments or bottlenecks along the flow path such as an EC2 web server that is responding slowly.

Logs are stored in S3 based on your data retention requirements. It is a best practice to use the S3 life-cycle manager to manage and reduce storage costs. The log file naming convention contains the IP address of the load balancer, AWS account number, load balancer's name and region, the date YYYY/MM/DD and a timestamp of the end of the logging interval, and a random number (to handle multiple log files for the same time interval). Logs are sent in intervals of 15 to 60 minutes.

See Figure 5.9 for the CloudWatch log displays for a network load balancer.

FIGURE 5.9 Network load balancer CloudWatch logs

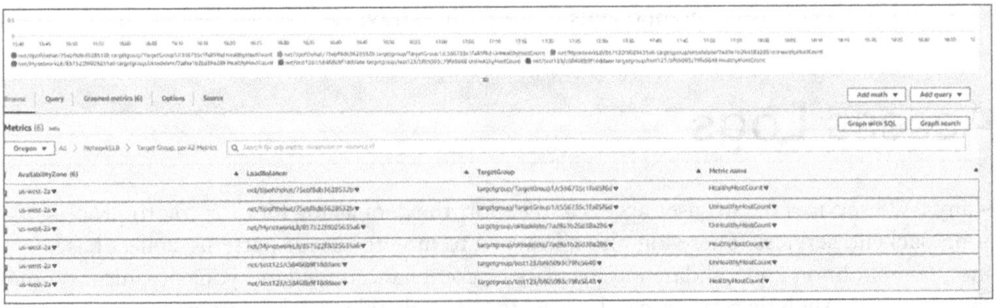

Route 53 Logs

Route 53 has service integrations for exporting events into CloudTrail and CloudWatch. DNS requests at the domain- and subdomain-level are logged into CloudWatch with metrics including what domain lookup was requested, the date and time, the record type such as CNAME or A records, the response code, and the edge location that responded to the query. CloudWatch also collects and analyzes Route 53 health-checking metrics.

The data can be stored and analyzed using AWS search and analysis tools or one of the many offerings from AWS partners. Log streams are categorized by each edge location that responds to a query and are formatted as *hosted-zone-id/edge-location-ID*. Since the logs can grow to be very large and are stored without a deletion date, it is a good practice to export query logs to a more cost-effective storage solution such as S3 with life-cycle policies applied.

CloudTrail collects console API actions made by a systems administrator, IAM role, or other AWS services. The CloudTrail records provide very detailed information such as who made the request, date/time, source IP address, and what the request was. All records are available in the event history tab of the CloudTrail console. It is important to remember that since Route 53 is a global service and not region specific, you must choose the us-east-1 Virginia region where the Route 53 data is stored, or if you chose Route 53 from the console, it will default to the global region.

For extended retention times, create a trail using the CloudTrail console to store the logs in S3, and use life-cycle policies to manage your storage requirements.

All domain records can be viewed in the Route 53 dashboard, which details registrations, domain transfers, and expiration dates of registered domains.

CloudFront Logs

Standard CloudFront logging, also called *access logging*, can be enabled in CloudFront and provides very detailed information on edge request activity. When it's enabled, you must specify the S3 bucket to store the log files in. The logging feature is provided at no charge by AWS; however, there is a charge associated with the S3 storage used. The logging feature is enabled when you create or update the CloudFront distribution. The standard log delivery time is several times per hour but can take up to 24 hours to appear. Real-time logging can also be enabled and sent to a Kinesis data stream for analysis or storage. The data from all of the edge locations is consolidated into the S3 repository.

CloudTrail Logs

CloudTrail records all API calls to AWS services. The API data can tell us who made changes to any of your services, where from, what time, what the change was, and a large amount of metric data. CloudTrail can also be configured to export the API logging to CloudWatch logs, as shown in Figure 5.10.

FIGURE 5.10   CloudTrail logs

X-Ray

The *X-Ray* service traces request and response actions between application workflows. By enabling X-Ray, you can view the actions inside your applications and services and how they interact with each other including microservices, databases, APIs, and other AWS services. By collecting this information, you can filter and view your data to locate problems and get insight into the interactions between the application and service flows.

X-Ray Traces

The X-Ray service receives inbound and outbound trace data that is collected from your applications.

X-Ray traces create a service map to give you a visual reference of the workflow and identify latency and performance issues, as shown in Figure 5.11.

X-Ray aggregates the collected trace information and metadata by installing the AWS daemon instrumentation code on the application servers to collect the information. The services do not export the data directly into the X-Ray service, but rather the client SDK exports the files to a collector that buffers the trace data from the clients and then uploads the data in its queue to the X-Ray service as a batch operation. The daemon is preinstalled in Lambda and Elastic Beanstalk and can be installed on Linux, macOS, and Windows platforms.

X-Ray collects the trace data and generates a detailed service map of the correlated traces. The map displays a complete path from the client to the application and its backend services. Bottlenecks and latency graphing allow you to identify and resolve performance issues. Developers can use X-Ray to look into their distributed applications and debug issues between microservices.

X-Ray will analyze the collected trace data and help to locate performance issues in your applications. It will assign these to root causes. Insights are created when the fault rates are out of normal operations, and the insight can be tracked through to resolution. This is a continuous background process that X-Ray is running.

FIGURE 5.11   X-Ray workflow map

X-Ray Insights

X-Ray Insights analyzes the data generated by the AWS X-Ray service, identifies anomalies, and generates notifications on what the anomaly is and why it was triggered. The service can be helpful in determining a root cause of a performance issue based on the trace data generated by the insights and can provide data on its impact to your operations. This is extremely helpful when troubleshooting distributed applications as it allows you to view the dependencies and responses between the microservices. It identifies other services and applications that may be affected by the issue so you can get a complete view of systems impacted and how it may be affecting users. The timeline view is helpful in determining when the issue began and how it has progressed over a definable timeline.

The service uses a statistical analysis to learn trends about your collected trace data. A band of acceptable values is calculated, and alerts are generated when trends exceed the baseline metrics. The alerts include information on the root service, other services that are affected, and any user impacts. A timeline is added with critical events listed along that timeline. The notifications can be posted to the AWS EventBridge service that allows you to forward the X-Ray Insights generated alerts to any AWS or external application for remediation or logging.

X-Ray is available in the CloudWatch console.

Flow Logs

Flow Logs capture data on IP traffic flows between interfaces in a VPC. You select the source and destination of the flow you want to analyze, and the service will show you the path between the two inside of AWS. The Flow Log captures are external to the actual data flow in your VPC, so the captures do not affect network latency or throughput of your production traffic. Flow Logs can be created from sources such as Elastic Load Balancer (ELB), Amazon Relational Database Service (RDS), Redshift, workspaces, NAT gateways, and Transit Gateways. Instances launched in a VPC after a Flow Log has been created are automatically added to the flow capture.

The Flow Log capture is configured; then you run the capture, and the data gets stored in CloudWatch logs or, optionally, in a S3 bucket or sent to Kinesis Firehose. Analyzing the logs is often used for monitoring traffic sent and received from an EC2 instance, analyzing traffic flows inside your VPC, and troubleshooting security group restrictions in addition to other uses. Logs can be created, deleted, or changed without any interference to your actual production traffic flows. Log monitor points can be at the VPC level, a subnet, or a network interface inside of a VPC. If the Flow Log is created for a VPC, each interface inside of that VPC is monitored. When creating a Flow Log, specify the resource to be monitored, whether you want to capture all accepted and rejected traffic, and where you want the data to be stored. Once the Flow Log is created, there is a delay of up to several minutes before the data is collected and stored. Flow logging is not considered a real-time service.

If you delete a Flow Log, the data collected is retained, and all log captures are suspended. If you do not want to preserve the capture logging data, then you will need to delete it from the storage locations you defined in the original configuration or through the use of life-cycle policies.

Flow Logs are created in the console in the VPC service. Select the VPC you want to enable logging, click the Flow Logs tab, and create the Flow Log, as shown in Figure 5.12. Traffic mirroring supports filters and packet truncation so that you extract only the traffic of interest by using the monitoring tools of your choice. When configuring traffic mirroring, you specify the source, destination, and a filter and then give it a session name.

Traffic mirroring is configured in the VPC section of the AWS console and allows you to filter the packets and truncate them to reduce the amount of data generated and to capture only traffic of interest. When Flow Logs are created, there are certain traffic types that are not logged including the following: AWS DNS server traffic (however, private internal DNS is logged), AWS instance Windows license activations, instance metadata to the 169.254.169.254 address, time sync traffic to 169.254.169.123, any DHCP-related traffic,

traffic from mirrored interfaces, VPC default gateway reserved IP address traffic, and traffic from endpoint interfaces, and a network load balancer.

Pricing for Flow Logs includes data ingestion of the logging traffic and storage charges. Check the CloudWatch console for detailed pricing information.

FIGURE 5.12   Creating a VPC Flow Log

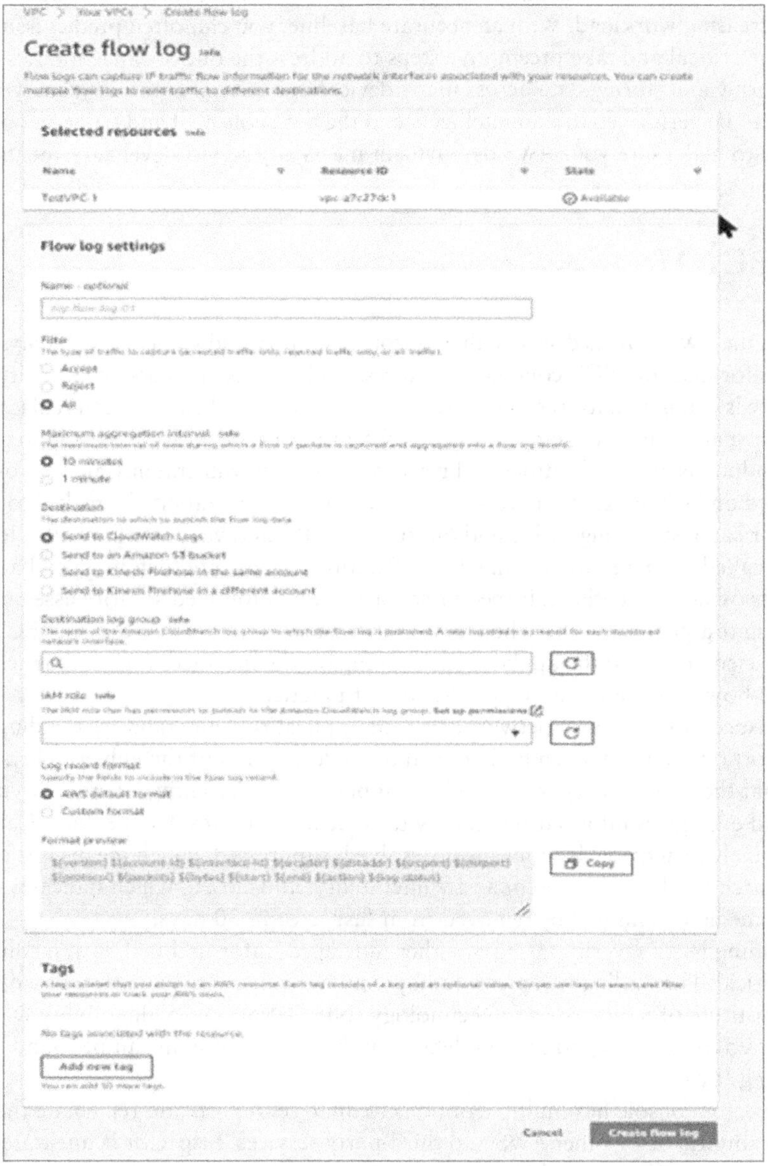

Baseline Network Performance

Baseline data collected from monitoring metrics and logs are used to understand your usage over time and to create a performance baseline. Baselines can help you understand what is considered a normal usage pattern. When the tracking data exceeds the baseline metrics, you will have visibility into what is out of range and work to resolve the issue or add capacity to meet an increasing workload. With an accurate baseline, you can often predict issues before they become critical and take preemptive steps to address the out-of-range metrics.

By capturing and storing data across many devices in a central repository, analytics and AI functions can be performed to add intelligence to the data collected and perform operations in real time to make sure your AWS deployment meets any service-level agreements.

Inspector

Inspector is the AWS managed service that performs security and vulnerability analysis and assessments for EC2 and ECR container instances, applications, network accessibility, and how security is configured for the applications on the instances. Inspector can replace scanning utilities, which are generally use-restricted by AWS inside a VPC. The service automatically discovers endpoints and applications and performs a security vulnerability analysis on each device; based on its findings, a report is generated, and the vulnerability is tracked to resolution.

Inspector can test routing inside and out of your VPC and validates firewall rules. Open ports, also called *listeners*, are identified per IP address. These are then mapped back to the host, and its owner is identified. Inspector can act as an automated security assessment service by using test packages. These host assessment packages report on the host/EC2, ECR/container-based hosts and the applications running on the instances for compliance, vulnerabilities, and how they compare to established best practices.

When Inspector discovers a network, host, or application vulnerability, a finding is created to report on the issue. Each finding includes a description of the vulnerability, logs the resource that the vulnerability was found on, applies a rating to how severe that vulnerability is, and even gives information on how to remediate and resolve the issue. Categories of findings include active, which means unresolved; suppressed, which means it is acknowledged and archived but still present as a vulnerability; and closed, which indicates the issue has been remediated and will be removed from Inspector in 30 days.

Each finding has a severity rating of either untriaged, informational, low, medium, high, or critical. The finding is represented by a numerical score. Scores are based on the National Institute of Standards and Technology (NIST) National Vulnerability Database at `https://nvd.nist.gov/vuln`, and details on the scoring system can be found at `www.first.org/cvss`.

The Inspector console has multiple options to analyze, report, and remediate the discovered vulnerabilities or by other AWS and third-party services. Inspector is integrated with many AWS service offerings including Amazon EventBridge and Security Hub. Pricing is per region and per container or EC2 image scanned.

Application Insights

Application Insights is an AWS managed service that can automatically perform discovery on resources and workloads that it supports. After the discovery process is completed, the service will configure a CloudWatch agent, alarms, metrics, and logs based on AWS best practices. The service helps you identify issues and resolve problems with your applications, databases, and workloads. Application Insights will provision the services required to record and visualize real-time application data in your account.

The collected data records what is accessing your services and how they are implemented and consumed. In the background, the services use Kinesis data streams and DynamoDB. The metrics captured include create, modify, and delete API calls for more than 60 AWS services.

Monitoring for this service is in real time. An Application Insights widget will be displayed on the CloudWatch overview home page in the console, and alerts and issues will be displayed on the Application Insights dashboard.

Config

AWS *Config* is a service configuration tracking service; it records and stores a detailed record of how your services are configured. The service continuously runs in the background and captures all configuration changes to your AWS resources. The management console includes a dashboard that allows for a complete and customizable view of the config status and results, as shown in Figure 5.13. Compliance guidelines can be configured in the Config service and compared to your actual configurations to audit your resource configurations for compliance and adherence to company policies. Config tracks AWS services, on-premise servers, and application changes.

FIGURE 5.13   Config dashboard

Config is a valuable change management tracking tool that provides a detailed record of all changes. It is also useful for troubleshooting as you can review what changes were made and roll back if necessary.

The configuration data can be analyzed and SNS messages generated based on the metric you define. Also, the data is stored in S3 for other applicants to analyze. The Config web console includes a query engine with preconfigured scripts that can be run, and granular results are returned, as shown in Figure 5.14.

FIGURE 5.14   Config query editor

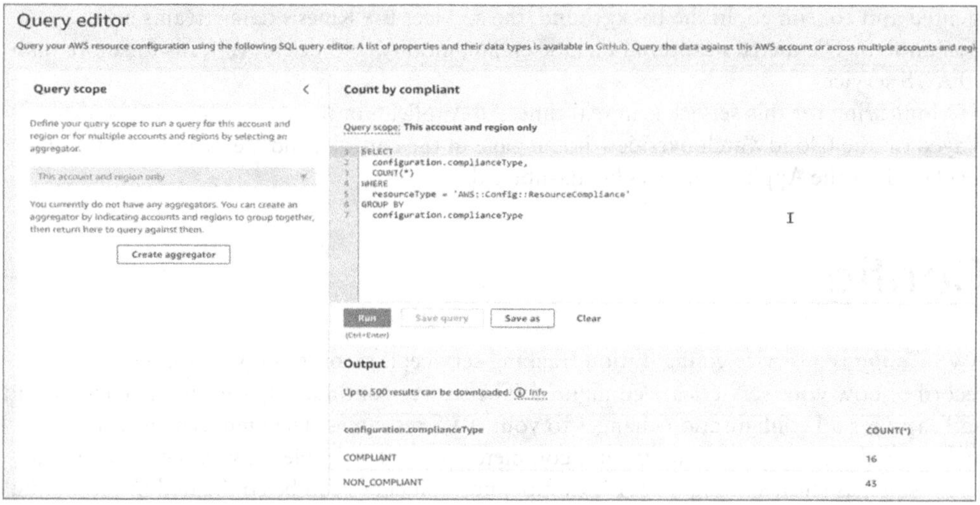

Summary

This chapter examined the AWS monitoring and management services available with a focus on networking. This is a broad subject with many services and features. We focused on CloudWatch as the primary network management application for AWS networking operations. There are many different features and applications that are part of CloudWatch. You learned about the primary CloudWatch features including metrics, monitoring, logging, Metric Insights, and dashboards.

The Transit Gateway Network Manager is used as the management application for the AWS Transit Manager service.

The VPC Reachability Analyzer is an important network troubleshooting utility where you define a source and destination and AWS gives you detailed analysis of the path between the two services and, if there is an issue, where the blockage is occurring.

Next you learned about many of the AWS networking services that provide access logging such as ELB, Route 53, CloudFront, and CloudTrail.

X-Ray is an application tracing service that gives you graphical insight and performance metrics of the interaction between applications. X-Ray Insights adds intelligence to the data using the AWS artificial intelligence services.

You then learned about Flow Logs, what they are, and how they are used to collect and troubleshoot networking issues. Baselines are used to determine what is considered normal activity and can be used to determine if there are issues when metrics exceed their baseline values.

The Inspector service performs security and vulnerability analysis and assessments for EC2 and ECR container instances, applications, network accessibility, and how security is configured for the applications on the instances. Inspector can replace scanning utilities that are generally use-restricted by AWS inside a VPC.

Remember that the Inspector service is an AWS managed service that can automatically perform discovery on resources and workloads that it supports. After the discovery process is completed, the service will configure a CloudWatch agent, alarms, metrics, and logs based on AWS best practices. The service helps you identify issues and resolve problems with your applications, databases, and workloads.

Exam Essentials

Know CloudWatch in detail.   CloudWatch is the key service in the AWS logging and monitoring suite of services. Know that it is a metric and logging collection service that has many additional utilities to manage, monitor, gain insights, and store the collected data. AWS and external applications export log and metric data into CloudWatch, and many of these services have integrations with CloudWatch that is as simple as enabling the service. Agents can be installed on compute instances to gather and export data with a great deal of customization options.

Understand access logs and which networking services generate them.   Many AWS networking services generate log files when they are accessed. For example, when a DNS query is made to Route 53, an access log is generated and forwarded to CloudWatch. For the exam, know these in detail and be able to identify them based on scenario questions. Access logs are created by networking services such as CloudFront, Route 53, and ELB.

Know that Transit Gateway Manager is used to monitor and manage the AWS Transit Gateway Service.   The Transit Gateway Service is an AWS SD-WAN offering that is used to integrate your company's software-defined wide-area network into AWS. The Transit Gateway Manager is an add-on management and monitoring service that graphs out your SD-WAN and is used to manage operations. There may be scenario-based questions about using an AWS service to control your SD-WAN, which would be referring to the Transit Gateway Manager application.

Understand what the VPC Reachability Analyzer does.   The Reachability Analyzer is used to validate your network connectivity, perform connectivity troubleshooting, identify network configuration issues, and automate validations for network connectivity after configuration changes or new deployments. The VPC Reachability Analyzer checks the network path taken by a packet from source to destination. The tool creates a logical model of the configuration and then checks for connectivity.

Understand the X-Ray service.   X-Ray traces request and response actions between application workflows. By enabling X-Ray, you can view the actions inside of your applications and services and how they interact with each other including microservices, databases, APIs, and other AWS services. By collecting this information, you can filter and view your data to locate problems and get insight into the interactions between the application and service flows. X-Ray Insights analyzes the data generated by the AWS X-Ray service, identifies anomalies, and generates notifications on what the anomaly is and why it was triggered.

Understand Flow Logs.   Flow Logs capture data on IP traffic flows between interfaces in a VPC. You select the source and destination of the flow you want to analyze, and the service will show you the path between the two in AWS. The Flow Log captures are external to the actual data flow in your VPC, so the captures do not affect network latency or throughput of your production traffic.

Know what AWS Inspector is and what it is used for.   Inspector is the AWS managed service that performs security and vulnerability analysis and assessments for EC2, ECR container instances, applications, network accessibility, and how security is configured for the applications on the instances. Inspector can replace scanning utilities that are generally use-restricted by AWS in a VPC.

Understand Insights.   Application Insights is an AWS managed service that can automatically perform discovery on resources and workloads that it supports. After the discovery process is completed, the service will configure a CloudWatch agent, alarms, metrics, and logs based on AWS best practices. The service helps you identify issues and resolve problems with your applications, databases, and workloads.

Written Labs

Written Lab 5.1: Enable CloudWatch Detailed Monitoring for an Instance That Has Already Been Enabled

1.   Open the Amazon EC2 console at `https://console.aws.amazon.com/ec2`.

2.   In the navigation pane, choose Instances.

3.   Select the instance and choose Actions, Monitoring, Manage, and Detailed Monitoring.

4.   On the Detailed Monitoring detail page, for Detailed Monitoring, select the Enable check box.

5.   Click Save.

Written Lab 5.2: Enable CloudWatch Logging from the Web Console

1. Open the AWS Management Console (`https://console.aws.amazon.com`) and sign in to your AWS account.

2. Navigate to the CloudWatch service by either searching for *CloudWatch* in the search bar or locating it under the Management & Governance section.

3. In the CloudWatch dashboard, click Logs in the left navigation menu to access the CloudWatch Logs interface.

4. Click the Actions button and select Create Log Group to create a new log group.

5. Enter a unique name for your log group in the Log Group Name field. For example, enter **MyApplicationLogs**.

6. Specify a Retention (Days) value to determine how long log data will be retained in the log group. The default retention period is indefinite, but you can set a specific number of days based on your requirements.

7. Click the Create button to create the log group.

8. Once the log group is created, you can click its name to access its details and configure log streams.

Written Lab 5.3: Enable CloudWatch Alarms from the Web Console

1. Open the AWS Management Console (`https://console.aws.amazon.com`) and sign in to your AWS account.

2. Navigate to the CloudWatch service by either searching for *CloudWatch* in the search bar or locating it under the Management & Governance section.

3. Click Alarms in the left navigation pane.

4. Click the Create Alarm button.

5. Select the metric for which you want to create an alarm. You can choose from a list of available services and metrics.

6. Specify the conditions for the alarm, such as the threshold value, comparison operator (greater than, less than, etc.), and the duration for which the condition must persist.

7. Select the metric for the alarm.

8. Choose the specific metric dimension for the alarm if applicable.

9. Define any additional filters or dimensions based on your requirements.

10. Specify the actions that should be taken when the alarm state is triggered. These actions can include sending notifications, triggering autoscaling actions, or invoking AWS Lambda functions.

11. Configure the appropriate action settings, such as email addresses for notification or selecting specific AWS resources to act upon.

12. Choose the notification options for the alarm. This includes specifying the Amazon SNS topic or an email address to receive the alarm notifications.

13. Review the alarm configuration to ensure all settings are accurate.

14. Provide a meaningful name and optional description for the alarm.

15. Click the Create Alarm button to create the alarm.

Written Lab 5.4: Create a VPC Reachability Analyzer from the Web Console

1. Open the AWS Management Console (`https://console.aws.amazon.com`) and sign in to your AWS account.

2. Navigate to the VPC Reachability Analyzer service by either searching for *Reachability Analyzer* in the search bar or locating it under the Networking & Content Delivery section.

3. Click Create Analyzer to begin the configuration process.

4. Provide a name and description for the analyzer.

5. Choose the AWS region where your resources are located and where you want the analyzer created.

6. Choose the source and destination components for analysis such as a VPC, subnet, security group, or instance.

7. Choose the traffic direction for analysis, either inbound, outbound, or bidirectional.

8. Specify the protocol and port range you want to analyze.

9. Select the VPC Flow Logs or AWS PrivateLink analysis method.

10. Review the analyzer configuration and review the settings.

11. Click Create Analyzer.

Review Questions

The following questions are designed to test your understanding of this chapter's material. For more information on how to obtain additional questions, please see this book's introduction.

1. Your development team is troubleshooting performance issues with a new distributed Docker architecture that processes product returns from your company's e-commerce site. There are many different microservices with dependencies on each other. They cannot locate the source of the performance bottleneck and ask you to see if the delays could be network related. What AWS service would you recommend they deploy to give visibility into the application flow?

    A. CloudTrail

    B. Flow Logs

    C. Config

    D. X-Ray

2. As a newly hired networking engineer, you are being tasked to document the company's AWS deployment and record its normal operational state. What would you create to understand normal and abnormal operations?

    A. Flow Logs

    B. Baseline

    C. Reachability Analyzer

    D. CloudTrail logs

3. Your company's AWS Cloud development team members are asking for advice in analyzing the interactions between their highly distributed application migration that uses the AWS Elastic Container Service. They want insights into detecting anomalies and why it was triggering with their instrumentation. What service would you suggest they implement to meet this requirement?

    A. Step Functions

    B. X-Ray Insights

    C. Identity and Access Manager

    D. X-Ray

4. You want to create an accurate assessment that you can use to predict issues before they become critical and take preemptive steps to address the out-of-range metrics. What would this be called?

    A. AWS Cloud Map

    B. Baseline

    C. X-Ray

    D. Route 53

5. What metric service allows you to visualize live data of your network and share your visualizations with outside entities even if they do not have an account with AWS or are not part of your organization?

A. AppFlow

B. EventBridge

C. CloudWatch dashboards

D. Cloud Search

6. Your DevSec developers have installed the X-Ray SDK on 25 macOS servers and have come to you to explain how to export the application metrics collected to the central repository. What is the next step after installing the macOS X-Ray SDK? (Select two.)

A. Edit the `export.conf` file with the CloudWatch destination on each server

B. Configure the SDK to export to a collector

C. Create a Docker sidecar and edit the SDK config files to export ECS

D. The SDK will automatically export all API calls to CloudTrail

7. Your team has been tasked with reducing the time it takes to create new Fargate containers when the connection count reaches 130 web users. You have configured alarms to trigger adding more containers based on metric reporting. However, the e-commerce team is still complaining about containers being slow to deploy. What can you recommend to increase Fargate performance when creating new containers?

A. Use standard monitoring metric reporting

B. Change the monitoring type to detailed monitoring

C. Configure Fargate service quota

D. Enable detailed logging in the Apache web server and export the metrics to an X-Ray collector

8. You have several Windows CRM servers in a collocated data center as part of your hybrid architecture. You are investigating a solution to consolidate monitoring and management into AWS. What needs to be done at the collocated data center to integrate network monitoring with AWS?

A. Install AWS Inspector on the remote servers

B. Enable custom detailed metrics on the CRM servers

C. Install the CloudWatch agent on the CRM servers

D. X-Ray Insights at the Colo gateway

9. As a senior network engineer for your company, you are investigating how to consolidate global network management monitoring and alerting and are looking for a multivendor integration with a graphical dashboard, utilization metrics, including packets and bytes sent and received, packet drops, changes in the network topology including routing and up/down connection events, and alerts generated. What AWS service would you evaluate that meets your design requirements?

A. Global Accelerator manager

B. Transit Gateway Manager

C. CloudWatch for SD-WAN

D. Direct Connect

10. What AWS service is used to collect values over time and display them along a graphical timeline and can be used for trend analysis and alerting?

   A. AppFlow

   B. EventBridge

   C. CloudWatch

   D. CloudSearch

11. You are assisting your software development team to maximize application performance by measuring delays on microservices between Docker containers running in the us-west-2 region. What would you install to accomplish this objective?

   A. X-Ray traces

   B. VPC Reachability Analyzer

   C. Inspector

   D. CloudWatch

12. What service would you use to see who made changes to your VPC configurations?

   A. CloudMon

   B. CloudWatch

   C. CloudTrail

   D. CloudTrace

13. You have been asked to provide analysis on ingress firewall flow acceptance. What AWS tool automates this testing and generates findings reports?

   A. Flow logging

   B. CloudTrail

   C. Inspector

   D. X-Ray

14. You have a requirement to create a dashboard that shows network utilization, packet drops, and topology changes. What service would provide this data in a graphical format?

   A. Global Accelerator manager

   B. Transit Gateway Manager

   C. CloudWatch for SD-WAN

   D. Direct Connect

15. Your team received a support case about a three-tier web stack having issues connecting to the backend SQL servers from the web application servers. What is a good tool to use to begin your troubleshooting?

   A. CloudFront logs

   B. VPC Reachability Analyzer

   C. CloudTrail

   D. Metric Insights

16. You need to implement an AWS managed service that performs security and vulnerability analysis and assessments for EC2 and ECR container instances, applications, network accessibility, and how security is configured for the applications on the instances. What's the recommended AWS managed service that can accomplish this requirement?

    A. Inspector

    B. Macie

    C. Control Tower

    D. X-Ray

17. The server administration team is troubleshooting a DHCP lease issue inside of the Ireland region. You have enabled flow logging in the VPC and exported the logs to an S3 bucket you created. However, after a testing session with the server admins, you look in the bucket and cannot find any data. What is the cause of this?

    A. There is a missing IAM role

    B. Kinesis Firehose does not support Flow Log streams

    C. DHCP data is excluded from Flow Logs

    D. The DHCP server is local to the availability zone, so Flow Logs would not capture the data

18. You are investigating a way to implement a change management tracking tool that limits your developers to creating only 45 EC2 instances per region. What service should you deploy?

    A. Config

    B. X-Ray

    C. CloudWatch

    D. Inspector

19. You are investigating deploying an AWS managed service that can scan and track vulnerabilities in your fleet of EC2 web servers. What service would meet this use case?

    A. X-Ray Insights

    B. Inspector

    C. CloudWatch

    D. Metric Insights

20. What AWS managed service can you use to generate a report of all changes made to your t2.medium instances over the past 2 years?

    A. Redshift

    B. Config query engine

    C. EC2 analytics

    D. CloudTrail

Network
Implementation

PART

II

Chapter 6: Hybrid Networking

Chapter 7: Connecting On-Premises Networks

Chapter 8: Inter-VPC and Multi-account Networking

Chapter 9: Hybrid Network Routing and Connectivity

Chapter

6

Hybrid Networking

**THE AWS CERTIFIED ADVANCED
NETWORKING - SPECIALTY EXAM
OBJECTIVES COVERED IN THIS CHAPTER
MAY INCLUDE, BUT ARE NOT LIMITED TO,
THE FOLLOWING:**

✓ **Domain 1: Network Design**

- ▪ Objective 1.5: Design a routing strategy and connectivity
  architecture between on-premises networks and the
  AWS Cloud.

- ▪ Objective 1.6: Design a routing strategy and connectivity
  architecture that include multiple AWS accounts, AWS
  Regions, and VPCs to support different connectivity patterns.

Hybrid Connectivity

In this chapter, you will review the lower two layers of the OSI model, which will help you to understand how the AWS network interconnects to the outside world. We will learn the fundamentals of interconnecting your on-premises network to the AWS cloud using Direct Connect and site-to-site VPN interconnects. A network that interconnects AWS with an on-premises data center is defined as a *hybrid network* and is the focus of this chapter and Chapter 7, "Connecting On-Premises Networks."

We will begin this chapter with a basic overview of the lower OSI networking layers of physical and data link are covered, and their implementation options when connecting to AWS are covered.

Next we discuss routing with a look at static and dynamic routing. You will learn about the different methods used to interconnect VPCs.

Since BGP is the primary routing protocol used to connect with AWS, a primer on how BGP operates is covered in this chapter to give you a base understanding of the protocol needed for AWS hybrid networking.

In the past, companies either hosted their compute resources in private enterprise data centers or leased space at a collocation facility. Now, with cloud computing, compute resources are migrating to AWS and other cloud providers, which then require connectivity from the corporate facilities into the cloud. Since it is common for many computer systems and applications to remain behind or distributed across many data centers and different cloud providers at many different locations, a knowledge of hybrid networking is required to interconnect these data centers.

OSI Layer 1

The *Open System Interconnect* model, as shown in Figure 6.1, defines a framework for networking that allows manufacturers to design products that can work with products from other manufacturers that also follow the specifications. This allows for competition and innovation in the networking industry. An understanding of the OSI model greatly assists you in understanding networking. This topic is out of scope for the AWS Advanced Networking exam and is taught in more fundamental networking studies. However, if you are not deeply familiar with the OSI model, taking the time to study and learn the concepts will make understanding networking much less challenging.

FIGURE 6.1   OSI model

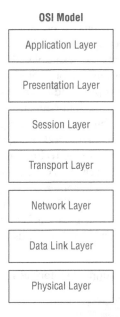

The exam blueprint does, however, specify that knowledge of layer 1 and 2 technologies as they relate to AWS may appear on the exam. So, in this section, we will cover what specifically applies to AWS networking deployments with a focus on the Direct Connect service.

OSI layer 1 is the physical layer, or PHY, and defines both the electrical/optical and physical specifications for devices. The physical layer standardizes the relationship between a device and a transmission medium, which is most often either copper, optical, or radio waves. The physical layer also includes the layout of pins, voltages, cable specifications, networking hubs, repeaters, adapters, and host bus adapters (used in storage networks), to name the most common specifications.

This layer is responsible for the actual physical connection between the devices and contains information in the form of bits, or ones and zeros. It's responsible for transmitting individual bits from one endpoint to the next. When receiving data, this layer will demodulate the signal back into zeros and ones and then send it up to the data link layer, which puts the data frame back together, and the flow continues up the OSI stack.

The primary tasks performed at the physical layer include synchronization of the bits by providing a clock. This clock controls both the sender and receiver providing synchronization at the bit level. The physical layer also defines the transmission rate, i.e., the number of bits sent per second. Physical topologies specify the way in which the different device endpoints and nodes are arranged in a network. Examples of this include bus, star, and mesh topologies. The transmission mode defines the way in which the data flows between the two connected devices, such as simplex, half-duplex, or full duplex.

Optics

Modern network interfaces include options for either electrical or optical media types. In this section, you will learn about fiber-optic networks. Fiber-optic media has many advantages over copper in most deployments. For example, fiber cables are not subject to electrical magnetic interference since they transmit optical, not electrical, signals. Fiber cables are much more difficult to tap into than copper and offer a higher level of security. Fiber optics support much higher transmission speeds than copper, with new breakthroughs of transmitting data over optical cable in the terabits per second range. With the use of laser technologies and the optical characteristics of single-mode fiber, the distances between repeaters are much greater than that of copper transmission technologies.

A vendor may ship hardware with open slots called *small form-factor pluggable* (SFP) options. The SFP port is a slot on a switch, router, or computer into which SFP transceivers are inserted. This allows us to purchase the SFP module that meets our requirements and slide it into the open SFP slot, as shown in Figure 6.2. SFPs are also called mini-GBICs and must match the cable type and wavelength at both ends.

FIGURE 6.2   Small form-factor pluggable interfaces

The AWS Direct Connect facilities use optical interfaces for the interconnection between their network equipment and yours, or your service provider's. AWS has three available connection speeds of either 1, 10, or 100 Gigabit Ethernet using single-mode fiber. 1 Gigabit uses the 1000BASE-LX (1310 nm) SFP transceiver, 10 Gigabit uses the 10GBASE-LR (1310 nm) SFP transceiver, and for 100 Gigabit, the 100GBASE-LR4 SFP transceiver is used. Remember that single-mode optics are the only type supported by AWS and that a single mode on one end will not establish a link to a multimode on the other end. The media type and optics must match on both ends. You must disable autonegotiation for each 10G and

100G interface. 1G interface autonegotiation configurations may vary based on location. If you have issues establishing a link, refer to the AWS online documentation about trouble-shooting layer 2 issues at `https://docs.aws.amazon.com/directconnect/latest/UserGuide/Troubleshooting.html#ts-layer-2`.

Other requirements for the DX interconnection are that 802.1Q VLAN encapsulation must be supported on each end of the interconnected interfaces at the DX location. This includes any intermediate devices at the DX. Your router connection from the premise data center to the Direct Connect facility must support the BGP routing protocol with MD5 authentication capabilities. Bidirectional forwarding can be enabled to detect asymmetric cable failures. AWS enables BFD on their interfaces, but the feature does not activate until your interface enables BFD.

OSI Layer 2

In this section, we will review layer 2 of the OSI model, which is commonly referred to as the *data link layer*. After the review, you will learn about the data link features that are specific for you to know for the exam including VLANs, link aggregation, and jumbo frames. The unit of data at layer 2 is called the *frame*. The layer 2 data link format is the frame, and the layer 3 data is called a *packet*. Layer 2, or data link layer, is concerned with local delivery of frames between nodes on the same local area network.

The frame flows down to the physical layer, or layer 1, and the data link relies on layer 1 to be operational and to send data to the remote end. Layer 2 networks can run over many types of layer 1 media including copper, fiber, coax, and wireless. There are several different layer 2 standards and protocols in use, with Ethernet being the most prevalent so it will be the focus of this section.

Layer 2 frames are addressed using a burned-in unique hardware address for each device. When using an Ethernet frame, this access is called a *Media Access Control* (MAC) address. Each MAC address is 48 bits long, is expressed in hexadecimal format, with the first 24 bits identifying the hardware vendor called the Organizationally Unique Identifier (OUI), and the last 24 are used to identify each device, or endpoint, as shown in Figures 6.3 and 6.4. The Ethernet hardware address on every interface in the world is required to be globally unique; there are no two devices with the same MAC address in the world.

If the MAC address is sent out on the network as all ones (all Fs in hexadecimal), then it is a broadcast sent to all listeners on that segment.

FIGURE 6.3 Ethernet MAC address

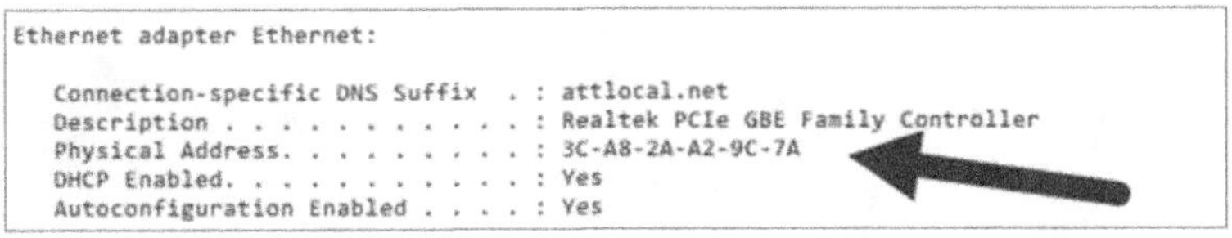

```
Ethernet adapter Ethernet:

   Connection-specific DNS Suffix  . : attlocal.net
   Description . . . . . . . . . . . : Realtek PCIe GBE Family Controller
   Physical Address. . . . . . . . . : 3C-A8-2A-A2-9C-7A
   DHCP Enabled. . . . . . . . . . . : Yes
   Autoconfiguration Enabled . . . . : Yes
```

FIGURE 6.4   Ethernet MAC address format

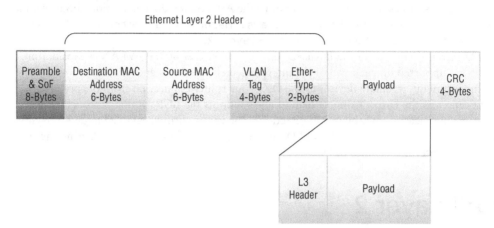

VLANs

Virtual local area networks (VLANs) are widely implemented in all types of data networks.
A *VLAN* is defined as being a logical overlay network on a LAN that has IEEE 802.1Q
addressing to group, a subset of devices, sharing a physical LAN with other devices, isolating
the traffic for each VLAN.

VLANs are used in most AWS network offerings including the DX interconnections
where they are used to stamp individual packets traversing between devices to identify which
layer 2 networks they belong to. VLANs range in identifiers from 1 to 4,095, which are
numbers that identify which network, or VLAN, a frame belongs to as it passes from one
piece of networking equipment to another, as shown in Figure 6.5.

FIGURE 6.5   802.1Q VLAN identifiers

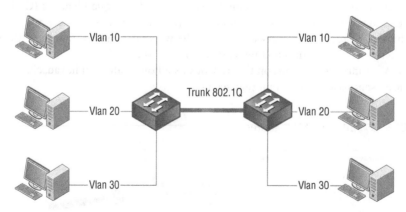

VLANs are defined in the IEEE 802.1Q standard, which is often shortened to "dot1q" in conversations. 802.1Q adds a VLAN header in the frame so that a single network interface can support thousands of different networks over the same media. In addition to the VLAN membership identifier, there is also a priority field to identify the quality-of-service requirements of the frame.

VLANs define the virtual interfaces (VIFs) in a Direct Connect facility.

Link Aggregation

The concept of bundling two or more interfaces into one single, faster channel is referred to as *link aggregation*. Some vendors call the links *link aggregation groups*, while others refer to them as *port aggregation* or *port channels*. LAGs are the actual grouping of interfaces, and LACP is the protocol used to create the groups. This may be a bit confusing, but just remember that there are LAG groups that get created using the *Link Aggregation Control Protocol* (LACP). LACP is defined in the IEEE 802.3ad standard as a method to control the bundling of two or more physical network links together to form a logical channel for increased bandwidth and redundancy purposes.

Bundling several physical links into a single logical link is used between switches in a DX facility to achieve higher speeds than a single interface could support and to provide link redundancy in the case of a physical link failure. Up to eight links can be aggregated into a LAG to create a single virtual link. LAGs are also used for resiliency. For example, if there are eight links in a group and two are lost, the other six will still be available to pass traffic. However, the total bandwidth will be less. You must use link aggregation to connect multiple ports between devices. Without using link aggregation, the spanning tree would shut down all but one link to prevent loops, defeating the purpose of creating the group.

Link aggregation can also be used between larger servers or blade chassis, network switches, and routers. LAG groups combine multiple links into a single logical link that is treated as a single logical connection. When configuring the LAG interface, the configuration applies to all interfaces in the bundle. As a rule, LAG groups are allowed only between switch-to-switch connections and not allowed to be split across multiple switches. There are exceptions and special architectures that support split LAG connections but are beyond the scope of the AWS Advanced Networking exam.

When traffic flows across the LAG, the packets for each flow will traverse only one of the active links. This implies that the frames do not get split up and are load balanced across all the interfaces in the group. This is done for several reasons, including the latency required to dissemble and reassemble the frames at each end, and if the load balancing is at the packet level, there is a possibility that the frames could arrive out of order at the receiving device. There are multiple methods to distribute the flows across the interfaces that are based on hashing the source/destination MAC or IP addresses, or a combination of the two and then assigning the flow to a specific physical interface. This implies that the maximum rate per flow is the rate of each individual interface and not the sum of the links in the LAG.

When configuring an LAG, make sure that all interfaces have the same settings before adding them to the group. Use the same link speeds, duplex settings, allowed VLANs (if it is layer 2), and the native VLAN. If there is a mismatch, the group may not form, or it may form and have issues. None of the ports in the channel should be manually shut down.

Jumbo Frames

Direct Connect supports *jumbo frames* on the customer interconnect point from 1,522 to 9,023 bytes (14 bytes Ethernet header + 4 bytes VLAN tag + bytes for the IP datagram + 4 bytes FCS) at the OSI link layer 2. Jumbo frame support allows for a more efficient transmission of frames over an Ethernet network by reducing the amount of framing overhead relative to the size of data in the frame. Jumbo support is most effective when large amounts of data must be transferred such as storage area networks, large video frames, or big data traffic. Jumbo frames reduce the number of frames sent across the network as there are fewer large frames compared to many smaller frames. The number of headers is reduced, which means there is less frame processing overhead to create and read on the interfaces. Also, network bandwidth is greater because of the fewer number of Ethernet frame headers needed.

Generally, you will see the maximum transmission unit (MTU) setting for jumbo frames set at 9,000 bytes.

AWS Direct Connect supports jumbos on private virtual interfaces connected to virtual private gateways, on a Direct Connect gateway, or on a transit virtual interface attached to a Direct Connect gateway.

You set the MTU of your private virtual interfaces; for more details, reference the AWS documentation site at `https://docs.aws.amazon.com/directconnect/latest/UserGuide/set-jumbo-frames-vif.html`.

Encapsulation and Encryption

Large data centers, such as AWS availability zones, support thousands or tens of thousands of customers. For security and management, these customer networks need to be segments and isolated from each other. This is the concept used by virtual private clouds (VPCs). While a VPC operates inside of AWS, it provides isolation from the other customer networks in the same data center. This is accomplished by using encapsulation techniques to create customer networks that "overlay" or run on top of the data center's switching fabrics commonly called the *underlay network*. In this section, you will learn about the most common encapsulation protocols. Then we will discuss some of the in-transit encryption techniques deployed in modern networks.

Overlay and Underlay Networks

The *overlay network* is a logical virtual network running on top of an existing physical network known as the underlay network.

Overlay and *underlay* are terms frequently used in SDN and network virtualization. In terms of the VxLAN protocol, the *underlay network* is the layer 3 routed IP network that routes VxLAN packets as normal IP traffic. The overlay refers to the virtual Ethernet segment created by this forwarding. Underlays are physical hardware, and overlays are logical and run above the underlay network.

Overlay networks use software to create layers of network abstraction that can be used to run multiple separate, discrete virtualized network layers on top of the physical network. This provides separation between networks even though they are traversing that same physical infrastructure. VPCs in AWS are the overlay, and the hardware in the AWS data centers is the underlay.

Overlays are created by taking networking endpoints and creating a virtual connection between them; multiple secure overlays can be built using software over existing networking hardware infrastructure. These endpoints could be actual physical objects, such as a network port, or they could be logical locations designated by a software address in the networking cloud.

Overlays use routing or switching software that applies software tags, labels, and sometimes encryption to create a virtual tunnel that runs on top of the physical network. When encryption is used, data is be secured between the endpoints so that the end users must be authenticated to use the connection.

The endpoints are designated by an identification tag or number. A device can be located by knowing its identification tag or number in the networking system. These tags are used to create the virtual connections.

VxLan

Virtual Extensible LAN (*VxLAN*) is a standardized encapsulation protocol that stretches layer 2 connections over a layer 3 routed network, and it is primarily used in larger enterprises, service providers, and cloud data centers. VxLAN is an overlay encapsulation protocol that scales up to 16 million logical networks by adding a 24-bit ID to the header, which allows for layer 2 connections over the top of IP networks. VxLAN allows multitenant networks to be isolated from each other but to run as an overlay over a common layer 3 switching fabric called the underlay network.

VxLAN is similar in concept to standard VLANs but is much more scalable beyond the relatively limited number 4,095 VLANs in the 802.1Q specification. Large cloud data centers require a much larger address space of thousands or tens of thousands of customers. This is much larger than traditional VLANs can support, making VxLAN the preferred protocol. The same VLAN concept applies with VxLAN in that only devices in the same VxLAN communicate with each other.

In its most basic form, VxLAN consists of an Ethernet frame put into a UDP packet, with a few extra bytes serving as a header and routed across a network. Layer 2 Ethernet frames are encapsulated into layer 4 UDP datagrams with a default port number of 4789. VxLAN endpoints are used to terminate VxLAN tunnels and can be either physical or virtual termination interfaces. These are referred to as *VxLAN tunnel endpoints* (VTEPs). The interface that performs the encapsulation and de-encapsulation of layer 2 traffic is the VTEP, as shown in Figure 6.6. This is usually a leaf Ethernet switch at the edge of the data center network and is where the connection between the overlay and the underlay networks are created.

FIGURE 6.6   VxLAN tunnel with endpoints

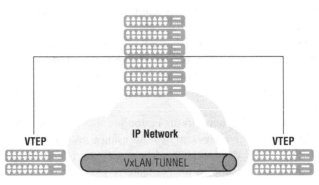

Generic Routing Encapsulation

Generic Routing Encapsulation (GRE) creates a tunnel over a network that allows for private paths to be created over public networks. This is accomplished by the encapsulation, or tunneling, packets using tunnel endpoints that encapsulate and then de-encapsulate traffic at each end of the tunnel. One major advantage of using GRE is that the tunnels can transport multicast packets where public networks cannot. Applications that require multicast such as routing protocols like OSPF, file distribution applications, and video streams benefit from using GRE. Non-IP protocols can now traverse IP-based networks by using this tunneling configuration.

Tunneling is the process of encapsulating packets inside other packets, as shown in Figure 6.7. GRE tunnels are established between two routers, where each router is one end of the GRE tunnel. These routers send and receive GRE packets between each other over the routed network. The intermediate routers only see the outside headers and not the original packet that is hidden inside the packet.

FIGURE 6.7   GRE header

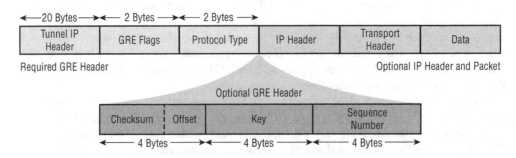

The GRE header is a new IP header wrapped over the original packet. The GRE header contains the new source and destination address of the network being traversed. The original IP packet enters a router, is inserted into a GRE tunnel, and is then routed over the network to the remote GRE terminating router, which then strips the header and forwards the original packet locally. It is important to note that GRE is not in itself a secure protocol. There is no encryption specification. It is common to use a VPN connection through the GRE tunnel for security.

IPSec

IPSec provides encapsulation of packets that are encrypted in transit between endpoint devices. IPSec is actually a family of protocols that work together for end-to-end encryption of data flows. IPSec will encrypt the packets and can authenticate the source of where the packets came from. It is the most common method used on networks to protect traffic from interception, snooping, and other malicious activity. Most VPN architectures use the IPSec protocol for transport.

There are two modes of IPSec encapsulation used: transport and tunnel modes. In transport mode, the transport layer and higher are encapsulated and encrypted. Transport mode protects only the original payload with no encryption for the IP header, as shown in Figure 6.8. The second method of IPSec encapsulation is tunnel mode, where the entire IP packet including the IP header is encrypted, as shown in Figure 6.9. The network layer IP payload is encapsulated with an application header (AH) or Encapsulation Security Protocol (ESP) header.

FIGURE 6.8   IPSec transport mode header

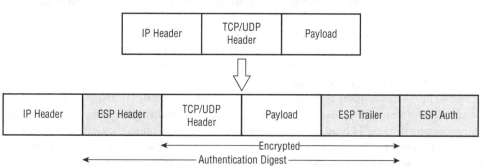

FIGURE 6.9   IPSec tunnel mode header

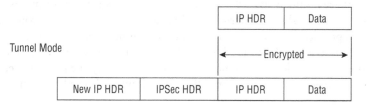

IPSec tunnel mode is used between two dedicated routers, with each router acting as one end of a virtual "tunnel" through a public or private corporate network. In tunnel mode, the original IP header that contains the final destination of the packet is encrypted, in addition to the packet payload. So, the intermediary routers know how to forward the packets, and IPSec adds a new IP header. At each end of the tunnel, the routers decrypt the IP headers and then deliver the packets to their destinations.

In transport mode, the payload of each packet is encrypted, but the original IP header is not. This approach allows the intermediary routers to view the destination address of each packet.

As noted earlier, IPSec is actually a family of protocols, and configurations vary widely with many different implementation and use cases. However, there are fundamental steps that we will cover here to give you a basic understanding of the protocol. IPSec can be very complex to understand and implement and is more part of the security realm. To gain a deeper knowledge, the AWS Security Specialty exam should be investigated.

The basic workflow of an IPSec session starts with the key exchange where a string of random characters is used to encrypt and decrypt the packets. IPSec standardizes the exchange of keys with a key exchange between the connected devices using many different protocols of your choice. The key exchange allows each device to decrypt the other device's messages. Data that is sent over a network is broken down into smaller pieces called *packets*. Each packet has a payload, which is the user data that is being sent, and headers, which contain the information about that data so intermediate routers know where to forward them as with any IP packet. The protocol adds headers to the original packets that contain the authentication, encryption information, and IPSec trailers are also added at the end. At each receiving endpoint, the packets are decrypted, usually by a VPN client or a router running IPSec software; then the data is forwarded to the application.

IPSec authenticates each packet, with a stamp to ensure that each packet is from a trusted source and not received or tampered with by a malicious third party. Each packet is encrypted using an encryption protocol you define and that is mutually negotiated by each endpoint when the connection is established.

The AH protocol ensures that data packets are from a known, validated, and trusted source. AH ensures that the data has not been modified in transit, and AH is considered to be tamper proof. The AH headers do not provide any encryption so they can be read by intermediary devices. ESP encrypts the IP header and the payload of each packet. However, the transport mode variant encrypts the payload only. ESP stamps its own custom header and a trailer to the data packet. The Security Association (SA) is a suite of different protocols that negotiate the encryption keys and algorithms during the initial session creation and is used for the negotiation of authenticated key material. Each SA is a grouping of security parameters that are mutually agreed upon and are used for sharing information between peers across an IP network. The Internet Key Exchange (IKE) is the most common security association protocol. There is also the common Internet Security Association and Key Management Protocol (ISAKMP) used for the IKE. Security associations are unidirectional, so for end-to-end full duplex communications, there will always be two SAs per session, one in each direction. IPSec runs on top of the IP protocol, which is used for routing across both private and public networks. For IPSec to traverse a firewall, it is required to open port UDP 500 and protocol number 50.

GENEVE

The GENEVE protocol was covered in Chapter 4, "Load Balancing," as part of the gateway load balancer. In this section, we will do a brief refresher of this standardized encapsulation protocol. The GENEVE protocol preserves the original packet by providing an encapsulation protocol that supports transparent routing. To make sure that the original packet remains intact, the GENEVE protocol encapsulates the original packet in a new header for transmission over the routed network. This preserves the headers that security appliances may need to process and allows for the separation of customer traffic, which may also have overlapping CIDR addresses. GENEVE is similar to VxLAN and GRE at layer 3 but does not have the fixed field size limitations of these protocols. This makes it more flexible for multitenant content analysis and for load balancing implementations that require that the original packet format not be modified.

Routing Fundamentals

Since this book is a study guide for the AWS Advanced Networking certification, there is an assumption that you are familiar with networking in general and routing protocols such as BGP. However, we will do a quick review of routing fundamentals to establish a baseline of understanding. If you are not familiar with routing protocols, networking architectures, design, implementation, and troubleshooting, you should take one of the many basic networking courses available on the market before taking this advanced-level certification exam. In this section, you will learn about the two general categories of routing: static and dynamic.

The primary function of a router is to receive a packet on one of its interfaces and know how to send it to its destination. Routers need to know the next hop router and which egress interface it is connected to. This information is stored in a routing table that is stored in each router in the network so the routers know how to send and receive packets so they can reach their destination. This routing table is populated with networks it learns from either static or dynamic routing configured on the router. When a packet that needs to be routed is received by the router, the process is referred to as *forwarding*. The destination IP address is looked up in the routing table and sent out the interface specified in the table. If there is a change in the network, the router needs to take note of the new route, update its routing forwarding table, and forward the packet out the new interface.

For the exam and interconnecting your internal networks with AWS, the focus will be on the Border Gateway Protocol (BGP). BGP is used to dynamically exchange routing information between your internal networks and external networks such as those in AWS. BGP can be quite complex, and large books have been written about its operation; here, we will cover the basics and what is specifically needed to interconnect your networks with AWS using BGP.

Static Routing

Static routing defines network reachability in a router where the network administrator manually configures the routes into the routing table to be used by the router to send packets to destination networks. A static route includes the destination network or host address, its corresponding network mask, and the IP address or egress interface of the next hop to the destination. The key point to remember is that static routing does not have the ability to automatically update the routing table based on changing network conditions. If a network topology change should occur, the static routes would have to be manually updated as compared to dynamic routing where the routing protocol would automatically be aware of the change and update the routing table.

The advantage of using static routes is that there is no routing protocol overhead that is required when using dynamic routing protocols. The administrator hard-codes the routes into each router, and there is no need for the routers to exchange routing information. In small networks, it's relatively easy to hard-code static routes with just a few routing statements. Static routing is best used in networks that will not change and do not need to be updated. It could be said that static routing is more secure since there are no routing updates sent over the wire between the routers, and there is no possibility of a router receiving a route that is not valid.

Dynamic Routing

Dynamic routing records all topology changes, updates automatically, and adjusts to changing networking conditions. Dynamic routing uses well-defined protocols such as OSPF internally or BGP between companies to exchange the routing information without ongoing administrative intervention. Internal routing methods used inside of a company's network are referred to as *Internal Gateway Protocols* (IGPs) and routing protocols used between organizations are called *External Gateway Protocols* (EGPs).

These routing protocols will learn of other routers in the network and exchange routes with the other routers in the network. Each router will learn about the networks that the others are connected to. When new networks are added or removed, the routers will update each other with the changes, and, for each router's route, the forwarding table will automatically be updated as required. Dynamic routing is the most used approach and is favored over static routing because of the ability to dynamically make changes without administrative intervention.

The BGP Routing Protocol

A deep understanding of the complexities of the BGP routing protocol is beyond the scope of the exam. However, AWS does use BGP for route exchanges for its hybrid networking implementations and many other services. An introduction to BGP is provided here to get you up to speed on the basics and how it is used in AWS. However, BGP can be a complex routing protocol to understand and master and it will require studies outside the scope of the AWS Advanced Networking exam.

The *Border Gateway Protocol* (BGP) is the standard dynamic network routing protocol that provides for loop-free interdomain routing between autonomous systems. BGP is used to propagate tens to hundreds of thousands of routes between networks (ASs) and to exchange network reachability information with other BGP systems. It is the only actively used EGP on the Internet. BGP is the primary protocol to exchange network reachability information between different organizations, such as AWS and your enterprise, known as autonomous systems. An *autonomous system* (AS) is described as a collection of connected Internet Protocol routing prefixes (networks) administratively controlled by a single administrative entity or domain, which presents a common and clearly defined routing policy to the Internet.

BGP is a classless distance-vector routing protocol, running over TCP port 179 for reliable connections, and uses the TCP error correction capabilities. BGP is a multivendor open protocol. The main design feature of BGP is to allow ISPs to richly express their routing policy to other connected autonomous systems, both in selecting outbound paths and in announcing internal routes to other entities. There are also BGP features that allow for administrative debugging, policy routing, and loop detection.

The purpose of BGP is to allow ASs to tell other ASs about routes (parts of the IP address space) that they are responsible for. BGP uses route advertisements or promises also called Network-Layer Reachability Information (NLRI). Networks are ASs identified in BGP by a number, called the Autonomous System Number (ASN). ASs are routers that are controlled by one entity such as a corporation, Internet service provider, or cloud company. ASNs are a collection of networks with the same policies and under the same administrative control. Each entity would own one or more publicly registered ASNs that would be managed by them and no other organizations. They are, as the name states, autonomous systems.

BGP exchanges routes between ASs. Figure 6.10 illustrates an AS deployed in a global network. The autonomous system is identified by its AS number that was assigned by the service provider. ASNs identify the organization managing a network space such as AWS or a private company. ASNs range between 0 and 65535 with 64512 through 65534 being reserved as private. There is no concept of pipe size, internal router hop-count, or congestion; its primary function is to provide information on how to reach networks between organizations.

AS networks can span the globe; routers in Los Angeles can be in the same AS as the systems in New York. The AS numbers are managed by the Internet Assigned Numbers Authority (IANA) at www.iana.org/numbers, which assigns ASNs to regional Internet registries (RIRs), which are organizations that manage Internet number resources in a particular region of the world. In the United States, the American Registry for Internet Numbers (ARIN) administers the ASNs at www.arin.net. Autonomous system numbers are how BGP distinguishes between different entities. When routes are exchanged, ASNs are stamped on the routes as they exit the AS, adding one "AS hop" per network traversed. BGP is often described as a path vector routing protocol as it advertises the path to remote network prefixes.

BGP route advertisement can be thought of as a "promise." For example, if we advertise the prefix 210.9.128.0/17, we promise that if you deliver traffic to me for anywhere in the 210.9.128.0/17 address space, we know how to deliver it at least as well as anyone else.

FIGURE 6.10   BGP ASs

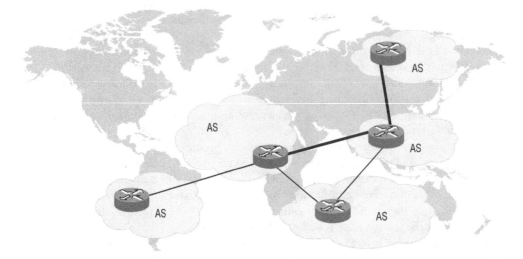

By making sure these routes, or "promises," are heard by all providers on the network, your provider ensures a return path for all your packets. Remember, sending packets out is easier than getting them back. Also, remember, sending routes out causes IP traffic to come in. When selecting a route to use, the most specific route wins, so if we advertise that we can reach the 210.9.240.0/24 network, all incoming traffic from other networks will start flowing in that pipe if there is not a more specific route advertised.

The advantages of using BGP include the ability for more control of your destiny when you speak BGP to the outside world. For example, you can break up your routes in an emergency or tune traffic flows. You can pad your announcements to de-prefer one or more upstream paths and fine-tune outbound traffic flow to the best upstream connected router.

BGP routes are exchanged over peering sessions, which run on top of TCP. Keepalives are used to avoid the need to re-send the whole routing table periodically. The routes are objects, or collections of "attributes." It can be helpful to think of BGP as a routing database. All peering sessions must be configured, and they are not automatically established. Once a peering session is established, the two autonomous systems can communicate and exchange network reachability information with each other.

BGP is often described as two protocols, Internal Border Gateway Protocol (iBGP), which is designed for internal routing within an AS, and External Border Gateway Protocol (eBGP), designed for routing between BGP autonomous systems. When BGP speakers in the same autonomous system form a BGP peering connection for the purpose of exchanging routing information, they are said to be running iBGP, or *internal BGP*. When BGP speakers in different autonomous systems from a BGP peering connection for the purpose of exchanging routing information, they are said to be running eBGP, or *external BGP*. eBGP peers are usually directly connected to each other.

You must inject routes into BGP to advertise them to the world, and someone else had to inject external routes that you get into BGP somewhere else in the first place. There is only one best BGP route for any given IP block at one time. There are two main ways of injecting routes; the first is to use network statements such as static BGP routes, and the second method is redistributing routes from OSPF, other internal routing protocols, or statics.

BGP routes are exchanged inside of BGP peering sessions. As we learned earlier, BGP uses TCP to ensure the reliable delivery of routing updates. If a TCP session dies, all associated routes must be withdrawn and removed from the router's forwarding table. BGP peers, or neighbors, must be specified explicitly in each router. Once a peering session is set up, both sides flood the other end with all their best BGP routes. Since there is only one best route per prefix, that is the route that is advertised. Periodic updates send new routes and/or withdraw old ones, and keepalives are sent every few seconds, generally 20 to 30 seconds. On a very stable network, very little or no traffic should flow besides keepalives.

BGP peering is designed for highly available network connections. Customers will typically peer with AWS at multiple places, either by peering with the same AS multiple times or between two or more ASs.

A multihomed interconnection can have several candidate paths to a given prefix. Figure 6.11 shows a sample of a routers peering table.

FIGURE 6.11   BGP peering table

```
RouterA# show ip bgp neighbors
  Total number of BGP Neighbors: 1
  IP Address   AS#   EBGP/IBGP  RouterID     PeerGroup
  1 1.1.1.2    200   EBGP       100.100.100.1 None
  State   Time     KeepAlive  HoldTime  RefreshCapability
  ESTABLISHED 0h16m32s 60       180       Received
  SendCommunity NextHopSelf DefaultOriginate ReflectorClient UpdateSource
  No      No      No         No        None
                  Open  Update KeepAlive Notification Refresh-Req
  Message Sent:    4    22    81    1      0
  Message Received: 4   3     85    0      0
  Last Connection Reset Reason:Reset All Peer Sessions
  Notification Sent:   Unspecified
  Notification Received: Unspecified
  TCP Connection state: ESTABLISHED
    Local host: 1.1.1.1, Local Port: 179
    Remote host: 1.1.1.2, Remote Port: 8027
    ISentSeq: 315455746 SendNext: 315456546 TotUnAck:    0
    TotSent:      800 ReTrans:     0 UnAckSeq: 315456546
    IRcvSeq: 302917150 RcvNext: 302917548 SendWnd:    16384
    TotalRcv:      398 DupliRcv:    0 RcvWnd:    16384
    SendQue:      0 RcvQue:      0 CngstWnd:    3102
```

Advertising networks into BGP is done using the network command that controls what networks are originated by this router. While the syntax can vary widely between vendors and versions of code, I am using a basic vendor command syntax that may be different from your command-line syntax.

```
!In this Example network 192.245.0.0 originates from this
!router
router bgp
local-as 3
network 192.245.0.0 255.255.0.0
```

continues

(continued)

```
!
ip route 192.245.0.0 255.255.0.0 null0
!
interface GigabitEthernet0/0/1.4
ip address 192.245.209.0 255.255.255.0
!
interface GigabitEthernet0/0/1.5
ip address 192.245.210.0 255.255.255.0
```

In the previous example, a static route is used to provide a matching entry in the routing table. The network command in BGP will only advertise networks that are already installed in its local IP route table. The prefix in the IP routing table must match the network command exactly, including the IP network and the subnet mask.

Another way of advertising networks is to redistribute dynamic IGP routes (such as OSPF) into BGP. Here is an example of redistributing OSPF *into* BGP:

```
router bgp
local-as 3
redistribute ospf match external2
```

In the previous example, all OSPF external type-2 routes will be advertised to external peers. Just like the network command, the `redistribute ospf` command will only advertise networks that are already installed in the IP route table. Use the distribute list to control what is advertised to external BGP neighbors from OSPF, in other words, to filter out unwanted routes being advertised to external peers.

The final way of advertising networks is to redistribute static routes into BGP. Here is an example of redistributing statics *into* BGP:

```
router bgp
local-as 3
redistribute static
!
ip route 12.64.13.0 255.255.255.0 149.172.18.1
ip route 191.166.153.0 255.255.255.0 150.100.100.11
ip route 210.201.102.0 255.255.255.0 150.100.100.11
```

In the previous example, all static routes defined in the router will be advertised to external peers. Just like the network command, the `redistribute static` command will only advertise networks that are already installed in the IP route table. Here we use the distribute list to control what is advertised to external BGP neighbors from the static routes in the IP route table.

To show the IP routes and BGP learned routes on a router, use the `show ip bgp` command, as shown here:

```
!AS 400
show ip bgp
Total number of BGP Routes: 14
Status codes: s suppressed, d damped, h history, * valid, > best, i internal
```

```
Origin codes: i - IGP, e - EGP, ? - incomplete
    Network             Next Hop        Metric LocPrf Weight Path
*>  100.100.100.0/24    0.0.0.0         0      100    32768  i
*>  150.100.100.0/24    20.20.20.1      0      100    0      100 i
*>  160.200.200.0/24    20.20.20.1             100    0      100 i
*>  160.1.1.0/24        20.20.20.1      0      100    0      100 300 i
*>  160.10.10.0/24      20.20.20.1      0      100    0      100 300 i
*>  160.100.100.0/24    20.20.20.1      0      100    0      100 300 200 i
*>  200.200.200.0/24    20.20.20.1             100    0      100 300 200 i
```

By default, the IP route table chooses and installs the best, most specific BGP route. However, providers along the way can use BGP local preference or weight attributes to override your path length. Also, it is important to remember that inbound and outbound traffic can be treated separately. Inbound traffic is affected by how the AS advertises its networks to the outside AS, and outbound traffic is affected by routing updates coming from outside of your AS. Asymmetric paths are common, and it is often impossible to control the end-to-end routing and paths traversed. Packets may not always traverse the same downstream path as they did when forwarded upstream.

Direct Connect

Direct Connect (DX) allows you to bypass the public Internet to connect directly between your data center and an AWS region. This is a private connection that gives you the benefit of security with a consistent speed at low latency. If you have large volumes of data to transfer, you may achieve lower costs using a direct connection than using the Internet.

AWS Direct Connect is currently available in more than 100 locations, which span nearly 70 cities in 30 different countries. These Direct Connect facilities contain AWS routers that interconnect with customer and telco networks. They are not AWS-owned data centers but hosted in collocation facilities or carrier hotels and serve as a common interconnection location. There are currently 99 partners including companies such as AT&T, CoreSite, Digital Realty, Equinix, and Lumen. The customer must install a router at the interconnection data center and provision a provider data circuit to the Direct Connect facility to complete the end-to-end provisioning. A current list of Direct Connect locations can be found at `https://aws.amazon.com/directconnect/locations`.

The interconnects are provisioned for either 1 Gbps, 10 Gbps, or 100 Gbps depending on your bandwidth requirements. Most interconnect service providers also offer subrate connections lower than 1 Gbps. The carriers will set up an interconnect with AWS at the peering locations and sell you a subset of that bandwidth. Also, the individual links can be combined or aggregated using the LACP protocol. LACP combines the multiple 1 G, 10 G, or 100 G connections into one logical connection for higher speeds. Link aggregation will be covered later in the chapter.

A DX connection is not inherently encrypted, and no in-flight data security is implied. However, a common security implementation is to use an IPSec site-to-site VPN connection over the DX link to provide encryption of data through the Direct Connect link.

The DX optics are either 1000-Base-LX, 10GBase-LR, or 100GBASE-LR4 for the optical cross-connects between the customer and AWS routers.

Once the physical connection has been made, VIFs are created that can be either private or public. A private VIF is shown in Figure 6.12, connecting to a single VPC using a Virtual Gateway (VGW). The VIF is an 802.1Q tagged VLAN with BGP routing for dynamic route exchange. The second type of interconnection is a public VIF, shown in Figure 6.13, that connects to AWS public services in any region, which includes all AWS public services such as DynamoDB, Route 53, S3, or CloudFront. The public VIF does not connect to the Internet, however. Customers cannot use Direct Connect for their Internet connections. A single Direct Connect can have multiple private VIFs to connect to multiple VPCs in a single region. Multiple accounts can share a VIF, which is referred to as a hosted VIF.

FIGURE 6.12   Direct Connect private VIF

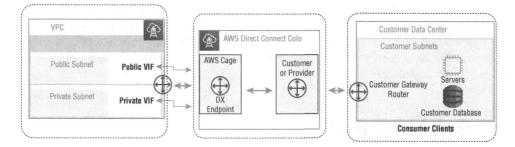

FIGURE 6.13   Direct Connect public VIF

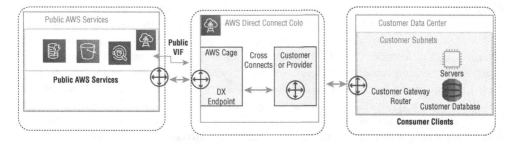

High availability is achieved by adding a Direct Connect backup link from your data center to the interconnection facility or, as a second option, using a VPN connection to back up the direct connection, as shown in Figure 6.14. When using this architecture, the capacity should not exceed 1 Gbps due to AWS VPN throughput limitations.

The AWS data circuits from the hosted interconnection facilities to the AWS regional data centers are redundant with BGP routing providing failover for high availability. It is your responsibility to architect the connection from your data center to the AWS cross-connect site for a dedicated backup link, if desired, or to configure a site-to-site VPN over the Internet to the AWS region terminating the primary DX data circuit. The second high availability connection you are responsible for is the connection in the hosting facility between your router and the AWS router, which is a single point of failure without a redundant cross-connection. Additionally, you need to take into consideration the possibility of router failures. To achieve high availability in this scenario, installing additional routers in your data center and at the collocation facility adds high availability at the router level, as shown in Figure 6.15.

FIGURE 6.14   VPN backup

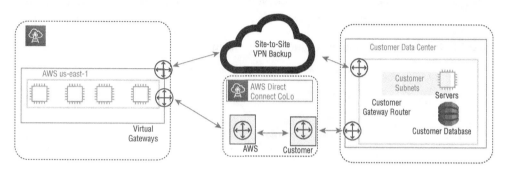

FIGURE 6.15   Hardware high availability connections

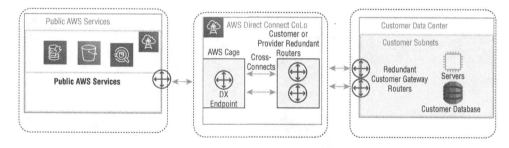

To set up a Direct Connect connection to AWS, start by going into the Networking and Content Delivery section of the web console and selecting Direct Connect at https://us-east-1.console.aws.amazon.com/directconnect/v2/home?region=us-west-2#. Notice that even though Direct Connect is a global service, it defaults to the region you specified as default for your account. A prerequisite is that you must pick the location you want to make the interconnection and the bandwidth you require, which will determine the data circuit capacity you provision for the carrier. Select Create Connection and give the connection a name and location. Select a port speed of either 1 Gbps, 10 Gbps, or 100 Gbps and if you are using your own on-premises routers or a service provider's router. You also can use *MACSec* for layer 2 encryption and add a tag for your internal tracking requirements.

There is also a wizard that you can use that steps you through the process including your desired resiliency level, as shown in Figures 6.16, 6.17, and 6.18. You can select the interconnect location and carrier if you use a service provider partner to create the connection. At this step, AWS will create a support case on your behalf to arrange for your equipment to be installed or work with the service provider to use their routing equipment. The support ticket contains information such as the AWS region to connect to, the connection ID, connection name, your account information, the port speed, jumbo frame capability, and who the service provider is. AWS will then provide you with a letter of authorization and connecting facility assignment that details how to do the actual interconnect, including the optic and connector types, the AWS cage information, your rack location, the optical patch panel, and port number details for the cross-connect.

FIGURE 6.16   Direct Connect configuration wizard

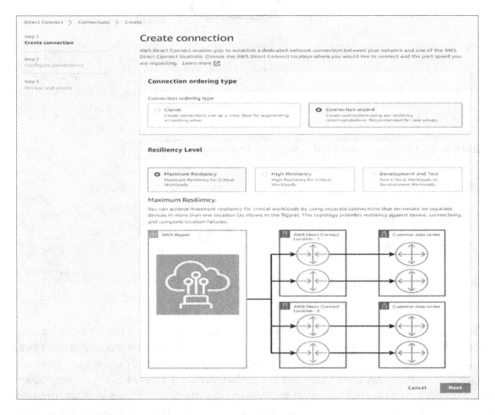

The next step is to create the VIFs between your equipment and the AWS routers, as shown in Figure 6.19. You will specify the VIF type and fill out the interface configuration, including physical interface, account information gateway type, VLAN ID number, and BGP ASN. The additional configuration setting includes the address family of either IPv4 or IPv6, your peer router and the AWS router IP addresses, a BGP authentication key value, and a jumbo frame MTU value.

FIGURE 6.17 Direct Connect configuration dialog

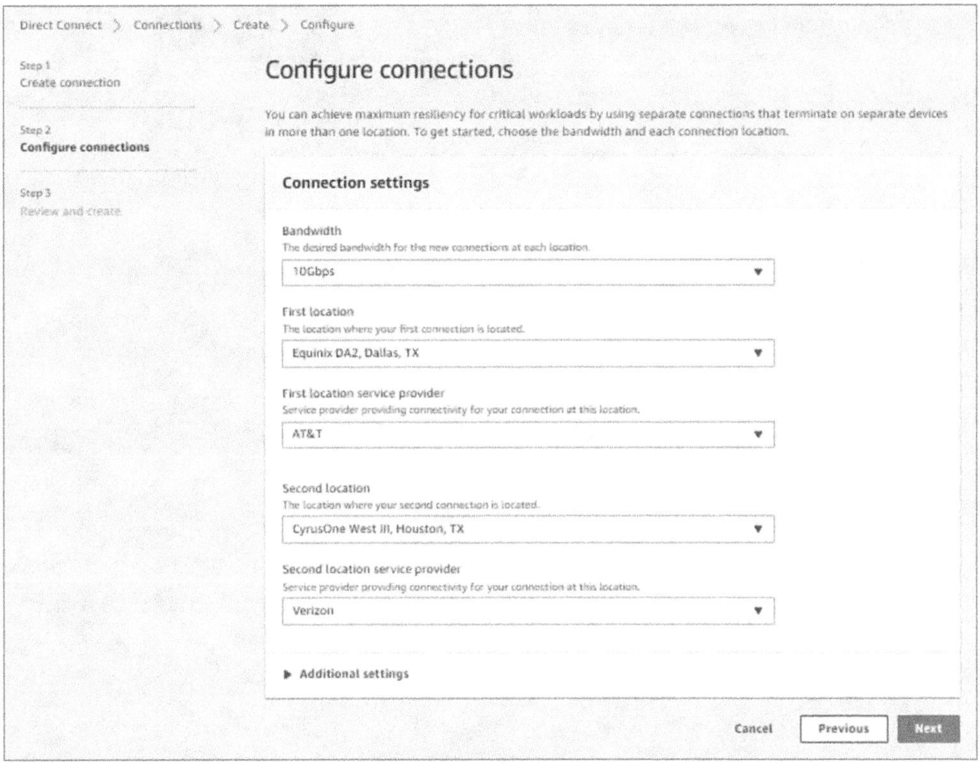

FIGURE 6.18 Direct Connect review and create dialog

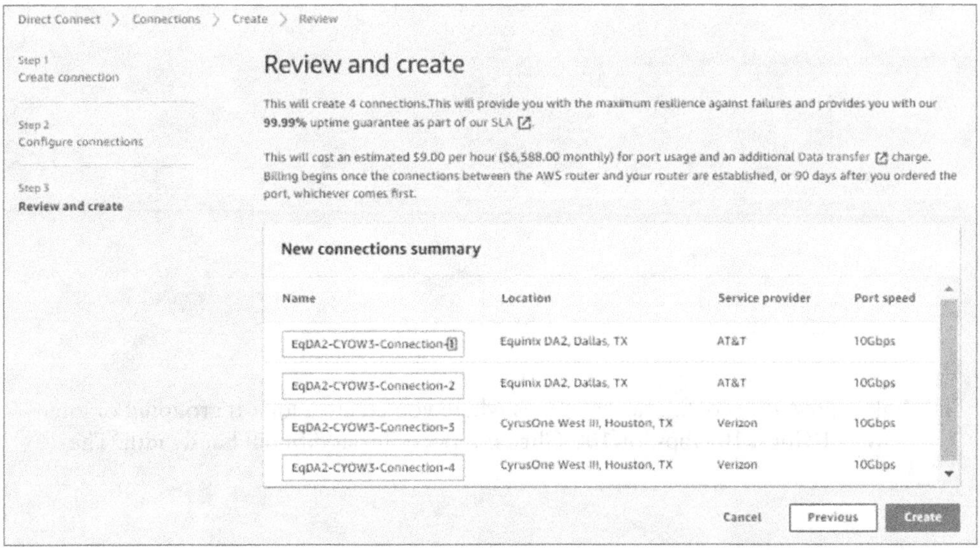

FIGURE 6.19 Virtual interface creation

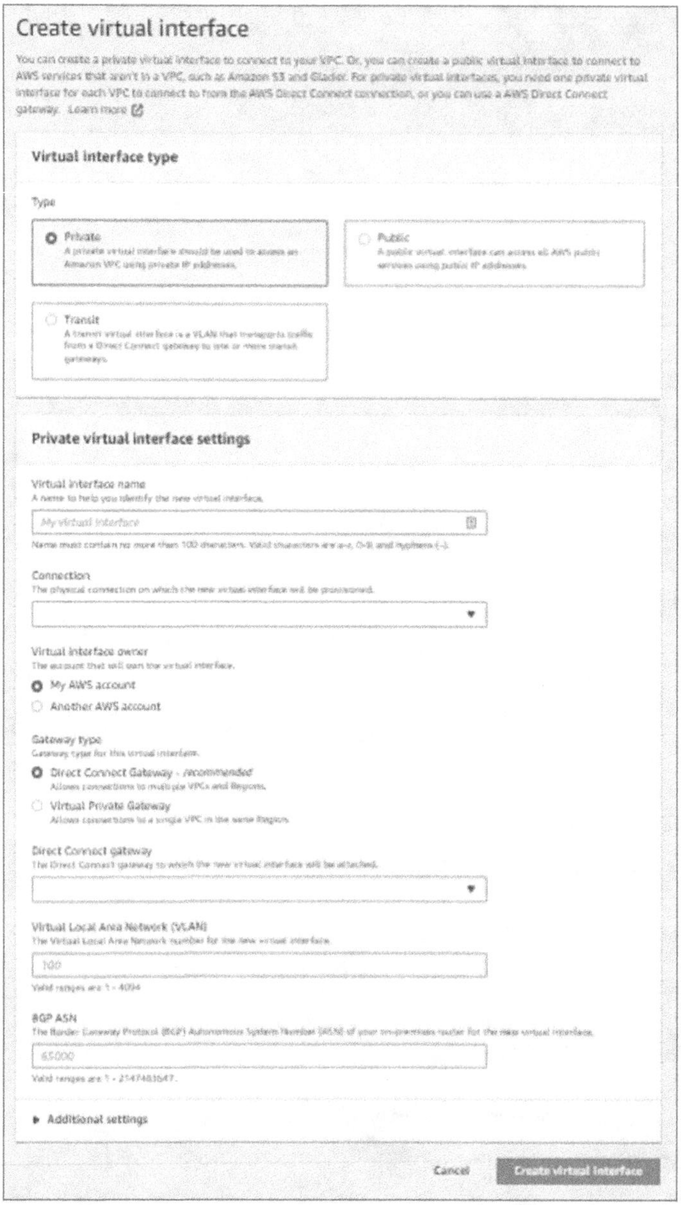

The link aggregation configuration area is where you create a logical grouping of interfaces of either 1 Gbps, 10 Gbps, or 100 Gbps interfaces for additional bandwidth. The grouping creates a single logical endpoint that is treated as one managed connection. Your options include using an existing connection or creating a new connection, the name of the link aggregation group, number of circuits in the group, and a minimum value that determines when to call the link down or unusable. See Figure 6.20 for an example of the LAG configuration dialog.

FIGURE 6.20   LAG creation

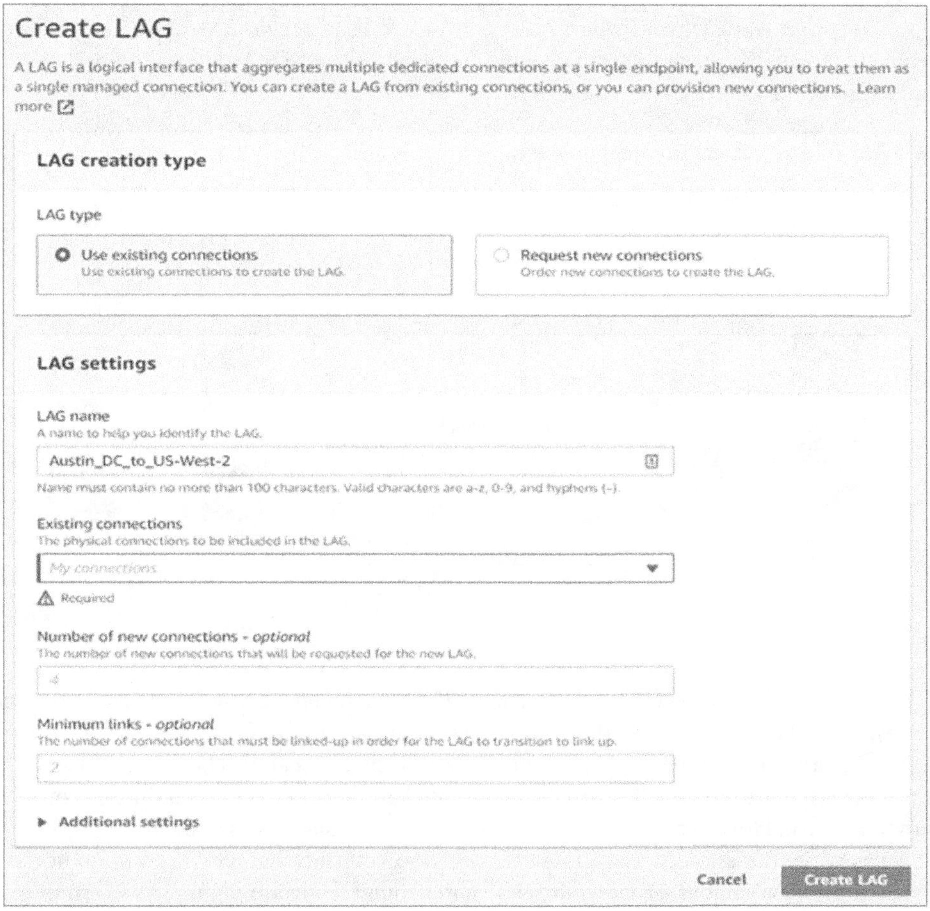

Direct Connect Gateway

The AWS *Direct Connect gateway* simplifies your Direct Connect architecture. Traditionally with Direct Connect, a separate connection would need to be established from your data center to each AWS region you wanted to connect to. If you needed to connect to two different regions, for example, since DX is a regional service, you would traditionally require two separate direct connections, one for each region. The gateway allows connections to global VPCs from a single DX connection location.

The Direct Connect gateway expands the private VIF capabilities over the standard DX interconnect capabilities. The Direct Connect gateway allows connections to global VPCs from a single DX connection location. Up to 500 VPC connections are supported from a single Direct Connect gateway. The Direct Connect gateway connects your AWS Direct Connect over a virtual interface to one or many VPCs in single or many accounts in any region. Note that while Direct Connect using private VIFs is a regional service, the gateway extends this to all AWS regions from a single connection. Figure 6.21 shows the basic architecture of the Direct Connect gateway.

FIGURE 6.21   Direct Connect gateway

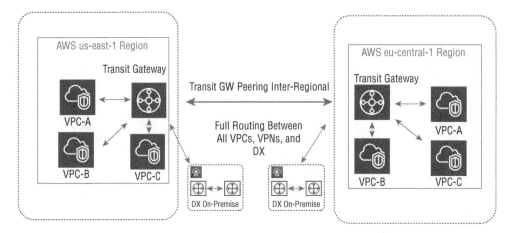

The service is enabled by creating a private VIF and associating it with a Direct Connect gateway, instead of a virtual private gateway, set up in any region. In the AWS cloud, the virtual gateways can now be associated with any VPC in any region. The VPCs connect to the gateway, which is associated with the private VIF that is routed to and from your internal network. However, inter-VPC communications through the same Direct Connect gateway are not allowed; the VPCs are routed to your internal network but do not get routed between each other via your data center router. Hairpinning inter-VPC routes through your on-premises router is not supported. Each DX gateway supports a private VIF connection and 10 virtual gateways per connection. So, 1 DX can have up to 50 private VIFs, which equal 50 DX gateways for up to 500 VPCs that can be connected.

To associate VPCs from different regions to a single DX facility, a private VIF is associated with a DX gateway in any region. This is the connection from your on-premises router to the DX gateway service. After this step has been completed, you can now associate virtual gateways that are attached to VPCs in any region in the world instead of the single region architecture prior to this implementation of your Direct Connect gateway. This allows all VPCs connected to the Direct Connect gateway to connect through the private VIF and into your on-premises network.

The Direct Connect gateway supports cross-account connections that allow you to associate VPCs from different accounts to the same DX gateway in a shared services account. All VPC IP address blocks must be unique and nonoverlapping. This service supports private VIF connections only and not public interfaces.

For the steps on creating a Direct Connect connection to a VPC using a Direct Connect gateway, refer to the AWS online documentation located at these locations:

```
https://docs.aws.amazon.com/directconnect/latest/UserGuide/create-vif
.html#create-private-vif
```

```
https://docs.aws.amazon.com/directconnect/latest/UserGuide/
WorkingWithVirtualInterfaces.html
```

```
https://docs.aws.amazon.com/directconnect/latest/UserGuide/direct-connect-
gateways-intro.html
```

Virtual Private Gateway

The AWS *virtual private gateway* is a virtual VPN endpoint that terminates a site-to-site VPN connection that attaches to a single VPC. A maximum of 10 external VPN tunnels that are not VPC networking locations per virtual private gateway are supported, and each of the tunnels connects using the IPSec protocol.

A virtual private gateway (VGW) is the VPN endpoint connector on the AWS side of the site-to-site VPN connection, as shown in Figure 6.22. This is an AWS managed logical gateway endpoint used to create the IPSec VPN tunnel from the AWS VPC to an on-premises customer gateway at the customer end of the connection. The maximum throughput through the gateway is 1.25 Gbps. However, that actual throughput is dependent on such factors as packet size, if the protocol is TCP or UDP, latency in the network, and the capacity of the connection. The maximum packets per second through the gateway is 140,000. The maximum number of BGP advertised routes is 1,000 dynamics and 100 statics.

FIGURE 6.22   Virtual private gateway

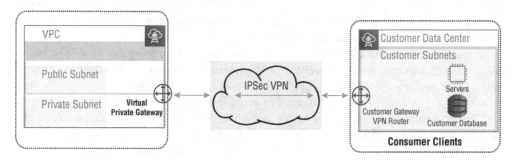

The VPN tunnel is established after traffic is generated from the customer side of the VPN connection.

Site-to-Site VPN

Site-to-site VPNs are created using encrypted tunnels over the Internet from your on-premises network to a VPC in an AWS region using the IPSec protocol suite to encrypt the in-flight traffic, as shown in Figure 6.23. In contrast to Direct Connect where it can take weeks or months to activate connectivity, a VPN can be created in less than an hour by using your existing Internet connections. The VPN can be used as the primary interconnection between your on-premises data center and AWS. VPNs can also be used to back up a Direct Connect link should it fail. Also, the site-to-site VPNs can traverse over the DX to provide an encrypted tunnel over the Direct Connect link.

FIGURE 6.23   Site-to-site VPN

The AWS site-to-site VPN is a managed IPSec VPN service from an AWS VPC to your corporate data center. Major components of an AWS site-to-site VPN include the VGW and the VPN router interface that resides in a AWS region at the VPC level that terminates the connection from your on-premise *Customer Gateway* (CGW), which is usually a physical router that the VPN connects to. The VPN connection is between the VGW and the CGW. The customer router is a physical device running VPN software.

Setting up a site-to-site VPN depends on how you are implementing the VPN; it can be either through Direct Connect or over the public Internet. You must record the IP address of the CGW router's outside-facing interface that is reachable from AWS over either Direct Connect or the Internet. You will also need to provide AWS with the subnets at your location that they will route to. The VPG is a highly available VPN router virtual machine that is created in your account and associated with a VPC that you want your remote site to connect to. The VGW has two outside interfaces that are connected as endpoint 1 and endpoint 2, and these interfaces have publicly reachable IPv4 addresses. This provides a high-availability

VPN design into AWS as each endpoint resides in a different availability zone. Note that if you have only one VPN router at your location, the connection will not be highly available as it will be a single point of failure. For full high availability, two separate VPN routers at the on-premises location and separate Internet or DX connections would be required.

In AWS there are two routing options for the VPN connections, static and dynamic. The static VPN uses hard-coded, static routing to advertise the routes or dynamic routing using the BGP as the routing protocol, which requires BGP support on your customer router. Static does not use any dynamic routing protocols and requires that you hard-code the static routes into the routing table. Static routing is useful over a single connection; however, with multiple paths between on-premise and AWS where failover or path load balancing is desired, BGP must be used for its ability to dynamically update the routing tables as the network conditions change. Inside the VPC, routes can automatically be updated based on the BGP route table by enabling route propagation. Later in this chapter we will cover static routing and BGP basic operations.

As we learned earlier, there is a maximum speed per VPG at the AWS location of 1.25 Gbps and a maximum of 140,000 packets per second (PPS) per VPN tunnel. This does not take into account the throughput capabilities of your on-site router and the speed of the Internet connection. The VGW speed limitation is the maximum speed regardless of how many VPN connections are configured. The total throughput will always be a maximum of 1.25 Gbps. Latency over the Internet will be inconsistent and based on the number of router hops, congestion, and distance. Internet latency can vary and cannot be controlled by the customer accessing the Internet.

The AWS VPN service is charged per hour, and AWS data transfer charges for all data transferred via the VPN connection are applied. Pricing varies per region and can be determined on the AWS web console.

VPN CloudHub

The AWS VPN *CloudHub* is an architecture for the AWS site-to-site VPN service. However, it's not an actual service that you can find in the console. CloudHub uses a VPG in a VPC to connect multiple remote sites each using a site-to-site VPN connection.

Building on the AWS managed VPN options described previously, you can securely communicate from one site to another using the CloudHub AWS VPN. The AWS VPN CloudHub uses a hub-and-spoke architecture that allows all spoke locations to communicate with each other. VPC services are not required but can be connected to CloudHub. Remote offices or small hubs can use VPNs and CloudHub as either their primary or backup networks.

AWS VPN CloudHub implements a VPC virtual private gateway and multiple customer gateways, and the gateways must use unique public or private BGP autonomous system numbers with no overlapping IP address ranges.

BGP route prefixes are advertised by the gateways over the VPN connections. The advertised routes are received and re-advertised by AWS to each BGP peer. This allows each VPN location to communicate with all other VPCs and the Internet if connected.

AWS Account Resource Sharing

Many organizations deploy multiple accounts in AWS and require them to share resources, administration, accounting, monitoring, and shared billing. This is often done for security, segmentation, accounting, and many other reasons such as mergers or departmental segmentation. We will cover the overview of resource sharing in this chapter and go into more detail in Chapter 8, "Inter-VPC and Multi-Account Networking."

When using the multiple organization approach to your AWS deployment, each account is often not an isolated island. AWS offers many options to manage multiple accounts and to share resources between these different accounts. When sharing a service or resource residing in your account to the outside world, you apply access policies and permissions in your account to allow these resources to be externally shared.

When the resource owner shares services with another account, that account accesses the resource as if they were the owners. All access techniques apply as if it were local to your account. This includes API calls, the CLI, or the GUI interface depending on the capabilities of the resources you are sharing and the granted permissions. Accessing a resource that is shared and when using that resource's services, the same abilities and limitations exist as for the AWS account that owns the resource. When the resource is regional, you can access it only from the AWS region where it was created by the account owner.

There are two types of resources to consider, global and regional. Both global and regional resources can be shared. If the resource is global, access is allowed from any AWS region that the resource's service console and tools support. While it may be confusing, global resources are displayed in the AWS console as either global or may show as being in the U.S. East Northern Virginia region, us-east-1, even though they are global. Examples of global services include IAM, Route 53, CloudFront AWS Organizations, Direct Connect, AWS Firewall Manager, AWS Web Application Firewall (WAF), and AWS Shield.

Summary

Hybrid networking and the underlying technologies that are used were the focus of this chapter. We covered the basics of the two lower layers of the OSI model. You learned about the optical connections at layer 1, and for layer 2 we covered link aggregation, VLANs, and jumbo frames.

There are several different types of encapsulation protocols that are used to create virtualized networks and separation over a common network fabric. You learned the difference between overlay and underlay networks and how they are integrated to create a modern networking architecture.

Next, we covered routing, and you learned about static and dynamic routing and the differences between the two approaches to populating the routing table. Static routing is used for basic networks that seldom change, while dynamic routing is more common in enterprise and service provider networks due to the changing network topologies and the need to automatically update the routing tables without human intervention.

When two different organizations interconnect and exchange routing information, the BGP protocol is used. You learned what BGP is and how it operates.

Hybrid network interconnects with AWS use either the Direct Connect, or DX, service or a site-to-site VPN connection. You were introduced to these architectures, and we will go deeper into them in Chapters 7 and 8.

Exam Essentials

Be able to identify and know the use cases of the lower two layers of the OSI model.   Know the different types of optical SFP interfaces and fiber types, as well as the types of optical cables such as single and multimode. Understand 802.1Q VLANs specifically and the other encapsulation types such as VxLAN generally. Be familiar with what jumbo frames are and why they are used. Also, understand link aggregation as it is used extensively in AWS Direct Connect environments.

Know the two main methods of populating a route table.   Route tables can be updated either statically or dynamically. Know that the static method hard-codes the routes and does not exchange any routing information with other devices on the network. Dynamic routing runs different types of routing protocols such as OSPF or BGP that allow for the routers to automatically update each other with changes in the network.

Understand the BGP routing protocol.   While the exam is not about routing protocol theory, you are expected to know how BGP operates in relation to interconnecting your on-premise network with AWS.

Understand the basic architectures of hybrid networking and Direct Connect.   Know the terminology, interface types, capabilities, and different architectures available such as DX and VPNs.

Know the difference between an overlay and underlay network.   The underlay network is the underlying hardware of switches and routers that form the switching fabric of the network. Overlays are virtualized networks that operate over the underlay using protocols such as VxLAN to create many independent virtual networks such as VPCs in AWS.

Exercises

1. Understand the OSI networking model. There are many online resources available for you to explore. YouTube has many excellent videos available.

2. Be familiar with SFP transceivers: www.youtube.com/watch?v=6m1xrTe22NY.

3. Read and understand the AWS Direct Connect user guide: `https://docs.aws .amazon.com/pdfs/directconnect/latest/UserGuide/dc-ug.pdf#Welcome`.

4. Review the AWS hybrid connectivity white paper and become familiar with the different architectures: `https://docs.aws.amazon.com/pdfs/whitepapers/latest/ hybrid-connectivity/hybrid-connectivity.pdf#hybrid-network- connection`.

5. Study the AWS site-to-site VPN user guide and become very familiar with connecting an on-premises data center to an AWS region: `https://docs.aws.amazon.com/pdfs/ vpn/latest/s2svpn/s2s-vpn-user-guide.pdf#VPC_VPN`.

6. Read the "Sharing Your AWS Resources" online documentation: `https://docs.aws .amazon.com/pdfs/ram/latest/userguide/ram-ug.pdf#getting-started- sharing`.

Written Labs

Written Lab 6.1: Simulate Creating a Direct Connection

1. In this exercise, we will look at the AWS GUI to view the steps to create a direct connection. However, this is only a review, and no connection will be created due to the large cost in doing so.

2. Log in to the AWS console, enter Direct Connect in the search box, and select the service.

3. Click the Get Started box to create a connection.

4. Select Classic Connection Ordering Type.

5. In Connection Settings, enter a name you want to give your test connection, and enter the location you want to use to make the connection. Select a port speed you want to use. Again, adding this information is only for your review, and we will not actually place an order for a direct connection.

6. Choose if you are using an AWS service provider partner to make the connection or if you are using your own networking hardware at the chosen interconnection facility.

7. Review the options under Additional Settings and notice this is where link aggregation and the tagging options are defined.

8. Stop here and do not click Create Connection.

Written Lab 6.2: Simulate Creating a Site-to-Site VPN Connection

1. In the AWS GUI service for VPC, enter the VPC configuration page.

2. In the left panel scroll down to the virtual private networks and select Site-to-Site VPN.

3. Click the Create VPN Connection box to get started.

4. Review the fields required to create the VPN including the name tag.

5. Under the gateway type, enter **virtual private gateway** and select the new customer gateway icon.

6. Review the information that is required for the gateway including the public IP address and BGP autonomous system number.

7. Notice the options to use either static or dynamic routing.

8. Review the tunnel options including IPv4 information, the pre-share encryption key fields, and the encryption algorithms under Advanced Options.

9. Stop here; do not click the Create VPN Connection box.

Review Questions

The following questions are designed to test your understanding of this chapter's material. For more information on how to obtain additional questions, please see this book's introduction.

1. You are exploring methods to interconnect your St. Louis data center to your long-term archival storage on Glacier. Your requirements are for a high-speed private connection to the AWS Ohio region. What options would you recommend? (Select two.)

    A. Private link

    B. Site-to-site VPN

    C. Direct Connect

    D. Global Accelerator

2. You are creating your router configuration template to load on your router being installed at a Reston, Virginia DX facility. Which layer 2 option must you configure for the interconnect to the AWS network interface?

    A. Jumbo

    B. LACP

    C. 802.1Q

    D. Bidirectional link detection

3. DX hybrid networks offer what advantages over traversing the Internet to access your AWS services? (Select three.)

    A. High bandwidth

    B. Dynamic routing resiliency

    C. Edge location access

    D. Low and predictable latency

    E. Global acceleration

    F. Native VxLAN support

4. You want to establish a direct connection to your VPC in the eu-west-3 Paris region. Your finance group does not want to purchase and ship a router to France for this project. What options do you have?

    A. Open a support ticket with the AWS European support desk and request they allocate a router port in the Paris region

    B. Use an AWS carrier business partner that offers interconnection services at a collocation facility shared by AWS in France

    C. Use your DX router you have installed at the Stockholm collocation facility to also connect to eu-west-3

    D. You must have your router hardware installed locally at the Paris DX facility to be able to connect to the AWS router to access the eu-west-3 region

5. Because of the large amounts of file transfers to your Redshift deployment running on Amazon, you are exploring options to increase your DX throughput to the maximum available. What is the best option available to meet this need?

    A. Upgrade to a VxLAN underlay for higher upload speeds to your DX availability zone connection

    B. Upgrade your port speed at the DX facility

    C. Use LACP to link aggregate multiple 100G interfaces between your customer interfaces and the AWS DX interfaces

    D. Remove the static routes and configure the interconnection to use BGP

6. Your corporate requirement is to encrypt all external WAN traffic at the Austin corporate data center. You notice that the DX connection through Equinix in Dallas is not encrypted. What options are available to remediate this issue?

    A. Enable SSL/TLS encryption on the DX interface at the Equinix facility

    B. Enable IPSec at each end of the connection

    C. Encryption is not supported over the Direct Connect link

    D. Use the CloudFront network to connect to instead of Direct Connect since it supports IPSec

7. You are exploring routing protocol options to dynamically exchange routes with AWS over your Direct Connect link in Denver. What options are available?

    A. iBGP

    B. OSPF

    C. IS-IS

    D. eBGP

8. You are configuring your Direct Connect interface into the us-west-2 region and want to access your EC2 fleet in availability zone 1. How would you configure the DX interface?

    A. Use GRE and point it to AZ-A

    B. Create an overlay network that includes us-west-2 and availability zone 1

    C. Create a private VIF

    D. Create a public VIF

9. What interface would you point your data center's VPN concentrator to for a site-to-site AWS VPN connection?

    A. DX interconnect

    B. Customer gateway

    C. Virtual private gateway

    D. Global Accelerator endpoint

10. For a router to forward an IPv4 packet to a remote location, what must be present?

   A. A static route

   B. A dynamic routing protocol that constantly updates the routing table

   C. A route in the routers routing and forwarding table showing the next hop egress interface

   D. Configure an 802.1Q tag pointing to the remote network

11. You have a small network that never changes. You have no desire to manage the complexity of setting up the Border Gateway Protocol. What options are available to you to populate your router's forwarding tables?

   A. Configure static routes.

   B. Use a less complex dynamic routing protocol such as OSPF.

   C. You must use BGP to route packets through a IPv4 network

   D. Networks that have fewer than eight subnets do not require routing to be configured.

12. You are setting up a direct connection between your New Orleans data center and the AWS Ohio region and want to use a dynamic routing protocol. What will be required to begin building the router configuration needed at the DX hosting center?

   A. AWS will assign you a unique VLAN ID

   B. A connection into your OSPF Area 0 backbone router

   C. A unique autonomous system number

   D. A list from AWS of what IPSec transforms they want to use and then you can use that data to build your tunnel parameters

13. BGP is known as a distance vector routing protocol; what characteristics give it this label?

   A. Next hop reachability based on latency, jitter, bandwidth, and reliability.

   B. AS path metrics.

   C. The use of the Bellman–Ford route calculation algorithm.

   D. Vector labels are exchanged by BGP to determine the best route to enter into the routing table.

14. Outgoing BGP router advertisements are used to effect what result?

   A. AS egress traffic flows

   B. Multi-exit discriminator values

   C. Traffic coming into the AS

   D. Best metric policies

15. You are setting up a site-to-site VPN from your corporate data center to AWS to access your EC2 fleet sitting behind application load balancers in multiple regions. You have been tasked with keeping the number of VPN tunnels low to reduce complexity and monitoring overhead. What is the best solution?

   A. Configure Route 53 to load balance between the application load balancers

   B. Configure CloudHub to connect to the required VPCs

   C. Configure a VPN connection to a VPG and use BGP routing in the data center.

   D. Use PrivateLink to connect to the application load balancers

16. What architecture uses only one autonomous system across the entire worldwide routed network infrastructure?

   A. OSPF

   B. Generic Routing Protocol

   C. iBGP

   D. VxLAN

17. Storage, video, and large file transfer traffic benefit from which layer 2 option being enabled?

   A. Spanning tree protocol

   B. LACP

   C. Jumbos

   D. Bidirectional forwarding

18. You are required to support multicast traffic over your VPN network. You learn that the IPSec tunnels do not forward multicast traffic, and you are searching for a solution that does not require you to replace your network architecture. What is a viable option?

   A. Use an underlay network

   B. Implement VxLAN

   C. Configure Generic Routing Encapsulation and send the multicast traffic through the GRE tunnel

   D. Implement the GENEVE protocol

19. You need a protocol that prevents bad actors from tampering with packets in flight. What would you suggest implementing?

   A. BGP

   B. Transport Layer Security

   C. Secure Sockets Layer

   D. IPSec

20. What are some of the use cases for account resource sharing? (Select three.)

   A. Departmental segmentation

   B. Support for VPN backup connections in case the primary DX connection fails

   C. Nonrepudiation

   D. Serverless container isolation

   E. Docker support

   F. Accounting

   G. Company resource sharing between accounts

Chapter 7

Connecting On-Premises Networks

THE AWS CERTIFIED ADVANCED NETWORKING - SPECIALTY EXAM OBJECTIVES COVERED IN THIS CHAPTER MAY INCLUDE, BUT ARE NOT LIMITED TO, THE FOLLOWING:

✓ **Domain 2: Network Implementation**

- Task Statement 2.1: Implement routing and connectivity between on-premises networks and the AWS Cloud.

On-Premises Network Connectivity

In this chapter, you will continue to learn about hybrid networking. In Chapter 6, "Hybrid Networking," we covered the underlying technologies used to interconnect networks with a focus on connecting to AWS from remote collocation and enterprise data centers to form hybrid networks.

In this chapter, you will go deeper into the VPN services AWS offers, review layer 3 of the OSI model, network connectivity testing, and the AWS Resource Manager. You will also learn about some of the utilities used to test and troubleshoot these hybrid networks.

VPNs

In Chapter 6, you learned about site-to-site VPNs, virtual private gateways, customer gateways, IPSec, and CloudHub. In this chapter, you will expand your knowledge of VPNs as they are used in connecting your on-premises networks into your AWS resources. VPNs are an integral component of hybrid networking, along with Direct Connect, which was also covered in Chapter 6. You should expect the exam to test your knowledge of VPNs, so I advise you to learn the material in this book and to read the AWS online documentation until you deeply understand VPN theory, implementation, and ongoing operations and support.

VPN Security

To understand VPN security, it is helpful to understand the big picture of AWS security, which is documented in the AWS *shared responsibility model*. It is important to know what your responsibility is and what security AWS takes care of for you. The AWS model views it as security *of the cloud* and security *in the cloud*.

Security of the cloud outlines what AWS takes responsibility for securing and what is the customer's responsibility. The model addresses protecting the AWS infrastructure that the services are running on inside of the AWS network. Both AWS and the customer have responsibility for maintaining both security and compliance in the AWS cloud. AWS operates, manages, and secures its data centers, the physical hardware, the virtualization layer, host operating systems, and, depending on the service, application support such as databases or big data services. This leverages the large resources of AWS to perform on your behalf and is a huge operational relief for customers by relieving them from having to configure, monitor, and maintain those components of their operations.

The customer will assume responsibility for maintaining the guest operating system in an infrastructure as a service (IaaS) model. AWS will manage the guest OS, if you are using a platform as a service (PaaS) or software as a service (SaaS) model, and their selected applications with current updates and patches. Security in the cloud is the AWS customer's responsibility and depends on the services you are using. You must take responsibility for the data you upload to AWS and any regulations or laws in your country or areas of business operations, as well as access and security group configurations in your VPCs, access control, firewalls, and any other security controls you want to enable.

VPN security consists of protecting the data traversing the VPN, applying Identity and Access Management (IAM) restrictions, and enabling logging and monitoring. Also, the VPN physical infrastructure must be secure.

Data protection includes securing account credentials by configuring user and group accounts with only the necessary permissions in IAM, setting up CloudTrail to record and archive AWS operations, and not exposing sensitive information in tags.

IAM is used to restrict user access in the AWS console when working with site-to-site VPNs. IAM allows you to limit access without sharing security credentials. Since the IAM default is to restrict the ability to create, view, or modify VPN configurations, you must explicitly enable user access and permissions. Create the IAM policies by granting user permissions to use the specific resources and API actions that they need; then attach the policy to the IAM group or user. Site-to-site VPNs share the API namespace with Amazon EC2 when working with site-to-site VPN connections, virtual private gateways, and customer gateways.

IAM policies for site-to-site VPN connections provide resource-level user limitations to VPN APIs. Actions supported include `ec2:CreateVpnConnection`, `ec2:ModifyVpnConnection`, and `ec2:ModifyVpnTunnelOptions`. The ARN format is `arn:aws:ec2:ap-east-1:123456789012:vpn-connection/vpn-0fac8372dab8ad6413`.

AWS VPN resiliency includes using diverse data centers with every regional availability zone physically separated from each other. This architecture allows VPN connections to failover should an availability zone go offline. This is because each site-to-site VPN uses two tunnels, with each tunnel terminating in a different availability zone, as shown in Figure 7.1.

The site-to-site VPN connects your VPC to your data center using Internet Protocol Security (IPSec) to encrypt all in-flight traffic through the VPN tunnels to maintain data confidentiality and integrity.

Accelerated Site-to-Site VPN Connections

There is an option to use the AWS *VPN Global Accelerator* to decrease the network latency and congestion experienced when routing your VPN traffic over the public Internet. The AWS accelerated site-to-site VPN is routed to the nearest Global Accelerator edge location and then traverses the internal AWS global network instead of the Internet, as shown in Figure 7.2. For more information on the Global Accelerator, refer to Chapter 1, "Edge Networking," or review the AWS web console at `https://aws.amazon.com/global-accelerator`.

FIGURE 7.1   Dual tunnel site-to-site VPN

FIGURE 7.2   Accelerated site-to-site VPN

In this chapter, we will cover how the AWS site-to-site VPN service is implemented to provide for faster response times than traversing the public Internet. VPN traffic gets routed to the nearest AWS edge location from your customer gateway VPN termination appliance.

All VPN traffic will traverse the Internet by default and bypass the Global Accelerator. You must manually enable the service at the time you create the VPN or later after it has been set up, by creating a new connection. The VPN tunnel endpoint IP address will change to point to the Global Accelerator endpoints. To review its configuration, read the AWS online documentation for the steps to create the accelerated VPN at `https://docs.aws.amazon.com/vpn/latest/s2svpn/create-tgw-vpn-attachment.html`.

There are some limitations and restrictions that you must know about when architecting or operating the accelerated site-to-site VPN. Acceleration must use a Transit Gateway since virtual private gateways do not support accelerated VPN connections. Accelerated VPNs are not able to connect to DX public virtual interfaces.

On existing site-to-site VPN connections, you must create a new site-to-site VPN connection with acceleration enabled. You are not allowed enable or disable acceleration on an existing connection. Next, configure your customer gateway VPN appliance to use the new site-to-site VPN connection. After the new connection is established, delete the old site-to-site VPN connection. You must enable NAT traversal in the configuration on both ends of the VPN connection. To keep the accelerated tunnels up, the Internet Key Exchange (IKE) must be re-keyed at the customer end of the VPN.

Layer 1 and Types of Hardware to Use

In Chapter 6 we covered the interconnection hardware required at the AWS Direct Connect locations. For a detailed lesson on AWS Direct Connect, refer to Chapter 6.

The AWS network interface to your equipment in the DX facility uses single-mode fiber with SFP transceivers.

For 1 Gigabit connections, the *1000BASE-LX* 1310 nm single-mode fiber SFP is used, for 10 Gigabit, we will use *10GBASE-LR* 1310 nm SFPs, and for 100 Gigabit Ethernet, the *100GBASE-LR4* connectors are utilized.

Direct Connect

In this section, you will learn about the physical interconnection at the DX facility. Auto-negotiation must be disabled on your router's interface connected to the AWS router when using port speeds higher than 1 Gbps. VLAN tagging using 802.1Q must be enabled. Also, there is jumbo frame support from 1,522 to 9,023 bytes.

Bidirectional forwarding is optional but enabled on the AWS end of the connection. This will remain inactive until AWS sees incoming BFD frames, and then the feature will automatically become enabled. The routing protocol used for peering with AWS is BGP with MD5 used for authentication. Both IPv4 and IPv6 protocols are supported.

Direct Connect Locations

AWS Direct Connect locations are located throughout the world and are not located in AWS facilities like availability zones are. Third-party data centers are used to house the AWS DX routers. Customers contract with service providers or supply their own network equipment located in the same data centers as the AWS DX equipment. Fiber patch cables, as discussed earlier, provide the interconnection.

For an up-to-date list of Direct Connect collocation facilities, go to the AWS online documentation at `https://aws.amazon.com/directconnect/locations`.

Letter of Authorization Documents

When requesting an AWS Direct Connect, you will fill out a *Letter of Authorization - Connecting Facility Assignment (LOA-CFA)* form that AWS will provide when you register for the service. This document is used to provide the details for establishing the connection at the DX facility and is used by the collocation partner to establish the cross-connect.

To begin the process, open the AWS console and enter Direct Connect in the search box. Then go to the Direct Connection menu. Next select Create A Connection on the Get Started screen. Enter a name for the connection and the location and choose Create A Connection.

After you download the LOA-CFA, the next step is to work with your provider to establish the connection to the AWS router installed in the DX facility. Once the physical connection has been made, use the AWS console to complete the logical configurations.

If you do not want to install your own network equipment at the facility, you can work with a member of the AWS Partner Network that will terminate the circuit from your location to their equipment installed at the DX facility.

To find an AWS Direct Connect partner, go to `https://aws.amazon.com/direct connect/partners/?partner-solutions-cards.sort-by=item.additional Fields.partnerNameLower&partner-solutions-cards.sort-order=asc&awsf .partner-solutions-filter-location=*all` and search the location you are using to find which partners offer connections at that site. It is recommended that you choose the AWS Direct Connect location and AWS region that is closest to your on-premises location to reduce data circuit costs and reduce latency. Link speed and MACSec support vary per location and provider, so make sure the site meets your requirements.

For additional details, refer to Chapter 6 and read the official AWS documentation at `https://docs.aws.amazon.com/directconnect/latest/UserGuide/Colocation .html`.

Layer 2 and Layer 3

In this section, we will review basic networking to provide you with the background needed when implementing hybrid networks with AWS. It is strongly suggested that if you are not clear on VLAN, routing, IP addressing, and other layer 2 and 3 concepts that you study basic networking before attempting the AWS Advanced Networking certification exam. This is not an entry-level certification, and it is expected that you have a solid background in networking before attempting to obtain this certification. We covered layers 1 and 2 in Chapter 6, will expand on layer 2 and layer 3 here, and then cover VPCs in Chapter 8, "Inter-VPC and Multi-Account Networking."

Switching

Layer 2 switching forwards Ethernet frames at the data link layer, which is layer 2 of the OSI model. The switch examines the Media Access Control (MAC) address of each frame and builds a forwarding table based on the source MAC address to determine the interface where the frames are to be forwarded. All layer 2 switches require that they learn the MAC address of the NIC on each connected node to transmit data. Ethernet switches break up one large collision domain into multiple smaller ones. The layer 2 switch learns which device is connected to which port and forwards a frame based on the destination MAC address in each frame. This reduces network traffic on the LAN and increases security since the frame is not sent out all its interfaces.

The layer 2 switch is a multiport bridge where each switch port is a separate collision domain. Layer 2 switches support the Spanning Tree Protocol (STP), and its many variants, which provides loop prevention when multiple switches are interconnected, to prevent switching loops. The switch builds and updates its own internal database of the known MAC addresses connected to each port. Switches reduce the amount of Ethernet frame flooding by sending out frames only to the interface of the connected destination MAC address. Management features include support for virtual LANs (VLANs), diagnostics, and metric collections. Some switches have layer 3 router support, making them layer 2/3 devices. Switches use hardware forwarding based on ASICs for wire, speed, and low-latency performance. Figure 7.3 shows a simple layer 2 switched network.

FIGURE 7.3   Layer 2 switch

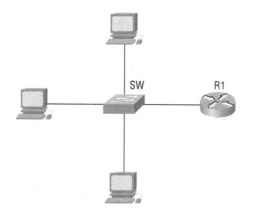

Switches increase the number of collision domains to one per interface, reducing the chances of a collision to zero.

Routing

While it is presumed that you have extensive prior knowledge of routing before taking the AWS Advanced Networking exam, we will briefly go over the basics here. A *router* is a network device that routes packets from one network to another. Routers are used to interconnect and forward traffic between two or more networks. Routers operate at layer 3 of the OSI model, and its forwarding decisions are based on the information present in layer 3, such as the destination IP address. Routers divide broadcast domains, provide full-duplex communication, and have traffic filtering capabilities.

When an IP packet arrives at a router's interface, the router reads the IP destination address information in the packet to determine on which port the packet will be sent out. Routers reference their locally stored forwarding table that is derived from its routing table that maps destination networks to outgoing ports.

When two endpoints that are on different networks need to send data between each other, a router is required to forward packets between the two different subnets. Figure 7.4 shows a simple routed network with three different subnets.

FIGURE 7.4   Basic routing

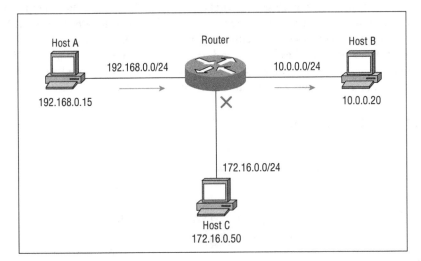

In this example, Host A is sitting on the 192.168.0.0 network with the host address of 192.168.0.15 and wants to send data to Host B at 10.0.0.20 on the 10.0.0.0 subnet. Host A will recognize that the network subnets are different, and it will need to hand the packet off to its locally connected router, which knows how to reach Host B. The router will receive the packet from Host A, do a lookup in its route forwarding table, and forward the packet out the correct egress interface to reach Host B. The process reverses itself when Host B replies to Host A. Host C will not see the traffic since it is on a different network, and the router does not forward to that segment since the network address is on a different subnet.

Gateways

A *gateway* is a device or software that interconnects dissimilar systems. A gateway translates between two networks with different protocols, as shown in Figure 7.5. *Routers* and *gateways* are terms that are often used interchangeably, and while there is a lot of overlap in functionality, there are also differences that distinguish the roles they are used for. Routers interconnect networks using the same communications protocol, usually TCP/IP. Gateways translate between different protocols and act as a "gate" from one network to another. Both devices forward traffic between different networks. The difference is that routers forward traffic between networks of the same communications protocol, whereas a gateway translates between two or more protocols. Since gateways operate with more than one protocol, they tend to be more complex than a basic router operating at layer 3 of the OSI model. Gateways do not run routing protocols like routers do. In basic TCP/IP host configurations, the IP address of the local router is often called the *default gateway*, which can be confusing as it's actually the default router.

FIGURE 7.5   Gateways

Gateway

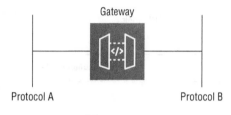

Protocol A   Protocol B

Software-Defined Networking

Networking equipment designs include a control plane and the forwarding plane. The control plane is the operational hardware and software that manages all the switch or router management functions, including configuration, monitoring, running the routing protocols, building the route, forwarding tables, and responding to network activity directed to it such as processing network management requests, routing updates, running spanning tree processes, SSH connections, and many other operations. The forwarding plane is the silicon and interfaces that forward the actual data through the device from the time it enters the ingress interface and performs the forwarding out the egress interface. This approach results in every networking device having its own control plane, which does not scale to hundreds or thousands of devices. Each switch or router needs to be individually configured, and the possibility of mistakes or out-of-synchronization configurations is very high. Software-defined networking removes the control plane from each device and abstracts all control functions to separate controllers that push configuration and updates to the network devices that are now functioning strictly as forwarding devices.

All configurations are implemented in an abstracted centralized control console or use API interfaces from a central controller without having to touch each individual switch or router.

Software-defined networking (SDN) is the physical separation of the network control plane from the forwarding plane and where a control plane controls all networking devices. The decoupling of the network control and forwarding functions enables the network control to become programmable from a central location and the underlying infrastructure to be abstracted from the applications and network services. SDN uses software-based controllers and application programming interfaces (APIs) to communicate with underlying hardware infrastructure that directs the traffic through the network.

The common representation of SDN architecture comprises three layers: the application, the control layer, and the infrastructure layer, as shown in Figure 7.6.

FIGURE 7.6   Software-defined networking

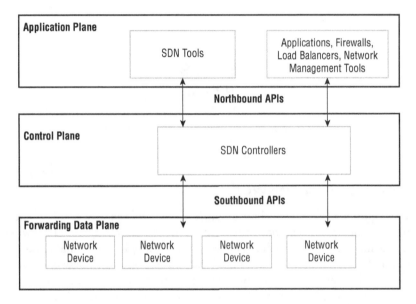

A typical SDN architecture consists of the controller, which is the core element of an SDN architecture; it enables centralized management and control, automation, and policy enforcement across the underlying physical and virtual network environments. Communications for the controller to the forwarding plane use southbound APIs that relay information to the individual network devices, such as switches, routers, and firewalls. Northbound APIs are used to exchange configuration and management information between the controller and application and policy engines, to which an SDN looks like a single logical network device.

Network control is directly programmable and is decoupled from forwarding functions. SDN provides for a centrally managed architecture that utilizes software- or hardware-based SDN controllers to maintain a global view of the network, which appears to applications and policy engines as a single, logical switch.

SDN allows for the configuration, management, security, and all other network operations to deploy quickly via dynamic, automated SDN programs and scripts.

Transit Gateway

The AWS *Transit Gateway* service is a central regional virtual router that is used to connect VPCs with on-premises facilities. The Transit Gateway service acts as a centralized core router for your hybrid network. The hub is designed to reduce the complexity of connecting multiple locations and VPCs by making only a single connection to the network and using the service to route to all connected VPCs and private data center locations. The gateway interconnects multiple regions to simplify VPC peering configurations as each VPC requires only a single connection to the gateway to reach all other connected VPCs. Software-defined wide-area networking (SD-WAN) allows third-party solutions to be integrated with the service so your enterprise network can be integrated with your Transit Gateway cloud-based network deployment. The Transit Gateway is a fully managed AWS service that scales based on the traffic load.

The AWS Transit Gateway is included in the VPC networking objectives and will be covered more extensively with interconnecting VPCs and multi-account networks in Chapter 8.

PrivateLink

The AWS *PrivateLink* service bypasses the public Internet to establish a direct connection from a VPC to AWS services as if they were inside of your VPC. It's an internal AWS connection from your private VPC subnets to AWS services that reside outside of the VPC. By restricting access to the Internet from the private subnets, you can control all external access to AWS services such as API endpoints, remote sites, and services. PrivateLink will be covered in greater detail in Chapter 8.

Resource Access Manager

The AWS *Resource Access Manager (RAM)* is an AWS management utility that allows you to share the AWS resources created in one AWS account and make them available to other AWS accounts. This makes your operations much more efficient, reduces overhead, and lowers costs by creating a resource one time and then using RAM to share it to other accounts instead of replicating the service in each account. External users can access the originating AWS service in the AWS console or use API operations as if those resources were native in the user's account.

When your accounts are managed by AWS organizations, you can share resources with other accounts in the organization or limit the scope to accounts contained in one or more organizational units (OUs) that you define. You can also share resources and services by using account IDs if you are not using organizations or an account is not part of an organization. The account that owns the resource is responsible for paying for the services used.

The Resource Access Manager is integrated with CloudWatch and CloudTrail for management and monitoring visibility. Security uses a single set of policies instead of many for the single, shared resource; this means users of the shared RAM resource are managed by a single set of policies and permissions. The resource owners can monitor which external entities have access to each individual shared resource.

If you need to share resources with accounts outside of your organization, the Resource Access Manager sends an invitation to the remote account. The recipient account then must accept the invitation before accessing the shared resources. Because of this initial step of sharing within your organization, all future sharing with those accounts in the organization doesn't require any additional invitations.

RAM supports many different AWS resources, but they will change over time and by region as AWS expands its capabilities. It's always a good idea to check the AWS online documentation for the latest list of services that RAM supports. The following are AWS resources that can currently be shared using the Resource Access Manager:

- App Mesh
- Amazon Aurora
- AWS Private Certificate Authority
- CodeBuild
- EC2
- EC2 Image Builder
- Glue
- License Manager
- Migration Hub Refactor Spaces
- Network Firewall
- Outposts
- S3 on Outposts
- Resource Groups
- Route 53
- SageMaker
- Service Catalog AppRegistry
- Systems Manager Incident Manager
- VPCs
- Cloud WAN

Testing and Validating Connectivity Between Environments

Network testing and validation is an important skill for any networking engineer, and in-depth knowledge is expected for you to pass the Advanced Networking exam. Network testing is an ongoing process that begins when you first configure the network. There are many monitoring, logging, and testing tools offered as services from AWS, and all host operating systems come with network testing utilities built in. In this chapter, we will expand on what you learned in Chapter 5, "Logging and Monitoring."

Route Analyzer

The AWS *Route Analyzer* is a utility that examines the routes in the Transit Gateway routing tables and analyzes the route path from the source and destination IP address that you specify. The utility can be used to validate that the route table is populated with the prefixes you are expecting, as well as validate your routing configurations. Also, it is used to troubleshoot routing issues in your network. The analyzer supports both IPv4 and IPv6 protocols and can analyze both the outgoing and return paths for traffic from the specified destination back to the source.

When working with the Route Analyzer, be aware of the following rules. The analyzer analyzes only the routes in the Transit Gateway route forwarding tables and not any other routing tables such as in the VPC or your internal routers; in addition, the Transit Gateway service must be registered on your network. VPC Flow Logs are needed to capture access control lists and security group rules; the analyzer does not provide that information. You will receive return path information only if there is a valid forward path.

Reachability Analyzer

The VPC *Reachability Analyzer* is used to validate your network connectivity, troubleshoot, identify network configuration issues, and automate validations for connectivity after configuration changes or new deployments. The VPC Reachability Analyzer checks the network path taken by a packet from source to destination. The tool creates a logical model of the configuration and then checks for connectivity. It is important to note that it does not actually send data over the forwarding plane; the reachability is analyzed in code only. Refer to Chapter 5 for an in-depth review of this AWS service.

ICMP *ping*

The *ping* utility is a command-line tool that tests for device reachability. You execute the ping command from the source using the IP address of the destination you want to test. If there is a reply, you know that there is a network path from the source to the destination. The ping utility has been around since 1983 and is included in all operating systems that support the IP protocol. Just like throwing a tennis ball against the wall and catching it after it bounces back to you, ping sends a packet using the Internet Control Message Protocol (*ICMP*) to a remote host and measures the time it takes for the echo to return.

ICMP is a network-level protocol that communicates information about network connectivity and sends data back to the source about compromised transmissions. It's a control message protocol that reports impairments such as destination network unreachable, source route failed, and source quench.

Most ping programs report round-trip times, errors, any packet loss, and a summary of the results. There are switches that can be used to modify their behavior, as shown in Figure 7.7 for Windows.

FIGURE 7.7 Windows ping

When running the ping command, a packet is sent to the remote IP address or domain name you specify. The remote device will respond with an ICMP reply packet that includes the original packet sent. If there are errors, codes are given, which vary based on the operating systems and the vendor's implementation of the utility. Here are some of the more common responses output from the command parser:

- A: Communication with destination network administratively prohibited

- C: Precedence cutoff in effect

- F: Fragmentation needed

- H, !N, or !P: Host, network, or protocol unreachable

- I: Source host is isolated

- Q: For this ToS destination network unreachable

- S: Source route failed

- T: For this ToS destination host unreachable

- U or !W: Destination network/host unknown

- V: Host precedence violation

- X: Communication administratively prohibited

- Z: Communication with destination host administratively prohibited

traceroute

traceroute is a useful command-line utility in your troubleshooting arsenal and is used to show the path taken over an IP network from source to destination. It will also tell us the delays to each router hop and, if configured, the DNS name of all the indeterminate routers. The utility is included in every operating system's IP stack. In Linux it is traceroute and in Windows, tracert. IPv6 is supported with the traceroute6 and tracert6 commands. PathPing is a utility introduced with Windows NT that combines ping and traceroute functionality. While ping is used to test the reachability of a specific device, traceroute will show the actual path taken. It's often used to determine where network hops are failing and to find network latency issues.

The traceroute utility will display three values including the hop count, which is the number of the hop along the route; the round-trip time (RTT), which is three columns that measure the round-trip time for the test packet to reach that point and return to your computer; and the domain/IP column, which shows the IP address or DNS name of the router.

Most Linux operating systems send a string of UDP packets with a range of port numbers from 33434 to 33534. There are Unix and Linux variants that allow you to specify that ICMP be used instead of UDP. Windows uses ICMP as its default. Be aware that firewalls along the path may block ping and traceroute as well as other utilities that will not send any replies.

Time-stamp values returned for each router in the source to destination path display latency values; these delay values are measured in milliseconds for each packet received by the utility. If a packet is not acknowledged within the expected interval, an asterisk will be used instead of the time value.

The time-to-live determines the hop limit and allows traceroute to find the intermediate routers. It sends packets with a TTL value set to 1 to the first router in the path. The router always decrements the TTL by 1; in this case it will be 0, which tells the router that the packet has expired. It also returns the ICMP error message "ICMP Time Exceeded" to the source and drops the packet. This allows the utility to record the router. Next it will send a packet with a TTL value of 2 and learn about the second router in the path as it will also reply with the ICMP reply since the first and second routers have decremented the TTL field in the packet and it's now 0. This process continues until the destination is reached.

In the Cisco IOS command line, `traceroute` also uses a UDP with the common incrementing TTL values and uses UDP 33434 as its default. Cisco also has an extended `traceroute` option where you can modify parameters such as the port number used by UDP.

Figure 7.8 shows an example of using the `tracert` utility with Windows PowerShell.

FIGURE 7.8   Windows `traceroute`

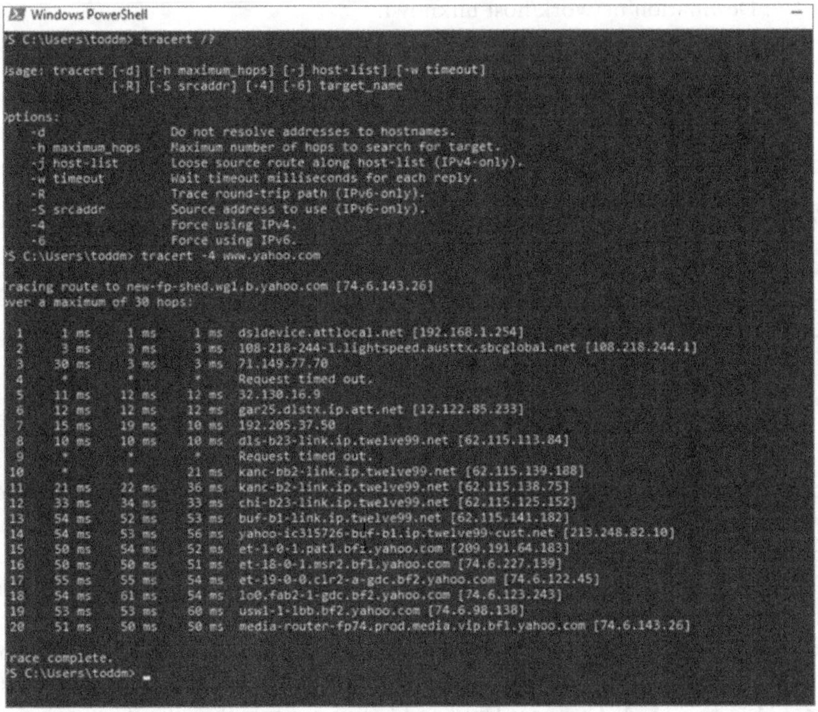

```
Windows PowerShell
PS C:\Users\toddm> tracert /?

Usage: tracert [-d] [-h maximum_hops] [-j host-list] [-w timeout]
               [-R] [-S srcaddr] [-4] [-6] target_name

Options:
    -d                 Do not resolve addresses to hostnames.
    -h maximum_hops    Maximum number of hops to search for target.
    -j host-list       Loose source route along host-list (IPv4-only).
    -w timeout         Wait timeout milliseconds for each reply.
    -R                 Trace round-trip path (IPv6-only).
    -S srcaddr         Source address to use (IPv6-only).
    -4                 Force using IPv4.
    -6                 Force using IPv6.
PS C:\Users\toddm> tracert -4 www.yahoo.com

Tracing route to new-fp-shed.wg1.b.yahoo.com [74.6.143.26]
over a maximum of 30 hops:

  1     1 ms     1 ms     1 ms  dsldevice.attlocal.net [192.168.1.254]
  2     3 ms     3 ms     3 ms  108-218-244-1.lightspeed.austtx.sbcglobal.net [108.218.244.1]
  3    30 ms     3 ms     3 ms  71.149.77.70
  4     *        *        *     Request timed out.
  5    11 ms    12 ms    12 ms  32.130.16.9
  6    12 ms    12 ms    12 ms  gar25.dlstx.ip.att.net [12.122.85.233]
  7    15 ms    19 ms    10 ms  192.205.37.50
  8    10 ms    10 ms    10 ms  dls-b23-link.ip.twelve99.net [62.115.113.84]
  9     *        *        *     Request timed out.
 10     *        *       21 ms  kanc-bb2-link.ip.twelve99.net [62.115.139.188]
 11    21 ms    22 ms    36 ms  kanc-b2-link.ip.twelve99.net [62.115.138.75]
 12    33 ms    34 ms    33 ms  chi-b23-link.ip.twelve99.net [62.115.125.152]
 13    54 ms    52 ms    53 ms  buf-b1-link.ip.twelve99.net [62.115.141.182]
 14    54 ms    53 ms    56 ms  yahoo-ic315726-buf-b1.ip.twelve99-cust.net [213.248.82.10]
 15    50 ms    54 ms    51 ms  et-1-0-1.pat1.bf1.yahoo.com [209.191.64.183]
 16    50 ms    50 ms    51 ms  et-18-0-1.msr2.bf1.yahoo.com [74.6.227.139]
 17    55 ms    55 ms    54 ms  et-19-0-0.clr2-a-gdc.bf2.yahoo.com [74.6.122.45]
 18    54 ms    61 ms    54 ms  lo0.fab2-1-gdc.bf2.yahoo.com [74.6.123.243]
 19    53 ms    53 ms    60 ms  usw1-1-lbb.bf2.yahoo.com [74.6.98.138]
 20    51 ms    50 ms    50 ms  media-router-fp74.prod.media.vip.bf1.yahoo.com [74.6.143.26]

Trace complete.
PS C:\Users\toddm> _
```

Summary

This chapter expanded on hybrid networks, which were introduced in Chapter 6. We went into more detail about how on-premises data centers and networks connect to AWS cloud services.

You learned about site-to-site VPN connections that use the public Internet to connect into AWS. An important part of using a VPN is to provide a secure tunnel to secure in-flight traffic. You learned about the AWS security model and what AWS assumes responsibility for and the security that you must manage. AWS is responsible for security "of" the cloud, and you are responsible for security "in" the cloud. VPN security protects the data as it traverses the Internet, and you learned about many of the VPN encryption technologies used.

To accelerate and provide additional security, accelerated site-to-site VPNs use the AWS Global Accelerator to direct VPN traffic off the sometimes-congested Internet and onto the higher-speed and lower-latency private AWS backbone as close to your location as possible.

To bypass the Internet and achieve higher-speed connections and lower latency, direct connections are used. You learned about the physical requirements of making a direct connection.

It is assumed that you already have a basic to advanced knowledge of layer 2 and 3 networks including how switches and routers operate. A review was included in this chapter to serve as a refresher. Gateways were reviewed, and the differences between gateways and routers were demonstrated.

Since AWS can be viewed as a very large software-defined network, you learned about the architecture of software-defined networks, how they are deployed, and how the SDN building blocks interact with each other.

The AWS central routing hub, Transit Gateway, was discussed, and you then learned about what AWS PrivateLink is and how it is used.

To share AWS resources between accounts, the Resource Access Manager service can be deployed to simplify ease of management, reduce overhead, and increase security.

We finished the chapter by learning about how to test and validate network connectivity. AWS tools that are used include the Route Analyzer and Reachability Analyzer. Public utilities that are also commonly used for testing and troubleshooting include `ping` and `traceroute`. How and when to use these utilities was explained by using examples.

Exam Essentials

Understand the AWS security model and best practices.   Read the AWS shared responsibility online documentation and understand the material before taking the exam.

Know the site-to-site VPN architecture and how to configure and operate site-to-site VPNs.   VPNs are an important component of hybrid networks. Focus on VPN security and how tunnels are created. Again, review this chapter's material and published AWS VPN documentation if you feel that you need additional knowledge of IPSec and the AWS implementation of VPNs. Know what AWS services make up the accelerated site-to-site VPN service and how it is implemented.

Understand the role of Direct Connect in hybrid networks.   Direct Connect is the second interconnect option. For the exam, know the physical interconnect optical options, speeds, types of fiber cable required, and base configurations. Also, review the process used to establish a direct connection.

Understand the basics of software-defined networking.   Have a good understanding of the software-defined networking architectural modes and their use of APIs. This conceptual understanding gives you a good high-level understanding of the AWS cloud and helps you see the "bigger picture" to help understand many of the exam questions.

Be familiar with the AWS Transit Gateway, PrivateLink, and Resource Access Manager. These services were introduced in this chapter and will very likely appear in at least a few exam questions. If you feel you do not have a thorough understanding of these services, review the sections in this chapter, the AWS online documentation pages, and the AWS web console before taking the exam.

Know the common network troubleshooting tools.   You will receive a few troubleshooting questions on the exam. Have a good understanding of the AWS Route and Reachability Analyzers, what they are, and how and when they should be used. Also, know the client-side utilities of `ping` and `traceroute` and have the commands memorized for both the Windows and Linux implementations. Expect a question or two where you will be required to distinguish between all the test utilities and where each one should be used.

Written Labs

Written Lab 7.1: Create a VPN Attachment on a Transit Gateway Using the Console

1. Using a web browser, open the Amazon VPC console at `https://console.aws` `.amazon.com/vpc`.

2. Select Transit Gateway on the right.

3. Select Create Transit Gateway in the AWS VPC console.

4. Fill in the name tag and description and use AS number 65000 for the autonomous system number (ASN).

5. Click Create Transit Gateway.

6. Select Site-to-Site VPN Connections on the right.

7. Click Create VPN Connection.

8. In the Name Tag box, enter a name for your site-to-site VPN connection. Doing so creates a tag with a key of Name and the value that you specify.

9. For Target Gateway Type, choose Transit Gateway, and choose the Transit Gateway instance just created to create the attachment.

10. For Customer Gateway, do one of the following:

    ▪ To use an existing customer gateway, choose Existing, and then select the gateway to use in the pull-down menu. If your customer gateway sits behind a NAT device that's enabled for NAT traversal, use the public IP address of your NAT device, and adjust your firewall rules to unblock UDP port 4500. If you do not have a public IP to use in this step, leave it blank and follow this lab until the end, but do not create the VPN as a public IP is required.

- To create a customer gateway, choose New.

11. For IP Address, enter a static public IP address of your device's outside interface. If you do not have a public IP to use in this step, leave it blank and follow this lab until the end, but do not create the VPN as a public IP is required.

12. For Certificate ARN, if you are using certificate-based authentication, choose the ARN of your private certificate. For the BGP ASN, enter the BGP ASN of your customer network. Reference `https://docs.aws.amazon.com/vpn/latest/s2svpn/ cgw-options.html` for additional information.

13. For Routing Options, choose whether to use Dynamic.

14. For Tunnel Inside IP Version, select IPv4. For Local IPv4 network CIDR, specify the IPv4 CIDR range on the on-premises customer gateway to specify which subnets are allowed to communicate over the VPN tunnels. Or open it to all networks by leaving this at the default of `0.0.0.0/0`.

15. In the Remote IPv4 Network CIDR dialog box, specify the IPv4 CIDR range on the AWS side that is allowed to communicate over the VPN tunnels. Or open it to all networks by leaving this at the default of `0.0.0.0/0`.

16. For the Tunnel 1 options, fill in the inside IPv4 CIDR range, which allows AWS to generate the pre-shared key for the tunnel, and review the tunnel options.

17. Review the advanced tunnel information, which includes the following:

- Encryption algorithms for phases 1 and 2 of the IKE negotiations
- Integrity algorithms for phases 1 and 2 of the IKE negotiations
- Diffie-Hellman groups for phases 1 and 2 of the IKE negotiations
- IKE version 1 or 2
- Phase 1 and 2 lifetimes in seconds
- Re-key margin time
- Re-key fuzz
- Replay window size
- Dead peer detection interval
- Dead peer detection timeout action
- Startup action

  For more information about these options, see `https://docs.aws.amazon.com/ vpn/latest/s2svpn/VPNTunnels.html`.

18. Choose Create VPN Connection. Note that if you do not have a public IP address to terminate the VPN connection, the connection will not be created.

19. When completed, delete the site-to-site VPN and the Transit Gateway instance.

Written Lab 7.2: Perform a *traceroute*

1. Open a command console on a client computer; it can be either Windows or Linux.

2. Enter **traceroute aws.amazon.com** (Linux) or **tracert aws.amazon.com** (Windows).

3. Observe the text output of the network route taken from your computer to aws .amazon.com using DNS.

4. Enter **traceroute 18.154.211.6** (Linux) or **tracert 18.154.211.67** (Windows).

5. Observe the text output of the network route taken from your computer to aws .amazon.com using its IPv4 address.

6. Explore the traceroute utility options using **tracert /?** for Windows or **man traceroute** for Linux.

Written Lab 7.3: Use *ping*

1. Open a command console on a client computer; it can be either Windows, Linux, or macOS.

2. Enter **ping aws.amazon.com** on either Linux, macOS, or Windows.

3. Observe the text output of the ping responses from aws.amazon.com using DNS.

4. Enter **ping 18.154.211.6** on your local computer.

5. Observe the text output of the network ping replies received from aws.amazon.com using its IPv4 address.

6. Explore the ping utility options using **ping /?** for windows or **man ping** for Linux.

Review Questions

1. As a network cloud engineer for your company, you are exploring options available to create a hybrid network from your Glasgow data center to the eu-west-1 region in Dublin, Ireland. What are viable connection options?

    A. DX

    B. Kinesis data stream

    C. Regional interconnect

    D. Site-to-site VPN

    E. VPC peering

2. What framework outlines responsibilities for security implementations in the AWS cloud?

    A. AWS Macie

    B. AWS Well-Architected Framework

    C. IPSec

    D. Shared responsibility model

    E. AWS security framework service

3. What data center technology centralizes control plane operations into a central controller?

    A. Routing

    B. CloudHub

    C. API Gateway

    D. SDN

    E. Control Tower

4. Which AWS networking service bypasses the public Internet to establish a direct VPC to AWS services connection?

    A. CloudHub

    B. PrivateLink

    C. AWS Direct Connect

    D. Control Tower

    E. App Mesh

5. Which operating system test utility is used to test connectivity?

    A. `ping`

    B. `traceroute`

    C. Reachability Analyzer

    D. Route Analyzer

    E. `nslookup`

6. What steps should be taken to enhance the security of your site-to-site VPN connection? (Select three.)

   A. Implement IAM restrictions

   B. Turn on KMS

   C. Enable CloudTrail

   D. Enable AWS Shield

   E. Prevent exposing sensitive information in tags

7. What networking device forwards traffic based on MAC addresses?

   A. Router

   B. Gateway

   C. Switch

   D. Direct Connect

   E. Load balancer

8. The software-defined networking architecture separates which networking functions from each other? (Select two.)

   A. Control plane

   B. Application plane

   C. Security plane

   D. Forwarding plane

   E. Route forwarding table

9. What is required by AWS to establish a DX cross-connection?

   A. Enable OSPF routing

   B. Multimode fiber

   C. Letter of Authorization

   D. Peering agreement

   E. CloudFront gateway

10. What networking device forwards traffic based on IP destination addresses?

    A. Router

    B. Gateway

    C. Switch

    D. Direct Connect

    E. Load balancer

11. You are troubleshooting a connection over the Internet from your client laptop in Austin to an DynamoDB database located in the Asia-Pacific Tokyo region. You suspect that there is no active route. What client utility can you use to see where the traffic is being dropped?

    A. Reachability Analyzer

    B. `traceroute`

    C. CloudTrail

    D. Route Analyzer

    E. `ping`

12. You are experiencing variable delays and congestion on your site-to-site VPN connection in the US West Oregon region. What alternative connection strategy is a viable solution?

    A. Accelerated site-to-site

    B. CloudHub

    C. Data center peering

    D. CloudHSM

13. What type of optical hardware does AWS use for Direct Connect interconnections?

    A. LC

    B. SC

    C. SFP

    D. SR

    E. Multimode

14. Your site-to-site VPN connections are dropping, and you suspect that there is a routing issue in your service provider's network. Which utility can be used to determine where the drops are occurring?

    A. Route Analyzer

    B. AWS Shield

    C. `ping`

    D. `traceroute`

    E. AWS Detective

15. What data center technology uses Northbound and Southbound API calls for configuration operations?

    A. Transit Gateway

    B. CloudHub

    C. API Gateway

    D. SDN

    E. Control Tower

16. What networking device translates protocols?

    A. Router

    B. Gateway

    C. Switch

    D. Direct Connect

    E. Load balancer

17. Which AWS service is used to interconnect VPCs and on-premises workloads using a central regional router?

    A. API Gateway

    B. SDN

    C. Transit Gateway

    D. Route 53

    E. CloudMap

18. You are investigating to see if there is a missing route in your Transit Gateway instance. Which AWS utility can provide you with source-to-destination routing information?

    A. Reachability Analyzer

    B. `traceroute`

    C. CloudTrail

    D. Route Analyzer

    E. CloudWatch

19. What AWS service is used to share resources between accounts?

    A. Resource Access Manager

    B. CloudHub

    C. CloudMap

    D. AppFlow

    E. CloudShell

20. What values does the `traceroute` utility display? (Select three.)

    A. Jitter

    B. Responding node IP/DNS name

    C. Autonomous systems path

    D. Hop count

    E. Round-trip time

Chapter

8

Inter-VPC and Multi-account Networking

THE AWS CERTIFIED ADVANCED NETWORKING - SPECIALTY EXAM OBJECTIVES COVERED IN THIS CHAPTER MAY INCLUDE, BUT ARE NOT LIMITED TO, THE FOLLOWING:

✓ **Domain 2: Network Implementation**

- Task Statement 2.2: Implement routing and connectivity across multiple AWS accounts, Regions, and VPCs to support different connectivity patterns.

Networking Services of VPCs

This chapter will focus on interconnecting AWS virtual private clouds (VPCs) and go into detail from a networking perspective about the different options, architectures, and services available from AWS. You will learn the specifics of enabling networking connections between VPCs and outside services as well as the wide-area networking services used to provide access and interconnects. VPC networking is a core component in the AWS Advanced Networking exam certification, and it is strongly suggested you really understand all the details before sitting for the exam.

VPC Sharing

VPC sharing connects resources from multiple accounts and groups into a common, shared network. Sharing VPCs uses internal AWS network links for added security and sharing of resources. By interconnecting VPCs and AWS resources such as RDS databases, DynamoDB, EC2 instances, or any other service, you are able to create a shared private network. VPC sharing gives you the ability to centrally manage your VPCs across multiple accounts.

VPC sharing gives AWS users the ability to share IP subnets with other AWS accounts in the same AWS organization. This gives us centralized control over routing, IP addressing, the sharing of security groups, larger and higher-density VPCs, less duplication of resources such as NAT gateways, endpoints, and cross-AZ traffic. It provides all this while allowing the application owners to continue to manage their own resources, security, and account structure.

The account VPC owners can create, manage, and delete VPC resources such as IP subnets, route tables, access control lists, VPC peering connections, service endpoints, PrivateLink endpoints, Internet gateways, NAT gateways, virtual private gateways, and Transit Gateway attachments. However, the owner of a VPC is not able to delete or modify other VPCs that they do not manage. They can view the network interfaces and security groups that are attached to other VPCs for troubleshooting and auditing.

When considering using VPC sharing, keep in mind that you must use AWS organizations. There is a limitation that sharing the default VPC and its subnets is prohibited. You can't launch resources using security groups that are owned by other participants or the owner.

Charges apply for data transfers associated with inter-availability zone data transfers, Internet gateways, VPC peering connections, data transfer through AWS Direct Connect, NAT gateways, virtual private gateways, Transit Gateway instances, AWS PrivateLink, and VPC endpoints.

VPC sharing uses the AWS Resource Access Manager (RAM) to define subnets that are shared between accounts. When RAM is enabled, sharing is enabled for your entire AWS organization. If you need to turn off RAM, you can create service control policies, which are discussed later in this chapter.

For more information on VPC sharing, reference the following link: `https://docs.aws.amazon.com/vpc/latest/userguide/vpc-sharing.html#vpc-share-unsupported-services`.

VPC Peering

VPC peering connections allow two or more VPCs to access resources in each VPC from the other, as shown in Figure 8.1. The AWS peering service has no bandwidth limitations, and there is no single failure point. It does not rely on gateways, Direct Connect, or VPN interconnections. This allows full IPv4 and IPv6 connectivity between services in each VPC. Peering connections can be in the same account or between separate accounts. Connections can be made across regions and availability zones. Instances running inside of a VPC, such as EC2 or Lambda, have full private network communications without the need to configure a gateway or NAT instance. All VPC-to-VPC traffic can use the private IP address space and transits the AWS internal global network.

FIGURE 8.1   VPC peer connection

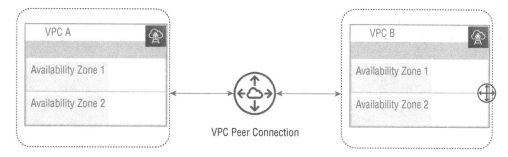

Figure 8.2 shows a multi-VPC peering architecture between VPCs A, B, and C. Since A is directly connected to B, they can exchange traffic. This is also true for the VPC B to C peering connection. However, since A is not directly connected to C, there can be no exchange of traffic; this is known as *nontransitive peering*. To route traffic from VPC A to VPC C, you must create a meshed peer connection between the two, as shown in Figure 8.3. VPC peering does not support transitive routing; for example, if a VPC has an Internet connection, the peered VPC cannot connect through it to reach the Internet. This is also true for NAT devices where, for example, VPC A peer is connected with VPC B and uses its NAT gateway

to exit the VPC to access services external to VPC B. Edge-to-edge routing is not supported through the peer connection to a gateway, VPN, or private Direct Connect. Gateway endpoints in a VPC such as for internal DynamoDB and S3 connections do not support transitive connections over a peer connection.

All peering connections represent a one-to-one connection between two VPCs. However, each VPC can have many peer connections to multiple VPCs. A VPC can route traffic only between VPCs that are directly connected; there is no transitive routing through an indeterminate peered VPC to another VPC that does not have a peer connection to the originating VPC. They must be directly connected.

FIGURE 8.2 Nontransitive peering

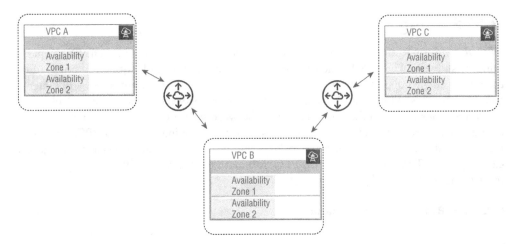

FIGURE 8.3 Meshed VPC peering

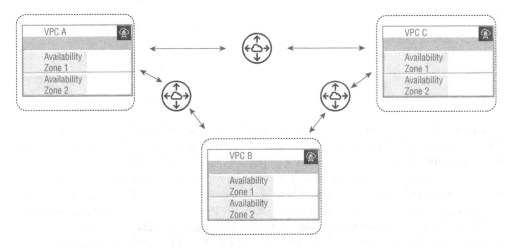

The default maximum number of peering connections is 50 per VPC. However, this can be increased to a maximum of 125 by contacting AWS Support and requesting an increase. There can be only a single peer connection between VPCs; tags are applied in the account only in a single region. DNS support can be enabled to resolve private domain names to the private IP address space if enabled. The IP CIDR blocks must be unique in each VPC. If there are overlapping or duplicate IP address spaces, routing is not possible.

Many of these limitations can be resolved by implementing the VPC Transit Gateway instances that are discussed later in this chapter.

AWS does not charge for VPC peer connections; however, standard data transfer charges still apply.

VPC peering between regions is supported and can be used, for example, for data replication and geographic proximity to reduce network latency. However, there are several limitations to be aware of when stretching a VPC peer between two different regions. Jumbo frames are not supported, so there is a basic maximum Ethernet frame size of 1,500 bytes that applies. However, jumbo frames are supported when peering inside a single region. You cannot use a security group in one region that references a security group in the other region. DNS resolution for private networks is supported across regions but must be enabled, as it is disabled by default.

It is a common architecture to create a central VPC for shared services. This allows you to create common resources in a single VPC and share them between the other VPCs, as shown in Figure 8.4.

The shared services VPC can be used as a central file sharing location to host management and monitoring applications such as Active Directory services or for a VPC you want to share with your customers but not allow the customers to see each other's data.

FIGURE 8.4   Shared resource VPC

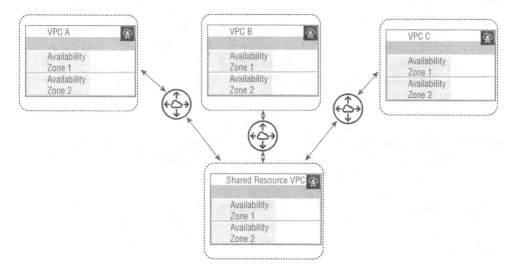

Multi-account VPC Sharing

VPCs can be shared between accounts and organizations by sharing management with AWS organizations and the Resource Access Manager. In this section, you will learn about how to accomplish sharing services in a VPC between accounts using the AWS PrivateLink service.

PrivateLink

In Chapter 7, "Connecting On-Premises Networks," you learned that the AWS PrivateLink service creates an internal direct connection from your VPC to AWS services outside of your VPC. Traditionally, when communicating with external sites, the traffic may traverse the public Internet, which exposes your data to the world when in transit and can introduce suboptimal routing, added latency, and jitter. PrivateLink does not allow this traffic to exit the AWS network and into the Internet. Instead, PrivateLink connects your private VPC subnets directly inside of the AWS network to select AWS services and allows you to use AWS security tools to control access to services running in your VPCs. Monthly costs may be reduced since there may no longer be a need for NAT gateways, firewalls, and data transfer charges if the VPC no longer requires Internet connectivity.

Since PrivateLink enables you to keep sensitive data internal to AWS, privacy concerns and regulatory requirements such as HIPAA, EU-US Privacy Shield, PCI, and other regulations can ensure compliance.

PrivateLink uses interface VPC endpoints to connect to services external from your VPC that are offered by AWS partner solutions in the AWS Marketplace at `https://aws .amazon.com/marketplace/privatelink`. PrivateLink provides private connectivity from your VPCs, AWS-Supported services, and on-premises networks.

The service creates internal, private connections from VPCs to AWS services that can be hosted by other AWS accounts or AWS Marketplace services. Since all traffic will remain inside of the AWS network, you do not need to use an Internet gateway, NAT device, AWS Direct Connect, or AWS site-to-site VPN connection. PrivateLink creates a VPC endpoint inside of your VPC, with a name tag of the service and subnet. An elastic network interface in the subnet that serves as an entry point for traffic destined to the service is created in your VPC. When you create your own VPC endpoint service, you can enable other AWS customers to access your service. Since PrivateLink network traffic never exits AWS to the public Internet, your in-transit traffic security is greatly enhanced. When using private IP CIDR blocks, traffic is not routable across the Internet. Security groups can be defined and attached to an endpoint policy to interface endpoints to manage service access policies. Since the traffic never exits to the Internet, there is no need to manage firewall rules, manage routing configurations, or add an Internet gateway to the VPC. Also, VPC peering is not a requirement to use PrivateLink.

Direct Connect connects your external on-premises networks to AWS where PrivateLink is an AWS internal connection to connect services and applications in one VPC, for example, a service offering from a service provider to their consumers' VPCs inside of an AWS region.

While this may sound like the same service as VPC peering, the difference is that VPC peering is used to securely interconnect VPCs. PrivateLink allows the capability to configure applications or services in VPCs as endpoints that your configured VPC peering connections can connect to.

PrivateLink is an AWS internal connection between VPCs to privately connect services and applications hosted in a VPC, usually by a service provider offering application services to customers, to other consumers' VPCs within an AWS region.

PrivateLink is generally used in client-server cases when multiple customers need to access a specific service or instance in a separate VPC. This is useful for providers offering a service to multiple customers. Customers can only initiate the connection into the service provider's VPC. Since PrivateLink uses Elastic Network Adapter interfaces in the customer's VPC, there are no overlapping subnets that the service provider must address. Also, you can access AWS PrivateLink endpoints via VPC peering connections, VPNs, and AWS Direct Connect.

AWS has integrated a very large number of services with PrivateLink that are updated at https://docs.aws.amazon.com/vpc/latest/privatelink/aws-services-privatelink-support.html.

VPC peering and Transit Gateway can be used in place of PrivateLink if direct layer 3 IP connections are required between VPCs.

To create and access services outside of your VPC using PrivateLink, you would create an interface VPC endpoint for the external service. This creates an elastic network interface (ENI) in your subnet that is assigned a private IP address. This is the entry point for traffic destined to the service.

When you need to share services over PrivateLink, you will create your own PrivateLink endpoint service and then enable your customers to access your service.

The PrivateLink endpoint configuration is in the VPC service of the AWS web console. In the left service pane, select Endpoints and then Create Endpoint as shown in Figure 8.5 for partner services and as shown in Figure 8.6 for AWS provided services.

Hub-and-Spoke VPC Architectures

The hub-and-spoke design is the most common topology used to connect multiple remote locations to one or more central locations such as a corporate data center, a third-party company, or a cloud provider over a wide-area network. Figure 8.7 shows a VPC hub-and-spoke architecture. The spoke locations all connect to the hub, and each spoke that communicates with other spokes must traverse the hub. The hub is the central interconnection location.

The hub-and-spoke, or star, wide-area networking model allows your organization to efficiently manage WAN connections by reducing the total number of carrier data circuits that would be required when using a mesh type of network.

The VPC hub model uses a central VPC to consolidate and centralize services such as Active Directory, DHCP, DNS, security, monitoring, and management applications.

FIGURE 8.5 PrivateLink VPC endpoint partner configuration

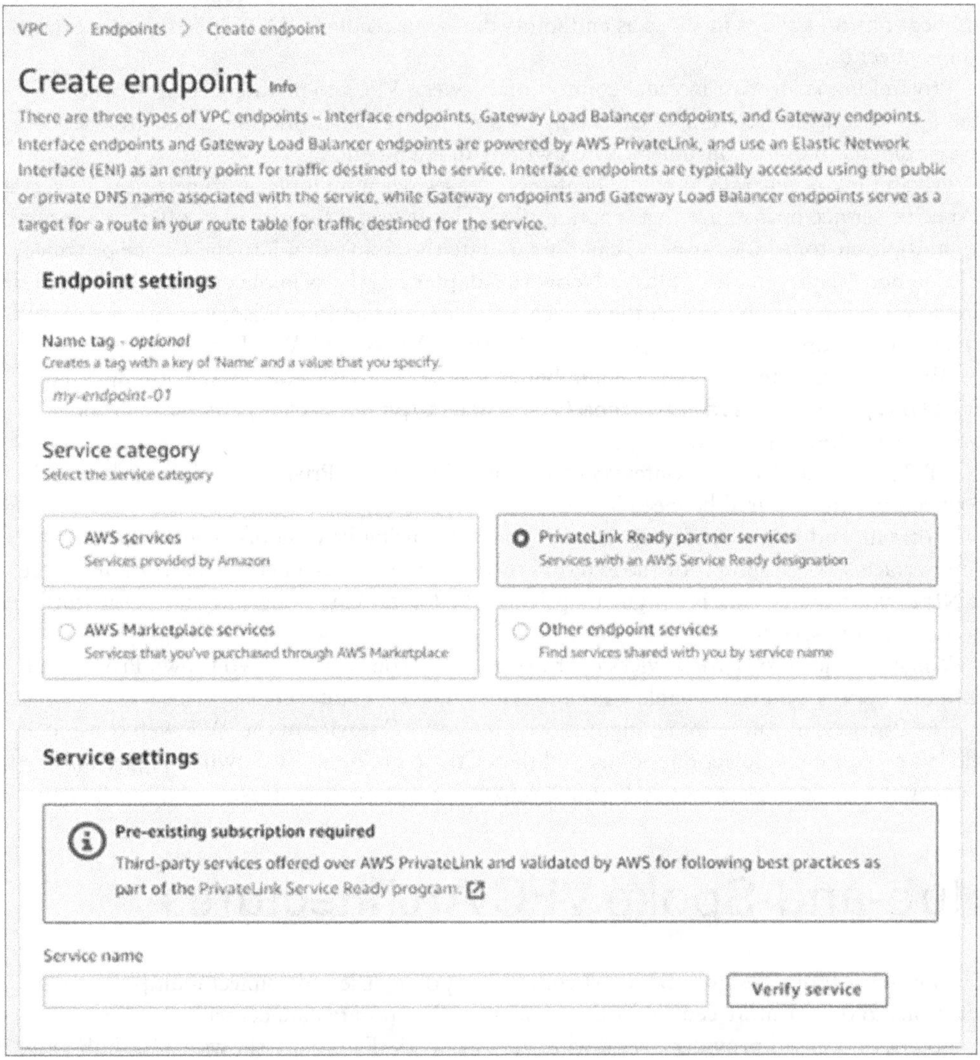

VPC > Endpoints > Create endpoint

Create endpoint Info

There are three types of VPC endpoints – Interface endpoints, Gateway Load Balancer endpoints, and Gateway endpoints. Interface endpoints and Gateway Load Balancer endpoints are powered by AWS PrivateLink, and use an Elastic Network Interface (ENI) as an entry point for traffic destined to the service. Interface endpoints are typically accessed using the public or private DNS name associated with the service, while Gateway endpoints and Gateway Load Balancer endpoints serve as a target for a route in your route table for traffic destined for the service.

Endpoint settings

Name tag - *optional*
Creates a tag with a key of 'Name' and a value that you specify.

    my-endpoint-01

Service category
Select the service category

○ AWS services
  Services provided by Amazon

● PrivateLink Ready partner services
  Services with an AWS Service Ready designation

○ AWS Marketplace services
  Services that you've purchased through AWS Marketplace

○ Other endpoint services
  Find services shared with you by service name

Service settings

(i) **Pre-existing subscription required**
Third-party services offered over AWS PrivateLink and validated by AWS for following best practices as part of the PrivateLink Service Ready program. ☐

Service name

[   ]   [Verify service]

In this section, you will learn about the most common AWS hub-and-spoke VPC architectural models including the Transit Gateway, Transit Gateway connect, and transit VPC.

Transit Gateway

The *Transit Gateway* is a virtual cloud routing service offering from AWS. The Transit Gateway is a regional service that is scalable and highly available and enables VPCs and on-premises networks to connect through a central hub over either site-to-site VPNs or

Direct Connect. The hub-and-spoke design allows any services connected to the gateway to talk to each other, which allows VPC-to-VPC routing in a region. The advantage of using a Transit Gateway instance is that only one connection needs to be made when adding new VPCs, VPNs, or on-premises networks, as shown in Figure 8.8. All traffic is routed at the Transit Gateway service. This allows for a single service to manage and monitor routing for the network.

FIGURE 8.6 PrivateLink VPC endpoint AWS Services configuration

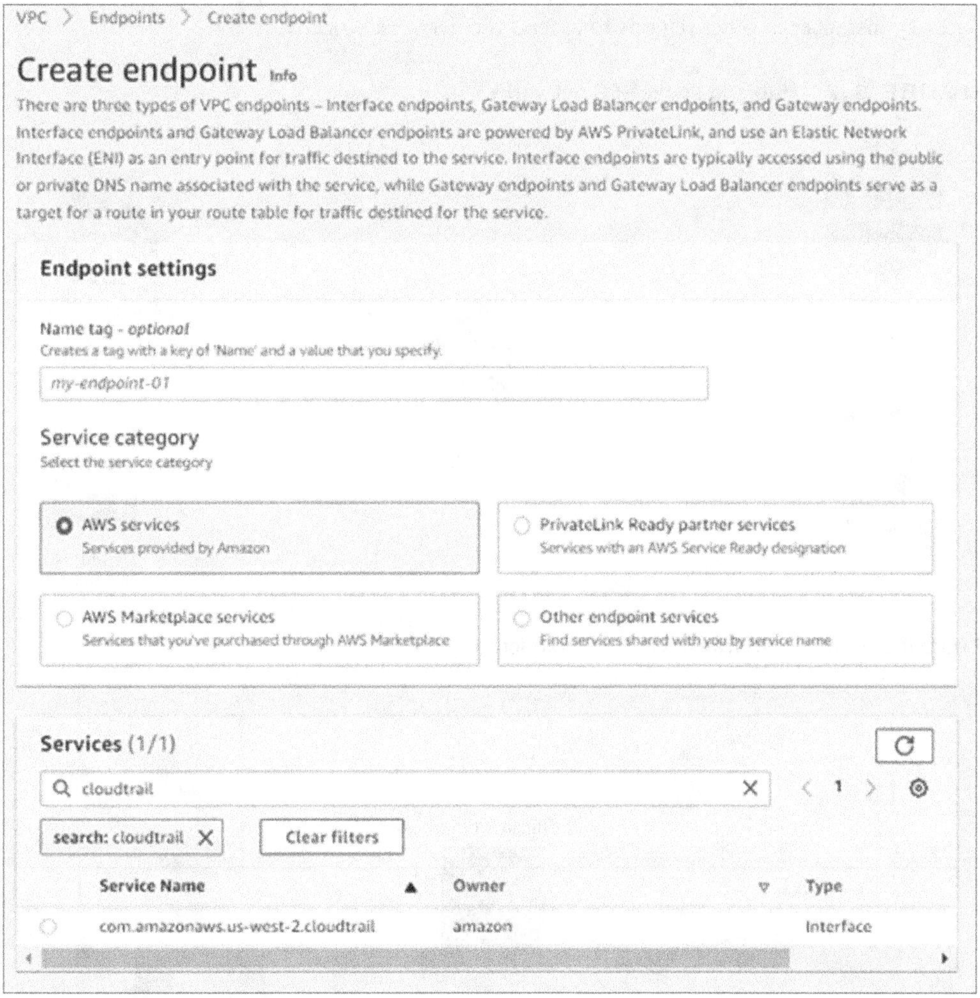

VPC > Endpoints > Create endpoint

Create endpoint Info

There are three types of VPC endpoints – Interface endpoints, Gateway Load Balancer endpoints, and Gateway endpoints. Interface endpoints and Gateway Load Balancer endpoints are powered by AWS PrivateLink, and use an Elastic Network Interface (ENI) as an entry point for traffic destined to the service. Interface endpoints are typically accessed using the public or private DNS name associated with the service, while Gateway endpoints and Gateway Load Balancer endpoints serve as a target for a route in your route table for traffic destined for the service.

Endpoint settings

Name tag - *optional*
Creates a tag with a key of 'Name' and a value that you specify.

| my-endpoint-01 |

Service category
Select the service category

⦿ AWS services	○ PrivateLink Ready partner services
Services provided by Amazon	Services with an AWS Service Ready designation

○ AWS Marketplace services	○ Other endpoint services
Services that you've purchased through AWS Marketplace	Find services shared with you by service name

Services (1/1)

| Q cloudtrail | ✕ | ‹ 1 › ⊚ |

| search: cloudtrail ✕ | Clear filters |

Service Name ▲	Owner	Type ▽
○ com.amazonaws.us-west-2.cloudtrail	amazon	Interface

The AWS Transit Gateway replaces VPC peering networks and reduces the complexity of establishing multiple VPC-to-VPC peering architectures. The Transit Gateway acts as a central virtual router where your VPC connects only once instead of having to establish many VPC peering connections. As you learned in Chapter 7, the Transit Gateway connects VPCs across regional boundaries and eliminates the need to create mesh networks to work around the limitation of VPCs not supporting transitive routing. Transit Gateway supports SD-WAN connections, peer-to-peer VPNs, and Direct Connections to connect your on-premises networks to the AWS cloud. The service is a highly scalable, AWS managed hub-and-spoke routing architecture. All spoke networks that are connected can route between each other in a single service offering to simplify the deployment, management, and monitoring of your network.

Transit Gateway instances residing in one region can be interconnected to other Transit Gateway instances in other regions to extend the network worldwide.

FIGURE 8.7 Hub-and-spoke VPC networks

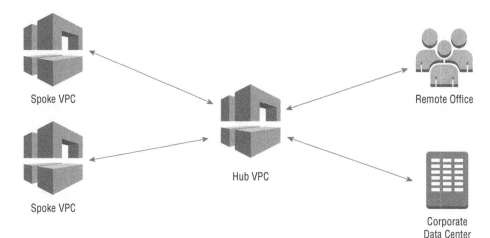

FIGURE 8.8 AWS Transit Gateway service

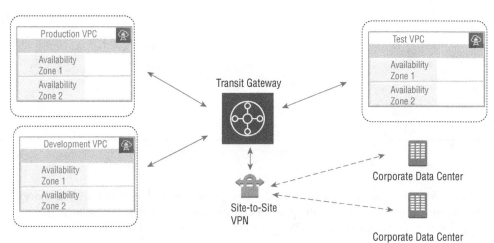

The Transit Gateway service allows you to manage connections across a large number, into the thousands, of VPCs while avoiding individual VPC peering connections. The Transit Gateway uses BGP to automatically update the routing table as networks are added or removed. Inter-region peering allows you to share common services such as DNS, Active Directory, and security services to your remote applications running in different AWS regions. New VPCs can be quickly added and removed with the service for fast responses to changes in your architecture. Multicasting is supported with Transit Gateway, and different multicast groups are supported that allow streaming of content using a one-to-many design, which is useful for streaming audio or video and for pushing software updates out to many devices simultaneously.

Identity and Access Management (IAM) is used to manage access into the Transit Gateway service, and users and groups can be applied to define access permissions. Automated provisioning is included with the service that automatically discovers site-to-site VPN connections and other remote networks connecting into your account. SD-WAN offerings from major vendors are also supported. These vendors offer preconfigured site-to-site VPNs to connect your remote networks into the gateway. The Gateway Network Manager utility gives you a complete view of your WAN including both AWS and on-premises networks. Comprehensive metrics are included in the monitoring capabilities.

The service uses BGP as its routing protocol for dynamic updates as networks are added or removed. Tunnels can be established using the Generic Routing Encapsulation (GRE) protocol. Multicast support is included, and different multicast groups can be used to deploy streaming audio, video, and software update content in one-to-many simultaneous data flows. Multicast is supported between VPCs but is not supported for Direct Connect; AWS site-to-site VPN endpoints, static multicast members, and IGMPv2 are all supported. The service works with both IPv4 and IPv6 using MP-BGP. There is a requirement that even if you are only routing IPv6 that IPv4 is used for the BGP peering connection and that the IPv6 prefixes are exchanged over IPv4 BGP peering using the MP-BGP protocol.

Network segmentation and isolation are provided by using multiple Virtual Router Forwarder (VRF) tables. Each VRF is a separate routing instance that supports multiple VPCs, and VPN connections associated with them, to create isolated networks. You can have multiple VRFs in each Transit Gateway. There remains a default routing table for un-assigned VPC, VPN, Direct Connect gateway, Transit Gateway connect, and Transit Gateway peered networks. Route prefixes are propagated using BGP, statics, or APIs from AWS for internal VPC networks. Transit Gateway routes do not populate the VPC route table; static routes must be created to send traffic to the Transit Gateway instance from your VPCs. When you peer Transit Gateways, route propagation is not supported, necessitating the use of static routes across the peering interconnections. For more information, see `https://docs.aws .amazon.com/vpc/latest/tgw/what-is-transit-gateway.html`.

Transit Gateway Connect

Transit Gateway Connect is a feature of the Transit Gateway service that integrates SD-WAN services to interconnect branch offices into the AWS cloud. AWS native SD-WAN support reduces the complexity and ongoing management of your wide-area network. The Transit Gateway Connect attachment creates an interconnection from the Transit Gateway service to services offered by AWS SD-WAN partners. Transit Gateway Connect uses two BGP peering sessions when connecting to AWS. The dual peer connections enable routing plane redundancy in case one peer is down due to maintenance or a network impairment. However, a single peer is allowed if desired.

Transit Gateway Connect integrates with the Transit Gateway Network Manager that allows you to view your network's performance by displaying network telemetry and metrics.

AWS partners with leading SD-WAN networking vendors for integration support and services. Vendors include Arista, Aruba, Alkira, Aryaka, Aviatrix, Cisco Systems, Citrix, Fortinet, Juniper, Palo Alto, Peplink, Silver Peak, Sophos, and Versa Networks. For details on each partner, reference the AWS Transit Gateway partner page at `https://aws.amazon.com/transit-gateway/partners`.

transit VPCs

The AWS *transit VPC* is used to create a global network transit hub that interconnects geographically separated remote networks and your VPCs. transit VPCs reduce the number of connections needed when interconnecting VPCs and remote networks by eliminating the need to create mesh connections between VPCs.

transit VPCs and Transit Gateway service instances have a lot in common with the difference being that Transit Gateway is an AWS service and the transit VPC is a network architecture.

The transit VPC acts as a central routed network hub to route traffic from your VPCs and on-premises networks. This hub supports networking features such as Network Address Translation (NAT) to address overlapping IP address blocks, packet inspection and filtering, cross-account connections, intrusion detection/prevention, and simplified integrated network management.

The architecture of a transit VPC is hub-and-spoke, where the transit is the hub and all the other VPCs and remote sites are the spokes that route through the hub. BGP is the common routing protocol, and the interconnects are IPSec-based VPNs. The transit VPN contains an EC2 compute instance running VPN software in the hub that is the overlay that performs the routing between the spoke VPCs. This enables VPC transitive routing and single regional support, which are limitations when using traditional VPC-to-VPC peer connections.

There are, however, limitations and potential downsides when implementing a transitive VPC architecture. You must absorb the cost of the EC2 instances needed to run the VPN applications. There is the VPN throughput limit of 1.25 Gbps per tunnel, which is a hard bandwidth limit. AWS does not manage the VPN service, so the configuration overhead becomes your responsibility. If you choose to implement a high-availability design, there will be a corresponding higher cost.

Wide-Area Networking

Wide-area networks are a key component in the AWS Advanced Networking objectives. We have touched on many different aspects of WANs so far in this book including Direct Connect, VPNs, BGP, and interconnecting VPCs over wide areas such as between AWS regions.

In this section, you will learn about some of the technology used in wide-area networks such as MPLS and SD-WANs.

These are not specific AWS services but are used behind the scenes when establishing WANs, and it is important for network engineers to understand these technologies.

Software-Defined Wide Area Networking

A software-defined wide-area network, or *SD-WAN*, is an automated, programmable wide-area network framework that can dynamically and securely route traffic based on network conditions, policies, or the priority of WAN circuits. The SD-WAN uses specialized SDN application technology to connect cloud, on-premises, and Internet sites that use automated, programmable functions that automate and manage your company's network connections and to enforce policies, manage security, and control costs.

The SD-WAN provides a single point of management, security monitoring, and visibility for your complete network that may comprise multiple WANs from different carriers.

AWS offers a managed SD-WAN as a service through its technology partners in the AWS Marketplace using its Transit Gateway Connect service covered earlier in the chapter.

WAN traffic is now able to automatically and dynamically be forwarded over the WAN path based on network conditions and defined policies such as application QoS requirements (low latency for voice, high bandwidth for video), security, circuit costs, or any other defined criteria. An example of the dynamic capabilities of an SD-WAN network would be where all your organization's Voice over IP (VoIP) traffic is sent over the company's MPLS network. However, if there is an impairment on that network, the SD-WAN Orchestrator can reroute the traffic over a 5G wireless or Internet connection. SD-WAN offers load balancing, congestion management, and forwarding over the lowest-cost paths.

While traditional WAN offerings usually have a fixed bandwidth capacity, SD-WAN services provide scalability and flexibility that can automatically adjust to traffic loads, network congestion, and outages. By implementing intelligent SD-WAN controllers, integrated security services, artificial intelligence monitoring your traffic flows, and dynamic real-time networking using automation can be achieved.

SD-WAN automates the operation of a WAN by decoupling the networking hardware from its control mechanisms. The SD-WAN is a virtualized WAN software layer that sits on top of your physical WAN network for a central point of control.

If your SD-WAN connections use the Internet as their transport, network performance cannot be guaranteed. However, using private MPLS VPN WAN services from service providers, your traffic will not traverse the Internet and comes with service-level agreements that define end-to-end performance metrics.

The SD-WAN architecture of an SD-WAN consists of the WAN edge, WAN gateway, SD-WAN controller, and SD-WAN orchestrator, as shown in Figure 8.9. The SD-WAN edge is either hardware or virtualized software that sits at the edge of the SD-WAN in central and remote enterprise locations, data centers, and cloud providers such as AWS. The SD-WAN edge connects multiple WAN connections, monitors link conditions, and determines how to route your traffic over the optimal link based on the current traffic conditions.

FIGURE 8.9   SD-WAN basic architecture

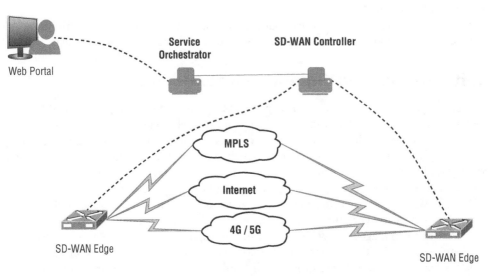

SD-WAN gateways provide access to the SD-WAN service and are a distributed network of gateways supplied by the SD-WAN service provider. The gateways are located at external locations that reduce back-haul traffic to your central site.

The SD-WAN orchestrator is the management tool for configuration, provisioning, and management operations.

The SD-WAN controller makes the forwarding decisions for each application flow in your network. The controller can reside in the orchestrator, in the SD-WAN gateway, on-premises, or hosted by an AWS SD-WAN partner.

The SD-WAN edge classifies incoming IP packets into application flows that are then grouped together. Once the traffic is classified, policies are applied to make SD-WAN traffic forwarding decisions. The classification process determines the route and performance requirements of each classification.

Multi Protocol Label Switching

Multi Protocol Label Switching (MPLS) is a networking architecture commonly used in telecommunications networks and has replaced traditional IP routing. Labels, or tags, are used to create a predefined path through the carrier's wide-area network.

MPLS networks are a common offering by service providers and telephone companies worldwide and are widely deployed and often the preferred WAN connectivity option.

Data is switched from node to node through the carrier's network from your source to destination using MPLS labels. MPLS uses predetermined paths using a label swapping push, pop, and swap method. This gives the operator significantly more flexibility and enables users to experience a greater SLA by reducing latency and jitter. RFC 3031 offers a good overview of MPLS.

MPLS is an encapsulation protocol that can be used by customers and managed service providers to establish a Direct Connect cross-connection from the AWS network to the existing enterprise WAN. Integrating AWS into existing customer MPLS networks prevents the enterprise from having to redesign its current WAN topology.

MPLS networks have several variants that support layer 3 (IP-based) or layer 2 (single broadcast domain) architectures. Layer 3 MPLS service provider networks implement routing inside their networks and appear to the customer as a WAN router. Layer 2 MPLS can be thought of as a distributed L2 Ethernet switch where the service provider forwards frames at layer 2 and does not participate in routing that is managed by the customer.

AWS does not directly offer an MPLS service. However, for the Advanced Networking exam, it is important that you understand the protocol as it is frequently used to interconnect customer networks with AWS Direct Connect facilities. However, the actual interconnect will still be Ethernet frames over a single-mode fiber connection.

The downsides of deploying MPLS networks are that they can be expensive to lease from the carriers, there are often long lead times to provision changes or add new locations, and long-term contracts are often required that may lock you into link speed commitments that make future topology changes difficult.

With traditional routing protocols, the routing tables are used to look up the next hop router to know where to send the packet based on the destination IP address. This operation is performed in every router in the path until the packet reaches its destination. Traditional routing requires each router to perform a header analysis at each hop that increases the processing needed in every router in the source-to-destination path. Since the route tables select the best path, some links may become congested, while others are lightly loaded or idle. This increases latency, degradation of throughput, and the potential for dropped packets. MPLS allows us to use traffic engineering in the routing of packets to utilize all paths available.

MPLS supports, as the name suggests, all network-layer protocols. The labels in the name tags are added to the top of the packet and are assigned when the packets enter the MPLS network. The packets are switched based on the labels and not the destination IP address. While MPLS supplements IP in the network, it does not replace it. The traffic is marked with the label and routed based on the assigned path to the destination. MPLS also has quality-of-service capabilities to identify traffic in the network, assign a classification, and forward traffic based on characteristics such as voice or video traffic taking precedence over web-based traffic. While IP routing is performed at each hop, label assignment and classification are performed only at the ingress router.

The key components of an MPLS network are the label edge router (LER) that performs the classification and assigns the label. Label switch routers (LSRs) are core routers in the network that switch packets based on the assigned MPLS label. Each router has a label information base (LIB) that maps incoming MPLS packets to outgoing interfaces. The end-to-end connection is the label switch path (LSP). There is a common protocol used called the Label Distribution Protocol (LDP). LDP communicates label information between MPLS-speaking neighbors to establish the LSP.

The Forwarding Equivalency Class (FEC) is a group of packets that require the same treatment over the same LSP. Packets are grouped based on either the IP address prefix, the host address, or quality of service markings. The FEC value assigned is then added to the label.

The LER receives the unmarked packet at the edge of the MPLS network, adds the MPLS label, and forwards the packet into the MPLS domain. The egress LER removes the label and delivers the packet to the external edge network.

The Label Switch Router (LSR) performs the backbone forwarding functions using label swapping. Each LSR examines the label at the top of the stack and references its LIB to find the outgoing path and the outgoing label to be used. The LSR removes the old label, attaches the new label, and forwards the packet on the predetermined path.

The LSP defines the path through the LSRs from the ingress point of the MPLS network to the egress router. All LSPs are unidirectional, so for each flow, there will be two paths, one in each direction. The LSPs do not need to take the shortest path in the routing table and can be assigned a predefined path using traffic engineering.

The MPLS label is fixed length at 32 bits and attached to each packet. The labels are local between two routers and not globally significant. Routers can have multiple labels in their tables referencing different connected routers and classes of service. The downstream, or originating, MPLS router creates the label value, binds it to the forwarding class, and informs the upstream router of the label binding value using the LDP protocol. The labels can be stacked to create a hierarchy where each packet can have several labels attached to it. This is useful when traffic crosses multiple networks allowing the packets to be tunneled through the intermediary networks.

MPLS route selection uses the LDP as the method of selecting an LSP for a particular flow. LDP is a defined set of procedures and messages that LSRs exchange to establish the LSP path. LPD can be either hop by hop or explicit. With hop by hop, each LSR independently selects the next hop, as is the mode of traditional IP routing, but without the processing overhead. Explicit routing is where a single router, which is usually the edge or ingress LER, specifies which LSRs the packet must traverse and is assigned as the packet enters the MPLS domain. By specifying the path, traffic engineering can be defined to explicitly specify the path you want the flow to traverse to its destination.

The LIB is a table in each LSR that contains the incoming label, the outgoing label, and prefix address.

MPLS forwarding works by using the underlay IP routed network to establish routes to destination networks just as traditional networks do. The LDP protocol creates labels to populate the LIB in each router. The ingress LER receives the incoming packet and adds the MPLS label to the frame. The LSRs then forward the labeled packets using label swapping. At the egress LER, the LER removes the MPLS label and delivers the standard Ethernet packet to the network attached to the MPLS domain.

Expanding AWS Networking Connectivity

AWS offers services that allow you to manage access into your cloud resources from outside accounts and authentication services. In this section, you will learn about AWS Organizations, which allows you to combine management and administration of multiple AWS accounts under a single administrative domain.

You will also review the Resource Access Manager service from AWS. This was covered in Chapter 7 and is used in configuring networking connections from one account to another.

Organizations

AWS Organizations is used to create and manage accounts, provision resources, manage security, govern access, centrally manage your accounts using policies, enforce compliance policies, control costs, consolidate billing, and configure AWS services over multiple accounts. AWS Organizations is an account management service that enables consolidating multiple AWS accounts into an organization that can be created and centrally managed. An organization is a collection of AWS accounts that are organized into a hierarchy for ease of management. The AWS Organizations service is available in all AWS regions worldwide and is a global service, meaning that accounts can reside in any region and be managed under a single organization. An organization is a single management location used to create new AWS accounts, link the existing accounts, and share resources among the accounts. It also allows you to centralize all your accounts logs and is a single point to set policies on how their AWS accounts will be managed. AWS Organizations is a no-charge offering, and users are only be billed for the resources utilized and consumed in each account.

By consolidating multiple accounts into a single organization, your company consolidates billing into a single payment for all your AWS accounts. Organizations can share and isolate resources between accounts, and the service centrally enforces security policies.

Each account is a container that contains your resources in AWS. The account structure allows you to create and manage AWS resources and provides administrative capabilities to use for access and billing.

There is added flexibility when a company creates multiple accounts and manages them with AWS Organizations, including billing boundaries, resource isolation, division of resources, and management of groups and teams.

The organization's management account is the master account used to create and administer the service. It allows you to create accounts, invite and manage invitations for other accounts to join your organization, and delete accounts from your organization. The management account is where you attach policies to entities such as root administrative accounts, organizational units (OUs), and other accounts within your organization, as shown in Figure 8.10. The management account is the master billing account for all accounts in the organization. It has ultimate control over the security settings, infrastructure operations, and financial policies that may be assigned. When you create the management account, you cannot change it later. Member accounts are all the accounts that are managed by the single management account in an organization. The administrator of the management account creates the member accounts by inviting existing accounts to join or by creating new accounts. Note that a member account is allowed to belong to only one organization. However, member accounts can be moved to other organizations by first removing them from the current organization and then migrating them to a different organization. The management account contains the administrative root. The administrative root sits at the top of the hierarchy and is used for all management activities such as creating organizational units. The OUs are used to group accounts. OUs are commonly used to group departments, business units, or application types such as security or monitoring together and allow all OU members to be managed as a single entity. OUs can be nested up to five deep for more granular functions such as development, test, and operations.

FIGURE 8.10   AWS organizations

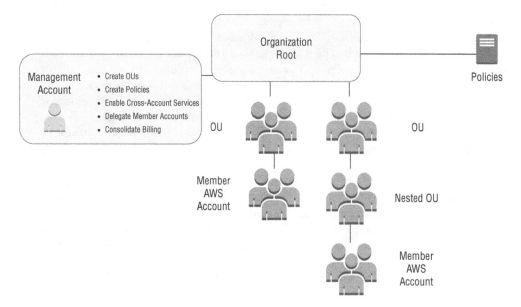

Organizations use policies to create controls that are applied to accounts. A policy is a document containing one or more rules. Standard policies are used for defining backups, tag keys with allowed values, how artificial intelligence services store and use content, and service control policies that we will discuss in this section. Policies can be applied at different levels in your OU hierarchy and flow downward. If you apply a policy at the root level, then that policy would be applied to all accounts in all OUs. However, if you apply a policy to a specific OU, then the policy would apply to all accounts contained in that OU including any nested OUs you may have created. A policy attached to one of the nodes in an organization's hierarchy flows down and affects all branches, OUs, and leaves. Accounts that are underneath policies are inherited from above and additive to policies at lower levels.

Service control policies (SCPs) are created to define and enforce what actions IAM users, groups, and roles can perform and are blocked from performing in the accounts in your organization that the SCP is applied to. SCPs are explicitly defined; if a right is not granted, it is by default denied. This works the same as IAM where an empty IAM policy is an implicit DENY. If you attach an empty SCP to an account, this is the same as attaching a policy that explicitly denies all actions. Permissions in an account that has an SCP attached are a combination of what the SCP allows and what is allowed explicitly in the permissions attached to the principal. For example, if an SCP applied to an account denies all S3 operations, then that account cannot manage S3. However, if the SCP permits S3 console operations, then the account would also have to configure rights and policies for S3 operations as if it were a non-organization–managed account. SCP allows the right for accounts to perform actions, but these actions still need to be defined in the account. When the organization account blocks access to a service or API action for a member account, a user or role in that account can't access any of the prohibited services or API actions, even if an administrator of a member account explicitly grants such permissions in an IAM policy. The organization account overrides all member accounts.

SCPs can be created and managed only at the root account, and any lower levels cannot modify, add, or delete SCPs. You can use the IAM policy simulator to test the effects of SCPs. The IAM policy simulator is helpful for analyzing effects of individual principals in an account.

To add an account into your organization, you must send out an invitation to the account owner to join. This can be issued only by the organization's management account and is extended to either the account ID or the email address that is associated with the invited account. When the invited account accepts the invitation, it then becomes a member account in the organization.

You can also send invitations to existing member accounts if you need to change from supporting only consolidated billing to supporting all features. Invitations work when accounts exchange handshakes, which is a multistep process of exchanging information between two parties. Handshake messages are passed between and responded to by the handshake initiator, which is the management account and the recipient or member account.

Resource Access Manager

As you learned in Chapter 7, the AWS Resource Access Manager (RAM) is an AWS management utility that allows you to share the AWS resources created in one AWS account and make it available to other AWS accounts.

You can create a resource in one account using the Resource Access Manager to make that resource usable in multiple other AWS accounts. This limits the duplication of resources in different accounts by sharing them using RAM.

RAM supports many different AWS resources including App Mesh, Amazon Aurora, AWS Private Certificate Authority, CodeBuild, EC2, EC2 Image Builder, Glue, License Manager, Migration Hub Refactor Spaces, Network Firewall, Outposts, S3 on Outposts, Resource Groups, Route 53, SageMaker, Service Catalog AppRegistry, Systems Manager Incident Manager, VPCs, and Cloud WAN. Additional resources are always being added. Check the online documentation for a current listing.

Authentication and Authorization

In this section, you will learn what authentication and authorization are and how they are used in AWS; then we will discuss some of the specific applications used in AWS to perform these functions.

Authentication is the method used to sign in to AWS or other systems using your login. Authentication is used to identify who you are, and based on this, you will be granted access to allowed services. It determines who is making the request, and authorization is what the user is allowed to do. Authentication is the combination of proving who the user is and that you are who you say you are.

The two primary methods used for access control are authentication and authorization. Open access to the public is called *anonymous access* and acts as "any access." If there are restrictions, which there almost always are, then a method is needed to identify who the user or service is, and based on that authentication, rights can be granted to permit or deny operations inside of AWS.

Authentication is accomplished when you sign in to your AWS account using an account created in the IAM service, which is usually a root user, IAM user, or role defined in IAM. Users have either usernames and passwords that are long-term credentials or a set of access keys.

Authentication verifies the identity of a user or service, and authorization determines the access rights used to protect systems and information.

For a user to authenticate from the AWS graphical web management console, you sign in using your username and password. There are other ways to authenticate such as with the AWS CLI or using an AWS API. The two primary methods here are to use access and secret keys or to use temporary credentials.

It is important to remember that IAM is both an authentication and authorization application. Once IAM determines who you are, you are granted access to approved services, which is the authorization process.

Authentication and authorization are the security systems that control all AWS API operations. Remember, all AWS console interactions use API calls even if you are working on a CLI, SDK, web console, or any other method to interface with AWS; underneath it is always an API call.

Once a user has been identified, *authorization* is used to determine what the identity is allowed to do and what it is restricted from doing. Authorization is defined in IAM and can be rather complex to configure and manage. IAM is beyond the scope of the Advanced Networking blueprint and is covered in the Security specialty certification. Authorization includes factors such as who is making the request, whether it is a user or other identity such as a software application, how the request was made, request data such as date and time, the source IP address, the operation that includes what operation is being requested, which service and policies are attached to the service, and which operations are allowed to be performed.

Security Association Markup Language

Security Association Markup Language (*SAML*) is used to simplify authentication services and allow for single sign-on operations.

SAML allows users to authenticate with the identity provider one time using a single set of credentials; they then get access to multiple applications and services without any additional sign-ins. SAML-enabled applications delegate authentication to an external identity provider (IdP), and AWS can automatically grant, revoke, or change a user's access to applications and services when an administrator adds, removes, or modifies the user's information in the IdP.

AWS offers SAML solutions to authenticate your internal users, outside contractors, and partners to AWS accounts and applications. SAML can be enabled for your mobile and web applications as well. It is a common user case to grant temporary access to services such as an S3 bucket to a user instead of having them log in to AWS.

The IAM SAML 2.0 identity provider is an entity in IAM that defines external IdP services that support the SAML 2.0 standard.

The IAM identity provider service is used to establish a trust relationship between an SAML-compatible IdP, such as Microsoft's Active Directory Federation Services and AWS. This enables users defined in Active Directory to access AWS resources with a single sign-on.

The identity federation establishes a trust relationship between AWS and an external system to authenticate users and receive the required rights to access AWS resources.

Once a user is authenticated, the IdP sends AWS a message, called an *assertion*, that contains the user's sign-in name and other attributes that IAM needs to create a user and to determine the AWS resources they are allowed to access.

Other identity applications in addition to SAML include Open ID Connect (OIDC) and OAuth 2.0.

Active Directory

Since most enterprises have existing Active Directory implementations, it is advantageous to integrate AD into AWS to simplify management and ongoing operations. The Microsoft *Active Directory* is a database and service used to connect users to network services and resources. The database, known as Active Directory, stores data about your environment including usernames and authentication and authorization credentials that manage user access and rights.

The domain controller is the Active Directory server that responds to authentication requests and stores a replica of the AD database. An AD site represents a physical or logical object that is defined in the domain controller. Every site is associated with an Active Directory domain that includes IP definitions for what IP addresses and blocks belong to that site. The domain controllers use this information to inform clients about proximity to the nearest domain controllers. The global catalog server is a Microsoft domain controller that stores partial copies of all forest Active Directory objects but stores a complete copy of all objects in the directory of your domain and a partial copy of all objects of all other forest domains.

The AD trust, or trust relationship, acts as a logical relationship established between Active Directory domains that allow authentication and authorization to shared services and resources. The Flexible Single Master Operation (FSMO) role in Active Directory is where critical updates are performed by the designated domain controller with a specific role and then get replicated to all the other DCs. These roles are assigned by the AD administrator to perform these tasks. You can also implement read-only domain controllers (RODCs). The read-only domain controllers hold a copy of the AD database and are used to respond to authentication requests, but applications or other servers cannot write to them.

Active Directory provides a centralized management application for Microsoft Windows computers and user administration. The AD architecture is a distributed hierarchical database for information about your IT infrastructure, containing configuration and management for users, user credentials, and access rights based on group memberships, DHCP, policy management, DNS zones and records, applications and devices, and application management.

AWS has multiple AD deployment options that meet different needs and use cases. These include the AWS Managed Microsoft AD, Active Directory on Amazon Elastic Compute Cloud, EC2 instances, and hybrid scenarios.

The AWS Active Directory service is an actual Microsoft Active Directory Server that is managed by AWS inside of the AWS cloud. Since it is a complete deployment of Active Directory running on a Windows server, you can manage all of the features and application integrations that AD supports. The service is fully managed by AWS, so you do not have to support the underlying server or manage backups, operating system, or application updates. AWS manages all the patching and software updates and automatic domain controller replacement. The managed service allows you to migrate AD-aware applications more easily into the AWS cloud by providing local directory services inside of AWS. The AWS Managed Microsoft AD comes in Standard and Enterprise editions. The editions have different storage capacities to fit your organization's size, and the Enterprise Edition also has multiregion support. In addition to user administration, the service supports access to the AWS management console and cloud services, connecting EC2 Windows instances to AD, managing Amazon RDS databases with Windows authentication, using FSx for Windows File Services, and using federated access in to productivity tools like Amazon Chime and Amazon WorkSpaces.

The AWS Managed Microsoft AD deploys a minimum of two domain controllers, each in a separate availability zone for high availability. The AWS managed domain controllers are not shared between accounts, so you have the complete server allocated to your account. However, Active Directory can share with any accounts or VPCs that you specify. Multiregion replication replicates your AD directory data across multiple regions. This puts directory services closer to your users for reduced latency and better performance.

Event logs can be exported to CloudWatch for integration with all other AWS service monitoring operations.

The AWS Active Directory service is a shared responsibility service where AWS manages the server, including the monitoring, firmware patch updates, backups, and recovery of domain controller instances should the virtual server fail.

Your responsibility is to administer Active Directory, including the users, groups, computers, and group policies using the Microsoft or add-on tools from all Windows computers joined to the Active Directory domain.

The replication service uses the native Microsoft AD replication tools. However, multi-region replication is only included in the Enterprise edition of the AWS Managed Microsoft AD service. See Table 8.1 for the differences between the Standard and Enterprise offerings.

TABLE 8.1   Standard vs. Enterprise

Edition	Storage Capacity	Approximate # of Objects	Approximate # of Users in Domain
Standard	1 GB	~30,000	Up to ~5,000 users
Enterprise	17 GB	~500,000	Over 5,000 users

The AWS Simple AD service is a lightweight directory service that is compatible with Active Directory. It can be used as a low-cost stand-alone alternative to a full Microsoft Active Directory deployment. Simple AD supports Samba 4 and Linux applications through LDAP directory services.

AWS also offers the Active Directory Connector (AD Connector) service that is a directory gateway proxy that redirects directory requests originating in AWS to your existing enterprise Active Directory deployment. The connector does not cache any data in AWS, and there is no trust or synchronization requirement for your AD user accounts. The connector can be used to sign in to AWS applications, such as Chime, WorkDocs, WorkMail, or WorkSpaces using corporate credentials stored in Active Directory.

If you choose to implement your own Active Directory service in your AWS account, there is the option of deploying Active Directory on an EC2 instance. This will not be managed by AWS, and you will be responsible for all server and Active Directory patching and maintenance.

All Active Directory services can be created and managed in the web console in the Security, Identity & Compliance section under Directory Services, as shown in Figure 8.11.

For a list of Active Directory services on AWS and feature differences, see the following resources:

```
https://docs.aws.amazon.com/whitepapers/latest/active-directory-
domain-services/directory-services-options-in-aws.html
https://docs.aws.amazon.com/directory-service/index.html
https://aws.amazon.com/directoryservice
```

FIGURE 8.11   AWS Directory Service configuration screen

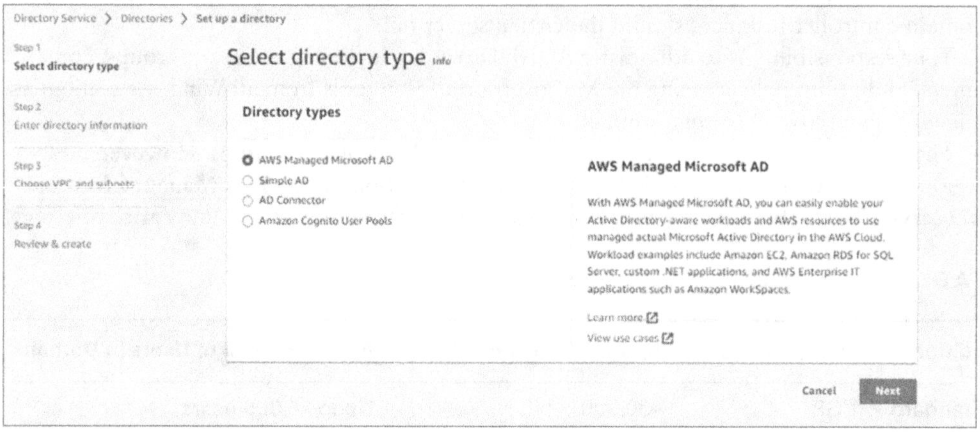

Summary

This chapter on inter-VPC and multi-account networking was a continuation of the previous chapter on hybrid networks. You learned about how to interconnect and access VPCs both inside and between accounts including VPC sharing, peering, and PrivateLink.

Common VPC network architectures were presented including the Transit Gateway, Transit Gateway Connect, and transit VPCs.

WAN was included as a refresher for the exam, and the specific topics of SD-WAN and MPLS were presented as network access technologies into the AWS cloud.

There are many higher-level issues that must be addressed beyond just interconnecting VPCs in your cloud deployment. To create, manage, and monitor inter-VPC and multi-account networks in AWS, management tools such as AWS Organizations and the Resource Access Manager are used. You learned about these services, their architecture, and how they can be used to manage your interconnected AWS networks.

Securing and controlling who can access your accounts is a critical concern in all networks, including multi-account networks where external entities may be allowed to access your VPC resources. The two primary methods used for access control are authentication and authorization, and you learned the differences and the functions they deliver. Specific authentication and authorization implementations were introduced, including the Security Association Markup Language, which is used to authenticate with an identity provider one time using a single set of credentials to enable single sign-on. The most prominent access control application is Active Directory services from Microsoft. AD is a database and service used to connect users to network services and resources. Active Directory stores data about your environment including usernames and authentication and authorization credentials that manage user access and rights.

Exam Essentials

Understand in detail the networking services options that are available for interconnecting VPCs. One of the most critical topics to understand for the Advanced Networking exam is how to access, interconnect, and manage VPCs. Know the topics presented in this chapter including how to share and peer VPCs and manage multi-accounts. Know that VPC sharing connects resources from multiple accounts and groups them into a common, shared network. Sharing VPCs uses internal AWS network links for added security and sharing of resources. VPC peering enables two or more VPCs to access resources in each VPC from the other. The AWS VPC peering service has no bandwidth limitations, and there is no single failure point.

Know the AWS services available for VPC sharing and managing multi-VPC deployments. VPCs can be shared between accounts by sharing management between accounts with AWS Organizations and the Resource Access Manager.

Be able to explain hub-and-spoke architectures. The Transit Gateway is a regional service that is scalable and highly available and enables VPCs and on-premises networks to connect through a central hub over either site-to-site VPNs or Direct Connect. The hub-and-spoke design allows any services connected to the gateway to talk to each other, which allows VPC-to-VPC routing in a region.

The transit VPC is used to create a global network transit hub that interconnects geographically separated remote networks and your VPCs. transit VPCs reduce the number of connections needed when interconnecting VPCs and remote networks by eliminating the need to create mesh connections between VPCs.

transit VPCs and Transit Gateways have a lot in common with the difference being that Transit Gateways are an AWS service and the transit VPC is a network architecture.

Know the details of WANs. Know what software-defined wide-area networking is and how it is used in modern wide-area networks. Understand that the SD-WAN provides a single point of management, security monitoring, and visibility for your complete network that may comprise multiple WANs from different carriers.

While MPLS is not an AWS service, you may see this WAN technology as part of a network access question. Know that MPLS is a networking architecture that replaces traditional IP routing. Labels, or tags, are used to create a predefined path through the carrier's network instead of IP next-hop routing that uses protocols such as OSPF, IS-IS, or BGP. Data is switched node to node through the carrier's network from your source to destination using MPLS labels.

Understand what authentication and authorization is and how it is implemented. Authentication and authorization are critical components in AWS. Understand at a deep level that they are used to grant users access to network resources. Know that SAML is used for single sign-on, and learn the different AWS implementations of Active Directory.

Exercises

1. Read and review the AWS VPC sharing documentation:

    `https://docs.aws.amazon.com/vpc/latest/userguide/vpc-sharing.html`

2. Read and review the AWS VPC peering documentation:

    `https://docs.aws.amazon.com/vpc/latest/userguide/vpc-peering.html`

3. Read and review the Transit Gateway Service documentation:

    `https://aws.amazon.com/transit-gateway`

    `https://aws.amazon.com/transit-gateway/faqs`

4. Read and review the AWS PrivateLink documentation:

    `https://docs.aws.amazon.com/whitepapers/latest/building-scalable-secure-multi-vpc-network-infrastructure/aws-privatelink.html`

    `https://aws.amazon.com/privatelink/features`

5. Know the details of the AWS Organizations service:

    `https://docs.aws.amazon.com/organizations`

6. Understand the Resource Access Manager service:

    `https://aws.amazon.com/ram`

7. Understand the AWS Active Directory services, their use cases, and how they are implemented:

    `https://aws.amazon.com/directoryservice`

Review Questions

The following questions are designed to test your understanding of this chapter's material. For more information on how to obtain additional questions, please see this book's introduction.

1. A group of developers in your Dublin office needs to access the AWS management console in your account. How can you provide access for each developer without having to create a separate IAM account for each developer?

    A. Implement VPC peering from the developer VPC into yours

    B. Add console rights for the Dublin developers into your AWS authorization account permissions table

    C. Use your on-premises SAML 2.0 identity provider

    D. Modify the VPC network ACL to allow access for the developers based on their authentication credentials

2. Carol is asking for help locating a single AWS utility that will enable her to access a single management location used to create new AWS accounts, link the existing accounts, and share resources among the accounts. Which service would you recommend she implement?

    A. Organizations

    B. Cognito

    C. AWS Authentication

    D. Macie

    E. Secrets Manager

3. Your finance and accounting manager has been reviewing the company's AWS spending and is asking you to reduce service duplication between the development, test, and production accounts. What tool could you use to consolidate your AWS services and share them between the three groups?

    A. Deploy MPLS and consolidate the multiple private link services

    B. Implement Active Directory Connector for federated access

    C. Use the Resource Access Manager tool

    D. Deploy a SAML 2.0 identity service provider

    E. Use the AWS Transit Gateway service

4. Many of your WAN links are underutilized, and certain company traffic flows are experiencing network jitter. You are looking for a technology that you can implement that offers a single point of control to optimize your backbone network. What technology would you explore to meet your needs?

    A. OSPF

    B. eBGP

    C. MPLS

    D. SD-WAN

    E. CloudWatch

5. You have been tasked to simplify your AWS Organizations structure in preparation for a new Service Control Policy rollout. Which technique would you use to accomplish this?

   A. Organizational units

   B. Simple Directory Services

   C. Workflow services

   D. Cloud HSM

6. You want to give your development and test teams the ability to share IP subnets between each other for less duplication of resources, such as EC2 instances, while allowing the application owners to continue to manage their own resources, security, and account structure. The requirement is for each VPC account owner to create, manage, and delete their own VPC resources but not in the other group's VPC that they do not manage. What would you implement to achieve the requirements?

   A. Cloud Connect

   B. VPC sharing

   C. Direct Connect

   D. Site-to-site VPN

7. Your company's AWS Organizations account is being audited by an outside security and compliance provider. They are asking you to implement restrictions assigned at the Organizations root level to block lower-level organization member accounts from implementing any Redshift services. What could you do to create a global policy that prohibits creating any Redshift services and apply it to all accounts in your organization?

   A. Service control policies

   B. IAM policies

   C. Label service policies

   D. Create the restrictions in Active Directory and apply it to all groups

8. You need to connect your SAN service provider's SD-WAN to access your AWS cloud services. You have implemented the AWS Transit Gateway service. What additional steps would you need to take to integrate the SD-WAN service?

   A. Implement VPC peering

   B. Use the Kinesis data pipeline

   C. Use the Transit Gateway attachment

   D. Deploy CloudFront

9. Due to federal governance restrictions, your sensitive customer data is not allowed to traverse the public Internet when in transit between certain AWS hosted applications. You need to interconnect two private VPCs in the Osaka region. What AWS network interconnect option would you use to meet these requirements?

   A. CloudWatch

   B. CloudTrail

   C. Direct Connect

   D. PrivateLink

10. What is the function of assigning user rights to resources?

   A. Authorization

   B. Cognito

   C. Authentication

   D. Step functions

11. MPLS networks are a common offering by service providers and telephone companies world-wide and are widely deployed and often the preferred WAN connectivity option. Which nodes are used in the core to forward frames based on label information?

   A. LER

   B. LSR

   C. LDP

   D. LSP

   E. LIB

12. You are investigating ways to connect your VPCs with three external business partners that also use AWS as their preferred cloud provider. What options can be considered to interconnect these accounts' VPC integrations? (Select two.)

   A. Organizations

   B. MPLS

   C. Resource Access Manager

   D. Kinesis Firehose

   E. Route 53

13. You have been tasked with establishing a logical relationship between your corporate and AWS Active Directory deployments to enable authentication and authorization services in a consolidated database. What service could you implement to achieve this objective?

   A. Implement Simple AD

   B. Establish an AD trust

   C. Read-only domain controllers

   D. Flexible Single Master Operation role

14. Jill has accessed her federated Active Directory servers and has been granted permissions to write to a SQL database in the AWS Milan region. What is the process that granted her the permissions to access the database?

   A. RDS

   B. Authentication

   C. Elastic Beanstalk

   D. Authorization

15. You want to create a hub for your VPC that connects your global networks. You have been tasked to keep VPC interconnections to a minimum and consider the ease of future VPC expansions. Which service would you investigate to meet this objective?

   A.   Transit Gateway

   B.   MPLS

   C.   Hub-and-spoke

   D.   AD Connector

   E.   AWS Global Accelerator

16. You are investigating upgrading your network to add real-time intelligence to route around impairments and manage traffic flows during times of congestion. You want the WAN traffic to automatically and dynamically be forwarded over the path based on network conditions and defined policies such as application QoS requirements (low latency for voice, high bandwidth for video), security, circuit costs, or any other defined criteria. What network technology would meet this requirement?

   A.   MPLS

   B.   SD-WAN

   C.   EIGRP

   D.   Intermediate system to Intermediate system

   E.   BPDU

17. What is the function of identifying a user entering your AWS cloud applications?

   A.   SWF

   B.   Cognito

   C.   Authentication

   D.   Organizational unit ID

   E.   Authorization

18. Which protocol enables applications to delegate authentication to an external identity provider so that AWS can automatically grant, revoke, or change a user's access to applications and services when an administrator adds, removes, or modifies the user's information in the IdP?

   A.   SAML

   B.   LDAP

   C.   AWS KMS

   D.   IAM

19. A basic user database needs to be created in the Stockholm region as a central source of user-names and which services they are granted based on their credentials. You are looking for a low-cost alternative to a full-featured user database. Which would be a good option?

   A.   Implement Simple AD

   B.   Establish an AD trust

   C.   Read-only domain controllers

   D.   Flexible Single Master Operation role

20. As an AWS solutions architect specializing in networking, you have been asked to trouble-shoot an issue where your private development and test VPCs are inter-connected with a peer connection and the test and production VPCs are peer interconnected to each other. The developers need to access an online development portal hosted by another cloud provider that uses the Internet gateway attached to the PROD VPC. What could be the issue prevent-ing developers from accessing their Internet-based tools?

   A. There is no route back to DEV in the PROD VPC

   B. The NAT gateway is missing

   C. The routing table in the TEST VPC needs statics assigned to PROD and DEV

   D. There is a nontransitive issue in the TEST VPC

   E. The security groups need to be modified to allow access to the Internet from the DEV PPC

20.

A.

C.

E.

Chapter

9

Hybrid Network Routing and Connectivity

THE AWS CERTIFIED ADVANCED NETWORKING - SPECIALTY EXAM OBJECTIVES COVERED IN THIS CHAPTER MAY INCLUDE, BUT ARE NOT LIMITED TO, THE FOLLOWING:

✓ **Domain 3: Network Management and Operations**

- Task Statement 3.1: Maintain routing and connectivity on AWS and hybrid networks.

Industry-Standard Routing Protocols Used in AWS Hybrid Networks

When creating a hybrid network with AWS, a standards-based routing protocol is required for interoperability between customer networks and AWS. You must use a routing protocol that is designed specifically to interconnect different accounts, or autonomous systems, together. The industry-standard routing protocol that is used in AWS hybrid networks is the Border Gateway Protocol (BGP), the protocol used to exchange network reachability information between your on-premises network and the Amazon cloud, which is typically to a VPC. BGP can be used for an organization's internal routing in which case it's referred to as the internal Border Gateway Protocol (iBGP). When two different entities, which are referred to as *autonomous systems*, interconnect their networks, the routing protocol used is external Border Gateway Protocol (eBGP). AWS has documented vendor configuration examples at https://docs.aws.amazon.com/vpn/latest/s2svpn/cgw-dynamic-routing-examples.html that have been tested and validated for the interconnections.

Amazon also supports the use of static routing, where routes are manually configured, and no dynamic routing protocol is required at the interconnection point. A static route is manually configured in the interconnected routers and is not learned through a dynamic routing protocol. Static routes are typically used when there is a need for a specific path to be taken for a specific destination, regardless of any other routing information that may be available.

Optimizing Routing

In this section, you will learn about ways to optimize routing inside of, and into, the AWS cloud. Optimization can improve performance, increase availability, improve security, and lower the cost of your network and AWS deployment. A number of tools, techniques, and best practices can help with optimization.

- Optimization is achieved by adjusting configuration parameters in various services such as the AWS Route 53 DNS service by taking advantage of its advanced routing policies to route traffic to the most optimal endpoints in your network.

- Content delivery networks such as CloudFront push content to worldwide edge locations for better response times to a globally dispersed client base.

- The AWS Global Accelerator utilizes the AWS high-bandwidth global network instead of traffic having to traverse the Internet to get to AWS services.

- Using Direct Connect bypasses the public Internet and uses a private connection to provide a reliable and secure connection.

- PrivateLink is used for private access to AWS services and VPC endpoint services over a private IP address and for all traffic to remain inside of the AWS network.

- AWS elastic IP addresses improve availability and allow you to assign a static IP address to your resources to improve availability.

- VPC peering and VPC endpoints can be implemented for inter-VPC communications inside of AWS to privately access services in an Amazon VPC without requiring a NAT gateway, VPN, or Direct Connect connection.

- The Transit Gateway is used to connect multiple VPCs, on-premises networks, and remote networks to a single gateway, which allows you to reduce costs and simplify the management of the network.

When you implement these best practices, routing is optimized to improve the performance, scalability, and security of your network infrastructure.

Optimizing Dynamic Routing

BGP route selection may not always be the optimal path to the destination as the protocol does not take into consideration latency, congestion, or jitter. As a result, your traffic may be routed over a suboptimal path. The path that BGP chooses may need to be overwritten with a better path. Path selection can be prioritized based on speed, latency, or cost. You may want to favor one ISP over another based on these metrics.

In Chapter 1, "Edge Networking," and Chapter 8, "Inter-VPC and Multi-Account Networking," software-defined wide-area networking (SD-WAN) was discussed, and you learned that SD-WAN offers automated dynamic routing. The AWS Cloud WAN is a single point of routing control that provides a single dashboard for monitoring and event displays. Cloud WAN offers dynamic routing that can be integrated with SD-WAN vendors such as Cisco, DXC, VMware Fortinet, and others in the AWS Marketplace.

Route 53 has DNS policy extensions that enable you to effect routing based on multiple criteria that you specify. When you create a record in Route 53, you choose the routing policy, which determines how Route 53 responds to queries including active-passive failover, geolocation that routes traffic based on the location of your users, and geo-proximity routes traffic based on the location of your resources that can shift traffic from resources in one location to resources in another. Latency-based forwarding directs traffic to the AWS region that provides the lowest latency from the user's location. When you want Route 53 to respond to DNS queries with up to eight healthy A records selected at random, use the multivalue routing policy. The weighted routing policy is used to route traffic to multiple resources based on weighted percentages that you specify in the configuration.

By optimizing dynamic routing in your enterprise and AWS, networks can help to improve the efficiency, scalability, and availability of your network. By using a combination of dynamic routing protocols, you can ensure that traffic is routed to the best possible destination, improving performance and reducing the risk of network congestion. The AWS Well-Architected Framework series of documents provides years of accumulated knowledge that is a valuable reference. This includes the performance efficiency pillars for network architecture selection at `https://docs.aws.amazon.com/wellarchitected/latest/performance-efficiency-pillar/networrk-architecture-selection.html`.

Optimizing Static Routing

AWS allows you to use static routing to optimize network routing. Static routing is a routing method where the network administrator manually enters the routing information into the routing table in place of using a dynamic routing protocol such as BGP. By using static routing, you can ensure that traffic is routed to the best possible destination and this improves the efficiency, scalability, and security of your network; enhances performance; and reduces the risk of network congestion.

Static routes are configured using the `ip route` command in most common router command parsers.

The command takes the following syntax:

```
ip route destination-network mask {next-hop-address | interface}
[administrative-distance]
```

For example, the following command configures a static route to the network 192.168.50.0/24, with a next hop of 172.16.1.1:

```
ip route 192.168.50.0 255.255.255.0 172.16.1.1 250
```

This command instructs the router that, if a packet has a destination IP address in the 192.168.50.0 subnet, it should forward it out its egress interface that is connected to 172.16.1.1 if it has the lowest administrative distance. Static routes are configured using the web interface, APIs, the CLI, or SDKs.

In a dynamic routing environment, static routes should be used as a last resort, since they can become stale or out-of-date quickly, and if they are not updated, they can cause routing loops or traffic blackholes. The configuring and maintaining many static routes can become a time-consuming and error-prone process, and dynamic routing protocols like OSPF or BGP are more appropriate.

Static routing configuration examples are available in various AWS documentation including how to set up static routing over a site-to-site VPN at `https://docs.aws.amazon.com/vpn/latest/s2svpn/cgw-static-routing-examples.html`.

Route Priorities and Administrative Distance

The administrative distance applies a priority value to a prefix in the routing table relative to other routing protocols that may be running on the router. A static route's administrative distance configuration is an optional value that is used to determine the trustworthiness of the route. The lower the administrative distance, the more trustworthy the route. The default administrative distance for a static route is 1, which is the most trustworthy of all routes except for directly connected interfaces, which have a value of either 0 or 1 depending on the router vendor. Direct Connect routes are preferred over site-to-site VPN routes. So, if the eBGP routes have a lower administrative distance of 200, they would take priority over the static with a higher administrative distance of 250. Using a static route to back up a dynamic route is achieved by assigning a higher administrative distance that is referred to as a *floating static route*. Should the eBGP route go away, then the static may have the lowest administrative distance and be installed in the route forwarding table.

Route Summarization

AWS route summarization is a useful technique to reduce the number of route entries in the routing table by using a single, larger subnet instead of many smaller routing entries. Summarization reduces the number of routes that are advertised and stored in the routing table but does not affect reachability. Route summarization is often referred to as *route aggregation*.

Summarization is supported by either dynamic or static routing. Route summarization is implemented using the AWS web management console, APIs, the command-line interface (CLI), or SDKs, all of which make it easy to configure and manage route summarization.

Route summarization groups multiple contiguous subnets into a single, larger subnet, known as the *summary route*. By implementing summarization, the number of routes that need to be advertised and stored in the routing table is reduced, making the network more efficient and reducing the risk of routing loops.

An example of how route summarization works is to consider a block of IP addresses in use in your VPC that are in the 10.10.x.x range. You may have many subnets assigned in your availability zones using smaller chunks of this address space. For example, AZ-A may use the 10.10.1.x through 10.10.49.x blocks, AZ-B has 10.10.50.x through 10.10.99.x, AZ-C has 10.10.100.x through 10.10.149.x, and AZ-D has 10.10.150.x through 10.10.199.x. You also have the address space of 10.10.200.x through 10.10.255.x set aside for future expansion. The standard approach would be to advertise each of these subnets using a mask of 25.255.255.0, or /24, into the routing table, which would create up to 255 address blocks, or, as they are commonly called, *prefixes*. This would be inefficient and consume route table entries. An alternative, by using route summarization, would be to advertise 10.10.0.0 /16. This tells your remote routers that if they have a destination IP address of any device from 10.10.0.0 through 10.10.255.254 to send it to this VPC, and the local routing will know the more specific subnets to forward the packet to. Since all of your prefixes are a subset of the 10.10.0.0 /16 summarization, all packets in the 10.10.x.x range would be forwarded to your router, which would then have the more specific subnets in its route forwarding table and know how to deliver the packet to the correct subnet in your VPCs.

The AWS routed network, and all other routers, will select the route in its forwarding table that has the most specific prefix to determine the next hop for a packet. For example, if a route table has two routes to the same destination prefix, one with a /24 prefix and another with a /16 prefix, the /24 prefix route will be used. 10.10.16.0 /24 is a better, or more specific, route than a table entry of 10.10.0.0 /16. This is often called the *longest match wins* route selection. This means that the route with the longer prefix will be chosen.

Route Propagation

A data packet originating from inside your VPC, for instance, a EC2 server, with a destination IP address outside of the subnet, the VPC routing table is consulted to determine where to forward the traffic. If the destination IP address of the packet matches the CIDR block of a route, the traffic is directed to the target specified in that route. If there is no route match, the traffic is either dropped or sent out a default gateway interface.

Routing tables are referenced to determine where to forward traffic to its destination network. Each VPC has a default routing table, and custom route tables can also be created to control the traffic flow of your VPC. There are multiple ways to populate the table with the routes in your network including using a dynamic routing protocol such as BGP, static routes, or importing routes using route propagation.

Route propagation allows a virtual private gateway to automatically import routes into the route tables. There is no need to manually enter external routes into your route tables. By enabling route propagation, the routes are automatically populated.

Route propagation is the process of advertising network reachability information between routers. In BGP, you will advertise your networks to the peer by using route propagation in different autonomous systems (ASs). In AWS, BGP route propagation is used to control the flow of traffic between your VPC and your on-premises data centers, or other VPCs in your AWS accounts.

Figures 9.1, 9.2, and 9.3 show the basic steps to enable route propagation on a gateway in a VPC. For more specific route propagation configuration information, reference the examples in the AWS VPC documentation for the options and steps for your specific use case.

FIGURE 9.1   Edit VPC route

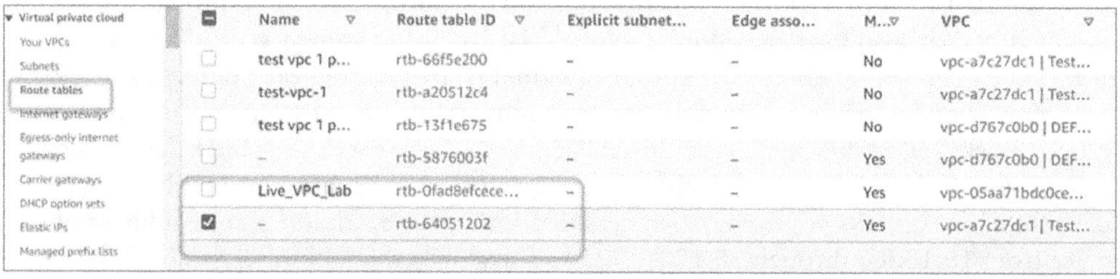

		Name	Route table ID	Explicit subnet...	Edge asso...	M...▽	VPC
▼ Virtual private cloud	☐						
Your VPCs							
Subnets	☐	test vpc 1 p...	rtb-66f5e200	--	--	No	vpc-a7c27dc1 | Test...
Route tables	☐	test-vpc-1	rtb-a20512c4	--	--	No	vpc-a7c27dc1 | Test...
Internet gateways	☐	test vpc 1 p...	rtb-13f1e675	--	--	No	vpc-d767c0b0 | DEF...
Egress-only internet gateways	☐	--	rtb-5876003f	--	--	Yes	vpc-d767c0b0 | DEF...
Carrier gateways	☐	Live_VPC_Lab	rtb-0fad8efcece...	--	--	Yes	vpc-05aa71bdc0ce...
DHCP option sets							
Elastic IPs	☑	--	rtb-64051202	--	--	Yes	vpc-a7c27dc1 | Test...
Managed prefix lists							

Overlapping Routes

It's important to have a well-planned and organized routing structure to avoid overlapping routes, as this can lead to unexpected traffic flows and potential security issues. With proper management, you can ensure that traffic is routed to the correct destination, improving network performance and security.

FIGURE 9.2   Route table configuration

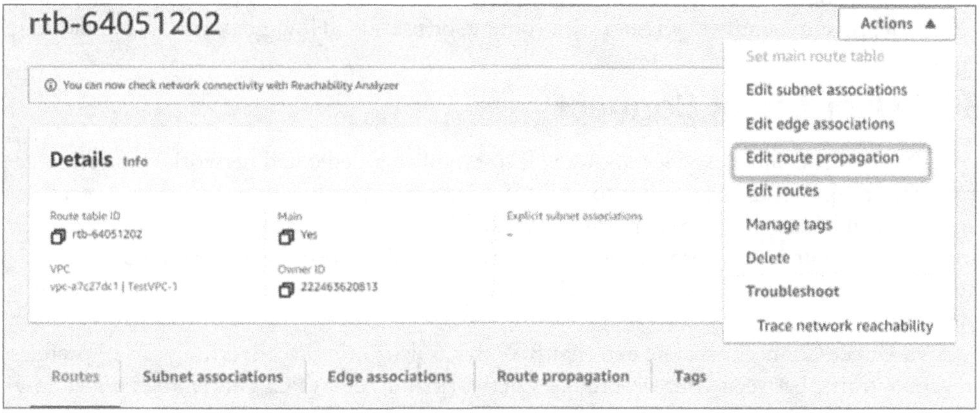

FIGURE 9.3   Enabling route propagation

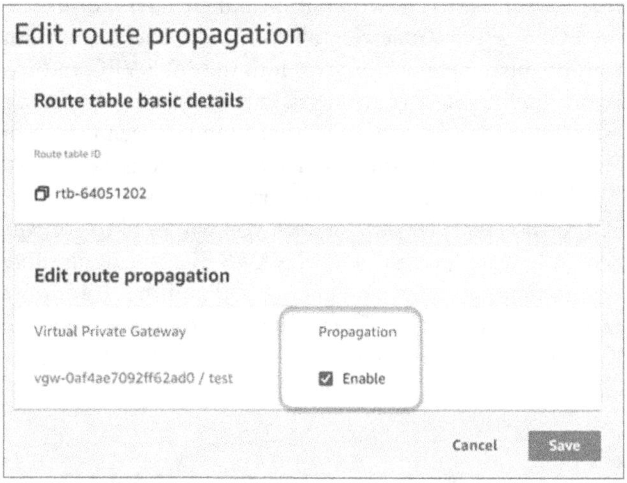

Overlapping routes occur when two or more separate routes in a route table have the same destination prefix. This can happen when you have multiple route tables advertising the same prefix or when you use VPC peering and each VPC was assigned the same block of IP addresses.

If you are experiencing issues with overlapping routes and subnets, you must resolve the issue to be able to route to those prefixes. You cannot traverse the routing process between two interfaces with the same subnet on each end. IP address blocks must be unique for proper routing to occur. You may need to re-address the duplicate subnets to rectify the issue. Another alternative is to implement a NAT device to translate the IP address block and basically hide the block from the rest of the network.

To help troubleshoot overlapping address blocks, you can review the individual VPC addressing configuration and identify duplicate addresses, use CloudWatch to monitor your VPC network and identify any issues with routing, or use VPC Flow Logs for troubleshooting.

BGP Over Direct Connect

The AWS Direct Connect service allows you to establish a dedicated network connection from your on-premises data center to an AWS Direct Connect location. By using Direct Connect, you bypass the public Internet and establish a more reliable and secure connection between your on-premises infrastructure and your AWS resources. Direct Connect was covered in detail in Chapter 6, "Hybrid Networking," when you learned about hybrid connectivity.

AWS Direct Connect uses the external BGP dynamic routing to advertise your IP prefixes and route traffic between your on-premises network and your VPC. This enables a fast, low-latency, and reliable connection provided by Direct Connect, while still maintaining the flexibility to use the public Internet as a backup path.

When using BGP over Direct Connect, a BGP peering session is established between the customer-owned or service provider router and the AWS Direct Connect router. *Peering* is a BGP management connection between two BGP speaking routers for use in exchanging routing information. The BGP peering connection allows you to exchange routing information and advertise your on-premises network *prefixes* into the AWS VPC and for the VPC to communicate its IP network prefixes into your internal network. This dynamic routing interaction enables you to create a seamless network connection between the on-premises network infrastructure and your AWS hosted resources. Your applications can access resources across both environments as if they were all part of the same network.

To establish a BGP session over Direct Connect, you will need to configure your on-premises router to communicate, or *peer*, with the AWS BGP speaking router. You will need values such as your autonomous systems number (ASN) and the IP addresses of the Direct Connect router you are interfacing with. Then you must configure the Virtual Gateway (VGW) with the BGP settings and the prefixes that you want to advertise to the on-premises network.

Connectivity Methods for AWS and Hybrid Networks

As you learned about in Chapter 6, hybrid connectivity allows you to securely connect your on-premises network to your VPC and enable your applications to access resources across both environments creating a single contiguous network.

Several connectivity methods can be used to establish a connection between an on-premises network and an AWS hybrid network, including using AWS Direct Connect, which establishes a dedicated network connection from your on-premises data center to an AWS Direct Connect facility. You can also create a virtual private network (VPN) connection between your on-premises network and your AWS Virtual Private Cloud using either AWS

VPN services or third-party VPN solutions. The AWS Direct Connect gateway enables you to connect your on-premises data centers to your VPCs and AWS accounts over AWS Direct Connect. The Direct Connect gateway allows you to simplify the network architecture and reduce the complexity of hybrid deployments by using a single connection and a set of virtual interfaces to access all your VPCs and AWS accounts. Another approach is to use the AWS Transit Gateway service. This is a service that enables customers to connect their VPCs and on-premises networks to a single gateway to simplify the management of the network, which can lower your operational costs. AWS App Mesh can be deployed to monitor and control microservices. This service makes it easy to connect, secure, and observe your microservices running AWS Fargate, Amazon Elastic Container Service (ECS), and Kubernetes on Amazon Elastic Container Service for Kubernetes (EKS).

Each of these connectivity methods has its own set of benefits and use cases, and the appropriate method will depend on the specific requirements of the organization and their network topology.

Direct Connect and Direct Connect Gateway

The Direct Connect gateway (DXGW) enables you to connect your on-premises data centers to your Amazon VPCs and accounts over AWS Direct Connect. DXGW simplifies the network architecture and reduces the complexity of managing hybrid deployments by using a single connection and a set of virtual interfaces to access all your VPCs and AWS accounts, as you learned in Chapter 6.

The Direct Connect gateway offers two connection methods. The Transit Virtual Interface allows you to connect your on-premises data center to multiple VPCs in the same AWS region using a single virtual interface. This allows you to create a hub-and-spoke network architecture where all VPCs connect to a central hub. The second method is to create a VPC association that allows the interconnection of your on-premises data center to a specific VPC in a different AWS region using a dedicated virtual interface. This enables you to create a full-mesh network architecture where each VPC connects directly to your on-premises data center.

Both methods enable you to use your existing network infrastructure and routing policies to connect your on-premises data center to your VPCs and AWS accounts. With a Direct Connect gateway, you can also use VPNs and CloudHub to connect your corporate network to your VPCs and AWS accounts in different regions.

The AWS Direct Connect gateway provides an easy and flexible way to connect your on-premises data centers to your VPCs and AWS accounts either using Transit Virtual Interface or using VPC associations, each with its benefits depending on the network topology and use case.

Direct Connect Virtual Interfaces

The Direct Connect Virtual Interface (VIF) establishes a dedicated, private network connection between your network infrastructure and your AWS resources, bypassing the public Internet. This provides a reliable, low-latency, high-bandwidth connection between your on-premises data center and the AWS cloud, enabling you to run latency-sensitive applications, migrate large data sets, and reduce Internet costs. When configuring a VIF, you must specify the bandwidth, the BGP ASN, the VLAN ID, and the IP prefixes that you want to advertise over the connection. The DX BGP routing has priority over any site-to-site VPN backup connections and is the preferred route.

The VIF is a logical connection that is created over an AWS DX interconnect between your data center and the DX Connect interface at the cross-connect facility. The VIF allows you to create a dedicated, private network connection between your network infrastructure and your AWS resources, bypassing the public Internet.

There are two types of VIFs; first there is the public virtual interface that is used to connect to the public IP address space of an AWS region and access the public AWS services such as S3, Elastic IP, and Route 53. Then there is the public virtual interface that is used to connect to the private IP address space of an Amazon VPC and access the private resources such as EC2 and RDS instances.

Site-to-Site VPN

In Chapter 6 you learned about creating hybrid networks using site-to-site VPN connections over the public Internet to create a direct connection from your on-site networks into AWS. Site-to-site VPNs are created using encrypted tunnels over the Internet from your on-premises network to a VPC in an AWS region using the IPSec protocol suite to encrypt the in-flight traffic. Site-to-site VPNs can serve as a primary interconnection between your on-premises data center and AWS or as a backup to a Direct Connect link should it fail. The site-to-site VPN route is a lower priority than the Direct Connect BGP route. If you have Direct Connect and the VPN as a backup, the VPN will be standby until the DX fails, and then BGP will reroute traffic over the VPN until the DX comes back online. Also, the site-to-site VPNs can traverse over the DX to provide an encrypted tunnel over the Direct Connect link.

App Mesh

The AWS *App Mesh* service is a fully managed AWS service mesh for Amazon Elastic Container Service (ECS) and Kubernetes that provides a consistent way to manage and secure microservices. It is useful when you need to control and monitor communication between your applications. App Mesh also enables you to troubleshoot and improve the performance of your AWS microservices.

App Mesh allows for automatic service discovery that automatically discovers and configures envoy proxies for new services and saves you from having to manually configure the mesh.

App Mesh also allows you to create and enforce rules for traffic routing between services, such as weight-based or percentage-based routing.

Observability, using built-in metrics, logging, and tracing for the services, enables you to monitor and troubleshoot your microservice applications. Also included is Transport Layer Security (TLS), used for encrypting traffic in-flight between services and integrating with AWS Certificate Manager (ACM) to create and manage certificates. There is also Cloud-Watch integration for collecting, monitoring, and troubleshooting the services.

AWS Networking Limits and Quotas

AWS networking services have limits and quotas that can affect their usage and performance. It's important to be aware of these limits and plan your network resources accordingly so they are not exceeded. If you hit any limits, you can request a service increase by contacting AWS Support. In this section, you will learn about some of the more important limits on AWS services. To review all service quotas, AWS has a dashboard in the console to track and manage quotas at `https://us-east-2.console.aws.amazon.com/service quotas/home?region=us-east-2`. Figure 9.4 shows the web GUI for the quota dashboard, Figure 9.5 shows the quota request form, and Figure 9.6 shows a history tracking dashboard.

FIGURE 9.4 Service quota dashboard

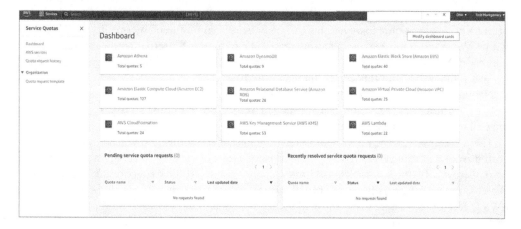

FIGURE 9.5 Service request

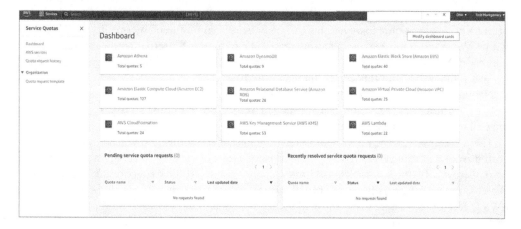

FIGURE 9.6 Quota history tracking

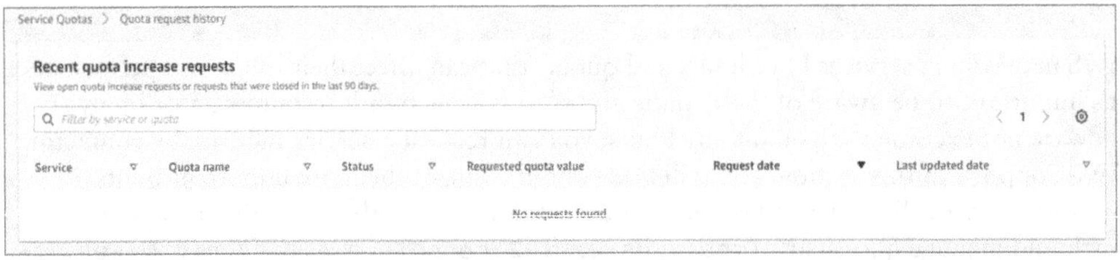

Some AWS services such as VPCs, Elastic IPs, Direct Connect, Route 53, Transit Gateway, and App Mesh can be used in conjunction with AWS Organizations, enabling the sharing of resources across member accounts and allowing for the increase of limits and quotas.

AWS places limits on the number of VPCs, subnets, and security groups that you can create per region. There are also limits applied to the number of elastic IPs and NAT gateways that can be allocated per VPC, as well as the number of IPs per subnet. There is a default of five VPCs per region. However, this can be increased to hundreds by opening a ticket with AWS Support and requesting an increase. The number of Internet gateways tracks the number of VPCs in each region. There can be up to 200 subnets in each VPC in up to 5 different CIDR blocks, and this can be increased to 50.

Network interfaces are variable based on the instance type selected. The table at `https://docs.aws.amazon.com/AWSEC2/latest/UserGuide/using-eni.html` outlines all the different network interface variables.

There are limits on the number of Direct Connect connections and virtual interfaces, both private and transit, per AWS Direct Connect gateway of 30 per account and per region. Also, there is a BGP route table hard limit of 1,000 routes, 10 link aggregation groups, 200 Direct Connect gateways per account, 10 virtual private gateways, 3 Transit Gateways per AWS Direct Connect gateways, and 100 route prefixes that can be advertised into AWS over transit virtual interfaces.

Table 9.1 shows the BGP limits.

TABLE 9.1 BGP Limits

AWS BGP Quotas	Value
BGP timers negotiate down to the lowest value between the routers.	
Default hold timer:	90 seconds
Minimum hold timer: A hold value of 0 is not supported.	3 seconds
Default keepalive timer:	30 seconds
Minimum keepalive timer:	1 second

continues

TABLE 9.1   BGP Limits *(continued)*

AWS BGP Quotas	Value
Graceful restart timer:	120 seconds
The BFD intervals are defined by the slowest device.	
BFD liveness detection minimum interval:	300 ms
BFD minimum multiplier:	3

Regarding Amazon Route 53, there are limits on the number of hosted zones and resource record sets that can be created per account, as shown in Table 9.2.

TABLE 9.2   Amazon Route 53

AWS Route 53 Quotas	Value
Maximum number of domains	20 (can be increased)
Default hold timer:	90 seconds
Hosted Zone quotas	
Hosted Zones	500 per AWS account (can be increased)
Hosted zones that can use the same reusable delegation set	100 (can be increased)
Amazon VPCs that you can associate with a private hosted zone per hosted zone	300 (can be increased)
Private hosted zones that you can associate a VPC	No quota*
Key signing keys (KSK) created per hosted zone	2
Record quotas	
Records	10,000 per hosted zone (can be increased)
Values in a record	400
Geolocation, latency, multivalue answer, weighted, and IP-based records	100 records that have the same name and type

continues

TABLE 9.2   Amazon Route 53 *(continued)*

AWS Route 53 Quotas	Value
Geoproximity records	30 records that have the same name and type
CIDR collections	5 per account (can be increased)
Resolver endpoints	
Endpoints per region	4 per account (can be increased)
IP addresses per endpoint	6 (can be increased)
IP addresses per rule	6
Rules per region	1,000 (can be increased)
Associations between rules and VPCs per AWS region	2,000 (can be increased)
Resolver Query logs	
Number of rule groups associated to a VPC for a single account per AWS region	5
Number of DNS Firewall domains in a single Amazon S3 file for a single account per AWS region	250,000 (can be increased)
Number of DNS Firewall domains in a single Amazon S3 file for a single account per AWS region	1,000 (can be increased)
Number of rules within a rule group for a single account per AWS region	100 (can be increased)
Number of domain lists for a single account per AWS region	1,000 (can be increased)
Number of domain specifications across all DNS Firewall domain lists for a single account per AWS region	100,000 (can be increased)
Health checks	
Health checks	200 active (can be increased)
Child health checks that a calculated health check can monitor	255

continues

TABLE 9.2 Amazon Route 53 *(continued)*

AWS Route 53 Quotas	Value
Maximum total length of headers in the response to a health check request	16, 384 bytes (16k)
Query Log configurations	
Query Log configurations	1 per hosted zone
Traffic flow policies and policy records	
Traffic flow policies and policy records	50 per account (can be increased)
Traffic policy versions	1,000 per policy
Traffic policy records	5 per account (can be increased)
Reusable delegation sets	
Reusable delegation sets	100 per account (can be increased)

There are limits on the number of Transit Gateways, attachments, and route tables that can be created per region and per account. A Transit Gateway cannot have more than one VPC attachment to the same VPC, as shown in Table 9.3.

TABLE 9.3 AWS Transit Gateways

AWS Transit Gateway Quotas	Value
Transit Gateways per account	5 (can be increased)
CIDR blocks per Transit Gateway	5
Routing	
Transit Gateway route tables per Transit Gateway	20 (can be increased)
Static routes per Transit Gateway	10,000 (can be increased)

continued

TABLE 9.3 AWS Transit Gateways *(continued)*

AWS Transit Gateway Quotas	Value
Dynamic routes advertised from a virtual router to a Transit Gateway Connect peer	1,000
Routes advertised from a Transit Gateway Connect peer on a Transit Gateway to a virtual router	5,000
Static routes for a prefix to a single attachment	1
Transit Gateway attachments	
Attachments per Transit Gateway	5,000
Transit Gateways per VPC	5
Peering attachments per Transit Gateway	50 (can be increased)
Peering peers per Transit Gateway	10 (can be increased)
Peering attachments within one Transit Gateway or between two Transit Gateway	1
Transit Gateway Connect peers (GRE tunnels) per Transit Gateway Connect attachment	4
Bandwidth	
Maximum bandwidth per VPC attachment, AWS Direct Connect gateway, or peered Transit Gateway connection	Up to 50 Gbps
Maximum packets per second per Transit Gateway attachment (VPC, VPN, Direct Connect, and peering attachments)	Up to 5,000
Bandwidth per VPN tunnel	Up to 1.25 Gbps
Maximum packets per second per VPN tunnel	Up to 140,000
Maximum bandwidth per Transit Gateway Connect peer (GRE tunnel) per Connect attachment	Up to 5 Gbps
Maximum packets per second per Connect peer	Up to 300,000

continues

TABLE 9.3 AWS Transit Gateways *(continued)*

AWS Transit Gateway Quotas	Value
Direct Connect gateways	
Direct Connect gateways per Transit Gateway	20
Transit Gateways per Direct Connect gateway	3
MTU	
VPC connections	8,500 Bytes
Direct Connect connections	8,500 Bytes
Peering connections	8,500 Bytes
VPC connections	8,500 Bytes
VPN connections	1,500 Bytes
Multicast	
Multicast domains per Transit Gateway	20 (can be increased)
Multicast network interfaces per Transit Gateway	1,000 (can be increased)
Members per Transit Gateway multicast group	100 (can be increased)
Multicast domain associations per VPC	20 (can be increased)
Sources per Transit Gateway multicast group	1 (can be increased)
Static and IGMPv2 multicast group members and sources per Transit Gateway	10,000
Static and IGMPv2 multicast group members per Transit Gateway multicast group	100
Maximum multicast throughput per flow	1 Gbps
Maximum aggregate multicast throughput per Availability Zone	20 Gbps

There are limits on the number of meshes, virtual nodes, and virtual services that can be created per account, as shown in Table 9.4.

TABLE 9.4   AWS App Mesh

AWS App Mesh Quotas	Value
Backends per virtual node	50
Connected Envoy processes per virtual gateway	50 (can be increased)
Connected Envoy processes per virtual node	50 (can be increased)
Gateway routes per virtual gateway	10 (can be increased)
Meshes per account	15 (can be increased)
Routes per virtual router	50 (can be increased)
Virtual gateways per mesh	3 (can be increased)
Virtual nodes per mesh	200 (can be increased)
Virtual routers per mesh	200 (can be increased)
Virtual services per mesh	200 (can be increased)
Weighted targets per route	10

Available Private and Public Access Methods for Custom Services

AWS services are either private or public. Private services reside inside your VPC, and you control access to them with access lists and security groups, with IAM, or by implementing many of the security services offered by AWS and external service providers in the marketplace. Public AWS services are reachable externally from your VPC and generally open to the world to access.

Private access to public services includes VPC endpoints that are secure private connections that do not require your traffic to traverse the Internet to access the public service. VPC endpoints are used to privately access services over an Amazon VPC without requiring a NAT gateway, VPN, or Direct Connect connection.

VPC peering allows you to privately connect two VPCs together and access resources in either of the VPCs as if they were in the same network. The PrivateLink service enables access to services over a private IP address, eliminating the exposure of your data to the Internet. Finally, VPN connections can be used to interconnect your on-premises networks to your AWS VPCs and access resources in either environment as if they were all part of the same network.

Public access to AWS services allows a service to be visible and accessed over the Internet by using elastic IP addresses, public subnets, and Internet gateways. Public access services in AWS include services that are accessible to the world such as the Elastic Load Balancer that allows you to distribute traffic to multiple servers behind the load balancer and can be configured to access AWS services over either public or private networks. The API Gateway enables you to publish APIs that you create and manage for your custom services. The API Gateway can be configured for public access. The AWS CloudFront content delivery network is a publicly accessible AWS service that is used to distribute content to users over the Internet. CloudFront is deployed at AWS edge locations throughout the world enabling proximity to your users to improve the performance and availability of your services. Route 53 is the AWS public DNS service.

PrivateLink

In Chapter 4, "Load Balancing," you learned that PrivateLink allows us to access AWS services and VPC endpoints using a private IP address, without the requirement for a NAT gateway, VPN, or Direct Connect connection. By using PrivateLink, your information is not exposed to the public over the Internet by creating a secure and private connection internal to AWS. PrivateLink meets many security, compliance, and data privacy requirements. PrivateLink, or endpoint services, allows outside accounts to share AWS resources with their customers and enables private access to AWS services and VPC endpoint services using a private IP address; this adds security and compliance and prevents exposing your data to the public Internet. It also provides a way to control access to the service by implementing endpoint policies.

To configure the service, you will create an endpoint in your VPC and then create the VPC endpoint service, which is a representation of the service in your VPC. After the creation of the VPC endpoint service, you will define a private endpoint in your VPC and associate it to the VPC endpoint service. A private connection between your VPC and the defined service is created, allowing you to access the service over a private IP address.

PrivateLink supports a large number of AWS services including S3, SNS, SQS, OpenSearch, DynamoDB, and a large list of other AWS services. A complete list is published in the AWS documentation at `https://docs.aws.amazon.com/vpc/latest/privatelink/aws-services-privatelink-support.html`.

The complete documentation set is at `https://docs.aws.amazon.com/vpc/latest/privatelink/aws-services-privatelink-support.html`.

VPC Peering

In Chapter 8, you learned that VPC peering is an interconnect that allows two or more VPCs to access resources in each VPC from the other allowing resources in either VPC to communicate with each other as if they were in the same network.

The AWS peering service has no bandwidth limitations, and there is no single failure point; it does not rely on gateways, Direct Connect, or VPN interconnections.

Peering connections can be in the same account or between separate accounts and across regions and availability zones. Instances running inside of a VPC, such as EC2 or Lambda, have full private network communications without the need to configure a gateway or NAT instance. All VPC-to-VPC traffic can use the private IP address space and transits the AWS internal global network.

To create a VPC peering connection, you need to specify the VPCs that you want to connect and accept the request on the other VPC. Once the connection is established, you can then route traffic between the VPCs using custom routes, or you can use the VPC's default route table. Peering does not provide a direct external network connection and does not provide transit connectivity between VPCs. A VPC cannot be used to route traffic to another VPC that it is not directly peered with. The Transit Gateway is used to provide transit connectivity between VPCs.

Available Inter-Regional and Intra-Regional Communication Patterns

AWS offers different networking architectures to connect your VPC resources internally, externally, within a region, and between regions.

Inter-regional communications refer to interconnecting AWS VPCs and services from one region to another, and intra-regional communications is the networking inside a specific AWS region. There are multiple AWS inter- and intra-communication options to choose from based on your specific requirements.

The communication approach you choose will be based on router requirements for security, compliance, bandwidth, latency, and cost. You are also not limited to just one option and can deploy these services in combination to meet your specific requirements.

Interconnecting your VPCs residing in different regions is referred to as *inter-regional communications*. The default method is to send your traffic across the public Internet. Since there are no bandwidth, delay, or quality of services guarantees using this approach, other methods are available that may be better suited to your requirements. A site-to-site VPN connection can be established over the Internet to add encryption for secure communications. Another option is to implement a Direct Connect between regions that allows traffic to be sent over a private high-bandwidth, low-latency, secure dedicated connection that bypasses the Internet.

As we discussed in Chapter 8, there are software-defined wide-area network solutions from AWS business partners available in the marketplace. Using the AWS Transit Hub allows you to route traffic between AWS regions as well as internally to your on-premises networks. You can also implement the Global Accelerator to offload traffic from the Internet onto the AWS backbone for increased backbone network performance.

When interconnecting your VPCs within an AWS region, your options include using VPC peering, using PrivateLink, traversing the public Internet, and using the AWS Transit Hub.

Summary

In this chapter, we expanded on routing technologies in general and focused on BGP specifically as it is the primary routing protocol used to interface with the AWS cloud. The topics covered were a continuation of earlier hybrid networking chapters where the services and concepts were introduced.

There was more detail given on how routing works and how to optimize routing configurations to meet your requirements. Topics such as optimizing dynamic and static routes, route summarization, propagation, and overlapping routes were presented.

AWS Direct Connect and site-to-site VPNs were reviewed as methods to connect on-site networks with AWS resources.

We also looked at the App Mesh service, which is the discovery and management service for AWS container services such as ECS and Kubernetes. App Mesh also allows you to create and enforce rules for traffic routing between services, such as weight-based or percentage-based routing.

Service limitations and quotas are important topics to be aware of as they can affect your production networks. You learned about the AWS values for many of the services such as BGP, Route 53, Transit Gateway, and App Mesh. The quota dashboard was introduced as a central point of management for tracking and managing AWS service quotas.

Methods to access AWS services that either are publicly exposed or are private in a VPC were covered, and the different connection methods were discussed.

Finally, you learned about inter and intra AWS connection options, which are the networking options to connect networks either inside of, or between, AWS regions.

Exam Essentials

Have a working knowledge of BGP routing.   Have a working knowledge of BGP routing and the terminology used. eBGP refers to the external use of the BGP routing protocol between organizations, or autonomous systems, in BGP terminology. iBGP refers to internal BGP and is used internally in an organization within a single autonomous system.

Know the difference between dynamic and static routing.   Know the difference between dynamic routing, where dynamic is an active protocol tracking and updating routing information in real time, and static routing, which is hard-coded nondynamic routing. Know that the administrative distance is used to set a priority of the route information with the lower administrative distance preferred and inserted into the route forwarding table over a similar route of a higher administrative distance value.

Know how to optimize routing in AWS.   Understand the different methods to optimize routing within AWS such as how to summarize routes, how to deal with overlapping routes, and the concept of route propagation. Hybrid connectivity methods are key to the advanced networking exam, and it is important that you understand Direct Connect and site-to-site VPNs thoroughly before sitting for the exam. Finally, know the different services and methods to interconnect AWS resources that are both private and public as well as internal to a region and between regions.

Written Lab

Written Lab 9.1: Enable Route Propagation in a VPC

1. Open the Amazon VPC console at `https://console.aws.amazon.com/vpc`.
2. In the left navigation pane, choose Route Tables.
3. Click the box of the route table to edit.
4. In the Actions pull-down, select Edit Route Propagation.
5. In the Edit Route Propagation dialog, check the Enable box.
6. Click Save.

Exercises

1. Search the VPC documentation page: `https://docs.aws.amazon.com/vpc/latest/peering/what-is-vpc-peering.html` and review the guide.
2. Review the Direct Connect BGP guide at `https://docs.aws.amazon.com/directconnect/latest/UserGuide/routing-and-bgp.html`.
3. Study the AWS site-to-site VPN documentation at `https://docs.aws.amazon.com/vpn/latest/s2svpn/VPC_VPN.html`.
4. Study the AWS PrivateLink documentation at `https://docs.aws.amazon.com/vpc/latest/privatelink/what-is-privatelink.html`.

Review Questions

The following questions are designed to test your understanding of this chapter's material. For more information on how to obtain additional questions, please see this book's introduction.

1. You are creating the architecture to connect your corporate data center to a VPC in the eu-south-1 Milan region. What routing solution would be best suited to interconnect your corporate network to the AWS VPC?

   A. Statics

   B. BGP

   C. OSPF

   D. Route propagation

   E. Use the AWS route table

2. How can you ensure that traffic is routed to the best possible destination to improve the efficiency, scalability, and security of your network; enhance performance; and reduce the risk of network congestion?

   A. Implement route propagation

   B. Use static routes

   C. Use the iBGP routing protocol

   D. Offload traffic to PrivateLink

   E. Enable App Mesh

3. What are common methods used to optimize routing in your network? (Select three.)

   A. Enable Elastic Beanstalk

   B. Use Route 53 routing options

   C. Implement CloudFront

   D. Use the AWS Global Accelerator

   E. Use the Web Application Firewall

   F. Enable CloudTrail

4. What routing method can be used to install a backup route into a routing table should the primary route fail? (Select two.)

   A. Implement CloudFront

   B. Use a floating static route

   C. Use a dynamic routing protocol such as BGP

   D. Use VPG route propagation

   E. Configure a backup route table for the subnets in your VPC

5. Jill is nearing the quota limits of BGP routes in her DX connection to AWS. She must import into her data center a new CIDR block that is being configured for the Redshift cluster in AWS. What can she enable to reduce the size of her routing table?

    A.   Use standby BGP peering

    B.   Configure static routes in place of BGP

    C.   Replace the direct connection with a site-to-site VPN, which has a larger BGP route table

    D.   Use iBGP in place of eBGP

    E.   Configure route summarization in BGP

6. What are the options to populate the table with the routes in your network? (Select three.)

    A.   Enable BGP

    B.   Enable CloudFront

    C.   Configure static routes

    D.   Configure Route 53 to inject the routes

    E.   Enable route propagation

7. You are setting up a VPC peering connection in the eu-central-1 Frankfurt region and are unable to create a connection between two EC2 Linux instances in each VPC. Upon further investigation you notice that when the VPCs were created, they were each assigned a CIDR block of IPv4 address in the 10.20.1.0 /24 range. What steps can you take to enable communications between the instances? (Select two.)

    A.   Implement static routes to override the route table entries

    B.   Use a NAT gateway in one of the VPCs

    C.   Enable route propagation in both VPCs

    D.   Readdress one of the VPCs to a different IP address block

    E.   BGP will route between the matching CIDR blocks

8. A DX connection between your Austin data center and the AWS us-west-2 Oregon region is being created to achieve reliable throughput with low latency and enhanced security. You are configuring the interconnect with AWS to dynamically exchange and update network prefixes. What steps would you need to take to send routing information from your data center into AWS and receive routes from your VPC?

    A.   Enable route propagation

    B.   Configure your router at the DX facility as an autonomous systems border router

    C.   Configure an eBGP peering connection with the AWS router at the DX facility

    D.   Use iBGP as your routing protocol to dynamically exchange routes

9. You are an AWS networking engineer that has been tasked to interconnect your company's Atlanta data center to 15 private VPCs in the us-central-1 Ohio region using a hub-and-spoke network architecture where all VPCs connect to a central hub to reach the data center. What type of interface will be required in your Direct Connect gateway?

   A. Configure a PrivateLink interface in each VPC

   B. Configure a transit virtual interface

   C. Configure individual VPC peering interfaces

   D. Use an application load balancer to front-end the AWS VPC and connect the virtual IP listener interface to the data center

10. You are configuring a Direct Connect virtual interface (VIF) that will be used to create a dedicated, private network connection between your Zurich data center infrastructure and AWS resources deployed in the eu-west-3 Paris region. What must be configured on the virtual interface at the DX facility? (Select three.)

    A. BGP peer domain name

    B. VLAN ID

    C. IPv4 address

    D. VxLAN endpoint

    E. BGP ASN

11. You require an encrypted data connection from your DR data center in Ottawa to your VPC resources in the Canada central region in Montreal. Because of the time constraints of installing a dedicated circuit into your data center, you have been tasked to look at alternatives. What can you deploy quickly to connect the data center to your VPC applications?

    A. CloudFront

    B. Site-to-site VPN

    C. Direct Connect

    D. BPG peering

    E. CloudHub

12. You are investigating methods to manage, control, monitor, and secure your microservices running on ECS and Kubernetes. What managed AWS service enables you to troubleshoot and improve the performance of your AWS microservices?

    A. App Mesh

    B. SageMaker

    C. Elastic Beanstalk

    D. Elastic Container Services

13. What can you do to maximize your VPC quota limits in your organization?

    A. Open a support ticket with AWS

    B. Enable quota history tracking in the AWS web console

    C. Automate the service quota dashboard to monitor limits

    D. Implement AWS Organizations

14. What tools can you use to monitor your service quota consumption? (Select two.)

    A. Search CloudTrail for quota metrics

    B. AWS service quota dashboard

    C. Search using the AWS Macie service

    D. Reference the CloudWatch metrics usage for each AWS resource

    E. Track using the AWS license manager

15. Your company hosts its production APAC CRM applications in the ap-northeast-1 Tokyo region. The development team is also based in Japan and has configured VPCs for test and development. A new CRM version is being developed in parallel with the existing application. The architecture requires that new VPCs be created for DEV, TEST, and PROD in the same region. When you run your CloudFormation scripts, the VPCs fail on creation. What do you need to do to remediate this issue?

    A. Set up a new VPC in another region and interconnect them

    B. Modify the CloudFormation template to use VPC override

    C. Request a VPC quota increase for the Tokyo region

    D. Use Elastic Beanstalk instead of CloudFormation

    E. Enable AWS Config

16. To optimize the routing tables between your company's data center in Bremen, Germany and your VPC applications running in the eu-central-1 Frankfurt region, you want to establish an alternate route over your custom VPN terminating on a EC2 non-BGP speaking instance in a public subnet. How can the routing table in your data center be updated if the DX BGP session drops?

    A. Enable AWS Config to track and update the configuration based on CloudWatch alarms

    B. Use a floating static route with a higher administrative distance value than the eBGP routes that will redirect traffic over the VPN connection if the primary BGP route is deleted from the routing table due to a circuit impairment

    C. The DX BGP routing process will automatically redirect traffic over the VPN connection

    D. Configure Route 53 custom metrics to redirect traffic over the VPN if the DX connection fails

17. Your company is required to be PCI compliant for its e-commerce financial operations. You must set up a connection from your VPC to public services running in the same region. How can you configure the VPC network to not egress financial traffic over the public Internet to access external AWS services?

    A. Configure VPC endpoints

    B. Enable transit routing

    C. Use a site-to-site VPN connection

    D. Configure VPC peering

    E. Enable CloudFormation

18. To meet your company's security requirements, you need to deploy a secure private connection internal to AWS that allows outside accounts to access a database you are hosting in your VPC on a private subnet. What networking service can you implement to allow outside accounts to privately access your data?

   A. Route traffic over the AWS Global Accelerator

   B. Configure VPC peering

   C. Enable CloudTrail interconnections

   D. Configure AWS Organizations

   E. PrivateLink

19. You are investigating methods to interconnect two of your test VPCs in the ap-southeast-2 Sydney region. The requirements include that they communicate with each other as if they were in the same network, that there be no bandwidth limitations, and that there is no single point of failure. What service would meet these requirements?

   A. CloudFront

   B. CloudWatch

   C. VPC peering

   D. Direct Connect

20. You are investigating options to interconnect your public Internet-facing VPCs in the us-east-2 Ohio and us-east-1 Northern Virginia regions. Which of the following methods would you use to accomplish this? (Select three.)

   A. Enable AWS Macie

   B. Send traffic over the Internet

   C. Create a DX between the VPC in the different regions

   D. Create a site-to-site VPN connection

   E. Enable IAM

Network Management and Operations

Chapter

10

Network Automation

THE AWS CERTIFIED ADVANCED NETWORKING - SPECIALTY EXAM OBJECTIVES COVERED IN THIS CHAPTER MAY INCLUDE, BUT ARE NOT LIMITED TO, THE FOLLOWING:

✓ **Domain 2: Network Implementation**

- Task Statement 2.4: Automate and configure network infrastructure.

Network Automation

In this chapter, you will learn about the process of automating your AWS and hybrid network deployment. Automation abstracts the physical network infrastructure into software, which describes the deployments. Automation can be used to automatically configure, provision, manage, and test network devices. It improves efficiency, reduces human error, and can lower your operating expenses. You will become familiar with the AWS tools and services offered to support automation and then learn about the different methods used to automate your AWS and on-premises networks.

Infrastructure as Code

Infrastructure as code (IaC) programmatically defines and creates AWS infrastructure using software instead of the traditional console-based configuration approach using a command-line interface, management console, or web GUI. Infrastructure as code is defined using a declarative code format that deploys your cloud resources automatically using automation tools to provision and manage your resources. Resources that are defined as code make it easier to ensure that configurations are consistently deployed the same way every time. IaC relies on creating code that defines the desired configuration you want to deploy. These files are version controlled like any other code and can be reused, creating a more efficient approach to deploying cloud infrastructure.

In this chapter, you will learn about the many tools and techniques available in AWS to automate your deployments such as AWS CloudFormation, which is a service that allows you to define infrastructure as code in either *JSON*, which is the most common format and is more of a machine format, or *YAML*, which is simplified and more of a human-readable format, and then automatically create and manage resources based on those definitions. The AWS Cloud Development Kit (CDK) is a software development framework that uses programming languages such as TypeScript, Python, Java, .NET, and Go to define AWS infrastructure as code. These tools enable you to create, change, and delete your AWS resources using automation. Infrastructure as code enables you to automate the provisioning and modifications of your cloud infrastructure. Misconfigurations can be reduced by reusing tested code. Deployment speeds are increased, and consistency is maintained. You can replicate your deployments across different accounts, regions, or environments such as DEV, TEST, and PROD.

IaC allows you to quickly scale up or down your AWS infrastructure resources on demand, as needed, enabling you to respond more quickly to changes in demand or to address new business requirements and reduce cost.

To ensure that your AWS infrastructure is reliable, scalable, and maintainable, it's critical that you follow AWS best practices such as using version control to track changes to the infrastructure over time, code validation, and detailed documentation of your deployments.

IaC is the best-approach practice for managing and scaling your AWS deployments. By using code to define your infrastructure, you guarantee that your resources are consistently deployed and configured and you can respond quickly to changes in demand or business requirements.

AWS Cloud Development Kit

The open-source AWS *Cloud Development Kit (CDK)* is a software development framework that allows for creating cloud infrastructure definitions and provisioning the code using AWS CloudFormation.

The AWS CDK enables developers to define their infrastructure in familiar programming languages such as TypeScript, Python, C#, and Java. The Cloud Development Kit provides a high-level object-oriented abstraction over CloudFormation resources, enabling developers to express infrastructure as code with fewer configuration files and lines of code.

The CDK enables developers to create a cloud infrastructure as a set of reusable code called *constructs*. These constructs are packaged into libraries and can be shared in your organization or published to the AWS CloudFormation registry for public access. This approach enables developers to use prebuilt constructs or create their own custom code for reusability across different projects. Figure 10.1 shows the CDK workflow. The CDK comes with a complete library of reusable AWS constructs to simplify the creation and management of commonly used infrastructure resources. By using the CDK, developers define and manage infrastructure resources, such as EC2 instances, S3 buckets, Lambda functions, the RDS family of databases, container clusters, DynamoDB, and many other AWS services using high-level constructs that are provided in the AWS Construct Library. CDK makes it easier to build and manage complex cloud infrastructures, by abstracting the underlying CloudFormation configuration code, and simplifies the tracking and management of dependencies between resources.

FIGURE 10.1   Cloud Development Kit workflow

CDK Compiler   Cloud Formation   Cloud Formation
                           Template

The CDK includes Integrated Development Environment (IDE) support with common IDEs, such as Visual Studio Code, IntelliJ, and PyCharm, that provide many features such as code highlighting, autocompletion, and error checking. Command-line tools, AWS Cloud-Formation templates, and AWS CodePipeline are natively supported. CDK stacks enable the creation and management of stacks, which are collections of AWS resources that can be updated and deployed together or deleted as a single unit.

The AWS Cloud Development Kit allows for cross-account and cross-regional replication of code. The CDK enables developers to quickly provision resources across multiple AWS accounts, projects, and regions, reducing the time and effort needed to manage AWS infrastructure resources. There is an extensive library of templates available to use to get started with your projects on Git at `https://github.com/aws/aws-cdk`.

The CDK allows developers to use familiar programming languages to define infrastructure, which reduces the learning curve for managing AWS resources. A high level of consistency is ensured in your deployments as the CDK automatically generates AWS CloudFormation templates. Productivity is increased by abstracting the often-complex AWS CloudFormation templates. The higher level of abstraction of CloudFormation when using the CDK enables developers to build and manage complex cloud infrastructure more efficiently and quickly.

AWS CloudFormation

The AWS *CloudFormation* service enables developers to define and manage AWS IaC by using templates, as shown in Figure 10.2. The CloudFormation service enables you to define and provision AWS infrastructure resources using code. The service creates models used to automate the creation, update, and deletion of AWS resources in a safe, predictable, and repeatable way.

FIGURE 10.2   CloudFormation workflow

| Create a New or Use an Existing Template | → | Save Template Locally or In a S3 Bucket | → | CloudFormation Creates a Stack Based on Your Template. | → | CloudFormation Constructs and Configures Resources Defined in the Stack |

When creating resources using CloudFormation, you can use either JSON or YAML to define the infrastructure resources in files called *templates*. The templates describe the architecture of your infrastructure and the resources required to run your application. There are many template samples and quick-start guides available on the AWS website, the CloudFormation public repository, Git repositories, or on the Web that can be used as a base configuration. AWS partners offer a wide range of configurations by the AWS service and industry sector. Templates are used to create and provision the resources necessary for your application to run. Developers can provision and manage a collection of AWS resources in single units, called *stacks*.

CloudFormation can be accessed using the browser console, command-line interface, or the AWS APIs to create a stack based on your template code.

A CloudFormation stack is a collection of AWS resources managed as a single unit with the resources in the stack defined using CloudFormation templates. The stack set is used to create, update, or delete stacks in multiple accounts and regions using a single operation. Change sets evaluate candidate changes to a stack to see how it will impact your running resources. The drift detection feature is used to identify configuration changes between your live resources and your templates. Drifts are detected on stacks and resources.

CloudFormation features include automating the provisioning and management of your infrastructure, which reduces manual interventions, that increase consistency and accuracy and reduce the risk of errors. Code can be stored as templates and reused in different environments and projects. Reusability enables the quick provisioning of resources. You can quickly add or remove resources as needed using CloudFormation, enabling infrastructure that is easily scalable. Most AWS resources are supported in CloudFormation, which enables you to define and provision almost any type of AWS infrastructure. Templates can be version controlled allowing for change management and the ability to roll back to previous versions if required. All templates are reusable, which enables you to create and manage multiple stacks of resources from a single template.

CloudFormation is integrated with many services to manage your infrastructure using a single tool. Services include IAM, CloudWatch, AWS Config, Elastic Beanstalk, CodeDeploy, and OpsWorks. The web interface includes a graphical designer to assist you in creating the JSON or YAML templates, as shown in Figure 10.3.

FIGURE 10.3   CloudFormation designer

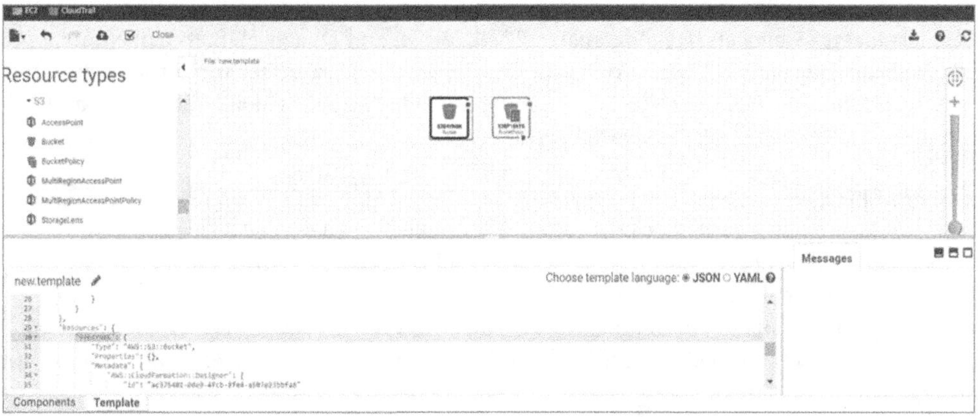

By using CloudFormation, your configuration changes can be validated prior to deployment. They are repeatable, which makes it easier to troubleshoot, detect, and remediate template errors.

CloudFormation is a powerful AWS tool used to define your infrastructure in code and automate your resources, deploy consistent configurations, and reduce errors.

The CloudFormation user guide includes an extensive explanation of the service at `https://docs.aws.amazon.com/AWSCloudFormation/latest/UserGuide/Welcome.html`.

EventBridge

A very useful AWS service to use when integrating networking functions is AWS *EventBridge*, which is a serverless service that provides real-time access to changes in data in AWS services, without having to create custom code. EventBridge uses events with triggers to connect application components together, and the service makes it easy to create scalable event-driven applications. For example, you can use it to route events from sources such as networking logs, AWS services, and on-premises network management applications. The EventBridge service offers you a simple and consistent way to receive, filter, transform, and deliver events so you can build new applications quickly. An EventBridge rule matches incoming events and sends them to targets for processing. EventBridge Pipes connects an event source to a target and enables you to filter or add content. The EventBridge Scheduler is similar to a Linux cron operation that invokes a target one time or at defined intervals. The EventBridge AWS console configuration steps are shown in Figures 10.4, 10.5, and 10.6.

AWS Command-Line Interface

The AWS command-line interface (CLI) enables you to manage AWS resources from the command line instead of the web GUI interface or using SDKs. The CLI includes an extensive set of commands used to interact with all AWS services and resources, including EC2 instances, S3 buckets, RDS databases, IAM, VPCs, and DynamoDB, to name only a few. You can manage IAM user groups, monitor operations, create security groups, monitor routes, and monitor DX interfaces. Files can be uploaded and downloaded from S3, and CloudFormation stacks can be created and managed.

Figures 10.7 and 10.8 show CLI examples of S3 bucket listings.

The CLI is a cross-platform tool that supports integration with Windows, macOS, and Linux shells including Bash and PowerShell. This reduces the learning curve and provides a consistent experience across different services and operating systems. The CLI is used to automate the deployment and management of resources in the AWS cloud and is often integrated with scripts to automate tasks and workflows. The AWS CLI integrates with other AWS services and tools, including AWS CloudFormation, Elastic Beanstalk, and Lambda, for managing AWS resources.

There is an extensive range of options and CLI commands that you can use to interact with AWS resources, which gives you a high degree of flexibility in managing AWS resources.

FIGURE 10.4   EventBridge scheduler

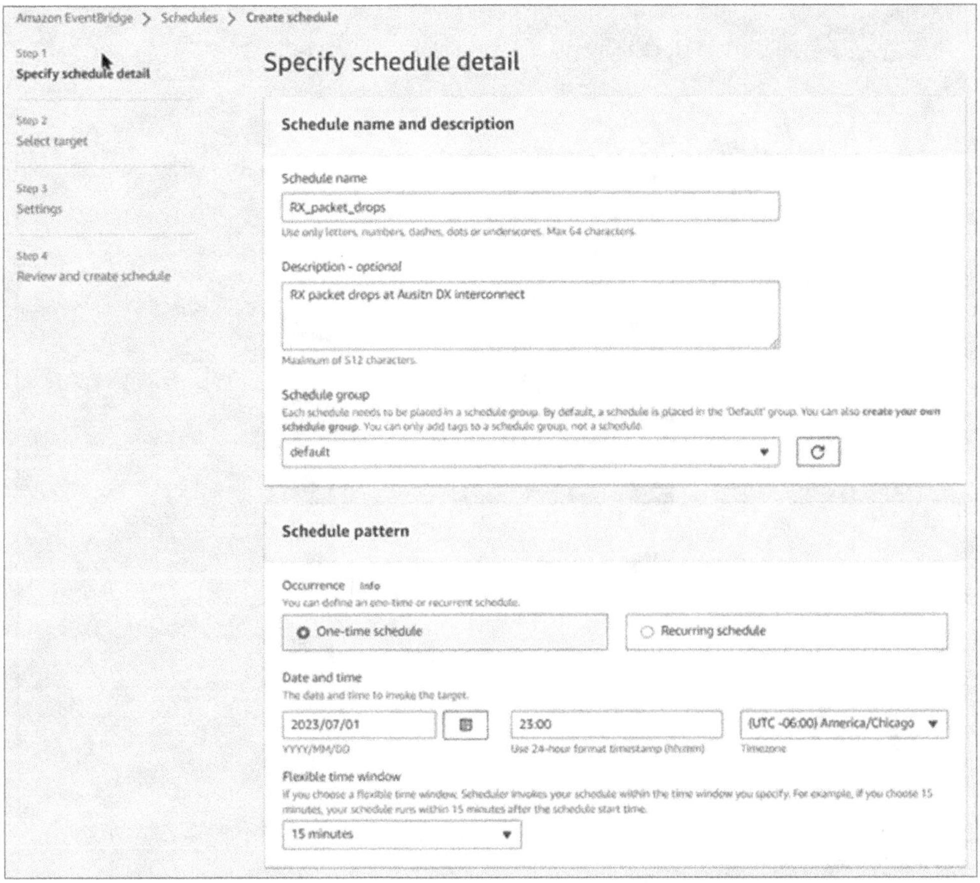

The CLI is an extremely powerful and flexible tool you can use to manage your AWS resources from the command line. The AWS CLI online reference guide provides additional details on how to set up and use the interface at https://docs.aws.amazon.com/cli/latest/userguide/cli-chap-welcome.html.

AWS Software Development Kit

The AWS *Software Development Kit* (SDK) is a collection of AWS-provided tools and libraries used to build applications that interact with AWS services. The SDK is a programming interface used by developers to access AWS services through their applications. The complexity of working with AWS services is hidden when using the SDK. This allows the developers to focus on building their applications instead of managing the interactions between the application and AWS backend services.

FIGURE 10.5 EventBridge target

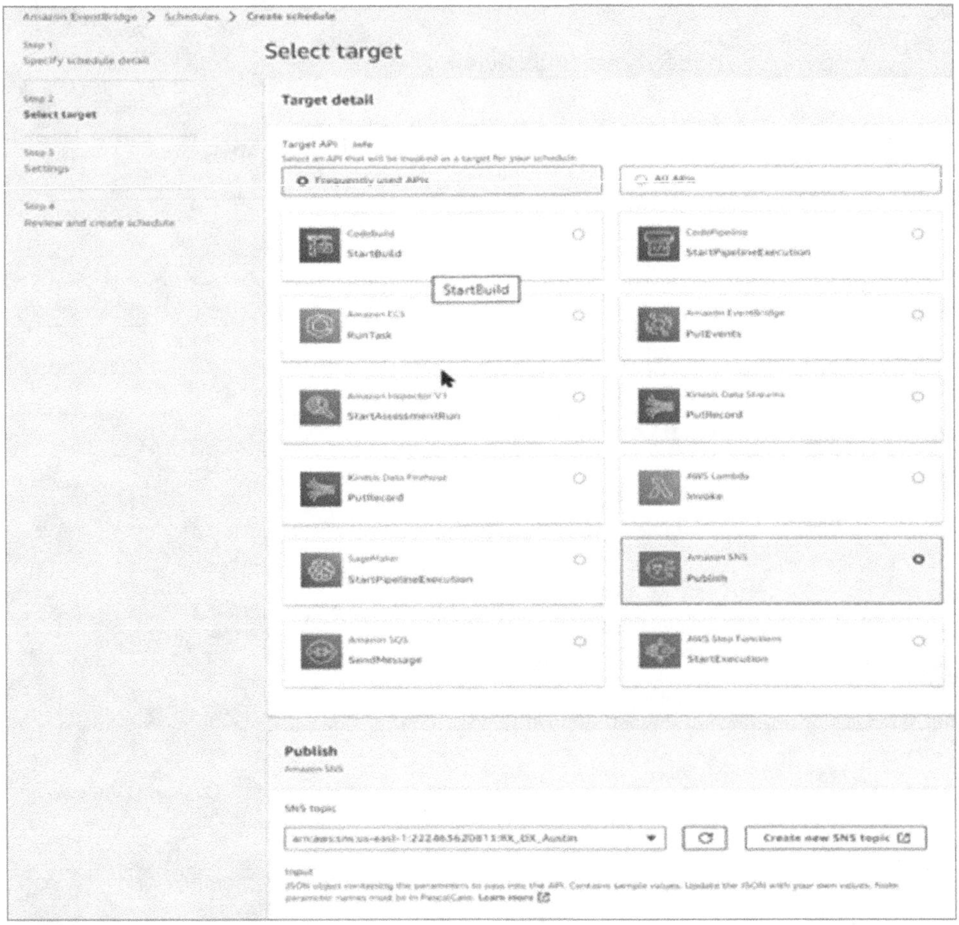

The AWS SDK is an AWS-provided software framework used for building applications that interact with AWS services. By providing simple APIs, authentication and security, error handling, resource management, and performance optimization, the SDK enables developers to build application integrations with AWS services that are reliable and efficient. The SDK provides libraries for the multiple programming languages, including C++, Go, Java, .NET, Ruby, Python, Java, JavaScript, Kotlin, .NET, Node.js, Rust, Swift, and PHP, and allows developers to integrate AWS services into their applications.

Developer environment integration is supported for the popular IDEs, including Cloud9, Eclipse, IntelliJ, and Visual Studio.

The SDK includes APIs that are used to interact with AWS services; this abstracts the complexity of the underlying services from developers, enabling them to focus on their applications. Libraries are included that integrate many of the AWS services with the SDK; for example, the services supported include S3, EC2, DynamoDB, and SQS. Libraries for secure authentication and authorization to access AWS services are integrated into the tool kit, which ensures that only authorized users can access AWS resources including support for IAM and Cognito authentication.

FIGURE 10.6   EventBridge create schedule

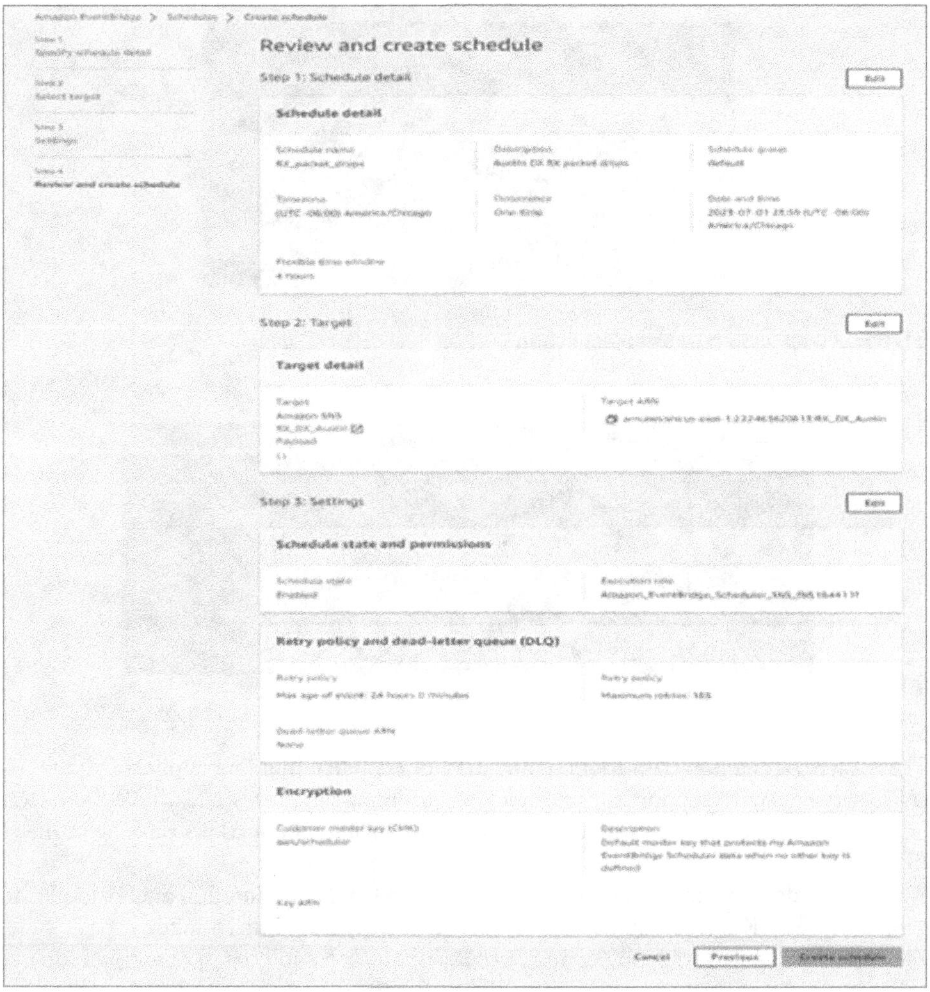

The SDK automatically manages AWS credentials, greatly simplifying the authentication process and abstracting the complexity away from the developers.

Management libraries are used to manage AWS resources, including launching and managing EC2 instances, creating and managing S3 buckets, from your applications, and many more functions. The SDK includes integrated error handling and retry logic to ensure that applications automatically recover from failures for enhanced reliability. Tools are provided for managing AWS resources, for example, the creation and deletion of resources, access control, and monitoring resource usage. The AWS SDK also provides performance optimization features, such as batch operations, request throttling, and caching.

FIGURE 10.7   S3 bucket listing

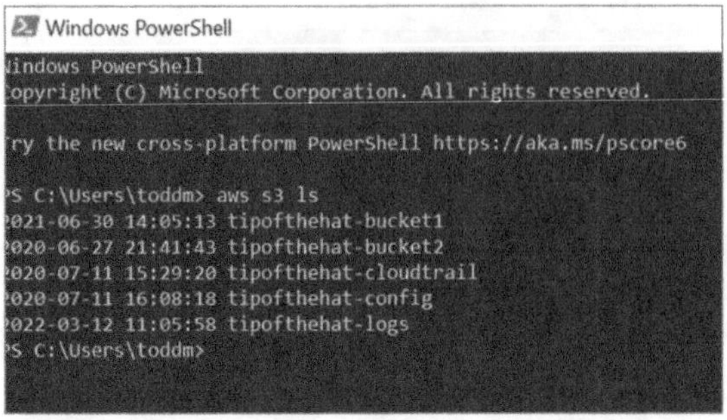

FIGURE 10.8   S3 bucket object listing

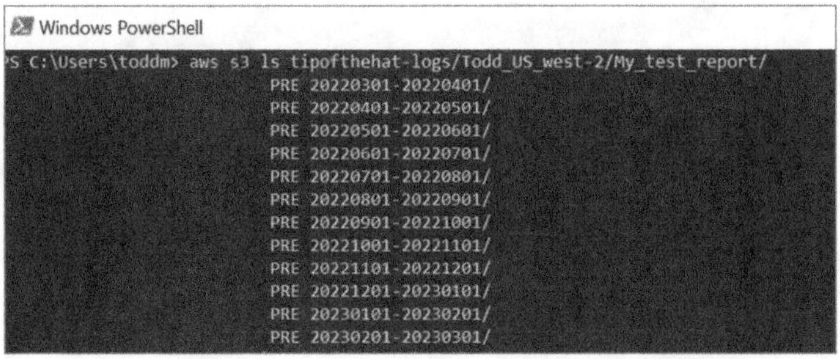

The AWS SDK is a powerful tool used by developers when building applications that use AWS services. With support for multiple programming languages and all AWS services, the SDK can be used to create scalable, reliable, and efficient applications running in the AWS cloud.

AWS online documentation provides extensive detailed documentation and examples for developers. The SDK documentation can be found at `https://aws.amazon.com/developer/tools` and `https://docs.aws.amazon.com/sdkref/latest/guide/overview.html`.

Application Programming Interfaces

The AWS *application programming interfaces* (APIs) are a set of tools, documentation, and protocols used by developers to interact with all AWS services programmatically. When using the web interface, CLI, or SDK to interact with AWS, underneath the interfaces is an API that is used to communicate with AWS. AWS APIs provide a standardized interface for accessing all AWS services, allowing developers to build applications that use AWS services without requiring direct access to the underlying infrastructure.

The API features provide a method to programmatically interact with AWS services enabling customers to create, manage, and monitor their cloud resources. APIs are used for all AWS automation services. The AWS APIs also allow third-party applications and services to be integrated with AWS. APIs are front-end portals used to configure, monitor, and troubleshoot AWS resources. The APIs provide standardized access to detailed metrics and logging information, making it easy to monitor and troubleshoot AWS resources.

AWS makes the APIs available for the most common programming languages, including Java, Python, .NET, Ruby, and PHP.

AWS APIs are designed to be highly available and scalable. They can support build applications delivering large amounts of traffic to AWS and scale up or down as needed.

Since the APIs provide a standardized interface for interacting with AWS services, customer development time and the effort required are reduced. AWS APIs support multiple formats including *Representational State Transfer* (REST). APIs use the HTTP protocol to send and receive data. Services using REST APIs include Amazon S3, Amazon EC2, and Amazon CloudFront. AWS APIs are used by developers to send requests to AWS services in a structured format, such as XML or JSON. The query APIs are used by services such as Amazon Simple Queue Service (SQS) and Amazon Simple Notification Service (SNS). API integrations are also included with the various AWS CLI and SDK offerings. The APIs can be used for data access to AWS services, allowing developers to receive real-time updates and data from their applications. Since the AWS APIs are standardized, the complexity is reduced.

AWS APIs offer a simple, consistent method to interact with AWS services; this helps reduce the complexity of building and maintaining applications and increases reliability.

The development cycle is reduced because the APIs make it easy to automate common tasks. The AWS APIs are highly scalable and offer a flexible method to interact with AWS services.

The AWS APIs support multiple programming languages and include a wide range of features. The AWS APIs offer developers a reliable, fully featured, and scalable method to interact with the AWS platform.

The AWS API gateway service allows you to create and publish your own APIs and was discussed in detail in Chapter 1, "Edge Networking."

AWS APIs are the primary interface used by applications to interact with AWS services. By using standardized formats, detailed documentation, and built-in security features, the AWS APIs make it easy for developers to write code that interacts with AWS services in a highly available, reliable, and efficient way.

AWS offers detailed API documentation that includes examples and use cases.

Integrating Network Automation Using Infrastructure as Code

In this section, we will investigate the different use cases for network automation in AWS including triggering automation based on events, automating cloud adoption, investigating the issues of hard-coding data into templates, creating repeatable configurations, using automation in hybrid networks, and learning how to reduce risks when implementing IaC deployments.

Event-Driven Network Automation

An event-driven architecture in AWS uses defined events to trigger and communicate between decoupled services. This is a common architecture used by modern applications built with microservices. An event is a change in state, or an update, based on these events, and automated actions can be performed in real time. Integrating event-driven networking functions into your AWS deployment enables you to automate monitoring, management, deployment, and networking functions.

The integration steps include defining infrastructure requirements; this includes documenting networking resources needed to support the event-driven functions such as your VPCs, subnets, security groups, or other network resources.

Next, you would create IaC templates using tools such as CloudFormation, the AWS CDK, or Terraform. The goal is to create IaC templates that include the necessary infrastructure resources, as well as any dependencies and configuration details.

Once those steps are completed, the next step is to create event-driven functions using AWS Lambda, EventBridge, SNS, CloudWatch, or other AWS services. Define the function code and specify the events that should trigger the function. The event trigger activates the networking function, allowing it to perform its intended task.

Once the event-driven functions are created, integrate them with the IaC template using the event sources that are offered by AWS such as a Lambda function being triggered by a new event object being written to an S3 bucket, an Amazon Kinesis stream, or an Amazon API gateway.

Before deploying the configuration to production, it is important to test and verify that the template is working as expected. Validation tools are usually included with the service you are using.

After everything is fully tested and debugged, the next step is to deploy the configuration into your AWS environment.

It is important to keep monitoring and managing the deployed configuration using tools like AWS CloudWatch and AWS Config. These tools provide real-time monitoring and alerting, as well as help track changes and ensure compliance with best practices and security requirements.

By combining IaC and networking event–driven triggers, you can create a scalable and flexible infrastructure that is adaptable to changes in your AWS deployment.

Use IaC to provide the ability to automate the deployment and management of your AWS cloud infrastructure. The event-driven networking functions provide the ability to respond to changes in real time; you can achieve quicker and more efficient processing of data and events. By combining IaC and event-driven functions, you can create a resilient, scalable, and cost-effective infrastructure in AWS.

Additional AWS documentation on creating an event-driven architecture can be found online here:

- https://aws.amazon.com/blogs/compute/getting-started-with-event-driven-architecture
- https://aws.amazon.com/blogs/compute/building-an-event-driven-application-with-amazon-eventbridge
- https://aws.amazon.com/event-driven-architecture

Automating the Process of Optimizing Cloud Network Resources with IaC

Automating is the process of optimizing cloud network resources by using IaC to reduce human error, increase operational efficiency, and achieve a highly optimized cloud network environment.

The following steps can help you to achieve this goal. First, determine what it is you want to achieve before the coding begins. Do you want to improve performance? Reduce latency? Are you looking for cost optimization? Define a detailed goal that you want to achieve first and then decide which AWS tools best fit your requirements. Tools such as CloudFormation, the AWS Cloud Development Kit, Terraform, Ansible, and commercial tools and services can be used to create IaC templates that define your network resources and the configurations required to achieve your defined goals. This includes resources such as virtual private clouds, IP subnets, routing tables, security groups, network access control lists, Internet gateways, and any others based on your requirements.

Reference AWS documentation that details the recommended best practices, investigate AWS recommendations for reducing the number of network hops, implement load balancing to distribute traffic, and optimize the routing of network traffic using Route 53, Direct Connect, Global Accelerator, and BGP. Automate the process of deploying network configuration updates. This includes updating the configuration of resources such as VPCs, subnets, routing tables, and security groups to optimize network performance and reduce costs.

AWS network monitoring and logging services such as Amazon CloudWatch and AWS CloudTrail should be implemented to track network performance and detect and resolve issues before they become major problems. Finally, document, test, and validate your changes made through the templates to ensure that they meet the optimization goals and do not introduce new issues or errors. Use versioning to enable rollbacks in case you encounter issues with new templates.

Using network automation for your AWS and on-premises deployment reduces the potential for human error, increases operational efficiencies, and enables your organization to achieve a highly optimized cloud network environment. IaC enables you to automate configuration updates, reducing the time and effort required to manage network resources and ensuring that the cloud network environment is always optimized for performance and cost and to achieve a more efficient and cost-effective cloud networking environment.

Common Problems When Using Hard-Coded Instructions in IaC Templates

When building your IaC deployments, there are some pitfalls to be aware of and steps that developers can take to improve the code quality and reusability. Hard-coding certain instructions reduces the flexibility of your templates. It also makes it difficult to modify, reuse, and update the templates where any changes you want to make will require that the templates be modified. This can be very time-consuming and increases the possibility of errors being introduced, which increases the risk of downtime or reduced performance. The hard-coding of certain instructions into the templates can make them more specific to certain operations in your environment and reduces their usefulness in reusing them for a broader scope of functions. An example would be where you hard-code IP address blocks or addresses in the templates, which then limits using that template outside of the VPC that is using that address block. Hard-coding data specific to your environment such as access keys, passwords, or other secure credentials can also increase security risks if the templates are exposed in public repositories or shared in forums hosted by AWS leading to a data breach or exposure of sensitive information. Hard-coding can also create inconsistencies in your environment if multiple templates are created because of the need for specific data in each environment. Over time these templates can suffer from configuration drift making each deployment different from the other and difficult to manage and troubleshoot.

AWS supports the use of variables and services to prevent the need to hard-code values in IaC templates, allowing you to reuse them in different deployments. Variables allow you to standardize your templates for reuse in different projects and environments. Using variables reduces security risks and makes templates easier to manage and troubleshoot. Services such as the AWS *Secrets Manager* allow you to separate specific parameters from your templates and store them in a secure repository. Use the Secrets Manager service for storing configuration information such as database passwords, API keys, or TLS certificates that are needed by an application at runtime. This allows you to remove sensitive and unique configuration data from your templates and store them in a secure repository.

Hard-coding instructions into IaC templates can be avoided by not implementing specific instructions and using parameterized and modularized IaC templates. Developers can reduce exposing sensitive security credentials, reduce errors, and improve template flexibility when provisioning cloud networking resources in AWS. This allows you to define and reuse variables, creating a standardized process when making changes. These templates separate the code into reusable building blocks, making it easier to reuse the same code across different projects and environments.

Creating and Managing Repeatable Network Configurations

To create and manage repeatable network configuration templates, it is important to follow IaC best practices and use AWS automation tools. Best practices include implementing version controls to track template changes for easy management and quick deployments. Leverage the features available in AWS services and tools such as CloudFormation, the AWS

Cloud Development Kit, or AWS CodeDeploy to ensure consistency and repeatable network configurations templates that can be quickly deployed and updated. Version controls enable the tracking of changes and the ability to roll back to earlier templates if necessary.

Create specific templates for your network infrastructure using the IaC tools of your choice. Specific templates based on function should be created for functions such as VPCs, IP subnets, routing tables, security groups, and any other network resources you need.

Use the network automation tools to automate the configuration of network settings that are best suited for your requirements including the AWS Systems Manager Automation.

Systems Manager enables you to make fast and efficient updates to network configurations and reduce the risk of human error. Automate your deployments by using tools such as AWS CodePipeline or AWS CodeDeploy. These tools make it easier to manage and deploy your network resources while also reducing risks.

Network management of multiple VPCs and VPC interconnection complexity can be reduced by using the AWS Transit Gateway service. The Transit Gateway service provides centralized management of VPC routing and allows for the isolation of network traffic between VPCs. Create a dedicated network connection between on-premises data centers and AWS by implementing Direct Connect. DX provides a consistent and reliable connection between the on-premises network and the AWS network, reducing latency and increasing data transfer rates.

Also, use AWS monitoring and logging services such as CloudWatch to monitor network performance, detect issues, and trigger alerts. CloudWatch offers the automation tools for quick troubleshooting and resolution of network issues. Configure CloudWatch to generate alerts and notifications to alert you to any issues or potential problems.

To ensure a consistent and reliable network infrastructure that can adapt to changes quickly, it is important you use the relevant AWS tools available to create and manage repeatable network configurations in AWS.

Following the steps to create manageable and repeatable network configurations enables you to create and manage your network resources in a consistent and automated way and makes it easier to scale your infrastructure and manage changes over time.

Integrating Event-Driven Networking Functions

The integration of IaC network functions into your AWS deployment enables you to automate the deployment and management of your infrastructure and network functions. Event-driven networking functions allow your organization to respond quickly and automatically to changing conditions.

The steps taken to integrate event-driven networking functions start with defining your requirements. Start by asking what it is you are wanting to accomplish. Determine which networking resources you need to support with automaton and that meet the use case for event-driven functions. This usually includes VPCs, subnets, security groups, and other network resources. Next, create templates using tools such as CloudFormation, the AWS CDK, or Terraform, to create modular IaC templates that include all the necessary infrastructure resources, dependencies, and configuration details for your environment. Add event-driven functions using AWS Lambda, SNS, SQS, EventBridge, or other AWS services that fit your requirements. The event trigger will activate the networking function, allowing it to perform its intended task. Specify the events that should trigger the function and create code to achieve your alerting requirements. After you create the event-driven functions, they are then integrated with templates using the appropriate event sources. For example, a Lambda function may be triggered by an object being stored in an S3 bucket, CloudTrail logs, network traffic, route table changes, or events captured in a Kinesis stream. Other services can include CloudWatch, SNS, SQS, and any other AWS event source. Then you will validate and deploy the configuration to production after testing to ensure the function works as expected. This includes testing the function's ability to process events, perform its intended task, and verify the network resources for connectivity and security. The final step is to monitor and manage the deployed configuration using tools like CloudWatch or AWS Config. Use release management best practices to manage updates and changes to the integration. The AWS-provided tools enable real-time monitoring and alerting to track changes to ensure compliance with your organization's security requirements.

Your organization can create a scalable and flexible network infrastructure that automatically adapts to changes in your environment by implementing event-driven networking functions in AWS. IaC provides automation for the deployment and management of your AWS network infrastructure, and the capabilities of the event-driven functions allow you to quickly respond to changes in real time, creating fast and efficient processing of data and events.

Integrating Hybrid Network Automation Options with AWS Native IaC

Integrating hybrid network automation options with AWS native IaC provides a complete network management solution. This includes both the network infrastructure that spans on-premises and AWS environments.

The steps taken to accomplish an integrated hybrid network automation objective begin by defining your objective. Ask what it is you want to accomplish. Define the network architecture, routing tables, security requirements, and all other objectives for both the AWS and on-premises networks.

Next you need to select the network automation tooling that best fits your requirements and integrates with your environment. Common hybrid network automation tools include open-source tools such as Ansible, Puppet, and Chef. There are many commercial tools on the market including Cisco DNA Center and VMware NSX, SaltStack, and SolarWinds.

Then define AWS native templates using tools such as CloudFormation, AWS Cloud Development Kit, or Terraform. These templates should include the necessary resources for the application, such as VPCs, subnets, security groups, and other network resources. The next step is to use the hybrid network automation tools to define the on-premises network infrastructure and integrate it with the AWS native IaC templates. This includes defining the network topology, security policies, and all hybrid network resources that span both on-premises and cloud environments. Use the AWS native tools and services to provision the infrastructure. This creates the necessary cloud resources in the specified AWS accounts and regions.

Once the provisioning has been completed, test the hybrid network automation to make sure that it functions as you expect it to. This will include testing the network connectivity between on-premises and cloud environments, verifying security policies, and testing the application's performance and testing. Test the on-premises device configuration interfaces using APIs or command-line interfaces that are provided by the hybrid network automation tool.

If the hybrid network automation or infrastructure needs to be updated, you will modify the templates and use the automation tooling and services to update the configuration. As we discussed previously, it is important to use version control tools and release management practices to track changes and ensure that all changes are properly tested and approved before production deployments occur.

By integrating hybrid network automation options with AWS native IaC, you can create a flexible and powerful way to manage network infrastructure that spans both on-premises and cloud environments. This approach allows users to take advantage of the benefits of both on-premises and cloud environments while providing a consistent and reliable way to manage network infrastructure across both environments.

Eliminating Risk and Achieving Efficiency in a Cloud Networking Environment

The goal of eliminating risk and achieving efficiency in AWS may sound contradictory; however, there are steps you can take to achieve this goal. Automation is a key factor in achieving efficiency and cost savings in your AWS networking environment. With automation, tasks such as network configuration, scaling, and monitoring reduce, but do not eliminate, human error and achieve a more efficient and reliable network infrastructure.

The first step is to take the time and effort to create an effective design based on your specific requirements. Many AWS services are available that are constantly being updated with new features. Amazon reduces service pricing regularly, and new reference designs are released. This step includes identifying the required resources, such as VPCs, subnets, routing tables, security groups, and NACLs, and then deciding on the most appropriate network architecture and connectivity options.

Your design should meet all your requirements and be scalable and secure; the network infrastructure must meet the needs of the application while minimizing costs.

Once the network architecture has been determined, you should investigate ways to optimize the network resources. Investigate where you can reduce costs. For example, if a resource is not needed or a feature is not required, disable it on the AWS console. By using AWS-provided management tools such as Cost Explorer and Trusted Advisor, you can operate your cloud deployment more efficiently.

As we have discussed throughout this chapter, use IaC to manage AWS network resources. There are many tools you can leverage, including CloudFormation, the AWS Cloud Development Kit, or Terraform, to define and manage your network IaC, enabling you to maintain, update, and reproduce infrastructure resources consistently and reliably.

Leveraging network monitoring for performance is essential to identifying potential issues and optimizing your AWS network resources. AWS services such as CloudWatch, Config, and AWS X-Ray can be implemented to monitor and identify areas for improvement.

AWS cost management tools that are used to optimize your AWS spending include the AWS Cost Explorer and AWS Budgets. These tools help identify areas where costs can be reduced and set up cost alerts to prevent unexpected expenses. Also, by implementing monitoring and alerting solutions, you can identify and resolve issues before they cause downtime or impact performance, which can save costs.

AWS users reduce risk, achieve greater efficiencies, and manage costs by following these steps. By using AWS best practices, using tools, and implementing network automation, you can create a secure, cost-efficient, and scalable network infrastructure. Regularly reviewing and updating your AWS networking environment ensures that it will continue to meet the needs of the application and stays up-to-date with the latest best practices and technologies.

Summary

In this chapter, you learned about network automation and the AWS tools available. Then we discussed how to use automation in your AWS infrastructure. IaC refers to the abstraction of AWS cloud hardware into software that is used to define your deployments. All interactions with AWS cloud services are defined in software. These software interfaces allow you to create, configure, monitor, and secure your deployments.

We started with a deep dive into the AWS tools available, including the Cloud Development Kit, CloudFormation, and EventBridge. Next you learned about the AWS CLI and the SDK and how to integrate them into your automation strategies.

We revisited the topic of APIs and how they are used to access all AWS services from various front-end applications such as web browsers, the CLI, and SDKs.

You learned about network automation using IaC. We investigated the different use cases for network automation in AWS including triggering automation based on events, automating cloud adoption, hard-coding data into templates, creating repeatable configurations, using automation in hybrid networks, and reducing risks when implementing IaC deployments.

Next, we went into detail on automating the process of optimizing cloud network resources by using IaC to reduce human error, increase operational efficiencies, and achieve a highly optimized cloud network environment.

When building your IaC deployments, there are some pitfalls to be aware of and steps that developers can take to improve the code quality and reusability. Hard-coding certain instructions reduces the flexibility of your templates. It also makes it difficult to modify, reuse, and update the templates where any changes you want to make will require that the templates be modified. Next you learned about methods to reduce hard-coding instruction in your templates.

Creating and managing repeatable network configuration templates using IaC best practices and AWS automation tools was discussed. The best practices include implementing version controls to track template changes for easy management and quick deployments. Leverage the features available in AWS services and tools such as CloudFormation, the AWS Cloud Development Kit, or AWS CodeDeploy to ensure consistency and repeatable network configuration templates that can be quickly deployed and updated.

Event-driven networking functions allow your organization to respond quickly and automatically to changing conditions. You learned about the architecture and methods used when setting up event-driven network automations. The capabilities of the event-driven functions allow you to quickly respond to changes in real time, creating fast and efficient processing of data and events.

You then learned about integrating hybrid network automation options with AWS native IaC and enabling a complete network management solution. This includes both the network infrastructure that spans on-premises and AWS environments.

Finally, you learned how to use IaC to achieve efficiency and cost savings in your AWS networking environment. With automation, tasks such as network configuration, scaling, and monitoring reduce, but do not eliminate, human error and achieve a more efficient and reliable network infrastructure.

Exam Essentials

Know what the Cloud Development Kit is used for and its basic functions.   The CDK enables developers to create a cloud infrastructure as a set of reusable code called *constructs*. These constructs are packaged into libraries and can be shared in your organization or published to the AWS CloudFormation registry for public access. This approach enables developers to use prebuilt constructs or create their own custom code for reusability across different projects. In the exam, there may be scenarios that describe IaC, and you must identify the tools required, such as the Cloud Development Kit, to complete the task.

Know what CloudFormation is, its various components, and how it is used for AWS automation projects.   CloudFormation service enables developers to define and manage AWS IaC by using templates. CloudFormation is the primary automation tool in AWS, and it is important that you understand how it is structured and how it deploys and rolls back configurations.

Know the AWS automation tools available such as EventBridge, the CLI, and the SDK.   EventBridge is a serverless service that provides real-time access to changes in data in AWS services, without having to create custom code. EventBridge uses events that you set triggers for in order to connect application components together; the service makes it easy to create scalable event-driven applications. The AWS CLI enables you to manage AWS resources from the command line instead of the web GUI interface or using SDKs. The CLI includes an extensive set of commands used to interact with all AWS services and resources. The AWS SDK is a collection of Amazon-provided software tools and libraries to assist your developers in building applications that interact with various AWS services. The SDK provides libraries for multiple programming languages, including C++, Go, Java, .NET, Ruby, Python, Java, JavaScript, Kotlin, .NET, Node.js, Rust, Swift, and PHP, which allows developers to integrate AWS services into their applications.

Understand the functions of APIs and how they are used when configuring AWS services.   APIs are sets of tools, documentation, and protocols used by developers to interact with all AWS services programmatically. When using the web interface, the CLI, or the SDK to interact with AWS, underneath the interfaces is an API that is used to communicate with AWS. AWS APIs provide a standardized interface for accessing all AWS services, allowing developers to build applications that use AWS services without requiring direct access to the underlying infrastructure.

Understand how network automation is accomplished using IaC.   Know the various use cases for AWS network automation and the steps taken to implement them. Some of the uses for AWS network automation include triggering automation based on events, automating cloud adoption, investigating the issues of hard-coding data into templates, creating repeatable configurations, using automation in hybrid networks, and reducing risks when implementing infrastructure as code deployments.

Exercises

1. Know how CloudFormation works in detail and explore the web user interface. Read the CloudFormation documentation at `https://docs.aws.amazon.com/cloudformation`.

2. Read and become familiar with the AWS Cloud Development Kit at `https://aws.amazon.com/cdk`.

3. Read and become familiar with the AWS Developer tools at `https://aws.amazon.com/developer/tools`.

4. Read and become familiar with the AWS API interfaces at `https://aws.amazon.com/what-is/api`.

Review Questions

The following questions are designed to test your understanding of this chapter's material. For more information on how to obtain additional questions, please see this book's introduction.

1. What abstracts the physical network infrastructure into software that describes the deployments?
   A. Automation
   B. Hypervisor type II
   C. AWS CloudTrail
   D. AWS Control Tower
   E. AWS Deployment Bridge

2. You have been tasked with defining your deployment using a declarative code format that deploys your cloud resources automatically using automation tools to provision and manage your resources. What design function are you performing?
   A. Resource Access Manager
   B. Amazon Aurora
   C. Infrastructure as code (IaC)
   D. Amazon Code Guru
   E. AWS LightSail

3. Name two code formats used by CloudFormation.
   A. XML
   B. Java
   C. YAML
   D. Python 3
   E. JSON

4. What's the AWS serverless service that provides real-time access to changes in data in AWS, without having to create custom code?
   A. AWS Macie
   B. AWS CloudTrail
   C. AWS CodeStar
   D. AWS EventBridge

5. Which AWS tool enables you to manage AWS resources without using the web GUI interface or using SDKs?
   A. AWS CLI
   B. Bash
   C. PowerShell
   D. AWS API

6. Which AWS command-line tool enables the creation and management of stacks that can be updated and deployed together or deleted as a single unit and integrates with CodePipeline and CloudFormation?

   A. CodeStar

   B. Amazon QuickSight

   C. Cloud Development Kit

   D. AWS Config

   E. AWS Code Guru

7. What is the open-source AWS tool used in software development frameworks that allows for creating cloud infrastructure definitions and provisioning the code using AWS CloudFormation?

   A. Amazon IQ

   B. AWS Config

   C. AWS AppSync

   D. AWS Cloud Development Kit

   E. AWS App Runner

8. When automating hybrid networks, what are common open-source tools used in enterprise data centers? (Select three.)

   A. SolarWinds

   B. Puppet

   C. Chef

   D. Ansible

   E. Config

   F. DNA Center

   G. SNMP

9. What tasks can be automated in your AWS deployment? (Select three.)

   A. Network configurations

   B. Account creation

   C. Security scans

   D. Monitoring

   E. Scaling

10. You are investigating ways to not hard-code sensitive information into your CloudFormation templates and store them in a secure repository. What AWS service would you investigate?

    A. Cognito

    B. Secrets Manager

    C. DynamoDB

    D. Config

    E. SWF

11. Which AWS toolkit provides software tools and libraries that are used by developers to build applications that interact with various AWS services?

    A. SDK

    B. CDK

    C. CLI

    D. API

12. What is the process called of using a declarative code format that deploys your cloud resources automatically?

    A. CodePipeline

    B. Infrastructure as code

    C. Elastic Kubernetes Service

    D. Representational State Transfer

    E. Event-driven automation

13. Which AWS tool provides a standardized interface for accessing all AWS services, allowing developers to build applications that use AWS services without requiring direct access to the underlying infrastructure?

    A. CDK

    B. Application programming interface

    C. SDK

    D. CloudFormation

14. Which AWS IaC service can be used to trigger automation pushes based on the date/time trigger?

    A. Config

    B. EventBridge

    C. Simple Queuing Service

    D. Application programming interfaces

15. What does the Cloud Development Kit create as sets of reusable code that can be packaged into libraries?

    A. AWS Step Functions

    B. Constructs

    C. Stack sets

    D. Application programming interface

16. What CDK enhancement provides many features such as code highlighting, autocompletion, and error checking?

    A. AWS Control Tower

    B. Integrated development environments

    C. CloudFormation

    D. AWS Code Guru

    E. AWS Config

17. Which AWS interface allows third-party applications and services to be integrated with AWS and act as front-end portals used to configure, monitor, and troubleshoot AWS resources?

   A. Application programming interfaces

   B. Macie

   C. RDS

   D. Outposts

   E. IAM

18. What automation tool is provided for managing AWS resources, such as the creation and deletion of resources, access control, and monitoring resource usage, and provides performance optimization features, such as batch operations, request throttling, and caching?

   A. Redshift

   B. Control tower

   C. SQS

   D. AWS SDK

   E. SWF

19. When automating hybrid networks, what commercial tools are used in enterprise data center IaC deployments? (Select four.)

   A. SolarWinds

   B. DNA Center

   C. NSX

   D. Ansible

   E. Puppet

   F. SaltStack

   G. Chef

20. Which AWS automation tool is integrated with multiple IDEs such as Visual Studio Code, IntelliJ, and PyCharm?

   A. Git Hybrid

   B. RDS

   C. DynamoDB

   D. CDK

   E. ECS

Chapter

11

Monitor, Analyze, and Optimize Network Traffic

THE AWS CERTIFIED ADVANCED NETWORKING - SPECIALTY EXAM OBJECTIVES COVERED IN THIS CHAPTER MAY INCLUDE, BUT ARE NOT LIMITED TO, THE FOLLOWING:

✓ **Domain 3: Network Management and Operations**

- Objective 3.2: Monitor and analyze network traffic to troubleshoot and optimize connectivity patterns.

- Objective 3.3: Optimize AWS networks for performance, reliability, and cost-effectiveness.

Monitoring, Analyzing, and Optimizing AWS Networks

In this chapter, you will learn how to use the Amazon networking tools and techniques to monitor your network, capture and analyze traffic to better understand your network, and troubleshoot issues as they arise. Based on the monitoring and logging data collected and a deep understanding of AWS networking, you can then optimize your deployment for maximum performance reliability and cost-effectiveness.

This chapter will cover a lot of ground on how to monitor, optimize, and use automation on your AWS network. We will also review many of the services and tools already covered in earlier chapters such as Route 53, elastic load balancers, the Reachability Analyzer, VPCs, logging, and others with a focus on how to apply them, where they can be used, and what tools and technologies are available to use from AWS, as well as from open-source and commercial companies.

Monitor and Analyze Network Traffic to Troubleshoot and Optimize Connectivity Patterns

Monitoring and analyzing network traffic in your AWS deployment requires a knowledge of the AWS services and tools available to you, as well as the techniques and skills to use to meet your objectives. In this chapter, you will learn about the AWS-provided, open-source, and public tools available to use. Many of the AWS services have options for tuning parameters to fit your requirements that we will cover. Some of the AWS services that can be utilized include VPC Flow logging, which captures information about IP traffic flows that are sent and received from network interfaces in a VPC. Flow Logs can be enabled at the VPC, subnet, or network interfaces. The logs are stored in S3 buckets and used to analyze traffic and for troubleshooting networking issues.

Flow Logs capture metadata about the IP traffic going to and from network interfaces in your VPC and capture information about the source and destination of the traffic, the protocol used, and the number of bytes transferred. You can use this information to troubleshoot connectivity issues and optimize network performance. CloudWatch provides a monitoring and logging service for a wide range of AWS services, resources, and device syslogs, including Flow Logs. The Amazon CloudWatch service is the tool used to collect and analyze metrics and log data, configure notifications, and trigger alarms when thresholds are reached. The AWS Network Firewall is an AWS managed service for network filtering and packet inspection. The Network Firewall can be used to monitor and analyze traffic, and rules can be configured to allow or block traffic that you define based on IP addresses, ports, protocols, and other values.

There is a wide variety of very useful public and vendor network optimization and troubleshooting tools that you can use for monitoring and analyzing network traffic in AWS. These tools help you to gain insights into your network traffic and resolve issues more quickly.

With a knowledge of how and when to use the various tools and services, you can monitor and analyze network traffic on AWS and use the findings to optimize connectivity patterns, enabling you to improve network performance and reliability. A deep understanding of how to monitor and analyze traffic in your cloud deployments is an important part of troubleshooting and optimizing connectivity patterns in AWS.

Some key steps to help you effectively monitor and analyze network traffic that we will cover in this chapter include the use of VPC Flow Logs to capture information about traffic flows going to and from network interfaces in your VPC. Enabling VPC Flow Logs can help you understand the traffic patterns and identify potential issues that may be impacting network connectivity.

- Monitor the CloudWatch Metrics service. CloudWatch Metrics provides a range of network-related data to monitor and analyze network traffic. These metrics can help you understand the performance of your network and enable you to identify potential issues that may be impacting connectivity.

- Implement the AWS X-Ray service discussed in Chapter 5, "Logging and Monitoring." X-Ray allows you to trace requests through your applications and helps you to identify the root cause of performance issues. By tracing requests through your applications, you can identify issues as seen from the communication patterns between applications to better understand where the impairments are located, and you can determine if they are network related.

- Use network load balancers to distribute traffic across multiple targets, improve application availability, and reduce the impact of network issues. Network load balancers provide high-throughput, low-latency load balancing for TCP and UDP traffic. Elastic load balancers provide load balancing for HTTP and HTTPS traffic. By using elastic load balancers, you can distribute traffic across multiple targets, improve application availability, and reduce the impact of network issues.

- The AWS Global Accelerator, covered in Chapter 1, "Edge Networking," can improve network performance and application availability by routing traffic to the most desirable AWS service endpoint. The Global Accelerator reduces latency, increases throughput, and improves the overall performance of your applications by directing traffic off the public Internet and onto the AWS internal network as close to the source as possible.

- The AWS-managed DNS service Route 53 generates logs that are useful for optimizing your network. Route 53 Resolver query logging enables you to log DNS queries that are made by all resources requesting name resolution. Route 53 Resolver query logs are used to monitor DNS traffic and troubleshoot connectivity issues related to hostname resolution.

- The Network Insights service provides visibility into the network traffic and connectivity of your VPC. By using Network Insights, you can troubleshoot connectivity issues, optimize network performance, and identify security threats by analyzing network flow data.

With a practical working knowledge of networking and the ability to monitor and analyze network traffic, you can troubleshoot and optimize connectivity patterns in AWS. This allows you to discover and resolve network-related issues that may be impacting network performance and to improve the overall performance and availability of your applications. This ensures your applications are running in the best configurations available and that your users can access them quickly and reliably.

Network Performance Metrics and Reachability Constraints

The various AWS reachability constraints, performance values, and metrics that can impact the connectivity patterns of an application are important to understand. You must be aware of what the network is and is not capable of.

Common constraints include network *latency*, which is the time it takes for data to travel from the source to the destination. *Packet loss* in the network occurs when data packets fail to reach their destination. This can be due to network congestion, routing issues, circuit impairments, and other factors. *Jitter* is the variance of time delay between when a packet is transmitted to when it is received; in other words, it's the change in delay. Jitter affects performance by injecting latency variations over time. Network *throughput* is the amount of data that can be transmitted over a network in each time period, and throughput is the speed of the network. High throughput is critical for applications that require fast data transfer, such as video streaming, big data, high-performance computing, and large file transfers.

High latency, network throughput limitations, jitter, and packet loss can all contribute to impairments in the network that slow down application performance.

Network routing protocols determine the best path for data to travel from the source to the destination. If the routing process is not optimal, then routing can cause delays and impact the performance of your network.

The size of the packets that are sent over a network can also impact performance. Large packets can increase throughput but may also cause congestion and packet loss.

To optimize your cloud connectivity patterns, it is critical to monitor and analyze these metrics and constraints to identify potential issues and areas for improvement. AWS provides various tools for monitoring network performance, such as CloudWatch, VPC Flow Logs, and network load balancer metrics that we will cover in detail in this chapter.

By using all available network services, tools, and proper monitoring of the network, you can optimize the performance and reachability of your AWS network resources. This helps increase the reliability and scalability of your applications and ensure a consistent and high-quality experience for your users.

Appropriate Logs and Metrics to Assess Network Performance and Reachability Issues

When monitoring network performance and reachability issues in AWS, you can leverage the various logs and metrics to gain insights into the health and performance of your network infrastructure.

There are multiple approaches you can take when monitoring logs generated by your network infrastructure for health and performance. As mentioned, VPC Flow Logs capture IP traffic information into and out of your VPC. CloudWatch is a primary AWS monitoring service that provides various metrics for monitoring network performance such as NetworkIn and NetworkOut frames, which record the amount of traffic in and out of your instances, and NetworkPacketsIn and NetworkPacketsOut, which measure the number of network packets sent and received by your instances. These metrics can help you identify baseline variations, trends, and anomalies in your network traffic.

AWS offers the Network Performance Monitor (NPM) tool that provides real-time visibility into the performance of your network. The NPM can help you diagnose and troubleshoot network issues by providing data on network topology, packet loss, latency, and other metrics.

Elastic load balancer access logs generate information about the requests and responses processed by your load balancer, including data such as the client IP address, request and response headers, and the HTTP response status code. Backend server logs include metrics such as ActiveFlowCount, TCP_Client_Reset_Count, and TCP_ELB_Reset_Count. These logs can help you identify issues such as failed requests and slow response times.

Route 53 provides detailed DNS query logs that contain information about the DNS queries received by Route 53, including the query type, domain name, and client IP address. Route 53 query logs can help you identify issues such as DNS resolution failures or excessive DNS latency.

Monitoring and analyzing the logging data generated in your deployment enables insight into performance and reachability issues and identifies where to take appropriate actions to optimize the health and performance of your network.

AWS Tools to Collect and Analyze Logs and Metrics

AWS provides native log collection tools and services, enabling you to gather and analyze logs and metrics generated internally or externally from AWS.

The most common AWS logging tools are CloudWatch logs, VPC Flow Logs, VPC traffic mirroring, CloudTrail, Lambda, and the Amazon Open Search Service (formerly Elasticsearch).

CloudWatch is the AWS monitoring and observability service that collects and displays metrics and logs from your AWS resources, such as EC2 instances, DynamoDB, Lambda, RDS databases, elastic load balancers, external servers, VPC Flow Logs, and many other services. CloudWatch Logs collects and stores logs from these resources and can be configured to generate alarms to be notified when metrics exceed certain thresholds enabling automated responses.

Flow Logs provide logging data about the traffic flowing into and out of your VPC, including the source and destination IP addresses, ports, and protocol. Flow Logs are helpful when troubleshooting network connectivity issues, when monitoring network performance, and for security analysis. Flow Logs can be analyzed by various third-party tools or with the AWS CloudWatch Logs service.

VPC Traffic Mirroring mirrors network traffic from a network interface of an EC2 instance to another network interface in the same VPC. The captured traffic can be sent to a destination, such as Amazon EC2 instances or S3 buckets, where it can then be analyzed using various tools and services.

CloudTrail provides logging of all the API calls made to your AWS account, including API calls made via the AWS Management Console, SDKs, and command-line tools. CloudTrail is useful for auditing, compliance, security operations, and troubleshooting.

AWS Lambda is a serverless compute service that can be used to process and analyze logging and metrics. Lambda is helpful when creating custom code to process and analyze logs and metric data in real time. Lambda can then send the results to various destinations, including S3, Amazon Kinesis streams, SQS, SNS, or third-party service offerings.

Amazon Open Search Service, originally called Elasticsearch, is a fully managed search and analytics engine that is used to search, analyze, and visualize your log data. The service is integrated with several AWS services, including CloudWatch Logs, VPC Flow Logs, and CloudTrail, that enable you to create custom dashboards to monitor your logs.

By leveraging these tools, you can collect and analyze logs and metrics data from various sources and gain insights into the performance and health of your AWS resources and applications.

AWS Tools to Analyze Routing Patterns and Issues

There are AWS-provided services and tools specifically used to analyze your network architecture.

The AWS Reachability Analyzer tool enables you to test whether traffic can reach a target resource from a specified source. The Reachability Analyzer uses a combination of `ping` and `traceroute` ICMP tests to determine the routing path, latency, and packet loss of the traffic. The analyzer is used to troubleshoot connectivity issues and verify the effectiveness of security groups and network ACLs. It can perform automated checks of your network infrastructure and provides a visual representation of your network topology and routing paths. It can also help identify the source of connectivity issues and suggest potential solutions. For more information on the Reachability Analyzer, refer to Chapter 5.

The Transit Gateway Network Manager tool provides a centralized view of your global network, including Transit Gateways and connected networks. With the Gateway Network Manager, you can analyze network traffic flows, troubleshoot connectivity problems, and monitor the health and performance of your network. The tool can be used to optimize routing and reduce operational complexity of your network. For more information on the Transit Gateway Network Manager, refer to Chapter 5, and Chapter 8, "Inter-VPC and Multi-Account Networking."

Elastic load balancers are an AWS service family that distributes incoming traffic across multiple targets, such as EC2 instances, containers, or IP addresses. They provide high availability, scalability, and low latency for your applications. Elastic load balancers can be used to optimize routing and improve the performance of your applications. For more information on the elastic load balancers, refer to Chapter 1.

The AWS Route 53 service provides DNS resolution for your domain names. It extends the DNS feature set by adding the ability to route traffic to the optimal endpoint based on geographic location, latency, and health of the endpoints. Enabling these Route 53 extended features enables you to improve the availability and performance of your applications. For more information on Route 53, refer to Chapter 2, "Domain Name Services," and Chapter 3, "Hybrid and Multi-Account DNS."

The AWS Global Accelerator service improves the availability and performance of your applications by directing traffic to the optimal AWS endpoint from the source. It uses anycast routing to automatically route traffic to the nearest endpoint based on geographic location and network health. The Global Accelerator reduces latency and improves application performance by directing traffic off the public Internet and onto the AWS global network. For more information on the Global Accelerator, refer to Chapter 1.

AWS VPC Flow Logs can also be used to collect metrics on routing patterns and issues. By analyzing the Flow Logs, you can identify the source and destination of traffic, along with the protocols and ports being used. Use this information to troubleshoot routing issues and monitor network traffic.

By using these tools, you can gain visibility and control over your network and identify and resolve routing issues.

Analyzing Logging Output to Assess Network Performance and Troubleshoot Connectivity

You can use several AWS services and tools to analyze collected data, evaluate network performance, and troubleshoot connectivity issues in your AWS environment. The available tools include VPC Flow Logs and Amazon CloudWatch Logs.

VPC Flow Logs provide information about the traffic flowing in and out of your VPC, including the source and destination IP addresses, ports, and protocol. By analyzing these logs, you can identify traffic patterns and monitor traffic volume. This information is useful when troubleshooting connectivity issues and identifying potential network security issues.

Amazon CloudWatch Logs are used to monitor, store, and access log files collected from your AWS and on-premises resources. By analyzing CloudWatch Logs, you can identify errors and issues in your environment, including network connectivity issues. Alarms can be created based on log metrics to alert you to potential problems.

When analyzing the output from your tools, start by looking for patterns and trends. Look for patterns in traffic volume, usage, and errors. Use this information to identify potential issues and connectivity problems. If you have established a performance baseline, compare current data with the expected metrics recorded in the baseline. Look for the source of the problem, whether it's a misconfiguration, a security issue, or a performance problem.

Use visual aids provided by AWS. Visualization tools can help you identify network patterns and issues, including VPC Flow Logs and CloudWatch Metrics. Create alarms based on CloudWatch metrics. Configure alarms using CloudWatch, which notifies you when certain conditions are met. Use these tools to gain a better understanding of your network, enable automation, and identify issues.

By analyzing the output of network monitoring tools like VPC Flow Logs and CloudWatch Logs, you can gain insights into your AWS environment and identify issues before they become serious problems.

Network Topology Mapping

Understanding your network topology and maintaining up-to-date documentation is essential for managing and troubleshooting any network including your AWS deployments. Creating detailed network diagrams to better understand your network topology is an important step in managing and troubleshooting your AWS environment.

A network topology diagram is the physical or logical structure of the network and the connections between the network components. Mapping the network topology can help greatly in identifying potential bottlenecks, fixing misconfigurations, and optimizing network performance. AWS provides tools that can help you map or understand the network topology of your environment.

As we have discussed throughout this book, a primary tool is the AWS Transit Gateway Network Manager, which provides a centralized view of your network topology and can help you visualize the connections between your network components. It allows you to track the health and performance of your Transit Gateways and attached resources, monitor your traffic, and troubleshoot connectivity issues.

Using the visual representation of your network topology allows you to see the connections between your Transit Gateways, VPN connections, VPCs, and other resources in a graphical format. You can view the status and configuration of each resource, as well as the traffic flow between them. Using information can help you identify misconfigurations, bottlenecks, and security issues, and take appropriate actions to optimize your network performance. In addition to providing a visual representation of your network topology, the

Transit Gateway Network Manager also allows you to track the performance of your network and analyze traffic patterns. It provides metrics such as packet loss, latency, and bandwidth utilization, which can help when troubleshooting connectivity issues and optimizing your network performance. The tool provides metrics that enable you to monitor the health and performance of your Transit Gateway network, including the number of active routes, the amount of traffic, and the latency of the connections.

By using the Transit Gateway Network Manager, you gain a better understanding of your network topology and identify potential issues that can affect network performance. This helps you to optimize your network performance and ensure that your network can support the requirements of your applications and users.

Analyzing Packets to Identify Issues

Knowing how to capture and analyze data at the packet level is a critical skill for any network engineer. By performing packet analysis, the most obscure and hard-to-identify issues can be resolved. AWS provides several tools that are used to capture and analyze packets, including VPC Traffic Mirroring. This tool is used to capture network traffic from an Amazon Elastic Compute Cloud (EC2) instance or Elastic Network Interface (ENI) by mirroring the traffic to a different instance for capture and analysis. This enables you to capture and analyze network traffic for security and troubleshooting purposes.

To perform a packet capture in a VPC, you will set up a traffic mirror session to capture the traffic you want to analyze. You can create the mirror by defining the instance interface or elastic network adapter you want to capture the data from and the destination to send it to for capture and for analysis. The destination interface must be set to promiscuous mode for packet capture capabilities.

You can use packet capture and analysis tools like Wireshark to analyze the captured packets. Wireshark is an open-source packet analyzer that allows you to view the details of each packet, including the source and destination IP addresses, the protocols used, and the data contained inside each packet.

By analyzing the packets, you can identify issues at the packet level, including dropped packets, delayed packets, or packets that have been modified. This information is very helpful in identifying and troubleshooting networking issues and to optimize the performance of your AWS network.

After the issue has been identified, you can take corrective action to address the problem. For example, you need to add quality-of-service configurations to place more critical or delay-sensitive voice traffic at a higher priority than storage traffic that is not delay-sensitive or to ensure that critical traffic has priority over noncritical data flows.

Using AWS VPC Traffic Mirroring and deep packet inspection tools like Wireshark enables you to capture and analyze packets to identify issues at the packet level and to troubleshoot network issues. Traffic mirroring helps you to troubleshoot and identify connectivity issues in your AWS environment. This enables you to optimize network performance and ensure that your applications are always available and responsive.

Using the Reachability Analyzer for Troubleshooting, Validating, and Automating Connectivity Issues

The Reachability Analyzer is a tool used to troubleshoot, verify network connectivity, and use automation for ongoing monitoring of your network.

Diagnosing network connectivity issues caused by misconfigurations can be a complex task, especially in large and hybrid networks such as AWS. Network misconfigurations can cause connectivity issues that impact application availability and performance. The troubleshooting complexity is reduced by using the tools provided by AWS, including the Reachability Analyzer that we covered in Chapter 5.

The Reachability Analyzer is a network diagnostic tool used for testing and troubleshooting network connectivity issues in your VPC. It uses a combination of traceroute and network probing to identify potential connectivity issues and pinpoint the source of the problem. You use the Reachability Analyzer to identify the resources that are having connectivity issues between the source and destination of the traffic.

You can use automation of the Reachability Analyzer to continuously verify the connectivity of your network as network configuration changes. This ensures that the network is functioning as intended and identifies any issues as soon as they arise.

To use the Reachability Analyzer for troubleshooting, the first step is to configure the test by specifying the source and destination interfaces of the test. You configure the test using the AWS Web Management Console, CLI, or SDKs. After the configuration parameters have been set up, initiate the test to identify potential connectivity issues. The test uses a combination of `traceroute` and network probing to help identify potential issues in the network path.

After the test completes its run, you can analyze the results to identify the source of the connectivity issue. The test data contains information on the network hops, the latency between the source and destination, and any network errors that were encountered in the path. The tool helps identify routing issues including misconfigured or missing network routes that may be causing connectivity issues and the routing configurations of your VPC. The Reachability Analyzer can be used to identify configuration errors in security group rules that may be blocking traffic to your resources.

The tool provides you with step-by-step instructions on how to fix the issues and restore network connectivity. Once you have determined where the issue resides, you can take steps to fix the problem, which may include changing device configurations, changing the routing tables, adjusting security group rules, modifying firewall rules or access control lists, or adding additional network capacity to optimize performance and reduce latency.

The Reachability Analyzer is often used when verifying your configuration during deployment or after changes have been made. You can run reachability tests to verify the changes are working as expected.

The Reachability Analyzer enables you to identify network connectivity issues and then to troubleshoot the identified issue quickly and easily. The tool helps to optimize your network for better performance and ensure that your applications are always available and responsive. Use the Reachability Analyzer to perform connectivity tests between different resources in your network, including VPCs, subnets, and endpoints. The tool can identify network misconfigurations that may be causing connectivity issues.

Optimize AWS Networks for Performance, Reliability, and Cost-Effectiveness

In this section, you will learn the different approaches available to maximize the performance of your AWS and hybrid network, enabling it to be reliable, secure, and cost-effective. We'll look at choosing the best approach to interconnect networks based on your requirements. You will learn about the use of multicast networks for one-to-many streaming architectures such as collaboration and video applications. We will look again at the AWS Route 53 DNS service and how its extensions can be used to optimize connectivity. Finally, we will cover the topic of frame sizes on the network.

VPC Peering vs. Transit Gateways

Communications between VPCs can be accomplished using peering or Transit Gateways. Both networking offerings from AWS allow your VPCs to communicate with each other. There are, however, specific use cases where one solution may be preferred over the other.

In situations where you want to interconnect two VPCs together and they are both in the same region, VPC peering would be more appropriate. VPC peering creates a direct connection between two VPCs and allows the instances in each VPC to have network connectivity between each other across two directly connected networks. VPC peering is used when you need to keep your network traffic inside the AWS network for compliance and security requirements, minimize network latency, and reduce costs.

VPC peering can be used in architectures when you want to create a hybrid cloud environment with multiple VPCs in the same region or when you need to connect multiple VPCs to share resources and workloads. VPC peering is a simple and cost-effective solution to connect VPCs in the same region to share resources such as databases, filesystems, and applications. For more information on VPC peering, review Chapter 8, and Chapter 9, "Hybrid Network Routing and Connectivity."

You would need to implement a Transit Gateway, when you have multiple VPCs that need to communicate across different AWS regions or accounts, or to create a hybrid network from your on-premises data center to AWS. The Transit Gateway acts as a central network hub that connects multiple VPCs, simplifies network management, improves security, and reduces complex peering designs. Use the Transit Gateway when you need to build a global network architecture that must be managed and be able to scale the network connections between AWS regions. For more information on Transit Gateways, review Chapter 7, "Connecting On-Premises Networks," and Chapter 8.

If you want to connect two VPCs within the same region, VPC peering is most likely going to be the best solution. However, to connect multiple VPCs that reside in different regions or accounts, you would need to use the Transit Gateway. You must analyze the network requirements of your environment to determine whether a VPC peering connection or a Transit Gateway is appropriate for your AWS environment.

Reducing Bandwidth Utilization with Multicast

Reducing the amount of traffic sent across the AWS network can result in better performance, lower costs, and reduced congestion. In this section, you will learn about using multicast in place of unicast transmissions, and we will review CloudFront, which was covered in Chapter 1.

Unicast is a one-to-one network communication between a single source and a single destination. Unicast is the most common data flow in a network but can be inefficient in certain use cases. A unicast data flow is shown in Figure 11.1.

FIGURE 11.1   Unicast data flow

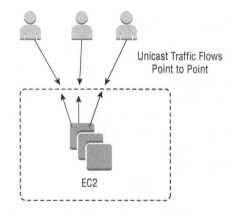

Multicast is one-to-many where data is sent to multiple destinations from a single source, as shown in Figure 11.2. This one-to-many architecture reduces the bandwidth required for sending data compared to unicast. An example of a multicast use would be if you are streaming a company video event with many participants viewing a speaker, the speaker would be the sender, and the participants would all be listening to the single multicast flow instead of the need for the speaker to send an individual data stream to each listener using unicast. This is a much more efficient use of network bandwidth.

Multicast traffic is supported when using the Elastic Network Adapter (ENA) or the Elastic Fabric Adapter (EFA) used in high-performance computing applications.

Implementing Multicast Capability Within a VPC and On-Premises Environments

Multicast is not enabled by default in a VPC. You enable multicast in the Transit Gateway console, as shown in Figure 11.3.

FIGURE 11.2   Multicast data flow

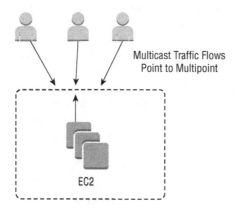

Multicast Traffic Flows
Point to Multipoint

EC2

FIGURE 11.3   Configuring Transit Gateway multicast

VPC > Transit gateway multicast domains > Create transit gateway multicast domain

Create transit gateway multicast domain   Info

A multicast domain controls how traffic flows for all associated subnets. A multicast domain can only be created in transit gateway with the multicast support option enabled.

Details

Name tag - *optional*
Creates a tag with the key set to Name and the value set to the specified string.

    transit-gateway-multicast-domain-01

Transit gateway ID   Info

    Select a transit gateway   ▼

Configure the transit gateway multicast domain

☐ IGMPv2 support   Info

☐ Static sources support   Info

☐ Auto accept shared associations   Info

Tags

A tag is a label that you assign to an AWS resource. Each tag consists of a key and an optional value. You can use tags to search and filter your resources or track your AWS costs.

No tags associated with the resource.

    Add new tag

You can add 50 more tags.

                                        Cancel   Create transit gateway multicast domain

Multicast is not enabled by default in AWS, so you'll need to enable it manually. You can do this by creating a multicast group in your VPC and associating it with a network interface. Enable *Internet Group Management Protocol* (IGMP) in your instances to enable them to join multicast groups. IGMP is used by hosts and adjacent routers to establish multicast group memberships. IGMP allows the network to direct multicast transmissions only to hosts that have requested joining a multicast group.

Enabling multicast routing between your VPC and on-premises environments requires enabling multicast on your routers to allow them to forward multicast traffic to AWS via either a Direct Connect or VPN connection. Once this has been completed, your next step will be to configure your VPC routers to forward multicast traffic to your on-premises routers.

To secure and optimize your multicast deployment, you should configure your VPC security groups and network ACLs to allow multicast traffic. Use the security groups to control traffic between instances in your VPC, and the network ACLs to control traffic between subnets.

Investigate optimizing your network interface configurations by enabling enhanced networking features such as ENA or EFA if supported on your instances.

Designing, implementing, and supporting multicast is complex and requires advance planning and design effort. Read the AWS design best practices and security guides to help during the planning process to make sure you have a reliable, cost-effective, and secure architecture.

In the AWS Marketplace, there are software-defined networking (SDN) solutions that support multicast, from vendors such as Aviatrix or Alkira. You may want to consider using multicast-to-unicast conversions to implement multicast-like capabilities within a VPC. This involves configuring a multicast-to-unicast gateway in your VPC that converts multicast traffic into unicast traffic, enabling you to send multicast traffic to multiple unicast destinations within your VPC.

Optimizing Route 53

The Amazon Route 53 DNS service was covered extensively in Chapters 2 and 3. In this chapter, we will cover several features of Route 53 that can be implemented to optimize your network.

Client connections that use Route 53 can use various extensions to the DNS service that Route 53 has added beyond basic name resolution.

The DNS load balancing feature of Route 53 distributes incoming traffic across multiple resources using DNS load balancing. This can be useful for global applications operating in multiple AWS regions, availability zones, or EC2 instances. Different load balancing policies such as round-robin, latency, geolocation, weighted, and failover are supported.

Route 53 can automatically route traffic to a healthy resource in the event of a failure. This can help to minimize downtime and improve the availability of your applications.

Latency-based routing directs traffic to the network endpoint that has the lowest latency from the user's location. This improves the hosted application's performance and reduces the time it takes to load the website.

Route 53 can be configured to route traffic to multiple resources by enabling weighted record sets. Each resource is assigned a weight, and Route 53 distributes traffic based on the weights assigned. This is useful when testing new versions of applications or when migrating from one resource to another.

Route 53 can monitor the health of the resources by periodically sending health check requests. The health check can be configured to test for various types of responses, such as HTTP, HTTPS, TCP, and SSL. If the health check fails, Route 53 can route traffic to a different resource that is healthy.

The Traffic Flow feature enables you to create complex Route 53 DNS routing policies based on multiple factors, such as latency, geolocation, and endpoint health. You create policies that route traffic to specific resources based on various criteria and dynamically change those policies based on real-time data.

Route 53 provides features such as DNS load balancing, health checks, latency-based routing, weighted record sets, and DNS failover to optimize your network. These features ensure that your applications are highly available and responsive to your users, even in the event of failures.

Frame Size Optimization Across Different Connection Types

The Ethernet frame size impacts bandwidth utilization, particularly when transmitting large amounts of data. Network interfaces on physical or virtual devices may have different *maximum transmission unit* (MTU) sizes that determine the maximum frame size that can be transmitted through an interface without fragmenting the frame and taking a performance hit.

As a network engineer, you should be familiar with the process and issues involved in optimizing frame sizes to improve the bandwidth utilization and overall network performance of your network.

MTU values vary depending on the interface type. Ethernet connections typically have a maximum MTU of 1,500 bytes, which is the standardized specification for the maximum size of an Ethernet frame. To reduce the possibility of fragmentation occurring, keep the frame size at 1,460 bytes or less to maximize the bandwidth utilization. The 1,460 value is recommended to account for extensions that may be added to the frame such as VLAN tags. Jumbo frames have a maximum transmission unit size of 9,000 bytes.

AWS Direct Connect defaults to 1,500 bytes and can be increased to an MTU of 9,000 bytes by modifying the configuration on both the customer and AWS DX interfaces. Transit Gateway MTU values vary depending on what the connection type is. For example, the Transit Gateway supports an MTU of 8,500 bytes for VPC-to-VPC flows, direct connections, the Transit Gateway Connect service, and peering attachments. The AWS VPN MTU is 1,436 bytes.

Wireless, or Wi-Fi, connections typically have a lower maximum MTU size compared to Ethernet with a frame size of 1,300 bytes or less to help reduce fragmentation and improve bandwidth utilization. WAN connections, such as VPNs, typically have a lower maximum

MTU size compared to Ethernet and can vary by vendor but are usually 1300 bytes or less. By default, the MTU for VPN connections in AWS is 1436 bytes.

Most newer network interfaces support jumbo frames, which are a larger MTU size than standard frame specifications. Implementing jumbo frames on your network improves bandwidth utilization, particularly when transmitting large amounts of data over high-speed networks. Jumbos work well in storage transfers, or any large blocks of data sent over the network.

When optimizing the frame size of your network, it is important that you test and monitor network performance to ensure the interfaces the frames traverse support the larger MTU sizes to prevent performance degradation because of the need to fragment the frame into smaller frames so they can traverse the network. This helps to ensure that the optimization is effective and doesn't negatively impact the network performance.

Overall, using a large frame size can help improve the bandwidth utilization and network performance across different connection types.

Jumbo Frame Support Across Different Connection Types

Jumbo frames improve network performance by reducing the number of frames that need to be processed by network devices. It's generally better to send a fewer number of large frames than a high number of smaller frames. Configuring jumbo frame support across different connection types in AWS can optimize network throughput and improve performance.

The following are some guidelines to keep in mind when enabling jumbo support on your AWS network.

- Enable jumbo support on the endpoint devices such as EC2 instances. You can enable jumbo frames on the EC2 instances by configuring each network interface to use a larger MTU size. Do this by modifying the network interface settings using the EC2 command-line interface.

- To enable jumbo MTU support on your VPCs, you must modify the MTU setting at the VPC's Internet Gateway, NAT Gateway, VPN Gateway, or Direct Connect Gateway depending on your configuration. Do this using the VPC console or the AWS CLI.

- For Elastic Network Interfaces, modify the MTU size of the ENI using the AWS CLI or the AWS Management Console. Configure jumbo frame support in your on-premises network. When you are creating a hybrid network that connects your VPC to an on-premises network, you must enable jumbo frame support. This would include modifying the MTU on all network devices, endpoints, switches, routers, firewalls, and any other network devices in the transmission path.

- Finally, you must test and monitor your network from end to end from your VPC and on-premises network to ensure that it is functioning correctly. This may involve performing network throughput tests and reviewing syslog files, Flow Logs, and packet captures to ensure that the larger frame sizes are being transmitted from end to end correctly.

Optimizing Network Throughput

In this section, you will learn about the different methods to maximize the amount of data that is transferred across the network. The goal of a properly designed network is to achieve high throughput with very low latency and minimal dropped packets. This includes selecting the proper network adapters to meet your requirements, choosing the most appropriate AWS services, and optimizing your subnet allocations.

The process of maximizing network throughput in AWS includes using high-performance network interfaces, grouping instances in placement groups, using advanced AWS networking services such as elastic load balancing and content delivery networks such as CloudFront to help improve network throughput by caching content closer to end users and reducing the amount of traffic that needs to traverse the Internet, and following the AWS recommendations to optimize your application architecture. By following AWS best practices, you can improve the network performance of your infrastructure.

Selecting a Network Interface for Best Performance

The performance of the different types of AWS network interfaces impacts how your applications perform and the overall operations of your network.

In this section, you will learn about the common network adapters used in AWS and when to best implement each one.

The Elastic Network Interface is a virtual network interface that attaches to EC2 instances in your VPCs. The ENI offers basic networking capabilities, such as connecting to the Internet and other instances within the VPC. Each ENI supports multiple IP addresses on each interface, which allows you to implement advanced networking configurations. The ENI is the most common interface and is the default network interface when you create most EC2 instances.

The Elastic Network Adapter is a high-performance network interface that offers up to 100 Gbps of network throughput on supported EC2 instance types. Note that not all EC2 instances support the ENA, and they require an instance-specific ENA driver. The ENA is used in compute-intensive workloads that require high network throughput with low latency, such as high-performance computing and big data applications.

The Elastic Fabric Adapter network interface provides ultra-low latency and high-bandwidth communication between instances in a cluster environment. The EFA is used in tightly coupled distributed applications, such as scientific computing and machine learning. The EFA requires special configuration and is only supported on a limited number of instance types.

Consider the specific needs of your application and infrastructure when selecting the right network interface adapter for the best performance. If you have compute-intensive workloads that require high network bandwidth and low latency, the ENA may be the best adapter to implement. If you require tightly coupled distributed applications that require ultra-low latency and high-bandwidth communication, EFA would be the best to implement. For most other use cases, the ENI is suitable.

It is important to note that not all instance types support ENA or EFI adapters. Always check the EC2 instance documentation and choose the right instance type for your needs. Also be aware that configuring and optimizing network interfaces can sometimes be very complex, and research may be required prior to implementation. Always read the documentation and best practices to make sure you are getting the optimal performance from your adapters.

Be aware of the additional costs you may incur based on your interface selection. ENIs are included in the price of the instance, while ENAs and EFAs usually have additional charges. Review the pricing for each type of network interface before making your selection.

Choosing the right network adapter for the best performance on AWS requires an understanding of the specific requirements of your workload. ENIs are a good option for general connectivity to a VPC, while ENA and EFA are better suited for high-performance computing workloads that require low-latency, high-bandwidth communication between instances. Be sure to select an instance type that supports the network interface you want to use and consider the cost of each type of network interface.

Select Network Connectivity Services That Meet Requirements

There are many options and decisions to make when designing your AWS network. Selecting the correct services will depend on your use case. Services include VPC peering, the Transit Gateway, VPN connections, Direct Connect, and others. You must have a clear and detailed understanding of what you want to accomplish and what the design requirements are. This includes the applications requirements, performance, security, regulatory, existing topology, and budget considerations. Factors such as the number of VPCs or on-premises networks that need to communicate, the level of security needed, and the expected traffic volume all must be taken into account.

In this section, you will get an overview of the more common network connectivity services in AWS and the best use cases.

As you learned in Chapter 8, VPC peering connects two VPCs within the same AWS region using private IP addresses. VPC peering allows traffic to flow directly between the VPCs without going over the Internet or a VPN connection. Use peering for simple network architectures that require low-latency communication between VPCs, such as those used for database replication or backup and disaster recovery.

The AWS Transit Gateway was covered in Chapter 7 and is the AWS managed service that allows you to connect multiple VPCs and on-premises networks using a hub-and-spoke model. The service allows you to centralize the management of your network and makes it easier to monitor and operate your network by reducing the number of VPC peering and VPN connections required. Transit Gateway is suitable for large-scale network architectures that require high scalability, security, and performance.

VPN connections are used to securely connect your on-premises network to your VPCs in AWS using an encrypted virtual private network connection. VPN connections are used to extend your on-premises network to the cloud and access resources securely. VPN connections are used in hybrid network architectures that require a secure encrypted connection between on-premises resources and resources in the AWS cloud.

When deciding which approach best fits your use case, consider the network requirements of your infrastructure and applications. If you have simple network requirements that require low-latency communications between VPCs, VPC peering may be a good fit. However, if you have large-scale network requirements that require high scalability, security, and performance, consider using Transit Gateway. If you have hybrid network requirements that require a secure connection between on-premises resources and resources in the cloud, then either a VPN or Direct Connect may be the most suitable solution.

VPC Subnet Optimization

Optimizing your VPC subnets can improve the performance, security, and scalability of your AWS deployments. In this section, you will learn about the best practices for managing your IP subnets, what options are available if you exhaust your address space and need to add more IP addresses for expansion, and subnetting issues when using autoscaling.

When architecting your VPCs, consider any specific needs your application may require. For example, if the application must support high availability and fault tolerance, you will most likely deploy them into multiple availability zones. Recall that subnets cannot span availability zones, so each AZ will require its own address blocks. You should create multiple subnets in each availability zone, enabling you to better distribute your resources across different failure domains to improve the availability and fault tolerance of your applications.

Design the subnets based on the VPC traffic flow. Look at your anticipated workflow patterns and create separate subnets for different tiers of your application, such as web servers, application servers, and database servers.

Choose an appropriate IP address range for each VPC subnet. This ensures that you have enough IP address space available to meet your application's needs, now and in the future, and you avoid conflicts with other IP address ranges in your network or partner networks you are connecting to. When deciding how to properly size your subnets, a good design guideline is that each subnet in a VPC should be large enough to accommodate the maximum number of resources you plan to deploy in that subnet with a buffer for unplanned expansions. However, you should avoid creating subnets that are too large, as this can lead to inefficient resource usage and potentially make it more difficult to isolate problems.

When designing your VPC subnets, consider using multiple smaller subnets instead of one very large subnet. Smaller subnets make it easier to isolate resources and limit the blast radius of security incidents. This may seem contradictory with my statement about planning for future growth. However, do not allocate CIDR blocks so large that you will never use all the space. Be reasonable and choose appropriate subnet sizes for your VPC. Ensure that you have enough IP addresses to meet your application's needs and you avoid conflicts with other IP address ranges you have assigned in your account and organization.

For backend resources that do not need to be publicly accessed, such as databases and application servers, use private RFC 1918 subnet blocks. This provides an additional layer of security by isolating these resources from the public-facing Internet.

For public-facing resources, you must use public subnets. Place resources that need to be publicly accessible, such as web servers and load balancers, in the public subnets. This allows them to communicate with the Internet and other resources in your VPC. Finally, use Network Address Translation (NAT) instances and gateways. Place the NAT instances and gateways in public subnets to provide outbound Internet connectivity to resources in private subnets.

Implement EIPs, which are public IP addresses that can be assigned to resources in your VPC, only as needed as public IPs are in limited supply and are an added expense if you do not actively use them. Consider implementing VPC endpoints to access your AWS services. VPC endpoints allow you to connect to public AWS services without going over the Internet to improve security and reduce costs compared to using public endpoints.

Implement network access control lists and security groups to control inbound and outbound traffic to your VPC subnets to meet your security requirements.

During ongoing system operations, monitor and optimize subnet traffic. Use VPC Flow Logs to monitor traffic to and from the VPC subnets to help you identify performance bottlenecks and optimize your subnet traffic.

Optimizing your VPC subnets can help improve the performance, security, and scalability of your AWS infrastructure. It is important to follow best practices and well-architected design recommendations to create an optimized and secure environment for your applications and services. Best practices include properly sizing your subnets, configuring multiple subnets across different AZs, placing resources in the appropriate public and private subnets, using NAT instances or gateways, using routing tables to control traffic flow, and considering the use of Elastic IP addresses. By following these best practices, you can help ensure the optimal performance, availability, and security of your AWS infrastructure.

Updating and Optimizing Subnets to Prevent the Depletion of Available IP Addresses in a VPC

You may need to update and optimize subnets to prevent the depletion of available IP addresses in a VPC. You should be planning for new services and deployments and then decide on the appropriate subnet expansion method (of creating additional subnets, resizing existing ones, or implementing secondary CIDR blocks); update the route tables, security groups, and DNS records; and test and monitor the updated subnets.

It's important to monitor your IP address usage to prevent the depletion of addresses in your VPC subnets. When the IP address space within a subnet is exhausted, new resources can no longer be launched within that subnet. The VPC web console or the AWS CLI can be used to view the number of available and used IP addresses within your subnets.

Review your current subnet usage to identify any subnets that are running low on available IP addresses. If you need to increase your address space, you have several options to consider, including creating additional subnets, resizing your existing subnets, or adding secondary CIDR blocks. You can create new subnets and allocate new IP address ranges that will be sufficient to meet your expected growth. Another method is to resize existing subnets to provide more addresses and to expand the subnet size to a larger CIDR block. The last option is to use a secondary CIDR block. This adds a new IP address block to your VPC.

If you have multiple VPCs in your AWS deployment, you may decide to implement VPC peering to allow resources in different VPCs to communicate with each other. This helps to reduce the number of IP addresses needed in a single subnet by distributing resources across multiple VPCs.

Using Elastic IP addresses can help you conserve IP address usage within your subnet. Elastic IP addresses are static, public IP addresses that are allocated to your account and are associated with resources in your subnet.

After expanding your subnets or creating new ones, you must update the route tables to ensure that traffic is properly routed to the new IP address ranges. Next, update your security groups to ensure that the new IP address ranges are allowed to communicate with the required resources. Finally, update any DNS records to reflect the new IP address ranges.

Test and monitor the updated subnets to validate everything is working as you expect.

Updating and Optimizing Subnets for Autoscaling

When configuring autoscaling in your VPC, attention must be given to your IP subnets to ensure that you do not deplete your IP address space.

To optimize your IP subnets for autoscaling deployments, review your current subnet configurations and identify the subnets that are associated with your current autoscaling groups. Review the size, capacity, and connectivity to other resources like load balancers or databases.

If an increased application load is anticipated, you may need to increase the capacity of your subnets to accommodate the additional instances that will be launched by the autoscaling group. This will require you to add to the number of available IP addresses in your subnets or increase the size of the current subnets. Subnets that are associated with your autoscaling group should be connected to other resources such load balancers or databases to ensure that traffic is properly routed and that your application can scale effectively. You optimize subnet connectivity by configuring route tables, network ACLs, and security groups to allow traffic to flow between subnets and other resources. Configure subnet placement groups that enable you to control the placement of instances within a subnet, optimize network performance, and reduce latency. You configure subnet placement groups to ensure that instances launched by your autoscaling group are placed in the same physical location, which improves network performance and reduces latency.

It is a good operational practice to proactively monitor and optimize subnet performance. After you've updated and optimized your subnets for autoscaling, you should configure CloudWatch to monitor their performance and adjust your configurations as needed. Use AWS monitoring and logging tools to track network traffic, latency, and other performance metrics, and adjust your subnet configurations as needed to ensure optimal performance.

Optimizing Network Performance and Availability Using Caching and Compression

Data compression can be implemented to reduce the amount of data that needs to be transferred between servers and clients to optimize network utilization. AWS offers several compression options, including Gzip compression for HTTP requests, S3 Select compression, and Amazon Redshift compression.

Amazon CloudFront is a content delivery network from AWS that pushes content to hundreds of AWS edge locations worldwide that caches the requested data closer to the consumers. CDNs serve content to end users with low latency and high transfer speeds by caching content at edge locations around the world, reducing the amount of data that needs to be transferred from the origin server to the end users. This reduces bandwidth utilization and improves the user experience. For more information on CloudFront, review Chapter 1. Edge caching is shown in Figure 11.4.

FIGURE 11.4   Edge caching

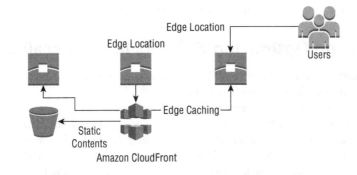

Bandwidth utilization can be reduced over the Internet by implementing the AWS Global Accelerator service. The accelerator uses CloudFront's globally distributed edge locations to accelerate transfer speeds for large data transfers. Traffic is automatically routed over optimized network paths, which reduces latency and bandwidth utilization. For more details, refer to Chapter 1.

There are also caching services that store frequently accessed data in a cache to reduce the need to fetch it repeatedly from the source servers. This can be application-specific such as with the AWS NoSQL database DynamoDB Accelerator (DAX), as shown in Figure 11.5. Other cache offerings include CloudFront and Amazon ElastiCache. By implementing these methods, you can reduce bandwidth utilization and optimize network performance in AWS.

FIGURE 11.5   DynamoDB Accelerator

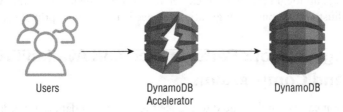

Summary

In this chapter, we applied many of the services and networking technologies covered in the earlier chapters to monitor and optimize your AWS network; you also learned about the tools available to analyze and troubleshoot network issues.

We began with monitoring and analyzing the data generated by network operations. The AWS, open-source, and commercial services and tools available to you and the operation techniques you can use were discussed. AWS services you can utilize include VPC Flow Logging that captures information about IP traffic flows that are sent and received from network interfaces in a VPC. Flow Logs can be enabled on VPCs, subnets, or network interfaces. The logs are stored in S3 buckets and used to analyze traffic and for troubleshooting networking issues. Flow Logs capture metadata about the IP traffic going to and from network interfaces in your VPC and capture information about the source and destination of the traffic, the protocol used, and the number of bytes transferred. CloudWatch provides a monitoring and logging service for a wide range of AWS services, resources, and logs. CloudWatch is used to collect and analyze metrics, log data, configure notifications and trigger alarms when thresholds are reached. The AWS Network Firewall is an AWS managed service for network filtering and packet inspection. The Network Firewall can be used to monitor and analyze traffic traversing through a VPC, and rules can be configured to allow or block traffic that you define based on IP addresses, ports, protocols, and other values.

AWS X-Ray is a service that allows you to trace requests through your application and identify the root cause of issues. By tracing requests through your applications, you can identify issues as seen from the communication patterns between applications to better understand where the impairments are located and enable you to determine if they are network-related. Using network load balancers, you can distribute traffic across multiple targets, improve application availability, and reduce the impact of network issues. Network load balancers provide high-throughput, low-latency load balancing for TCP and UDP traffic. Elastic load balancers provide load balancing for HTTP and HTTPS traffic. By using elastic load balancers, you can distribute traffic across multiple targets, improve application availability, and reduce the impact of network issues.

The Route 53 DNS service generates logs that are useful for optimizing your network. Route 53 Resolver query logging enables you to log DNS name resolution queries. Route 53 Resolver query logs are used to monitor DNS traffic and troubleshoot connectivity issues related to DNS resolution. You also learned about the many extensions to Route 53 that can be implemented to enhance your network, including DNS load balancing for global applications operating in multiple AWS regions, availability zones, or EC2 instances. Different load balancing policies such as round-robin, latency, geolocation, weighted, and failover are supported. Route 53 can automatically route traffic to a healthy resource in the event of a failure. This can help to minimize downtime and improve the availability of your applications. Latency-based routing directs traffic to the resource that has the lowest latency from the user's location. This improves the hosted application's performance and reduces the time it takes to load the website. Weighted record sets are where each resource is assigned a weight, and Route 53 distributes traffic based on the weights assigned. This can be useful for testing new versions of applications or when migrating from one resource to another. Route 53 can monitor the health of the resources by periodically sending health check requests. Traffic flow features enable you to create complex Route 53 DNS routing policies based on multiple factors, such as latency, geography, and endpoint health.

The Network Insights service provides visibility into the network traffic and connectivity of your VPC. By using Network Insights, you can troubleshoot connectivity issues, optimize network performance, and identify security threats by analyzing network flow data.

The AWS Global Accelerator helps you improve network performance and application availability by routing traffic over the AWS internal global network to the optimal end-point. Global Accelerator can reduce latency, increase throughput, and improve the overall performance of your applications by directing traffic off the public Internet and onto the AWS internal network as close to the source as possible.

Network latency is the time it takes for data to travel from the source to the destination. Packet loss in the network occurs when data packets fail to reach their destination. This can be due to network congestion, routing issues, circuit impairments, and other factors. Jitter is the variance of time delay between when a packet is transmitted to when it is received, the change of delay. Network throughput is the amount of data that can be transmitted over a network in each time period; throughput is the speed of the network.

The AWS Reachability Analyzer tool enables you to test whether traffic can reach a target resource from a specified source. The Reachability Analyzer can be used to troubleshoot connectivity issues and verify the effectiveness of your security groups and network ACLs.

The Transit Gateway Network Manager network management tool provides a centralized view of your global network, including Transit Gateways and connected networks.

The network load balancer is an AWS service that distributes incoming traffic across multiple targets providing high availability, scalability, and low latency for your applications. Network load balancers improve the performance of your applications.

AWS VPC Flow Logs can also be used to analyze routing patterns and issues. By analyzing the Flow Logs, you identify the source and destination of traffic, along with the protocols and ports being used. This information is used to troubleshoot routing issues and monitor network traffic.

Understanding your network topology and maintaining up-to-date documentation is essential for managing and troubleshooting any network, including your AWS deployments. Creating detailed network diagrams to better understand your network topology is an important step in management and troubleshooting. A network topology diagram is the physical or logical structure of the network and the connections between the network components. Mapping the network topology can help greatly in identifying potential bottlenecks and misconfigurations and can help to optimize network performance.

Communications between VPCs are accomplished using peering or Transit Gateways. Both networking offerings from AWS will allow the VPCs to communicate with each other. There are, however, specific use cases where one solution may be preferred over the other. If you want to connect two VPCs within the same region, VPC peering is most likely going to be the best solution. However, to connect multiple VPCs that reside in different regions or accounts, you would need to use the Transit Gateway. You must analyze the network requirements of your environment to determine whether a VPC peering connection or a Transit Gateway is appropriate for your AWS environment.

Reducing the amount of traffic sent across the AWS network can result in better performance, lower costs, and reduced congestion. Unicast is a one-to-one network communication between a single source and a single destination. Unicast is the most common data flow in a network but can be inefficient in certain use cases. Multicast is one-to-many where data is sent to multiple destinations from a single source. This one-to-many architecture reduces the bandwidth required for sending data compared to unicast.

Ethernet frame sizes impact the bandwidth utilization, particularly when transmitting large amounts of data. Network interfaces on physical and virtual devices may have different maximum transmission unit (MTU) sizes, which determine the maximum frame size that can be transmitted through an interface without fragmenting the frame.

Choosing the right network adapter for the best performance on AWS requires an understanding of the specific requirements of your workload. ENIs are a good option for general connectivity to a VPC, while ENA and EFA are better suited for high-performance computing workloads that require low-latency, high-bandwidth communication between instances. Be sure to select an instance type that supports the network interface you want to use and consider the cost of each type of network interface.

Next, you learned about optimizing VPC subnets to improve the performance, security, and scalability of your AWS deployments. You learned the best practices for managing your IP subnets, as well as your options if you exhaust your address space and need to add more IP addresses for expansion, and we covered the subnetting issues when using autoscaling.

Finally, you learned about caching and data compression and how it can be implemented to reduce the amount of data that needs to be transferred between servers and clients to reduce network utilization. CloudFront provides content caching at edge locations around the world, reducing the amount of data that needs to be transferred from the origin servers to end users. Bandwidth utilization can be reduced over the Internet by implementing the AWS Global Accelerator service. There are also caching services that store frequently accessed data in a cache to reduce the need to fetch it repeatedly from source servers. This may be application-specific such as with the AWS NoSQL database, DynamoDB Accelerator, or DAX. Other cache offerings include Amazon ElastiCache.

Exam Essentials

Understand the tools and processes used to monitor, analyze, and optimize AWS networks. Based on a given scenario, you should be able to eliminate the wrong answers and identify the correct tools and technologies that fit the requirements of the question.

Know the services that generate logs and the services that store and process log information. This would include CloudTrail and CloudWatch. You must have a detailed understanding of logging and monitoring services to be able to determine the correct answers in scenario-based exam questions. Look closely for key words in the question and wording that would eliminate answers in the selection.

Know all of the options available to optimize your network using Route 53 service extensions.   These includes the DNS load balancing feature that distributes incoming traffic across multiple resources using DNS load balancing. Different load balancing policies such as round-robin, latency, geolocation, weighted, and failover are supported. Route 53 can automatically route traffic to a healthy resource in the event of a failure. Latency-based routing directs traffic to the network endpoint that has the lowest latency from the user's location. Route 53 can be configured to route traffic to multiple resources by enabling weighted record sets. Each resource is assigned a weight, and Route 53 distributes traffic based on the weights assigned. Route 53 can monitor the health of the resources by periodically sending health check requests. The health check can be configured to test for various types of responses, such as HTTP, HTTPS, TCP, and SSL. If the health check fails, Route 53 can route traffic to a different resource that is healthy.

Know the different types of network interfaces and their use cases.   ENIs are for general connectivity to a VPC, while ENA and EFA are better suited for high-performance computing workloads that require low-latency, high-bandwidth communication between instances. Be able to select the correct adapter type based on the requirements given in the question.

Be able to determine what steps you need to take to manage your subnet address allocations.   Create multiple subnets in each availability zone enabling you to better distribute your resources across different failure domains, to improve the availability and fault tolerance of your applications. Design the subnets based on the VPC traffic flow. Choose an appropriate IP address range for each VPC subnet to ensure you have enough IP address space available to meet your application's needs now and, in the future, and you avoid conflicts with other IP address ranges in your network or partner networks you are connecting to. Each subnet in a VPC should be large enough to accommodate the maximum number of resources you plan to deploy with a buffer for unplanned expansions. However, you should avoid creating subnets that are too large, as this can lead to inefficient resource usage and potentially make it more difficult to isolate problems.

Understand VPCs and Transit Gateways.   Know that VPC peering is only used in a single region and that you can use Transit Gateways globally to interconnect many different types of networking connections.

Understand the Global Accelerator.   Know how it works and that it is used to get traffic from the Internet into the AWS global network as close to the source as possible to offer better performance and lower latency than traversing the Internet to the intended AWS region.

Know the different types of compression and caching services in AWS.   Be prepared to identify the best solution given the requirements presented in a question.

Understand jumbo frames.   Know the details and implementation issues of jumbo frames and identify solutions based on what the question is asking for.

Written Labs

Written Lab 11.1: Create a VPC Flow Log

1. Log in to the console.
2. Open the Amazon VPC console at `https://console.aws.amazon.com/vpc`.
3. Select Your VPCs. Select the check box for the VPC.
4. Choose Actions and Create Flow Log.
5. For Filter, specify the type of traffic to log. Choose All to log accepted and rejected traffic. You can optionally select Reject to log only rejected traffic or Accept to log only accepted traffic.
6. For Maximum Aggregation Interval, select the maximum period of time during which a flow is captured and aggregated into one Flow Log record.
7. For Destination, select Send to CloudWatch Logs.
8. For Destination Log Group, choose the name of an existing log group or enter a new log group name that will be created when you create a Flow Log.
9. For IAM Role, specify the name of a role that has permissions to publish logs to Cloud-Watch Logs. For Log Record Format, select the format for the Flow Log record. To use the default format, choose AWS Default Format.
10. To use a custom format, choose Custom Format and then select fields from Log Format.
11. You can optionally select Add New Tag to apply tags to the Flow Log.
12. Choose Create Flow Log.

Written Lab 11.2: Add a New Subnet to a VPC

1. In the AWS console, select Services, Networking, and Content Delivery and VPC at `https://console.aws.amazon.com/vpc`.
2. Select the region the VPC is in.
3. In the navigation pane, choose Subnets.
4. Choose Create Subnet.
5. For VPC ID, choose the VPC for the subnet.
6. For Subnet Name, enter the name of the new subnet. Doing so creates a tag with a key of Name and the value that you specify.
7. Choose an availability zone for your subnet, or you can leave the default of No Preference and AWS assigns one for you.
8. Enter the IPv4 CIDR block you want to use for your subnet.
9. Choose Create Subnet.

Written Lab 11.3: Change the MTU on a Linux EC2 Interface

1. Open a SSH CLI session to your EC2 Linux instance.

2. Enter **sudo ip link show eth0**.

3. Verify the current MTU:

    ```
    eth0: <BROADCAST,MULTICAST,UP,LOWER_UP> mtu 1500 qdisc mq state UP mode DEFAULT
    group default qlen 1000
    link/ether 02:0b:01:14:de:cd brd ff:ff:ff:ff:ff:ff
    ```

4. Change the MTU to 9000 with this command:

    ```
    sudo ip link set dev eth0 mtu 9000
    ```

5. Verify that the MTU has changed from 1500 to the following:

    ```
    9000: 2: eth0: <BROADCAST,MULTICAST,UP,LOWER_UP> mtu 9000 qdisc mq state UP
    mode DEFAULT group default qlen 1000
    link/ether 02:0b:01:14:de:cd brd ff:ff:ff:ff:ff:ff
    ```

Exercises

1. Review the CloudWatch Logs user guide: https://docs.aws.amazon.com/pdfs/ AmazonCloudWatch/latest/monitoring/acw-ug.pdf.

2. Review the CloudWatch Metrics documentation: https://docs.aws .amazon.com/pdfs/AmazonCloudWatch/latest/monitoring/acw-ug .pdf#working_with_metrics.

3. Review the Getting Started with Reachability Analyzer user guide: https://docs .aws.amazon.com/pdfs/vpc/latest/reachability/reachability-ug .pdf#getting-started.

4. Read and understand the How Traffic Mirroring Works AWS documentation: https://docs.aws.amazon.com/pdfs/vpc/latest/mirroring/vpc-tm .pdf#traffic-mirroring-how-it-works.

5. Read the VPC Flow Logging document: https://docs.aws.amazon.com/pdfs/ vpc/latest/userguide/vpc-ug.pdf#flow-logs.

6. Read the AWS network performance user guide: https://docs.aws.amazon .com/pdfs/network-manager/latest/infrastructure-performance/ infrastructure-performance.pdf#what-is-nmip.

7. Review the AWS VPC Subnets user guide: https://docs.aws.amazon.com/pdfs/ vpc/latest/userguide/vpc-ug.pdf#configure-subnets.

8. Read the Enhanced Network Adapter documentation: `https://docs.aws.amazon` `.com/pdfs/AWSEC2/latest/UserGuide/ec2-ug.pdf#enhanced-networking-` `ena`.

9. Read the Enhanced Fabric Adapter documentation: `https://docs.aws.amazon` `.com/pdfs/AWSEC2/latest/UserGuide/ec2-ug.pdf#efa`.

10. Read the Enhanced Network Interface documentation: `https://docs.aws.amazon` `.com/pdfs/AWSEC2/latest/UserGuide/ec2-ug.pdf#using-eni`.

Review Questions

The following questions are designed to test your understanding of this chapter's material. For more information on how to obtain additional questions, please see this book's introduction.

1. Your development team is testing a collaboration application that requires real-time audio and videoconferencing high-definition capabilities. The network must support high throughput with little packet loss and minimal jitter. What network architecture feature would you recommend that supports the application requirements?

   A. Enable enhanced networking

   B. Use Lambda instances for videoconferencing

   C. Use the largest frame size supported

   D. Enable LACP interface teaming

2. You are working on the architecture of a new high-performance computing project at your company. You need to choose a network interface that supports HPC clustering with very high throughput and ultra-low latency. What would be the best fit for this application?

   A. ENI

   B. ENA

   C. Enable jumbo frames

   D. EFA

3. You are collecting metadata on your network to troubleshoot connectivity issues and optimize network performance. What capture types would include data such as IP traffic flows from network interfaces in your VPC and capture information about the source and destination of the traffic, the protocol used, and the number of bytes transferred?

   A. CloudTrail logging

   B. Flow Logs

   C. CloudWatch Metrics

   D. Wireshark packet captures

4. You are troubleshooting a database performance issue and need to perform deep packet inspections on bidirectional server traffic hosting a read replica. You suspect that the client is sending malformed packets when making certain SQL queries. What tool would allow you to capture and inspect the database traffic on a Windows virtual server?

   A. CloudTrail logs

   B. AWS CLI

   C. VPC traffic mirroring

   D. Wireshark

   E. VPC Flow Logs

5. You are troubleshooting a network connectivity issue in a VPC that includes a fleet of application servers that store customer data in a MySQL RDS back-end database in a private subnet. The application servers are reporting time-outs when attempting to query the database. What connectivity tool can you use to verify that there is connectivity to the RDS servers?

    A. Look at the App Mesh logs

    B. Reachability Analyzer

    C. Configure a Step Functions connectivity test

    D. Search the CloudTrail logs

    E. Run the Amazon application discovery service

6. What AWS service can automatically reroute traffic away from unhealthy EC2 web servers?

    A. CloudFront

    B. CloudTrail

    C. CloudWatch

    D. Route 53

    E. Web Application Firewall

7. You have been investigating AWS managed services to apply security rules against the flow of traffic between your VPCs. Which AWS offering would provide the ability for you to apply network security policies?

    A. Amazon Guard Duty

    B. AWS Network Firewall

    C. Viptella manager

    D. CloudFront

    E. Identity and Access Manager

8. You have deployed the AWS Transit Gateway to route traffic throughout your on-premises and AWS regional locations. The application team is installing a new Redshift data warehouse in the ap-northeast-1 Tokyo region, and you have added the connection to the Transit Gateway. During validation you are unable to reach any services in the Tokyo AZ. What steps should you take to troubleshoot the issue? (Select two.)

    A. Investigate if the ap-northeast-1 networks are in the Transit Gateways routing table

    B. Investigate that the MTU is set to the standard Ethernet frame size

    C. Verify that there are no overlapping CIDR blocks

    D. Enable remote access for the Redshift cluster

    E. Make sure you are running Enhanced Fabric Adapter

9. What tool is provided by AWS that provides monitoring and observability service that collects and displays metrics and logs?

    A. CloudTrail

    B. Amazon Athena

    C. Amazon Syslog

    D. CloudWatch

    E. Amazon Systems Manager

10. A public-facing Nginx web server is being installed in the Paris region, and you are tasked with configuring HTTPS Internet access on the outside-facing interface. What configuration options should you enable?

    A. Configure Elastic Network Interface in the 10.x.x.x IP address space

    B. Use an instance type that supports the Elastic Fabric Adapter

    C. Use an instance type that supports the Elastic Network Adapter

    D. Configure an Elastic IP in the public VPC subnet and a route to the Internet gateway

    E. Enable the Global Accelerator

11. Your development team is planning on testing a new version of a custom application on your public-facing web fleet. They plan on using the canary approach that allows a small subset of connections to access the new version of the application while the remaining connections access the original version. What can you enable to accomplish the developer's request?

    A. Enable the Route 53 weighted policy

    B. Use Route 53 geolocation

    C. Enable Route 53 latency-based routing

    D. Configure the firewall to redirect some of the connection requests to the test web server

12. What feature can you enable to optimize block storage transfers in your VPC?

    A. Network load balancing

    B. 802.1p quality of service

    C. Jumbo frames

    D. VPC subnet optimization

    E. Traffic mirroring

13. The us-west-2 region is hosting your company's development operations. You have a single VPC that is used by the development team. They have a new project that needs a larger number of isolated host addresses than are available. What would be a good option to meet their requirements?

    A. Use CloudFront

    B. Create the application front end with an AWS ELB network load balancer

    C. Create a new VPC in us-west-2 and peer it to the existing development VPC and use access control lists for isolation

    D. Create a simple workflow service in the region and add the new project to the workflow

    E. Use AWS config to create the new network space

14. Your global client base is complaining about long network delays when accessing a web-based scheduling application. You have distributed the web app to AWS regions spread evenly around the globe. What would be the best next step to optimize the application's response time to all users regardless of location?

    A. Enable CloudTrail

    B. Use the AWS Global Accelerator

    C. Enable Route 53 latency-based routing

    D. Front-end the web servers with an application load balancer

    E. Implement AWS Step Functions

15. Your company is expanding and has decided to open a development office in Europe using the AWS data centers in the Ireland region. All the current VPCs reside in the United States' Virginia region. What option would you suggest for interconnecting the VPCs on different continents?

    A. Use VPC peering

    B. Deploy a Transit Gateway

    C. Enable CloudFront

    D. Use the AWS Elastic Beanstalk feature in both locations

16. You are investigating methods to optimize network utilization using compression. With which services can you leverage compression to reduce the load on the network? (Select three.)

    A. HTTP GZip

    B. S3 Select

    C. Elastic Map Reduce

    D. Amazon Data Pipeline

    E. Redshift compression

17. You have been tasked to provide an up-to-date network diagram to the Operations Center. What is a good tool to accomplish this?

    A. Transit Gateway Network Manager

    B. Wireshark network discovery

    C. Tableau

    D. Control Tower

    E. CloudWatch

18. You are investigating network performance issues and suspect that an IPS service is fragmenting packets over 1,500 bytes. What tool could you use to ensure that the larger frame sizes are being transmitted end to end correctly?

    A. Monitor the Control Tower dashboard

    B. Review the OpsWorks network logs

    C. Review the CloudTrail logs

    D. VPC Flow Logs

19. Your DevOps VPC needs 1,024 new IP addresses for a new project, and you have discovered that your existing address scheme will not accommodate the growth. What options are available to you to prepare for the new project? (Select three.)

    A. Deploy CloudFront

    B. Create a new VPC in the same region

    C. Resize your existing subnet

D. Add a new CIDR block

E. Modify Route 53 to add new IP address ranges to the VPC

20. You are deploying an Ubuntu jump box for remote secure shell access in the eu-south-1 Milan region. The t2.medium instance type will be used, and the requirements dictate that costs be kept to a minimum. What would be the best network adapter to attach to the instance?

A. Elastic Network Interface

B. Elastic Fabric Adapter

C. Elastic Network Adapter

D. Network load balancer

E. Global Accelerator

Network Security, Compliance, and Governance

Chapter

12

Security, Compliance and Governance

THE AWS CERTIFIED ADVANCED NETWORKING - SPECIALTY EXAM OBJECTIVES COVERED IN THIS CHAPTER MAY INCLUDE, BUT ARE NOT LIMITED TO, THE FOLLOWING:

✓ **Domain 4: Security, Compliance and Governance**

  ▪ Task Statement 4.1: Implement and maintain network features to meet security and compliance needs and requirements.

Security, Compliance, and Governance

In this chapter, you will learn about security in the AWS cloud including both network security and AWS security in general.

Security compliance is a critical topic that cloud network engineers must be familiar with to meet requirements internal to your organization, your country's laws, regulations in countries your organization or customers operate in, and any specific industry requirements for the marketplace you are in such as finance and healthcare.

The topic of network security is very complex and has its own area of expertise. There is an AWS security specialty certification that goes into much more detail than we can here. In this chapter, we will follow the exam topics outlined in the AWS Advanced Networking exam blueprint and address the specific security, compliance, and governance topics for the exam.

The security of your AWS deployment is an ongoing process that must be diligently monitored and audited. To meet ongoing compliance and governance requirements, you must constantly monitor and audit your network. There is a wide range of monitoring and logging services offered by AWS to assist you in identifying security issues and responding quickly to potential threats that we will cover in this chapter.

Security, compliance, and governance of the network are critical aspects of maintaining a secure and compliant cloud infrastructure. AWS provides an extensive range of tools and services to help organizations ensure that their network security follows regulatory requirements, industry best practices, and corporate security policies including the best practices to configure, monitor, and maintain network security compliance and governance.

The steps AWS recommends for protecting your cloud deployment starts with the need to identify and assess your compliance requirements. You should define in detail what it is you want to accomplish. Based on these findings, review what your current level of compliance is and then develop a plan to reach your desired security requirements. You should leverage AWS, open-source, and commercial services, compliance tools, and reporting utilities. AWS can help you understand what compliance requirements you must meet and provide you with the services to help you meet those requirements.

During the implementation of the security controls, you can leverage the AWS tools to help you secure your network. Many of these we have covered in this book, including virtual private clouds (VPCs), security groups, and access control lists to restrict access and secure your network resources.

Automation can be used extensively for compliance checking. You can use AWS-provided tools and services to automate the compliance checking and enforce your security policies. Examples of security automation include using the AWS Config service to monitor resource configurations and track configuration changes and compliance. A best practice for enforcing secure configuration consistency is to use CloudFormation to deploy resources in a secure, repeatable, and compliant manner.

You must maintain detailed documentation and reporting to meet your specific compliance and governance requirements. You can leverage a range of AWS reporting and analytics services. Services such as Audit Manager, Detective, Inspector, GuardDuty, CloudTrail, Security Hub, and CloudWatch can help you track and analyze network activity.

Leveraging these and other AWS services helps your organization comply with relevant security standards and regulations. This helps improve your overall security posture and reduce the risk of security incidents and breaches.

There are many tools and services that support network security, compliance, and governance offered by AWS, open source and commercially. AWS integrates security into all its services and is constantly updating and releasing new security products and services. In addition to the native AWS security services, many companies offer custom tools and professional services in the AWS Marketplace.

Some of the most common AWS security tools and services include the AWS Identity and Access Management (IAM) system. IAM is a core security service used to securely manage access to AWS resources. IAM enables you to define granular control over user access and permissions, allowing organizations to enforce the principle of least privilege.

The AWS Config service provides a detailed inventory of AWS resources and maintains a configuration history that tracks changes to your environment. AWS Config also supports rule-based compliance checks, which can be used to automatically detect noncompliant resources. Config is also used for monitoring compliance with security standards and regulations such as HIPAA, PCI DSS, and GDPR.

VPCs enable you to define and control your own virtual cloud-based network that is logically isolated from other AWS resources, user accounts, and from the Internet. VPCs provide a range of security features, such as security groups, network access control lists (ACLs), and traffic routing controls, which can be used to restrict access and prevent unauthorized traffic.

The AWS Firewall Manager service enables centralized management of firewall rules across multiple AWS accounts and VPCs. The Firewall Manager provides a range of compliance and security controls, including automated policy enforcement and audit trail logging.

Security Hub is an AWS unified dashboard that provides visibility into security alerts and compliance issues across multiple AWS accounts and services. Security Hub collects data from various AWS services, such as AWS GuardDuty and AWS Config, and provides recommendations for remediation.

The Amazon Inspector service enables organizations to improve the security and compliance of their applications deployed on AWS. Inspector performs automated workload security assessments for application software vulnerabilities. Inspector generates findings and provides recommendations for remediation.

There are many components that make up a comprehensive security strategy, and they can vary between organizations and technology areas. Some of the critical steps organizations can take to maintain network security compliance and governance on AWS include implementing the AWS security best practices. Organizations should follow these best practices to ensure that their network security follows industry standards. AWS publishes a wide range of best practices for network security, including network segmentation, access control, and encryption.

Organizations should conduct ongoing audits of their AWS infrastructure to identify potential vulnerabilities and ensure that their network security maintains compliance with regulatory requirements.

Your organization should continually monitor network activity for suspicious activity, unauthorized changes, and vulnerabilities. There are a wide range of tools and services, including Amazon CloudWatch, CloudTrail, and GuardDuty, that enable organizations to monitor network activity and detect potential security threats.

You must implement network security compliance frameworks based on your company's markets. AWS provides compliance frameworks such as HIPAA, PCI DSS, and SOC 2 that organizations can implement to ensure that their network security follows regulatory requirements.

By following these steps, and others that we will cover in this chapter, organizations can maintain network security compliance and governance on the AWS platform and ensure that their cloud infrastructure is secure and compliant with industry standards and regulatory requirements.

Threat Models

Threat models help you to identify and take steps to mitigate potential security threats to the network, applications, and services. You can identify your threat models by reviewing the specific architecture you have deployed.

There are several relevant threat models in AWS that depend on your applications and cloud architecture. The different architectures each have a different threat model that is based on the application's components, communication protocols, and the data that flows between them.

The *monolithic architecture* is where all application components are tightly coupled and often run on the same EC2 instance or server, as shown in Figure 12.1. When evaluating the security of a monolithic architecture, a threat model might focus on vulnerabilities in the operating system, privilege escalations, cross-site scripting, any middleware running, or databases. Evaluate threats such as denial-of-service attacks, SQL injection, or cross-site scripting.

FIGURE 12.1   Monolithic architecture

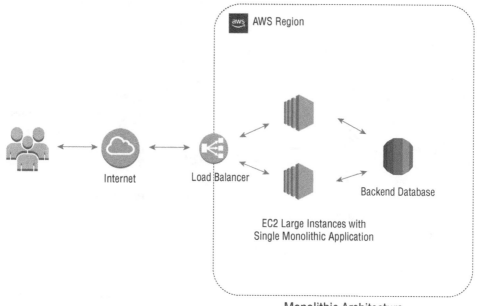

Monolithic Architecture

The *microservices architecture* is where the application is broken down into smaller, discrete components that interact with each other often using API calls, as shown in Figure 12.2. The individual microservices work together to make a complete application. The microservices architecture threat model might focus on the service mesh that manages the communication between the services and any vulnerabilities in the APIs.

The *serverless architecture* is where the application is broken down into individual functions that are executed in response to specific events, as shown in Figure 12.3. This enables developers to build and run applications without managing servers. A threat model might focus on vulnerabilities in the serverless application code, insecure serverless configurations, insufficient access controls, limited application visibility, and the security of the APIs that trigger the functions.

The *containerized architecture* is when the application is broken down into smaller components that are packaged as containers that run on container orchestration platforms such as Kubernetes. A containerized threat model focuses on vulnerabilities in the container images, the Kubernetes cluster, and the network connections between the containers. Figure 12.4 shows a common containerized architecture.

The *edge computing architecture* is when the application runs on compute resources located at the edge of the network, close to end users. The threat model for an edge computing architecture includes distributed denial-of-service (DDoS) attacks, data exfiltration, and unauthorized access to edge computing resources. Figure 12.5 shows an example of the edge computing architecture.

FIGURE 12.2   Microservices architecture

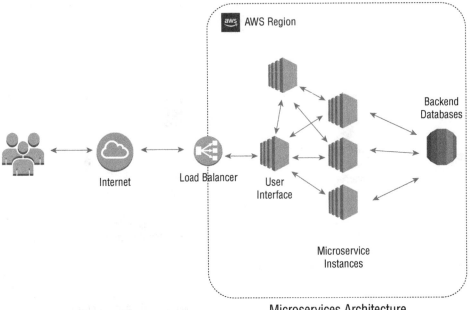

Microservices Architecture

FIGURE 12.3   Serverless architecture

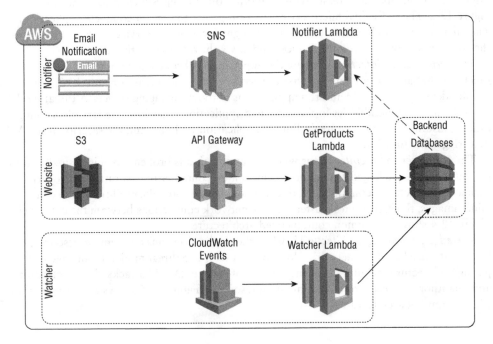

FIGURE 12.4 Containerized architecture

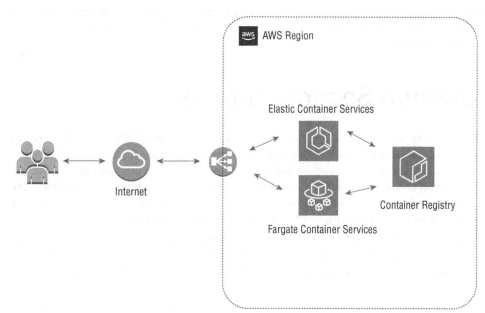

FIGURE 12.5 Edge architecture

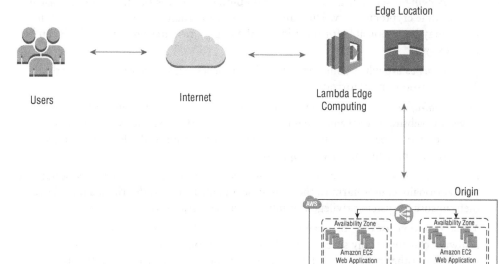

Threat models for application architectures need evaluations of the security of the underlying infrastructure, libraries, APIs, and services used by the application. Because of changes in the threat landscape and updates to the application code, threat models should be evaluated and updated regularly.

Common Security Threats

There are many security threats that organizations face when using AWS. Cloud computing has many of the same threats you face in your on-premises operations and should be treated with the same importance. Also, with hybrid networks with a common architecture, security vulnerabilities that are exposed in the cloud can infiltrate your on-premises operations, and on-premises vulnerabilities can traverse the network and affect your cloud operations. In this section, you will learn about many of these common security threats.

- *Account hijacking* is when an attacker gains access to an authorized user's account and uses it to access data or systems in your cloud environment. Account hijacking can be accomplished with phishing attacks, brute-force attacks, man-in-the-middle exploits, and other methods.

- *Advanced persistent threats* (APTs) are long-term, targeted attacks intended to steal data or disrupt operations over an extended time. Advanced persistent threats are typically carried out by sophisticated attackers with significant resources.

- *Cryptojacking* is when attackers use the computing resources of the victim's infrastructure to mine cryptocurrency. This can cause the infrastructure to slow down, and the victim may be responsible for the additional compute resources required which can be very costly.

- *Data breaches* are when your company's data is accessed, stolen, or exposed without your permission or authorization.

- The *denial-of-service* attacks attempt to disrupt the normal functioning of a network, server, or website by overwhelming it with traffic or other malicious activity. DoS attacks may overload the system and cause it to become unavailable or to significantly slow down. This can impact your operations.

- *Insider threats* occur when an employee or other authorized user either intentionally or unintentionally causes harm to the system or organization. Insider threats include data theft, misuse of system privileges, or introducing vulnerabilities into the system.

- *Malware* and viruses are programs designed to cause harm to systems and networks. Malware can commonly spread over the Internet through email attachments, malicious websites, or other methods, and can cause significant damage to data, software, and infrastructure.

- *Misconfigured security controls* create openings for attacks to your AWS infrastructure. Misconfigured security controls include improperly configured access controls, network security groups, or improperly configured encryption settings.

- Many organizations deploy third-party services and software that may expose your company to additional security risks, such as data breaches, malware infections, or ransomware if the third-party providers do not follow proper security practices.

- *Unauthorized access* occurs when an attacker gains access to your operations' sensitive data and systems without permission. Unauthorized access can occur with phishing attacks and exploiting vulnerabilities in software or infrastructure.

AWS services such as IAM GuardDuty, Inspector, the Web Application Firewall (WAF), and many others can be leveraged to reduce your risk to vulnerabilities in your operations. By performing ongoing security audits and vulnerability assessments, you can identify and address potential vulnerabilities in the infrastructure.

It's very important that your organization be aware, monitor, and take steps to mitigate these and other common security threats to reduce risk to your operations. AWS provides a broad range of security tools and services that can help to secure your cloud infrastructure and data against these threats. It is your responsibility to use these tools and implement a comprehensive security strategy for your company.

Securing Application Flows

Network security includes making sure that the traffic flow that traverses the network is secure from tampering and theft. AWS supports the standard security protocols found commercially and offers services that assist in securing your network traffic. In this section, you will learn about the most common mechanisms used to secure different application flows.

The most common method of securing traffic in flight is the Secure Sockets Layer/Transport Layer Security, SSL/TLS, family of protocols. Encrypting data in transit over the Internet is the recommended transport method for web traffic. SSL/TLS is a networking protocol designed for securing connections between web clients and web servers over an insecure network such as the Internet. AWS provides several services, such as Elastic Load Balancing, CloudFront, and API Gateway, that support SSL/TLS encryption for application traffic. AWS includes an SSL security certificate at all CloudFront edge locations that is bound to the `cloudfront.net` domain, which is the global domain name for CloudFront. If you choose to connect to the edge nodes using this default domain, all you need to do is enable it in the CloudFront distribution configuration settings.

An AWS VPC is a private, isolated network within AWS. VPCs allow your organizations to control network traffic between their resources and the Internet, hybrid network, or other networks that enable you to enforce network security controls, such as access control lists, security groups, and firewalls, to protect your applications.

AWS *security groups* act as a virtual firewall that controls inbound and outbound traffic, for instance, inside of a VPC. Security groups enable you to specify the type of traffic that is allowed to access your resources and are configured to allow traffic from specific IP addresses, protocols, or ports.

Network Access Control Lists (NACLs) are network filters that are applied at the subnet level within a VPC. NACLs filter inbound and outbound VPC traffic at the network level and can be used to block specific IP addresses or protocols. NACLs are stateless and provide granular control over traffic.

The WAF is a managed AWS service used to protect web and other common applications running in AWS. The WAF detects and blocks common web application attacks, such as SQL injection and cross-site scripting, and can be customized to block specific types of traffic.

IAM is a primary AWS security service that enables organizations to control access to AWS resources. IAM is used by administrators to manage users, groups, and roles, and to set granular permissions for different types of resources.

AWS offers a range of encryption options to secure data in transit and at rest. These include encrypting with the Amazon Elastic Block Store (EBS) encryption, Simple Storage Service (S3) encryption, and AWS Key Management Service (KMS). EBS and S3 encryption provide encryption of data at rest, while KMS allows you to create and manage encryption keys that protect your data. The AWS *Key Management Service* (KMS) is an AWS managed service used to create and control the encryption keys used to secure data. KMS enables organizations to encrypt their data at rest or in transit and controls access to the encryption keys. The AWS *Certificate Manager* creates, stores, and rotates digital certificates as a managed AWS service. The certificates can be used for both AWS services and internal connected resources. The Certificate Manager automates the process of purchasing, uploading, and renewing SSL/TLS certificates. You use the Certificate Manager to generate key pairs without the steps usually required such as generating a certificate-signing request, generating the key pair, and downloading it locally for installation. The AWS Certificate Manager handles all the backend steps required to install the certificate on the application devices. In addition to locally generated certificates, the Certificate Manager allows you to import certificates from outside certificate authorities for central management and logging.

Application security managed services offered by AWS include GuardDuty and Inspector that detect and remediate vulnerabilities in applications running on AWS. AWS Lambda can also be used to build and deploy secure serverless applications.

AWS logging and monitoring services include CloudTrail, AWS Config, and CloudWatch, which enable users to monitor and log user activity and resource changes in their AWS account and trigger alarms and respond to events.

Organizations can secure their services, applications, and data flows and protect their resources from common security threats by implementing these security services.

Network Architectures That Meet Security and Compliance Requirements

To create an AWS network architecture that meets your security and compliance requirements, you must consider security items such as data protection, access control, monitoring, logging, and compliance. When architecting an AWS network architecture that will meet your security and compliance requirements, consider the following factors.

Network isolation is important when protecting sensitive data and resources. This includes isolating network segments, applications, and data using the AWS VPC and subnetting to isolate your resources from other AWS customers and the outside world.

Restricting access to resources using security groups and network access control lists is a core security measure. Security groups are stateful, which means they automatically allow return traffic if permitted outbound. Implementing proper IAM policies should also be used to control user and application access.

Data encryption in transit and at rest is important for data protection. AWS provides multiple options for encryption including AWS Key Management Service, Certificate Manager, SSL/TLS support, Amazon S3 server-side encryption, RDS database encryption, and security support options for many other AWS services.

There are AWS tools and services for logging and monitoring network traffic, including VPC Flow Logs, CloudWatch, CloudTrail logs, API calls and events, and Amazon Config, which tracks resource configurations and changes.

PrivateLink is used to securely access services over an internal private connection that does not expose your traffic to the Internet. PrivateLink enables you to access services within your VPC without using public IPs, Internet gateways, NAT devices, or VPN connections.

These services enable visibility into network traffic patterns and help identify potential security issues.

Compliance is an important consideration when designing a secure network architecture. AWS provides compliance resources for major regulatory frameworks such as HIPAA, PCI, and GDPR. Amazon *Artifact*, AWS Config, and AWS Control Tower are used to ensure compliance and governance requirements. Artifact provides access to AWS compliance reports and agreements, Config tracks configuration changes, and *Control Tower* offers central governance and management of multiple AWS accounts, which creates a multi-account architecture using preconfigured security and access settings, plus a dashboard to monitor and manage your AWS deployments.

Addressing your company's disaster recovery plans is critical for ensuring business continuity in case of unexpected events such as natural disasters or man-made events. AWS offers several disaster recovery service support options, including cross-region replication of S3 objects and database failover between different availability zones. The AWS Marketplace is a good source to locate companies that can assist in creating and managing your disaster recovery plans.

Your AWS network design should be scalable to handle changing traffic patterns and business growth. Using elastic load balancing and autoscaling groups can help to ensure resources are available when needed.

By considering these factors, you can design an AWS network architecture that meets security and compliance requirements. The networking team must work with the security, application, development, and compliance groups in your organization to ensure your architecture meets the specific requirements of your company.

Securing Inbound Traffic Flows

This section is about securing inbound traffic flows into AWS and your cloud-hosted applications. Inbound security is critical to protect your cloud assets and data and to maintain your compliance requirements. Traffic flows into AWS can be secured using a combination of AWS services and best practices.

AWS provides the tools and services to secure inbound traffic flows, including the AWS Web Application Firewall, Shield, access control lists, security groups, and the Network Firewall.

In addition to the AWS services covered in this section, it is important to implement other security best practices including restricting access to resources, encrypting sensitive data, and regularly monitoring and logging network traffic. It is recommended to work with your security and application teams to implement a complete security strategy that addresses your company's specific needs and requirements.

Web Application Firewall

The AWS Web Application Firewall protects web applications from common web exploits. WAF provides a layer of security between the Internet and your AWS-hosted web applications. The firewall is used to monitor and control incoming and outgoing Internet traffic to your web-based services. The firewall can be deployed globally to protect against SQL injection, HTTP header modifications, cross-site scripting (XSS), and DDoS attacks.

The WAF is integrated with CloudFront, the Application Load Balancer, and API Gateway. These integrations enable the Web Application Firewall to protect the applications running on these services.

The WAF includes preconfigured rules that you can implement to protect your applications against common exploits and attacks. These rules are regularly updated by AWS to keep up with new threats. You can also create custom rules that allow or block requests based on the content of the request, such as the requesting URL, query parameters, or data in the request body. WAF firewall rules can be created to block malicious traffic and filter requests based on source or destination IP addresses, geographic locations, port numbers, and other attributes.

The detailed logging and monitoring capabilities of the service allow you to monitor and analyze traffic patterns to your web applications. The Web Application Firewall is a managed service that provides an additional layer of security for your applications running on AWS. It is cost-effective, with no up-front costs or long-term commitments for the service, and you pay only for what you use.

The Web Application Firewall is a powerful tool that protects your web applications from common web exploits and attacks. It provides a layer of security between the Internet and your web applications and allows you to monitor and control incoming and outgoing traffic to your web applications. It has integrations with other AWS services and supplies detailed monitoring and logging data.

Network Firewall

The AWS *Network Firewall* is a managed firewall service used to secure incoming network traffic by providing network traffic filtering and monitoring. The Network Firewall can be deployed in your VPC or as a perimeter firewall in front of your VPCs. It operates at the network level and provides both stateless and stateful protection, as shown in Figure 12.6.

The *stateless firewall* rules engine inspects each packet in isolation and does not consider the direction of the flow or if it is part of an existing allowed connection. Stateless firewalls offer high throughput where rules are processed in the order that you configure them and stop evaluations when a match is found. The AWS Network Firewall stateless operation is the same as a VPC network access control list.

FIGURE 12.6   Network Firewall traffic flow

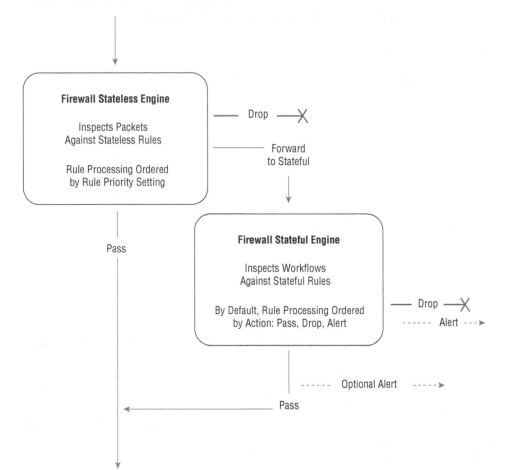

Stateful firewalls track individual sessions to analyze each flow. This allows for the analysis of more complex rules and the logging of traffic alerts. Stateful rules take into consideration the direction of the traffic flow and can group packets together for evaluation. Rules are evaluated with permit rules first and then drop and, finally, alert rules. The stateful processing engine stops when a match is found, and no further matches are considered. The stateful rules engine uses Suricata code, which is an open-source intrusion prevention system that provides a standard rules language to stateful packet inspection.

Shield

Shield is the AWS-managed DDoS protection service that protects your applications from common DDoS attacks, including volumetric-, protocol-, and application-layer attacks. Figure 12.7 shows the AWS web console Shield dashboard. The service comes in Standard and Advanced tiers with Advanced adding expanded support for 24/7 access to the AWS DDoS response team, real-time visibility, and automated mitigation.

FIGURE 12.7   AWS Shield DDoS protection

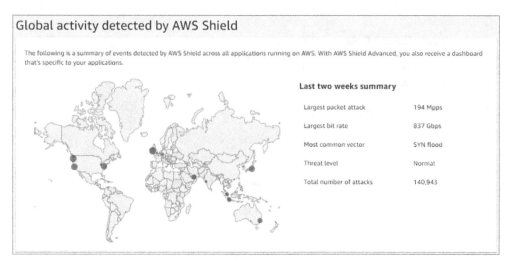

AWS Shield is used in front of Elastic Load Balancers, CloudFront, Global Accelerator, EC2, and Route 53 to protect your applications against DDoS attacks.

AWS Shield Standard provides protection for all AWS customers from common, frequent network- and transport-layer DDoS attacks and is a standard no-charge AWS services offering that is automatically operational; there is no need to enable the service. *Shield Advanced* is a chargeable service providing enhanced protection for Internet-facing applications running on EC2, ELBs, CloudFront, Global Accelerator, and Amazon Route 53. Shield Advanced is available to all customers but requires Enterprise or Business AWS Support levels.

Security Groups

Security groups control the inbound and outbound traffic of your VPC and the resources inside the VPC. Security groups are stateful, meaning that they automatically allow return traffic if the inbound is permitted. You use security groups to control traffic at the instance level by allowing traffic only from specific IP addresses and ports. Figure 12.8 illustrates a common inbound security group configuration enabling access to web and secure shell access to servers in a public subnet. Figure 12.9 shows an outbound security group configuration that allows all SSL and SSH traffic to exit the VPC to the Internet.

FIGURE 12.8 AWS VPC security group inbound

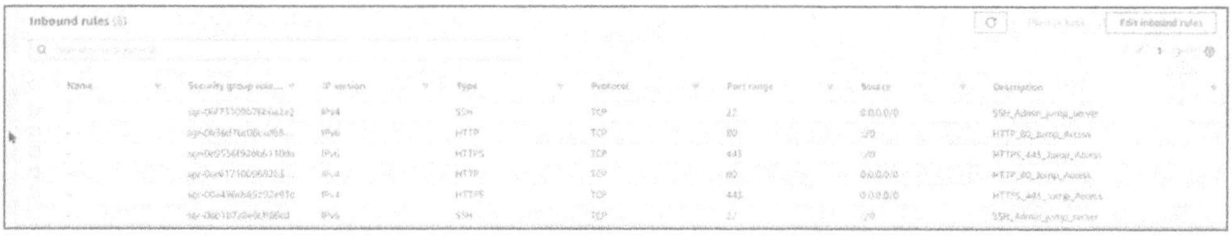

FIGURE 12.9 AWS VPC security group outbound

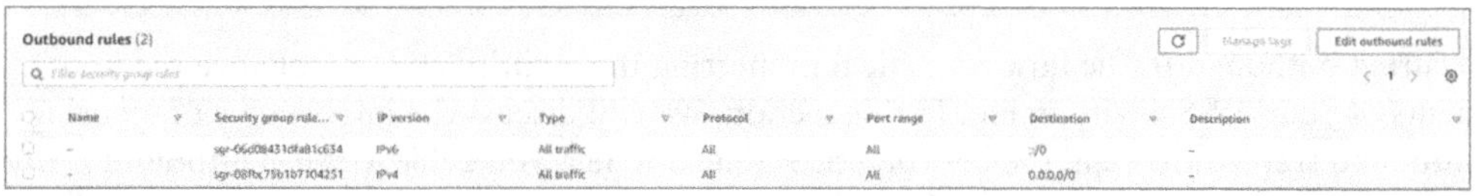

Network Access Control Lists

NACLs control inbound and outbound VPC traffic at the subnet level. NACLs are stateless, which means rules are required for both for both inbound and outbound traffic. You create NACLs to control traffic at the subnet level by allowing or denying traffic based on source and destination IP addresses and port numbers.

Figure 12.10 illustrates an inbound NACL security group configuration enabling access to web and secure shell access to servers in a public subnet. Figure 12.11 shows an outbound security group configuration that allows all SSL and SSH traffic to exit the VPC to the Internet.

FIGURE 12.10 AWS VPC NACL inbound

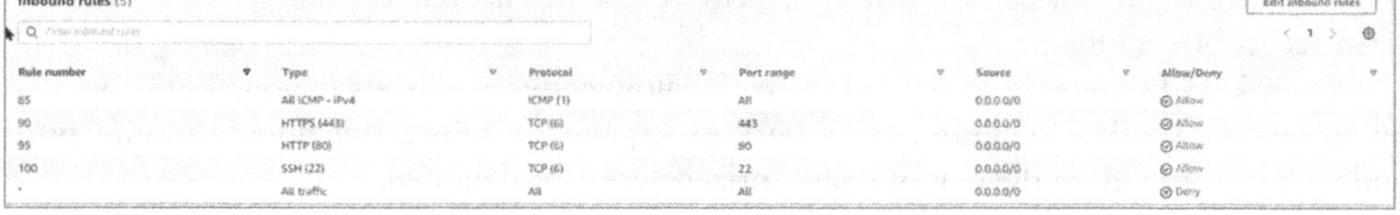

FIGURE 12.11   AWS VPC NACL outbound

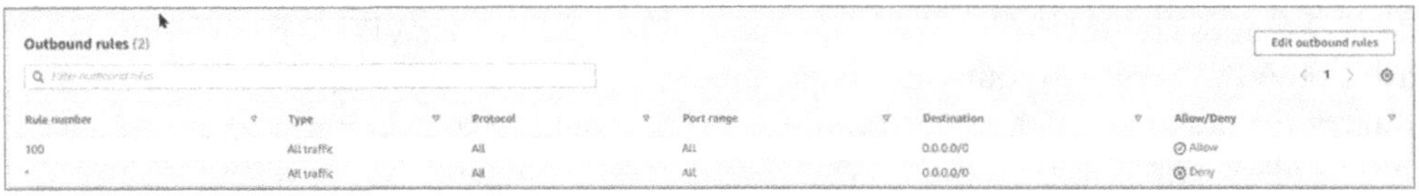

After the NACL has been created, the next step is to associate it with a subnet, as shown in Figure 12.12, for it to take effect.

FIGURE 12.12   NACL subnet associations

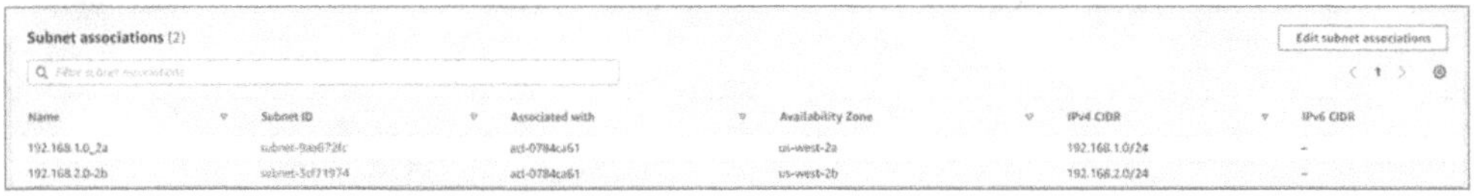

Securing Outbound Traffic Flows

Securing outbound traffic flows is critical in meeting the security and compliance requirements of your AWS environment. In this section, we will discuss the importance of securing outbound traffic flows and the best practices that can help you achieve this. Outbound traffic filtering gives you control over outbound traffic flows from your AWS environment. By filtering outbound traffic, you can prevent unauthorized data transfers, malware infections, and other security threats.

Compliance regulations often require organizations to monitor and control outbound traffic flows, block unauthorized access, and prevent data loss and other security breaches. Securing outbound traffic flows is important for compliance, data protection, and threat prevention.

Outbound traffic flows can include sensitive data such as medical records, financial information, personal data, and corporations' intellectual property. Securing these flows is essential to protect this data from unauthorized access or theft. Outbound traffic may also contain malware or threats that can infect other systems or networks. Securing outbound traffic flows can help prevent these threats from spreading.

The best practices for securing outbound traffic flows include implementing network segmentation that isolates sensitive data that enables you to granularly control the flow of traffic between different parts of your AWS environment. This reduces the risk of unauthorized access or data loss.

Network ACLs are used to control the traffic flow between subnets in your VPC. By implementing detailed and granular network ACLs, you limit the traffic flow to specific ports and protocols to reduce the risk of unauthorized access or data loss.

Implementing a proxy server provides an additional layer of security that can filter and monitor outbound traffic flows. A proxy server can also help you enforce your organization's security policies and control access to external resources.

The AWS Route 53 DNS resolver provides domain name resolution within your VPC. The Route 53 Resolver can be used to block traffic to known malicious domains and allow traffic only to trusted domains.

The PrivateLink service prevents your traffic from being exposed to the Internet and enables secure access to your services hosted on AWS from within your VPC. PrivateLink secures outbound traffic by enabling private communication between your VPC and other AWS services.

A gateway load balancer is used to distribute incoming traffic across multiple targets such as EC2 instances, containers, and IP addresses. You can also use the gateway load balancer to secure outbound traffic by configuring health checks, SSL/TLS encryption, and access control policies.

Monitoring outbound traffic enables you to detect and prevent security threats and data breaches. By using tools such as Amazon VPC Flow Logs, you can monitor outbound traffic flows and identify any suspicious activity.

Securing outbound traffic flows is an essential aspect of maintaining the security and compliance of your AWS environment. By implementing network segmentation, network ACLs, egress filtering, proxy servers, and monitoring outbound traffic, you can help reduce the risk of data loss, unauthorized access, and security breaches. These best practices can help you achieve a secure and compliant AWS environment while ensuring that your sensitive data is protected from threats and vulnerabilities.

Network Firewall

The Network Firewall was discussed in the previous section on securing inbound traffic. It allows you to create rules to filter and inspect both inbound and outbound traffic. Use Network Firewall to set up stateful rules that inspect traffic at the application layer, block traffic from known malicious sources, and filter traffic-based IP addresses, port, protocol, geolocation, or other factors.

You can use Network Firewall to create rules to block or allow outbound traffic based on IP address, port, protocol, and other factors.

Proxies

An AWS *proxy server* is a network security server that acts as an intermediary between client devices and other servers or services such as the Internet or applications in the AWS environment.

By routing outbound traffic through a proxy server, an extra layer of security is added that enables you to inspect traffic for suspicious behavior, filtering, event logging, and blocking traffic from known malicious sources.

In this section, we will discuss what AWS proxy servers are, how they work, and their benefits.

The AWS proxy server sits between client devices and upstream servers or services. It acts as an intermediary that forwards requests from client devices to other servers or services, such as the Internet, other AWS services, external APIs, and other web applications. It receives the responses from these servers or services and forwards them back to the client devices.

The AWS proxy servers work by intercepting requests from the client devices, inspecting the flows and forwarding them to the appropriate server or services. When a client device makes a request, the request is forwarded to the proxy server instead of the intended destination. The proxy server evaluates the request and forwards it to the destination server or service on behalf of the client if the forwarding conditions are met. The response from the destination server or service is then evaluated by the proxy server and forwarded back to the client.

Proxy servers provide additional security by filtering and monitoring inbound and outbound traffic. They block unauthorized access, prevent malware infections, and enforce security policies. Performance of your AWS environment can be improved by caching frequently accessed data. This helps reduce the latency and response times of your applications. AWS proxy servers enable you to scale your applications by distributing traffic across multiple servers or services. This can help you handle increased traffic loads and reduce the risk of downtime. The proxy server enables you to control the traffic flows in your AWS environment. You can control access to external resources, filter outbound traffic, and enforce security policies.

The proxy server provides an additional layer of security, helps to improve application performance, and enables you to scale your applications. AWS proxy servers are a tool used for improving the security, performance, scalability, and control of your AWS environment.

Gateway Load Balancers

The AWS Gateway Load Balancer service enables you to deploy, scale, and manage third-party virtual appliances such as firewalls, intrusion detection and prevention systems, and deep packet inspection systems. With gateway load balancers, you can deploy and manage these appliances in a highly available manner, and route outbound traffic flows through them. For more information, refer to Chapter 1, "Edge Networking."

Route 53 Resolvers

The Route 53 Resolver is an AWS managed DNS service that provides domain name resolution within your VPC and globally. You can use the resolver to block traffic to known malicious domains and to allow traffic only to trusted domains. In this section, we will discuss how you can manage outbound traffic with Route 53 Resolvers, what they are, and their benefits.

Route 53 is Amazon's DNS service that allows you to manage the domain names and routing policies of your applications running on the AWS environment. Route 53 Resolvers are a feature of the Route 53 DNS services that enable you to resolve domain names in your VPC without the need for public IP addresses. By enabling resolvers, you can route DNS queries for private domain names to specific DNS servers within your VPC, which enables the management and security of the outbound traffic.

Route 53 Resolvers forward DNS queries from inside your VPC to a specific set of DNS servers. You then configure the resolver to route DNS queries to specific IP addresses or DNS endpoints. When a query is received by the resolver, it checks its cache for the domain name resolution. If the resolver does not have the resolution, it sends the query to the specified DNS server and caches the result.

The resolvers secure your outbound traffic by allowing you to route DNS queries to specific DNS servers. This helps prevent unauthorized access and data exfiltration. Resolvers can help with compliance of regulatory requirements that mandate controlling outbound traffic flows. By routing DNS queries to specific servers, you can ensure that your traffic is being monitored and controlled.

Route 53 Resolvers are managed by AWS and highly available to improve the reliability of your applications by ensuring that DNS queries are resolved quickly, accurately, and with a reduced risk of downtime.

Route 53 Resolvers are used to manage the outbound traffic flows in your AWS environment. They can help you improve the security, compliance, scalability, reliability, and cost-effectiveness of your applications. By routing DNS queries to Route 53 Resolvers, you ensure that your traffic is being monitored, controlled, and in compliance with regulatory requirements. For more information, refer to the discussion on resolvers in Chapter 2, "Domain Name Services."

Virtual Private Networks

You can implement an AWS virtual private network (VPN) to secure outbound traffic flows. VPNs create an encrypted tunnel between your VPC and a remote endpoint usually over the Internet, ensuring that all data transmitted between the two locations is secure. The VPN connection supports industry standard security and encryption protocols.

Using a VPN to secure outbound traffic flows in AWS ensures that all data transmitted between your VPC and the remote network sent across the Internet is encrypted and secure. VPNs also enable you to control and monitor all outbound traffic from your VPC. Finally, VPNs provide an additional layer of security for your VPC by preventing unauthorized access to your in-flight data.

Using an AWS VPN to secure outbound traffic flows from your VPC is an effective solution that provides the benefits of using an encrypted connection across the Internet to ensure that all data transmitted is secure. For detailed information on site-to-site VPNs, refer to Chapter 6, "Hybrid Networking."

VPC Endpoint Services: PrivateLink

When it comes to securing outbound traffic flows from your VPC, AWS endpoint services, also called PrivateLink, can be used to secure outbound traffic from your VPC. PrivateLink allows you to privately access services hosted on the AWS infrastructure, without your VPC traffic traversing the public Internet.

To use PrivateLink to enable secure outbound VPC traffic flows, create a VPC endpoint for the service you want to access. This endpoint will provide a secure and private connection between your VPC and the service internal to AWS. Configure your VPC's routing table to send traffic destined for that service through the endpoint. This will ensure all VPC outbound traffic is forwarded through the secure and private connection provided by PrivateLink.

The service allows you to control and monitor outbound traffic from your VPC to the service. It also provides additional layer security for your VPC by preventing unauthorized access to your data. For a review of PrivateLink, refer to Chapter 4, "Load Balancing."

Securing Inter-VPC Traffic

Securing inter-VPC traffic within an account or across multiple accounts involves a combination of network-level security measures such as security groups and network ACLs, and application-level security measures such as VPC endpoint policies and PrivateLink. By implementing layered security measures, you ensure that your inter-VPC traffic is protected from potential threats.

Network ACLs

Network ACLs act as a stateless firewall and are used to control inter-VPC traffic at the subnet level. Network ACLs can be used to control traffic flows between VPCs within the same account or across multiple accounts. You can implement network ACLs to create rules to allow or deny traffic based on IP addresses, port numbers, or protocols.

VPC Endpoint Policies

VPC endpoints allow you to privately connect your VPC to supported AWS services without requiring an Internet gateway, NAT device, VPN connection, or AWS Direct Connect. You define the VPC endpoint policies to control access to VPC endpoints within your account or across multiple accounts. Endpoint policies are rules to allow or deny access to specific VPC endpoints. VPC endpoint policies are essential for securing inter-VPC traffic across multiple accounts.

Security Groups

AWS security groups act as a firewall for your instances. They filter inbound and outbound traffic at the instance level. Security groups allow or deny traffic from other VPCs within the same account or across multiple accounts and allow traffic only from trusted sources and block traffic from known malicious sources. Security groups allow you to specify the ports and protocols allowed and from which IP addresses traffic is allowed.

Transit Gateway

Transit Gateway is a network transit hub that simplifies inter-VPC connectivity. You can use Transit Gateway to connect VPCs within the same account or across multiple accounts. You can also use Transit Gateway to control access between VPCs by creating route tables and security policies. Transit Gateway enables you to route traffic internally in the AWS network between VPCs to ensure low-latency and high-bandwidth connections. For more information on Transit Gateway, see Chapter 8, "Inter-VPC and Multi-Account Networking."

VPC Peering

VPC peering allows you to connect two VPCs within the same account or across multiple accounts with private IP addresses. VPC peering enables you to route traffic between VPCs using the internal AWS network, which ensures low-latency and high-bandwidth connections. For a detailed look at VPC peering, review Chapter 8.

Implementing an AWS Network Architecture to Meet Security and Compliance Requirements

Implementing an AWS network architecture that meets your security and compliance requirements involves designing a secure and scalable network architecture that meets the specific needs of your organization. Here are some common AWS network architectures that can help you meet security and compliance requirements.

By using AWS services and best practices for security and compliance, you can create a secure and scalable network architecture that protects your data and resources.

Untrusted Networks

The untrusted network architecture as shown in Figure 12.13 is also commonly referred to as a demilitarized zone (DMZ). It will contain a VPC that hosts resources that are accessible from the public Internet, such as web servers, and the Internet traffic can only access the DMZ and not the internal, protected network. You can use security groups, network ACLs, and VPC endpoint policies to limit access to your resources, and you can implement data encryption to protect your data in transit and at rest.

FIGURE 12.13   Untrusted VPC

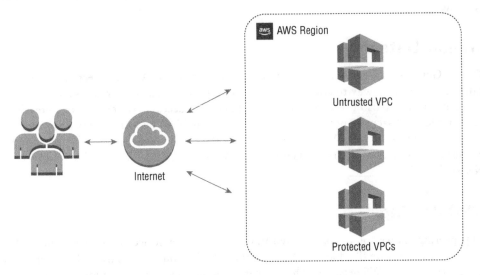

Perimeter VPC

The perimeter VPC architecture uses a dedicated VPC that acts as a perimeter around your other VPCs, as shown in Figure 12.14. The perimeter VPC is isolated from the rest of the VPCs in your environment and contains resources that are responsible for protecting your environment from external threats. You might decide to use the AWS Transit Gateway to connect your perimeter VPC to your other VPCs; you can also use security groups, network ACLs, and VPC endpoint policies to control access to your resources.

FIGURE 12.14   Perimeter VPC

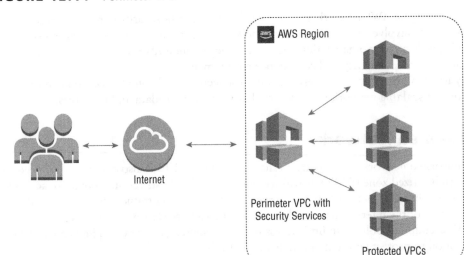

Three-Tier Architecture

The three-tier architecture uses three separate networks for your web, application, and database tiers. Each tier is placed in a separate subnet in the VPC, and access between the tiers is restricted using security groups and NACLs, as shown in Figure 12.15. You implement security groups, network ACLs, and VPC endpoint policies to control access to your resources, and you can implement data encryption to protect your data in transit and at rest.

FIGURE 12.15   Three-tier architecture

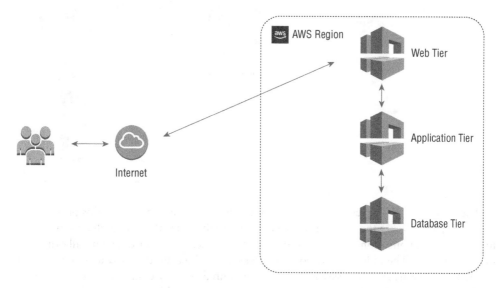

Hub-and-Spoke Architecture

Figure 12.16 shows the hub-and-spoke architecture, which uses a central hub VPC that acts as a central point of control for your other VPCs. You can use AWS Transit Gateway to connect your hub VPC to your other VPCs, and you can use security groups, network ACLs, and VPC endpoint policies to control access to your resources.

Develop a Threat Model and Identify Mitigation Strategies

The process of developing a threat model and then identifying appropriate mitigation strategies for the network architecture involves understanding the potential threats to your network and implementing security controls to reduce the likelihood and impact of those threats.

FIGURE 12.16   Hub-and-spoke architecture

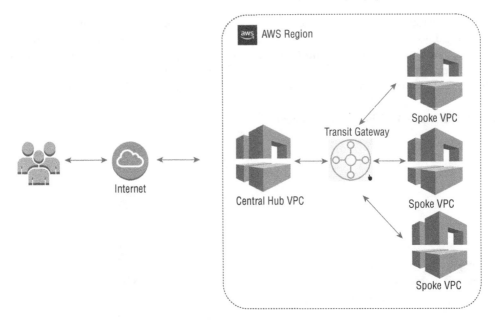

The following best practices outline the steps you can take to complete this process.

Start by identifying the assets in your network architecture; this will include servers, microservices, applications such as databases and web servers, your data, and all other items to protect. Then identify the potential risks and vulnerabilities of your assets, such as unpatched software, weak passwords, or misconfigured security controls. Assess the potential impact and likelihood of each threat occurring. This should include unauthorized access, data breaches, denial-of-service attacks, malware, phishing attacks, and any threats specific to your environment.

Research and analyze potential threat actors, which may include internal or external attackers, nation-state actors, and hacking organizations. When you have a list of threats, the next step is to investigate the likelihood and impacts of each threat based on your assets and the potential threat actors involved. Next, identify the mitigation strategies for each threat based on the likelihood and impact, including access controls, encryption at rest and in flight, network segmentation, monitoring and logging, and disaster recovery planning.

After the background research and planning steps have been completed, you will implement the security steps, services, and controls that were identified in your mitigation strategy planning. This may include configuring security groups, network ACLs, VPC endpoints, firewall rules, intrusion detection, and other AWS or partner service offerings. You may need to prioritize your mitigation steps based on your assessment and available resources. Focus on addressing the most critical threats and vulnerabilities first.

Finally, there needs to be ongoing testing and monitoring to validate the effectiveness of security controls. This may include penetration testing, vulnerability scanning, security audits, and log analysis.

When you complete the steps outlined, you can develop a threat model and identify appropriate mitigation strategies for your specific network architecture. You must review and update your threat model and mitigation strategies on a regular basis as your network architecture, corporate security policies, and threat landscape will evolve over time.

When developing the threat model and identifying appropriate mitigation strategies for your network architecture, a comprehensive understanding of the assets, threats, and vulnerabilities in the architecture is required. Follow the structured approach; using the available AWS security services and best practices enables you to create a secure network architecture that meets the needs of your organization.

Compliance Testing

Compliance testing is an important step in ensuring that your AWS environment meets your organization's security compliance requirements.

You can use the AWS tools when conducting compliance testing, such as CloudFormation, CloudWatch, Config, Lambda, and Trusted Advisor. There are also many third-party partners that offer tools and services that conduct penetration testing, vulnerability assessments, and compliance audits. You must also monitor your network architecture and associated services for any changes or anomalies that may indicate a security or compliance issue. AWS monitoring and alerting tools include CloudWatch and CloudTrail, which can help you detect and respond to security incidents in a timely manner.

Some common types of compliance tests that can help you validate compliance with the initial requirements include failover testing, resiliency testing, compliance audits, penetration tests, and backup and restore testing.

Failover testing involves intentionally triggering a failure to test the effectiveness of your disaster recovery and high-availability configurations. For example, you could simulate an outage in one availability zone and verify that your database or web application automatically fails over to another availability zone without interruption.

Resiliency testing involves testing the ability of your environment to withstand and recover from security threats and attacks. This may include the simulation of a DDoS attack on your environment to verify that your network and application security controls can detect and mitigate the attack.

Compliance audits include a comprehensive review of your environment against the specific requirements that you are required to meet, such as HIPAA, PCI DSS, or SOC 2. You can use AWS services such as AWS Config and CloudTrail to monitor and report on compliance-related activities in your environment.

Penetration testing is the simulation of an attack on your environment to identify vulnerabilities that could be exploited by an attacker. It is good to use Amazon Inspector to automate these vulnerability assessments, or you can engage third-party security firms to perform penetration testing on your environment.

Backup and restore tests involve testing the effectiveness of your backup and restore strategy in the event of a data loss or corruption. An example would be to restore a backup of your database to a separate environment to verify that the data is consistent and recoverable.

It is important to regularly conduct compliance testing to validate that your AWS deployment meets your initial compliance requirements and to identify any areas where improvements are needed. Use the test results to update your environment and address the issues that are identified.

Testing compliance with your requirements requires a combination of different tests to ensure that your infrastructure meets your organization's compliance and security needs. You can use the AWS services and best practices, and by following a comprehensive testing strategy, this enables you to create a secure and resilient infrastructure that meets the needs of your organization.

Automating Security Incident Reporting and Alerting

AWS and business partners offer many tools and services to automate security incident reporting and alerting. Enabling reporting and alerting operations on AWS starts by collecting logging data from your various AWS services such as CloudTrail, VPC Flow Logs, Config, and others, as well as from your own applications and servers.

You can use CloudTrail to capture API activity across your AWS accounts, including the Web Management Console, software development kits, the command-line tools, and higher-level AWS services. CloudTrail stores the logs in an S3 bucket, which can be used as a central log repository. You can also use CloudWatch to collect system-level logs from EC2 instances, Elastic Load Balancers, (RDS), Lambda, microservices, DynamoDB, and other AWS services.

The logs are forwarded to a centralized logging service like Amazon CloudWatch Logs or an external security information and event management (SIEM) tool like Splunk or ELK.

Once the logs are collected and stored in a central location, you can use tools like Amazon CloudWatch Logs, Config, GuardDuty, Insights, or Amazon Athena to query and analyze them. CloudWatch can monitor logs in real time and trigger alerts when certain patterns or events are detected. CloudWatch Logs Insights can be used to query and analyze log data, and CloudWatch alarms can be set up to trigger actions when specified thresholds are crossed. GuardDuty is a threat detection service from AWS that continuously monitors for malicious activity and unauthorized behavior in your environment. GuardDuty generates alerts for potential security incidents and can be integrated with other AWS services, such as Lambda, to automate incident response. Lambda is a serverless computing service from AWS that you can use to run code in response to specific events or triggers. Lambda can be used to automate incident response by triggering specific actions when security incidents are detected. AWS Config enables you to assess, audit, and evaluate the configurations of your AWS resources. Config can be used to detect and alert on changes to security configurations that could indicate a security incident. Amazon *Detective* helps automate your security investigations and assists your security group in incident investigations. Detective uses pre-built data aggregations, summaries, and context to analyze security events. Detective makes it easier for log analysis, security, and investigations, and it helps identify the root cause of potential security issues or suspicious activities.

You can look for specific patterns or events that indicate a security incident such as failed login attempts, unusual network traffic, etc.

Once you've identified a potential security incident, you must alert the appropriate people or systems. AWS provides several options for alerting, which include Amazon Simple Notification Service (SNS), AWS Lambda, or CloudWatch Events. You can configure these services to send notifications to automation applications, email addresses, Slack channels, or other applications.

Automated remediation is the ability to automate the remediation processes when responding to a security incident. For example, you can set up an alarm to trigger automation tools when a certain number of failed login attempts are detected within a certain time period. You could then automatically block the source IP address using the Web Application Firewall or Network Firewall and disable logins for that account in AWS Active Directory Services.

Once an alert is triggered, you need to have a process in place to investigate and respond to the incident. There are many tools you can use to automate this process, including Lambda, Step Functions, and Amazon SNS. An example would be to use Lambda to trigger a script that disables a compromised AWS resource, such as an EC2 instance or RDS database. You could use Step Functions to automate an incident response workflow, such as escalating the incident to a security operations center or launching an AWS CloudFormation stack to remediate the issue. You can use SNS to send notifications to security teams or other stakeholders.

AWS also gives you the tools to track and report on security incidents over time including Athena and QuickSight. Athena can be used to query and analyze log data stored in S3, and QuickSight is used to create interactive dashboards and visualizations.

Using these tools, you can create a comprehensive security incident reporting and alerting system that can help you quickly detect and respond to security threats in your AWS environment.

Summary

We started this chapter by discussing network security compliance and governance and gave examples of many of the security automation services, including using the AWS Config service to monitor resource configurations and track configuration changes and compliance. AWS reporting and analytics services include the AWS Audit Manager, Detective, GuardDuty, CloudTrail, Security Hub, and CloudWatch; they can help you track and analyze network activity. The Identity and Access Management system enables you to define granular control over user access and permissions, allowing organizations to enforce the principle of least privilege.

The AWS Config service provides a detailed inventory of AWS resources and maintains a configuration history that tracks changes to your environment. The VPC service enables you to define and control your own virtual cloud-based network that is logically isolated from other AWS resources, from user accounts, and from the Internet. The AWS Firewall Manager service enables centralized management of firewall rules across multiple AWS accounts and VPCs. Security Hub collects data from various AWS services, such as AWS GuardDuty and AWS Config, and provides recommendations for remediation. Amazon Inspector performs automated workload security assessments for application software vulnerabilities.

AWS publishes a wide range of best practices for network security, including network segmentation, access control, and encryption.

Organizations should conduct ongoing audits of their AWS infrastructure to identify potential vulnerabilities and ensure that their network security maintains compliance with regulatory requirements.

Threat models help you to identify and take steps to mitigate potential security threats to the network, applications, and services. You can identify your threat models by reviewing the specific architecture you have deployed. Examples of the various models were introduced and discussed.

The monolithic architecture is where all application components are tightly coupled and often run on the same EC2 instance or server. The microservices architecture is where the application is broken down into smaller, discrete components that interact with each other often using API calls. The serverless architecture is where the application is broken down into individual functions that are executed in response to specific events. The containerized architecture is when the application is broken down into smaller components that are packaged as containers that run on container orchestration platforms such as Kubernetes, and the edge computing architecture is when the application runs on compute resources located at the edge of the network, close to end users.

Next you learned about the common security threats in the network. Account hijacking is when an attacker gains access to an authorized user's account and uses it to access data or systems in your cloud environment. Advanced persistent threats are long-term, targeted attacks intended to steal data or disrupt operations over an extended time. Cryptojacking is when attackers use the computing resources of the victim's infrastructure to mine cryptocurrency. Data breaches are when your company's data is accessed, stolen, or exposed without your permission or authorization. The denial-of-service attacks attempt to disrupt the normal functioning of a network, server, or website by overwhelming it with traffic or other malicious activity. Insider threats occur when an employee or other authorized user either intentionally or unintentionally causes harm to the system or organization. Malware and viruses are programs designed to cause harm to systems and networks. Misconfigured security controls create openings for attacks to your AWS infrastructure. Misconfigured security controls include improperly configured access controls, network security groups, or improperly configured encryption settings. Unauthorized access occurs when an attacker gains access to your operation's sensitive data and systems without permission.

Next, we went into detail on securing application flows including encrypting data in transit over the Internet using SSL/TLS services. We went into detail on the tools and services used to secure inbound and outbound traffic flows, including the AWS Web Access Firewall, Shield, ACLs, security groups, and the Network Firewall.

The AWS Web Application Firewall is used to monitor and control incoming and outgoing Internet traffic to your web-based services. The firewall can be deployed globally to protect against SQL injection, HTTP header modifications, cross-site scripting, and DDoS attacks. The AWS Network Firewall is a managed firewall service used to secure incoming network traffic by providing network traffic filtering and monitoring. Shield is the AWS managed DDoS protection service that protects your applications from common DDoS attacks, including volumetric-, protocol-, and application-layer attacks. Security groups control the inbound and outbound traffic of your VPC and the resources inside the VPC; you use security groups to control traffic at the instance level by allowing traffic only from specific IP addresses and ports. NACLs control inbound and outbound VPC traffic at the subnet level. Proxies sit between client devices and upstream servers or services. A proxy acts as an intermediary that forwards requests from client devices to other servers or services, such as the Internet, other AWS services, external APIs, and other web applications. Gateway load balancers enable you to deploy, scale, and manage third-party virtual appliances such as firewalls, intrusion detection and prevention systems, and deep packet inspection systems. The Route 53 Resolvers are an AWS managed DNS service that provides domain name resolution within your VPC and globally. You can use the resolver to block traffic to known malicious domains and to allow traffic only to trusted domains. VPNs create an encrypted tunnel between your VPC and a remote endpoint usually over the Internet, ensuring that all data transmitted between the two locations is secure.

The AWS Endpoint services, also called PrivateLink, can be used to secure outbound traffic from your VPC. PrivateLink allows you to privately access services hosted on the AWS infrastructure, without your VPC traffic traversing the public Internet.

Network ACLs act as a stateless firewall and are used to control inter-VPC traffic at the subnet level. Network ACLs can be used to control traffic flows between VPCs within the same account or across multiple accounts. Define the VPC endpoint policies to control access to VPC endpoints within your account or across multiple accounts. Endpoint policies are rules to allow or deny access to specific VPC endpoints. VPC endpoint policies are essential for securing inter-VPC traffic across multiple accounts.

AWS security groups act as a firewall for your instances. They filter inbound and outbound traffic at the instance level. Security groups allow or deny traffic from other VPCs within the same account or across multiple accounts, allow traffic only from trusted sources, and block traffic from known malicious sources. Transit Gateway is a network transit hub that simplifies inter-VPC connectivity. You can use Transit Gateway to connect VPCs within the same account or across multiple accounts. You can also use Transit Gateway to control access between VPCs by creating route tables and security policies. VPC peering allows you to connect two VPCs within the same account or across multiple accounts with private IP addresses. VPC peering enables you to route traffic between VPCs using the internal AWS network, which ensures low-latency and high-bandwidth connections.

We discussed the common AWS network architectures that can help you meet security and compliance requirements.

The untrusted network architecture is also commonly referred to as a DMZ. It will contain a VPC that hosts resources that are accessible from the public Internet, such as web servers, and the Internet traffic can only access the DMZ and not the internal, protected network. You can use security groups, network ACLs, and VPC endpoint policies to limit access to your resources, and you can implement data encryption to protect your data in transit and at rest. The perimeter VPC architecture uses a dedicated VPC that acts as a perimeter around your other VPCs. The perimeter VPC is isolated from the rest of the VPCs in your environment and contains resources that are responsible for protecting your environment from external threats. The three-tier architecture uses three separate networks for your web, application, and database tiers. Each tier is placed in a separate subnet in the VPC, and access between the tiers is restricted using security groups and NACLs. The hub-and-spoke architecture uses a central hub VPC that acts as a central point of control for your other VPCs. You can use AWS Transit Gateway to connect your hub VPC to your other VPCs, and you can use security groups, network ACLs, and VPC endpoint policies to control access to your resources.

We then learned about the process of developing a threat model. Identifying appropriate mitigation strategies for the network architecture involves understanding the potential threats to your network and implementing security controls to reduce the likelihood and impact of those threats. You first start by identifying the assets in your network architecture; this will include servers, microservices, applications such as databases and web servers, your data, and all other items to protect. Next, identify the potential risks and vulnerabilities of your assets, such as unpatched software, weak passwords, or misconfigured security controls. Assess the potential impact and likelihood of each threat occurring. This should include unauthorized access, data breaches, DoS attacks, malware, phishing attacks, and any threats specific to your environment. Research and analyze potential threat actors, which may include internal or external attackers, nation-state actors, and hacking organizations. When you have a list of threats, the next step is to investigate the likelihood and impacts of each threat based on your assets and the potential threat actors involved. Next, identify the mitigation strategies for each threat based on the likelihood and impact, including access controls, encryption at rest and in flight, network segmentation, monitoring and logging, and disaster recovery planning. After the background research and planning steps have been completed, you will implement the security steps, services, and controls that were identified in your mitigation strategy planning. Finally, you must perform ongoing testing and monitoring to validate the effectiveness of security controls. This may include penetration testing, vulnerability scanning, security audits, and log analysis.

Compliance testing uses AWS tools such as CloudFormation, CloudWatch, Config, Lambda, and Trusted Advisor. There are also many third-party partners that offer tools and services that conduct penetration testing, vulnerability assessments, and compliance audits. AWS monitoring and alerting tools include CloudWatch and CloudTrail, which can help you detect and respond to security incidents in a timely manner. Testing compliance with your requirements requires a combination of different tests to ensure that your infrastructure meets your organization's compliance and security needs. You can use the AWS services and best practices, and by following a comprehensive testing strategy, this enables you to create a secure and resilient infrastructure that meets the needs of your organization.

Automating security incident reporting and alerting operations on AWS starts by collecting logging data from your various AWS services such as CloudTrail, VPC Flow Logs, Config, and others, as well as from your own applications and servers. The logs are forwarded to a centralized logging service like Amazon CloudWatch Logs or an external SIEM tool like Splunk or ELK. Once the logs are collected and stored in a central location, you can use tools like Amazon CloudWatch Logs, Config, GuardDuty, Insights, or Amazon Athena to query and analyze them.

Automated remediation is the ability to automate the remediation processes when responding to a security incident. AWS also gives you the tools to track and report on security incidents over time including Athena and QuickSight.

Exam Essentials

Know the steps to achieve network security compliance and governance.   These include threat models, common security threats, application flows, and designing secure network architectures.

Understand how to implement security automation at a high level.   Implement security with AWS services such as the Web Application Firewall, Network Firewall, Shield, security groups, and NACLs.

Know the reporting and analytics services.   These include Audit Manager, Detective, GuardDuty, CloudTrail, Security Hub, and CloudWatch.

Know the details of the IAM system and how to identify the services in scenario-based questions.   IAM is a core security service used to securely manage access to AWS resources. IAM enables you to define granular control over user access and permissions, allowing organizations to enforce the principle of least privilege.

Know the AWS Config service and how it is used to monitor resource configurations and track configuration changes and compliance.   The AWS Config service monitors resource configurations and tracks configuration changes and compliance.

Be able to identify and answer questions about the AWS Firewall Manager service.   The AWS Firewall Manager service enables centralized management of firewall rules across multiple AWS accounts.

Know the basics of the AWS Security Hub.   Security Hub collects data from various AWS services and provides recommendations for remediation.

Understand the AWS Inspector service.   The AWS Inspector service performs automated workload security assessments for application software vulnerabilities.

Know the different threat models and be able to identify each one based on a scenario question.   They are monolithic, microservices, serverless, containerized, and edge computing architectures.

Be able to identify common security threats.   Common security threats include account hijacking, advanced persistent threats, cryptojacking, data breaches, denial of service, insider threats, malware, misconfigured security controls, and unauthorized access.

Know the different AWS security services and how to implement them to secure application flows.   The most common method of securing traffic in flight uses the SSL/TLS family of protocols. Know in detail the AWS services used to secure inbound and outbound flows: AWS Web Application Firewall, Network Firewall, Shield, security groups, NACLs, proxy servers, the gateway load balancer, Route 53 Resolvers, VPNs, VPC endpoint services such as PrivateLink, Transit Gateway, and VPC peering. Expect there to be exam questions on these services, what they accomplish, and when to use each one.

Be able to interpret and answer scenario questions on threat models and mitigation strategies.   These include identifying appropriate mitigation strategies including identifying the assets in your network architecture, and then identifying the potential risks and vulnerabilities of your assets.

Be able to answer questions based on reporting and alerting operations.   These include collecting logging data from AWS services such as CloudTrail, VPC Flow Logs, Config, and others, as well as from your own applications and servers.

Know the AWS centralized logging services.   Centralized logging includes CloudWatch Logs or an external SIEM tool like Splunk or ELK.

Analyze the logs using AWS services.   Use CloudWatch Logs, Config, GuardDuty, Insights, or Amazon Athena to query and analyze logs. Alerting services include Amazon SNS, SQS, Lambda, and CloudWatch Events. Tools to track and report on security incidents over time include Athena and QuickSight.

Exercises

1. Read the online documentation concerning compliance at `https://aws.amazon.com/compliance/resources`.

2. Read the AWS Well Architected Framework Security Pillar documentation at `https://docs.aws.amazon.com/pdfs/wellarchitected/latest/security-pillar/wellarchitected-security-pillar.pdf#welcome`.

3. Review the AWS Security Hub user guide at `https://docs.aws.amazon.com/pdfs/securityhub/latest/userguide/securityhub.pdf`.

4. Review the AWS GuardDuty user guide at `https://docs.aws.amazon.com/pdfs/guardduty/latest/ug/guardduty-ug.pdf`.

5. Review the AWS Inspector user guide at `https://docs.aws.amazon.com/pdfs/inspector/latest/user/inspector-guide.pdf`.

6. Review the AWS CloudWatch user guide at `https://docs.aws.amazon.com/pdfs/AmazonCloudWatch/latest/monitoring/acw-ug.pdf`.

7. Review the AWS Network Access Control List and Security Group documentation at `https://docs.aws.amazon.com/pdfs/vpc/latest/userguide/vpc-ug.pdf`.

Written Labs

Written Lab 12.1: Download an Artifact Report

1. Sign in to the AWS Management Console, select your region, in the services box search for *artifact*, and open the AWS Artifact console.

2. On the AWS Artifact home page, choose View Reports in the upper right of the browser display.

3. On the Reports page, leave the defaults on the AWS Reports tab.

4. Enter a keyword in the search field to locate a report such as **Cyber Essentials Plus Certification**.

5. Select Cyber Essentials Plus Certification Report, and then choose Download report in the upper-right corner.

   Note: You might be asked to accept the terms and conditions that apply to the specific report you are downloading.

   The download will begin in Adobe format.

6. Open the downloaded file using Adobe Acrobat Reader. Read the terms and conditions section. When you are finished, follow the instructions to view the downloaded report.

   Note: When you sign up for AWS Artifact, your account is automatically granted permission to download some reports. If you are having trouble accessing AWS Artifact, follow the guidance on the `https://docs.aws.amazon.com/service-authorization/latest/reference/list_awsartifact.html` page.

Written Lab 12.2: Request a Public SSL/TLS Certificate from the Aws Console

1. Sign in to the AWS Management Console, select your region, and in the services box search for *ACM* to open the ACM console.

2. Choose Request A Certificate on the right side of the browser window.

3. Select a public certificate and click Next.

4. Enter your domain name. If you do not own a domain name, then follow along without creating a certificate.

5. Validate using DNS.

6. Select a key algorithm. RSA 2048 is the default and a good option.

7. Verify the "Successfully requested certificate" message. A certificate request with a status of pending validation has been created. Further action is needed to complete the validation and approve the certificate.

8. Click View Certificate and review your new public certificate.

9. Delete the certificate if you do not plan on using it.

Written Lab 12.3: Review a Security Group Configuration from the AWS Console

1. Sign in to AWS, select your region ,and search for *EC2* in the services box.

2. In the left pane, scroll down to Network And Security and select Security Groups.

3. Select the default security group and review the inbound and outbound rules.

4. Select tags and enter a Key value of **SG** and a Value of **Default**.

5. Click Save Changes.

6. Validate that the security group has the new tag attached to it.

Review Questions

1. What service can you implement to monitor logs in real time and trigger alerts when certain patterns or events are detected? (Select two.)
   - **A.** CloudTrail
   - **B.** CloudWatch Insights
   - **C.** CloudWatch Logs
   - **D.** GuardDuty
   - **E.** Lambda

2. Which threat model focuses on the communications between the services including API vulnerabilities? (Select two.)
   - **A.** Monolithic
   - **B.** Microservices
   - **C.** Containerized
   - **D.** Serverless
   - **E.** Edge services

3. You are tasked with implementing a change management tracking system to document all changes made to your AWS cloud environment. Which Amazon tool would best meet this requirement?
   - **A.** CloudTrail
   - **B.** IAM
   - **C.** Config
   - **D.** CloudWatch
   - **E.** Splunk

4. Your company's operations center is reporting sustained probing from Internet bots to your company website hosted in the AWS eu-north-1 Stockholm region. The security team is concerned that this is malicious activity and has captured 500 source IP addresses to block. Which approach best ensures both security and scalability in blocking the threat?
   - **A.** Deploy the AWS Web Application Firewall to block the IP addresses
   - **B.** Add the IP addresses to the inbound security group rules to block the IP addresses
   - **C.** Use Linux IPTables to filter the IP addresses at the instance interface
   - **D.** Implement inbound NACL rules to block the IP addresses

5. Your three-tier web application is deployed in the ap-northeast-3 Osaka region, and you are setting up an automated notification system if there is suspected malicious activity detected on the application tier's network interfaces. What AWS services can you use to build an automated notification system? (Select two.)

   A. CloudTrail

   B. Lambda

   C. Shield

   D. Inspector

   E. VPC Flow Logs

6. Which AWS service collects data from various AWS services and provides recommendations for remediation?

   A. GuardDuty

   B. Security Hub

   C. Insights

   D. Config

7. The server admin team at your e-commerce company has created a new VPC with a CIDR block of 172.16.1.0/16 using RFC 1918 private subnets in their DevOps VPC. They access the AWS resources over a site-to-site VPN connection from your company's on-premises offices in Austin. Now the admins want you to set up SSH access to the EC2 instances in AWS from their office building. How would you enable SSH access?

   A. Enable inbound traffic on port 80 from the public subnet's security group having a bastion host

   B. Enable inbound traffic on port 22 from the public subnet having a bastion host security group

   C. Enable inbound traffic on port 443 to allow the user to connect to a private subnet over the Internet

   D. Allow inbound traffic on port 22 from the on-premises network

8. What are the most common methods of encrypting web traffic in transit over the Internet? (Select two.)

   A. Deploy CloudFront

   B. Secure Sockets Layer

   C. IPSec

   D. Transport Layer Security

   E. Use the `secure.cloudfront.net` domain endpoint

9. You are investigating log files stored in an S3 bucket in the us-west-2 Oregon region for network errors. What AWS tools would you most likely use to search the logs? (Select three.)

    A. CloudWatch

    B. Splunk

    C. QuickSight

    D. Athena

    E. OpenSearch

10. Which AWS service can automate and assist in security investigations? It uses prebuilt data aggregations, summaries, and context to analyze security events and makes it easier for log analysis, security, and investigations, and to identify root causes of potential security issues or suspicious activities.

    A. Detective

    B. Artifact

    C. Shield

    D. GuardDuty

    E. EKS

11. Which administrative vulnerability creates openings for attacks to your AWS infrastructure?

    A. Misconfigured security controls

    B. DMZ

    C. Shield

    D. Proxy

    E. Unauthorized access

12. What AWS service can you use to query and analyze log data?

    A. Inspector

    B. CloudTrail

    C. Insights

    D. Splunk

    E. DynamoDB

13. What attack type is when your company's data is accessed, stolen, or exposed without your permission or authorization?

    A. Account hijacking

    B. Data breach

    C. Advanced persistent threats

    D. Denial-of-service

    E. Malware

14. You are required to implement an AWS managed service that can continuously monitor malicious activity and unauthorized behavior in your environment. Based on the findings, the service must generate alerts for potential security incidents and can be integrated with other AWS services, such as Lambda, to automate incident response. What service should you investigate?

    A. GuardDuty

    B. Security Hub

    C. Athena

    D. Insights

15. What threat is a long-term, targeted attack that is intended to steal data or disrupt operations over an extended time?

    A. Account hijacking

    B. Cryptojacking

    C. Advanced persistent threat

    D. Unauthorized access

    E. Data breach

16. Which AWS serverless service can be used to create custom event triggers that runs code in response to specific events or triggers?

    A. Artifact

    B. Lambda

    C. Config

    D. Athena

    E. GuardDuty

17. Which service provides access to AWS compliance reports and agreements?

    A. CloudTrail

    B. GuardDuty

    C. Artifacts

    D. CloudWatch

    E. Secrets Manager

18. Which AWS tools assist you in creating a comprehensive security incident reporting and alerting system that enables you to query and analyze log data stored in S3 and creating interactive dashboards and visualizations over time? (Select two.)

    A. Inspector

    B. Athena

    C. CloudTrail

    D. QuickSight

    E. Shield

19. Which AWS service can you use to create, store, deploy, and rotate public and private SSL/ TLS digital certificates?

   A. Secrets Manager

   B. AWS Certificate Authority

   C. SSL manager

   D. Certificate Manager

20. You have been tasked to create a graphical dashboard for the Operations Center that shows network status. What is the best tool available to accomplish this?

   A. CloudWatch

   B. Splunk

   C. QuickSight

   D. Athena

   E. OpenSearch

Chapter

13

Network Monitoring and Logging

THE AWS CERTIFIED ADVANCED NETWORKING - SPECIALTY EXAM OBJECTIVES COVERED IN THIS CHAPTER MAY INCLUDE, BUT ARE NOT LIMITED TO, THE FOLLOWING:

✓ **Domain 4: Security, Compliance and Governance**

  ▪ Task Statement 4.2: Validate and audit security by using network monitoring and logging services.

Network Monitoring and Logging Services in AWS

In this chapter, you will learn about the services that generate logging data and the services that store, process, and manage logging data to properly manage and secure your AWS cloud infrastructure.

AWS offers native network logging and monitoring services that enable you to monitor, troubleshoot, and secure your network infrastructure. Some of the key services that we will cover are as follows.

CloudWatch is a key Amazon monitoring service that provides real-time visibility into the operation of your AWS resources, that allows you to monitor, store, and access log files, and it manages metrics, logs, and alarms from resources in AWS and externally in hybrid networks. CloudWatch can monitor EC2 instances, EBS storage volumes, RDS instances, S3, load balancers, microservices, and many other AWS and external resources. CloudWatch can be configured to monitor user defined custom metrics, generate alarms, troubleshoot issues, create dashboards for visualizing performance data, monitor applications and Internet health, and enable automations in your environment. CloudWatch Insights can monitor Lambda instances and containers, and provides metrics for ECS, EKS, and Kubernetes clusters.

You use CloudWatch Logs to monitor application and system logs, track application performance, monitor for compliance and security, and troubleshoot issues.

VPC Flow Logs captures information about the IP traffic going to and from network interfaces in your VPC. The Flow Logs are used for troubleshooting connectivity issues, investigating security incidents, and monitoring network performance. Flow Logs can be stored in S3 buckets or Kinesis for analysis using tools such as Amazon Athena, GuardDuty, Elastic Map Reduce, and many third-party offerings in the Amazon Marketplace.

CloudTrail is the Amazon service that records API calls and events in your AWS account. CloudTrail logs can be used to detect and investigate security incidents and comply with audit requirements. CloudTrail provides a complete audit trail of API calls in your AWS account, including calls made by users, services, and AWS resources.

The AWS Config service provides a detailed inventory of your AWS resources and is also used to track changes to these resources over time. Config is used to monitor compliance, troubleshoot issues, and identify resource dependencies. Config can also be used to enforce security policies and create rules to restrict resource configurations and deployments.

Amazon GuardDuty is a threat detection service that uses machine learning to identify potential security threats in your AWS environment such as unauthorized access attempts, compromised instances, and data exfiltration attempts. GuardDuty enables you to continuously monitor your network for security threats and respond to them in real time. The service can also be used to analyze VPC Flow Logs, DNS logs, and other data sources to detect security threats, such as unauthorized access attempts, malicious activity, and reconnaissance activity. GuardDuty provides detailed alerts and integrates with CloudWatch and CloudTrail for monitoring and analysis.

Amazon Inspector is a security assessment service that identifies security issues and vulnerabilities in your EC2 instances and applications. Inspector scans your instances for common security issues, such as insecure network configurations, missing patches, and exposed ports and generates findings that can then be investigated.

The Amazon Network Firewall has monitoring capabilities in addition to its granular network traffic control for your VPCs. The Network Firewall is used to create custom security rules, monitor traffic flows, and detect and block malicious traffic. The Web Application Firewall allows you to control access to your web applications and protect them from common web exploits. Use the AWS Web Application Firewall (WAF) to monitor and block suspicious web traffic, such as bots and scrapers.

AWS provides a range of network monitoring and logging services that we will cover in this chapter. They can help you monitor and troubleshoot your network infrastructure, detect security threats, and maintain compliance. By implementing these Amazon services and best practices, you will be able to create a secure and resilient network environment in AWS.

AWS CloudTrail

The AWS CloudTrail service provided by Amazon logs all API actions taken by users, services, or resources in an AWS account. CloudTrail was covered in Chapter 5, "Logging and Monitoring," and will be covered in more detail in this chapter. CloudTrail helps your organization monitor and audit their AWS infrastructure and provides visibility into user activity, resource changes, and system events.

CloudTrail is enabled in all AWS regions and captures and logs API calls made by or on behalf of an AWS account and provides an audit trail of activity that can be used for operational and risk auditing, regulatory compliance, security analysis, and troubleshooting. The service provides a log history of AWS API calls for an AWS account, including the identity of the caller, the date and time of the API call, the source IP address of the caller, the resources affected, the parameters of the API call, and the response returned by the AWS service. This information can be used to understand what actions were taken in your AWS account, who took them, and when they were taken.

The logs are formatted as follows:

```
AccountID_CloudTrail_RegionName_YYYYMMDDTHHmmZ_UniqueString.FileNameFormat
```

The YYYY, MM, DD, HH, and mm are the digits of the year, month, day, hour, and minute when the log file was delivered. Hours are in 24-hour format. The Z indicates that the time is in UTC.

The 16-character UniqueString component of the log file name prevents the overwriting of files. It has no meaning, and log processing software should ignore it. The FileNameFormat is the encoding of the file. This can be either .json or .gz, which is a JSON text file in compressed .Gzip format.

CloudTrail logs are delivered to an Amazon S3 bucket, where they can be analyzed and monitored using AWS services such as Amazon Athena, Glue, QuickSight, Amazon OpenSearch (originally Elasticsearch), third-party tools such as Splunk, or other custom applications.

CloudTrail logging data can be used to monitor for unusual or unauthorized activity in AWS resources. The data tools accessing CloudTrail logs can be configured to detect and respond to security incidents and ensure compliance with internal policies or external regulations by providing an audit trail of all API activity in your AWS account. The CloudWatch API log analysis assists in your troubleshooting efforts by analyzing detailed information contained in the API calls, including error messages, and the context in which they occurred. You can optimize usage of your AWS resources by analyzing API calls to identify opportunities to reduce costs or improve performance.

CloudTrail is enabled by default in all AWS accounts and is provided at no charge for the basic service. However, there are charges for storing and accessing the CloudTrail logs. CloudTrail can be integrated with other AWS services such as Config and Security Hub to provide a detailed view of your AWS environment and its security posture.

CloudTrail logs are stored in an S3 bucket and can be accessed and analyzed using a variety of AWS tools and third-party solutions. CloudTrail logs can be used for a range of use cases, including for compliance and audits. CloudTrail logs can help organizations meet regulatory compliance requirements by providing a record of all API calls and events in their AWS environment. They are also used for security and governance. CloudTrail logs are used to detect and investigate security incidents, such as unauthorized access attempts or changes to security configurations. CloudTrail logs can help organizations troubleshoot issues by providing a detailed record of resource changes and API calls made in an AWS environment. CloudTrail logs are used to track resource usage and identify cost optimization by analyzing usage patterns and trends.

CloudTrail is the log collection service that helps organizations collect, monitor, and audit their AWS infrastructure, and provide visibility into user activity and resource changes. CloudTrail enables your organization to improve its security, ensure compliance with regulatory requirements, and optimize AWS usage and costs. CloudTrail provides a comprehensive and centralized solution for monitoring and logging API activity in your AWS account.

VPC Traffic Mirroring

The Amazon VPC Traffic Mirroring service enables you to copy network traffic from Elastic Network Interfaces (ENIs) within your VPC and forward that traffic to monitoring and security tools for storage and analysis. Traffic Mirroring enables you to capture and analyze network traffic in real time, without impacting the performance or availability of the applications running in your VPC. Traffic Mirroring replicates the network traffic from EC2 network interfaces running inside your VPC to destination Amazon Elastic Network Interfaces, allowing you to monitor and analyze the network traffic in real time. Traffic Mirroring is used for auditing, troubleshooting, security analysis, and optimizing the performance of your operations.

The service enables you to mirror network traffic from an individual EC2 instance, or from an entire subnet, and sends the traffic to a destination ENI, which can be located in the same or a different VPC. The mirrored traffic can then be viewed and analyzed using third-party network monitoring and analysis tools that support the PCAP format such as Wireshark. The key features and benefits of VPC Traffic Mirroring include flexible target options that allow you to mirror traffic to EC2 instances, network load balancers, third-party appliances, or services that support packet capture decoding and analysis applications. When configuring Traffic Mirroring, you specify the source and destination ENIs and apply filter rules that define the types of traffic that will be mirrored.

You can filter the traffic that you mirror by specific criteria, such as the direction of the flow, source IP address, destination IP address, protocol, and port number. By using the granular filtering capabilities, you can drill down to the data of interest and filter out what is not needed.

Traffic Mirroring is integrated with other AWS services, such as Amazon CloudWatch and Lambda, enabling you to automate the analysis and alerting of captured traffic. Traffic mirroring uses the AWS high-performance networking stack that supports low-latency, high-bandwidth network mirror capabilities under all loading conditions.

Common VPC Traffic Mirroring use cases include conducting compliance audits where you mirror traffic to compliance monitoring tools to ensure that your network traffic is in compliance with regulatory requirements and industry standards such as PCI DSS, HIPAA, and GDPR. VPC Traffic Mirroring is also used to perform basic network monitoring operations where you mirror traffic to monitoring tools, such as intrusion detection systems, intrusion prevention systems, and analysis tools, to detect and respond to security threats. This tool is very valuable for network troubleshooting by mirroring traffic of interest to diagnostic tools, such as packet capture tools and network analyzers, that help to diagnose network issues and troubleshoot application performance problems. Performance optimization allows you to analyze network traffic to identify and diagnose performance issues such as network congestion, packet loss, and latency. Mirroring is also used for performing security analysis by monitoring traffic to and from EC2 instances to detect and investigate security threats such as malware, unauthorized access, and data breaches.

Traffic Mirroring provides a powerful and flexible solution for monitoring and analyzing network traffic within your VPC, enabling you to improve security, troubleshoot issues, and ensure compliance. It is a useful tool that gives you greater visibility into the network traffic within your VPC and enables you to better monitor, analyze, and secure your AWS resources.

VPC Flow Logs

The VPC Flow Logs feature allows you to capture metadata about the IP traffic going to and from network interfaces inside your VPC. It is important to understand that the logs are not complete packet captures, only the metadata about each packet. The VPC Flow Logs are generated at the network interface level and capture the source and destination IP addresses, ports, and protocol numbers for each packet that flows through the interface. You can also configure VPC Flow Logs to capture additional information such as the VPC ID, the subnet ID, and the network interface ID. You can create logs either for individual network interfaces or for the entire VPC. Figure 13.1 shows the basic architecture of a Flow Log.

FIGURE 13.1 VPC Flow Logging

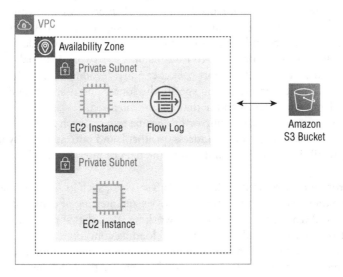

The captured logs are used for troubleshooting network issues, security analysis, and monitoring network activity, and for meeting compliance auditing and compliance requirements. To troubleshoot network connectivity issues, Flow Logs is useful to identify dropped or rejected packets and application issues, and you can identify if packets are being dropped or rejected by security groups or network ACLs; and to perform compliance audits by tracking data transfers between your VPC and external networks. Flow Logs is used to monitor network traffic for security purposes, such as identifying and mitigating security threats, detecting unauthorized access attempts, and identifying unusual patterns of network activity.

To set up VPC Flow Logs, you first must create the Flow Log configuration and then specify the VPC, subnet, or network interface that you want to monitor. You then select where to deliver the Flow Logs including S3, CloudWatch Logs, AWS OpenSearch, or to third-party logging solutions. Once created, the Flow Logs are generated and updated in near real-time.

You can use various tools to analyze the logs, such as Amazon Athena, which allows you to query the data using standard SQL query formats, and Amazon Kinesis Data Firehose, which enables you to stream the data to other services for real-time analysis.

Flow Logs are created in the VPC service of the AWS console. First you select the VPC that you want to create the logs in, as shown in Figure 13.2. Then you fill out the details, as shown in Figure 13.3. Next you create the Flow Log with the results, shown in Figure 13.4.

Then you review the Flow Log in the VPC Flow Log tab, as shown in Figure 13.5. Finally, Figure 13.6 shows an actual Flow Log.

FIGURE 13.2   Creating a VPC Flow Log

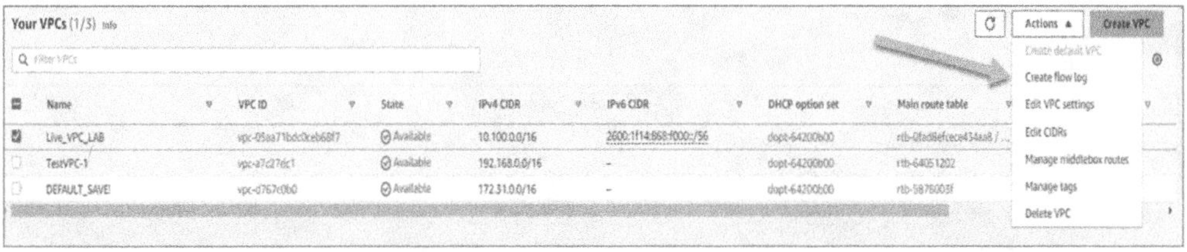

Flow Logs are not enabled by default, so you will need to manually enable them for each network interface or VPC that you want to monitor. Be aware that there may be additional charges for data storage, retrieval, delivery, and the tools used to analyze the Flow Logs, so be sure to check the AWS pricing documentation for details.

The Amazon Flow Logs service collects the log records, consolidates them into log files, and exports the file to external collectors at 5-minute intervals. Each log file contains Flow Log records for the IP traffic recorded in the previous 5 minutes. The maximum file size for a log file is 75MB. If the log file reaches the file size limit within the 5-minute period, the Flow Log stops adding Flow Log records to it, publishes the Flow Log to the Amazon S3 bucket, and creates a new log file. In Amazon S3, the Last Modified field for the Flow Log file indicates the date and time when the file was uploaded to the Amazon S3 bucket. This is later than the time stamp in the filename and differs by the amount of time taken to upload the file to the Amazon S3 bucket. You must specify one of two formats for the log files. Plain text is the default format or the Apache Parquet, which is a columnar data format. Parquet has a performance advantage of being 10 to 100 times faster compared to queries on data in plain text. The Parquet files are formatted with Gzip compression and use 20 percent less storage space than plain text with Gzip compression.

Analyzing Flow Logs enables you to gain insight into network traffic patterns and identify potential security threats. For example, you can use Flow Logs to identify traffic from suspicious IP addresses, monitor traffic between different VPCs, and detect potential data exfiltration attempts.

Transit Gateway Logging

The Transit Gateway service was covered in Chapter 5. In this section you will learn about its logging capabilities. The AWS Transit Gateway Network Manager is a managed network service from AWS that simplifies the management of global networks by providing a centralized view of network resources across multiple AWS accounts and on-premises data centers. The service enables you to visualize, monitor, and manage the entire network topology in a single place.

FIGURE 13.3   Creating a VPC Flow Log

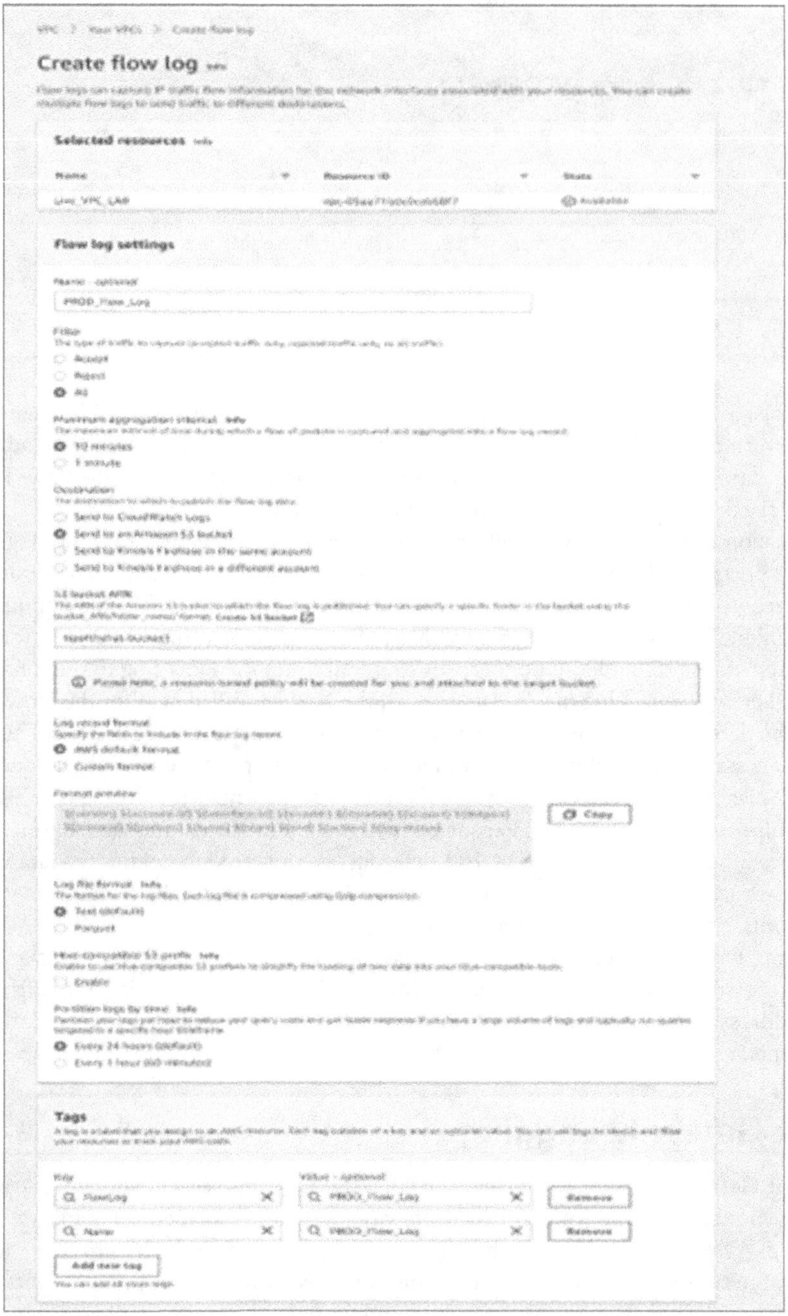

FIGURE 13.4   Created VPC Flow Log

FIGURE 13.5   Flow Log tab

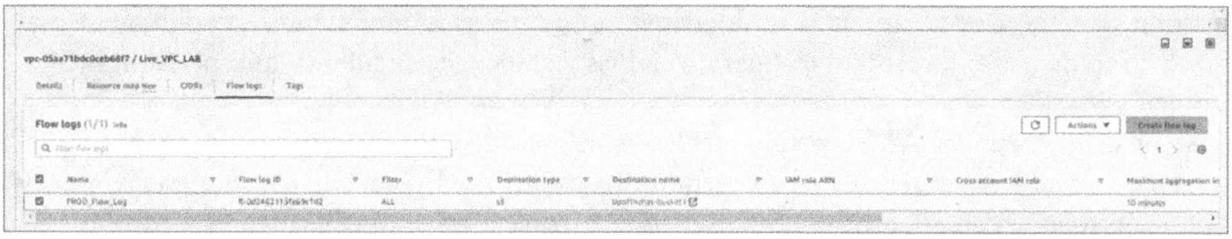

FIGURE 13.6   Flow Log data

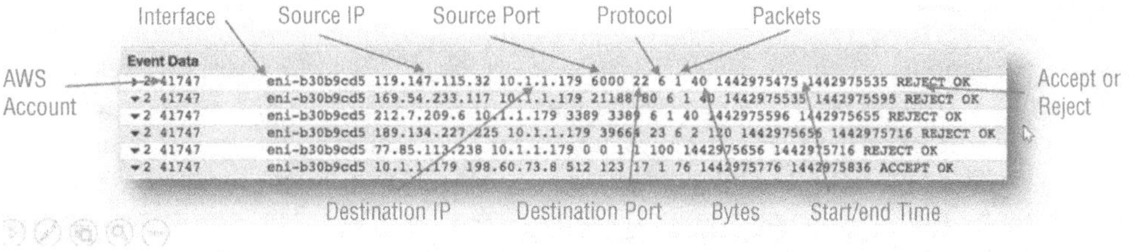

The Transit Gateway Network Manager is a fully managed Amazon service, which means that AWS manages the underlying infrastructure and software, including upgrades and maintenance. This allows you to focus on managing your network resources and improving network performance, without worrying about the underlying infrastructure.

Flow Logs for Transit Gateways allow the visibility of network traffic patterns in the Transit Gateway. The Transit Gateway can export detailed information, including the source and destination IP addresses, port numbers, the protocol type, counters, time stamps, and a collection of metadata on every network flow traversing through the Transit Gateway. This enables you to gain end-to-end network visibility. The Flow Logs enable flow-level visibility for all the traffic traversing between VPCs and on-premises networks using one central gateway.

Flow Logs provide an AWS native tool to export and inspect flow-level information for all traffic flows between AWS and customer's on-premises networks including over Direct Connect gateways or VPN connections without any external tools in your data center's operations center.

The Transit Gateway Flow Logs generate network metrics at an individual flow level; this is in addition to the Transit Gateway attachment-level metrics.

The logs provide information into their traffic flows for protocols, applications, and individual end users that access AWS resources from on-premises networks across the transit gateway.

Alerting Mechanisms

Alerting services in AWS are used for alerting and monitoring in your AWS deployment that help to detect and respond to operational issues, security incidents, and performance problems.

Some of the primary AWS alerting mechanisms include CloudWatch alarms that monitor metrics and trigger actions when certain thresholds are breached. You can create alarms that notify you via email, SMS, or SNS when a metric crosses a specified threshold. The Personal Health Dashboard provides customized information about the health of your AWS resources. You can configure notifications for changes to the status of your resources, such as when a resource becomes impaired or unavailable. AWS Config rules enable you to create rules that evaluate the configuration settings of your AWS resources. Then you configure alerts to be sent via SNS when resources are not compliant with your organization's policies, industry regulations, or if a rule is violated. CloudTrail provides a record of API calls made to your AWS account. CloudTrail can be configured to send alerts via SNS when specific API calls are made or when new API activity is detected. CloudTrail Insights records unusual API activity. The AWS Security Hub provides a view of your security posture across multiple AWS accounts. You can configure notifications to be sent via SNS when security findings are detected. SNS is an Amazon managed messaging service that enables you to send messages or notifications to a variety of destinations, such as email, SMS, mobile push notifications, and HTTP endpoints. EventBridge provides a serverless event bus that routes events between AWS services or from your own applications. You configure EventBridge to trigger AWS Lambda functions or send notifications via SNS when specific events occur. AWS Lambda is a serverless compute service that enables you to run code in response to events. Lambda can be used to create custom alerting workflows that respond to CloudWatch alarms or other events. For example, you can use Lambda to automatically scale resources in response to changes in demand. It can be used to send notifications of any planned or unplanned service disruptions, and to provide guidance on how to remediate issues. The AWS Service Health Dashboard provides a global view of the health of AWS services, regions, and availability zones. It can be used to monitor the status of AWS services and to receive alerts about any service disruptions.

By using these AWS alerting mechanisms, you can monitor your environment, detect issues, and respond to them in a timely manner.

CloudWatch Alarms

AWS CloudWatch alarms monitor metrics and generate alerts when certain thresholds are breached. CloudWatch is a monitoring service that provides you with real-time visibility into your AWS resources and applications performance and health. With CloudWatch alarms, you can proactively detect and respond to issues before they impact your operations. CloudWatch provides a wide range of metrics that you can monitor, including networking, operating systems, applications, and custom metrics.

By setting up alarms for critical metrics, you can take proactive action to prevent outages or performance issues. The flexible notification options and integration with other AWS services make it easy to stay on top of your infrastructure and maintain the availability and performance of your applications.

CloudWatch alarms include customizable thresholds that enable you to define metrics such as CPU usage, network traffic, and disk usage. You configure the threshold values to trigger an alarm when a metric exceeds or falls below a certain threshold for a specified duration. For example, you can set a CPU utilization threshold of 90 percent, so that an alarm is triggered when the CPU utilization of an EC2 instance reaches 90 percent. When an alarm is triggered, you choose how to process the notifications, for example, via email, running an AWS Lambda function, generating SMS texts, or the AWS Simple Notification Service features. You can configure multiple notification options for a single alarm, ensuring that you receive notifications in multiple formats. CloudWatch alarms are integrated with many AWS services such as EC2, DynamoDB, S3, RDS, and Lambda. This allows you to monitor key performance metrics for these services and take action based on the alerts generated by CloudWatch. CloudWatch alarms are also used to automate scaling of your infrastructure. For example, you can set up an alarm to trigger a scaling policy when CPU usage exceeds a certain threshold to automatically add or remove instance compute capacity to maintain performance. In addition to sending notifications, CloudWatch alarms can also trigger custom actions, such as invoking a Lambda function or stopping an EC2 instance.

To configure a CloudWatch alarm, you select the metric you want to monitor, configure the threshold value, and specify the notification options. Once the alarm is set up, CloudWatch will continuously monitor the metric and trigger alerts if the threshold is breached. By setting up alarms to monitor key metrics, you can quickly detect and respond to issues, ensuring that your applications remain available and perform optimally.

Simple Notification Service

The AWS Simple Notification Service (SNS) is an Amazon managed messaging push service that enables you to send and receive messages between applications or distributed systems. SNS is used to decouple application components and enable asynchronous communication between them. SNS enables you to publish messages from various sources, such as applications, microservices, and cloud resources, and deliver them to multiple subscribers or endpoints, such as email, SMS, HTTP endpoints, and Lambda functions.

The key features and use cases of AWS SNS include the publish/subscribe messaging pattern, enabling you to publish messages to SNS topics and deliver them to multiple subscribers asynchronously. Subscribers can be other applications, Lambda functions, or even mobile devices. SNS supports messaging protocols, such as HTTP, HTTPS, email, SMS, and mobile push notifications. This enables SNS to deliver messages to various types of endpoints. SNS can fan out messages to multiple subscribers for use cases where a single message needs to be delivered to multiple recipients, such as broadcasting system-wide alerts or notifications. SNS is highly scalable and can send messages to millions of recipients in real time, without requiring any additional infrastructure or management overhead. The service includes message security by encrypting all messages at rest and in transit using industry-standard encryption protocols.

The service is managed by Amazon and is designed to handle high volumes of messages and provides durability and fault tolerance by replicating messages across multiple availability zones. It is also integrated with other AWS services, including CloudWatch, CloudFormation, Elastic Beanstalk, SQS, and Lambda. This allows you to use SNS to trigger actions based on events or alerts generated by these services.

Typical use cases for AWS SNS include implementation into event-driven architectures where events are published to topics and subscribers receive notifications when events occur. This enables loosely coupled and scalable architectures. It's also used to enable communication between applications and microservices deployed in different regions or accounts. SNS is used to send push notifications to mobile devices running iOS, Android, or Kindle Fire operating systems. It can also send email or SMS notifications to subscribers based on specific events or triggers.

The AWS Simple Notification Service is a flexible and scalable Amazon managed messaging service that is used to enable asynchronous communications between distributed systems and applications. Its integration with other AWS services and support for multiple messaging protocols make it a widely used tool for building highly scalable and fault-tolerant architectures. SNS pricing is based on usage, with no up-front charges or minimum commitments, making it a cost-effective messaging solution.

Log Creation with Different AWS Services

Logging is essential for the secure and reliable operations of any production IT system; this, of course, includes systems deployed in the cloud. AWS provides many different services that include logging options to help you monitor, audit, secure, analyze, and troubleshoot your infrastructure.

Some common AWS services that provide logging capabilities include EC2 instances that have two types of logs: system logs and instance logs. EC2 system logs contain information about the instance's boot process and other operating system data and are stored in the /var/log directory. The second type, instance logs, are specific to the application or services running on the instance and are configured by the application or service. For example, the Amazon Relational Database Service (RDS) provides a variety of logs, including database logging, error logs, slow query logs, and general logging. These logs can be accessed using the RDS console, AWS CLI, or API calls. When you launch an EC2 instance, you can choose to enable CloudWatch Logs, which allows you to monitor and store logs generated by the EC2 instances. EC2 instances can be configured to send logs to Amazon S3 or other log analysis tools using a logging agent installed at the operating system level and provided by Amazon.

S3 provides access logs that record all requests made to the S3 bucket. These logs are used to monitor bucket activity and troubleshoot access issues. S3 provides server access logging, which logs all requests made to the S3 bucket, including the requester's IP address, the time of the request, and the requested object. S3 also supports object-level logging, which logs specific actions performed on the objects, such as object creation, deletion, or retrieval. S3 Server Access logs are stored in an S3 bucket that you specify.

The CloudFront content distribution service provides access logs that contain detailed information about the requests made to your distribution, including the time of the request, the edge location that served the request, and the requested object.

Lambda is a serverless compute service that enables you to run code in response to events. Lambda provides logging through Amazon CloudWatch Logs. You can use the AWS Lambda console or AWS CLI to view and analyze Lambda function logs. Lambda generates logs to help you monitor the function's execution and to diagnose any issues. These logs contain information such as function invocation details, function execution duration, and error messages. You can also use custom logging libraries, such as Winston or Bunyan, to log custom messages.

CloudTrail is the service that logs all API calls made to your AWS account. These include API calls made by users, roles, and AWS services. CloudTrail logs are often used for security analysis, compliance auditing, troubleshooting, resource change tracking, and compliance auditing. CloudTrail automatically creates and stores logs in an S3 bucket that you specify. You can also configure CloudTrail to send logs to CloudWatch Logs for longer-term retention and analysis, which enables you to analyze and search logs in real time. Logs stored in S3 can take advantage of AWS life-cycle management services to automate your company's data retention policies.

The VPC Flow Logs feature enables you to capture information about the traffic flowing through your VPC. Flow Logs are used to monitor network activity, detect and investigate security incidents, and troubleshoot connectivity issues.

The Amazon API Gateway provides logs for every API request made through the service, which includes information about the request, response, and the integration with backend services.

Elastic Load Balancing (ELB) provides access logs that capture detailed information about every request made to the load balancer, including the client IP address, the requested path, and the response time.

AWS provides services that have integrated logging capabilities that are used to monitor and troubleshoot your infrastructure. Each service has its own logging capabilities, and you can access the logs using the AWS Management Console, CLI, or API. It's important that you enable and configure logging on your AWS services to ensure that you can effectively monitor and troubleshoot your infrastructure. It's important to understand how logging works in each service to effectively monitor and troubleshoot applications and infrastructure in the cloud.

Load Balancer Access Logs

Chapter 4, "Load Balancing," was dedicated to the different types of load balancers in the Amazon ELB family. These load balancers will generate access logs that are used for analysis, troubleshooting, and security auditing. You can use this information to identify trends, troubleshoot issues, and optimize your application's performance.

The ELB classic load balancer is a legacy load balancer service that can be used to distribute traffic across EC2 instances. ELB classic load balancer generates access logs that record details such as the time of the request, the client's IP address, the requested URL, and the response code. These logs can be stored in an S3 bucket that you specify. The classic load balancer has been deprecated by AWS, and you will most likely not ever use it.

The application load balancer (ALB) is a layer 7 load balancer that can route traffic to targets based on content such as HTTP headers or URLs. The ALB generates access logs that record details such as the time of the request, the client's IP address, the requested URL, and the HTTP response codes. These logs are stored in the S3 bucket that you specify. You can enable access logging using the AWS Management Console, the AWS CLI, or the AWS SDK.

The network load balancer (NLB) is the Amazon layer 4 load balancer that routes traffic to targets based on IP address and port. The NLB generates access logs that record details such as the time of the request, the client's IP address, the target IP address, the HTTP response codes, and the size of the reply. These logs are stored in the specified S3 bucket. As with the other types of load balancers, you enable access logging using the AWS Management Console, AWS CLI, or AWS SDK.

To enable the load balancer to write access logs to your S3 bucket, you will need to grant appropriate permissions to the load balancer. This typically involves creating an S3 bucket policy that allows the load balancer to write logs to the specified bucket. You have the option to configure the load balancer to create new logs in daily, hourly, or per-minute intervals, and to optionally compress the logs using Gzip compression.

You can use various AWS services and tools to analyze and visualize these logs, such as Amazon Athena, OpenSearch, or third-party log analysis tools such as Elastic Stack, Splunk, or Loggly from SolarWinds.

By enabling and analyzing load balancer access logs, you can gain valuable insights into your application's traffic patterns and identify issues that may impact the performance or security of your infrastructure. ELB access logs can help you identify traffic patterns, detect security issues, and troubleshoot issues related to your load balancer and its targets.

CloudFront Access Logs

In Chapter 1, "Edge Networking," you learned that Amazon CloudFront is a content delivery network service that caches and delivers content to AWS edge locations around the world.

CloudFront generates access logs that detail every request made to your CloudFront distribution. The logging data includes the time of the request, the request method, the requested URL, the status code of the response, and the IP address of the requester.

Standard CloudFront logging, also called *access logging*, provides detailed information on edge request activity. The logging feature is enabled when you create or update the CloudFront distribution and is enabled in the CloudFront console or by using the AWS CLI. Once you have enabled CloudFront access logging, the logs are stored in the S3 bucket you specified. You can access the logs using the S3 console, AWS CLI, or any other S3-compatible tool. When it's enabled, you must specify the S3 bucket you want to store the log files in. The logging feature is provided at no charge by AWS; however, there are charges associated with the S3 storage used. The standard log delivery time is several times per hour but can take up to 24 hours to appear. Real-time logging can also be enabled and sent to a Kinesis data stream for analysis, forwarding, or storage. The data from all the edge locations is consolidated into the S3 repository. To enable access logging, you need to specify or create an S3 bucket to store the logs and then configure your CloudFront distribution to write the logs to that bucket.

The access logs contain a great deal of information about requests made to your Cloud-Front distribution. This data is used to identify trends, troubleshoot issues, and optimize your application's performance. For example, you can use logs to identify the most frequently accessed objects, the geographic distribution of your users, or the source of excessive requests.

To analyze the logs, you can use a variety of tools such as Amazon Athena, OpenSearch (formally Elasticsearch), and open-source analysis tools that can work with S3 data. For example, you can use Amazon Athena to run SQL queries against the log data to extract insights and identify patterns.

Amazon CloudFront provides access logs that are used to monitor and optimize the performance of your distribution. By enabling logging and analyzing the access logs, you can gain insights into the usage of your distribution, identify issues, and optimize performance.

Log Delivery Mechanisms

AWS offers log delivery mechanisms for different services, including CloudWatch Logs, that enable you to monitor, troubleshoot, and analyze your log data in real time. This is a managed service that allows you to monitor, store, and access log files from many AWS resources and custom applications. CloudWatch Logs can also be used to create alarms and automatically respond to specific log events. Amazon Lambda is a serverless computing service that can be used to collect, process, and trigger downstream actions based on specific log events from various sources, such as CloudWatch Logs, or streams such as Kinesis or S3, and send it to other AWS services for analysis or storage. The Kinesis Data Firehose service is a fully managed streaming data service that lets you capture, transform, and load streaming data into AWS storage services like S3, Redshift, and OpenSearch. Customers can use Firehose to receive, temporarily store, and process large volumes of log data in near real time.

Log data that requires either temporary or long-term storage is commonly stored in the S3 object storage service that enables you to store and retrieve data from inside AWS or remotely. You can use S3 to store log data from various sources, such as CloudWatch Logs and AWS Lambda, for short-or long-term retention or for backups. The AWS Direct Connect service can be used to transfer large amounts of log data from your on-premises infrastructure to AWS for analysis or storage. The OpenSearch service is used to index, search, and visualize log data from various sources, such as CloudWatch logs, S3, Kinesis data streams, or Kinesis Data Firehose. You can use Kibana, a web-based user interface, to create dashboards, alerts, and reports based on your log data. For Internet of Things deployments, use the AWS IoT Core service to collect log data from IoT devices and send it to other AWS services for analysis or storage.

AWS offers a range of log delivery mechanisms that are used to collect and analyze your log data. The choice of delivery mechanisms depends on your specific use case, the type of log data, the desired level of scalability, the reliability, and the cost-effectiveness. Depending on your specific requirements and use case, you can combine multiple delivery services to create a customized logging solution.

Kinesis

The Amazon Kinesis family is a fully managed service for real-time data streaming and processing. Kinesis can collect data from thousands of different sources including CloudWatch Logs, VPC Flow Logs, or custom log files and consolidate them into data streams that can then be analyzed or forwarded to other Amazon services such as S3 for object storage. Kinesis acts as middleware that integrates and interconnects with other AWS services, such as Lambda, S3, OpenSearch, and Redshift. These integrations allow you to use Kinesis to stream log data to other services for further processing or analysis.

Kinesis is used for collecting and analyzing log data in real time. Kinesis is often used as the primary Amazon service to process log data in real time, allowing you to monitor and respond to events as they occur. Kinesis can manage high volumes of data in real time, making it ideal for log processing applications that generate large amounts of data. The Kinesis service scales up and down automatically based on the volume of data being processed. Amazon manages the infrastructure provisioning and provides multiple levels of data durability to ensure that your log data is safe and secure.

Kinesis streams create performance metrics for the service that can be viewed and analyzed using Amazon CloudWatch. The Kinesis stream metric data includes the number of incoming records, the number of put and get operations, and the latency and throughput of your stream. With this information, you can set up alarms and notifications to detect and respond to anomalies or performance issues in real time.

Kinesis Data Streams supports a feature called enhanced fan-out (EFN) that allows you to replicate data in real time to multiple locations, customers, or services. Fan-out metrics include the number of active EFN consumers, the number of active connections, and the data processing rate for each consumer. You can use these metrics to monitor the performance and availability of your consumers and to optimize the stream processing. For example, you can use Lambda, the Amazon serverless compute service, to process log data in real time. Lambda can filter, transform, or enrich log events before sending them to Kinesis Data Streams or Kinesis Data Firehose. For example, you can use Lambda to extract fields from log messages or enrich log events with metadata such as geolocation or user context, transform your data before storing it in S3, or use OpenSearch to index and search your data for real-time insights.

Kinesis Data Analytics analyzes streaming data in real time using SQL queries. You can use Kinesis Data Analytics to perform windowing, filtering, aggregation, and join operations on log data streams. For example, you can use Kinesis Data Analytics to detect anomalies in your log data.

Using Amazon Kinesis for log collection and consolidation, you will set up Kinesis data streams to receive and process log data from various sources, such as CloudWatch Logs, syslog servers on Linux, or custom applications. The *Kinesis Data Firehose* option is used to automatically deliver log data to destinations such as S3 or OpenSearch for additional processing, analysis, or storage. The Kinesis Analytics service is used to perform real-time analytics on your log data, such as filtering, aggregating, or enriching log events. The various Kinesis services enable you to collect log data from thousands of sources, process, store, and analyze log data in real time. Depending on your specific requirements, you can use one or more of the Kinesis features to monitor and analyze your streaming data.

Route 53

The Amazon Route 53 DNS service provides multiple logging mechanisms to help you monitor and troubleshoot your DNS traffic. You can refer to Chapter 2, "Domain Name Services," for more detail on the Route 53 DNS logging services.

Route 53 can log all DNS hosted zone queries that it receives for your domain names in near real time and forward them to CloudWatch logs. The logs are used to monitor DNS traffic patterns, troubleshoot DNS resolution issues, and detect security threats such as DNS-based attacks or malware. DNS query logging can help you troubleshoot DNS-related issues, such as misconfigured DNS records, DNS server errors, and DNS cache poisoning attacks. It can also help you monitor DNS traffic and identify unusual patterns or trends that may indicate security threats or performance issues.

DNS query logging with CloudTrail provides additional logging of Route 53 API calls made to create, update, or delete resources. The logs include information about the user or service that made the API call, the source IP address of the API call, and the result of the API call. You must enable CloudTrail logging by selecting Route 53 as one of the services to monitor. The logs are then delivered to the specified S3 bucket.

Route 53 also logs information about the DNS queries that it receives and how it routes them to your AWS resources. This includes the source IP address, the type of query, the response code, and the latency. Route 53 traffic Flow Logs can be stored in Amazon S3 or Amazon CloudWatch Logs for further analysis. Route 53 also logs data about the health checks that it performs on your resources. Health check logs include type of health check, resource status, and response times. Route 53 health check logs are used to troubleshoot health check failures, monitor the availability of your resources, or detect performance issues. If you have VPC flow logging enabled for your VPCs, you can enable DNS query logging to capture DNS queries that originate from within your VPCs. This allows you to associate DNS queries with specific resources in your VPCs.

The Route 53 logging options give you data on your DNS infrastructure. This information is used to optimize your DNS configuration, troubleshoot issues, and ensure high availability and performance of your applications.

Route 53 has native integration with CloudTrail for recording API calls from the console, CLI, SDK, and applications directly to Route 53, and exporting the records to CloudTrail. Users, roles, and services of AWS will capture the API calls occurring in Route 53 and record them in CloudTrail. If you create a trail in CloudTrail, then all Route 53

IP records can be stored in an S3 storage bucket for analysis, troubleshooting, and historical archives. This will collect data on who made the request, what the request domain was for, and the IP address, date/time, and more. Since CloudTrail is enabled when you create your AWS account, Route 53 records DNS logs in event history by default. API access information can be globally collected from all AWS regions and stored in a single consolidated CloudTrail S3 bucket.

CloudWatch

CloudWatch is the Amazon monitoring and logging service that enables you to monitor, store, access, and analyze logs generated by AWS and external resources, applications, and services. CloudWatch logging is used to collect and track metrics, monitor log files, and set alarms. You can also use the CloudWatch SDKs to send logs from your applications running on EC2 instances or on-premises servers, and the logs can be collected from any text-based log file.

CloudWatch logs are used for troubleshooting, monitoring, automation, and compliance auditing. The benefit of CloudWatch logging includes a centralized logging repository to store and access logs from multiple sources. The service collects logs from your AWS resources, applications, and services, and stores them in a single location for access, retention, and analysis. You can use CloudWatch for real-time streaming of logs, which enables you to monitor and analyze logs as they are generated in real time. CloudWatch logging can be used to set alarms based on log data to trigger automated actions based on log events. This helps to identify and resolve issues quickly.

CloudWatch logging is a fully managed AWS service that can scale to handle large volumes of logs, so you can collect and store logs from even the largest applications and services. The service includes powerful search and query capabilities, so you can easily find and analyze relevant logs. CloudWatch Logs Insights enables administrators to run ad hoc queries using SQL-like syntax to analyze and visualize log data in graphs and charts.

To configure CloudWatch logging, you need to create a log group, which is a collection of log streams that share the same retention, monitoring, and access control settings. The log data collected by CloudWatch logging is stored in durable storage, and you can choose to store logs indefinitely or set retention policies to automatically delete logs after a specified time. You can then use the CloudWatch logging API or console command-line utilities to send logs to your log group. Once logs are stored in your log group, you can use CloudWatch Logs Insights to search and analyze your logs and set up alarms based on log metrics. For example, you can set up an alarm to notify you when a certain error message appears in your logs.

CloudWatch logging is a powerful tool for monitoring and troubleshooting your AWS environment, and it can help you identify and resolve issues quickly to improve the availability and reliability of your applications.

Mechanisms to Audit Network Security Configurations

AWS provides native services to audit network security configurations, including the Config service that allows you to track changes of your AWS resources and your network security configurations over time to identify any deviations from your desired state. AWS Config also provides prebuilt and custom rules that you can use to evaluate the compliance of your resources against industry standards and best practices. You can use Config rules to define compliance rules and evaluate the compliance of your network security configurations against these rules.

The Config service can be helpful in auditing changes to your network security groups, network ACLs, and other network-related resources.

As we learned earlier in this chapter, the VPC Flow Logs service allows you to capture information about the traffic flowing in and out of your VPC. You can use Flow Log data to monitor network traffic and identify security threats, as well as to troubleshoot connectivity issues.

Amazon *GuardDuty* is a threat detection service from Amazon that uses machine learning and anomaly detection to identify potential security threats in your AWS environment. GuardDuty identifies network-based threats, such as suspicious network traffic or unauthorized access to your resources.

The AWS CloudTrail service provides a record of actions taken by users, services, and systems in your AWS account. CloudTrail logs can include information about network security configuration changes, such as changes to VPC settings, security group rules, and network ACLs. Use CloudTrail to audit network security configurations and track changes over time.

The AWS Security Hub is a centralized security service that provides a detailed view of your security stance across accounts and services. Security Hub provides a customizable dashboard that displays your compliance status, security alerts, and other security-related information, and provides automated compliance checks to ensure that your network security configurations meet regulatory and industry standards. Security Hub automatically aggregates and prioritizes security findings from various AWS services, including Config, GuardDuty, and Inspector. Security Hub also provides a set of prebuilt compliance standards that you can use to evaluate your security posture against industry benchmarks and best practices. Security Hub integrates with AWS Config and CloudTrail to provide a complete overview of your security posture. Use Security Hub to monitor network security configurations and receive alerts when security issues are detected.

The Amazon Inspector is a security assessment service that helps identify security vulnerabilities and compliance issues in your applications and network configurations. Inspector automatically examines your resources against industry standards and best practices and then provides detailed reports with recommendations for remediation.

There are also offerings from third-party service providers in the AWS Marketplace that can help you audit and monitor your network security configurations. These service offerings and tools provide additional features and functionality in addition to what is available from AWS's native services, including automated compliance checks, vulnerability scanning, and security assessments.

Using these tools and services enables you to have detailed visibility into your network security configurations, gives you the ability to identify potential security threats, and ensures that your network security is configured in compliance with best practices and industry standards.

Security Groups

AWS security groups are virtual firewalls used to control inbound and outbound traffic to AWS resources, such as EC2 and ECS instances or RDS databases, to name just a few examples. Figure 13.7 shows an example of an inbound security group. Security groups operate at the instance level, and each instance can be associated with one or more security groups. They act as a protective layer that restricts access to your resources from only the necessary traffic by creating traffic filters, making it easy to secure your infrastructure from potential threats. AWS service integrations include VPCs and AWS Identity and Access Management (IAM). You can create IAM policies that control access to security groups and VPCs, and you can use VPC Flow Logs to monitor traffic to and from security groups. You can use security groups to control access across VPCs or between accounts and to control network access. Security groups provide logging capabilities that allow you to track changes to security group rules and monitor network traffic.

FIGURE 13.7   VPC security group inbound

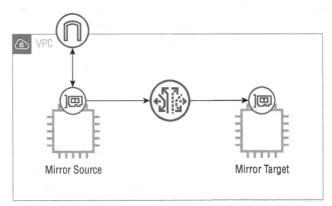

Security groups can be associated with single or multiple AWS resources.

Security groups are stateful filters, which means they track the state of network connections and allow traffic to flow only to authorized ports and protocols. Security groups give you granular control over inbound and outbound traffic, allowing you to specify the IP addresses, protocols, and ports that are allowed or denied. When an outbound traffic flow is allowed, the return traffic into AWS is automatically allowed, regardless of any rules in the associated security group.

You can create separate rules for inbound and outbound traffic. This enables you to create specific rules for each type of traffic and limit access to only the necessary ports and protocols. Security groups are easy to create and manage through the AWS Management Console, AWS CLI, or AWS SDK. You can dynamically add, remove, or modify security group rules in real time and as needed to meet your security requirements and they take effect immediately. They are integrated with many AWS services including ELBs, autoscaling, and Lambda.

Implementing security groups in your infrastructure reduces the risk of unauthorized access and ensures that your resources are protected from potential threats.

Security groups enable you to control inbound and outbound traffic to AWS resources. Security groups act like a virtual firewall that controls traffic to and from the AWS resources you apply them to.

Firewall Manager

AWS *Firewall Manager* is a security management service that allows you to centrally manage AWS WAF and AWS Shield Advanced across AWS accounts and resources. The Firewall Manager enables you to deploy and manage firewall rules across your entire AWS infrastructure to ensure consistent security policies across multiple firewalls. You can use preconfigured or custom firewall rules. Creating custom security policies defines the rules and actions that can be applied to your resources. These policies are based on resource types, accounts, or tags.

The Firewall Manager is integrated with AWS Organizations, Config, and CloudWatch to provide a consolidated view of your security posture across all your accounts.

Firewall Manager includes monitoring and reporting capabilities to track compliance with your security policies and identify security risks.

The Firewall Manager is a fully managed AWS service that is used to centrally monitor and manage your WAF and Shield Advanced infrastructure.

You can enforce your organization's security policies, detect, and respond to security threats, and ensure consistent and effective security in your AWS deployment.

Trusted Advisor

Trusted Advisor is an AWS managed service that provides real-time guidance to help you manage performance and costs of your AWS deployment by continuously analyzing your accounts and providing you with recommendations based on the best practices in the AWS Well-Architected Framework guidelines. Trusted Advisor performs a series of checks that identify ways to optimize your AWS infrastructure, improve security and performance, reduce costs, and monitor service quotas. Trusted Advisor analyzes your AWS usage patterns and offers recommendations from more than 200 checks across five categories, including cost optimization, performance, security, fault tolerance, and service limits.

Trusted Advisor provides recommendations on how to optimize your AWS usage to reduce costs by identifying underutilized resources, providing recommendations for using the most cost-effective instance types, identifying idle resources, optimizing your storage usage, recommending reserved instance purchases, and suggesting options to reduce the cost of other AWS services.

The service can also analyze your deployed infrastructure and, based on its findings, it will provide you with recommendations on how to improve performance. For example, it can identify EC2 instances with high CPU utilization, recommend changes to your load balancer configurations, give you recommendations on how to optimize network throughput, and identify bottlenecks to improve application performance. The service can help you optimize your RDS database configurations and increase your EBS storage volume performance.

Trusted Advisor also provides recommendations on how to improve security by identifying security groups with overly permissive rules, recommendations on configuring IAM policies, enforcing encryption, identifying exposed access keys and unencrypted data, providing suggestions on the use of multifactor authentication, and improving network security.

The service offers recommendations on how to improve fault tolerance by identifying single points of failure in your architecture, offering recommendations for implementing load balancing, configuring backups, improving disaster recovery, and suggesting the use of multi-availability zone deployments. Trusted Advisor monitors your AWS service usage and alerts you if you are approaching service limits and gives you suggestions on how to improve your AWS operations. Trusted Advisor includes integrations with AWS Support services, which enables you to create support cases directly from Trusted Advisor recommendations.

Trusted Advisor also allows you to create and deploy custom checks to evaluate your resources against your specific requirements and best practices.

The AWS Trusted Advisor service provides valuable real-time insights into your AWS infrastructure and helps you optimize your usage, improve performance, increase security, and reduce costs. By using Trusted Advisor, you can ensure that your AWS environment is running efficiently and effectively, reducing the risk of downtime or cost overruns.

Traffic Mirroring and Flow Logs

Traffic Mirroring and Flow Logs are Amazon managed services used to gain visibility into network traffic and to help monitor and troubleshoot your AWS network infrastructure.

The Traffic Mirroring service enables you to copy network traffic from an Elastic Network Interface (ENI) on an EC2 instance and send it to a monitoring appliance, such as an intrusion detection system or a network analyzer tool such as *Wireshark*, as shown in Figure 13.8. Traffic Mirroring enables the inspection of network traffic in real time to detect security threats, monitor network performance, and troubleshoot network issues. Traffic Mirroring provides real-time monitoring of network traffic, while Flow Logs provides logs that are generated after the fact.

Flow Logs captures metadata about the IP traffic going to and from network interfaces in your VPC, subnet, or network interface. Flow Logs does not capture the complete packet, but the data about the packet, including the source and destination IP addresses, ports, protocols, time stamps, and packet counts. This data is sent to Amazon CloudWatch Logs or Amazon S3 for storage and analysis. Flow Logs enables you to monitor network traffic patterns, troubleshoot connectivity issues, and perform security analysis. Both services provide real-time visibility into network traffic, allowing you to monitor and analyze your network traffic as it occurs. They are relatively easy to set up and configure in your VPC or on EC2 instances.

FIGURE 13.8 VPC Traffic Mirroring

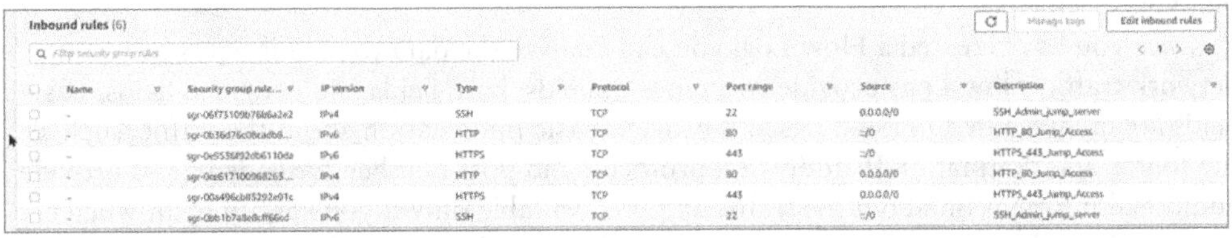

The services are customizable and allow you to select the network interfaces and traffic that you want to monitor or mirror. Both the mirroring and logging services are integrated with AWS monitoring and storage services such as CloudWatch Logs and S3, for additional monitoring and analysis capabilities. They can help you to meet security and compliance requirements by providing visibility into network traffic and helping you identify security threats and anomalies.

You should implement these services as a best practice, to detect security threats, troubleshoot network issues, and optimize network performance. Remember that Traffic Mirroring provides a more detailed view of network traffic, including the packet payloads, while Flow Logs provides metadata about the traffic. In addition, Traffic Mirroring allows you to mirror traffic from any network interface, while Flow Logs only captures traffic from specific network interfaces. Traffic Mirroring is more expensive than Flow Logs, as it requires additional network resources and processing power, while Flow Logs provides more basic information in a cost-effective way.

Creating and Analyzing VPC Flow Logs

Some common use cases for Flow Logs include troubleshooting network connectivity by using Flow Logs to identify the source of connectivity issues, such as blocked traffic or misconfigured security groups, and to monitor traffic patterns, such as traffic volume and the types of traffic flowing through your VPC. Network security can be analyzed by using Flow Logs to identify potential security threats, such as unauthorized access or network attacks.

Creating and analyzing a VPC Flow Log in AWS enables insights into your network traffic flows and helps to troubleshoot connectivity issues, monitor traffic patterns, and improve network security. By analyzing the base and extended fields of Flow Logs, you have the capability to have a deeper understanding of your network traffic and then use this information to optimize your AWS deployment.

To create and analyze a VPC Flow Log in AWS, first create a Flow Log for your VPC. To do this, go to the Amazon VPC console, select your VPC, and then select the Flow Logs tab. Click the Create Flow Log button.

Next, specify the destination for your Flow Logs, which can be a CloudWatch Logs log group, an Amazon S3 bucket, or an Amazon Kinesis Data Firehose delivery stream. Apply a filter to specify the traffic that you want to log, which can be all traffic or traffic that matches specific criteria, such as a specific subnet, network interface, or traffic type. You must apply an IAM role that allows Amazon VPC to publish Flow Logs to the destination that you specified.

Once you have created a Flow Log, you can analyze the data to gain insights into your network traffic. Flow Logs provide two types of fields: base fields and extended fields. Base fields are included in all Flow Logs and provide basic information about the traffic, such as the source and destination IP addresses, protocol, and port number. Extended fields provide additional information about the traffic and are available only if you specify them when creating the Flow Log. Some common extended fields include packets, bytes, start, and end.

The base fields of VPC Flow Logs include the following information:

- *Version*: The version of the Flow Log format

- *Account ID*: The ID of the AWS account that owns the network interface or subnet

- *Interface ID*: The ID of the network interface or subnet

- *Source/Destination IP Address*: The IP address of the source or destination of the traffic

- *Source/Destination Port*: The source or destination port number of the traffic

- *Protocol*: The protocol of the traffic (TCP, UDP, ICMP, etc.)

- *Packets*: The number of packets in the flow

- *Bytes*: The number of bytes in the flow

- *Start Time*: The time when the flow started

The extended fields of VPC Flow Logs include additional information about the traffic, such as the following:

- *Action*: The action that was taken on the traffic (ACCEPT or REJECT)

- *Log Status*: Indicates whether the log record represents the start or end of a flow

- *TCP Flags*: The TCP flags that were set in the packet

- *Flow Direction*: Indicates the direction of the flow (INGRESS or EGRESS)

- *ICMP Type/Code*: The ICMP type and code of the packet

- *Packet Source Type*: Indicates the source of the packet (AWS or Customer)

- *VLAN ID*: The VLAN ID of the packet

By analyzing the base and extended fields of VPC Flow Logs, you can gain insights into the traffic flowing through your network interfaces and subnets, troubleshoot connectivity issues, monitor network performance, and perform security analysis. You can use tools such as Amazon Athena or Amazon CloudWatch Logs Insights to analyze the Flow Logs and generate insights.

Creating and Analyzing Network Traffic Mirroring

To create and analyze network traffic mirroring in AWS using VPC Traffic Mirroring, the first step is to create a Traffic Mirror target, which is the destination for mirrored traffic. This can be an Amazon Elastic Compute Cloud (EC2) instance or a network interface in your VPC. Then you will create a Traffic Mirroring filter, which determines the traffic to be mirrored. The filter can be set by source or destination IP address, port, protocol, or other criteria. Finally, you create a Traffic Mirroring session, which specifies the source and destination of the mirrored traffic, and the Traffic Mirroring filter you want to apply.

After you have created the mirror session, you then can analyze the mirrored traffic using a network analysis tool. A common open-source analysis tool is Wireshark or `tcpdump`. You install and configure Wireshark to capture traffic on the network interface or EC2 instance that is the destination for the mirrored traffic. To capture Traffic Mirroring traffic in Wireshark, select the interface or adapter that you configured to capture the mirrored traffic. After you have captured the traffic, you can apply filters in Wireshark to narrow down the scope of the analysis. You can use filters to focus on specific protocols, source or destination IP addresses, or other criteria. Once you have captured and filtered the traffic, you will begin to analyze it using Wireshark's built-in analysis tools. You can analyze traffic by protocol, traffic volume, packet size, and more.

Oher tools include the CloudWatch Logs console, or you can export the data to Amazon S3 and use third-party tools such as OpenSearch or Kibana to analyze the data. Amazon tools include Athena and Amazon QuickSight that can be used to query and visualize traffic data.

You can also leverage machine learning. AWS provides several machine learning services that can be used to analyze network traffic. For example, GuardDuty uses machine learning to analyze network traffic and detect threats, such as port scanning and reconnaissance activity.

Once you have analyzed the mirrored traffic and have detected possible anomalies or threats, you will need to take action to mitigate them. You can implement any number of security services such as WAF, Shield, and the Firewall Manager to protect your network resources.

By using VPC Traffic Mirroring tools, you can capture and analyze network traffic in your VPC for security and compliance purposes. This information can be used to detect and respond to security incidents, troubleshoot network issues, and optimize network performance.

CloudWatch

As we have covered extensively in this book, CloudWatch is the monitoring and observability service provided by AWS. It allows you to collect, view, and analyze metrics, logs, and events from various AWS services, resources, and applications. It can be used to monitor resources and applications that are running on AWS, as well as on-premises resources.

CloudWatch collects various types of data, such as metrics, logs, and events. Metrics are numerical values that represent the performance of a resource over time, such as CPU usage or network traffic. Logs are textual data that represent events or activities that occur within a resource, such as server access logs or application logs. Events are notifications of significant changes or actions within a resource, such as the creation or deletion of an EC2 instance.

The key features of CloudWatch include CloudWatch Metrics that enable you to collect and monitor data in real time of objects such as CPU utilization, network traffic, and request latency. Metrics are viewed in the dashboard or used to generate alarms when thresholds you define are crossed. CloudWatch Logs allows you to collect and store log data from applications, services, and AWS resources. Use the logs to search, filter, and analyze log data in real time and create alarms based on specific log events. CloudWatch Events is used to respond to events and trigger actions in real time. You create rules to match incoming events and use targets such as AWS Lambda or Amazon SNS to trigger actions.

CloudWatch alarms are used to monitor metrics and respond to changes in your environment. You set up alarms based on metric thresholds or CloudWatch Logs events, and take automated actions when alarms are triggered. The dashboards allow you to create custom views of your metrics and log data. You can create and apply widgets to display specific metrics, logs, or events, and customize the layout and formatting of dashboards. CloudWatch integrates with a variety of AWS services and tools, including EC2, RDS, Lambda, and Elastic Load Balancing. You can also use CloudWatch with third-party tools such as Datadog or Grafana.

The logs in CloudWatch allow users to collect, monitor, and store log files from any log generating resources such as Amazon EC2 instances, CloudTrail, and Route 53, among others. These logs can then be analyzed using *CloudWatch Insights*, a feature that enables users to search and analyze log data using a query language.

CloudWatch is a powerful monitoring and observability tool that allows you to gain insights into your AWS environment and take proactive actions to maintain the performance, health, and security of your resources.

Implementing Automated Alarms Using CloudWatch

CloudWatch enables you to automate alarms to monitor and react to events in your AWS resources.

To implement automated alarms in CloudWatch, begin by selecting the resource you want to monitor. This can be resources such as EC2 instances, RDS databases, Lambda functions, or any other AWS service.

Each resource has a set of predefined metrics that can be monitored in CloudWatch. You select the metric you want to monitor, for example, the CPU utilization of an EC2 instance, network traffic, or RDS database connections. To create an alarm, you will define a metric filter that will search for specific patterns in your log data and create a metric based on that pattern. After you create the metric filter, you then create an alarm based on that metric. If we use the example of CPU utilization, you will then set a threshold value that triggers an alarm. For example, you may want to receive a notification when CPU utilization exceeds 80 percent. You can create an alarm in CloudWatch that monitors the metric you selected and triggers a notification when the threshold is exceeded. You must choose the notification mechanism such as sending an email or text message, using SNS topics, or even an automated action such as triggering a Lambda function or adding web server capacity to a load balancer.

You should always test and validate the alarm before implementing it in a production environment to make sure it is working as expected when the metric breaches the threshold. You can simulate an alarm breach by manually setting the metric value to the threshold limit. Once the alarm is deployed, make sure to monitor it regularly to ensure it functions correctly. If necessary, you can also modify or delete the alarm as needed. CloudWatch also provides data such as alarm histories, which helps you track the alarm state over time. CloudWatch Logs Insights is used to analyze the logs and metrics data to identify the root cause of the alarm breach.

By following these steps, you can implement automated CloudWatch alarms to monitor your resources to ensure their availability and performance.

Implementing Customized Metrics Using CloudWatch

CloudWatch allows cloud administrators and SysOps engineers to create custom metrics that monitor specific aspects of their application or infrastructure that are not covered by the predefined metrics. You can create customized metrics in CloudWatch to monitor and track specific applications or infrastructure performance data.

The basic steps to take to implement customized metrics for CloudWatch include identifying the data source that you want to monitor and track. This can be any source such as application logs generated on servers, custom scripts, or any other data source that can be programmatically accessed. The next step is to define the metric that you are going to track. This will include the metric name, the metric namespace, the units of measurement, and the metric dimensions. Dimensions are used to filter the metric data by different attributes, such as instance ID, region, or environment. Next, define the custom metric dimensions. Custom metric dimensions are key-value pairs that are used to identify the metric. For example, you might use the dimension key-value pairs to identify the specific instance or resource that is being monitored.

Then you publish the metric data to CloudWatch using the CloudWatch API or SDK. You have the option to publish data in real time or batch mode, using various data formats, such as JSON or CSV.

After the metric data has been captured and loaded into CloudWatch, you can proceed to set up alarms that will trigger when the metric data crosses above or below your defined threshold. You can define the alarm actions, such as sending notifications, triggering AWS Lambda functions, or scaling resources. The next step is to test the custom metric to verify that what you configured is being collected by the CloudWatch agent. You can do this by using the CLI or CloudWatch console to query the metric data and ensure that it is being recorded.

Monitor the metric data and troubleshoot any issues that arise. You can use CloudWatch Logs Insights to search and analyze logs related to the metric data or use CloudWatch Metrics Explorer to visualize the metric data.

By following these steps, users can create customized metrics to monitor and track specific applications or infrastructure performance data. CloudWatch provides a powerful tool for custom monitoring and management of AWS resources, and customized metrics can help users gain greater visibility and insights into their systems.

Users can create and publish their own custom metrics that give them the capability to monitor the health and performance of their resources with metric filters they create. Custom metrics provide a more detailed view of your resources and can help you identify and address issues before they become critical. By leveraging custom metrics, you can customize your monitoring to the specific needs of your application or infrastructure.

Correlating and Analyzing Information Across Single or Multiple AWS Log Sources

As has been discussed throughout this book, AWS and their partners provide multiple services for logging, such as CloudWatch Logs, CloudTrail, Splunk, and the OpenSearch service.

These services can generate a large volume of log data that can make it difficult to correlate and analyze all the information that is stored in single or multiple log sources. In this section, we will investigate several tools provided by AWS that can help users manage this data.

The general steps you can take to correlate and analyze information across single or multiple AWS log sources include centralizing the log data from multiple sources into a single destination such as CloudWatch Logs, OpenSearch, or Splunk to make it easier to search and analyze log data from a single location.

Next, the log data structure must be defined. Using a common log data structure across all log sources makes it easier to perform actions on the data such as correlation and analysis. The structure should include standard fields, such as time stamps, source IP address, and HTTP method, and can follow one of the various standard log formats.

Next, use one of the log analytics tools from AWS or its partners in the marketplace. These log analytics tools help to correlate and analyze log data. Event correlation enables you to use a query language to compare data received across multiple log sources and identify trends. For example, you can correlate CloudTrail logs with load balancing access logs to identify the source of a security breach.

The AWS tools include CloudTrail Insights, CloudWatch Logs Insights, and the Amazon OpenSearch Service. These tools allow users to search and analyze log data using advanced query capabilities.

AWS also provides machine learning services that can be used to analyze log data. These tools include SageMaker and Kinesis Data Analytics. These services can identify patterns and anomalies in log data, providing insights into potential issues. *QuickSight* or *Kibana* are used to create visualizations that make it easier to understand log data. Data can be displayed in dashboards, charts, and graphs.

Your operations team should continuously monitor and refine the log data analysis to identify new insights and improve the accuracy of log data correlation and analysis. AWS and their partners provide a variety of tools and services for logging and log analytics.

By leveraging these tools and services, you can correlate and analyze information across single or multiple AWS log sources to gain deeper insights into the performance and security of their AWS infrastructure, hybrid clouds, and applications. This helps you to improve resource optimization, enhance security, and ensure compliance with industry standards and regulations.

Implementing Log Delivery Solutions

Implementing log delivery solutions is a key component in the management and monitoring of your cloud infrastructure and applications. AWS provides services that you can use to collect, store, and analyze logs from various sources.

The components of a log delivery solution in AWS include identifying which log sources you need to collect. These can be from the many sources we have covered in this chapter such as CloudTrail logs, VPC Flow Logs, ELB access logs, Route 53 query logs, or application logs. This may also involve configuring your application code to enable logging or installing an agent on your EC2 instances. You must decide which log sources are most critical for your organization.

Next you will choose the log collection method that best meets your requirements. AWS provides several options, including CloudWatch Logs, Kinesis Data Streams, and Kinesis Firehose. Configure the log sources to send their log data to your log collection destination. This will involve modifying resource settings or installing log agents on your instances.

Then, you need to define the rules that determine how log data is delivered and stored. These rules may include filters, transformations, or aggregations that help organize and analyze log data. You may want to modify the log delivery configurations to specify the frequency of log delivery, the maximum log size, or the compression format.

Configure a log storage solution that suits your requirements. Storage options include Amazon S3 that can be used to store log data for long-term retention. There are also the OpenSearch Service, used to store and analyze log data in real time, and Amazon Redshift, which is a fully managed data warehouse that can be used to store and analyze large volumes of log data. Define the retention policy for your log data. The retention policy specifies how long the log data should be retained before it is deleted. Your log retention policies should take into consideration any data retention regulations and should minimize storage costs.

Define the access policies for your log data. The access policies specify who can access the log data and what actions they can perform on it.

As with any new deployment, you must test the log delivery architecture to ensure that logs are being delivered to the log management service as expected. Use your log management service's tools to query and visualization tools to verify that the logs are being correctly parsed and indexed.

After you have set up your log delivery solution, you can monitor and analyze your log data to gain insights into the performance and health of your infrastructure and applications. Use the visualization and analytics tools provided by your log storage solution to create dashboards and alerts that help you monitor log data in real time.

Implement a log delivery solution that allows you to collect, store, and analyze log data from your deployed source applications and services. This can help improve resource optimization, enhance security, and ensure compliance with industry standards and regulations.

Implementing a Network Audit Strategy

Your organization may need to implement network audits across single or multiple AWS network services and accounts. This is often an important step to ensure that your cloud or hybrid infrastructure is secure and meets compliance requirements.

To implement a network audit strategy, consider the following steps. You should begin by defining your network audit goals and scope of the audit, including the AWS network services, your hybrid connections, and accounts that will be audited. Next, identify the AWS network services that will be audited, such as IAM policies, firewall configurations, security groups, network ACLs, VPCs, and subnets.

Create a plan for how you will conduct your network audit; this should include the tools and processes you will use to evaluate your network services. This can include using AWS Config rules to evaluate compliance, using CloudTrail to track activity, or using third-party tools to conduct vulnerability assessments.

Collect the network configuration data for the AWS network services and accounts that you plan to audit. Execute your audit plan and evaluate your network services against your defined audit criteria.

The AWS *Audit Manager* service is helpful in conducting network audits by using preconfigured frameworks to help you conduct and automate assessments for specific standards and regulations. The frameworks let you select from preconfigured controls that include documentation and instructions on how to implement the tests. You can customize these frameworks and controls to meet your specific requirements.

The AWS Config service is useful when you want to capture the configuration data, use AWS CloudFormation templates to deploy network resources, and use the AWS *Systems Manager* service to gather inventory data. Use tools such as AWS Config rules, AWS Trusted Advisor, or third-party tools to automate this analysis.

After the project definitions and collections are completed, you can review and assess the network configurations of the identified network services and accounts to identify any misconfigurations or security gaps in your network infrastructure. Ensure that the configurations are compliant with security best practices, regulations, and industry standards. Identify security gaps in the network configurations and prioritize their criticality based on severity and risk to your operations and regulatory requirements. Once this has been completed, you will need to develop a remediation plan for the identified security gaps, including timelines, resources, and responsibilities for each remediation task. Implement the remediation plan, including fixing misconfigured network resources, updating security group rules, configuring network ACLs, or implementing additional security controls such as AWS WAF or AWS Shield.

Monitor the network activity to identify any suspicious or unauthorized activity. Use AWS CloudTrail to capture API activity, use VPC Flow Logs to capture network traffic, or use third-party network monitoring tools to detect anomalies. It is important to monitor and audit the configurations of your network services and accounts on an ongoing basis to ensure that they remain compliant with security best practices and industry standards.

It's good practice to continuously improve the network audit strategy and processes based on lessons learned and feedback from all sources.

Your organization should implement a detailed and complete network audit strategy across single or multiple AWS network services and accounts to ensure your infrastructure is secure and compliant with relevant industry standards and regulations. By performing regular and ongoing audits, you minimize security risks, reduce the likelihood of data breaches, and ensure business continuity. Audits help identify and remediate security issues in a timely manner, reduce the risk of security breaches, and maintain compliance with industry standards and regulations.

Summary

This chapter's focus was on the monitoring of your AWS and hybrid deployments. Logging was covered extensively, and you learned about the common network services that generate log files, how they are collected and stored, and the options available to analyze the collected data. Audits are a critical security and regulatory compliance practice, and you learned about the audit process from generation to analysis to remediation.

AWS offers native network logging and monitoring services to help you monitor, troubleshoot, and secure your network infrastructure. The key network monitoring and logging services provided by AWS were covered in this chapter.

CloudWatch is an Amazon monitoring service that provides real-time visibility into the performance of your AWS resources and allows you to monitor, store, and access log files and manage metrics, logs, and alarms from resources in AWS and externally in hybrid networks. CloudWatch can monitor EC2 instances, EBS storage volumes, RDS instances, S3, load balancers, microservices, and many other AWS resources. CloudWatch can be configured to monitor custom metrics, generate alarms, troubleshoot issues, create dashboards for visualizing performance data, monitoring applications, and the health of the Internet. Cloud-Watch Insights can monitor Lambda instances and containers and provide metrics for ECS, EKS, and Kubernetes clusters. Use CloudWatch Logs to monitor application and system logs, track application performance, and troubleshoot issues.

VPC Flow Logs enables you to capture information about the IP traffic in your VPC. They are used for troubleshooting connectivity issues, investigating security incidents, and monitoring network performance. Flow Logs can be stored in S3 buckets for analysis using tools such as Amazon Athena, GuardDuty, Elastic Map Reduce, and many third-party offerings in the Amazon Marketplace or stored in Amazon CloudWatch Logs and Amazon Kinesis Data Firehose.

CloudTrail is the service that records API calls and events in your AWS account. CloudTrail logs can be used to detect and investigate security incidents and comply with audit requirements. CloudTrail also provides a complete audit trail of API calls in your AWS account, including calls made by users, services, and AWS resources.

The AWS Config service provides a detailed inventory of your AWS resources and tracks changes to these resources over time. Config is used to monitor compliance, troubleshoot issues, and identify resource dependencies. Config can also be used to enforce security policies and create rules for resource configurations.

GuardDuty is a threat detection service from Amazon that uses machine learning to identify potential security threats in your AWS environment, such as unauthorized access attempts, compromised instances, and data exfiltration attempts. GuardDuty enables you to continuously monitor your network for security threats and respond to them in real time. The service can be used to analyze VPC Flow Logs, DNS logs, and other data sources to detect security threats, such as unauthorized access attempts, malicious activity, and reconnaissance activity. GuardDuty provides detailed alerts and integrates with CloudWatch and CloudTrail for monitoring and analysis.

Inspector is a security assessment service from Amazon that can identify security issues and vulnerabilities in your EC2 instances and applications. The Inspector service scans your instances for common security issues, such as insecure network configurations, missing patches, and exposed ports.

The Network Firewall has monitoring capabilities in addition to its granular network traffic control for your traffic. The Network Firewall is used to create custom security rules, monitor traffic flows, and detect and block malicious traffic. The Web Application Firewall allows you to control access to your web applications and protect them from common web exploits. Use AWS WAF to monitor and block suspicious web traffic, such as bots and scrapers.

You learned about the alerting services and options such as CloudWatch alarms and the Simple Notification Service that is used to implement actions and automations based on events in your AWS deployments.

Logs can be generated from many different sources, and you learned about the AWS networking log generation capabilities of Route 53, Load Balancers, Kinesis, Transit Gateway, and CloudWatch. You can also generate log data using traffic mirroring and Flow Logs.

Network security audits were discussed with a focus on the AWS security services including security groups, the AWS Firewall Manager, and Trusted Advisor.

Finally, you learned how to collect logging data from many sources and store it in a centralized data store to perform correlation and analysis on the collected information. With the data collected and formatted, auditing can take place, and we discussed the steps taken when performing network audits.

Exam Essentials

Know the various networking sources that generate log data.   AWS services that generate logging data include CloudTrail, VPC Traffic Mirroring, logging from Transit Gateway, Route 53, CloudFront, and the different types of elastic load balancers.

Understand the AWS CloudWatch service. CloudWatch is the core AWS logging and security service that fits into many use cases. You should be very familiar with CloudWatch logging, what CloudWatch metrics are, and how CloudWatch can generate alarms and trigger automations such as autoscaling of services. Know that CloudWatch logs are used for troubleshooting, monitoring, automation, and compliance auditing. CloudWatch Logs Insights enables administrators to run ad hoc queries using SQL-like syntax to analyze and visualize log data in graphs and charts. The visualization tools that are commonly used include Kibana and Splunk.

Know the key features of CloudWatch. Key features of CloudWatch include metrics that enable you to collect and monitor data in real time of objects such as CPU utilization, network traffic, and request latency. Metrics are viewed in the dashboard or used to generate alarms when thresholds you define are crossed. CloudWatch Logs allows you to collect and store log data from applications, services, and AWS resources. Use CloudWatch Logs to search, filter, and analyze log data in real time, and create alarms based on specific log events. CloudWatch Events is used to respond to events and trigger actions in real time. You create rules to match incoming events and use targets such as AWS Lambda or Amazon SNS to trigger actions. CloudWatch alarms are used to monitor metrics and respond to changes in your environment. You set up alarms based on metric thresholds or CloudWatch Logs events and take automated actions when alarms are triggered. The dashboards allow you to create custom views of your metrics and log data. You can create and apply widgets to display specific metrics, logs, or events, and customize the layout and formatting of dashboards. CloudWatch integrates with a variety of AWS services and tools, including EC2, RDS, Lambda, and Elastic Load Balancing. You can also use CloudWatch with third-party tools such as Datadog or Grafana. CloudWatch Logs allows users to collect, monitor, and store log files from any log-generating resources such as Amazon EC2 instances, CloudTrail, and Route 53, among others. These logs can then be analyzed using CloudWatch Insights, a feature that enables users to search and analyze log data using a query language.

Know that there are multiple log delivery mechanisms that can be implemented. Log delivery services include Kinesis Data Streams and Firehose. The Amazon Kinesis family is a fully managed service for real-time data streaming and processing. Kinesis can collect data from thousands of different sources including CloudWatch Logs, VPC Flow Logs, or custom log files and consolidate them into data streams that can then be analyzed or forwarded to other Amazon services such as S3 for object storage. Kinesis acts as middleware that integrates and interconnects with other AWS services, such as Lambda, S3, OpenSearch, and Redshift. These integrations allow you to use Kinesis to stream log data to other services for further processing or analysis. Log data can be stored in CloudWatch or S3 as the primary two locations.

Know the details about Flow Logs, including some common use cases for Flow Logs. Common use cases include troubleshooting network connectivity by using Flow Logs to identify the source of connectivity issues, such as blocked traffic or misconfigured security groups, to monitor traffic patterns, such as traffic volume and the types of traffic flowing through your VPC. Network security can be analyzed by using Flow Logs to identify potential security threats, such as unauthorized access or network attacks. Creating and analyzing a VPC Flow Log in AWS enables insights into your network traffic flows and helps to troubleshoot connectivity issues, monitor traffic patterns, and improve network security. Analyzing the base and extended fields of Flow Logs gives you the capability to have a deeper understanding of your network traffic and then use this information to optimize your AWS deployment. Flow Logs provide two types of fields: base fields and extended fields. Base fields are included in all Flow Logs and provide basic information about the traffic, such as the source and destination IP addresses, protocol, and port number. Extended fields provide additional information about the traffic and are available only if you specify them when creating the Flow Log. Some common extended fields include packets, bytes, start, and end. Remember that Flow Logs are not complete packet captures but are the metadata and information about each packet.

Know how to create and analyze network traffic mirroring in AWS.   AWS Traffic Mirroring allows you to capture complete packets for analysis. You specify the traffic mirror source and target; then you create a filter, which determines the traffic to be mirrored. After you have created the mirror session, you then can analyze the mirrored traffic using a network analysis tool. A common open-source analysis tool is Wireshark or `tcpdump`. Oher tools include the CloudWatch Logs console, or you can export the data to Amazon S3 and use third-party tools such as OpenSearch or Kibana to analyze the data. Amazon tools include Athena and QuickSight that can be used to query and visualize traffic data.

Know the security services that are used to remediate security vulnerabilities.   These include using security groups, access control lists, Identity and Access Manager, and the different firewall services Amazon offers such as Web Application Firewall and Firewall Manager. Understand the capabilities of the Trusted Advisor services and how they are implemented.

Understand the basics of a network audit strategy.   Define your network audit goals and scope of the audit, including the AWS network services, your hybrid connections, and the accounts that will be audited. Next, identify the AWS network services that will be audited, such as IAM policies, firewall configurations, security groups, network ACLs, VPCs, and subnets.

Understand the steps to create a plan for how to conduct a network audit.   This should include the tools and processes you will use to evaluate your network services. This can include using AWS Config rules to evaluate compliance, CloudTrail to track activity, or third-party tools to conduct vulnerability assessments. Collect the network configuration data for the AWS network services and accounts that you plan to audit. Execute your audit plan and evaluate your network services against your defined audit criteria.

Exercises

1.   Study the AWS CloudWatch user guide, focusing on logs, alarms, metrics, and exercises, at `https://docs.aws.amazon.com/pdfs/AmazonCloudWatch/latest/ monitoring/acw-ug.pdf`.

2. Study the AWS CloudTrail user guide, focusing on the logging sections, at `https://docs.aws.amazon.com/pdfs/awscloudtrail/latest/userguide/awscloudtrail-ug.pdf`.

3. Review the Traffic Mirroring documentation at `https://docs.aws.amazon.com/pdfs/vpc/latest/mirroring/vpc-tm.pdf`.

4. Review the VPC Flow Log section of the VPC user guide at `https://docs.aws.amazon.com/pdfs/vpc/latest/userguide/vpc-ug.pdf`.

5. Review the logging section of the Transit Gateway user guide at `https://docs.aws.amazon.com/pdfs/vpc/latest/tgw/vpc-tgw.pdf`.

6. Familiarize yourself with the SNS basic concepts at `https://aws.amazon.com/sns`.

7. Review the basics of Kinesis Data Streams, Firehose, and Data Analytics at `https://docs.aws.amazon.com/kinesis/index.html`.

8. Familiarize yourself with the basics of security groups at `https://docs.aws.amazon.com/vpc/latest/userguide/vpc-security-groups.html`.

9. Review the basics of Trusted Advisor at `https://docs.aws.amazon.com/awssupport/latest/user/trusted-advisor.html`.

Review Questions

The following questions are designed to test your understanding of this chapter's material. For more information on how to obtain additional questions, please see this book's introduction.

1. You have configured CloudTrail to store API logs in an S3 bucket. You want to analyze the data to look for a specific user's access and the changes they have made. What are three tools you can use to analyze log data? (Select three.)

    A. Wireshark

    B. DynamoDB

    C. Athena

    D. Splunk

    E. OpenSearch

2. You are configuring VPC mirroring to do a packet capture for a network audit. You are interested only in the flow between two application servers in your VPC. What can you configure to focus only on the interesting traffic?

    A. Application Firewall

    B. VPC Traffic Mirroring filters

    C. Access control lists

    D. Security groups

    E. CloudTrail logs

3. You need to capture FTP transfer data in your VPC. Your requirements are to analyze high-level information about the packet flows. What should you implement to view the metadata of the traffic?

    A. Traffic Mirroring

    B. VPC Flow Logs

    C. CloudWatch metrics

    D. `tcpdump`

    E. Kinesis Data Firehose

4. You are required to monitor and inspect flow-level information for all traffic flows between AWS and your on-premises networks including over Direct Connect gateways or VPN connections without any external tools in your data center's operations center. What AWS service can you implement to accomplish this?

    A. VPC Flow Logs

    B. VPC Traffic Mirroring

    C. CloudTrail

    D. Transit Gateway Network Manager

    E. CloudWatch

5. What service can you implement that can alert you of unusual API activity in your AWS Ireland region?

    A. Config

    B. Security Hub

    C. CloudTrail Insights

    D. SNS

    E. EventBridge

6. You are troubleshooting an FTP authentication issue on an EC2 instance running in your Sydney region. The support vendor is requesting a packet capture of the handshake from the client to the server when the failure occurs. You need to capture traffic from the EC2 instance's Elastic Network Interface. What Amazon tool can you use to accomplish this?

    A. IAM Access analyzer

    B. VPC Traffic Mirroring

    C. AWS Config

    D. GuardDuty

    E. WAF traffic logs

7. Your company is required to keep a record of all changes to AWS resources to provide an audit data source for regulatory compliance. Which AWS service provides a record of all API changes made to your account?

    A. Config

    B. CloudWatch

    C. CloudTrail

    D. GuardDuty

    E. Kibana

8. You need to decouple your AWS monitoring and alerting services and push the alerts received from various monitoring sources to subscriber endpoints, via email, text, and Lambda functions. What service would best meet this requirement?

    A. CloudTrail

    B. SNS

    C. SQS

    D. CloudWatch Insights

    E. QuickSight

9. You are investigating storage options for CloudTrail logging. Where can the logs be stored? (Select two.)

    A. S3

    B. RDS

    C. CloudWatch

    D. Redshift

    E. OpenSearch

10. You have performed a packet capture in your VPC and need an open-source packet analysis tool to review the data. What are two tools you can use? (Select two.)

   A. OpenSearch

   B. Wireshark

   C. VPC Flow Logs

   D. tcpdump

   E. Athena

11. Which AWS service can be used to store logs for troubleshooting, monitoring, automation, and compliance auditing? The service is a centralized logging repository used to store and access logs from multiple sources. The service can collect logs from your AWS resources, applications, and services, and stores them in a single location for access, retention, and analysis.

   A. CloudFront

   B. CloudWatch Logs

   C. CloudTrail logs

   D. Kinesis Data Analytics

   E. VPC Flow Logs

12. What destination repositories can Kinesis Data Firehose stream data to? (Select three.)

   A. Control Tower

   B. Redshift

   C. S3

   D. DynamoDB

   E. RDS

   F. OpenSearch

13. Which AWS service is a centralized security service that provides a detailed view of your security stance across accounts and services; displays your compliance status, security alerts, and other security-related information; and provides automated compliance checks to ensure that your network security configurations meet regulatory and industry standards?

   A. Control Tower

   B. CloudWatch

   C. Security Hub

   D. GuardDuty

   E. Inspector

14. You have created a custom alarm in CloudWatch and are coding an automation application that will run an on-demand Python serverless system to remediate the alarm condition. You configure the alarm in CloudWatch that monitors the metric you selected that triggers a notification when the threshold is exceeded. You must choose an AWS managed service that can run the Python code on demand. What service would you implement?

A. GuardDuty

B. EC2 reserved instance

C. VMware virtual machines

D. Kibana

E. Lambda

15. Which security assessment service from Amazon can identify security issues and vulnerabilities in your EC2 instances and applications by scanning instances for common security issues, such as insecure network configurations, missing patches, and exposed ports?

A. Control Tower

B. CloudWatch

C. Security Hub

D. GuardDuty

E. Inspector

16. You need to replicate your logging data in real time to multiple locations, including S3, OpenSearch, and Redshift. What AWS managed service should you implement?

A. Simple Workflow Service

B. Kinesis Data Streams

C. AWS EventBridge

D. Splunk

E. Traffic Mirroring

17. Which AWS machine learning services can be used to analyze log data and identify patterns and anomalies in log data, providing insights into potential issues? (Select two.)

A. SageMaker

B. Kibana

C. Kinesis Data Analytics

D. Splunk

18. Which tools can be used to visualize data? (Select two.)

A. SageMaker

B. Kibana

C. QuickSight

D. Systems Manager

E. Trusted Advisor

19. Which AWS service continually audits your AWS usage to manage risk and compliance with regulations and industry standards?

    A. GuardDuty

    B. Kinesis Data Analytics

    C. Audit Manager

    D. QuickSight

    E. Redshift

20. What AWS tool can you use to analyze streaming data in real time using SQL queries?

    A. Kinesis Data Analytics

    B. tcpdump

    C. Wireshark

    D. Kinesis Data Streams

    E. Splunk

Chapter

14

Confidentiality and Encryption

THE AWS CERTIFIED ADVANCED NETWORKING - SPECIALTY EXAM OBJECTIVES COVERED IN THIS CHAPTER MAY INCLUDE, BUT ARE NOT LIMITED TO, THE FOLLOWING:

✓ **Domain 4: Network Security, Compliance, and Governance**

- Task Statement 4.3: Implement and maintain confidentiality of data and communications of the network.

Confidentiality and Encryption

In this final chapter, you will learn about confidentiality and encryption in AWS. The focus will be on network security and the underlying technologies being used.

Protecting data in the cloud, both at rest and in transit, is critical for your cloud deployments. It is important for enterprises utilizing AWS services to protect their data from unauthorized access. Confidentiality and encryption are two important cybersecurity concepts that enable organizations to safeguard their data. AWS offers a range of tools and services to help ensure the confidentiality and encryption of its customers' data.

Confidentiality is the protection of information from unauthorized disclosure, and only authorized entities should have access to the information, which will be secure and protected from unauthorized access. AWS provides multiple services to ensure the confidentiality of customer data including network isolation, access controls, and encryption.

Encryption transforms your information into an unreadable format, known as *ciphertext*, by using an encryption algorithm and a secret key. This prevents unauthorized parties from accessing or reading the information if they do not have the encryption keys, even if they gain access to the data. AWS offers multiple encryption options, which include encryption at rest and in transit. *Encryption at rest* is the encryption of data that is stored in AWS services such as S3, EBS, and RDS. *Encryption in transit* refers to the encryption of data as it travels between AWS services or between AWS and customer environments.

AWS encryption services include AWS *Key Management Service* (KMS), AWS *CloudHSM*, and the AWS *Certificate Manager*. KMS allows customers to create and manage encryption keys, and CloudHSM provides secure key storage and management. The AWS Certificate Manager enables customers to provision, manage, and deploy SSL/TLS certificates for use with AWS services and resources.

Confidentiality and encryption are the key components to secure your organization's resources. AWS offers a range of tools and services to help you protect your data and ensure its confidentiality and encryption. By using these services, you can ensure that your sensitive information remains secure and protected from unauthorized access.

Network Encryption Options Available on AWS

Network encryption is a critical component in securing your AWS computing environment. Encryption ensures that data transmitted over the network is protected from bad actors accessing your data. AWS provides multiple network encryption options that are used to encrypt data in transit between your resources inside and externally to the AWS network. We will also review encryption at rest in storage systems or databases. In this section, we will discuss the various network encryption options available on AWS.

Transport Layer Security (TLS) is the most common encryption protocol used to secure data in transit over the Internet and across your internal networks. TLS is used to secure web traffic using the *HTTPS* and email communication using *SMTPS*, *IMAPS*, and *POP3S*.

AWS provides several services that support TLS encryption, including the elastic load balancer that uses TLS encryption for incoming and outgoing client traffic. The AWS Certificate Manager (ACM) can be used to generate and manage SSL/TLS certificates for your ELB and other AWS services or you can upload and implement your own certificates. The AWS ACM service makes it easy to provision, deploy, and renew SSL/TLS certificates to encrypt your web traffic. KMS is the Amazon Key Management Service that securely stores your keys. CloudFront supports TLS encryption for incoming and outgoing data, and the ACM can be used to generate and manage SSL/TLS certificates for your CloudFront distribution.

The AWS API Gateway supports TLS encryption for in-flight traffic, as with the other AWS services; you can use the ACM service to generate and manage SSL/TLS certificates for your API gateways. A virtual private network (VPN) creates a secure, encrypted tunnel between your on-premises network and your AWS resources. A site-to-site VPN enables you to connect your on-premises network to your AWS deployments over encrypted VPN tunnels. The site-to-site VPN supports Internet Protocol Security (IPSec) encryption for all traffic between your on-premises network, and your AWS resources. The client VPN supports Open-VPN, an open-source VPN protocol that provides secure communications.

Amazon Direct Connect supports IPSec encryption if configured to use VPN tunnels, to encrypt traffic between your on-premises network and your AWS resources. Data transmitted over a Direct Connect circuit does not traverse the public Internet, so it reduces your security exposure and helps maintain data privacy. Encryption is recommended but optional for Direct Connect. PrivateLink uses AWS-managed SSL/TLS encryption keys to encrypt traffic between your resources and the AWS network. The AWS Transit Gateway supports IPSec encryption for all traffic between your VPCs and on-premises networks.

The Network Firewall supports SSL/TLS decryption and inspection, which enables you to inspect encrypted traffic for threats at the entry point into your network. You can use custom certificate authorities (CAs) to encrypt traffic between your internal resources and the AWS network.

The AWS S3 object storage service has multiple encryption options including *SSE-C* encryption. Amazon S3 data at the object level can use server-side encryption with customer-provided keys, or SSE-C. This encrypts data in transit and at rest and allows you to manage the encryption keys. However, network encryption is handled automatically by Amazon S3. S3 client-side encryption is the strongest network encryption you can implement. This method is when you encrypt data at the client before ever sending it across the network. The data is then decrypted at the receiving client. AWS never sees your unencrypted data. There is a downside to this approach due to the complexity in implementing and managing the encryption.

By implementing these encryption options, you can secure your network traffic to protect it from interception and unauthorized access. It is important to remember that encryption is only one component of a comprehensive security strategy. You should also follow other security best practices, such as configuring firewalls, monitoring, auditing your resources, and implementing access controls, to ensure the security of your AWS resources. Using a combination of these encryption techniques ensures that your sensitive data and communications remain private as they traverse AWS networks and the public Internet.

VPN Connectivity Over Direct Connect

In Chapter 6, "Hybrid Networking," we covered the options for connecting your on-premises network to your AWS resources. One option is to use an Amazon Virtual Private Network (VPN) connection, which provides secure, encrypted tunnels between your on-premises network and your AWS resources. Another option we covered was to use the AWS Direct Connect service, which provides a dedicated, private network connection between your on-premises network and your AWS resources. In this section, we will discuss how to combine the two services to establish an AWS VPN connection over a Direct Connect circuit.

The site-to-site VPN configuration enables you to connect your on-premises networks to your AWS resources over an encrypted VPN tunnel. Site-to-site VPN supports both IPSec and Transport Layer Security (TLS) protocols. You can implement the VPN using either the Internet or Direct Connect as the transport.

Direct Connect bypasses the public Internet and provides a private, low-latency connection that is ideal for large data transfer and mission-critical applications. AWS Direct Connect provides a secure private connection as it is not routed through the public Internet. By combining the two, you can gain all of the benefits of Direct Connect and add the encryption capabilities of a site-to-site VPN. The VPN tunnels traverse the Direct Connect circuits. The Direct Connect service provides dedicated bandwidth, which is faster than a VPN connection.

To set up an AWS Direct Connect connection over a VPN, you must configure both the AWS Direct Connect connection and the VPN connection. On the AWS side, you will create a virtual private gateway (VGW) and attach it to your Direct Connect connection. Then create a customer gateway on the VPC subnet that will host the VPN endpoint. Configure the IP address and BGP information of the customer gateway device. You will then interconnect the two gateways using the dedicated connection.

The first step is to create a Direct Connect connection between your on-premises network and your AWS resources. Then create a VPN connection between your on-premises network and your AWS resources using the Direct Connect circuit as the transport. This involves creating the VPN tunnel between the VGW and the CGW and configuring the security settings on both sides of the tunnel, such as encryption and authentication. The final setup step is to configure the VPN connection to use Direct Connect. To do this, you need to create a virtual private gateway, or VGW, and attach it to your Direct Connect connection. You will also need to configure the VPN connection to use the virtual gateway.

At your data center or local network side, you will need a customer gateway device, such as a firewall, router, or VPN concentrator. Configure its IP address, and the BGP information you used when creating the AWS virtual private gateway. Enable the IPSec VPN encryption protocol and set up the VPN tunnel using the details from your AWS VPN connection profile, such as the security associations, DHCP options, and IKE version 2 configurations.

Once the VPN tunnels are fully configured on both networks, the VPN traffic will traverse over your dedicated Direct Connect link, providing secure connectivity between your on-premises network and the AWS cloud. The high bandwidth and low latency of Direct Connect combined with the encryption of IPSec VPN provides a robust and secure connectivity solution for hybrid cloud deployments.

The high performance of Direct Connect provides a private, low-latency connection that is ideal for large data transfer, sensitive data, and mission-critical applications. By using AWS VPN over Direct Connect, you can ensure that your VPN traffic is transmitted over the fast and reliable Direct Connect service.

In this section, we discussed the benefits of connecting an AWS site-to-site VPN over Direct Connect. By using AWS VPN over Direct Connect, you can establish a secure, encrypted connection between your on-premises network and your AWS resources that protects your data from interception and unauthorized access. By using the high-performance and simplified management of Direct Connect, you can ensure that your VPN traffic is transmitted over a fast, reliable network connection.

Encryption Methods for Data in Transit

In this section, you will learn about the encryption methods used to protect your data in transit within the AWS cloud and between your internal networks and AWS. Encryption is used to protect data in transit from being accessed by unauthorized parties. Encryption is the process of transforming data into a form that is unreadable to anyone except those who have the appropriate encryption keys to decrypt the data back to its original, unencrypted form. By encrypting the network traffic, you can ensure that your data is secure and not decipherable to unauthorized parties as it is traverses insecure networks.

Data in transit is data being sent or received over a network. This includes data that is sent over the Internet, such as email messages, web pages, and file transfers. It also includes data that is sent over private networks, such as a company intranet or corporate data network.

Implementing VPNs to take advantage of IPSec encryption capabilities is a popular method for encrypting traffic between your on-premises network and AWS. This design establishes an encrypted VPN connection that wraps all the traffic within the VPN tunnel to provide end-to-end encryption. You can use the AWS VPG and VPN connections to set up an IPSec VPN from your network to AWS. For more details, refer to Chapter 6.

For traffic internal to the AWS network such as between AWS availability zones, you can implement encryption at the transport layer using TLS security. TLS is a widely used encryption protocol that provides secure communication over the Internet and private networks. HTTP traffic can be encrypted using Hyper Text Transfer Protocol Secure (HTTPS), which is based on the SSL/TLS protocols by simply changing the URL from HTTP to HTTPS. This encrypts web traffic using TLS encryption and uses port 443 instead of the standard port 80 for unencrypted traffic.

You may have the option to encrypt traffic at the application layer using proprietary encryption methods built into your applications. For example, if you develop custom applications that transmit sensitive data, you can build your own encryption algorithms and keys to encrypt the inter-application traffic.

AWS offers server-side encryption options for data stored at rest within AWS services such as Amazon S3 and EBS. This enables you to encrypt your data on the servers using AWS-managed encryption keys. Though the data is encrypted at rest, you must also configure the encryption options for data in transit when accessing or transmitting that encrypted data.

The AWS Key Management Service (KMS) enables you to create and control your own encryption keys instead of using AWS-managed keys. This gives you full control and flexibility over the encryption of your data in transit and at rest within AWS.

In this section, we discussed the various encryption methods available on AWS for securing data in transit. By using these encryption methods, you protect your network traffic from being intercepted and from unauthorized access. AWS provides multiple options to encrypt your data in transit, including IPSec VPNs, TLS, HTTPS, and proprietary application-level encryption. When these are combined with server-side encryption of data at rest, you have complete control and protection of your encrypted data in the AWS cloud. Remember that encryption is only one component of a complete security strategy. You should follow other security best practices, such as configuring firewalls, monitoring and auditing your resources, and implementing access controls, to ensure the security of your AWS resources.

Network Encryption and the AWS Shared Responsibility Model

In this section, we will provide an overview of network encryption under the AWS shared responsibility model. Encryption is the process of converting plain text into a coded message that cannot be read without the proper decryption key. Network encryption is the process of securing data that is transmitted over a network. Network encryption is used to protect sensitive data such as login credentials, credit card numbers, and other personally identifiable information (PII) from being intercepted and accessed by unauthorized individuals.

The AWS shared responsibility model is a security model that defines the security and division of responsibilities between AWS and its customers. As a customer, it is important to understand your cloud security responsibilities when it comes to network encryption.

Under the shared responsibility model, AWS is responsible for the security of the underlying infrastructure that supports the AWS cloud operations. This includes securing their physical data centers, network infrastructure, and the hardware components installed in the AWS facilities. AWS deploys multiple layers of security to protect its infrastructure, including perimeter security, firewalls, intrusion prevention systems, and other security mechanisms to protect its network perimeter from unauthorized external access.

AWS implements secure network protocols and encryption to protect data in transit between AWS resources, customers, partners, and the public Internet. AWS uses security groups and access control lists to control access to its EC2 instances containers and other resources.

Customers are responsible for securing their data and applications that run on top of the AWS infrastructure. This includes implementing appropriate network encryption measures to protect data in transit between their resources and the AWS network. Customers can implement various encryption options provided by AWS to protect their data in transit, including TLS. TLS is a widely used encryption protocol that provides secure communication over the Internet. Customers can use TLS to encrypt data in transit between their resources and AWS services such as Elastic Load Balancers, Amazon CloudFront, and Amazon API Gateway. AWS offers SSL/TLS HTTPS encryption as a default for all Amazon S3 and Amazon CloudFront communications. TLS will be discussed later in this chapter.

Customers use VPNs to create a secure, encrypted tunnel between their on-premises network and AWS resources. This enables them to securely transmit data over the public Internet and protect it from interception and unauthorized access. Direct Connect is used to establish a dedicated network connection between their on-premises network and their AWS resources. Direct Connect provides a private, low-latency connection that bypasses the public Internet and supports encryption for all traffic between the customer's network and AWS resources. IPSec is a protocol that encrypts data at the IP layer of the network stack. AWS offers managed IPSec VPN services such as the AWS client VPN and site-to-site VPNs that allow customers to create secure VPN connections to their VPCs.

To ensure the security of their data in transit, customers should use appropriate encryption protocols such as TLS, IPSec, and OpenVPN to protect their data in transit. Customers should also implement firewalls, intrusion detection and prevention systems, and other appropriate security services to protect their network perimeter from unauthorized access. Customers should implement access controls such as security groups, access control lists, and restrictive Identity and Access Management (IAM) policies to control access to their resources. You must continually monitor and audit your security posture to detect any security breaches or unauthorized access attempts. Follow all the compliance standards that apply to your business such as the Payment Card Industry Data Security Standard (PCI DSS), the Health Insurance Portability and Accountability Act (HIPAA), or any of the other industry or governmental compliance standards that your company must adhere to.

In this section, we discussed network encryption under the AWS shared responsibility model. Under this model, AWS is responsible for securing the underlying infrastructure that supports the AWS cloud, while customers are responsible for securing their data and applications that run on top of the AWS infrastructure. Customers can use various encryption options provided by AWS to protect their data in transit, including TLS, VPNs, and AWS Direct Connect. It is critical that you, as the customer, configure the encryption options correctly. AWS provides documentation and best practices for configuring encryption, but it is the customer's responsibility to ensure that the encryption is configured correctly. By following best practices such as securing your network perimeter, using effective access controls, and monitoring and auditing your resources, you can ensure the security of your data in transit under the AWS shared responsibility model.

Security Methods for DNS Communications

Securing DNS was covered in Chapter 2, "Domain Name Services." In this chapter, covering network security, we will discuss some of the DNS security methods that are commonly used to protect against DNS attacks.

The Domain Name System (DNS) is a critical component of the Internet infrastructure. It is responsible for translating domain names into IP addresses that can be used to locate web servers and other network resources. DNS security is essential to ensure that users can access legitimate websites without interference from bad actors attempting to hijack DNS queries or redirect users to fake websites.

DNS Security Extensions (DNSSEC) is a security protocol designed to add an additional layer of protection to DNS queries. DNSSEC uses digital signatures to verify that DNS records have not been tampered with, ensuring that users are directed to the intended website. DNSSEC is supported by most modern browsers and operating systems. DNSSEC can be used only for public hosted zones in Amazon Route 53. This allows you to provide origin authentication and data integrity for DNS queries and responses.

DNS filtering inspects DNS queries and blocks known malicious or suspicious requests. This is accomplished using a variety of methods, such as applying blacklists of known malicious domains or using machine learning algorithms to detect suspicious DNS traffic patterns.

DNS over HTTPS (DoH) encrypts DNS queries and responses using HTTPS, with the same protocol used by web browsers to encrypt web traffic that uses SSL/TLS as the encryption protocol. DoH prevents eavesdropping on and tampering with DNS queries by encrypting them, preventing attackers from modifying DNS queries. *DNS over TLS (DoT)* is a protocol that encrypts DNS requests and responses using TLS. It provides similar security and privacy benefits as DoH but does not use the HTTP protocol for transport. DoT is used to protect against DNS hijacking and can be configured to use trusted DNS resolvers.

Response Policy Zones (RPZs) is a DNS server feature that enables administrators to block DNS requests to known malicious domains, and IP addresses, prevents malware infections, and blocks access to undesirable content.

Threat intelligence feeds are a source of information about known malicious domains and IP addresses and can be implemented in your DNS deployments as a blacklist. They are used to update DNS filters and firewalls to block access to known malicious domains. Threat intelligence feeds can be obtained from multiple sources, including commercial vendors, open-source projects, and government agencies.

Response Rate Limiting (RRL) limits the rate of DNS responses to prevent DNS amplification attacks. It involves limiting the rate of responses to a DNS query from a single source, making it more difficult for an attacker to use DNS amplification to flood a target with traffic.

The *DNS firewall* is a specialized type of firewall designed to protect against DNS-based attacks. DNS firewalls analyze DNS queries and block requests that are known to be malicious, preventing attackers from redirecting users to fake websites or hijacking DNS queries.

DNS security is an essential component of network security. DNS attacks can be devastating and deny all legitimate access to your resources. However, there are many security options available to protect against DNS attacks. DNSSEC, DNS filtering, DNS over HTTPS, DNS over TLS, Response Policy Zones, and DNS firewalls are all effective methods for protecting against DNS attacks.

By implementing these security methods, you can protect your DNS servers and queries enabling users to access legitimate websites without interference from malicious actors.

Implementing Network Encryption Methods to Meet Application Compliance Requirements

AWS has multiple security offerings to help you meet application compliance requirements and protect your data. By implementing encryption methods that meet all corporate and regulatory compliance requirements, you protect your data from unauthorized access and disclosure. AWS also offers public sector customers exclusive regions that include specialized security services such as FedRAMP.

RDS is the AWS family of cloud-based relational databases that provides managed database instances for various database engines, such as MySQL, PostgreSQL, Oracle, and others. RDS provides various encryption options, such as SSL/TLS encryption for data in transit and SSE for data at rest. RDS also provides the option to use *SSE-KMS*, which provides the added benefit of using AWS KMS to manage your keys.

AWS provides various encryption options for S3 data, such as Server-Side Encryption (SSE), Server-Side Encryption with AWS KMS (SSE-KMS), or Server-Side Encryption with Customer-Provided Keys (SSE-C).

KMS Encryption is a managed service that provides key management and encryption for various AWS services and custom applications. KMS provides multiple encryption options, including symmetric and asymmetric encryption, and supports various encryption algorithms, such as AES and RSA. KMS is integrated with many AWS services, including S3, RDS, and EBS, allowing for the central management of encryption keys.

The AWS Certificate Manager (ACM) service provides SSL/TLS certificates for use with AWS services. ACM enables customers to request, manage, and deploy SSL/TLS certificates for use with AWS services, including Elastic Load Balancers, CloudFront, and API Gateway. ACM also integrates with other AWS services, such as Elastic Beanstalk and EC2 instances, to automate certificate deployment and renewal.

The AWS *CloudHSM* service provides customers with dedicated hardware security modules (HSMs). HSMs are specialized hardware devices used to store, manage, and perform operations of crypto keys. CloudHSM enables you to manage your own encryption keys and guarantees the encryption keys are never exposed to AWS or other customers.

IPSec

The IPSec protocol suite enables secure communications over IP networks. IPSec is a widely used standard for securing communication across the Internet or from your on-premises data center to a VPC, as shown in Figure 14.1. The protocol secures a wide range of in-flight network traffic, including data sent between two computers, between a computer and a network, and between two networks. The protocol is a suite of tools that provide a range of features including confidentiality, integrity, authentication, and nonrepudiation. IPSec encrypts the data being transmitted between two parties, ensuring that the data is protected with encryption algorithms such as the *Advanced Encryption Standard* (AES). It verifies that the data has not been tampered with during transmission. This is accomplished with a digital signature added to each IP packet, which is then verified by the recipient. IPSec can also guarantee that the parties involved in the communication are who they claim to be. This is accomplished with digital certificates, which are issued by trusted certificate authorities who vouch for the authenticity of the certificate owner.

FIGURE 14.1   IPSec VPN

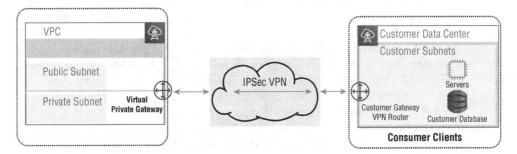

IPSec is a family of different protocols and components that work together to secure network communications. These protocols include *Authentication Header* (AH), *Encapsulating Security Payload* (ESP), *Internet Key Exchange* (IKE), and Key Management Protocol (KMP). These protocols work together to secure communication over IP networks.

Figure 14.2 shows the simplified IPSec handshake process.

FIGURE 14.2   IPSec handshake

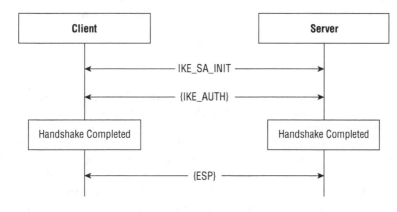

The AH protocol provides integrity and authentication for IP packets. AH is used to ensure that the data being transmitted has not been tampered with during transmission and that it originated from a trusted source. It is important to remember that AH does not provide confidentiality, and the contents of the packet are not encrypted. The ESP protocol provides the confidentiality, integrity, and authentication functions for IP packets. ESP encrypts the contents of the packet and provides authentication and integrity protection, ensuring that the data has not been tampered with during transmission. The IKE protocol negotiates and establishes a secure communication channel between two endpoints. IKE is used to negotiate the security parameters for each IPSec session, including the encryption algorithms, authentication methods, and key exchange mechanisms that will be used for the session using either IKE version 1 or IKE version 2. The *Key Management Protocol* (KMP) manages the keys that are used by IPSec. KMP is responsible for generating and distributing the keys used for encryption and decryption during the IPSec session.

IPSec creates a secure communication channel between two parties over an insecure network such as the Internet by creating security associations. A *security association* is a description of how two or more entities will use security services to communicate securely. IPSec requires at least two SAs to be configured to enable a secure tunnel. The SA is a set of security parameters that are negotiated between two endpoints during the negotiation process of a new session. These parameters include the encryption algorithm, the authentication algorithm, the key length, and the lifetime of the security association. Once the parameters have been agreed upon, they are used to secure communications between the two endpoints.

The secure channel is established using IKE, which negotiates the security parameters for the IPSec session. Once the security parameters have been established, AH or ESP is used to secure the data being transmitted. The data is transmitted between the two parties using the IPSec tunnels. The receiving endpoints use information in the AH or ESP packets to verify the integrity and authenticity of the data and to decrypt the contents of the packet if necessary.

In summary, IPSec provides a standardized suite of protocols used to secure IP communications over a nonsecure network such as the Internet by authenticating and encrypting each packet in a data stream. IPSec allows for the confidential and secure networking between locations.

TLS

The TLS protocol is a standardized communications protocol that provides security for in-flight traffic flows over an insecure network such as the Internet. TLS is used to secure communication between a client and a server. TLS encrypts the data being transmitted between a client and a server to protect the data from unauthorized access or disclosure and protects against man-in-the-middle attacks that alter messages. It is most noticeable in HTTPS communications between a web browser and a web server. TLS has replaced SSL and is an upgrade of SSL 3.0. The TLS protocol is similar to SSL 3.0 but was redesigned to fix security issues found in previous versions of SSL. The current version of TLS is 1.3, released in 2018. The term SSL is still commonly used when, in fact, it is TLS that is being used. Table 14.1 compares IPSec and TLS features.

TABLE 14.1 IPSec TLS Comparison

Feature	IPSec	SSL/TLS
Configuration	Complex	Simple
Preshared key	Mandatory	Optional
Interoperability	Complex	Simple
TCP support	All applications	Some applications
UDP support	Supported	Not supported
Client authentication key	Mandatory	Optional
Throughput	High	High
Compression	Yes	OpenSSL
Negotiation delay	Slow	Fast

TLS provides confidentiality, integrity, and authenticity services for the data being transmitted between a client and a server. TLS provides endpoint authentication using X.509 certificates and *symmetric encryption* for the protection of traffic. TLS symmetric encryption uses the same key for both encryption and decryption, which makes it more efficient than asymmetric encryption that uses different keys. The TLS handshake is designed to set up a shared symmetric encryption key between the client and the server, which is then used to encrypt and decrypt the data. TLS symmetric encryption can be used for various applications, not just web browsing, such as email, file transfers, videoconferencing, instant messaging, and Voice over IP. TLS symmetric encryption provides confidentiality and integrity of data, which protects it from eavesdropping and tampering.

The encryption algorithms are negotiated, and most use the current Advanced Encryption Standard. TLS uses the *Diffie-Hellman key exchange* algorithm to establish symmetric keys and ensure perfect forward secrecy. This ensures that the encryption keys are unique for each session.

TLS is used to verify that the data has not been tampered with during transmission by adding digital signatures to each TLS message, which are then verified by the recipient. TLS provides authentication services to ensure that the client and server involved in the communication are who they claim to be by using digital certificates, which are issued by trusted certificate authorities or the AWS Certificate Manager, which can be used to manage SSL/TLS certificates for Amazon Elastic Load Balancer, Amazon CloudFront, API Gateway, and other services.

TLS is a modular protocol suite that can be configured to meet many different security requirements. The two main components of the TLS architecture are the TLS Handshake Protocol and the TLS Record Protocol. The *TLS Handshake Protocol* is used to negotiate and establish a secure connection between the client and the server. The Handshake Protocol provides the negotiation of the security parameters that will be used during the session. TLS sessions can be resumed using session IDs to improve performance. A full handshake does not need to be performed after an initial handshake. The *TLS Record Protocol* is used to transmit encrypted data between a client and a server. The Record Protocol encapsulates data into TLS records and then encrypts and authenticates the records before transmitting them.

The TLS handshake process in AWS involves the following steps, as shown in Figure 14.3:

1. The client sends a ClientHello message to the server, indicating the supported TLS version, cipher suites, and compression methods.

2. The server responds with a ServerHello message, selecting the TLS version, cipher suite, and compression method for the session.

3. The server sends its certificate to the client and optionally requests the client's certificate.

4. The client verifies the server's certificate and optionally sends its own certificate to the server.

5. The server verifies the client's certificate if provided.

6. The client and the server use asymmetric encryption to generate a shared secret key for the session.

7. The client sends a Finished message to the server, encrypted with the shared secret key.

8. The server sends a Finished message to the client, encrypted with the shared secret key.

9. The client and the server can now exchange application data using symmetric encryption with the shared secret key.

FIGURE 14.3 TLS handshake

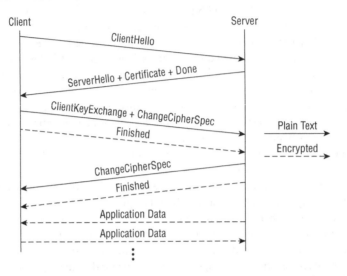

In summary, TLS is the replacement for the SSL protocol. You will still hear the SSL term used even when it is TLS that is being used. TLS is most often used to secure communication over the Internet. It provides multiple security services, including confidentiality, integrity, and authentication. TLS is a modular protocol suite that can be configured to meet different security requirements. The protocol is widely used for web browsing, email, file transfer, and real-time communication such as VoIP and video conferencing. TLS connections are established using a handshake procedure. This enables the client and server to authenticate each other, negotiate a cipher suite, and establish shared keys before the application protocol transmits or receives its first byte of data.

Implementing Encryption Solutions to Secure Data in Transit

It's important to secure data in transit over the Internet and hybrid networks to prevent unauthorized access, prevent the interception of your sensitive data, and comply with corporate and regulatory requirements.

AWS offers a range of encryption and security solutions to secure data in transit, including Transport Layer Security, IPSec, Certificate and Key Management Services, and AWS PrivateLink.

TLS and IPSec are used to provide encryption and authentication of data transmitted over a network. AWS PrivateLink enables customers to access AWS services securely over a private network connection, eliminating the need to expose services to the Internet. Amazon VPC provides several features to help secure data in transit within a VPC, including Network ACLs, security groups, and endpoint groups.

CloudFront

CloudFront and its security options were covered in Chapter 1, "Edge Networking." We will review its encryption offerings again here in this chapter about data security and encryption.

AWS includes a TLS security certificate at all CloudFront edge locations that is bound to the `cloudfront.net` domain that is used globally by AWS as the default domain name for its CloudFront service. If you choose to connect to the edge nodes using this default domain, all you need to do is enable it in the CloudFront distribution configuration settings.

Figure 14.4 shows TLS encrypted communications from the client to a CloudFront edge location.

FIGURE 14.4   CloudFront edge TLS encryption

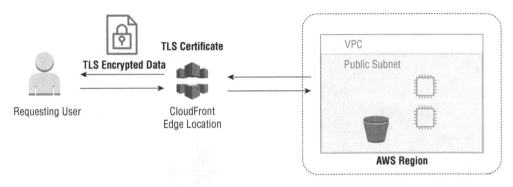

It's common to use your own domain and map it to the CloudFront domain in DNS using a CNAME. This allows you to use your company's descriptive domain name and hide the rather convoluted AWS CloudFront domain that is in the format of `https://a123456789abcd.cloudfront.net`, as an example. By default, the `*.cloudfront.net` certificate is installed at all edge locations.

To use your own certificate, such as `www.tipofthehat.com`, for example, you can create it at any of the security authorities or choose to use the Amazon Certificate Manager. Regardless of how you create the certificate for your domain, you will need to import it into ACM. ACM certificates are usually AWS region dependent, which means you must create the certificate in the AWS region you intend to use it in if you are using the AWS ACM service to create the certificates. Since CloudFront is a global service, all CloudFront certificates are managed in the AWS us-east-1 region in Northern Virginia.

Incoming traffic to the edge location can be either HTTPS and use a certificate or the unencrypted HTTP. There is a commonly used configuration option that automatically redirects unencrypted connection requests using HTTP port 80 to HTTPS port 443 to force the use of encrypted communications regardless of if the client is making an HTTP or HTTPS request. This forces the user's connection to be encrypted. It is important to understand that the certificate being used must match the domain name of the distribution. If they are different, the SSL/TLS handshake will fail.

Application Load Balancers and Network Load Balancers

The AWS Elastic Load Balancer family of products supports the termination of encrypted TLS connections by acting as the hosting server. TLS client session termination acts as an SSL offload for the backend targets, removing the processing overhead from the backend servers. TLS security policies are predefined and offer a large selection of options to meet your specific security requirements and allow for older browser support. This requires the ELBs to have TLS certificates directly installed on them since the load balancer acts as the target server and is terminating the encrypted TLS connections. The Amazon Certificate Manager can be used to manage your digital certificates.

Figure 14.5 shows the TLS encrypted communications from the client to an ELB.

FIGURE 14.5   Encrypted load balancing

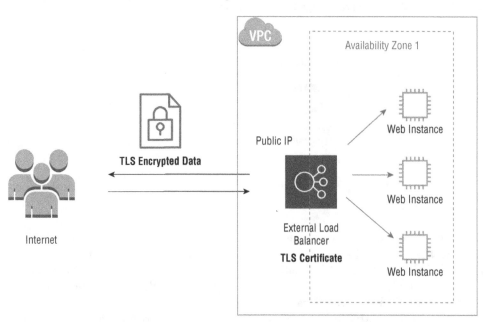

Elastic Load Balancers can be configured to also encrypt TLS/SSL connections from the load balancer to the backend servers to provide end-to-end encryption between the client and target server. The incoming TLS session will be terminated on the ELB for inspection and processing. Then, a second secure connection is created between the ELB and the target servers on the back end of the load balancer. In this case, the ELB will be acting as the client, and the servers store the TLS certificate.

Securing AWS Managed Databases

AWS offers a range of managed databases in the Relational Database Service (RDS), which allows you to create and manage relational databases in the cloud, and AWS manages all the underlying infrastructure, resiliency, and ongoing database maintenance.

RDS is a fully managed database service that makes it easy to set up, operate, and scale a relational database in the cloud. While AWS manages the security and maintenance of the service, it's important for you to take extra steps to make sure your data is properly secured and protected.

With the shared responsibility model, it is your responsibility to secure the databases you deploy in AWS. Databases often contain sensitive information and steps must be taken to secure access and protect the data.

RDS managed databases are often targets for attackers because they may contain sensitive information such as PII, medical records, or financial data. Unauthorized access to such information can lead to identity theft, financial loss, and damage to your organization's reputation. It's important that you secure your RDS databases against unauthorized access and data breaches.

When you secure an AWS RDS managed database that is accessed remotely via RDP for management, you must implement strong authentication mechanisms such as complex passwords and *multifactor authentication* to ensure that only authorized users can access the database. Enabling MFA adds an extra layer of security and prevents attackers from gaining access to the database even if they have the user's password. You may also decide to implement a *bastion host*. A Bastion host is a jump server that is a specially configured EC2 instance that acts as a proxy server and allows secure remote access to your RDS instances. The Bastion host is used to enforce access control policies and provide additional logging and monitoring capabilities. By implementing a Bastion host, you can restrict direct access to your RDS instances and limit the exposure of your database to the Internet. Figure 14.6 shows encrypted communications from a remote administrator connecting to a Bastion host.

FIGURE 14.6   Bastion host

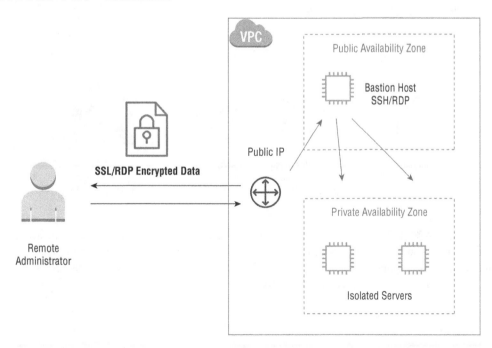

Configuring IAM access policies is a critical step in securing your AWS RDP managed databases. Use IAM to control access to RDS instances. IAM enables you to create and manage AWS users and groups, and you can assign them roles and permissions that grant them access to specific AWS resources.

Security groups are also used to secure your AWS RDS managed databases accessed via RDP. Security groups act as a virtual firewall that filter inbound and outbound traffic to your RDS instance. You configure security groups to restrict access to specific IP addresses such as from your corporate network, specific protocols, and port numbers.

Enabling TLS encryption for your RDS instances ensures that data in flight between your client application and the database is encrypted. TLS encryption is enabled using the AWS Management Console, API calls, or the CLI.

Keeping your database applications patched and updated to current revision levels maintains the security and integrity of your RDS deployment. AWS automatically patches and updates the database engine version of your RDS instance, but you are responsible for patching and updating the operating system and any applications or custom software you may have installed on your RDS instances. Regular patching and applying bug fixes reduces vulnerabilities and exploits from being used to compromise your database.

Securing AWS-managed RDS databases accessed remotely maintains the confidentiality, integrity, and availability of your data. By implementing RDS security best practices, you protect your data from unauthorized access, data breaches, and other security incidents. It is important to regularly review and update your security policies and procedures to ensure that your RDS instances are secure and compliant with standards and regulations.

RDS supports encryption for data at rest using the AWS Key Management Service (KMS), as shown in Figure 14.7. You leverage the KMS to manage and control the encryption keys that protect your data. When you enable encryption, AWS RDS automatically encrypts your data before storing it on disk and decrypts it when you access it.

FIGURE 14.7 RDS encryption

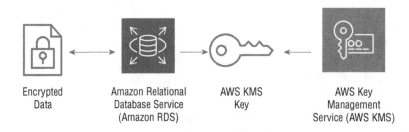

| Encrypted Data | Amazon Relational Database Service (Amazon RDS) | AWS KMS Key | AWS Key Management Service (AWS KMS) |

Securing AWS RDS managed databases includes access control, encryption, monitoring, and logging. You should always follow the AWS best practices. It's important to remember that security is an ongoing process, and you should regularly review and update your security measures to ensure they remain effective.

Securing Amazon S3 Buckets

Amazon Simple Storage Service is an object storage service that enables users to store and retrieve data stored in AWS from anywhere on the Web. While AWS S3 is designed with many security options, you must take steps to implement the options to meet your requirements. In this section, we will review the different options available for securing AWS S3.

Server-side encryption encrypts data at rest and ensures that data stored in S3 is protected from unauthorized access. There are three different SSE options available: SSE-S3, SSE-KMS, and SSE-C. S3 encryption options for data in transit and at rest are shown in Figure 14.8.

FIGURE 14.8   S3 encryption

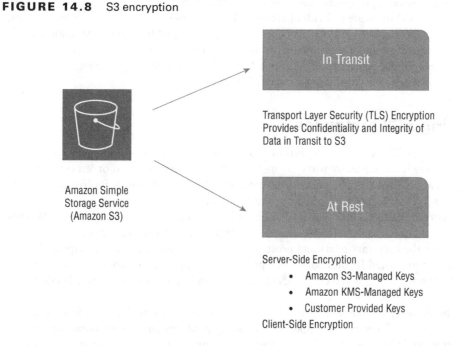

SSE-S3 encrypts data at rest using AES-256 encryption and is enabled by default for all S3 buckets, providing an easy way to encrypt data stored in S3. SSE-KMS encrypts data at rest using the AWS Key Management Service and allows you to manage your own encryption keys, provides you greater control over data with generated access and audit trails, and allows you to track who is accessing your data, and provides additional security features like access controls, key rotation, and auditing.

SSE-C allows you to use your own encryption keys to encrypt data stored in S3 providing an additional layer of control over data access. Client-side encryption is when you encrypt your data before it is uploaded to an S3 bucket. AWS provides an S3 encryption client that features an interface for encrypting and decrypting data stored in S3. AWS provides a client-side encryption SDK for Java and .NET.

Transfer encryption encrypts your data while it is being transferred between the client and S3. Transfer encryption provides protection against man-in-the-middle attacks, ensuring that data is encrypted while in transit. SSL/TLS transfer encryption is enabled by default on all S3 buckets. S3 Transfer Acceleration uses TLS to encrypt data in transit. Amazon S3 Transfer Acceleration provides faster data transfer speeds than traditional transfer methods.

Bucket policies and access control lists are tools you can use to control access to S3 buckets. Bucket policies and ACLs enable you to define access controls based on IP addresses, user agents, and more. You can use bucket policies to require that data uploaded to S3 is encrypted, ensuring that all data stored in S3 is protected by encryption. You can use AWS IAM to manage access to your S3 buckets and objects. IAM allows you to create and manage users and groups, assign permissions, and manage access to AWS resources. You can configure IAM to create individual accounts for each user, rather than sharing accounts. Limit access to S3 buckets and objects based on the principle of least privilege, granting access only to the minimum set of permissions required for a user's job responsibilities.

By implementing the encryption solutions outlined in this section, you create a secure and reliable environment for your data stored in AWS S3.

Securing EC2 Instances

EC2 instances in AWS have a great deal of configuration flexibility options. This creates a situation where there are many ways the instances can be misconfigured or left open for security breaches. You must be knowledgeable and follow the AWS security best practices to ensure your EC2 instances are locked down and secure.

It's important that you follow the principle of least privilege when configuring IAM roles and policies that are required for your users and applications to do their work.

Only open the necessary ports and protocols when configuring security groups and restrict access to trusted IP addresses when possible. You should monitor security groups regularly for any unauthorized changes, ensuring that only the necessary traffic is allowed to access your EC2 instances.

You should have a patch management process in place to ensure that your instances are up-to-date with the latest security updates. Regularly apply patches to minimize any vulnerabilities that could be exploited. You can automate your patch management operations by using the AWS Systems Manager or third-party tools available in the Amazon Marketplace. You should monitor your patching process and maintain logging records of applied patches for auditing purposes.

Also, apply encryption where possible to protect sensitive data and communications. This includes encrypting EBS volumes and snapshots to protect data at rest and implementing SSL to encrypt network traffic. You can implement data encryption at rest on your EBS storage volumes by using AWS-managed keys or customer-managed keys.

SSH or RDP access should be restricted only to trusted administrators. This includes using strong passwords or SSH keys to log in and disable root logins via SSH and instead use the sudo command and deploy Bastion hosts to proxy SSH access. Deploy NAT gateways or NAT instances to control outbound Internet access and use routing tables, network ACLs, and security groups to filter traffic. Use the AWS monitoring tools for your EC2 deployments.

Use log analysis, metric collection, and alerting to detect threats and unauthorized access. Regularly check for vulnerabilities in your EC2 instances.

Architect your VPC subnets to segregate resources based on their purpose and security requirements. Always use private subnets for instances that do not require direct access from the Internet, and public subnets for those that do. Implement network address translation (NAT) gateways for outbound Internet access from private subnets.

CloudWatch can be used to monitor EC2 instances, EBS volumes, and other AWS resources to collect and track metrics, logs, and generate alarms for your EC2 resources. You can enable detailed monitoring for your critical EC2 instances that collect and analyze data at a higher frequency. Create CloudWatch alarms to notify you of any unexpected behavior or potential security threats. Implement the AWS Trusted Advisor service to provide real-time guidance that helps you optimize your EC2 infrastructure and improve security. The Trusted Advisor will continuously monitor your environment and provide recommendations to improve security. You should review Trusted Advisor security checks regularly and implement the recommended actions. You can use CloudTrail to record API activity on your EC2 instances and forward the logs to CloudWatch.

Use the AWS Config service to assess, audit, and evaluate the EC2 configurations. Config continuously monitors and records your resource configurations and enables you to automate the evaluation of recorded configurations against desired baseline configurations. You can create custom rules for AWS Config to evaluate your resources against your organization's specific security requirements. Also, use Config to maintain a history of your resource configurations for compliance and auditing.

The AWS GuardDuty service continuously monitors your EC2 instances for threats, malicious activity, and unauthorized behavior patterns. GuardDuty will analyze and process VPC Flow Logs, AWS CloudTrail event logs, and DNS logs to identify potential security threats. Create a schedule to review the GuardDuty findings and remediate any security threats. You can integrate GuardDuty with your existing security tools and incident response processes.

Back up your EC2 instances using EBS snapshots and encrypt them in case you need to recover from a security failure or disaster. Use access controls on your snapshots.

Follow the AWS best practices in all these areas to ensure security controls and to protect your AWS EC2 resources to enhance the security of your EC2 instances and protect your data and resources. Always review and update your security configurations and stay informed about the latest security threats and best practices. Monitor and audit your EC2 instances to identify and respond to security threats in a timely manner. You should configure your monitoring and auditing tools to provide the necessary visibility into your EC2 instances and associated resources.

Transit Gateway

The Transit Gateway service was covered in Chapter 5, "Logging and Monitoring," Chapter 7, "Connecting On-Premises Networks," and Chapter 8, "Inter-VPC and Multi-Account Networking," and we will do a quick review here. The Transit Gateway is an AWS service that enables VPCs and on-premises networks to connect through a central hub over either site-to-site VPNs or using Direct Connect. Transit Gateway Connect is a Transit Gateway attachment that creates the interconnections from a Transit Gateway to SD-WAN services.

The hub-and-spoke design allows any services connected to the gateway to talk to each other. This allows VPC-to-VPC routing. The advantage of using a Transit Gateway is that only one connection to the hub needs to be made when adding new VPCs, VPNs, or on-premises networks. All traffic is then routed at the Transit Gateway. This allows for a single service to manage and monitor routing for your entire network.

To secure a Transit Gateway, you can implement security groups and NACLs. Security groups provide stateful filtering of traffic at the instance level, and NACLs provide stateless filtering at the subnet level. Both security groups and NACLs can be used to control inbound and outbound traffic.

Create encrypted VPN tunnels through your AWS Direct Connect connections. VPNs use IPSec encryption to secure traffic over the Internet, while DX uses 802.1Q VLAN tagging to isolate traffic over a private network connection. These two services can be combined to enhance the security of your hybrid network connections. To encrypt the traffic between VPCs, you can create a VPC attachment for each VPC that you want to connect to the Transit Gateway and enable PrivateLink to encrypt the traffic between the VPC attachments and the Transit Gateway.

You can also use the AWS Firewall Manager as a central management console of firewall rules for your VPCs. Implement the Firewall Manager to manage the firewall rules for your Transit Gateway. The Web Application Firewall (WAF) provides protection against web-based attacks. You can implement the AWS WAF service to protect your Transit Gateway from web-based attacks.

GuardDuty is a threat detection service from AWS that continuously monitors for malicious activity in your AWS accounts. You can configure GuardDuty to detect and respond to threats in your Transit Gateway.

Monitoring can be implemented using the AWS Transit Gateway Network Manager that enables you to monitor and control AWS Transit Gateway connections. It provides visibility into network topology, traffic flow, and network health, and it also allows you to trouble-shoot network issues and optimize network performance. Use the Gateway Network Manager to enforce security policies and to detect and prevent unauthorized access and network attacks. You can also use the Transit Gateway Network Manager to monitor and manage your network security policies and traffic flow. The Transit Gateway Network Manager also supports Amazon CloudWatch Logs and Amazon CloudWatch Events for logging and alerting.

Implement security and encryption on your AWS Transit Gateway deployment to ensure the confidentiality, integrity, and availability of your data transmitted across multiple Amazon VPCs and hybrid on-premises networks. AWS Transit Gateway offers you the ability to create a secure method to interconnect your VPCs and remote networks. How-ever, to ensure the security of the traffic passing through the Transit Gateway, you need to implement encryption and other security measures. You can implement Network ACLs, security groups, AWS Firewall Manager, AWS WAF, and AWS GuardDuty to secure your Transit Gateway and use IPSec or PrivateLink to encrypt traffic between VPCs and VPN connections.

Certificate Management Using a Certificate Authority

Digital certificates are a key component used in securing communications over the Internet. They are used to verify the identity of a website or server, to encrypt the data in transit, and to provide assurance that the information being transmitted is secure. *Certificate management* is the process of creating, distributing, revoking, and renewing certificates. A *certificate authority* (CA) is a trusted third-party organization that issues digital certificates, verifies that the person holding the certificate is who they claim to be, and is central to managing the life cycle of a certificate. In this section, we will discuss the implementation of a certificate management solution using certificate authorities.

A certificate management solution consists of the certificate authority, the certificate requesting organization, and revocation lists. The certificate authority issues certificates, verifies the identity of the certificate requester, and manages the certificate life cycle. The certificate requester is the organization that requests a certificate from the certificate authority. The *certificate revocation list* (CRL) is a list of revoked certificates that is maintained by the certificate authority and distributed to all parties that rely on the certificates issued by the authority to identify certificates that are no longer active.

They verify the identity of an individual or organization requesting a certificate as the rightful owner of the domain and then signs the certificate with its own digital signature and creates a chain of trust between the certificate holder and the recipient of the certificate, enabling secure communication and data exchange. Popular certificate authorities include AWS, DigiCert, GlobalSign, GoDaddy, and Entrust, to name a few of many.

When implementing a certificate management process, you would use a certificate authority to create and manage your certificates. The CA can be a private self-signed implementation using open-source software such as OpenSSL or commercial software such as Microsoft Certificate Services. The CA generates a public-private key pair and uses the private key to sign certificates. The CA's public key is distributed to all parties that rely on the certificates issued by the authority. The CA also maintains a record of all certificate requests, and issued and revoked certificates under its administrative control. The CA database contains the secret private keys, and steps should be taken to secure them by using access controls and encryption to prevent unauthorized access.

To obtain a certificate from the CA, the certificate requester submits a *certificate-signing request* (CSR) that is a text document used to define the parameters of the certificate. The CSR contains the requester's public key and identifying information. The CSR is signed by the requester's private key to provide proof of ownership of the public key. The CSR is a generated text file that you submit to the CA to give it the information it needs to sign the certificate. The CA uses the CSR information to verify the identity of the certificate requester using one of several methods, such as verifying the requester's identity using a government-issued ID, verifying the requester's employment status, or verifying the requester's domain ownership. Once the identity is verified, the CA signs the CSR using its private key, generates a digital certificate that includes the requester's public key, identifying information, and the CA's digital signature.

The certificate revocation list (CRL) is a list of revoked certificates that is maintained by the CA and distributed to all parties that query the certificates issued by the authority. Certificate revocation can occur for several reasons, such as a compromised private key, or the expiration of the certificate. The CRL is updated regularly to reflect certificate revocations.

Finally, set up a monitoring and reporting system to track the usage and validity of digital certificates issued by the certificate authority. This helps identify potential security issues and ensure compliance with regulatory requirements.

A certificate management solution using a certificate authority is a component of securing your communication on the Internet. The CA is responsible for issuing certificates, verifying the identity of certificate requesters, and managing the certificate life cycle. The certificate requester obtains a certificate by submitting a CSR and verifying their identity. The CRL is a list of revoked certificates that is maintained by the CA and distributed to all parties that rely on the certificates issued by the authority. By following best practices and keeping all certificates current, you can ensure the security and integrity of your communication over insecure networks.

AWS Certificate Manager and Private Certificate Authority

A CA is a trusted third-party organization that issues digital certificates. The digital certificate is an electronic document that is used to verify the identity of a person, device, or organization. The CA verifies the identity of the requester and issues a digital certificate that is used to authenticate the requester. The certificate contains information about the requester's identity, such as the requester's name, public key, and expiration date of the certificate.

Creating and administering SSL/TLS digital certificates is often a challenge. AWS has a certificate management service called the AWS Certificate Manager (ACM) that eases your ongoing certificate management duties.

The ACM service enables you to create, manage, and deploy SSL/TLS certificates for use with AWS services and your enterprise resources. With ACM, you can create either public or private SSL/TLS certificates that are trusted by AWS services and integrated with AWS resources, such as ELBs, CloudFront, and API Gateway. ACM also enables you to renew and revoke your certificates automatically, so you don't have to track expiration dates and create renewed certificates manually.

The first step is to request a certificate by providing the fully qualified domain name that you want to secure the connection for. ACM will verify that you own the domain by sending an email to the domain's administrative contact or by performing a DNS validation such as reading a key from your domain's TXT file. Once the verification is complete, ACM will issue the certificate.

You can now install the certificate to your AWS resources. ACM makes it easy to deploy the certificate to all your resources in just a few clicks. For private certificates, ACM stores the certificates within AWS KMS for additional security.

Finally, you must renew the certificate before its expiration date. ACM can manage the certificate's renewal and updates it automatically. This ensures that your certificates are always up-to-date and reduces the risk of service disruptions due to expired certificates.

ACM is easy to use and masks much of the complexity associated with digital certificates.

A private CA is used to issue digital certificates for internal resources. It is a trusted entity that is used to authenticate the identity of internal resources within an organization. A private CA is usually used to issue certificates for resources that are not publicly accessible, such as internal servers, applications, or devices.

The AWS Certificate Manager private CA provides a secure and private way to issue and manage digital certificates within an organization. The private CA can be used to issue certificates for internal resources. By using the ACM private CA, organizations can ensure the security and privacy of their internal resources, while also complying with industry standards. A public CA publishes certificates that will be exposed to the public such as over the Internet. The public certificates can be verified as legitimate to the requesting client querying the CA to validate that the owner of the certificate is who they claim to be.

There are no additional charges for using ACM, and it reduces administrative overhead by automating the renewal and deployment process.

The AWS Certificate Manager is a valuable service that makes it easy to provision, manage, and deploy SSL/TLS certificates for use with AWS services and your internal connected resources. ACM reduces the complexity of managing certificates, improves security, and integrates seamlessly with AWS services. With the ACM service, you pay only for the AWS resources used to manage and deploy your certificates, and you don't pay up-front or ongoing fees for the certificates themselves. The certificates are free.

Summary

This chapter's focus was on confidentiality and encryption. Protecting data in the cloud, both at rest and in transit, is critical for your cloud deployments. It is very important for enterprises utilizing AWS services to protect their data from unauthorized access. Confidentiality and encryption are two important cybersecurity concepts that enable organizations to safeguard their data.

Confidentiality is the protection of information from unauthorized disclosure; only authorized entities should have access to the information, and that information will be secure and protected from unauthorized access. AWS provides multiple services to ensure the confidentiality of customer data including network isolation, access controls, and encryption.

Encryption transforms your information into an unreadable format, known as ciphertext, by using an encryption algorithm and a secret key. This prevents unauthorized parties from accessing or reading the information if they do not have the encryption keys, even if they gain access to the data. AWS offers multiple encryption options, which include encryption at rest and in transit. Encryption at rest is the encryption of data that is stored in AWS services such as S3, EBS, and RDS. Encryption in transit refers to the encryption of data as it travels between AWS services or between AWS and customer environments.

AWS encryption services include AWS KMS, AWS CloudHSM, and the AWS Certificate Manager. KMS allows customers to create and manage encryption keys, and CloudHSM provides secure key storage and management. The AWS Certificate Manager enables customers to provision, manage, and deploy TLS certificates for use with AWS services and resources.

TLS is the most common encryption protocol used to secure data in transit over the Internet and across your internal networks. TLS is used to secure web traffic using HTTPS and email communication using SMTPS, IMAPS, and POP3S.

AWS provides several services that support TLS encryption, including the Elastic Load Balancer service that uses TLS encryption for incoming and outgoing client traffic. The AWS Certificate Manager (ACM) can be used to create and manage TLS certificates for your ELB and many other AWS services, or you can implement and use your own certificates. The AWS ACM service makes it easy to provision, deploy, and renew TLS certificates to encrypt your web traffic. KMS is the Amazon Key Management Service that securely stores your keys. CloudFront supports TLS encryption for incoming and outgoing data, and the ACM can be used to generate and manage TLS certificates for your CloudFront distribution.

AWS provides several services that support TLS encryption, including the Elastic Load Balancer service that uses TLS encryption for incoming and outgoing client traffic. The AWS Certificate Manager (ACM) generates and managesTLS certificates for your ELB and other AWS services, or you can implement your own certificates.

The AWS API Gateway supports TLS encryption for in-flight traffic and, as with the other AWS services, you can use the ACM service to generate and manage SSL/TLS certificates for your API gateways. A virtual private network (VPN) creates a secure, encrypted tunnel between your on-premises network and your AWS resources. A site-to-site VPN enables you to connect your on-premises network to your AWS deployments over encrypted VPN tunnels. The site-to-site VPN supports Internet Protocol Security (IPSec) and encryption for all traffic between your on-premises network and your AWS resources. The client VPN supports OpenVPN, an open-source VPN protocol that provides secure communications.

Amazon Direct Connect supports IPSec encryption, if configured to use VPN tunnels, to encrypt traffic between your on-premises network and your AWS resources. The AWS Transit Gateway supports IPSec encryption for all traffic between your VPCs and on-premises networks. The Network Firewall supports SSL/TLS decryption and inspection, which enables you to inspect encrypted traffic for threats at the entry point into your network.

The AWS S3 object storage service has multiple encryption options including SSE-C encryption. Amazon S3 data at the object level can use server-side encryption with customer-provided keys, or SSE-C. This encrypts data in transit and at rest and allows you to manage the encryption keys. However, network encryption is handled automatically by Amazon S3.

DNS Security Extensions (DNSSEC) is a security protocol designed to add an additional layer of protection to DNS queries. DNSSEC uses digital signatures to verify that DNS records have not been tampered with, ensuring that users are directed to the intended website. DNS filtering inspects DNS queries and blocks known malicious or suspicious requests. DNS over HTTPS encrypts DNS queries and responses using HTTPS, which is the same protocol used by web browsers to encrypt web traffic that uses SSL/TLS as the encryption protocol. DoH prevents eavesdropping on and tampering with DNS queries by encrypting them, preventing attackers from modifying DNS queries. DNS over TLS is a protocol that encrypts DNS requests and responses using TLS. Response Policy Zones is a DNS server feature that enables administrators to block DNS requests to known malicious domains, and IP addresses, prevent malware infections, and block access to undesirable content. Threat intelligence feeds are a source of information about known malicious domains and IP addresses and can be implemented in your DNS deployments as a blacklist. They are used to update DNS filters and firewalls to block access to known malicious domains. Response rate limiting limits the rate of DNS responses to prevent DNS amplification attacks. The DNS firewall is a specialized type of firewall designed to protect against DNS-based attacks. DNS firewalls analyze DNS queries and block requests that are known to be malicious, preventing attackers from redirecting users to fake websites or hijacking DNS queries.

Next, we covered the AWS shared responsibility model, which is a security model that defines the security and division of responsibilities between AWS and its customers. Under the shared responsibility model, AWS is responsible for the security of the underlying infrastructure that supports the AWS cloud operations. This includes securing their physical data centers, network infrastructure, and the hardware components installed in the AWS facilities. AWS deploys multiple layers of security to protect its infrastructure, including perimeter security, firewalls, intrusion prevention systems, and other security mechanisms, to protect its network perimeter from external unauthorized access. Customers are responsible for securing their data and applications that run on top of the AWS infrastructure. This includes implementing appropriate network encryption measures to protect data in transit between their resources and the AWS network.

The IPSec protocol suite enables secure communications over IP networks. IPSec is a widely used standard for securing communication across the Internet. The TLS protocol is a standardized communications protocol that provides security for in-flight traffic flows over an insecure network such as the Internet. TLS is used to secure communications between a client and a server. TLS encrypts the data being transmitted between a client and a server, to protect the data from unauthorized access or disclosure and protects against man-in-the-middle attacks that alter messages.

There are many AWS services that use encryption; in this chapter we covered the most common networking services that use TLS and IPSec, including CloudFront, the AWS family of load balancers, Transit Gateway and securing EC2 instances and S3 storage buckets.

We ended the chapter with a review of the certificate authority services that are offered by AWS.

Exam Essentials

Understand the security protocols and services at a high level.   Know the definitions of confidentiality and encryption as these topics are core to understanding network security. Focus on networking encryption options of TLS and IPSec and how they are implemented for in-flight data. Review all the protocols used by IPSec and understand them at a high level; this includes the Diffie-Hellman key exchange, Encapsulation Security Protocol, Application Headers, Internet Key Exchange, the Key Management protocol, and security associations. For TLS, know that it is the replacement for SSL, and know the basics of the TLS handshakes.

Review how security is implemented in the primary Amazon networking services.   Review the security sections on DNS, CloudFront, WAF, VPNs, load balancers, and the Transit Gateway.

Review the documentation on certificate authorities and what they are used for.   Understand the difference between public and private certificates and the process used to create digital certificates such as using certificate signing requests. Then review the AWS service offerings for public and private certificate management.

Exercises

1. Review the AWS Data Protection and Privacy documentation at `https://aws.amazon .com/compliance/data-protection`.

2. Read the AWS documentation on Network and Application protection at `https://aws .amazon.com/products/security/network-application-protection`.

3. Know what the division of responsibilities is under the AWS Shared Responsibility model: `https://aws.amazon.com/compliance/shared-responsibility-model`.

4. Review the AWS Certificate Manager documentation: `https://docs.aws.amazon .com/acm`.

5. Read the AWS documentation on CloudHSM: `https://aws.amazon.com/cloudhsm`.

6. Read the AWS documentation on the IPSec protocol: `https://aws.amazon.com/ what-is/ipsec`.

7. Read the AWS documentation on the TLS protocol: `https://aws.amazon.com/ what-is/ssl-certificate`.

8. Review the AWS Route 53 DNSSEC configuration guide: `https://docs.aws.amazon .com/Route53/latest/DeveloperGuide/dns-configuring-dnssec.html`.

Review Questions

The following questions are designed to test your understanding of this chapter's material. For more information on how to obtain additional questions, please see this book's introduction.

1. Which AWS service enables you to create, manage, and deploy SSL/TLS certificates for use with AWS services and your enterprise resources?

   A. SSL

   B. ACM

   C. CRL

   D. CSR

   E. TLS

2. Which cybersecurity process transforms your information into an unreadable format, known as ciphertext, by using an algorithm and a secret key?

   A. Confidentiality

   B. Authentication

   C. Authorization

   D. Encryption

3. Which AWS service allows you to create, manage, and control cryptographic keys across your applications and is integrated with many AWS services?

   A. RDS

   B. HSM

   C. SSE

   D. KMS

4. To meet regulatory compliance requirements, you need to provide a hardware-based secure key storage and management solution in the Frankfurt region. Which AWS service processes cryptographic operations and provides secure storage for cryptographic keys?

   A. Security Hub

   B. CloudHSM

   C. KMS

   D. Control Tower

   E. Macie

5. Transport Layer Security (TLS) is the most common encryption protocol used to secure data in transit over the Internet and across your internal networks. What common protocols commonly implement TSL for securing in-flight network traffic? (Select three.)

   A. KMS

   B. HTTPS

   C. IMAPS

   D. ACM

   E. SMTPS

6. Your company has an AWS Direct Connect connection between its on-premises data center and an Amazon VPC. The ERP application that is running on an Amazon EC2 instance in the VPC needs to access confidential data stored in a RAID array located in the on-premises data center. Because of the nature of the application, a low-latency, high-speed connection is required. To meet compliance requirements, you must encrypt the data in transit. How would you meet these requirements?

    A. Establish a Direct Connect connection and configure a site-to-site VPN between the customer gateway and the virtual private gateway in the VPC

    B. Establish a Direct Connect connection from your on-premises data center and the AWS VPC and enable the native DX encryption

    C. Create an Internet gateway in the VPC and establish a software VPN between the customer gateway and an EC2 instance in the VPC

    D. Create an Internet gateway in the VPC and then configure an AWS site-to-site VPN between the customer gateway and the virtual private gateway in the VPC

7. Which of the following options can be used to encrypt data in transit between an Amazon EC2 instance and an Amazon S3 bucket?

    A. Create a virtual private gateway

    B. Use client-side encryption

    C. Create a network access control list

    D. Use a security group

    E. Implement a virtual private cloud endpoint

8. What AWS process outlines what security roles AWS is responsible for?

    A. CloudFront

    B. Shared Responsibility Model

    C. Well-Architected Framework

    D. CloudWatch

    E. CloudTrail

9. Which of the following options is true about using DNSSEC with Amazon Route 53?

    A. DNSSEC is not supported in Amazon Route 53

    B. DNSSEC can only be used for private hosted zones

    C. DNSSEC can only be used for public hosted zones

    D. DNSSEC can be used for both private and public hosted zones

    E. DNSSEC can only be used for VPC peering connections

10. Which of the following options is true about using a Bastion host for security in a VPC?

    A. A Bastion host is not necessary for security in a VPC

    B. A Bastion host provides an additional layer of security by acting as a gateway to instances in a private subnet

    C. A Bastion host can be used for instances only in a public subnet

    D. A Bastion host can be used for instances only in a private subnet

    E. A Bastion host can be used only for VPC peering connections

11. Which of the following options is true about using AWS Certificate Manager?

    A. AWS Certificate Manager can be used only to manage SSL/TLS certificates for Amazon CloudFront distributions

    B. AWS Certificate Manager can be used only to manage SSL/TLS certificates for Elastic Load Balancers

    C. AWS Certificate Manager can be used only to manage SSL/TLS certificates for Amazon API Gateway

    D. AWS Certificate Manager can be used to manage SSL/TLS certificates for multiple AWS services, including Amazon CloudFront, Elastic Load Balancer, and Amazon API Gateway

    E. AWS Certificate Manager can be used only to manage SSL/TLS certificates for VPC peering connections

12. Which of the following is true about using AES encryption with IPSec for a VPN connection between a VPC and an on-premises network?

    A. AES encryption with IPSec is not supported for VPN connections

    B. AES encryption with IPSec can be used only for site-to-site VPN connections

    C. AES encryption with IPSec can be used only for client VPN connections

    D. AES encryption with IPSec can be used for both site-to-site and client VPN connections

    E. AES encryption with IPSec can be used only for VPC peering connections

13. Which of the following statements is true about TLS symmetric encryption?

    A. TLS symmetric encryption uses different keys for encryption and decryption

    B. TLS symmetric encryption is more efficient than asymmetric encryption

    C. TLS symmetric encryption does not require a shared key

    D. TLS symmetric encryption is only used for web browsing

    E. TLS symmetric encryption is not secure against eavesdropping

14. Which of the following options is true about using encryption with the AWS Transit Gateway service?

    A. Encryption is not supported for AWS Transit Gateway

    B. Encryption can be used only for site-to-site VPN connections

    C. Encryption can be used only for VPC peering connections

    D. Encryption can be used for both site-to-site VPN and VPC peering connections

    E. Encryption can be used only for Direct Connect connections

15. Which of the following statements is true about private certificate authorities (CAs) in AWS?

   A. AWS Certificate Manager (ACM) is the only service that can issue and manage certificates from CAs

   B. AWS Key Management Service (KMS) can be used to create and manage private CAs in AWS

   C. AWS CloudFormation can be used to create and manage public certificates in AWS

   D. AWS Directory Service can be used to integrate with external CAs for authentication and encryption

   E. AWS IAM can be used to control access to CAs in AWS

16. Which cybersecurity term describes the protection of information from unauthorized disclosure and that only authorized entities should have access to the information, and the information will be secured and protected from unauthorized access?

   A. Confidentiality

   B. Authentication

   C. Authorization

   D. Encryption

17. Which of the following options is a security feature available in Amazon Route 53?

   A. DNS response rate limiting

   B. DNSSEC

   C. IPSec

   D. Bastion host

   E. VPC peering

18. Which of the following options is true about using IPSec with IKE for a VPN connection between a VPC and an on-premises network?

   A. IKE is not supported for VPN connections

   B. IKE can be used only for site-to-site VPN connections

   C. IKE can be used only for client VPN connections

   D. IKE can be used for both site-to-site and client VPN connections

   E. IKE can be used only for VPC peering connections

19. What is the file that contains a list of deleted or cancelled certificates that is maintained by the certificate authority and distributed to all parties that rely on the certificates issued by the authority to identify certificates that are no longer active?

   A. CA

   B. CRL

   C. Certificate Manager

   D. Certificate Management

   E. CSR

20. Which of the following statements is true about the TLS handshake process in AWS?

    A. The client and the server exchange certificates and verify each other's identity

    B. The client and the server negotiate the cipher suite and the session key using the Diffie-Hellman algorithm

    C. The client and the server use a preshared key to encrypt and decrypt the data

    D. The client and the server send a FIN packet to each other to terminate the connection

    E. The client and the server use AWS KMS to generate and manage the encryption keys

Appendix

Answers to Review Questions

Chapter 1: Edge Networking

1. C. To remove a cached object before its TTL timer expires, you need to invalidate the file to force the edge to request a new file from the origin. Setting the TTL to zero is not a valid option, and replacing the file at the origin does not automatically force an update at the cache since the cache has TTL timers that define how long that locally stored data is fresh. There are no file management utilities in the CloudFront console.

2. C. When cached data in CloudFront becomes stale, it reaches out to the nearest edge cache location for updates. Edge locations do not query other edges for content refresh. Edge locations check the regional cache and not the origin for basic content in S3. TTL values of cached data do not automatically rest.

3. B. By deploying CloudFront, the application files will be cached closer to users worldwide and not have to go back to the origin region to pull the downloads. By using geo-restrictions, users can be restricted to their local edge locations to meet encryption regulations. Global Accelerator could improve performance, but the user request would still need to traverse the AWS network to the region where the data is stored. Stringing the data in all AWS regions worldwide would not be optimal and would incur costs for each region. An RDS multi-AZ configuration would not meet the requirements as all the data would be stored in a single region and not be optimized for download speeds.

4. C. This is a good use case for Global Accelerator as users can traverse the faster AWS global network and not the Internet to access the data stored in the us-west-2 region. CloudFront nodes at edge locations do not support the FTP protocol. While using a load balancer may speed up responses if the FTP servers are overloaded, the users would still need to traverse the public Internet from very remote locations to access the data. Using API Gateway would not resolve the issue Global Widgets is trying to resolve.

5. A. The company could leverage the use of the AWS global network for transport of data from customers worldwide. Global Accelerator supports the use of customer-owned public IP addresses used as an Anycast access point to the network to allow customers connecting over the Internet to access the nearest edge location and transfer the data over the AWS global network. Using AWS-assigned Anycast addresses does not meet the Global Widgets security policy. Options C and D are not valid options.

6. A. This is a good use case for the custom Global Accelerator instance to have the flexibility to make connections internal to the AWS network and offer faster data transfer times to the remote users. A standard Global Accelerator instance does not have the advanced feature set for this customer's requirements. Implementing API gateways would not address the issue the customer is reporting. Classic load balancers are no longer available and would not meet this requirement.

7. A. This is a classic use case for SNI; the ALB terminating the TLS connection can read the destination domain name in the header and terminate it using the correct certificate. URL mapping would not resolve the issue the customer is having. Network load balancers operate at layer 4 and do not inspect header information. SNI is not used in CloudFront.

8. C. To modify HTTP headers, a virtual server or microservice will be needed with code to make the changes needed. Of the options presented, this is a perfect use case for Lambda@ edge, which can host code to modify the headers at the CloudFront edge location. API gateways and EC2 instances do not fit this requirement as only Lambda is available as an edge service. ALBs do not meet this requirement.

9. C. Deploying a network load balancer will be able to service a high session count and burst rates with very high performance. While the Lambda and RDS solution could improve performance, you are being asked to provide a networking-based solution and not the applications. API gateways have capacity limits that may affect this solution's requirement for high performance and connection rates.

10. B. API Gateway is an application front end based on standard protocols. By also implementing WebSockets on API Gateway, a single connection can support multiple client sessions, which will improve the transfer of financial trading data. While Global Accelerator could decrease the network latency, this does not address how to design the application front-end architecture. Using an application load balancer would distribute the load across multiple backend servers and increase performance; the use of WebSockets was not given, so it would not be the best solution offered. Because of the rapidly changing data inherent in financial trading deployments, caching at the CloudFront edge would not give us any performance improvements.

11. A, C. Sticky sessions, also known as session affinity, retain user connections to the same backend server. In this case, since the shopping carts are hosted at the server level, the user must always connect to the same server, making this the solution to the problem. Target groups and health checking do not accomplish this.

12. B, D. The Web Application Firewall (WAF) and many third-party firewalls can be combined with CloudFront for application-level perimeter security. AWS uses its Shield service in front of all edge locations. Shield will protect the edge from distributed denial-of-service (DDoS) attacks. Shield includes automatic inline attack mitigation support to protect your site from common attacks at no additional charge. Control Tower does not meet these requirements, and there is no such service as CloudFront DDoS.

13. A. IAM requests are sent from the requester to the API Gateway using Sigv4 security headers that contain the IAM credentials, which are then passed to IAM from API Gateway. User pools are part of Cognito, and the AD connector is not a valid solution for this design.

14. E. Listeners support HTTP and HTTPS connections on a port that you define between 1 and 65535? TCP offload can be set to decrypt SSL/TLS connections on the ELB to eliminate the server decryption workload. Listeners support WebSockets HTTP/2 and can service up to 128 parallel requests per connection. When configuring listeners, you set how the connection requests are processed and sent to the backend services called *targets*. Cognito is an AWS authentication service that uses user pools, and the transfer accelerator is not related to the load balancer virtual listening interface.

15. D. The gateway load balancer listens across all ports in an IP flow and forwards the traffic you define in a listener rule to target groups. The original packet is not modified. All of the other ELB family types modify the original packet.

16. B. API Gateway caching can be configured to locally store frequent requests in the stage on the gateway. The API Gateway will cache response for the time-to-live, or TTL, period. The gateway will then first check the cache for the response before making an endpoint request if there is a cache miss. The other options do not meet this requirement.

17. B. The GENEVE protocol is used by the gateway load balancer and uses a header that contains system state information and is extensible so it can evolve over time to meet future use cases. VxLAN is a similar technology but is not used in this scenario. Proxy protocol and WebSockets do not apply to this architecture.

18. A, C. Geographical locations and political regulations should be taken into consideration when designing a CloudFront content distribution network. The BGP policy implementation on the Internet cannot be controlled by most enterprises, and while encryption is important, CloudFront offers the same cipher suites at all of its edge locations.

19. A, D. When a server is being taken offline or disabled, connection draining can be implemented to allow existing connections to complete their operations and prevent any new connections being made to the server. This allows for a nondisruptive operation that is transparent to the end users. Connection draining is sometimes called a deregistration delay. Session affinity and proxy connections would not accomplish what is required.

20. B. The AWS Lambda authorizer service is integrated with API Gateway and provides authentication services that can be customized based on the code you download to run on Lambda. None of the other offered choices can accomplish this requirement.

Chapter 2: Domain Name Services

1. D. A round-robin routing policy would sequentially deliver an IP address to client requests, allowing each FTP server to get an equal number of requests. Simple routing would not work since it would deliver only a single address, and in this case, four are needed. Latency-based routing would deliver IP records based on neatwork response times but not evenly across the servers as is being requested. Weighted routing would work in this case, but round-robin is the simpler solution.

2. B. This is a perfect solution for Route 53 failover. It will monitor the Jakarta primary site and, if it should fail, route traffic to the standby in Mumbai. CloudWatch can trigger events, but the failover can be automated using Route 53 failover routing. Multivalue responses would deliver multiple IP addresses for the domain but do not have the intelligence to perform an automatic failover. Configuring an Alias record would not be automatic for a fast failover to the standby region. CloudTrail is an API recording service but would not be a fit for automatic DNS routing changes as is required here.

3. B. Option B is correct as both `enableDnsHostnames` and `enableDnsSupport` must be set to true. The BIND server should get the A records from Route 53 and not locally. This is a direct connection and not an Internet firewall architecture. IAM roles would not apply in this use case.

4. B, E. Alias records are internal to Route 53 and AWS; they can be used to map one domain name to another. CNAME records are a standard DNS record type and are not location dependent. Alias records are internal only to Route 53. Zone apex records are supported in Alias records but not CNAME records. TTL values cannot be changed in Alias records; they inherit the original value.

5. C. An Alias record would need to be configured since it supports zone apex records; none of the other options offered have that ability.

6. A, C. The name server hierarchy includes the root server to resolve to the top-level domain (.edu, .com, .io, etc.) and the top-level domain server resolves to the domain of tipofthehat.com. The Alias and apex are not servers but records. The public zone server is a distractor and does not apply.

7. D. In this case, weighted routing would allow you to define the percentage of load delivered to each server and would be the optimal solution to resolve this issue. Latency could work as the old servers would be slower and receive less connection but does not allow you to hard-code the distribution as was required in the question. Simple routing would deliver only a single IP record and not work here. Multivalue would deliver multiple IP addresses for the client to choose from and not facilitate a defined load distribution. Round-robin would evenly distribute the load between the slow and fast servers, which is not what we want to accomplish here.

8. B, D. The EC2 instances must know how to connect the resolver, so the DHCP scope needs the Route 53 address to give to the new servers. The Route 53 private zones must be associated to the new VPC for name resolution from that VPC. Option A is incorrect because this is a common configuration. Option C is incorrect because host files should not be used in place of DNS, if possible, which it is in this case. This scenario does not mention a requirement for name resolution in the corporate data center, so option E is irrelevant.

9. E. CloudFront collects and reports on metric values in AWS and is the solution to this request. CloudTrail records API calls to Route 53 but not metric and performance information. Macie is a security service and is not a valid solution to this request from operations. CloudFront is for content distribution and not monitoring and logging operations.

10. B. ICANN is responsible for managing and tracking domain information for the Internet worldwide and is the correct answer. IANA is the Internet Assigned Numbers Authority that manages public IP addressing. ARIN is the American Registry for Internet Numbers and is responsible for IP address and autonomous system number registration in the Americas. ENISA is the European Network and Information Security Agency and does not manage domain names.

11. A, C. Route 53 supports public hosted zones for Internet DNS resolution and private hosted ones for internal VPC DNS resolution. Single AZ zones and Internet zones do not exist.

12. B. Application Recovery Controller is a feature of Route 53 that monitors your endpoints and is used to determine if they have the ability and are ready for recovery. You can use the routing control and readiness checking to manage failover using DNS responses to queries. The feature can be used in all regions and availability zones as well as your on-premise applications. It acts as a single control point in the AWS console to manage Route 53's recovery

features. Recoveries can be either active-active and/or active standby. Recoveries can be automated or manually executed. Route 53 failover does not have the extended feature sets as requested in the question. Hybrid Route 53 does not meet the recovery requirements, and transfer acceleration is not a Route 53 feature.

13. A. When resolving a DNS query, each DNS server that answers the queries needs a path to every zone in that namespace. Delegations provide this purpose. The delegation is a record stored in the parent zone that lists authoritative name servers at the next level down in the hierarchy. This allows for servers in one zone to direct clients to servers in other zones. For example, the root zones delegate to the `.com` servers below them that in turn delegate to the company domain below such as `tipofthehat.com`. Zones are record sets themselves and not references, multivalue is a type of response, and health checking does not apply to the question.

14. C. Redshift is a data warehouse offering by AWS that can analyze Route 53 data in the data lake, and queries can be run to gain intelligence on the data. Redshift can store petabytes of data and perform machine learning on records exported from Route 53. Redshift is self-learning and self-tuning and has robust third-party support services available in the Amazon Marketplace. Redshift uses standard SQL to analyze and visualize the data from Route 53 and other sources. Hadoop, EMR, and Spark are all big data services but are not AWS data lake SQL offerings.

15. B. Multivalue responses are an extension to the simple routing policy. Instead of returning just a single record's IP address, multivalue will return any number up to eight responses of IP addresses for the same domain name. This allows the client to choose which IP address to use as the domain is active on all of the IP addresses.

16. B. Resource records are at the core of DNS functionality. They contain the actual data about DNS resources. Each record contains a name, type, and time-to-live (TTL) information. While there are more than 90 different types of resource records, most are rarely seen. Alias records are pointers, resolvers are not specifically individual resource records, and host files contain host-to-IP address mapping but are not used in Route 53.

17. B. Hybrid DNS with Route 53 allows you to interconnect your DNS systems from your corporate on-premise servers with Route 53 running in the AWS cloud for end-to-end name resolution. DNS queries originating from AWS can be sent to your corporate DNS for resolution, and corporate DNS requests can be sent to a Route 53 Resolver to access your AWS VPC resources. This allows DNS to work across your entire network. Public hosted zones are used to define Internet-accessible Route 53 records, and a private zone is for AWS VPC internal records. AWS multi-account is not applicable to the question.

18. D. The Route 53 Resolver allows for seamless interconnection of your Route 53 and on-premise systems. The Route 53 Resolver is a fully managed AWS service that supports 10,000 queries per second both inbound and outbound. CloudFront is an AWS management and monitoring service. While the question is about hybrid DNS, it is specifically about the resolver function. Control Tower is a policy dashboard and a resolver.

19. B. The AAAA, or quad A, record is the IPv6 address mapping in DNS. The A record is used for IPv4, MX is for mail servers, and CNAME is a domain mapping record.

20. B. Geo-proximity routes traffic based on location just as geolocation with enhancements allows you to adjust how the traffic gets routed based on a bias value. The bias increases or decreases the geographical size of the region that traffic gets routed. Geo-proximity works for both AWS and non-AWS resources. If the resource resides in an AWS region, then the region is defined in the policy. If the resource is in a non-AWS location such as a corporate data center, then latitude and longitude values are used. Once the resources are defined in the policy, the size of the region can be expanded by adding a positive number between 1 and 99; it can be shrunk with a negative value between -1 to -99. Regional routing and geo-zones are not terms used in Route 53. Geolocation does not use a bias setting to determine query responses.

Chapter 3: Hybrid and Multi-account DNS

1. A. In this case, the raw, or zone, apex domain needs to forward to the virtual IP of the load balancer. This is what the Alias record was created by AWS to do since it is not supported using a CNAME. Using the IPv4 or IPv6 addresses is not a domain name, and the alias requires the destination domain name, so using an Alias is the best solution over IP addresses.

2. B. To locally resolve DNS names in a private VPC, a Route 53 private zone needs to be created to hold the resource records for the development servers. A public hosted zone would not be used in this case as the IP records are private in the AWS Stockholm region. Both geolocation and multivalue would not meet the requirements of the development team as this is not a geographic issue and there was no stated need for multivalue traffic management.

3. C. To balance the connection count between the front-end web servers using Route 53, multivalue routing would need to be deployed. All the other options do not meet the requirement.

4. B. To redirect email SMTP traffic to the new server, the MX record needs to be modified. The other options given would not work.

5. B. To create IPv6 resource records, choose the AAAA type. All the other answers given do not work.

6. B, D. Both a direct connection and inbound endpoints would be required to allow the corporate DNS servers to query the Route 53 hosted zones. Zone delegations and specific resources do not apply when interconnecting DNS servers.

7. E. By deploying a failover-based routing solution, Route 53 will serve the IP address of the standby if the primary fails. The other options do not meet this requirement.

8. C. Route 53 health checking is designed just for this type of use case. The other options given will not meet the requirement.

9. C. By configuring weighted routing, you can statically configure the connection allocation between your web servers that takes into consideration the different processing capabilities.

10. C. The optimal solution would be to divide the Route 53 hosted zone configuration responsibilities to the specific groups responsible for managing those domains by delegating authority. Forwarding rules do not apply here, public and private hosted zones do not address configuration management, and forwarding rules are for hybrid DNS architectures.

11. A. Latency-based routing is configured at the record level in the Route 53 console. AWS calculates the delay, or latency, over the Internet from the requesting device to the endpoint in the AWS cloud. However, latency-based routing does not calculate the applications delay such as the latency inherent in a database or backend application. Delay and proximity are not policies in Route 53, and geolocation does not take network latency into consideration as a metric.

12. C. Name Authority Pointer, or NAPTR, records are commonly used for Internet Telephony applications when mapping servers and user addresses in the Session Initiation Protocol (SIP) to convert phone numbers to URIs. SPF is used to prevent email spoofing, the GENEVE protocol is for network encapsulation, and SIP is a Voice over IP.

13. B. Certificate Authority Authorization, or the CAA, record limits the certificate authorities that can create TLS/SSL certificates in the domain. This is a whitelist of CAs that you allow to issue certificates for this domain or subdomain. The TLS is a type of data encryption, NAPTR is a mapping record often used for VoIP services, and ICANN is the Internet Corporation for Assigned Names and Numbers and is not used to whitelist certificate authorities in DNS.

14. B. The service, or SRV, record redirects sessions for specific service types, such as VoIP or instant messaging sessions, to specific hosts and port numbers. The syntax is in the format of [priority] [weight] [port] [server host name] such as 1 10 5269 xmpp-server1.tipofthehat.com. The CAA record whitelists certificate authorities, AAAA is a IPv6 host record, and NAPTR is not used for mapping.

15. B. Conditional forwarding rules are required to tell the Route 53 Resolver what domain names you want to forward to remote resolvers such as an on-premise DNS server. A forwarding rule is needed for each domain to which you want queries to be forwarded. While the question refers to hybrid DNS, that is not the specific answer. Zone transfer and PTR records do not apply to forwarding policies.

16. B. Route 53 sends the logs to CloudWatch Logs, and they are not directly accessible through the Route 53 console; you must use the CloudWatch console to view them. CloudWatch displays the logging data in near real time and provides search, filter, and export capabilities. CloudTrail records API management calls to all AWS services but not query logs, and API Gateway and Redshift are services that are not related to Route 53 query logging.

17. B. Data specific to the resolver endpoints is exported to and monitored by CloudWatch. The raw data is collected at 5-minute intervals and converted into readable near real-time data and displayed in dashboards and tables you create. You can use Amazon CloudWatch to monitor the number of DNS queries that are forwarded by Route 53 Resolver endpoints.

Amazon CloudWatch collects and processes raw data into readable, near real-time metrics that are stored for 14 days by default. The other options are not specifically AWS Route 53 monitoring types.

18. B. SOA, or Start of Authority, records contain basic information about the domain and hosted zone, including the Route 53 name server that created the SOA record, the email address of the administrator for your organization, and a serial number that can be incremented whenever you update a record. There is a value that tells the secondary DNS servers how often to refresh their zone records and a retry interval the secondary server must wait to retry a failed transfer. The TXT, PTR, and CAA records do not contain this information.

19. B. Outbound endpoints allow DNS resolutions originating inside your VPC to your on-premise DNS deployment or to another VPC. As with all DNS endpoint architectures, a direct connection is required and can be either using the DX, Direct Connect, service or using a VPN connection. Outbound DNS queries require forwarding rules to define the domains hosted on-premise, and the rules define what will be forwarded to the on-premise resolver when a query is made in your VPC. Public and private hosted zone endpoints do not exist, and inbound is only for DNS resolutions originating outside of the VPC such as from another VPC or from your internal network.

20. A. The most common DNS record type is the A record, which maps a fully qualified domain name to an IPv4 address. The A records contain the domain name, the IP address, and the TTL value. The CNAME maps to another domain name, AAAA is used for IPv6 addressing, and an Alias record can map a zone apex domain to another domain.

Chapter 4: Load Balancing

1. B. This is a perfect solution for this e-commerce site. The network load balancer can handle the high connection count and throughput to meet the load during the flash sales. The classic load balancer is no longer available. While the application load balancer could be used here, the connection counts and throughput of the network load balancer would be a better solution in this case.

2. D. This is the exact use case the gateway load balancer was designed to address. The GLB sits inline to the customer's traffic flow, but the packets are not changed in any way, the traffic is passively processed with no packet modifications, and the ingress and egress packets are not changed in the process.

3. B. The X-Forwarded-For header records the source IP address of all the devices in the packet's path from source to destination. Even if this address gets modified, the header will show the original IP address. Geo-proximity would not prevent the IP modifications, SSL/TLS passthrough would not guarantee that the source IP was not changed in flight, and the use of an external load balancer would still change the source IP address as it would act as a proxy.

4. C. The application load balancer operates at layer 7 of the OSI model and can inspect the HTTP/HTTPS headers to determine the device type; rules can be applied to direct the request to the appropriate web servers. The other options given do not support this capability.

5. B. Load balancers that do not connect to the public Internet or have a public IP address attached are classified as internal load balancers. In this case, the LB sits internally between the application and database tiers and would use a private IP address, making it an internal load balancer.

6. D. This is a perfect solution for the AWS Web Application Firewall. The WAF can be placed in front of the ALB listener port to filter traffic and prevent attacks originating from the Internet.

7. D. Global Accelerator will redirect traffic from Europe off the Internet and onto the AWS private network, which has less network delays and increased performance for this deployment. Route 53 is a DNS service that would not reduce network delays, CloudTrail is an API repository, and the gateway load balancer would not have any effect on latency.

8. C. This is a case of the ALB client session moving from one server to another. If the shopping cart is running on a specific server for the user, then it could lose the user connection as it moves to another server. Session affinity will resolve this. The GENEVE protocol is used for packet transparency on a gateway load balancer and does not apply. The network load balancer would not support session affinity, and cross-zone load balancing would not change the LB routing to pin sessions to a single target.

9. A. The design calls for the use of a public-facing listener on a load balancer, which would classify it as being an external load balancer.

10. D. This is when you want to use connection draining to stop new sessions going to the server and allow existing connections to gracefully complete before taking down the server. There is no such thing as a slow stop, health checking will not perform a graceful shutdown, and deletion protection is used to stop anyone from deleting a complete load balancer.

11. D. TLS passthrough is the more traditional design for load balancers that do not process SSL/TLS traffic on port 443. The load balancer does not have any digital certificates locally installed and just passes all encrypted traffic to the backend servers for them to perform the encryption and decryption functions. In this case, the load balancer is not aware of and does not look into the encrypted traffic; it just load balances the connections to the servers in the defined target groups. Offload refers to the load balancer processing the encrypted traffic, GENEVE is a packet encapsulation protocol, and deregistration does not pertain to SSL/TLS.

12. A. Load balancer deletion protection prevents a load balancer from being deleted when this feature is enabled. Deletion protection is disabled by default, and it's a good practice to enable it. The only way to delete a load balancer when deletion protection is enabled is to disable the feature and then perform the deletion steps. Session affinity and deregistration are not deletion protection features, and forward proxy protection does not exist.

13. B. The proxy protocol header is a feature that inserts the original source IP address for the target servers and applications to reference. When enabled, a human-readable header is added to the request header that contains detailed connection information such as source and destination IP addresses and the application port number. This header is sent to the target instance as part of the request and is in a human-readable format. The proxy protocol works with the TCP protocol to identify the IP address of the clients to the backend servers. Session

affinity preserves connections to target group servers, the GENEVE protocol is a packet encapsulation technique, and TLS is an encryption protocol.

14. B. To prevent a new target from being overwhelmed with connection requests when it is first brought online, the slow start feature allows the server to gradually process new requests after the new target passes its health checking and comes online. This gives the server time to "warm up." The ELB will increase connection requests in a linear manner until the time window is met and the server is fully online. Session affinity is a sticky session feature. Offload is not a specific ELB feature, and connection limiting does not exist.

15. D. The ELB will send out periodic connection requests to each server and listen for a healthy response code to be returned from the server. If the server responds positively, then the ELB will forward connections to it. However, if the server does not respond, it will be taken out of the rotation and alarms generated for remediation. Kubernetes is a microservice, round-robin is a target group distribution type, and offload is used for SSL/TLS operations.

16. B, C. You can secure your public-facing listener and reduce the load by using CloudFront as a front-end service and restricting access to the ELB listener only to the CloudFront service. When using an application load balancer, you can take advantage of its layer 7 capabilities to have CloudFront insert custom HTTP header values before sending the request to an application load balancer. Then the ALB needs to be configured to only process requests that contain that header. This prevents users from bypassing CloudFront and going directly to the ALB. The Web Application Firewall can be placed in front of the ELB's listening interface for public Internet-facing deployments. The WAF can reduce the impact of denial-of-service attacks, allows you to define access filtering, and is a fully managed and monitored service from AWS. CloudTrail and CloudWatch are monitoring services from AWS.

17. A, B, D. When a target group is created, a target type must be defined and cannot be changed after creation. Target types include instance, IP, and lambda.

18. C, D. Depending on your design, you can configure either a round-robin or least outstanding request algorithm to distribute the load to the backend servers in a target group. Latency and affinity are not available load distribution selections.

19. B. With TLS offload, the load balancer takes responsibility for encrypting and decrypting in-flight traffic as it sits in the direct path of the traffic flow and is the listener interface that accepts all traffic form the outside. With the offload on the load balancer, the traffic can then be sent to the backend servers for processing without the need for those servers to perform any encryption functions. The other options presented do not specifically perform this function.

20. A. Autoscaling is an ELB feature that enables you to dynamically add and remove capacity based on your workload. This feature matches the compute servers offered to the current workload to save costs by using the compute service you need at any given point in time. If your server workload grows as the site becomes more heavily used, autoscaling can automatically add services to meet the workload. Later, when the load drops, those servers will be removed, saving you the cost of paying for unused capacity. Autostandby and autoredundancy are not valid AWS features, and target groups do not natively perform autoscaling functions.

Chapter 5: Logging and Monitoring

1. D. In this scenario, deploying X-Ray would show the application interactions between the microservices and any delays or performance issues in a graphical format. CloudTrail would show API configuration data but not necessarily accomplish what the development team needs. Flow Logs would provide packet capture data but not a complete graphical view that X-Ray offers. Config tells them the history of configuration changes but not performance data.

2. B. A baseline will document your operations under normal operational conditions and can be used to determine if current metrics exceed those values. This gives insight into your operations for troubleshooting and growth planning. Flow Logs can be used to create a baseline but is not a good end solution. The Reachability Analyzer tests connectivity paths but cannot provide the detailed services and application-level metrics that a baseline provides. Cloud-Trail documents API calls to AWS services but not performance data.

3. B. X-Ray Insights analyzes the data generated by the AWS X-Ray service, identifies anomalies, and generates notifications on what the anomaly is and why it was triggered. The service can be helpful in determining a root cause of a performance issue based on trace data generated by insights and provide data on its impact to your operations. X-Ray collects and displays the data, but the better answer would be X-Ray Insights as that is the application that analyzes the X-Ray data. Step Functions is a serverless function orchestrator that creates event-driven, checkpointed workflows. IAM securely controls access to AWS services.

4. B. Data collected from monitoring metrics and logs is used to understand your usage over time and to create a baseline. Baselines can help you understand what is considered a normal usage pattern. When the tracking data exceeds the baseline metrics, you will have visibility into what is out of range and work to resolve the issue or add capacity to meet an increasing workload. Cloud Map is a resource discovery service that is not used in trending analysis, X-Ray is a distributed application performance mapping service, and Route 53 is the AWS DNS service.

5. C. Dashboards allow for a single view of your operations and can present the data in graphical form of many different metrics such as performance, utilization, and errors. Cloud-Watch dashboards are fully customizable and are created based on your requirements. Dashboards are helpful in giving operations personnel a quick overview of the collected metrics of your services. AppFlow automates your data transfers, EventBridge is a serverless event bus that ingests data from your apps and AWS services and routes the data to targets. Cloud-Search is an AWS search index service.

6. B, C. When using the X-Ray SDK on any operating system, the local service does not export directly to the AWS X-Ray services but to a collector, which can be a Docker sidecar or run on a virtual server. The collector buffers the trace data from the clients and then uploads the data in its queue to the X-Ray service as a batch operation. X-Ray does not export to Cloud-Watch or CloudTrail.

7. B. Detailed monitoring measures metrics with a 1-minute interval, which improves the response time to create new containers over using the standard 5-minute window of standard monitoring. Fargate service quotas do not collect web connection counts. Detailed monitoring in Apache to X-Ray is not a valid configuration option.

8. C. The CloudWatch agent is code that can be installed on your Windows or Linux servers to collect data and forward it to the CloudWatch service. The agent is installed on your servers and runs in the background. The agents collect logs from EC2 instances and on-premises Linux and Windows servers. Once the agent is installed, internal system metrics are collected using the EC2 instance metrics and custom guest metrics. AWS Inspector does not provide the metrics requested in the question and, while custom detailed metrics is an option in the agent, the best answer is to install the agent on the remote servers. X-Ray is an application performance monitor that runs at the server level and not the remote gateway router.

9. B. The AWS Transit Gateway Manager is an AWS service used to manage and monitor your global network when using the Transit Gateway service to route your company WAN traffic over the AWS network. Transit Gateway Manager integrates with SD-WAN branch office devices and gives us network visibility across the AWS network and your private corporate-connected networks in a single dashboard. There is no such service as the Global Accelerator manager or CloudWatch for SD-WAN. Direct Connect is a WAN interconnect offering from AWS but is not a WAN network monitoring and management application.

10. C. CloudWatch is the AWS serverless monitoring service used to monitor and manage your AWS deployments. It plays a critical role in providing insights with a wide range of metrics including resource usage and errors that can be used to make sure your services are optimized and, if something should go wrong, generate alarms to trigger remediation steps to restore down or performance-impacted services. AppFlow automates your data transfers, EventBridge is a serverless event bus that ingests data from your apps and AWS services and routes the data to targets. CloudSearch is an AWS search index service.

11. A. X-Ray collects the trace data and generates a detailed service map of the correlated traces. The map displays a complete path from the client to the application and its backend services. Bottlenecks, latency graphing allows you to identify and resolve performance issues. Developers can use X-Ray to investigate their distributed applications and debug issues between microservices. The VPC Reachability Analyzer is useful for evaluating connectivity between servers and other services in the VPC but does not measure application performance. While CloudWatch allows you to collect and analyze metric data, in this scenario, X-Ray is the best solution.

12. C. CloudTrail records all API calls to AWS services, and the API data can tell us who made changes to any of your services. CloudMon and CloudTrace are not valid services, and CloudWatch does not record API calls to AWS service management.

13. C. Inspector can test routing in and out of your VPC and validates firewall rules. Open ports, also called *listeners*, are identified per IP address. These are then mapped back to the host, and its owner is identified. Inspector can act as an automated security assessment service by using test packages. Flow logging is a data capture service that can be used for analysis but does not include the requirements in the question, CloudTrail is an API logging service that tracks changes to your service configurations, and X-Ray is an application performance measuring tool and does not apply to this requirement.

14. B. The Transit Gateway Manager includes a graphical dashboard, utilization metrics, including packets and bytes sent and received, packet drops, and alerts. Global Accelerator is am Internet offload service that does not pertain to this question, CloudWatch for SD-WAN is not a valid service, and Direct Connect is used to interconnect AWS regions to your in-house data center and is not relevant to this question.

15. B. The VPC Reachability Analyzer provides a hop-by-hop analysis of the path a packet traverses given the source, destination port, and protocol information you define when you set up a trace test. If the test fails, the analyzer will identify where the data is being blocked to assist in troubleshooting. CloudFront logs are collected at the edge and not near a backend database. CloudTrail records configuration API calls and would not be helpful in troubleshooting the given issue. Metric Insights would be useful here, but the Reachability Analyzer is the most specific troubleshooting tool in this scenario.

16. A. Inspector can replace scanning utilities that are generally use-restricted by AWS in a VPC and perform vulnerability scans. Inspector automatically discovers endpoints and applications and performs a security vulnerably analysis on each device; based on its findings, a report is generated, and the vulnerability is tracked to resolution. Macie is a security-based service, Control Tower is an integrated dashboard, and X-Ray is a distributed application monitoring/troubleshooting tool.

17. C. When Flow Logs are created, there are certain traffic types that are not logged including DHCP-related traffic. IAM does not apply here since DHCP Flow Log captures are not supported, the Kinesis service does support Flow Log streams, and Flow Logs can capture intra-availability zone data flows.

18. A. Config is a service configuration tracking service; it records and stores a detailed record of how your services are configured, a log of changes over time. The service continuously runs in the background and captures all configuration changes to your AWS resources. Config is a valuable change management tracking tool. X-Ray, CloudWatch, and Inspector do not track configuration changes.

19. B. When Inspector discovers a network, host, or application vulnerability, a finding is created to report on the issue. Each finding includes a description of the vulnerability, logs the resource that the vulnerability was found on, applies a rating to how severe that vulnerability is, and even gives information on how to remediate and resolve the issue. X-Ray Insights is an application performance analysis tool, CloudWatch is a network management application, and Metric Insights do not scan for vulnerabilities.

20. B. AWS Config is a valuable change management tracking tool that provides a detailed record of all changes. The Config web console includes a query engine with preconfigured scripts that can be run and granular results returned. While Redshift could provide this information, it is not the best solution as this capability is included with AWS Config. EC2 analytics is not a service offering. While CloudTrail will log all API changes to EC2 instances, it does not include native query capabilities.

Chapter 6: Hybrid Networking

1. **B, C.** Both Direct Connect and site-to-site VPNs are viable options to connect your data center to an AWS region. PrivateLink and Global Accelerator are not designed for data center hybrid network interconnects.

2. **C.** The layer 2 frame format between the AWS interface and your DX interface must be VLAN tagged using the 801.1Q standard. Jumbo frame support, LACP, and bidirectional link detection are all optional.

3. **A, B, D.** High bandwidth of over 100 Gbps, BGP dynamic routing support, and low latency are all advantages of using a direct connection to AWS over the Internet. Edge access, global acceleration, and VxLAN support are not components of a Direct Connect architecture.

4. **B.** AWS business partners offer options where they supply the network hardware in the local collocation facility to interconnect to AWS. This eliminates the need for your company to install their own network gear locally at the DX location. The other options offered are not valid solutions.

5. **C.** Since the question is asking for the maximum speed available, the correct answer is to use LACP link aggregation groups on the highest speed interfaces available, which are the 100G interfaces. Using just one of the highest speed interfaces supported does not provide the maximum available throughput available when using LAGs. The other options either do not exist as is the case with VxLAN at the DX facility or with BGP, which does not increase the network throughput.

6. **B.** Creating an IPSec VPN through the DX link will provide the needed encryption over the wide-area network. There is no TLS option on DX links, encryption is not native to DX interfaces, but the link can be encrypted using IPSec VPNs. The CloudFront content distribution network is not part of Direct Connect and not an option in this scenario.

7. **D.** External BGP is designed to interconnect autonomous systems owned by different companies for the purpose of exchanging routing information. The Open Shortest Path First (OSPF), Intermediate System to Intermediate System (IS-IS), and Internal BGP routing protocols are only for internal routing and not designed to interconnect different organizations' networks.

8. **C.** A private virtual interface (VIF) is required to connect your data center to the VPC in an availability zone where your EC2 fleet resides. GRE and overlay networks are not supported in the AWS Direct Connect service. Public VIFs are for public services such as Route 53 and not private services such as VPC access.

9. **C.** The virtual private gateway terminates the customer site-to-site VPN tunnels. DX sites do not terminate the VPN session, the customer gateway is located at the customer's VPN location, and Global Accelerator is not a VPN solution.

10. C. For the router to forward a packet through the network, there must be an entry in the routing table instructing the router which interface to send the packet to its final destination. Either dynamic or static routes can work, but there must be a route in the table to reach the remote network. 802.1Q is a layer 2 protocol and does not apply to layer 3 routing.

11. A. In this scenario where complexity needs to be kept to a minimum and the network does not change, configuring static routes is a viable option. Using OSPF still entails a fair amount of complexity, and knowledge of how the protocol operates BGP is not mandatory in this case. No matter the number of subnets, if you need to forward packets from one network to another, then you are routing.

12. C. To connect two networks managed by different organizations, eBGP is required and it must have different and unique autonomous system numbers between the ASs. VLAN IDs are not assigned by AWS and are not part of routing. OSPF is an internal routing protocol and not used to exchange routes with AWS. IPSec and its encryption negotiation transforms are not part of any routing protocol.

13. B. BGP uses path metrics based on AS numbers to determine its default routing information. BGP route determination is not influenced by metrics such as speed, jitter, bandwidth, or reliability. The Bellman-Ford route calculation algorithm is used by another routing protocol and not BGP; there is no such thing as vector labels.

14. C. BGP-advertised outgoing traffic tells the remote network how to send traffic into the autonomous system. AS egress traffic flows are determined by the received routing information from the remote peer router. The MED is used to select outgoing interfaces but not the actual routes advertised by BGP to the remote AS. BGP metrics are used to determine outgoing traffic flows.

15. B. CloudHub allows you to use a single VPN connection from your location and access multiple VPCs in multiple regions. Route 53 can be used, but CloudHub is the preferred solution. BGP routing at the data center is suboptimal due to hairpinning the connections. PrivateLink is not used in site-to-site VPNs.

16. C. Internal BGP (iBGP) does not cross autonomous systems and uses only one AS number. OSPF uses areas and not autonomous systems. GRE and VxLAN are tunneling protocols that do not use autonomous systems.

17. C. By enabling jumbo frame support and using a frame size of 9,000 bytes, there will be less Ethernet frame overhead, fewer frames, and more link bandwidth available for user traffic. Spanning tree, LACP, and bidirectional forwarding do not apply in this scenario.

18. C. This is a primary use case for GRE since it allows multicast traffic to traverse the tunnels over a VPN network. Underlay networks do not apply. VxLANs ad GENEVE encapsulations will work but add a lot of complexity if all that is needed is transporting multicast traffic.

19. D. IPSec provides support to detect if a packet between the sender and receiver has been tampered with. BGP is a routing protocol and not security protocol; SSL and TLS provide encryption only.

20. A, F, G. Departmental segmentation, corporate accounting, and sharing company services between accounts are all common use cases for resource sharing in AWS. VPN backup is not related to account sharing. Resource sharing is not a requirement for serverless and Docker deployments.

Chapter 7: Connecting On-Premises Networks

1. A, D. The two primary methods of creating a hybrid interconnection are to use either a site-to-site VPN or a direct connection, or a combination of the two. Kinesis streaming is not a workable solution for data center interconnections, regional interconnects is not a service offered by AWS, and VPC peering is internal to AWS and does not extend to private data centers.

2. D. The AWS shared responsibility model outlines what AWS takes responsibility for securing and what is the customer's responsibility. Macie is a security service but not a framework; the Well-Architected Framework documentation is valuable in the case but not the best answer. IPSec is an encryption protocol but does not apply to the question. There is no actual AWS security framework service.

3. D. Software-defined networking uses controllers as a central control plane function and communicates with the forwarding plane devices using APIs. Routing, CloudHub, API Gateway, and Control Tower are not software-defined networking controllers.

4. B. PrivateLink is an AWS service that creates a direct connection from your VPC to internal AWS services and bypasses sending traffic over the Internet. CloudHub, Direct Connect, Control Tower, and App Mesh are all valid AWS services but do not serve the function that PrivateLink does.

5. A. The ICMP `ping` utility is present on all modern operating systems and is used to test remote node reachability. `traceroute` will also verify reachability; however, `ping` is the most commonly used utility for reachability testing. The Route Analyzer and Reachability Analyzer are not operating system utilities, and `nslookup` is for checking DNS resolution.

6. A, C, E. VPN security management includes IAM restrictions; collecting, analyzing, and archiving CloudTrail logs; and not exposing VPN configuration information in tags.

7. C. Layer 2 switches forward traffic based on the frame's MAC address. Routers forward on layer 3 addresses. Gateways translate between protocols and load balancers use layer 3–7 data.

8. A, D. The SDN architecture abstracts the control plane and separates it from the underlying forwarding plane. There is no such thing as application or security planes in SDN, and the route tables are part of the control plane.

9. C. A letter of authorization document must be filled out when registering for the DX service. BGP is the routing protocol used, and OSPF is not supported. Single-mode fiber is used, not multimode, and there is no such thing as a peering agreement. CloudFront is not part of Direct Connect.

10. A. A router examines layer 3 destination IP addresses to make forwarding decisions. Layer 2 switches forward traffic based on the frame's MAC address. Gateways translate between protocols, and load balancers use layer 3–7 data.

11. B. `traceroute` will display the network path taken from your laptop to the destination and, if it is being dropped, show where the path stops. Reachability Analyzer and Route Analyzer cannot test from the client, CloudTrail tracks API calls in AWS, and `ping` can test end-to-end reachability, but it does not provide information on where the drops may be occurring.

12. A. Using the Global Accelerator feature of an accelerated site-to-site VPN will allow your traffic to traverse the private AWS backbone network and bypass the congestion of the public Internet. CloudHub is not a solution for this use case. There is no service called data center peering, and CloudHSM is a security feature.

13. C. AWS uses SFP transceivers to terminate cross-connects. LC and SC transceivers are not supported. Long-range (LR) optics are used instead of short range, and single-mode fiber is required, not multimode.

14. D. `traceroute` displays the network path taken from source to destination and will show where on the path the route is failing. Route Analyzer, Shield, and Detective are AWS services that would not provide path impairment information. `ping` validates reachability but does not display where the connection drops.

15. D. Software-defined networking uses Northbound and Southbound API calls to communicate configuration information between the underlying hardware forwarding plane's southbound and application's northbound traffic. Transit Gateway, CloudHub, API Gateway, and Control Tower do not apply to this question.

16. B. Gateways translate between protocols; a router examines layer 3 destination IP addresses to make forwarding decisions; layer 2 switches forward traffic based on the frame's MAC address; and load balancers use layer 3–7 data.

17. C. The Transit Gateway is a centralized AWS regional virtual router that interconnects VPCs to on-premises facilities. API Gateway, SDN, Route 53, and CloudMap do not meet the requirements given in the question.

18. D. The AWS Route Analyzer is used to investigate routing issues in your Transit Gateway router. `traceroute` will display the network path taken from your laptop to the destination but is not an AWS utility. CloudTrail tracks API calls in AWS, and the Reachability Analyzer can be used but the Reachability Analyzer is specific to the Transit Gateway service. Cloud-Watch is an AWS monitoring and management service.

19. A. The Resource Access Manager is used to simplify management, reduce overhead, and increase security by sharing resources between AWS accounts. CloudHub is a hub-and-spoke VPN offering from AWS, CloudMap is a resource discovery service, AppFlow is used to transfer data between SaaS applications, and CloudShell is a web-based CLI tool in the AWS console.

20. B, D, E. The `traceroute` utility displays the responding node, hop count, and round-trip time (RTT). AS path and jitter are not recorded or displayed.

Chapter 8: Inter-VPC and Multi-account Networking

1. C. An SAML 2.0 identity provider can grant your developers federated access to the management console using single sign-on. VPC peering is a way to connect one VPC to another but does not address user access permissions. There is no authorization account permissions table to modify, and network ACLs do not address account access rights.

2. A. Organizations is the service that would provide her with the account management operations that she is looking for. Cognito is used for federated access using external provider accounts, and AWS authentication is not a valid service. Macie is a sensitive data discovery tool, and Secrets Manager is used to securely store passwords.

3. C. You can create a resource in one account and use the Resource Access Manager to make that resource usable in multiple other AWS accounts. This limits the duplication of resources in different accounts by sharing them. There is no such thing as Multiple Private Link Services. The AD connector and SAML are used for authentication services but do not enable VPC access between accounts. The Transit Gateway does interconnect VPCs but is not a management tool like the Resource Access Manager that is being requested in this question.

4. D. An SD-WAN is an automated, programmable wide-area network framework that can dynamically and securely route traffic based on network conditions, policies, or the priority of WAN circuits. Routing protocols such as OSPF and BGP determine reachability but do not inherently offer quality-of-service tools that are asked for in the question. While MPLS has QoS capabilities, it is not a single automated configuration application. CloudWatch is a monitoring utility and not a tool that would work for the SD-WAN requirement as is the case in this question.

5. A. Organizational units (OUs) are used to group accounts together in the AWS Organizations service. The AWS Simple Directory Service is a user account database that is not part of AWS Organizations. Workflow services chain services together to create a flow and do not pertain to the question. The CloudHSM is an AWS certificate store offering that does not apply to the question being asked.

6. B. VPC sharing gives AWS users the ability to share IP subnets with other AWS accounts in the same AWS organization. This gives us centralized control over routing, IP addressing, the sharing of security groups, larger and higher-density VPCs, less duplication of resources such as NAT gateways, endpoints, and cross-AZ traffic, while allowing the application owners to continue to manage their own resources, security, and account structure. Cloud Connect is not a valid AWS service. Direct Connect and site-to-site VPNs are used to interconnect private enterprise resources to the AWS cloud, not to interconnect two VPCs as is the case in this question.

7. A. SCPs are created to define and enforce what actions IAM users, groups, and roles can perform or are blocked from performing in the accounts in your AWS Organizations service. In this case, an SCP would be created and applied that blocks all accounts from creating any Redshift services. IAM could be used here, but the question is asking for a globally assigned policy at the root, which is what an SCP is. There is no such label service policy. Active Directory is not useful in this case as the question asks for the functions provided by SCPs.

8. C. The Transit Gateway attachment creates an interconnection from a Transit Gateway instance to SD-WAN services. The Transit VPC creates a global network transit hub that interconnects geographically separated remote networks and your VPCs. VPC peering interconnects VPCs but not external carrier-based networking services. Kinesis data pipeline is a streaming service that does not apply to the question. CloudFront is the AWS content distribution network and does not apply to the question being asked.

9. D. PrivateLink does not allow private VPC traffic to exit the AWS network and travel into the Internet. Instead, PrivateLink connects your private VPC subnets directly inside of the AWS network to select AWS services and allows you to use AWS security tools to control access to services running in your VPCs. Both CloudWatch and CloudTrail are monitoring and management offerings from AWS and do not apply to the question. Direct Connect is for connecting hybrid networks from external networks into AWS VPCs.

10. A. Authorization determines what the identity is allowed to do and what it is restricted from doing. Cognito is used for federated access using external provider accounts. Authentication determines who the user is. Step Functions is workflow service used by developers.

11. B. The key components of an MPLS network are the LER that performs the classification and assigns the label. LSRs are core routers in the network that switch packets based on the assigned MPLS label. Each router has the LIB that maps incoming MPLS packets to outgoing interfaces. The end-to-end connection is the LSP. There is a common protocol used called LDP that communicates label information between MPLS-speaking neighbors to establish the LSP.

12. A, C. VPCs can be shared between accounts with AWS Organizations and the Resource Access Manager. MPLS is a carrier WAN technology that does not apply to the question. Kinesis Firehose is an AWS real-time data streaming service, and Route 53 is the AWS DNS service and does not apply to the question.

13. B. The AD trust, or trust relationship, acts as a logical relationship established between Active Directory domains that allow authentication and authorization to shared services and resources. The Flexible Single Master Operation (FSMO) role in Active Directory is where critical updates are performed by the designated domain controller with a specific role and then it gets replicated to all the other DCs. These roles are assigned by the AD administrator to perform these tasks. You can also implement read-only domain controllers (RODCs). The read-only domain controllers hold a copy of the AD database and are used to respond to authentication requests, but applications or other servers cannot write to them.

14. D. Authorization determines what the identity is allowed to do and what it is restricted from doing. RDS is the AWS database service being accessed; however, the question asked how the rights are assigned to access the SQL server in RDS. Authentication determines who the user is. Elastic Beanstalk is an application deployment offering.

15. A. The Transit Gateway is a virtual cloud routing services offering from AWS. The Transit Gateway is a regional service that is scalable and highly available and enables VPCs and on-premises networks to connect through a central hub over either site-to-site VPNs or Direct Connect. The hub-and-spoke design allows any services connected to the gateway to talk to each other; this allows VPC-to-VPC routing in a region. The advantage of using a Transit Gateway is that only one connection needs to be made when adding new VPCs. The hub-and-spoke option describes an architecture and not a specific service asked for in the question. MPLS is a wide-area networking technology. The AD connector connects two Active Directory services, and the Global Accelerator is used to route traffic over the AWS global backbone instead of using the Internet for improved performance.

16. B. SD-WAN traffic is automatically and dynamically forwarded over the WAN path based on network conditions and defined policies such as application QoS requirements, security, circuit costs, or any other defined criteria. SD-WAN offers load balancing, congestion management, and forwarding over the lowest-cost paths. SD-WAN automates the operation of a WAN by decoupling the networking hardware from its control mechanisms. MPLS, EIGRP, IS-IS, and BPDUs are all networking protocol for layer 2 and layer 3 forwarding of network traffic but do not have the capabilities asked for in the question.

17. C. The user authentication process determines identity; based on the identity, access rights are assigned. The Simple Workflow Service chains services together but is not an identity service. Cognito is used for federated access using external provider accounts. Organizational units are logical groupings of objects and do not have any relation to what the question is asking.

18. A. SAML allows users to authenticate with the identity provider one time using a single set of credentials; they then get access to multiple applications and services without any additional sign-ins. SAML-enabled applications delegate authentication to an external identity provider (IdP) and AWS can automatically grant, revoke, or change user's access to applications and services when an administrator adds, removes, or modifies the user's information in the IdP. LDAP is directory access protocol, and KMS is an AWS Key Management Service that is used to store digital certificates. IAM is not an identity service provider.

19. A. Simple AD is a low-cost, lightweight directory service that would meet the requirements in the question. The AD trust relationship acts as a logical relationship established between Active Directory domains. The Flexible Single Master Operation role in Active Directory is where critical updates are performed. Read-only domain controllers hold a copy of the AD database and are used to respond to authentication requests, but applications or other servers cannot write to them.

20. D. Traffic crossing a VPC peering connection can connect to services and applications in each other's VPCs. However, traffic cannot transit from the DEV VPC to the PROD VPC through the TEST VPC. There is a nontransitive issue in the TEST VPC. All the other options do not apply.

Chapter 9: Hybrid Network Routing and Connectivity

1. B. You must use a routing protocol that is designed specifically to interconnect different accounts or autonomous systems together. The industry-standard routing protocol that is used in AWS hybrid networks is the Border Gateway Protocol (BGP). This is the protocol used to exchange network reachability information between your on-premises network and the Amazon cloud, which is typically to a VPC. While static routes may be a solution, the question asks for a dynamic routing protocol. OSPF is not supported by AWS and not used to interconnect customer networks; route propagation and the AWS route table are not valid solutions or actual routing protocols.

2. B. Static routes let you override dynamic routes to forward traffic to the best possible destination. Route propagation does not allow you to determine whether the route traffic is forwarded; iBGP, PrivateLink, and App Mesh are not static methods of routing.

3. B, C, D. Route 53 routing options, content distribution networks such as CloudFront, and the AWS Global Accelerator are all methods available to optimize routing in the AWS network. Elastic Beanstalk is for application deployments, and CloudTrail logs API calls to the console and will not optimize any network operations. The Web Application Firewall is a security service that does not modify the route tables.

4. B. Using a static route to back up a dynamic route by assigning a higher administrative distance is referred to as a floating static route. Should the eBGP route go away, then the static route may have the lowest administrative distance and be installed in the route forwarding. BGP can install a backup route if the primary route goes down. CloudFront and VPGs do not have this capability. You cannot assign more than one route table to a subnet in a VPC.

5. E. Route summarization combines multiple contiguous subnets into a larger CIDR clock to reduce the number of prefixes in the routing table and will resolve the issue. Standby BGP peering is not a valid configuration. Static routes do not necessarily reduce the route table entries unless summarization is configured on the statics. Replacing the DX connection with a VPN will not resolve the issue. iBGP is used internally to an organization or autonomous system and not to interconnect with AWS.

6. A, C, E. Dynamic and static route entries are used to populate the route tables. Route propagation is the process of advertising network reachability information between routers. In BGP, you will advertise your networks to the peer by using route propagation in different autonomous systems. In AWS, BGP route propagation is used to control the flow of traffic between your VPC and your on-premises data centers, or other VPCs in your AWS accounts. CloudFront and Route 53 do not populate or modify route tables.

7. B, D. Routing cannot occur between overlapping subnets in different VPCs. By implementing NAT or readdressing one VPC CIDR block, routing will work properly. Static or BGP routing or route propagation will not resolve the issue.

8. C. Peering is a BGP management connection between two BGP speaking routers for use in exchanging routing information. The BGP peering connection allows you to exchange routing information and advertise your on-premises network prefixes into the AWS VPC and for the VPC to communicate its IP network prefixes into your internal network. This dynamic routing interaction enables you to create a seamless network connection between the on-premises network infrastructure and your AWS hosted resources. Route propagation is not a dynamic routing protocol. Autonomous system border routers (ASBRs) are part of the OSPF routing protocol and not applicable to this use case. To interconnect two different organizations, or autonomous systems, an external Border Gateway Protocol router is required; iBGP is internal BGP routing in an organization.

9. B. The transit virtual interface allows you to connect your on-premises data center to multiple VPCs in the same AWS region using a single virtual interface. This allows you to create a hub-and-spoke network architecture where all VPCs connect to a central hub. PrivateLink and VPC peering cannot be used to directly connect an external network such as a data center. Using an ALB as a front end to an external data center is not valid for this application.

10. B, C, E. When configuring a virtual interface, you must specify the bandwidth, the BGP ASN, the VLAN ID, and the IP prefixes that you want to advertise over the connection. BGP peers do not use domain names, and VxLAN endpoints are not used at the DX interconnect.

11. B. Site-to-site VPNs are created using encrypted tunnels over the Internet from your on-premises network to a VPC in an AWS region using the IPSec protocol suite to encrypt the in-flight traffic. Since the VPN traverses the Internet, there is no requirement to install a dedicated circuit and the potential implementation delays. CloudFront is a content distribution network and is not used to connect your networks to a VPC. Direct Connect requires a carrier circuit and does not natively encrypt traffic. BGP peering is not a physical interconnection method, and CloudHub does not directly address the connection type asked about in the question.

12. A. App Mesh service is a fully managed AWS service mesh for Amazon Elastic Container Service (ECS) and Kubernetes that provides a consistent way to manage and secure microservices. It is useful when you need to control and monitor communication between your applications. App Mesh also enables you to troubleshoot and improve the performance of your AWS microservices. SageMaker is a machine learning tool, Elastic Beanstalk is used to automate application deployments, and ECS is a microservices AWS offering but does not address the use case in the question.

13. D. AWS services like VPCs, Elastic IPs, Direct Connect, Route 53, Transit Gateway, and App Mesh can be used in conjunction with AWS Organizations, enabling the sharing of resources across the member accounts and allow for the increase of limits and quotas. AWS Support can be contacted to increase quota limits; however, that is not what this question is asking. The quota dashboard tracks your quota values but does not natively enable the resource-sharing the organization provides to maximize the use of your services.

14. B, D. AWS networking services have limits and quotas that can affect their usage and performance. It's important to be aware of these limits to plan your network resources accordingly so they are not exceeded. If you hit any limits, you can request a service increase by contacting AWS Support. The service quota dashboard and CloudWatch console can be

used to track usage. CloudTrail does not track usage, Macie is a security service, and the license manager is not used for tracking service quotas.

15. C. AWS places limits on the number of VPCs, subnets, and security groups that you can create per region. There are also limits applied to the number of Elastic IPs and NAT gateways that can be allocated per VPC, as well as the number of IPs per subnet. There is a default of five VPCs per region. However, this can be increased to hundreds by opening a ticket with AWS Support and requesting an increase. Creating VPCs in another region will work but does not meet the requirements in this question. There is no such VPC override option in CloudFormation. Elastic Beanstalk and AWS Config do not modify VPC quotas.

16. B. The administrative distance applies a priority value to a prefix in the routing table relative to other routing protocols that may be running on the router. Direct Connect routes are preferred over site-to-site VPN routes. So, if the eBGP routes have a lower administrative distance of 200, they would take priority of this static with a higher administrative distance of 250. Using a static route to back up a dynamic route by assigning a higher administrative distance is referred to as a floating static route. Should the eBGP route go away, then the static may have the lowest administrative distance and be installed in the route forwarding table. AWS Config and Route 53 will not modify the route forwarding table, and BGP would need to be running over the VPN connection for option C to be valid.

17. A. AWS services are either private or public. Private services reside inside your VPC, and you control access to them by using access lists and security groups, by using IAM, or by implementing many of the security services offered by AWS and external service providers in the marketplace. Public AWS services are reachable externally from your VPC and generally open to the world to access. Private access to public services includes VPC endpoints that are secure private connections that do not require your traffic to traverse the Internet to access the public service. VPC endpoints are used to privately access services over an Amazon VPC without requiring a NAT gateway, VPN, or Direct Connect connection. The other options offered do not allow for private to public service access.

18. E. AWS PrivateLink does not expose your data to the public Internet by creating a secure and private connection internal to AWS. PrivateLink meets many security, compliance, and data privacy requirements. PrivateLink allows outside accounts to share AWS resources with their customers. Using private IP addressing adds to the security and compliance and prevents exposing your data to the public Internet. It also provides a way to control access to the service by implementing endpoint policies. Global Accelerator is for Internet offload onto the AWS network and does not apply to this question. VPC peering and AWS Organizations will work but are not the best solutions for this use case. There is no such service as CloudTrail interconnections.

19. C. VPC peering is an interconnect used to allow two or more VPCs to access resources in each VPC from the other allowing resources in either VPC to communicate with each other as if they were in the same network. The AWS peering service has no bandwidth limitations, and there is no single failure point; it does not rely on gateways, Direct Connect, or VPN interconnections. CloudFront and CloudWatch do not enable networking between VPCs, and Direct Connect is used for hybrid access.

20. B, C, D. Interconnecting your VPCs residing in different regions is referred to as inter-regional communications. The default method is to send your traffic across the public Internet. Since there are no bandwidth, delay, or quality of service guarantees using this approach, other methods are available that may be better suited to your requirements. A site-to-site VPN connection can be established over the Internet to add encryption for secure communications. Another option is to implement a Direct Connect between regions that allows traffic to be sent over a private high-bandwidth, low-latency, and secure, dedicated connection that bypasses the Internet. Macie and IAM are not networking services.

Chapter 10: Network Automation

1. A. Automation abstracts the physical network infrastructure into software that describes the deployments. Automation can be used to automatically configure, provision, manage, and test network devices. It improves efficiency, reduces human error, and can lower your operating expenses. Hypervisors are a less specific answer. The AWS services of CloudTrail and Control Tower do not directly perform automation functions. Deployment Bridge is not a valid AWS service.

2. C. IaC creates code that defines the desired configuration you want to deploy. IaC enables you to automate the provisioning and modifications of your cloud infrastructure. Resource Access Manager is used to create resources centrally and share them to benefit from a simplified resource management experience in a multi-account environment. Aurora PostgreSQL is Amazon's enterprise-class PostgreSQL-compatible database. Code Guru evaluates and recommends application improvements for performance, efficiency, and code quality for Java and Python applications. LightSail is packaged deployment service and not a design function.

3. C, D. When creating resources using CloudFormation, you can use either JSON or YAML to define the infrastructure resources in files called templates. XML, Java, and Python 3 are not used in CloudFormation definitions.

4. D. EventBridge delivers a stream of real-time data from your applications, SaaS applications, and AWS services to targets such as AWS Lambda functions, HTTP invocation endpoints using API destinations, or event buses in other AWS accounts. AWS Macie is a security service that uses machine learning and pattern matching to discover and protect sensitive data. CloudTrail tracks console activity and API usage, and CodeStar is a cloud-based development service that provides the tools you need to quickly develop, build, and deploy applications on AWS.

5. A. The AWS CLI enables you to manage AWS resources from the command line instead of the web GUI interface or SDKs. Bash and PowerShell are Linux and Microsoft command parsers and do not belong to Amazon. An API is an interface into AWS and not a management tool.

6. C. The AWS Cloud Development Kit (CDK) is an open-source tool that enables developers to create a cloud infrastructure as a set of reusable code packaged into libraries that can be shared in your organization or published to the AWS CloudFormation registry for public access. AWS CodeStar enables you to develop, build, and deploy applications on AWS and is not an infrastructure as code service. QuickSight is a business analytics and visualization tool. AWS Config creates resource inventory, configuration history, and configuration change notifications for security and governance. Code Guru evaluates and recommends application improvements for performance, efficiency, and code quality for Java and Python applications.

7. D. The AWS Cloud Development Kit (CDK) is an open-source tool that enables developers to create a cloud infrastructure as a set of reusable code called *constructs*. These constructs are packaged into libraries and can be shared in your organization or published to the AWS CloudFormation registry for public access. Amazon IQ connects users with AWS Certified freelancers and AWS partners. AWS Config creates a resource inventory, configuration history, and configuration change notifications for security and governance. AppSync uses the GraphQL data language to enable client apps to fetch, change, and subscribe to data from servers. App Runner is a service that makes it easy for developers to deploy from source code or container images directly.

8. B, C, D. Puppet, Chef, and Ansible are open-source automation tools. SolarWinds and DNA Center are commercial. Config and SNMP are not IaC products.

9. A, D, E. Implementing IaC is a key factor in achieving automation tasks such as network configuration, scaling, and monitoring. Security scans are not permitted by AWS without prior consent and should not be automated.

10. B. The Secrets Manager service stores configuration information such as database passwords, API keys, or TLS certificates that are needed by an application at runtime. Secrets Manager removes sensitive and unique configuration data from your templates and stores them in a secure repository. Cognito is an AWS user authentication and authorization service, DynamoDB is the AWS NoSQL database offering, Config tracks AWS configuration changes, and Simple Workflow Service is for coordinating application interactions.

11. A. The AWS Software Development Kit is an AWS-provided software tool used for building applications that interact with AWS services. By providing simple APIs, authentication and security, error handling, resource management, and performance optimization, the SDK enables developers to build application integrations with AWS services that are reliable and efficient. The CDK is used for IaC deployments and not for application integrations; the CLI does not contain the feature sets of the SDK, and APIs are a software interface and not a development kit.

12. B. IaC defines resources in code making it easier to ensure that configurations are consistently deployed the same way every time. IaC relies on creating code that defines the desired configuration you want to deploy. CodePipeline is an AWS developer's tool, Kubernetes is a microservice management tool, REST is an API protocol, and event-driven automation is a category of using network-based automation.

13. B. The AWS application programming interfaces (APIs) are a set of tools, documentation, and protocols used by developers to interact with all AWS services programmatically. When using the web interface, the CLI, or the SDK to interact with AWS, underneath the interfaces is an API that is used to communicate with AWS. AWS APIs provide a standardized interface for accessing all AWS services, allowing developers to build applications that use AWS

services without requiring direct access to the underlying infrastructure. The CDK, SDK, and CloudFormation tools do not directly access the underlying AWS architecture.

14. B. EventBridge Pipes connects an event source to a target and enables you to filter or add content. The EventBridge Scheduler is similar to Linux cron operations that invoke a target one time or at defined intervals. Config is an AWS configuration tracking service, and SQS is a pull-based queue for interconnecting distributed applications. APIs do not fit this use case and are not a configuration management tool.

15. B. The CDK enables developers to create a cloud infrastructure as a set of reusable code called constructs. These constructs are packaged into libraries and can be shared in your organization or published to the AWS CloudFormation registry for public access. The CDK comes with a complete library of reusable AWS constructs to simplify the creation and management of commonly used infrastructure resources. AWS Step Functions is a serverless function orchestrator used to sequence AWS Lambda functions and multiple AWS services into business-critical applications. Stack sets are used in CloudFormation to extend the capability of stacks by enabling you to create, update, or delete stacks across multiple accounts and AWS regions with a single operation. APIs are a set of tools, documentation, and protocols used by developers to interact with all AWS services programmatically.

16. B. The CDK includes integrated development environment (IDE) support with common IDEs, such as Visual Studio Code, IntelliJ, and PyCharm, that provide many features such as code highlighting, autocompletion, and error checking. The AWS Control Tower service enables you to enforce and manage governance rules for security, operations, and compliance. CloudFormation, Code Guru, and AWS Config are not CDK enhancements.

17. A. APIs are used for all AWS automation services and allow third-party applications and services to be integrated with AWS. APIs are front-end portals used to configure, monitor, and troubleshoot AWS resources. The APIs provide standardized access to detailed metrics and logging information, making it easy to monitor and troubleshoot AWS resources. Macie is a security service, RDS is a database service, Outposts is a remote on-premise compute service, and IAM is for Identity and Access Management, none of which are relevant to the question.

18. D. The AWS SDK is an AWS-provided software tool used for building applications that interact with AWS services. By providing simple APIs, authentication and security, error handling, resource management, and performance optimization, the SDK enables developers to build application integrations with AWS services that are reliable and efficient. The SDK provides libraries for the multiple programming languages, including C++, Go, Java, .NET, Ruby, Python, Java, JavaScript, Kotlin, .NET, Node.js, Rust, Swift, and PHP that allow developers to integrate AWS services into their applications. Redshift is a data warehouse service, and AWS Control Tower orchestrates multiple AWS services on your behalf while maintaining the security and compliance needs of your organization. SQS decouples services using queuing, and SWF is a workflow tool for application integration.

19. A, B, C, F. SolarWinds, DNA Center, NSX, and SaltStack are commercial automation tools. Puppet, Chef, and Ansible are open-source automation tools.

20. D. The AWS open-source CDK includes integration with common IDEs such as Visual Studio, IntelliJ, and PyCharm. Git Hybrid does not exist, RDS and DynamoDB are AWS database services, and ECS is the Amazon container service and not a development toolkit.

Chapter 11: Monitor, Analyze, and Optimize Network Traffic

1. A. Enhanced networking on EC2 would support the high throughput with low latency and jitter requirements of the application. Lambda would not have the performance requirements needed. Most video and voice transmissions use smaller frame sizes. Teaming interfaces would not be better than using enhanced networking.

2. D. The key factor is that the HPC deployment will be in a cluster. The Elastic Fabric Adapter (EFA) network interface provides ultra-low latency and high-bandwidth communication between instances in a cluster. The Elastic Network Adapter (ENA) network interface meets the requirements of high-performance computing (HPC), and the EFA is intended for use in clustering designs.

3. B. Flow Logs capture metadata about the IP traffic going to and from network interfaces in your VPC and capture information about the source and destination of the traffic, the protocol used, and the number of bytes transferred. CloudTrail logs API calls to AWS services and would not apply here, CloudWatch Metrics does not include network Flow Logs, and Wireshark is used for deep packet inspection and not for collecting metadata.

4. D. The key to answering this question is that it is asking for deep packet inspection. Of the answers given, only the Wireshark network analyzer offers this capability.

5. B. The Reachability Analyzer is a network diagnostic tool provided by AWS for testing and troubleshooting network connectivity issues in your VPC. It uses a combination of traceroute and network probing to identify potential connectivity issues and help pinpoint the source of the problem. Use the Reachability Analyzer to identify the resources that are having connectivity issues and the source and destination of the traffic. The App Mesh service monitors and controls microservices, Step Functions is a serverless orchestrator. CloudTrail records API calls and is not a network tracing tool. The Application Discovery Service determines application dependencies and not connectivity.

6. D. Route 53 can automatically route traffic to a healthy resource in the event of a failure. This can help to minimize downtime and improve the availability of your applications. All the other services listed including CloudFront, CloudTrail, CloudWatch, and WAF do not provide networking failover capabilities.

7. B. The Network Firewall can be used to monitor and analyze traffic, and security rules can be configured to allow or block traffic that you define based on IP addresses, ports, protocols, and other values. GuardDuty is an AWS threat detection service that does not offer packet filtering. Viptella is a commercial SD-WAN product, CloudFront provides content distribution but not firewall services, and Identity and Access Manager controls access to your AWS resources.

8. A, C. Since this is a new installation that is unreachable, the routing table should be checked to see if your network's forwarding table has the prefix information to reach the new region. You should also verify that the CIDR address block is not in use elsewhere in your network.

MTU size would not affect reachability, Redshift does not have a remote access enable option, and the fabric adapter type would not affect the ability of routing in the Transit Gateway.

9. D. CloudWatch is the AWS monitoring and observability service that collects and displays metrics and logs from your AWS resources such as EC2 instances, DynamoDB, Lambda, RDS databases, elastic load balancers, and all other services. CloudTrail records API calls to AWS, Athena is a database service, there is no product called Amazon Syslog, and Systems Manager is an Amazon management tool and dashboard.

10. D. For public-facing resources, use public subnets. Place resources that need to be publicly accessible, such as web servers and load balancers, in the public subnets. This allows them to communicate with the Internet and other resources in your VPC. Implement elastic IP addresses (EIPs) which are public IP addresses that you can assign to the Elastic Network Interface. This question concerns the assignment of a publicly reachable IP address so the adapter type used would not be relevant to the question. Also, the 10.x.x.x address block is an RFC 1918 private address that is not reachable from the Internet.

11. A. The DNS load balancing feature of Route 53 distributes incoming traffic across multiple resources. By using a weighted policy, you can direct a subset of connections to the test servers to perform the canary test. Round-robin, latency, and geolocation policies would not fit the testing requirements of the question. Using a firewall for network redirects is not a feature found in most firewalls.

12. C. Block storage transfers would benefit from the low overhead of a large packet size. Storage frames are usually at the maximum MTU available for the network so enabling jumbo frames in your VPC would optimize file transfer performance. Load balancing, enabling quality of service, changing the subnet size, and mirroring of the traffic would have no effect on data transfer rates.

13. C. Since the existing VPC is running out of IP address space, the best option given is to create a new VPC with the new address block and use VPC peering to connect them together. You can also take advantage of the network access control to address the team's security requirements. CloudFront, load balancing, SWF, and Config do not configure VPC address blocks.

14. C. Route 53 latency-based routing directs traffic to the resource that has the lowest latency from the user's location. This improves the hosted application's performance and reduces the time it takes to load the website. CloudTrail records AWS API calls, and the Global Accelerator may improve the latency but is not the best solution. Elastic Load Balancer implementations would not be the best solution as you have already distributed the web servers globally. AWS Step Functions is a serverless orchestration tool that does not apply to the question.

15. B. Transit Gateway allows you to peer VPCs across regional boundaries and acts as a centralized networking hub for your operations. Standard VPC peering is available in a single region, CloudFront does not interconnect VPCs, and Elastic Beanstalk does not fit what the question is asking for.

16. A, B, E. Data compression can be implemented to reduce the amount of data that needs to be transferred between servers and clients to reduce network utilization. AWS offers several compression options, including Gzip compression for HTTP requests, S3 Select compression, and Amazon Redshift compression. Elastic Map Reduce is a big data Hadoop service, and Data Pipeline is a workflow orchestrator.

17. A. The AWS Transit Gateway Network Manager tool provides a centralized view of your network topology, which can help you visualize the connections between your network components. Wireshark does not generate network diagrams, and Tableau can generate graphical representations but does not support automated network discovery. Control Tower and CloudWatch do not generate network diagrams either.

18. D. Use VPC Flow Logs to test and monitor your network from end to end to ensure that it is functioning correctly. This includes reviewing Flow Logs to ensure that the larger frame sizes are being transmitted end to end correctly. Control Tower, OpsWorks, and CloudTrail are not packet analysis tools.

19. B, C, D. If you need to increase your VPC address space, you have several options to consider including creating additional subnets, resizing your existing subnets, or adding secondary CIDR blocks. You can create new subnets and allocate new IP address ranges that will be sufficient to meet your expected growth. Another method is to resize your existing subnets to provide more addresses, to expand the subnet size to a larger CIDR block. Another option is to use a secondary CIDR block. This adds a new IP address block to your VPC. You can also add a new VPC and use peering to interconnect the existing VPC.

20. A. The Elastic Network Interface (ENI) is a virtual network interface that attaches to EC2 instances in your VPCs. The ENI offers basic networking capabilities, such as connecting to the Internet and other instances within the VPC. The ENI is the most common and cost-effective interface. The Elastic Fabric Adapter (EFA) network interface provides ultra-low latency and high-bandwidth communication between instances in a cluster and would not run on this low-end instance type. The Elastic Network Adapter (ENA) is a high-performance network interface, which offers up to 100 Gbps of network throughput and meets the requirements of high-performance computing and big data applications and would not support this instance type and would not be as cost-effective as the basic ENI. A network load balancer and Global Accelerator are not network interfaces.

Chapter 12: Security, Compliance and Governance

1. C, E. CloudWatch Logs enables you to monitor logs in real time and trigger alerts when certain patterns or events are detected. CloudTrail captures API activity across your AWS accounts, including the AWS Management Console, SDKs, and command-line tools. CloudWatch Insights can be used to query and analyze log data. GuardDuty is a threat detection service that monitors malicious activity and unauthorized behavior in your environment. Lambda is a serverless compute offering that can run applications to monitor logs and generate alarms based on configured conditions.

2. B, D. The microservices architecture is where the application is broken down into smaller, discrete components that interact with each other often using API calls. The microservices architecture threat model might focus on the service mesh that manages the communication between the services and any vulnerabilities in the APIs.

The serverless architecture is where the application is broken down into individual functions that are executed in response to specific events. A threat model might focus on vulnerabilities in the serverless application code, insecure serverless configurations, insufficient access controls, limited application visibility, and the security of the APIs that trigger the functions. A containerized threat model focuses on vulnerabilities in the container images, the Kubernetes cluster, and network connections between the containers. The threat model for an edge computing architecture includes DDoS attacks, data exfiltration, and unauthorized access to edge computing resources.

3. C. The AWS Config service monitors resource configurations and tracks configuration changes and compliance. CloudTrail will document API calls used to make changes but does not specifically track configuration changes in the manner of Config. IAM does not track the changes to configurations, and CloudWatch is a network management application but does not have the specific change management feature sets of the AWS Config service. Splunk is a logging analysis tool but is not an AWS service and does not specifically track configuration changes.

4. A. This is an ideal use for the Web Application Firewall to block the probes before they enter your network and can scale to handle well over the 500 IP addresses needed for this question. Security groups, NACL groups, and filtering at the Linux instance level are not scalable. They are internal to your VPC and may sit behind an ELB if you have one deployed. Of the options given, the WAF is the best solution.

5. B, E. VPC Flow Logs can collect the network traffic data at the instance interface level, and then you can use Lambda to code network automation and alerting routines. CloudTrail tracks system configuration changes but not production network traffic. AWS Shield sits on the Internet outside of your VPC so it would not fit this requirement. Inspector performs automated workload security assessments for application software vulnerabilities.

6. B. Security Hub is an AWS-provided unified dashboard that provides visibility into security alerts and compliance issues across multiple AWS accounts and services and collects data from various AWS services, such as AWS GuardDuty and AWS Config, and provides recommendations for remediation. CloudWatch Insights is a log query service and is too limited for the requirements in the question. The AWS Config service monitors resource configurations and tracks configuration changes and compliance.

7. D. The VPC security group default setting is to deny all inbound traffic and allow all outbound traffic and allow all traffic between the instances assigned to the security group. In this case, you would need to open port 22 SSH access into the VPC from the site-to-site VPN connection to access the server in the question. Ports 80 and 443 are for HTTP/HTTPS traffic and not SSH. The traffic is not arriving on the public Internet connection but over the VPN.

8. B, D. The SSL and TLS services are security protocols designed for securing connections between web clients and web servers over an insecure network such as the Internet. SSL/TLS is used to secure communications traffic in flight between clients and servers. SSL has been deprecated, and TLS is currently the active protocol. CloudFront terminates SSL/TLS sessions but is not a security protocol. IPSec is used by SSL/TLS but is not the actual in-flight security implementation used; it is a subset. There is no such `secure.cloudfront .net` URL.

9. A, D, E. CloudWatch has naïve log searching capabilities, and Splunk can search log files but is a commercial tool and the question is asking for AWS services. QuickSight is used to create interactive dashboards and visualizations. Athena can be used to query and analyze log data stored in S3. OpenSearch, formally called Elasticsearch, is an AWS search tool that can be used to search log files stored in an S3 bucket.

10. A. Detective automates security investigations and assists your security group in incident investigations. Detective uses prebuilt data aggregations, summaries, and context to analyze security events. Detective helps identify the root cause of potential security issues or suspicious activities. Artifact provides access to AWS compliance reports and agreements. Shield is a DDoS protection service that protects your applications from common DDoS attacks. GuardDuty generates alerts for potential security incidents and can be integrated with other AWS services, such as Lambda, to automate incident response. EKS is the AWS-managed Kubernetes container management service.

11. A. Misconfigured security controls create openings for attacks to your AWS infrastructure. Misconfigured security controls include improperly configured access controls, network security groups, or improperly configured encryption. Untrusted network architectures are also commonly referred to as a DMZ. DMZs contain a VPC that hosts resources that are accessible from the public Internet, such as web servers. The Internet traffic can only access the DMZ and not the internal, protected network. Shield is a DDoS protection service that protects your applications from common DDoS attacks. A proxy server sits between client devices and upstream servers or services. It acts as an intermediary that forwards requests from client devices to other services. A proxy server provides an additional layer of security that can filter and monitor traffic flows. A proxy server can also help you enforce your organization's security policies and control access to external resources.

Unauthorized access occurs when an attacker gains access to your operation's sensitive data and systems without permission. Unauthorized access can occur with phishing attacks and exploiting vulnerabilities in software or infrastructure.

12. C. CloudWatch Insights can be used to query and analyze log data. Inspector performs automated workload security assessments for application software vulnerabilities. CloudTrail logs API calls and events, and Amazon Inspector automates vulnerability assessments. Splunk is a commercial monitoring and searching product that is not managed by AWS; DynamoDB is a NoSQL database that does not fit the requirements of the question.

13. B. Data breaches are when your company's data is accessed, stolen, or exposed without your permission or authorization. Account hijacking is when an attacker gains access to an authorized user's account and uses it to access data or systems in your cloud environment. Advanced persistent threats are long-term, targeted attacks intended to steal data or disrupt operations over an extended time. The DoS attack attempts to disrupt the normal functioning of a network, server, or website by overwhelming it with traffic or other malicious activity. Malware and viruses are programs designed to cause harm to systems and networks. Malware and viruses can commonly spread over the Internet through email attachments, malicious websites, and other methods.

14. A. GuardDuty generates alerts for potential security incidents and can be integrated with other AWS services, such as Lambda, to automate incident response. Security Hub is a unified dashboard that provides visibility into security alerts and compliance issues across multiple AWS accounts and services. Amazon Athena is an interactive query service that makes it easy to analyze data in a data lake using standard SQL but is not a continuous real-time monitoring service. CloudWatch Insights is a log query service and is too limited for the requirements in the question.

15. C. Advanced persistent threats are long-term, targeted attacks that are intended to steal data or disrupt operations over an extended time. Advanced persistent threats are typically carried out by sophisticated attackers with significant resources. Account hijacking is when an attacker gains access to an authorized user's account and uses it to access data or systems in your cloud environment. Account hijacking can be accomplished with phishing attacks, brute-force attacks, man-in-the-middle exploits, and other methods. Cryptojacking is when attackers use the computing resources of the victim's infrastructure to mine cryptocurrency. This can cause the infrastructure to slow down, and the victim may be responsible for the additional compute resources required, which can be very costly. Unauthorized access occurs when an attacker gains access to your operation's sensitive data and systems without permission. Unauthorized access can occur with phishing attacks and exploiting vulnerabilities in software or infrastructure. Data breaches are when your company's data is accessed, stolen, or exposed without your permission or authorization.

16. B. Lambda can be used to automate incident responses. Lambda is a serverless computing service from AWS that you can use to run code in response to specific events or triggers. Lambda can be used to automate incident response by triggering specific actions when security incidents are detected. Artifact provides access to AWS compliance reports and agreements. AWS Config enables you to assess, audit, and evaluate the configurations of your AWS resources. Athena is an interactive query service that uses standard SQL to analyze data directly in Amazon Simple Storage Service. GuardDuty is an AWS threat detection service that continuously monitors for malicious activity and unauthorized behavior in your environment. GuardDuty generates alerts for potential security incidents and can be integrated with other AWS services, such as Lambda, to automate incident response. While GuardDuty is close, it is not a serverless service that runs custom code.

17. C. Artifact provides access to AWS compliance reports and agreements. CloudTrail logs API calls to AWS services, and GuardDuty is a threat detection service from AWS that continuously monitors for malicious activity and unauthorized behavior in your environment. CloudWatch is an AWS network management application, and Secrets Manager is used as a secure vault to store authentication and authorization credentials.

18. B, D. Athena can be used to query and analyze log data stored in S3, and QuickSight is used to create interactive dashboards and visualizations. Inspector is a reporting tool, CloudTrail tracks API calls to AWS services, and Shield is a network security service.

19. D. Certificate Manager is the AWS service that creates, stores, deploys, and rotates public and private SSL/TLS digital certificates. Certificate Manager automates the process of purchasing, uploading, and renewing SSL/TLS certificates. Secrets Manager is used as a password vault to protect credentials, AWS is a certificate authority, but that service does not deploy and manage user certificates as required in this question. There is no such service called SSL Manager.

20. C. QuickSight is the AWS tool used to create dashboards and visualizations. CloudWatch is a network management application that can display metrics in a graphical format but is not as extensive as QuickSight. Splunk is a search and analytic application but does not have the dashboard capabilities that QuickSight does. Athena and OpenSearch can query and analyze data but do not generate graphical dashboards.

Chapter 13: Network Monitoring and Logging

1. C, D, E. Log data can be analyzed using tools offered by Amazon, open-source, and commercial applications. Athena, Splunk, and OpenSearch can search log files in S3. Wireshark is used for packet capture and analysis, and DynamoDB is a NoSQL database that does not perform this function.

2. B. You can filter the VPC traffic that you mirror by specific criteria, such as the direction of the flow, source IP address, destination IP address, protocol, and port number. By using the granular filtering capabilities, you can drill down to the data of interest and filter out what is not needed. Access control lists, firewalls, and security groups can filter traffic flows but will block traffic and not perform packet captures. CloudTrail is a logging service with no packet capture capabilities.

3. B. The Amazon flow logging feature allows you to capture metadata about the IP traffic going to and from network interfaces inside your VPC. It is important to understand that the logs are not complete packet captures, only the metadata about each packet. The logs from VPC Flow Logs are generated at the network interface level and capture the source and destination IP addresses, ports, and protocol numbers for each packet that flows through the interface. Traffic Mirroring captures the complete packet, and CloudWatch Metrics does not provide the information on flows required in this question. tcpdump is a packet capture utility, and Kinesis Data Firehose is an Amazon streaming service that is used to deliver data to destinations such as S3 or OpenSearch for additional processing, analysis, or storage.

4. D. Transit Gateway Network Manager Flow Logs provide an AWS native tool to export and inspect flow-level information for all traffic flows between AWS and customer's on-premises networks including over Direct Connect gateways or VPN connections without any external tools in your data center's operations center. VPC Flow Logs and Traffic Mirroring will not capture remote data center traffic. CloudWatch and CloudTrail are logging services that do not meet the requirements of this question.

5. C. CloudTrail Insights records unusual API activity. Config monitors and enforces configuration changes. The AWS Security Hub provides a view of your security posture across multiple AWS accounts. Notifications can be sent via SNS when security findings are detected. EventBridge provides a serverless event bus that routes events between AWS services or from your own applications.

6. B. The Amazon VPC Traffic Mirroring service enables you to copy network traffic from Elastic Network Interfaces (ENIs) within your VPC and forward that traffic to troubleshooting, monitoring, and security tools for storage and analysis. The IAM access analyzer evaluates permissions and security controls, and Config tracks configuration operations in your account, not packet-level analysis. GuardDuty and Web Application Firewall are security-related services and are not network analysis tools.

7.   C. CloudTrail logging data can be used to monitor for unusual or unauthorized activity in AWS resources by providing an audit trail of all API activity in your AWS account. While Config tracks configuration changes on your AWS resources, it does not specifically record API calls, which is required in the question. CloudWatch and GuardDuty do not generate API records. Kibana is a visualization tool that does not apply to the question.

8.   B. The AWS Simple Notification Service is an Amazon managed messaging push service that enables you to send and receive messages between applications or distributed systems. SNS is used to decouple application components and enable asynchronous communication between them. SNS enables you to publish messages from various sources, such as applications, microservices, and cloud resources, and deliver them to multiple subscribers or endpoints, such as email, SMS, HTTP endpoints, and Lambda functions. CloudTrail is an API logging service, SQS is also a queuing service but is based on a pull model, CloudWatch Insight is an analysis tool, and QuickSight is a visualization application.

9.   A, C. CloudTrail is the service that logs all API calls made to your AWS account. These include API calls made by users, roles, and AWS services. CloudTrail logs are often used for security analysis, compliance auditing, troubleshooting, resource change tracking, and compliance auditing. CloudTrail automatically creates and stores logs in an S3 bucket that you specify. You can also configure CloudTrail to send logs to CloudWatch Logs for longer-term retention and analysis, which enables you to analyze and search logs in real time. Forwarding CloudTrail logs to a relational database is not an option. Redshift and OpenSearch can analyze logs stored in S3 but do not natively store information from CloudTrail.

10.   B, D. Wireshark and `tcpdump` are network packet analyzers that allow the user to display TCP/IP and other packets being transmitted or received over a network. OpenSearch, VPC Flow Logs, and Athena do not perform native packet analysis.

11.   B. The logs generated by CloudWatch Logs are used for troubleshooting, monitoring, automation, and compliance auditing. The benefit of CloudWatch logging includes a centralized logging repository to store and access logs from multiple sources. The service collects logs from your AWS resources, applications, and services, and stores them in a single location for access, retention, and analysis. You can use CloudWatch for real-time streaming of logs, which enables you to monitor and analyze logs as they are generated in real time. CloudWatch logging can be used to set alarms based on log data to trigger automated actions based on log events. This helps to identify and resolve issues quickly. CloudFront is a content distribution service, CloudTrail records API calls to AWS, Kinesis Data Analytics is a streaming network analysis tool, and VPC Flow Logs captures metadata about traffic in your VPC.

12.   B, C, F. The Kinesis Data Firehose service is a fully managed streaming data service that lets you capture, transform, and load streaming data into AWS storage services such as S3, Redshift, and OpenSearch. Customers can use Firehose to receive, temporarily store, and process large volumes of log data in near real time. Control Tower, DynamoDB, and RDS are not supported endpoints for the Kinesis Data Firehose service.

13. C. The AWS Security Hub is a centralized security service that provides a detailed view of your security stance across accounts and services. AWS Control Tower is a service used to configure and manage a secure, multi-account AWS environment. CloudWatch is an AWS monitoring service used to collect, access, and provide insight into all AWS and on-premises resources, applications, and services. GuardDuty is a threat detection service. Inspector generates findings and provides recommendations for remediation.

14. E. CloudWatch alarm notification mechanisms can include sending emails, text messages, SNS topics, or trigger an automated action such as a Lambda function. Lambda is the best choice since it can run Python code on demand, and you are charged only for the time the Lambda instance is active. None of the other options can run Python code on demand or are serverless.

15. E. Inspector scans your instances for common security issues, such as insecure network configurations, missing patches, and exposed ports. Inspector performs automated workload security assessments for application software vulnerabilities and generates findings and provides recommendations for remediation. AWS Control Tower is a service used to configure and manage a secure, multi-account AWS environment. CloudWatch is used to collect, access, and provide insight into all AWS and on-premises resources, applications, and services. Security Hub provides a customizable dashboard that displays your compliance status, security alerts, and other security-related information, and it provides automated compliance checks to ensure that your network security configurations meet regulatory and industry standards. GuardDuty is a threat detection service that monitors for malicious activity and unauthorized behavior in your environment.

16. B. Kinesis Data Streams supports Enhanced Fan-Out that allows you to replicate data in real time to multiple locations, customers, or services. Simple Workflow Service is used by developers to build, run, and scale background jobs. EventBridge Pipes can receive records in a Kinesis data stream but it is not an actual data pipeline. Splunk is used for monitoring, reporting, analyzing, and performing security information and event management and is not a pipeline service. Traffic Mirroring enables you to copy network traffic from an Elastic Network Interface (ENI) on an EC2 instance and send it to a monitoring appliance.

17. A, C. SageMaker and Kinesis Data Analytics are machine learning tools from AWS that can identify patterns and anomalies in log data, providing insights into potential issues. Kibana and Splunk are not machine learning services.

18. B, C. QuickSight and Kibana are AWS services that create visualizations of data. SageMaker is a machine learning tool. Systems Manager enables you to gather inventory information and make fast and efficient updates to network configurations. Trusted Advisor is an AWS managed service that provides real-time guidance to help you manage performance and costs of your AWS deployment by continuously analyzing your accounts and providing you with recommendations that help you follow AWS best practices and AWS Well-Architected Framework guidelines.

19. C. Audit Manager conducts network audits by using preconfigured frameworks to help you conduct and automate assessments for specific standards and regulations. The frameworks let you select from preconfigured controls that include documentation and instructions on how to implement the tests. GuardDuty is a threat detection service from Amazon that uses machine learning to identify potential security threats in your AWS environment, such as unauthorized access attempts, compromised instances, and data exfiltration attempts. Quick-Sight is a visualization application, and Kinesis Data Analytics and Redshift are not risk and compliance tools.

20. A. Kinesis Data Analytics analyzes streaming data in real time using SQL queries. You can use Kinesis Data Analytics to perform windowing, filtering, aggregation, and join operations on log data streams. For example, you can use Kinesis Data Analytics to detect anomalies in your log data. It is a network packet analyzer that allows the user to display TCP/IP and other packets being transmitted or received over a network. Wireshark is an open-source network analyzer that does not fit the use case in the question. Kinesis Data Streams is a real-time data streaming service. Splunk is a commercial log management application.

Chapter 14: Confidentiality and Encryption

1. B. The AWS Certificate Manager service enables you to create, manage, and deploy SSL/TLS certificates for use with AWS services and your enterprise resources. A certificate revocation list (CRL) is a list of revoked certificates that is maintained by the certificate authority and distributed to all parties that rely on the certificates issued by the authority to identify certificates that are no longer active. The CSR is a generated text file that you submit to the CA to give it the information it needs to sign the certificate. SSL and TLS are both encryption protocols.

2. D. Encryption transforms your information into an unreadable format, known as cipher-text, by using an encryption algorithm and a secret key. Encryption prevents unauthorized parties from accessing or reading the information if they do not have the encryption keys, even if they gain access to the data. Confidentiality is the protection of information from unauthorized disclosure and only authorized entities should have access to the information, and that information will be secure and protected from unauthorized access. AWS provides multiple services to ensure the confidentiality of customer data including network isolation, access controls, and encryption. Authentication is the method used to sign in to AWS or other systems using your login and is used to identify who you are, and based on this, you will be granted access to allowed services. Authorization determines what the identity is allowed to do and what it is restricted from doing. Authorization includes factors such as who is making the request, how the request was made, which can include the date and time, the source IP address, what operation is being requested and what service, and the policies attached to the service and what operations can be performed.

3. D. AWS KMS is the service that enables you to create, manage, and control cryptographic keys across your applications. All of the other options do not apply; RDS is an AWS database service, HSM is a key storage hardware module, and SSE is server-side encryption and not a key manager.

4. B. CloudHSM provides AWS hardware security modules secure key storage and management in the AWS cloud. The HSM is a computing device that processes cryptographic operations and provides secure storage for cryptographic keys. Security Hub, KMS, Control Tower, and Macie do not offer the capabilities required in the question.

5. B, C, E. Transport Layer Security (TLS) is the most common encryption protocol used to secure data in transit over the Internet. TLS is used to secure web traffic using the Hyper Text Transport Protocol Secure (HTTPS), Simple Mail Transport Protocol Secure, (SMTPS), Internet Mail access Protocol Secure (IMAPS), and Post Office Protocol 3 Secure (POP3S). ACM is the AWS Certificate Manager, and KMS is the key manager and they are not Internet transport encryption applications.

6. A. Traffic is not encrypted on a DX connection; you must also create a site-to-site VPN across the DX connection. Using a site-to-site VPN over the public Internet will not meet the latency and throughput requirements; DX does not offer native encryption.

7. B. The client-side encryption option allows you to encrypt data at the client before uploading it to Amazon S3. The other options are not directly related to encrypting data in transit between an Amazon EC2 instance and an S3 bucket. Use of a virtual private gateway is incorrect because it is used to connect a VPC to an on-premises network using a VPN or direct connection. Using a network access control list is incorrect because it is used to control traffic in and out of a subnet within a VPC but does not perform any encryption. A security group is incorrect because it acts as a virtual firewall for your instance to control inbound and outbound traffic and using virtual private cloud endpoints is incorrect because it enables you to privately connect your VPC to supported AWS services and VPC endpoint services with PrivateLink but does not encrypt the data in transit.

8. B. The AWS shared responsibility model is a security model that defines the security and division of responsibilities between AWS and its customers. Under the shared responsibility model, AWS is responsible for the security of the underlying infrastructure that supports the AWS cloud operations. This includes securing their physical data centers, network infrastructure, and the hardware components installed in the AWS facilities. CloudFront is for content distribution, the Well-Architected Framework is a series of AWS white papers of suggested designs, CloudWatch collects and reports on metric values in AWS, and CloudTrail records API activity.

9. C. DNSSEC can be used only for public hosted zones in Amazon Route 53. This allows you to provide origin authentication and data integrity for DNS queries and responses. DNSSEC is supported for public hosted zones in Route 53. DNSSEC is not supported for private hosted zones in Route 53. VPC peering does not use DNS technology and does not support the use of DNSSEC.

10. B. The correct answer is that a Bastion host provides an additional layer of security by acting as a gateway to instances in a private subnet within a VPC. This allows you to securely access instances without exposing them directly to the Internet. A Bastion host is not necessary for security in a VPC is incorrect because while it is not strictly necessary, it does provide an additional layer of security by acting as a gateway to instances in a private subnet. A Bastion host is typically used to access instances in a private subnet. A Bastion host can only be used for instances in a private subnet is partially correct because while it is typically used to access instances in a private subnet, it can also be used to access instances in other subnets within the VPC. VPC peering does not use Bastion hosts and does not require their use.

11. D. The AWS Certificate Manager can be used to manage SSL/TLS certificates for multiple AWS services, including Amazon CloudFront, Elastic Load Balancer, API Gateway, and

others. This enables you to provision, manage, and deploy public and private TLS certificates for use with these services. AWS Certificate Manager can be used only to manage TLS certificates for Amazon CloudFront distributions, Elastic Load Balancer, and API Gateway only are all incorrect because AWS Certificate Manager can also be used to manage TLS certificates for multiple AWS services. VPC peering does not use TLS encryption and does not require the use of TLS certificates.

12. D. AES encryption with IPSec can be used for both site-to-site and client VPN connections. This allows you to securely connect your VPC to your on-premises network.

A, B, and E are invalid because AES encryption is supported on many different services.

13. B. TLS symmetric encryption uses the same shared key for both encryption and decryption, which makes it more efficient than asymmetric encryption that uses different keys. The TLS handshake is designed to set up a shared symmetric encryption key between the client and the server, which is then used to encrypt and decrypt the data. TLS symmetric encryption can be used for various applications, not just web browsing, such as email, file transfers, video/audioconferencing, instant messaging, and Voice over IP. TLS symmetric encryption provides confidentiality and integrity of data, which protects it from eavesdropping and tampering.

14. B. The correct answer is that encryption can be used only for site-to-site VPN connections with an AWS Transit Gateway. This allows you to securely connect your VPCs and on-premises networks. VPC peering does not use VPN technology and encryption is not supported. Direct Connect does not use VPN technology unless configured to do so and does not offer native support for encryption.

15. B. The AWS Key Management Service can be used to create and manage private certificate authorities in AWS. Private CAs are used for issuing certificates for internal resources that are not exposed to the public Internet. The AWS Certificate Manager is a service that can issue and manage certificates from CAs, but it is not the only one. You can also use KMS or third-party CAs to issue and manage certificates in AWS. CloudFormation is a service that can automate the creation and management of AWS resources, but it cannot create or manage CAs in AWS. Public CAs are external entities that issue certificates for public-facing resources that need to be trusted by browsers and clients. AWS Directory Service is a service that can integrate with external CAs for authentication and encryption, but it cannot be used to create or manage CAs in AWS. IAM is a service that can be used to control access to CAs in AWS, but it cannot be used to create or manage CAs in AWS.

16. A. Confidentiality is the protection of information from unauthorized disclosure, and only authorized entities should have access to the information. The information will be secure and protected from unauthorized access. AWS provides multiple services to ensure the confidentiality of customer data including network isolation, access controls, and encryption. Authentication is the method used to sign in to AWS or other systems using your login and is used to identify who you are, and based on this, you will be granted access to allowed services. Authorization determines what the identity is allowed to do and what it is restricted from doing. Authorization includes factors such as who is making the request and how the request was made, which can include the date and time, the source IP address, the operation, the policies attached to the service, and what operations can be performed. Encryption transforms your information into an unreadable format, known as ciphertext, by using an encryption algorithm and a secret key. This prevents unauthorized parties from accessing or reading the information if they do not have the encryption keys, even if they gain access to the data.

17. B. The correct answer is DNSSEC, which is a security feature available in Amazon Route 53 for public hosted zones. This allows you to provide origin authentication and data integrity for DNS queries and responses. DNS response rate limiting, IPSec, Bastion hosts, and VPC peering are not security features available in Amazon Route 53.

18. B. IKE is only implemented in site-to-site VPN connections. This allows you to securely connect your VPC to your on-premises network. A, C, D, and E are incorrect because IKE is used on many different AWS services. VPC peering does not use VPN technology and does not support the use of IKE.

19. B. The certificate revocation list is a list of revoked certificates that is maintained by the certificate authority and distributed to all parties that rely on the certificates issued by the authority to identify certificates that are no longer active. A certificate authority is a trusted third-party organization that issues digital certificates, verifies that the person holding the certificate is who they claim to be, and is central to managing the life cycle of a certificate. The AWS Certificate Manager service enables you to create, manage, and deploy SSL/TLS certificates for use with AWS services and your enterprise's resources. Certificate management is the process of creating, distributing, revoking, and renewing certificates. The certificate-signing request (CSR) is a generated text file that you submit to the CA to give it the information it needs to sign the certificate.

20. A. The correct answer is that the client and the server exchange certificates and verify each other's identity. The Diffie-Hellman algorithm is not used in the TLS handshake process in AWS. The Diffie-Hellman algorithm is used in the Internet Key Exchange (IKE) protocol for establishing IPSec VPN tunnels. Preshared keys are not used in the TLS handshake process in AWS. Preshared keys are used in IPSec VPN tunnels or WPA2 wireless security protocols. The FIN packet is not part of the TLS handshake process in AWS. FIN packets are used in TCP to indicate the end of data transmissions. AWS KMS is not used in the TLS handshake process in AWS. AWS KMS is a service that provides encryption and key management for AWS resources such as S3, EBS, RDS, etc.

Index

D

E